The Life and Letters of
Emily Chubbuck Judson
{Fanny Forester}

—◠ Volume 3 ◡—

1846-1847

EDITED BY
George H. Tooze

Published in cooperation with the American Baptist Historical Society

Mercer University Press
Macon, Georgia

MUP/H791

© 2010 Mercer University Press
1400 Coleman Avenue
Macon, Georgia 31207
All rights reserved

First Edition.

Books published by Mercer University Press are printed on acid free paper that meets the requirements
of American National Standard for Information Sciences—Permanence of Paper for Printed Library Materials.

Mercer University Press is a member of Green Press Initiative (greenpressinitiative.org), a nonprofit program dedicated
to supporting publishers in their efforts to reduce their impacts on endangered forests, climate change,
and forest dependent communities. This book is printed on recycled paper.

ISBN 13: 978-0-88146-156-5

Copyrights for the original letters and pictures are held and reserved as listed below.
No part of this publication may be reproduced without the prior permission of the copyright owner.

Letters:
The American Baptist Historical Society, Atlanta, Georgia (1,217 letters)
The Hanna family files, Dr. Stanley Hanna, Palo Alta, California (384 letters)
Jerome Walker Chubbuck Collection, Wisconsin Historical Society Archives, Madison, Wisconsin (24 letters)
The First Baptist Church of Malden, Massachusetts (3 letters, 1 poem)
Franklin Trask Library, Andover Newton Theological School, Newton Centre, Massachusetts (3 letters)
Special Collections, Colgate University, Hamilton, New York (1 letter)
James Fields Collection, Houghton Library, Harvard University

Pictures:
The New York Public Library, New York, New York (12 portraits)
The Hanna family files, Dr. Stanley Hanna, Palo Alta, California (16 pictures)
The American Baptist Historical Society, Atlanta, Georgia (14 pictures)

Cataloging-in-Publication Data is available from the Library of Congress

Book design by Burt&Burt

—m—

To George Andrew Tooze, Janet Austin Tooze,
Alexander Austin Tooze, and Grace Amanda Tooze,

With boundless thanks for all that you bring to our life together.
You light up our lives!

—m—

MERCER
UNIVERSITY PRESS

Endowed by
TOM WATSON BROWN
and
THE WATSON-BROWN FOUNDATION, INC.

CONTENTS

We note that volume one, *The Life and Letters of Emily Chubbuck Judson (Fanny Forester)* has biographies of all the letter writers and of those mentioned in the letters; it also has descriptions of places and events.

Additionally, it has timelines of Emily's life and events important to her life story. Volume one is a descriptive companion to all the other volumes.

PREFACE

—ɱ—

⟶ This is volume 3 of *The Life and Letters of Emily Chubbuck Judson.*

This volume begins with a letter from Emily E. Chubbuck to Anna Maria Anable telling in awestruck tones that her innocent flirtation with Adoniram Judson has blossomed into something much more serious than either of them had intended, and she did not know where it would take them. That was resolved rather quickly, for he proposed formally on January 20 with a letter in which he said, "I hand you, dearest one, a charmed watch." He had come on Christmas Day 1845 to the home of the Reverend Abram Dunn Gillette, intending to ask her to consider writing the memoir of his second wife, the late Sarah Hall Boardman Judson. Within a short period of time, Adoniram Judson resolved to ask her to take Sarah's place in his heart and life. Over the next several months, the letters reflect her great joy in this wonderful love that both came to believe was ordained by God. They also reflect Emily's personal angst as she fought with her perception of what she had been in her "worldly" period. This darkness focused on letters she wanted N. P. Willis to return to her. If made public, these letters would have been, in her judgment, detrimental to the reputation of the great missionary and his "secular" wife. Probably their public discovery, she thought, would also bring rejection by executives of the mission board and the church public at large, for they would con-clude that her secular credentials were not strong enough to elevate her to the sacred stratosphere of missionary endeavor. Then, in the midst of all of this joy and angst, both continually expressed in the letters, there finally came resolution; N. P. Willis first refused, but then he acquiesced. The letters were returned and destroyed, though interestingly Emily kept the letters that N. P. Willis had sent to her, and they are included in this correspondence. Emily and Adoniram were mar-ried on June 2, 1846 and embarked from Boston to Burmah on July 11.

The next section of this volume contains letters and poetry from the five-month voyage, from their landing in Burmah at the end of November, and from their settling into missionary life. The new year of 1847 opens with the desire to go and establish a mission in Rangoon (a stepping stone, they hoped, to a later mission in Ava), the separation from mission friends, the fire that destroyed all their worldly possessions (many valuables that had been left behind in Maulmain), the tribulation of a house full of bats ("bat castle" as Emily was to call it), and the rejection of the mission to Ava by the mission board. They return to Maulmain in fall 1847 to continue work on the Burmese dictionary and to settle into the mission community that was so strong there.

Volume 3 closes with the birth of Emily Frances Judson and the beautiful poem "My Bird," which Emily wrote to commemorate this blessed event.

These letters portray two people who discovered a love of great depth and who allowed that love to bind them together in the common task of mission and of a life together to which they had been called. Many of these letters are extraordinarily personal, and many of them have never before been published at all or in their entirety. They significantly change our perceptions of Adoniram Judson.

We pray, dear reader, student, scholar, mission supporter, and pilgrim—whoever you may be, whatever you may be about—that in these lives and lines you may indeed be blessed by the God who called them and who indeed calls us all.

May they bring blessings to enrich your life and experience.

George H. Tooze
Indianapolis, Indiana

Acknowledgment

⟨⟩ The editor wishes to express his deepest appreciation to the following for granting permission to use original letters and pictures for these volumes.

Letters   The American Baptist Historical Society, Atlanta, Georgia

The Hanna family files, Dr. Stanley Hanna, Palo Alta, California, and David Hanna, Phoenix, Arizona

Jerome Walker Chubbuck Collection, Wisconsin Historical Society Archives, Madison, Wisconsin

The First Baptist Church of Malden, Massachusetts

Franklin Trask Library, Andover Newton Theological School, Newton Centre, Massachusetts

Special Collections, Colgate University, Hamilton, New York

James Fields Collection, Houghton Library, Harvard University

Pictures   The New York Public Library, New York, New York

The Hanna family files, Dr. Stanley Hanna, Palo Alta, California

The American Baptist Historical Society, Atlanta, Georgia

LETTERS

———

JANUARY 1846

Emily E. Chubbuck to Anna Maria Anable, January 2, 1846[1]— Philadelphia

So Ninny[2] darling, I have had quite a "set down" up there at Utica, hav'nt [*sic*] I? Anything but a "*gospel*" way of doing things that.[3] But never mind, it was quite refreshing—I have been praised till it makes me sick at the stomach. Doct. Judson says the paragraph is "brutal"—the dear, *dear* doctor!

Do you know, Ninny, that the *Mirror* people have dissolved—Morris[4] and Willis[5] withdrawn and left Fuller sole editor and proprietor. It is a strange move and I fancy a very sudden one; for Willis in his last letter gave as a reason for hurrying home that the *Mirror* needed him.[6] I rec'd a letter from Mary Adams[7] yesterday. It had rained for three weeks and she had been very blue but she wrote in excellent spirits. Mr. Roman[8] was dangerously ill which made it doubtful about

---

[1] Emily had first met Adoniram Judson on December 25, 1845; they had been introduced to each other by the Reverend A. D. Gillette for the purpose of talking about the memoir to be written of Sarah Hall Boardman Judson. Years later, Emily would remember that Judson made the "ask" on January 5, 1846; her letter of January 6, 1846 stated that Judson had been with her the prior evening and most of that day and that the "ask" had been made, and she was on the edge of acceptance.

This letter is undated. It speaks of a growing relationship between Emily and Adoniram, but Emily clearly states that she does not know where the doctor intends to take it. The letter also contains a response to information that Anna Maria had included in her letter of December 30, 1845; allowing several days for Anna Maria's letter to go from Utica, New York, to Philadelphia, Pennsylvania, we date this reply on January 2. The next letter from Anna Maria, which is in response to this letter, is dated January 5, 1846.

[2] "Ninny" was a name of endearment given to Anna Maria Anable by her most intimate friends at the Utica Female Academy. Emily was "Nemmy."

[3] This is in response to what Anna Maria Anable had written on December 30, 1845: "Some folks here think you are getting transcendentalist. What do they mean do you suppose? I guess it's because you say "God-gifted" and "inner light." If a body advances an original idea now-a-days one is transcendentalist."

[4] General George P. Morris was a partner with N. P. Willis at the *New Mirror* and a prominent literary figure in New York and Philadelphia. The original founder of the *New York Mirror* in 1823, beginning in 1843 with the *New Mirror*, he entered into a succession of publication enterprises with N. P. Willis. A writer, poet, and songwriter, Morris published a number of anthologies of both prose and poetry. When Willis went to Europe in 1845 after the death of his wife, he asked General Morris to guide Emily in her literary endeavors. Known universally as General Morris, his title came from his rank as a brigadier-general in the New York Militia.

[5] Nathaniel Parker Willis was the editor, with General George Morris, of the *New Mirror*, a prominent literary magazine in New York. His "discovery" of Emily in the June 8, 1844 edition of the *New Mirror* catapulted her into literary fame and enabled her to command the highest prices for her articles and stories from the major magazines of that period. It began a new and glorious chapter in her life. Over the next two years, he became her friend, mentor, and confidant. His black-bordered letter of March 21, 1846, made it abundantly clear that her engagement to Adoniram Judson had come as a "death blow" and that he had expected to marry Emily upon his return that month from England. He returned several letters to Emily to demonstrate to her, lest she had forgotten, why he had felt right in that expectation. In vol. 1, there is a timeline that presents in some detail the substance of their developing relationship, all from the letters Willis had written to Emily. When she received her letters back from Willis, she destroyed them, feeling that they would cast a negative shadow on her life and, because of that, the life and ministry of Adoniram Judson.

[6] See the letter from N. P. Willis to Emily E. Chubbuck dated November 28, 1845.

[7] See the letter of Mary Adams to Emily E. Chubbuck dated December 16, 1845. Mary Adams had been related to the Utica Female Academy. Her letter to Emily in October 1845 was almost a whimsical piece of fantasy with literary pretensions. It would reflect a fairly close relationship. A second letter in December 1845 was similar. The letters were written from New Orleans, and she spoke of Hatty Anable as being nearby. On January 29, 1849, Anna Maria Anable wrote, "Hatty says Mary Adams is going to marry Gardner Green of Norwich,—a very fine young man, of invention, fortune, piety and all that Mary's heart ever sighed for." On July 8, 1850, Mrs. Urania Sheldon Nott spoke of attending this wedding in New York.

[8] Hatty Anable was situated with the family of Mr. Roman.

their removing into the city. Hatty[9] had not been very well for a few days, but had taken an emetic and was getting better. Lou was quite well.

And now, Ninny, I have something to say to you which will very likely make you laugh and stare both; but indeed it is no laughing matter. I set out to have a little fun with my good Doct. J. just as I do with other men and will you believe me when I tell you that it has grown into quite a serious matter. I love him a great deal better than I ever loved W.[10] or H.[11] or any body else on earth. He has all their poetry, all their sensitiveness, and delicacy, far more tenderness and gentleness combined with a strong active intellect and it seems to me almost measureless wisdom. And, above all, Anna Maria,—his piety!—a pure holy-hearted man, that I could rest my own wicked heart on, and be made better. Do I frighten you? Well, I am frightened myself, for I don't know what it is all coming to. I ought either to stop here or make up my mind to—what I cannot. He knows how wicked I am as much as anyone can know, for I have told him—I have told him that I was a great trifler and world-lover and that I never could be serious and sober-minded as a missionary ought to be. And so he has picked out a nice niche for me to fill. He will furnish the material for a history of the mission which it will take about three years to write; and several other things of the kind. I may have a nominal connection with the school just to satisfy the board but do nothing but write. Some times [*sic*] I think it is more pity for me than love, and yet I think he loves me very much as a father does a child, for he takes me to his heart so gently and his voice is so soft and tender while he tells me what a sad thing it is to be wasting my life so. You must not think however that he has made formal proposals to me, and I am trying to decide the matter. We have known each other but a very little time, and though there was a kind of magnetism in our first meeting, it has not come to that. It will

---

[9] Harriet, "Hatty," "Hattie," or "Hat" Anable was one of nine children born to Joseph and Alma Anable and was a niece to Miss Cynthia Sheldon and Mrs. Urania Sheldon Nott. In 1841, she added a note to a letter written by Miss Cynthia Sheldon to Emily. As early as November 1842, she was away, and a letter from Emily to Catharine Chubbuck said that "she (Miss Sheldon) expected that Hat would return as accomplished as Anna Maria." Her trips were both educational and employment, as she worked as a private tutor in families that would bring her into their homes. In August 1843, she returned from Beonsen, in the vicinity of New Orleans, and was engaged to go again. A letter from Anna Maria on January 6, 1845 said that she would stay in the South for another year. About this time, Miss Cynthia Sheldon mentioned her concern for Hatty's spiritual health. In May 1845, she was in New Orleans. She was home again in summer 1846, but a September 27 letter from Anna Maria said she had been asked by Mr. Roman with some urgency to return and she thought that she should. She was to return home from New Orleans in January 1849 after Anna Maria Anable had started the Misses Anable's School in Philadelphia in fall 1848. Harriet was fluent in French, having placed herself earlier in a French environment in New Orleans. Hatty died in 1858.

[10] Emily's mentor and friend, Nathaniel Parker Willis was the editor of the *New Mirror*.

[11] Charles Fenno Hoffman was a prominent literary figure in Philadelphia and New York, who was well known as an adventurer, an editor, a poet, and a writer of exceptional talent. In fall 1843, he wrote three letters to Emily Chubbuck addressed to "Laura Linden," for Emily had written to him under that name, asking his advice about love, fame, and fortune. Only one of these letters is in the correspondence. Hoffman was not to learn of Emily's identity until spring 1845; in a letter dated approximately April 7, 1845, he spoke of Laura having taken off her mask and revealing herself to him. There were four letters from Hoffman in April when Emily was in Philadelphia. There were another three in December 1845 when Emily again was in Philadelphia. [See vol. 1, "Cast of Characters," s.v. "Hoffman, Charles Fenno," and vol. 1, "Places and Events," s.v. Laura Letters."] Anna Maria Anable frequently intimated in her letters that Emily was interested in "Hoffy" as a beau.

though if I don't prevent it; and I cannot bear to do it—the dear noble old man! What shall I do Ninny? I am not fit to be a missionary and I would not call myself one if I went. And yet I should be one—in the employ of the board—obliged to do as they bade me. He has (or had before it was broken up) a pleasant home at Maulmain, and I could have just as much English society as I could wish. He has kept up only a calling acquaintance with the families of the provincial officers because he had'nt [sic] time, but they would be very glad of his society. I can't sleep o'nights thinking of it, and yet once in a while ridiculous things come into my head and I laugh aloud all by myself. Married to my father! (he is fifty-seven.) F. F.[12] a missionary's wife! Choosing between the funny "halt between two opinions"—the holy Doct. J. that everybody considers more of an angel than a man, and the scape-grace N. P. W.! Is'nt [sic] it funny? Ridiculous? Would'nt [sic] the world split its sides? Don't I have the funniest set of lovers that ever any mortal did? W. "developed" me—made me what I am in more senses than one, and I feel as though I belonged to him. If he were here he sh'd decide the matter—he has a right—but for him Doct. J would not have loved me, but—oh Ninny, tell me what to do. Is'nt [sic] it a funny case? I know I sh'd be better—a more rational and useful creature, more satisfied with my own doings, and better fitted for the world that comes after, if I sh'd say to a noble man who loves me dearly, "be my guide"—I sh'd even be happier in this world-but, how *can* I do it? You may tell Aunt C.[13] about this if she will be very *very* private and learn what she thinks; and do my darling Ninny write me the minute you have done so. If I turn [written in the right margin of the address page] missionary you must do it too. Would'nt [sic] we be a rare couple? Stop wondering and laughing and write me this minute. Ten kisses in sweet good night. (the doctor kisses, oh, *so* sweetly!) from your own

Nemmy[14]

---

[12] Emily Chubbuck wrote under the *nom de plume* Fanny Forester. Asked about it once, she said, "Would anyone buy a book written by Emily E. Chubbuck?"

[13] Miss Cynthia Sheldon was in charge of the administrative and financial departments of the Utica Female Academy. Miss Sheldon and her sister Urania, who was literary principal, gave Emily Chubbuck a place at the academy in October 1840. They had deferred any cost to a future time when Emily could afford to reimburse them. Upon Miss Urania Sheldon's marriage in the late summer 1842 to the Reverend Doctor Eliphalet Nott, the president of Union College, and her subsequent move to Schenectady, Miss Cynthia Sheldon assumed a larger leadership role at the academy. Active and well-known in Baptist circles, Miss Cynthia was to become an important mentor, advisor, and friend to Emily until the time of Emily's death in 1854. She was the aunt of Emily's best friend, Anna Maria Anable, and was addressed by most as "Aunt Cynthia." In 1848, Miss Sheldon moved to Philadelphia to help Miss Anable with the startup of the Misses Anable's School.

[14] "Nem" or "Nemmy" was a name of endearment given to Emily by a small group of her intimate friends at the Utica Female Academy. Anna Maria Anable was "Ninny."

Written in the bottom margin of the address page: "Augusta[15] is to leave this afternoon, C. K. says. She spends a week in N. Y. I fancy my letter will be *ripe* by the time you get it."

Written in the left margin of the address page: "Mr. Denio, C. Kirkland and Rosa were here this morning. C. R. send [*sic*] love. I have just rec'd a sweet letter from my darling brother W.[16] Ninny he *is* a brother in reality. He thinks me an angel—rather different from the opinion of my good doctor, I fancy. However the D. D. knows how to flatter a little. He says, 'I could not wish you more beautiful, more accomplished, more fascinating, more sweetly amiable' (didn't my vanity open its big ears to all the words?) 'but I do my dearest Emily, wish that you loved my Saviour better! The 'one needful thing'—oh, Ninny, if I were only good!"

Written in the left and top margins of page 1: "I gave Mr. Inman[17] a blasting[18] for what he said in the paper about me and yesterday rec'd a very beautiful letter from West[19] throwing all the blame on Inman. No reply from Mr. I. though West says he promised it. West used to be a Methodist preacher. Mr. G.[20] advises me to

---

[15] Augusta Crafts is mentioned frequently in the letters written from the Utica Female Academy. A number of references chronicle her very strong opinions; many of these were spoken against N. P. Willis and Emily's relationship to him (Mrs. Crafts did not approve of either). In an April 30, 1845 letter Anna Maria Anable said, "The Dr. is not engaged nor isn't going to be to Mary Spencer I imagine, and tho' Mrs. Crafts intimated very strongly that there was *some one* he had his eye upon, he denied it to me strongly and scolded about Mrs. Crafts gossiping tongue."

[16] This could be either her older brother Walker, who was a newspaperman in the Wisconsin Territory, or her younger brother Wallace, who worked at various jobs and was in and out of their home in Hamilton Village, New York. From the reading, this also could be a reference to N. P. Willis (he *is* a brother in reality).

[17] John Inman was the editor of the *Commercial Advertiser* and the *Columbian Magazine*, responsibilities that failing health forced him to give up early in 1845. He was Emily Chubbuck's initial contact with the *Columbian Magazine*, which began to publish some her stories early in 1844. He strongly encouraged Emily in her writing, said that they would publish everything they could get from her, hoped that she would consider writing exclusively for them, and when she asked for it, gave her the unheard of rate of five dollars a page for her articles. When he did that, he candidly stated that with this, they would not consider it fair if she continued to write for N. P. Willis and the *New Mirror* without charge.

[18] Emily had not appreciated what Mr. Inman said of her recent publication *Trippings in Author-land*.

[19] Mr. West, at the age of thirty-five, took over the position of editor of the *Columbian Magazine* following the serious illness of John Inman. In an extensive letter written April 28, 1846, Mr. West revealed to Emily that he was a Methodist lay minister, sidelined for the present by illness. He went on to list all of the clergy in his family, including his father and his brother, and said that his wife was the daughter of missionaries to Ceylon. Wishing Emily many blessings and an abundance of God's grace, he said in part, "I knew not until recently that my valued correspondent was one whose heart was turned to serve the Lord and for [ ] hour an inscrutable but ever wise providence has prepared for so inconvenient a station." He said that he had met Adoniram Judson at a convention and hoped to meet him again and gain an introduction at a major convention in New York.

Mr. West wrote to Emily on December 17, 1845, but the letter had not been posted until December 28. Mr. Inman was the chief editor of both the *Columbian Magazine* and the *Commercial Advertiser*. He was an ardent promoter of Fanny Forester and her writing.

[20] Following several successful pastorates, the Reverend A. D. Gillette was the founding pastor of the flourishing Eleventh Baptist Church in Philadelphia in 1839. With his wife Hannah and several children (they would eventually have six), they graciously opened their home to Emily Chubbuck at the end of March 1845 for her health. The connection had been made through Miss Cynthia Sheldon, a family friend of Mr. Gillette and his parents. A prominent Baptist, Mr. Gillette journeyed to Boston in December 1845 to accompany Adoniram Judson to Philadelphia for meetings, and on Christmas Day, he introduced Dr. Judson to Emily Chubbuck with the hope that Fanny Forester could be persuaded to write the memoir of Sarah Hall Boardman Judson. A. D. Gillette and his wife Hannah remained valued and trusted friends, not only with Emily, but with the Sheldon and Anable families. He moved from Philadelphia to New York in 1852.

go eat and Mr. Robarts[21] says I would die in a year but neither of them know anything except as they guess. What shall I do? Love to all, and to yourself, dear Ninny, love immeasurable—"

Source: Hanna family files.

Miss Sarah J. Hinckley[22] to Emily E. Chubbuck January 3, 1846— Utica Female Academy

My dear darling friend

Your kindest of kind notes is before me now, and my pen almost refuses to "*bend an inch*" for the gratitude *it* feels—not I certainly. But indeed I am more than grateful that you have been so very kind; if there is a feeling that is deeper, more abiding than gratitude, it is that which makes me sit down now (almost some nights) to thank you. You can tell I think from experience what my feelings are, and my wishes that you may entertain towards *your friends*, such do I cherish in my heart of hearts for you my dear—supply the blank with the most endearing expressive sound you can—no danger of my coming out grand. That is not what I wish—only let me see the effect of my murders of the kings English in hard round "*roots*" and it will be all my present ambition aspires to. It is very grovelling [*sic*], is it not, to have no higher aspiration than this—shall I say I have and read you another leaf in a certain red bound volume? No—that will turn of itself soon enough—All the "shyness" I have, need so much alteration, correction, and revision that I hardly know what to send; but I will dispatch a package as soon as I can get it ready; and then if you will look over and if possible save me from *appearing ridiculous* I shall be for ever [*sic*] grateful—Oh! if you were only here—Selfishness! no. I will not wish you back—for I fear our cold winter would be any thing [*sic*] but *gallant* to our Fanny Forester.[23] But when we up north, that is earth and elements

[21] Mr. and Mrs. W. S. Robarts were active in Philadelphia Baptist circles. They were frequent visitors to the home of the Reverend and Mrs. A. D. Gillette and later to the Misses Anable's School, which Anna Maria Anable and her extended family had started in Philadelphia in 1848. In his biography of his father, Edward Judson mentioned that Adoniram Judson stayed at the Robarts' home when he came to Philadelphia in December 1845 when he met Emily Chubbuck. A. C. Kendrick said, "(Mr. Gillette and Dr. Judson) arrived in (or out of) due time in Philadelphia, and Dr. Judson was welcomed to the house of Mr. and Mrs. W. S. Robarts, who became warm personal friends, as they were already active friends of the mission cause." In 1846, with the engagement of Adoniram Judson and Emily Chubbuck, the correspondence indicates some hard feelings toward Mrs. Robarts for comments disparaging the coming marriage and missionary service. This is found in Emily's letter to Adoniram dated February 6, 1846; Mrs. Robarts seemed to be accusing Emily of worldliness when all the time, Emily was quick to say, Mrs. Robarts was engaging in the same activity of which she was accused. The correspondence also indicates a satisfactory healing of the relationship. In January 1849, Miss Sheldon told Emily that Mrs. Robarts had placed their daughter Mary in the Misses Anable's School.

[22] Sarah Hinckley was one of the girls from the Utica Female Seminary and a student of Emily's; there are some letters from her in the collection. In an 1849 letter Miss Hinckley reminisced about that time and brought Emily up to date on many of those who were there with her. She also spoke of the sad farewell when Emily left for Boston and then Burmah.

[23] Emily Chubbuck as Fanny Forester. See vol. 1, "Cast of Characters," s.v. "Chubbuck, Emily." Also "Forester, Fanny."

and girls are clothed in summer smiles once more then you will come won't you? And now for a sentiment a-la Fuller—the very birds [ ] [ ] [ ] [ ] [ ] [ ] our *"graceful little self"* was here to echo them; the very airs forget to "balmify" if Fanny was not here to breath [*sic*] them—the flowers forget to bloom if she was not here to love them—and all the girls and boys cease to become *characters at all* if Fanny's *pen, that wonderful* pen, *either steel* or *gold*, was not here to paint them—Such an accumulation of disasters would surely plunge Utica into a state of nonentity from which nothing could restore her—Then as you love us—set your face towards home. But I must say you good night, ask you to forgive any absurdities, accept my warmest thanks, love me if you can, write to me a good long note—(I should treasure it so) and believe me your friend

    Sarah J. Hinckley

I shall expect a reply soon [ ] *I pause for it.*

Source: American Baptist Historical Society, AJ 24, no. 1183.

Anna Maria Anable to Emily E. Chubbuck January 5, 1846[24]

My dear *dear* Nemmy[25]

    Your earnest heartful letter which I rec'd this afternoon I cried over till I almost made myself sick and then I laughed, till Aunt C.[26] who stood by begged to know what was the matter and then I read it to her and Lydia,[27] and we all cried and laughed alternately. What should we do? What *can* I say to you? I never felt so at a loss in all my life—I am struck dumb.

---

[24] This letter is wonderfully sensitive, filled with expressions of profound theological thought and purpose, different from the usual newsy or gossipy letters typical of Anna Maria. It is also a momentous letter, a gut response to Emily's letter about her new relationship with Adoniram Judson.

On a personal note, the letter copy has a lot of bleed-through, so it looked to be a difficult transcription as the work started. At about the fifth line it began to dawn on me that this could be unusual. At about the tenth line I felt like singing the "Hallelujah Chorus" for I knew what I had before me. It is such discoveries that make a project like this not only worthwhile, but soul-stirring.

This letter was written in response to Emily Chubbuck's letter we have dated January 2, 1846. We would give it several days to travel from Philadelphia to Utica, New York, and we expect that Anna Maria would have responded to it immediately.

[25] Emily Chubbuck. See vol. 1, "Cast of Characters," s.v. "Nemmy, Nem, or Nemmy Petty (Nemmie Pettie)." Also the chapter "Names of Endearment."

[26] See vol. 1, "Cast of Characters," s.v. "Sheldon, Miss Cynthia."

[27] Lydia Lillybridge was one of Emily's closest friends at the Utica Female Academy. When Emily made the decision to go to Burmah as the wife of Adoniram Judson and as a missionary, Lydia wanted to go with them. Emily spoke to Adoniram Judson of Lydia's extraordinary abilities, and Adoniram advocated her appointment before Dr. Solomon Peck and the Board of the American Baptist Missionary Union. Lydia was commissioned to go with them, in spite of the fact that she remained single. Always independent, outspoken, and unafraid to cause ripples in the missionary community, Lydia served on the mission field for twenty-eight years. She married missionary Thomas Simons in May 1851. See the timeline on the life and service of Lydia Lillybridge Simons in vol. 1.

I see clearly that you love your dear good old Dr. for your few expressions of interest have interested me more than I have ever been in any of your lovers—Willis[28] not excepted. How is that possible now? Tell me, you who has so much better versed in heart love than I am.

I did think once that Willis had a hold on your heart that no one could *loosen*; but your "noble minded holy old man" has done it I see, and it seems to me that he is sent from God, and we should not say a word. Oh, Emily, it is a sacred subject for me to write upon and I feel utterly incapable—yet I cannot help telling you that it seems to me this is the way in which you will be fulfilling the destiny which the God who gifted you so highly marked out for you.

What a different phase will your character present to the world—what a holy interest will it not awaken in the hearts of your numerous friends.

And the dear sweet old man who takes you so to his heart, and gives you such good counsel, I feel as if I could bless him for his interest in you. I love him dearly already, and am *so* sorry I did not see him when he was here.[29] You know I was in P when he visited us. O, Nemmy, I cannot be still I want so to go to P. and see you all.

But how can we let you go clear off to Burmah. What will this poor forlorn child do without her darling? O, I cannot think of it,—and yet it does not seem to me so much worse than the thought of your spending the rest of your days in Europe.[30] We shall see you in a few years again—O, I shall not think of it. You must come home right off and then we will talk it all over.

In the meantime write me all about the Dr.—all he says to you and what your plans are—for I feel quite confident as to how the whole will terminate. It seems as if this would be one of the *heavenly matches*.

Can it really be? O how I wish I could be there this night to hear you tell me from your own lips all about it. The Dr. must be very fascinating. Does not your heart relent when you think of all those sweet letters your papa[31] writes you? What will he say? It may be the means of making him a *good man*.

I do not believe that you will repent if you decide in favor of the D. D. for with Willis you feel that you will always have to take the lead—but to the Dr. you will bow to his superior judgment and strength of character as to its natural lord and master. Is it not so? Am I right in thinking it all settled as far as you are concerned?

[28] See vol. 1, "Cast of Characters," s.v. "Willis, Nathaniel Parker."

[29] In his November travels, Adoniram Judson stopped at the Utica Female Academy.

[30] After the death of his wife in March 1845, N. P. Willis took his daughter Imogen to Europe to meet many of his wife's relatives in England. After spending close to two weeks in New York in May and seeing N. P. Willis almost every day, Emily Chubbuck began to think of taking a trip to Europe. She spoke with George Graham of *Graham's Magazine* and with Robert West of the *Columbian Magazine* to see if they would pay her for articles from her European travels that she would send to them for publication. There is little doubt that the relationship between N. P. Willis and Emily was growing increasingly stronger; later, Willis returned several of Emily's letters with passages underlined in red, and he said that if she would reread them, she would find evidence that encouraged him in his plan to marry her upon his return to the United States.

[31] Both Emily and Anna Maria Anable made references to N. P. Willis as Emily's "papa."

Or have I taken the alarm too easily? O no! I feel it way down in my heart's core that you are going away from us.—When it is all *fixed*, give my love to the dear old man and tell him I think he ought to come up here and get Mama's[32] consent. That's the usual way of doing things in this country whatever they may think in *heathen* lands.

O Nem—if I could kiss you one two three five twenty times tonight, would not I then look way down into your heart and fish up some of its secrets. Do write me the minute you get this and tell all about it to

Ninny[33]

Lydia wants to know if the Dr. has said anything about your writing the memoirs of the late Mrs. J.!!![34] By the way you ought to send one of your missionaries after L.[35] The old plan would then be carried out admirably. I would give anything to kiss good night instead of writing it. Give love to Fanny[36] and tell her I shall write soon.

What will the folks say! I cannot help thinking on that, and I laugh at the funny of the thing as much as I cry at its milancholy [*sic*]. Willis Morris[37] Hoffman[38] and all the scape-graces [*sic*] who have taken you under their special protection and stare their eyes out—and most with vexation.

Source: American Baptist Historical Society, AJ 23, no. 1137

---

[32] A self-reference; Anna Maria often referred to herself to Emily as "mother" or "mother-in-law."

[33] Anna Maria Anable. See vol. 1, "Cast of Characters," s.v. "Ninny."

[34] The possible memoir of Sarah Hall Boardman Judson was what originally brought Emily Chubbuck and Adoniram Judson together. Emily eventually wrote that memoir.

[35] Lydia Lillybridge would, in fact, be going to the mission field with Adoniram and Emily, embarking with them from Boston in July 1846. She remained single for several years, and in 1851, she married longterm missionary Thomas Simons.

[36] Fanny Anable was one of nine children born to Joseph and Alma Anable and was a niece of Miss Cynthia Sheldon and Mrs. Urania Sheldon Nott. The correspondence indicates that in April 1845 she was away from home studying and taking music lessons. These spring letters indicate that she was in Philadelphia, working in the home of and with the family of the Reverend A. D. Gillette. See Miss Sheldon's letter to Emily of November 30, 1845, in which she spoke of all that Fanny was doing to improve herself in the field of music, but also her concern for Fanny's interest in the party life and the "vanitie" which surround her. A March 30, 1847 letter from Anna Maria Anable told of Fanny's conversion following her grandmother's death. In September 1847, she was listed as one of the teachers at the Utica Female Academy. Fanny became a teacher with her sisters in the Misses Anable's School in Philadelphia.

[37] General George Morris. See vol. 1, "Cast of Characters," s.v. "Morris, General George Pope."

[38] See vol. 1, "Cast of Characters," s.v. "Hoffman, Charles Fenno."

Emily E. Chubbuck to Catharine Chubbuck, January 6, 1846—Philadelphia

Dear Kitty,

I write to inform you of a matter which will set both your little eyes a-staring at a great rate. I have actually and for-sure this blessed day—this 6 of Jan. 1846, rec'd proposals of marriage from the darlingest man on earth—and who? Who do'ye guess? Ask father[39] and mother[40] how they would like a minister for a son-in-law, and that minister a missionary and that missionary the Rev. Adoniram Judson D. D. Just ask them. Well, he wants me to go out with him in July and I sort of want to go myself. Did you see him at Hamilton? He says it is all fudge about the life of a missionary being so hard. I could live just as pleasantly as though I sh'd marry a minister in this country, and he will take just the nicest care of me, and I need'nt [*sic*] do anything if I don't want to. He thinks too that the sea-voyage and the delightful climate there together would make me healthy. Shall I go? What would the Hamiltonians say? Not *Willis*[41] exactly—eh? Ask father and mother what they think about the matter. They would be well taken care of—the doctor has some money of his own, and he says that I sh'd be better able to help them than I am now. I pause for reply!!!!—What do you say? Fanny Forester[42] missionary to Burmah!!!!! What would Willis say? What would Hoffy[43] say? Mr. Gillette[44] is perfectly delighted. Write the very day you get this for I shall have to say yes or no very soon. In the meantime I keep a-being

Nem[45]

Source: Hanna family files.

---

[39] Emily's father, Charles Chubbuck, was born at Bedford, New Hampshire on March 3, 1780; he was married to Lavinia Richards in Goffstown, New Hampshire on November 17, 1805. They were to have seven children. Though he held varying jobs over the years, he failed at many of them, and Emily was the main support of the family after she purchased a home for her family in fall 1842.

[40] Emily's mother, Lavinia Richards Chubbuck, was born June 1, 1785, at Goffstown, New Hampshire, the eldest of thirteen children. She married Charles Chubbuck on November 17, 1805, at Goffstown, New Hampshire. Four of her children were born at Goffstown, and moved with Charles and Lavinia Chubbuck to Eaton, New York in September 1816; they were Lavinia, Benjamin, Harriet, and John Walker. Sarah Catharine, Emily, and Wallace were all born in Eaton.

[41] See vol. 1, "Cast of Characters," s.v. "Willis, Nathaniel Parker."

[42] Emily Chubbuck as Fanny Forester. See vol. 1, "Cast of Characters," s.v. "Chubbuck, Emily." Also "Forester, Fanny."

[43] See vol. 1, "Cast of Characters," s.v. "Hoffman, Charles Fenno."

[44] See vol. 1, "Cast of Characters," s.v. "Gillette, The Reverend Abram Dunn."

[45] Emily Chubbuck. See vol. 1, "Cast of Characters," s.v. "Nemmy, Nem, or Nemmy Petty (Nemmie Pettie)."

Emily E. Chubbuck to Anna Maria Anable, January 6, 1846—
Philadelphia

Dear Ninny,[46]

I have waited impatiently for an answer to my last letter, but—darling, darling Anna Maria,[47] I am afraid your opinion will have but little weight with me, if it should happen not to correspond with *his*. I love the dear man with all my heart, and he has been with me all the morning and all day yesterday and so I have almost said the yes. Think of it! Don't [sic] it seem infatuation? What will Mrs. Grundy say? What will H.[48]—what will W.[49] say? Mr. Wallace[50] called last night, and so the doctor had to stop teazing [sic] me to say yes and go away. W. spoke of his being such a holy old man and said the sight of such people made him feel most deeply how utterly worthless was his own trifling way of living. Thinks I, *miboy*, if you knew what the old fellow was at would'nt [sic] you storm? I believe the very spirit of lying or lie-acting was in me for what do you think I did but sit and form a plan for another incognito.[51] I am to write the stories and W. will copy and dispose of them for me. And there we sat and laughed at the nice trick as though I had really enjoyed it. It would be a grand thing if I did'nt [sic] intend to turn missionary.

Now, Anna Maria, you must'nt [sic] think that I have looked on but one side of the question. In the first place[52] the doctor says he has no doubt but the sea voyage and the climate together will establish my health entirely and be the means of prolonging my life. Then he promises the tenderest care such as mothers usually give, but husbands seldom. In the next place I am not to be confined to any course of life, I shall not be under any kind of control, but shall spend my time just as I choose. If I wish to write I may do so—if not I need never take up the pen. I shall of course wish to learn the language, but shall do it as leisurely as I choose and he will be my teacher. They have servants to do all their work, and I could be freer

---

[46] Anna Maria Anable. See vol. 1, "Cast of Characters," s.v. "Ninny." Also the chapter "Names of Endearment."

[47] Anna Maria Anable was the niece of the Misses Urania and Cynthia Sheldon and the daughter of Joseph and Alma Sheldon Anable. Emily first met Anna Maria in fall 1840 when she went as a student to the Utica Female Academy; both Emily and Anna Maria became members of the faculty there. In these years, Anna Maria became Emily's dearest friend, and the extensive correspondence between the two reflects sensitive, flirtatious spirits and a deep intimacy. Emily was "Nemmy" to Anna Maria's "Ninny." In 1848, Anna Maria Anable, with the help of her extended family, moved to Philadelphia and started the Misses Anable's School in Philadelphia. At Emily's death in 1854, Anna Maria was given guardianship of Emily Frances Judson, daughter of Emily and Adoniram Judson.

[48] See vol. 1, "Cast of Characters," s.v. "Hoffman, Charles Fenno."

[49] See vol. 1, "Cast of Characters," s.v. "Willis, Nathaniel Parker."

[50] Mr. Wallace was the nephew of Horace Binney Wallace. An attorney, whom Emily called aristocratic and privileged, he called on her regularly during winter 1845 when she was in Philadelphia, and then after her engagement to Adoniram, he became a trusted friend and advisor.

[51] Beginning in late 1843, Emily had written a number of letters incognito to Charles Fenno Hoffman, identifying herself as Laura Linden. There were several letters written by "Laura," and it was not until early 1845 that the truth was revealed.

[52] Here Emily repeats Adoniram Judson's promises to her as she enumerated them to her sister Catharine in another January 6, 1846 letter, but then she adds at least another three beyond what she had told her sister.

from care than the wife of a clergyman in this country. He is pastor of a little church and when not engaged with that he is in his study preparing his dictionary of the language. He says I must not think that the missionaries [*sic*] wives usually live so pleasantly, but if I will go I shall be made an exception, though I believe he has marked out a kind of incidental good (for the sake of not having me entirely useless) which he expects me to accomplish—something in the way of refining and polishing I believe. Then he promises that father[53] and mother[54] shall be taken care of, for he has some money and—oh, I don't know what. There is a dark side of the picture he shows too, but nothing worth repeating to you—nothing but what you know already or will be able to paint for yourself. There are other things too— oh, Ninny it will break my heart to go away from the dear friends I love—why can't you go with me? My head and heart are both aching tonight. I have cried till I can hardly see from my eyes—and yet I almost want to go. I have been a great deal troubled lately about Willis. I think he loves me and I am afraid I sh'd marry him, and just think what a life I sh'd lead! How much more rational the other! I firmly believe that I sh'd be happier the wife of a Burman missionary than in the position he would place me. Don't you believe I would—happier and most certainly better. The doctor says he would try to influence me for good—will you give your consent, Ninny? Have not yet decided past [ ]cal, and don't mean to, if I can help it till I hear. He sails in July—that is his present intention, but it seems to me very soon and I sh'd hope to be able to induce him to wait.

I rec'd your letter through Fan[55] yesterday. Thank you for your New Year's present. It is beautiful and I shall wear it, missionary or no missionary. Mr. Gratiot[56] called yesterday and left my dictionary and Fan's flowers. Fan attended a party at the Mitchells[57] last night, and I had agreed to go, but I got in such a worry over the Doct.'s proposal that I had to give it up. If I conclude to become Mrs. J. you will

---

[53] See vol. 1, "Cast of Characters," s.v. "Chubbuck, Charles."

[54] Emily's mother. See vol. 1, "Cast of Characters," s.v. "Chubbuck, Lavinia Richards."

[55] See vol. 1, "Cast of Characters," s.v. "Anable, Fanny."

[56] Charles Gratiot grew up in St Louis, where his father was an army engineer responsible for developing the Port of St. Louis. He married Ann Sheldon, who was a cousin of Miss Cynthia Sheldon, Mrs. Urania Sheldon Nott, and Alma Sheldon Anable. Together, Charles and Ann Gratiot had six children. Because they often lived with the Sheldon family, their letters contain a great deal of him. Letters in 1847 speak of his religious awakening; those of 1849 speak of his leaving for the California gold fields. In 1853, Charles Gratiot applied for a grant of 400 acres in Illinois, and he already owned 148 acres.

[57] Mr. and Mrs. Mitchell lived in Philadelphia; Mrs. Tyndale, Mrs. Mitchell's mother and the owner of a prosperous china shop in downtown Philadelphia, lived with them. In November 1845, as Emily was thinking of prolonging her stay in the city to last through the winter, the Mitchells generously offered to open their home to her, promising that they would do everything in their power to take good care of her: her own room, solitude or company as desired, the ability to write, and all of the comforts they could provide. Emily did express appreciation, saying that many of her friends told her what wonderful people they were and how sensitive they were to the needs of an invalid such as Emily was at that time. Her one serious reservation was that they were Unitarians. In the end Emily decided that she would stay with the Reverend and Mrs. Gillette, knowing from her past experience that she would be more than comfortable with them.

probably see me soon.[58] In the meantime write darling—do. Mr. G.[59] will write to Aunt C.[60] tonight.

Written in the right margin of the address page: "Don't be scared about this matter, deary, but think and talk it over with Aunt C. (nobody else, for the world) and if you can't go it, why, maybe you need'nt [*sic*]. The dear old teaze [*sic*] is going to Washington soon and 'out of sight out of mind' maybe. So people call me transcendental—they will consider this freak the super-refinement of transcendentalism, won't they?[61]

"Good-night, darling. Think of little peaked-chin's[62] nestling in a man's bosom, and such a man. Well, his bosom has got a heart in it, and my head has lain there more than once, not caring for a better pillow. He knows how to pet sweetly. But,—Ninny, I would give a great deal if you could be here tonight, and I would snuggle down on your shoulder and sleep more soundly than I have slept in one fortnight. A kiss darling—another—another. Good night."

Nem.[63]

Written in the top margin of page 1: "I meant to have sent Lydia's[64] shawl and your *Trippings*[65] by Mr. Bright[66] but the scamp never called. Tell Lydia patience—maybe I will bring them myself."

Source: Hanna family files.

---

[58] Emily was able to return to Utica by the middle of February.

[59] See vol. 1, "Cast of Characters," s.v. "Gillette, The Reverend Abram Dunn."

[60] See vol. 1, "Cast of Characters," s.v. "Sheldon, Miss Cynthia Sheldon."

[61] This is a reference to some comments made in the letter of Anna Maria Anable to Emily E. Chubbuck dated December 30, 1845. Emily mentioned them as well in her letter to Anna Maria of January 2, 1846.

[62] Emily E. Chubbuck used a number of different names over the course of her life and career. She wrote often under the name Fanny Forester, her argument being "who would buy a book authored by Emily Chubbuck?" At other times, she used Amy Scribbleton (July 6, 1841); Amy S. (September 28, 1841); Nem or Nemmy (Emily was always Nem or Nemmy to Anna Maria Anable who was Ninny); Pithy to Anna Maria (April 29, 1845); Peaked chin (See Anna Maria Anable, November 12, 1845); Sister Peakedchin (See Emily Chubbuck, February 28, 1846); Miss Peakedchin (Adoniram Judson, March 7, 1846); Miss Nemmy Petty (Adoniram Judson, March 7, 1846); Petty (April 13, 1846).

[63] Emily Chubbuck. See vol. 1, "Cast of Characters," s.v. "Nemmy, Nem, or Nemmy Petty (Nemmie Pettie)." Also the chapter "Names of Endearment."

[64] See vol. 1, "Cast of Characters," s.v. "Lillybridge, Miss Lydia." Also the timeline "Lydia Lillybridge Simons."

[65] *Trippings in Author-land*, Emily's book that had been released by the publisher November 22, 1845.

[66] At this time, Dr. Edward Bright was affiliated with the *Baptist Register*, a prominent regional newsletter. Prior to this, Mr. Bright, in 1838, had been the founding pastor of the Bleecker Street Baptist Church in Utica; Cynthia Sheldon, her parents Isabell and Asa Sheldon, and her sister Alma Anable, had been involved as well. The Bleecker Street Church was to have a close relationship over the years with the residents of the Utica Female Academy. Bright was, in 1846, appointed as the corresponding secretary of the American Baptist Missionary Union.

Mrs. E. T. Josslyn[67] to Emily E. Chubbuck, January 7, 1846—Nottsway

My dear Emily

To-night I am *all alone*—an event so unusual that I have resolved to celebrate it by writing you. Had I room and inclination I could fill this sheet with excuses for not writing sooner—which after all you would construe to mean I have been careless and negligent and probably always shall be—so adieu to the whole catalogue.

I was indeed glad to hear from you by letter—and have since been almost equally pleased to hear from you by our mutual friends—and through the public journals. The fame and (I trust) the *golden* rewards you are receiving by your literary labours [sic] give me a pleasure I cannot express. You cannot doubt that every thing [sic] which comes from your pen that I can get I read [ ]. Indeed Em I am almost a star by shining in your light. I am quite a wonder when I say I correspond (pray don't tell any body [sic] I have had but *one* letter from you) with Fanny Forester!!![68] They want to know how you *look* and how you *sit* and what you *say*. I describe you as I knew you—trusting that you have not been spoiled by the unparalleled praises of even N. P. Willis.[69]

Now that the Holidays are passed I suppose you are again at your duties in school.[70] I wish I could look in upon you, and see you all engaged in your various departments. But as that may not be I will tell you about "me and my house" hoping you will do likewise very speedily.

From the time I last [sic] to Utica—until two months ago I have suffered almost constantly from the ague. My "seasoning" has been a severe one—but I believe it is finally done with. It has taken off a little of my fat—but has left me with my usual quantity of spirits and colors—tho' for a time it deprived me of both. Oh how busy I have had to be since I have been well. Besides the usual quantum of fall sewing there was quilting—and "helling time" and soap-boiling—and candle making—and sausage making etc. etc. Then I have made three or four dinner—dinner—*parties* (is most to be a name for a Michigan *fixin*) and had some to attend—and then the winter evenings visiting must not be forgotten. All of these things bring their own wares and pleasures—I have only *one* unmitigated trouble and that is, this confounded *stiff steel pen*.

Upon her return to America in 1851, Emily Judson had a very close relationship with Dr. Edward Bright. He helped Emily with many of her business affairs, he carried on the publishing details of the Judson memoir because of a serious illness in Dr. Wayland's family, and he and his wife took in Henry and Edward Judson for a year, beginning in October 1851. He, with Dr. Edward Granger, was the executor of the estate of Emily Chubbuck Judson.

[67] Mrs. Josslyn was associated with Emily at the academy in Utica. Her letters are filled with references to people they both knew.

[68] Emily Chubbuck as Fanny Forester. See vol. 1, "Cast of Characters," s.v. "Chubbuck, Emily." Also "Forester, Fanny."

[69] See vol. 1, "Cast of Characters," s.v. "Willis, Nathaniel Parker."

[70] This letter was mailed to Emily at the Utica Female Academy. Apparently, Mrs. Josslyn was not aware that Emily had been in Philadelphia for her health since the first of November.

Will has finally sold his farm so we shall be farmers no more. Where we shall go in the spring is yet undecided tho' I hope and rather think back to Centreville. The villagers all manifest a great anxiety to have us go back—I make quite a fuss if we talk of going elsewhere, from which you well should infer we are very popular there. Whether I meant to convey that impression or not when I began the sentence I will leave you to judge. Will is carrying on the whiplash business pretty largely yet—so that our house had eight or nine in the family all winter. I have had the [ ] girl living with me for a year, so that she can take charge of the house now as well as I can. We have had sleighing now for a few weeks and I assure you we have improved it. I was at Marshall last week. Whilst there I met a Mrs. Shearman formerly from Utica, and as she frequently hears from there she told me a great deal of Utica news. I cannot tell you how much I want to see my friends at the Seminary. If Will could leave his business so as to go with me I could go east next summer. Sometimes I think I will conclude to go without him—and you need not be surprised to see me, not exactly going "foot and alone, crosslots [*sic*] and crying"—but poping [*sic*] in upon you without any husband. Just now Will's head is so full of land speculations, that I can't get him to lay a plan more than a week a head [*sic*]—but perhaps it will not last long. All Marshall is crazy about the Lake Superior copper mines—and as he has been up there several times lately I am not sure that he may not be a little affected by it.

Oh how many many questions I want to ask you about the old teachers. From most of them I have not heard in *one*, *two*, and *three* years. Could I draw forth an immediate answer I would ask, for Jane Damaux, Eugenia,[71] Sarah and Soph Hastings, Lucy Look, Mr. [ ], Molly Barber, Jane K,[72] Anna Maria,[73] Hat,[74] Miss Cynthia,[75] Grandpa and Grandma[76] and which of all the loved ones would I forget.

---

[71] Eugenia Damaux had been part of Emily's intimate circle of friends at the Utica Female Academy. Living in New York City, Eugenia suffered from some kind of eye problem that made life difficult at times; this was a matter of comment in many of the letters exchanged between the girls themselves and with Miss Cynthia Sheldon. In 1848, Eugenia was in New York living "at Mrs. Brown's—the same warm-hearted French girl as ever." In 1849, she married Johnny Edmonds, described as rich and pious, and they lived in Utica.

[72] Miss Jane Kelly was Emily Chubbuck's friend at the Utica Female Academy, and then she became a teacher with Emily at that institution. Miss Kelly became the literary principal in 1844 with the retirement of Mr. and Mrs. James Nichols from that position. During a period of Miss Kelly's illness in 1844, Emily filled in the position for her. Then, in 1848, when Miss Cynthia Sheldon moved to Philadelphia to help start the Misses Anable's School, Miss Kelly became the "headmistress" of the academy and successfully brought it into the future, though not without some initial disparagement from the Sheldon-Anable families.

[73] See vol. 1, "Cast of Characters," s.v. "Anable, Miss Anna Maria."

[74] See vol. 1, "Cast of Characters," s.v. "Anable, Harriet."

[75] See vol. 1, "Cast of Characters," s.v. "Sheldon, Miss Cynthia Sheldon."

[76] Deacon Asa Sheldon was the father of Miss Cynthia Sheldon, Urania Sheldon Nott, and Alma Sheldon Anable. Deacon and Mrs. Isabell Sheldon lived with their daughters and grandchildren as a part of the Utica Female Academy community. Mrs. Sheldon died January 29, 1847. Deacon Sheldon continued to have a room at the Utica Female Academy, where he died in March 1848. For many years, he led mealtime prayers for the academy family, and Deacon and Mrs. Sheldon were popular with the students, who often looked in on them.

Tell Julia Look[77] if she would endure my everlasting affection to sit down within 48 hours and write me something of all for whom I have enquired of the teachers now there. Think you that my heart does not sometimes go out towards you all as if it would over come [*sic*] impossibility to clasp at least some of you in my arms. I feel at times [Note: A section of the paper bottom has been torn out, accounting for the following blanks.] [ ] I *must* see you and from your lips hear of your welfare. [ ] [ ] indulgence of such homesick feelings are worse than [ ] [ ] to banish them and am heartily thankful for even a letter. Tell Miss C. that Mr. Josslyn saw Abby Bagg Austin yesterday [ ] her Father-in-laws [Note: Text continues in the right margin of the address page.] "near Bal[ ]. She was well. Will says her little girl is a beautiful child, and almost idolized by its grandparents. Eliza Carpenter is marrying and lives in Marshall—I saw her there this fall.

I have heard several times that your health is not good. I wish I could induce you to make your plans to visit Mich in the spring or summer. Any time after the middle of May to the first of Sept the country is beautiful. Anything that I can do to render a stay of a few days, weeks, or months pleasant to you, I will most gladly promise to do.

Written in the left margin of the address page: "Please tell Jane Kelly her letter has been read and shall be answered one of these days. [Note: This is the back side of the page with the tear.] Tell her she must not get vain by being so much flattered by the Principal. Dear dear what are you and Jane coming too [*sic*]. [ ] [ ] were as much puffed up by praise as are, you [ ] [ ] perfect mountains. But who cares for praise—*I do*[ ] [ ] have got a good husband with a big nose and you [ ] [ ] good. But then I don't want to brag over you for (you *can't*) *help it if you have not got husbands.*"

Written in the bottom margin of the address page: "Where is Molly Barker? Eugenia said she was not in Utica but did not say where she was.

"Em do please write me soon—for you know—you are loved by your sincere friend"

E. T. Josslyn

Source: American Baptist Historical Society, AJ 24, no. 1172.

[77] Julia Look was a student of Emily's at the Utica Female Academy and later a fellow teacher. A November 22, 1845 letter from Anna Maria encouraged Emily to stay in Philadelphia for the winter for her health and remarked that Julia had the hardest part because she was teaching Emily's composition class, and the students kept asking for Emily. In a September, 1847 letter, she was listed as one of the teachers at the Utica Female Academy. On September 23, 1849, Anna Maria wrote that Julia and Albert B. Casswell were married and came to visit with her. In one 1849 letter Julia spoke of another teacher who was teaching "our composition class." On October 27, 1850, Anna Maria Anable noted that she had had a son. She was one of a small number of people who addressed Emily as "Nemmy" in her letters.

Miss Cynthia Sheldon to Emily E. Chubbuck, January 9, 1846

Friday E'g

Dear dear Emily,

Your letter this aft[78]—together with Mr. Gillette's[79]—has relieved us, yes I will say relieved, for altho' I could not tender to you any advise on this subject, my whole heart was intent on your favoring the wishes of the best of Men.[80] I know you have said yes before this. Therefore my girl your new situation is what I want to talk about—your letter will probably reach your Mother[81] tomorrow. I shall if possible send one to her by the same mail—my heart is full to overflowing—if it were possible for me to leave home I would take the stage tomorrow—then write you that we all felt to subscribe to this wonderful providence.

I hope you will not suffer anxiety about home, because they will be sustained—nor about any settlement, preparations etc—Is it not the duty, and privilege of people to work, when the Lord in great condescension opens the way in which they may do some good—I trust you will have some evidence of willing hearts—I have written to Mr. Gillette father's[82] feelings on the subject—must write some to dear Fanny[83]—Courtland[84] goes back tomorrow—we have kept this from Urania[85] a whole week—I must tell her knowing full well she and the Doct.[86] will be greatly interested—they would if possible go quite to Philadelphia to see Dr. Judson—if you were out of the question—they go to Albany tomorrow—return Monday, you cannot get her letter before the last of the week—do Emily make the Dr. think well of us here—but I beg you will not send any Missionaries here—father says he would not give his consent to any other than your Dr.—

---

[78] See the letter of Emily E. Chubbuck to Anna Maria Anable dated January 6, 1846.

[79] See vol. 1, "Cast of Characters," s.v. "Gillette, The Reverend Abram Dunn."

[80] The reference would be to Adoniram Judson.

[81] Emily's mother. See vol. 1, "Cast of Characters," s.v. "Chubbuck, Lavinia Richards."

[82] Deacon Asa Sheldon, Cynthia Sheldon's father.

[83] See vol. 1, "Cast of Characters," s.v. "Anable, Fanny."

[84] Courtland Anable was a younger brother of Anna Maria Anable. He held several positions over the years, and he studied at Hamilton College while he boarded for a time with Emily's parents. In 1853, he returned to Philadelphia where he preached his first sermon at the Eleventh Baptist Church. He was "Uncle Court" to Emily Frances Judson. In 1880, Courtland Anable was listed in the Massachusetts Census as an ordained minister serving in a church.

[85] Urania Sheldon had been the literary principal of the Utica Female Academy in fall 1840 when Emily Chubbuck came to study there. Emily was able to afford this wonderful education through the generous offer of Miss Sheldon and her sister Cynthia, the executive and financial head of the academy, to defer tuition. Urania Sheldon left in late summer 1842 upon her marriage to the Reverend Doctor Eliphalet Nott, the president of Union College in Schenectady, New York. Because of the distance separating them, Emily's relationship with Urania Sheldon Nott did not develop the intimacy that grew between Emily and Miss Cynthia Sheldon. Urania Sheldon Nott remained a mentor, advisor, and friend to Emily in the years of her writing, her missionary endeavors, and upon her return to America in 1851. She was also the aunt of Anna Maria Anable.

[86] The Reverend Doctor Eliphalet Nott was the president of Union College in Schenectady, New York. An ordained Presbyterian minister, he was married to Urania Sheldon Nott, the sister of Miss Cynthia Sheldon and Mrs. Alma Anable and the aunt of Anna Maria Anable.

I cannot write more—Heaven bless you my girl—indeed I feel assured you will enjoy the presence of Him "who dwelt in the bush"[87]

Yours ever C. S.

Source: American Baptist Historical Society, AJ 26, no. 1266B.

Anna Maria Anable to Emily E. Chubbuck, January 9, 1846

Friday eve'g 11 o'clock

Dear Nem[88]

I have been dying of impatience to hear from you all the news—have scarcely slept a wink. I don't really believe you have been much more excited than I have been. I have devoured the memoirs of Mrs. Judson, and everything else relating to the mission, and have almost become a baptist [sic] and determined to go too. Couldn't the Dr. take two wives—for I have quite lost my heart with your account of him! How sorry I am that I did not see him![89] I hope he will come here early in the Spring. You must make him. If you have seriously talked yet about being married you must not listen to the idea being married any where but here.

You would laugh to see Lydia[90] and me. We sit and wonder and wonder—and then exclaim, and then we fall to talking the matter over. When I think of all the dear old man has suffered I wonder more and more that he should think it possible—that it should even have entered his head that you *could* go out with him. I don't believe it will strike the world as much stranger that you should go than that he should think of asking you. I guess Mrs. Grundy hasn't heard any thing in the while that will make her storm so. Has Hoffman[91] gone to P? I expect the D. D. will have to fight somebody yet.

What will Willis[92] say indeed!! Do you know I am [ ]ed most to death at the thought of him [ ]full of his vanity—much as I pity and like him. I suppose it has never entered his brain that if he had a mind to propose you would not jump to get him.

---

[87] This reference is to the biblical story of Moses, when Yahweh spoke to him from the burning bush.

[88] Emily Chubbuck. See vol. 1, "Cast of Characters," s.v. "Nemmy, Nem, or Nemmy Petty (Nemmie Pettie)." See also the chapter "Names of Endearment."

[89] In a January 5, 1846 letter Anna Maria said that she was away when Dr. Judson had been in Utica. He would have made a visit to the Utica Female Academy, as it was such a prominent institution in Baptist circles.

[90] See vol. 1, "Cast of Characters," s.v. "Lillybridge, Miss Lydia," also the timeline on Lydia Lillybridge Simons.

[91] See vol. 1, "Cast of Characters," s.v. "Hoffman, Charles Fenno."

[92] See vol. 1, "Cast of Characters," s.v. "Willis, Nathaniel Parker."

Have you seen the criticism on his "Dashes" in the Edinburgh Review? Twill do him good won't it. It takes those foreign reviewers to hit on the *very failure* of a man, and show it up. Poor fellow, I do really pity him.

Now Nem I have a great favor to ask. I would give more to see the letter you write him telling him of this matter than any thing [*sic*] else I can think of at present. So please don't destroy it, that is unless you really don't want me to see it.

Jimmy[93] has been here tonight and we had really a *very* pleasant call. He wants to know what you are doing now—Wouldn't he split his fat sides if he knew.

Oh, Nemmy, how can I bear to have you go. I cannot bear to think of it. Not that from my soul I do not believe you would be happier—for you never could find your happiness in the world, and the influence of that "holy man"[94] will make you emminently useful, and you will of course be happier as you grow better—but how can I let you go? What shall I do without you? Why I have felt all Winter as desolate and forlorn as a bird without her mate and can I be so unselfish as to be *willing* you should go. O do come back here as quick as you can and let us have all the time we can before you go. I cannot realize it and it seems the strangest thing in the world to be writing seriously about it. I can think of nothing else tho'; so do write me very often, just as often as you can possibly find time—and tell me all about the dear good man that has so infatuated you. You must not be afraid of saying too much, for as I have never seen him I can form an opinion only from your letters. I do *so* want to see him.

The clock has struck twelve and I must go to bed. Oh that I could see you one little while first, or that you *could* "snuggle down on my shoulders" and go to sleep as in old times. Those times will never come again. I must not say more but kiss good night.

Ninny[95]

---

[93] Jimmy Williams was often mentioned in Anna Maria Anable's letters, mostly simply as "Jimmy." He was around the Utica Female Academy, and she spoke of their conversations, what he was doing, and his interests. She often referenced him as being with "Helen." Writing to Emily on April 29, 1845, Anna Maria had some interesting comments to make. In a paragraph of gossip she said, "(and now) I'll turn to Jimmy and Helen." She went on to talk about a party:

> It was one of the most elegant parties that has been given in a long time. Jimmy's three sisters were there—all elegant women. (Also) all the flowers of Utica Society—and among them—no not among *them* but in the rooms was [*sic*] poor dowdy looking little Helen giggling when she showed any animation with [ ] and girls of that class and stamp. Jimmy tried to bring her forward as much as he could—but it would not do. She will never shine in society, and what is worse Jimmy will feel her deficiency in that respect very much. He would like very much to have a wife but would entertain his guests handsomely—and yet—he loves Helen very much I have no doubt and the one hundred thousand will make up for some deficiencies or ought to. I may abuse my pity I dare say."

Then on November 14, 1845, Anna Maria said to Emily: "Do you know Jimmy is really engaged to Helen M? He hasn't been to see me yet, and he came home last Sat. Oh, love! love! Even a seven year friendship must fade before thy potent spell. Little did I think tho' that Jimmy would be faithless."

[94] In her initial letter about Adoniram Judson on January 2, 1846, Emily had referred to him as "a pure holy-hearted man."

[95] Anna Maria Anable. See vol. 1, "Cast of Characters," s.v. "Ninny."

Written in the left margin of the address page: "Do you know Emily that Grandpa has thought and told Grandma[96] it seems from the first that if Dr. J. went to P. you would go back with him to Burmah. He is so pleased that I left him at ten o'clock wide awake and in a very facetious mood. He says Sarah Bell[97] shan't have Mr. Abbott[98] but I guess he thinks Lydia may—Isn't that a grand idea? But [Written in the right margin of the address page] I'll never try to make a match again in my life, for I firmly believe they are all made in heaven.

Lydia says "never think of my shawl again—she is going to be a missionary and ought to have everything."[99] By the way how soon may we get up a *Sewing* Society for you?

Don't send the *Trippings*.[100] I have a copy and have had two or three besides Aunt C's[101] collection of them. They are all over the house.

Written in the left margin of page 1: "What can be the occasion of your letter being so long on the wing."

Written in the top margin of page 1: "Do write. Write immediately. It seems as if I can't wait to see you. Miss Crafts[102] has returned from S. She had and a delightful visit. *She* don't [sic] think there is any great disparity [ ] in Dr. and Aunt U.'s[103] age.

"Do you know in[ ] your Dr. is very much like hers, only with perhaps more strength of intellect."

Source: American Baptist Historical Society, AJ 23, no. 1159.

[96] See vol. 1, "Cast of Characters," s.v. "Sheldon, Deacon Asa."

[97] Sarah Bell Wheeler was a teacher at the Utica Female Academy, an intimate of Emily Chubbuck, and one of the few who addressed Emily as Nemmy. In a September 1847 letter, she was listed as one of the teachers at the Utica Female Academy. There are a number of letters from Sarah Bell before and after her marriage to Charles Gould of Boston in October 1850. There are several letters clustered in the year or two after Emily left for Burmah and a number at the time of her return to America. Emily stayed with Charles and Sarah Bell Gould in October 1851 when she arrived in Boston after the long sea voyage from Burmah and then England. She stayed there a number of times following that. In 1851, Anna Maria Anable wrote of Sarah Bell: "Sarah is grown so lovely in person as well as character that she must assert a blessed influence on all with whom she comes in contact."

[98] This no doubt is a reference to Elisha Litchfield Abbott, missionary to Burmah. Born in 1809, Elisha Abbott was ordained in 1835, and he first arrived in Calcutta in 1836, finally arriving in Maulmain on April 4, 1837. His wife Ann died in Burmah on January 27, 1845, and he had returned to the United States, arriving on November 14, 1845. Elisha Abbott was from Cazenovia, New York, which was not far from Utica and the Utica Female Academy. He returned to Burmah on August 16, 1846, about nine months after Emily, Adoniram, and Lydia Lillybridge arrived. There were some efforts in Burmah at that time to match Lydia Lillybridge with Elisha Abbott.

[99] Writing on January 6, Emily asked Anna Maria to tell Lydia that she had meant to return her shawl to her.

[100] Emily's recent book, released by the publisher on November 22, 1845, was *Trippings in Author-land*.

[101] See vol. 1, "Cast of Characters," s.v. "Sheldon, Miss Cynthia."

[102] Speaking of Miss Crafts in November 1845, Anna Maria Anable reflected, "What a blessing to society it is, that she was never married. What a shame it would have been for *her* to have settled down into a mere *me* and *my husband* and *my children*! I wonder if I should ever make such a good old maid!"

[103] See vol. 1, "Cast of Characters," s.v. "Nott, The Reverend Doctor Eliphalet and Urania Sheldon." At the time of their marriage in 1842, Urania Sheldon was thirty-five years old, and Eliphalet Nott was sixty-nine years old. A comparison is being made here to the fact that Emily was twenty-nine to Adoniram Judson's fifty-seven years of age.

In her initial letter of January 2, 1846, Emily herself had referenced her age difference with Adoniram: "Married to my father! (he is fifty-seven.)"

Mrs. Urania Sheldon Nott to Emily E. Chubbuck, January 14, 1846—Union College

My dear Emily

Letters from Utica within a few days have informed me of the struggle which has recently taken place in your condition and prospects, a change in which all your friends feel deeply interested—and none more than myself. You have no doubt my child weighed the matter and I trust looked to Him, who alone is able to direct all your steps—I have only to say that if you have done so in sincerity and in truth—you will neither regret your decision nor should it bring you to a premature grave—But we will hope for better things—and as I do not wish to cast even the shadow of a cloud on your pathway—I must stop—I cannot say more to you now, I could not say less—When you have a moment for me, let me hear something of your plans.

Hoping and expecting to see you soon, I subscribe myself as [ ] your friend
U. E. Nott

Source: American Baptist Historical Society, AJ 25, no. 1231.

Miss Lydia Lillybridge to Emily E. Chubbuck, January 17, 1846—Utica[104]

Oh the liberties that some people will take when they are elevated in the scale of existence a little above their fellows!! Now, Miss Emily (I suppose you'd like to be called Mrs. D. D.[105] but I think it not wise to add to your vanity) I'd thank you to send my shawl to me by the first express. No matter if I have got yours, and have had it all the time, I could let my sister wear it if I only had my own.[106]

As it regards going with you—I would sooner go than not if you had, instead of telling your "Ninny"[107] to ask me, spoken to me yourself,[108] just as you did about

---

[104] This letter is part of a dual letter; after Lydia's note, Anna Maria Anable added a brief note of her own (See January 17, 1846, Anna Maria Anable to Emily E. Chubbuck).

[105] This is a reference to the growing relationship between Adoniram Judson ("the Doctor") and Emily Chubbuck.

[106] Apparently, the shawl was a topic of conversation between Lydia and Emily.

> May 1, 1845 from Anna Maria: "Lydia wants me to remind you to send home her shawl."

> January 6, 1846: Emily to Anna Maria: "I meant to have sent Lydia's shawl."

> January 9, 1846 from Anna Maria: "Lydia says 'never think of my shawl again—she is going to be a missionary and ought to have everything.'"

> January 17, 1846: Lydia to Emily: "I'd thank you to send my shawl to me by the first express. No matter if I have got yours, and have had it all the time, I could let my sister wear it if I only had my own."

[107] Anna Maria Anable. See vol. 1, "Cast of Characters," s.v. "Ninny."

[108] It is obvious that Emily desired Lydia Lillybridge to accompany her to Burmah as a missionary, and instead of asking her personally, Emily asked Anna Maria Anable to bring the matter to her.

going to Europe.[109] Instead, I did make up my mind to go when I first heard your letter read and even went so far as to shed some tears in anticipation of parting with my friends; but after thinking a little longer on the subject, I have concluded not to "run before I am sent," at least before I'm plainly asked. "So there! Now."[110]

From your most faithful servant

And "humble companion"

L. Lillybridge

Source: American Baptist Historical Society, AJ 25, no. 1251.

Mrs. Urania Sheldon Nott to Emily E. Chubbuck, January 17, 1846—Union College

My dear Emily,

I have just received a letter from Utica saying that you are anxious to return to us again and are waiting for an opportunity.[111] A gentleman from this place returned from [Note: "There" is written and crossed out.] P. this week and there are frequent opportunities. If Mr. Gillette[112] would enquire of Mr. Potter I think he might hear of company for you, but were I in your place, I would not wait for company. Mr. G. can put you on board the train for N. York and some of Mr. Colgate's[113] will find a traveling companion from there. There are always some gentlemen from Albany staying at the Croton, or Franklin House—as well as at all the others—who would be glad to take care of you.

Mr. Delevan has been in New York this week, and for aught I know is to be there several days longer. He would be delighted to bring you here, and I will go up to Utica with you. If Mr. D. is in the city he will be at the Croton Hotel. You would be more likely to find company from a hotel in N. York than you would from a pri-

---

[109] Emily spoke of going to Europe, supported by the magazines for which she was writing stories. She talked to George Graham of *Graham's Magazine* and John Inman, the editor of the *Columbian*, to see about their supporting her passage and stay, in exchange for letters to the magazine about her experiences. There was some talk of Anna Maria Anable accompanying her. That Lydia Lillybridge was also asked is new information. In the end, Emily was unable to make the European tour because of her continually failing health.

[110] Lydia Lillybridge, in fact, went to Burmah with a special appointment from the mission board. She accompanied Emily and Adoniram when they left Boston in July 1846, and Lydia served as a missionary for twenty-eight years. In 1851, she married veteran missionary Thomas Simons.

[111] With the thought of her marriage to Dr. Judson, Emily began to make plans to get back to Utica and Hamilton, New York, to arrange not only for the marriage itself, but for purchasing and packing all that she would need to set up a household in Burmah. Weather and health worked against her; she was finally able to leave Philadelphia on February 17.

[112] See vol. 1, "Cast of Characters," s.v. "Gillette, The Reverend Abram Dunn."

[113] This is the William Colgate who, according to the *Baptist Encyclopaedia*, was one of the most prosperous men in the city of New York, creating his wealth through the manufacturing of soap and other products (249–50). He was a devout Christian and a prominent Baptist. He married Mary Gilbert and had three sons, Samuel, James, and Robert. A letter written in January 27, 1846, by James shows that there were two daughters, Mary and Sarah.

vate family. You will arrive at Albany late in the eve'g—and should go to Mr. Delevan's house which you know is close by the R. Road—and which you must take at 11 past 7 and we will be at the cars for you—You had better make up your mind dear E. to undertake this journey alone as a kind of preparatory exercise to the future. I would not hesitate were I in your place about coming on—and really you have no time to lose.

My Doc't[114] says your books must come out in a new edition[115] this winter or as soon as possible—and that you may realize something handsome[116] from them. He thinks with me, that you are wise in your decision—and that if God should spare your life, you may be more eminently useful in *that far off world* than you could be here[117]—I am very sorry that I wrote you this week[118] under the influence of deep feeling a short and [ ] you will think abrupt letter—it was meant in kindness and written soon after the first intelligence burst upon me. I have very much to say to you and shall look for you with the greatest anxiety. Let me know when you are to leave P. that we may be on the lookout for you. If your good Doctor is with you remember me kindly to him, and I was going to send a message to him, but shall wait until I see him here at my own house.

Give my best love for Fanny[119]—How sadly she will miss you—she must write us by you—kind regards to Dr. and Mrs. Gillette.

And believe me—ever your most affectionate

Urania E. Nott

Say to Doct Judson [ ] have a son of Mr. Sam. Nott in [Note: Rest of line fades.].

Source: American Baptist Historical Society, AJ 25, no. 1230.

Mr. Colgate had some contact with missions and Adoniram Judson. When Emily was preparing for the Judson memoir in December 1851, she wrote to William Colgate for possible resources, and he responded to her. Mr. Colgate was one of the founders of the American Bible Society, removing himself from a previous Bible society because it would not print the Bibles as translated by missionaries on the field.

[114] See vol. 1, "Cast of Characters," s.v. "Nott, The Reverend Doctor Eliphalet."

[115] *Trippings in Author-land*, a collection of Emily's stories, had been published in November 1845. A later collection was published under the title *Alderbrook*.

[116] Emily had said in a November 23, 1845 letter that she would receive a sixpence for every copy of *Trippings in Author-land* that was sold and that many advised her that this was a generous royalty.

[117] If Emily were to marry Adoniram Judson, her life would change dramatically, for she would leave shortly for Burmah as a missionary.

[118] See the letter of Mrs. Urania Sheldon Nott to Emily E. Chubbuck dated January 14, 1846.

[119] See vol. 1, "Cast of Characters," s.v. "Anable, Fanny."

Nathaniel Parker Willis to Emily E. Chubbuck,[120] January 17, 1846—London

Dearest Emily

I learned a moment since, that the *Massachusetts* sails tomorrow, and have hurriedly sat down to write essential business letters. First, however, a word to you.

Yours came yesterday—most welcome, but complaining of the *coldness* of my letters. What can you mean, my dear Emily? I have sent you always a warm leaf from my heart, and you and my child live there now alone. Your own eyes must have colored what I wrote. You were sad. But we shall meet soon—please God. I sail on the 24th and when you read this shall be tossing on the ocean, ill and sorrowful. By the 20th of February look for me. The "Prince Albert" [*sic*] is the name of the ship. My Imogen comes home with me.

My projects for the future are dark and limited.[121] I am half inclined to abstract a year from the *noon* of my mind to write some poems that will repair my neglected fame. Think over this, and give me advice. Where should I live for such a respite. How can I see you? I fear I *must* stay in New York. Will you write me a journal of you *thoughts for me* till I return. I am so changed a man since Death has struck down so many that I loved.[122] The value of all things in this world seems gone. I shall be a dull companion to you. And—by the way—you have seen very little of me, and you have too much genius not to idealize and over-color that which your mind dwells on. I am a poor erring creature, dear Emily, and you may be disenchanted. Don't expect me to keep up to your ideal. My heart has ebb'd, but I still shall appear *outwardly* at full tide mark. Pride and scorn of the world, will always make me *seem* gay and careless. Love alone shall ever read me truly.

I have no more time. A kiss on your dear lips from my lips—tho' they are steeped in most unattractive sadness.

Ever yours affectionately

N. P. Willis

Source: Hanna family files.

[120] Written on the address page in the handwriting of Emily Chubbuck: "W 36." This was the thirty-sixth letter she had received from Willis.

[121] See the letter Emily wrote to Anna Maria Anable on January 2, 1846, in which she mentioned that Willis and his partner, General George Morris, had left the *New Mirror*, the publication that had been so successful in promoting her as Fanny Forester.

[122] In March 1845, N. P. Willis lost his wife quite unexpectedly. In early June, he left for Europe with his daughter Imogen, hoping that some time with his wife's family in England would be helpful to their healing.

Anna Maria Anable to Emily E. Chubbuck, January 17, 1846[123]

Dear Nem[124]

Is this article which is in the "Daily" by *your* Hoffman?[125] If it is *God help him*! You ought to give him a dozen kisses for it at least. It shows a heart-felt appreciation of you that I like. I do hope the poor fellow is not going to be among the *disappointed ones*.[126] If he is I should think it high time you would be taken off to some heathen country.

Mr. Morris[127] is starting a new paper—what can Willis[128] be about?

Do write

Ninny[129]

Source: American Baptist Historical Society, AJ 25, no. 1251.

Mrs. Urania Shelton Nott to Emily E. Chubbuck, January 20, 1846[130]

Dear Emily,

I am truly obliged to you for your kind letters and wish they were more frequent. Your books are having a pretty nice circulation here[131]—as much so as I can bring about—and gain for you I will not say "golden opinions" for that would be miraculous these hard times—though I hope even this reward will be forthcoming before long. [ ] very says you must write—and Mr. Gotten or my gude [*sic*] man will be its god father[*sic*]—though I forgot you Baptists don't believe in such naughty things.

The last sentence in your letter sounded to me rather portentous. [ ] garde! dear E. Runes garde! it is a serious thing—do let me know my child if there is any thing [*sic*] in this—if you can make confidence—perfect confidence—you are safe—but if not—beware—once taken the step can never be retraced.[132] If I were

---

[123] This letter was an addendum to one from Lydia Lillybridge to Emily, dated January 17, 1846.

[124] Emily Chubbuck. See vol. 1, "Cast of Characters," s.v. "Nemmy, Nem, or Nemmy Petty (Nemmie Pettie)." See also the chapter "Names of Endearment."

[125] See vol. 1, "Cast of Characters," s.v. "Hoffman, Charles Fenno."

[126] Anna Maria Anable saw a number of potential "beaus" whose hearts would be broken with the news of Emily's engagement to be married to Adoniram Judson. These included Charles Fenno Hoffman, Nathaniel Parker Willis, and Joseph Neal, all literary elites.

[127] See vol. 1, "Cast of Characters," s.v. "Morris, General George."

[128] See vol. 1, "Cast of Characters," s.v. "Willis, Nathaniel Parker."

[129] Anna Maria Anable. See vol. 1, "Cast of Characters," s.v. "Ninny."

[130] This letter is undated. Its contents fit the January 20 date.

[131] *Trippings in Author-land*, a collection of Emily's stories, was released by the publisher on November 22, 1845.

[132] The letter of Mrs. Urania Sheldon Nott to Emily Chubbuck dated January 14, 1846 indicates that Mrs. Nott had been informed of the relationship between Emily and Adoniram Judson.

sure you would find your anticipations realized one half as much as I have done—
I would say to you—do not falter.[133]

Write me by the first opportunity—and tell me (you may in strict confidence
do so) all about the matter.

That you may be guided by Him who alone is able to protect you from all harm
is the prayer of your forever friend,

Urania E. Nott

Source: American Baptist Historical Society, AJ 25, number 1242.

Adoniram Judson to Emily E. Chubbuck,[134] January 20, 1846— Philadelphia

I hand you, dearest one, a charmed watch. It always comes back home and
brings its wearer with it. I gave it to Ann,[135] when a hemisphere divided us,[136] and
it brought her safely and surely to my arms—I gave it to Sarah, during her husband's life-time,[137] (not then aware of the secret), and the charm, though slow in
its operation, was true at last.

Were it not for the sweet indulgences you have kindly allowed me, and blessed
understanding that "love has taught us to guess at," I should not venture to pray

---

[133] In this touching personal commentary, Mrs. Nott was referring to her own life story. In 1842, she had been an extremely effective leader, the literary principal of the Utica Female Academy, working with her sister, Miss Cynthia Sheldon, who was in charge
of the financial side of the school. She had given up all of this in late summer 1842 to marry the Reverend Doctor Eliphalet Nott,
the president of Union College in Schenectady, New York. At that time Miss Sheldon was thirty-five years old and Dr. Nott was
sixty-nine. They were to have twenty-one happily married years together before Dr. Nott suffered a debilitating stroke in 1863;
Urania Sheldon Nott was to devotedly take care of him until his death in 1866.

[134] Of this letter, Dr. A. C. Kendrick said in *The Life and Letters of Mrs. Emily C. Judson* (New York: Sheldon and Company, 1831):
"The following little note contains Dr. Judson's formal avowal of attachment. It seems half like sacrilege to lift the veil upon a
thing so sacred as a marriage proposal; but this interweaves so ingenious and graceful a memorial of his former wives, and in its
delicate playfulness illustrates so admirably a large element in his character which found little scope in his ordinary correspondence, that the reader will pardon its publication" (146).

[135] Of his mention of Ann and Sarah in this proposal of marriage to Emily Chubbuck, Dr. A. C. Kendrick said in *The Life and
Letters of Mrs. Emily C. Judson* :

It is beautiful to see Dr. Judson ever linking in memory his third wife with his former ones, and even in his first avowal
of affection blending the three in sacred association. Nor did Emily feel that love for her demanded any restraint
upon his expressions of affectionate remembrance of them. His unforgetting regard for them was her surest guaranty
of her own permanent place in his heart, and she writes with equal truth and beauty:

For death but lays his mystic spell
Upon affection's earthliness;
I know that though thou lov'st me well
Thou lov'st they sainted none the less. (147)

[136] In August 1822, Ann Hasseltine Judson returned to America because of her declining health; she returned to Burmah in
December 1823.

[137] After the death of Ann Hasseltine Judson, Adoniram Judson, terribly distraught over the sense of his loss, gave away many of
their possessions. Ann's watch had gone to Sarah Hall Boardman, the missionary wife of George Boardman; they had come to
Burmah in April 1827 to Tavoy to work with the Karens. George Boardman had died in 1831.

you accept my present, with such a note.[138] Should you cease to "guess" and toss back the article, saying—"Your watch has lost its charm. It comes back to you, but brings not its wearer with it!" O first smash it to pieces, that it may be an emblem of what will then remain of the heart of

Your devoted

A. Judson   (See Appendix for sample of original letter.)

Source: A. C. Kendrick, *The Life and Letters of Mrs. Emily C. Judson*, 148–49; Hanna family files.

Emily E. Chubbuck to Cynthia Sheldon, January 21, 1846

I am so thankful to you dear Miss C.[139] for favoring this wild-looking project of mine![140]

My good doctor has just gone away and I have just said to him the irrevocable *yes*, though I must acknowledge that I had acted it before a little bit.[141] It was most kind and thoughtful in you to write to mother[142]—it will soften the matter to her greatly and even then, I fear the result. You think there is a mysterious Providence in this queer proceeding and so does Mr. Gillette.[143] As for the doctor he thinks there is a combination of circumstances about it which almost gives one an idea of supernatural agency. He is a blessed man—you cannot begin to dream how good he is, and I suppose that I have a good share of it yet to learn. Well, I shall have years of at least partial loneliness to learn in.

Dear aunt C. I have not undertaken this without a *great deal* of thought, and I would'nt [*sic*] do it but that I believe the blessing of God is on it, but I must acknowledge that I have but little of what is called a missionary spirit. Perhaps it will increase. I hope so. I should like to be useful, and that has influenced me very much in my decision, but I do not wish to make any professions, and you will find me the same as ever. But one thing it may be well to say to you now. What ever [*sic*] may happen—if I should die on the *passage I should not* be sorry I went.

---

[138] It was obvious from the first moment of their meeting that something was "happening" between Adoniram Judson and Emily Chubbuck. As early as January 6, Emily had written to Anna Maria Anable and Catharine Chubbuck that she had almost said the "yes." In those letters, she spelled out all the arguments that Adoniram Judson had given to her as to why they should be married. Then, in letters we have dated January 21 and January 22, Emily said that she had made the "irrevocable" commitment.

[139] See vol. 1, "Cast of Characters," s.v. "Sheldon, Miss Cynthia."

[140] Having heard of the possibility of Emily being married to Adoniram Judson, on January 9, 1846, Miss Sheldon had written, "For altho' I could not tender to you any advise on this subject, my whole heart was intent on your favoring the wishes of the best of Men." In that same letter, she also said, "Is it not the duty, and privilege of people to work, when the Lord in great condescension opens the way in which they may do some good."

[141] As early as January 6, Emily had written that she was almost ready to give Adoniram Judson her "yes."

[142] Emily's mother. See vol. 1, "Cast of Characters," s.v. "Chubbuck, Lavinia Richards."

[143] See vol. 1, "Cast of Characters," s.v. "Gillette, The Reverend Abram Dunn."

I shall not mind anything about preparations for I know there are enough kind, good, friends to attend to that. Mr. G.[144] will, (as he says) "beg the privilege," and I shall leave it to you and him; but I have several debts at Utica[145] and I am anxious to get back and see about them. I do not know exactly my resources, but I know I am in a pretty bad state. For that reason, I have refused to go to Washington and I am very anxious to get back to Utica. I do not even know just how much is due on my place. I shall have enough to make out my April payments, but beyond that, I am very destitute.[146] I shall collect all my F. F.[147] stories and make as good a bargain as I can. I should like B. B. & H.[148] to get out a new edition of my other books with my name (E. Chubbuck) but I don't know how they can be induced to do it immediately.[149] The books would meet with an immense sale to come out just on the announcement of this affair. I suspect there will be a great buzz all over the country—some very unpleasant things, likely, but I don't care—the doctor has a right to marry as he chooses, and so have I.

My good doctor is as attentive to my comfort as though he had been accustomed to luxuries instead of self-denial and suffering; and he proposes to me to take out a woman in the *capacity* of servant or humble companion if I wish it. The native servants are not to be depended on and I should of course manage a house very poorly. I thought of Mercy Thomas if she is not engaged to be married. You will understand that the situation will be an easy one, more overseeing than laboring. One thing the doctor says if I take a pretty girl I must make her agree to pay back the passage money in case of getting married, for some of the provincial officers will take her in spite of herself. Please look about you some and help me to somebody.

If you can contrive any way to get me home please do it, for I am in great haste to be among you. Give my love to Grandpa and Grandma.[150] Tell grandpa that he

---

[144] Reverend A. D. Gillette, pastor of the Eleventh Baptist Church in Philadelphia. Emily stayed with them when she came to Philadelphia in spring 1845 for her health, and she returned in November. In the parlor of their home, she met Adoniram Judson on Christmas Day 1845. Mr. and Mrs. Gillette became strong friends and supporters; Mrs. Gillette played an important part in getting Emily's outfit together for her life in Burmah.

[145] Emily had invited her sister Catharine to take several terms at the Utica Female Academy and still had some of that cost as outstanding debt.

[146] Emily purchased a home for her parents in Hamilton, New York; at four hundred dollars, she made four yearly payments of one hundred dollars each. In listing the reasons why she should marry Adoniram Judson in January 6, 1846 letters to Anna Maria Anable and her sister Catharine, she said that Judson had promised to take care of her parents and could do so better than she could.

[147] Emily Chubbuck as Fanny Forester. See vol. 1, "Cast of Characters," s.v. "Chubbuck, Emily." Also "Forester, Fanny."

[148] The publishing firm of Bennett, Backus, and Hawley. Mr. Hawley was helpful to Emily in publishing her earlier books.

[149] This eventually became the two-volume series titled *Alderbrook*, which was published in 1847 by Ticknor, Reed and Fields of Boston.

[150] See vol. 1, "Cast of Characters," s.v. "Sheldon, Deacon Asa."

would have been burned for his prophecy if he had lived at Salem.[151] Take warning from my case and don't let any of your girls go away to spend a winter.

I am anxious to hear what aunt U.[152] will say.[153] Keep the matter as whist as possible—there will be a great staring soon.

Love to all, yourself especially,

Emily

Source: A. C. Kendrick, *The Life and Letters of Mrs. Emily C. Judson*, 148–49; Hanna family files.

Emily E. Chubbuck to Catharine Chubbuck, January 21, 1846[154]

Well Kit you do take the [news] of my turning missionary in a mighty [ ] manner. There [ ] no fun about it and I just [know] [you] wouldn't think so if you knew what a state [of] excitement this house has been in for a few [weeks]. [ ] am really in earnest and said the irrevocable yes yesterday. I love the good doctor with all [ ] [heart] and you will love him too when you [ ] him in a different way. As for me, unless [some] unexpected disease should take me off I have no doubt but the sea voyage and the residence in a tropical climate would be the means of pre-serving and prolonging my life. The doctor is as gentle and kind to me as tho I were an infant and I am fully persuaded would take the most tender care of me under all circumstances. I shall die sometime wherever I am; and I have lived and remained unmarried till the family is comfortable and I can make an arrangement by which it may still be so.[155] If I were to marry Willis[156] I might flourish in gay society and be happy *occasionally*, but—not half as happy as with my good doctor. Willis would dress me handsomely and surround me with elegancies, but I sh'd not always be sure of the comforts. You must'nt [*sic*] think that the Dr. chose me because he thought I would make a good missionary—he has seen hundreds and hundreds who would do much better than I; but he loves me and [wants me for] a *wife* and

---

[151] In her letter of January 9, 1846, Anna Maria Anable told Emily that Grandpa Sheldon had predicted, when he heard that Adoniram Judson would be going to Philadelphia, that he and Emily would meet and that they would be smitten with each other.

[152] See vol. 1, "Cast of Characters," s.v. "Nott, Urania Sheldon."

[153] In a letter to Emily on January 20, 1846, Mrs. Nott wrote, "If you can make confidence—perfect confidence—you are safe—but if not—beware—once taken the step can never be retraced. If I were sure you would find your anticipations realized one half as much as I have done—I would say to you—do not falter."

[154] This letter is undated. It is placed on January 21 because she mentions that the day before she had said the "irrevocable yes." This is a reference to Adoniram Judson's letter of January 20, 1846, and duplicates what she said in a January 21 letter to Miss Cynthia Sheldon. The original copy has several large areas covered by ink blots, and this accounts for the large number of letter/word omissions.

[155] Emily still owed some debt on the home she had purchased for her family in Hamilton. When he proposed to her, Adoniram Judson said that he would take care of those matters. Emily listed this as one of his arguments for marriage in her letters of January 6, 1846 to Anna Maria Anable and her sister Catharine.

[156] See vol. 1, "Cast of Characters," s.v. "Willis, Nathaniel Parker."

not a m[ ] missionary. [ ] old man true—fifty seven—but he [ ] people generally imagine sickly. He has [ ] [ ] and so have hundreds of young m[ ] [ ] you wouldn't think of calling sickly, and [ ] [ ] has been so long accustomed to a warm climate that he can't bear our savage winters [ ] [ ] [ ] to live twenty years a [ ] man [ ] [ ]. But if I sh'd chance to outlive [him] there [ ] [ ]—[ ] than getting aboard some [ ] and coming [ ] [ ] board would pay the passage money. Moreover we talk of taking out a servant. I shall try to find some good faithful creature who will go merely because she loves me and take care of my house. Going to Burmah is not what it used to be and since the communication with China vessels are constantly passing and re-passing. Maulmain, the Doct.'s place of residence, belongs to the English and is full of Europeans. Ava where Mr. Kincaid[157] has flourished so much is in possession of the Burmese and of course quite a different affair. The doct. has not deceived me—he has told me the bright side and the dark, and there will be a great many unpleasant things, but, in some shape or other, they will come in all situations of life. I would rather live in a barn with the doctor and have him love me as I am confident he will, than in a palace with Willis and be sometimes petted and sometimes neglected.

As for living at home, mother[158] could'nt [*sic*] expect [ ]. I sh'd [*sic*] probably have [ ] [ ] in the course of [ ] year if I had not met the good doctor for I think I am quite old enough and circumstances would have separated me as much [ ] [ ] as distance will now. And as far as [ ] [ ] ambition is concerned she could'nt [*sic*] wish [ ] [ ] better. I shall be admired all over the country. It [ ] [ ] of an honour [*sic*] let me tell you for a man like [ ] [ ] from the [ ] he has seen and people will [ ] [ ] it so. [ ] this as I would argue for [ ] [ ] [ ] but he [ ] [ ] something more. He is a [ ] [ ] pious and though he sh'd fail to make [ ] [ ] himself, [ ] one could live with him without growing bitter. I have spent a long time in fun and frolicking and now I sh'd like to be a little useful if I can. The truth is with Willis on one side and this best of noble-hearted men on the other—rational and sober usefulness on the right and folly and fashion on the left, I feel pretty much as when first called on— "Choose ye this day whom ye will serve." As for excitement you will find me less excited than anyone else—I have weighed every side of the question and decided

[157] Born in 1797, educated at the seminary in Hamilton, New York, and ordained in 1822, the Reverend Eugenio Kincaid served several churches before being appointed as a missionary to Burmah in February 1830. His first wife died soon after their arrival. His second wife was Barbara McBain, and they were married in 1833. In these years, they served in Rangoon, Ava, Saduja, and Akyab. The Reverend and Mrs. Kincaid returned to the United States in 1843; because of her persistent health problems, they were not reappointed in 1846. While in the United States, Rev. Kincaid became instrumental in the establishment of the University of Lewisberg (later Bucknell University). Upon Mrs. Kincaid's restoration, they returned to Burmah, arriving in February 1851 just as Emily Judson was embarking for her return voyage. With his knowledge of the language and customs, Rev. Kincaid was able to establish himself in work with the Burmese government at Ava. With one more trip home (in 1857, on an official mission for the King of Burmah to President Buchanan of the United States), they retired to Gerard, Kansas, in 1866. Of Rev. Kincaid, the correspondence indicates a man of convictions and occasional independent action.

[158] Emily's mother. See vol. 1, "Cast of Characters," s.v. "Chubbuck, Lavinia Richards."

deliberately—as deliberately as though I had taken two years. We shall probably be married about the first of June and leave home immediately to sail in a month after. You must'nt [sic] lisp a word of this to any one. I am ready to split my sides with laughter when I think of the mighty sensation that it will make. I sh'd like to stay at home long enough to hear all about it. I shall manage some way to have you a nice portrait. The dinner bell has rung.

Written in the right margin of the address page: "One thing to show you that a life in the east is not so very [ ] [ ]. Mr. and Mrs. Hough[159] went [ ] with the [ ] missionaries, but they had [ ] religion [ ] [ ] the mission. They have since become [ ] [ ] but you couldn't induce Mr. and Mrs. H. to return [ ] [ ]. (They like) the east too well. Mr. G.[160] is waiting for my [ ] [ ] [ ] must close. Write the moment you receive this.—Nem."[161]

Written in the left margin of the address page: "P.S. What will the Morrisville old maids and the Hamiltonians and the rest of the people say to my snatching up the lion as soon as he came to P.—What will they?—Soberly, I have but a few more years to live at best and I *should* like to spend them to the best advantage. I shall be home as soon as I can get there. Would start today but for the river."

Source: Hanna Family files.

Adoniram Judson to Emily E. Chubbuck[162] January 25, 1846—Washington, DC

My dearest love,

Thank God, and is it my sweet privilege to commence a letter with such an address—*to you?* You may be sure I had a pleasant ride from Phil. to Baltimore in the cars, sitting at the window, with nobody to disturb the bubbling up of the well-spring of love, "sparkling bright in its liquid light,"[163] or prevent my leisurely

[159] George and Phoebe Hough were the first missionaries to be wholly called by the American Baptist Missionary Union. They worked in Burmah with Adoniram and Ann Judson. They arrived in Burmah in October 1816 and retired from missionary service in 1826; George Hough subsequently worked for the government as an interpreter and school superintendent, and Mrs. Hough worked as an educator. They remained friends with Adoniram Judson and many of the other missionaries. Their independence was problematical for many of the missionaries.

[160] See vol. 1, "Cast of Characters," s.v. "Gillette, The Reverend Abram Dunn."

[161] Emily Chubbuck. See vol. 1, "Cast of Characters," s.v. "Nemmy, Nem, or Nemmy Petty (Nemmie Pettie)." Also the chapter "Names of Endearment."

[162] This letter is the first in a series written by Adoniram Judson between the time of his engagement to Emily E. Chubbuck and the time of their marriage on June 2,1846.

[163] These are lines from a poem by Charles Fenno Hoffman:

> SPARKLING and bright in liquid light,
> Does the wine our goblets gleam in,
> With hue as red as the rosy bed
> Which a bee would choose to dream in.
>
> *Then fill to-night, with hearts as light,*
> *To loves as gay and fleeting*
> *As bubbles that swim on the beaker's brim,*
> *And break on the lips while meeting.*

contrasting the icy new face of the ground with the warm "muddy dew of a woman's dear lips." But at the latter place, we were detained three hours, the train not starting till 8 o'clock, so that I had a tedious cold ride in the evening, and did not reach "Parson Brown's" till 8 o'clock. And then to be thrown among strangers and obliged to rub roughly against the variety of characters to be encountered in a new place—O I wish I was safely stowed away in the loggery[164] of a certain place, south of Utica, or still better, in a snug little cabin bouyant on the blue sea. I have just been exhibited at Parson's Brown's meeting house, and expect to be done again at Parson Samson's this evening, and that I trust will give me the freedom of the city, or at any rate, I intend to take it. I snatch a few minutes after dinner to write you a line, which, they say, must be mailed tonight or it will not reach you tomorrow. Perhaps I shall get a return the next day or the day after, (directed At Rev. O. B. Brown's Washington DC). Your *first letter!* What will be its tenor? What spirit will it breathe? It would be unjust to your truthfulness to doubt that it will be deliciously confirmatory of all those darling little "guess"es,[165] [sic] that have sprung up, like so many tender plants in the hot-bed, which, during the cold winter, we have happily contrived to raise to a tolerable degree of temperature by the steady application of the stream of kisses at bloodheat, and the perpetration of other "innocent blisses." The latter phrase from Wordsworth,[166] but the jingle from Lilla Lilbourne I guess.

But after all, there is a deeper sweetness, and more substantial, permanent happiness, than that of any earthly love,—and blessed be God, we feel and enjoy that too.

> "As down in the sunless retreats of the ocean,
> Sweet flowers are springing no mortal can see,
> So, deep in my heart the still prayer of devotion,
> Unheard by the world, rises silent to Thee—
> Pure, warm, silent to Thee."[167]

---

[164] From A. C. Kendrick, *The Life and Letters of Mrs. Emily C. Judson:* "Emily reached home—'the loggery,' as she playfully styled her father's humble but very comfortable dwelling—the first week in March" (166).

[165] See the proposal letter of Adoniram Judson to Emily E. Chubbuck dated January 20, 1846. Judson had concluded his letter with these words: "Were it not for the sweet indulgences you have kindly allowed me, and blessed understanding that 'love has taught us to guess at,' I should not venture to pray you accept my present, with such a note. Should you cease to 'guess' and toss back the article, saying—'Your watch has lost its charm. It comes back to you, but brings not its wearer with it!' O first smash it to pieces, that it may be an emblem of what will then remain of the heart of Your devoted A. Judson"

[166] From "The Sun Has Long Been Set," by English poet William Wardsworth.

> On such a night of June
> With that beautiful soft half-moon,
> And all these innocent blisses?
> On such a night as this is!

[167] These lines are from a poem, a sacred song to a Haydn tune: "As Down in the Sunless Retreats" by Sir Thomas Moore.

I really have not time to write more and must hastily close saying, dearest, sweetest one—

Yours ever—

A. Judson

Source: Hanna family files.

Adoniram Judson to Emily E. Chubbuck, January 25, 1846[168]— Washington, DC

My dearest Love,

Since closing my last, I have attended evening meetings and had a most interesting time. There was a crowded house, and young Lamson is a truly eloquent preacher. It all passed off well, except that the most appalling praises were poured out on me—so that I felt obliged to get up and disclaim the praise and confess my sins, and beg the people to join me in praying for pardon. But they will not understand me—They will take everything the wrong way, and I cannot help it. As to *you*, I am afraid you will find me out too soon and understand me too well. And perhaps you will go to the other extreme, as is frequently the case, though it would be no more that just retribution, how could I bear to see your scanty sources of happiness in distant Burmah so grievously curtailed? I can only promise to try to alleviate your disappointment by being as kind to you as my poor nature will permit. But I beg you will endeavour to put your happiness on a better foundation than my love. There is, you know, one that loves you infinitely more than I can. His love is unchanging and endless, for with him is no variableness, nor shadow of turning. And when he has once set his love upon a soul, he will ever draw that soul to himself. Have you not found this to be true, from the day you first loved the Saviour, though your love may have been low and dim and subject to occasional fluctuations, or eclipses—yet have you not found that the magnetic influence would never leave you; with it you can truly say:—

> "As true to the star of its worship, though clouded,
> The compass points steadily o'er the dim sea,
> To dark as I rove through this wintry world shrouded,
> The hope of my spirit turns trembling to Thee.[169]
> True, fond, trembling to thee."

Source: Hanna family files.

[168] This is the second letter written by Adoniram Judson to Emily Chubbuck on January 25, 1846. The first was written in the morning; this was written in the evening at the end of the day. An addendum (see January 26, 1846) was written the next evening.

[169] This is a poem/sacred hymn to a Haydn tune written by Sir Thomas Moore titled: "As Down in the Sunless Retreats." The first stanza was quoted in the letter that Adoniram Judson wrote in the morning of January 25, 1846. This poem was added to the letter he wrote that evening, and it is a paraphrase of the second verse.

Adoniram Judson to Emily E. Chubbuck,[170] January 26, 1846

I have spent all day in the Senate and House of Representatives, great curiosities to me, and the evening, in a large party at Mr. Lamson's where I met Dr. Bacon, the president of the college and his lady, and Gov. Marcy, now Secretary of war and his lady, who is, I find, a pious woman and a member of Dr. Welch's church, Albany. Dull formalizing, this,—but really I am so tired in body and mind, that my pen is at fault.

Perhaps I shall get a letter from you tomorrow. Your first letter. I am sure it will be "confirmatory" so—But I shall feel more sure, when I actually get it.

I have been praying for every blessing to rest on you, that I think you need,—especially that your mind may be gradually drawn from every thing [sic] that is *dubious* or *barely good*—to the *better* and the *best*, and that in promising the "more excellent way," you may not be repelled or deterred by the company you may occasionally meet on that way. Christ went about doing good—May it be our glory to imitate his example! And in order to do this, we must do good to the evil and the unthankful. Herein is true glory, as the light of eternity will show—

"My spirit clings to thine, love." So, dear, let me add the next line and remain Thine ever,

A. Judson

Source: Hanna family files.

Emily E. Chubbuck to Miss Cynthia Sheldon, January 26, 1846[171]

My dear Miss C.

Although in very, *very* great haste, settling up some little affairs which must be attended to before I leave, I must drop you a line begging you not to say a word of my engagement to Eliza or Mr. Raymond.[172] Any other secret they can keep better than this and both Doct. J and myself would feel very badly to have it known before it is absolutely necessary. Of course those profs's at Hamilton have no secrets from each other and the Doct. told me the last thing before he went away that he [Note: Written and crossed out is "would rather."] dreaded having them get hold of it more than anybody else. His wife died in August[173] only, and it is

---

[170] This letter was an addendum to Adoniram Judson's second (evening) letter of January 25, 1846.

[171] This letter is undated. It is postmarked January 27, 1846; the "Monday" heading would place it on January 26.

[172] In 1846, Dr. John Howard Raymond was a professor of rhetoric and English language at Madison University. Apparently, Miss Cynthia Sheldon told him very early of the budding relationship and impending engagement of Emily Chubbuck and Adoniram Judson, and Mr. Raymond is frequently mentioned as a source of the information getting into the community, much to the consternation of Emily and Adoniram, who wanted to keep the matter a "secret" for as long as possible. This warning to Miss Sheldon came too late.

[173] Adoniram Judson was to write (as quoted in Courtney Anderson, *To the Golden Shore*, 440) "On the evening of the 31st of August she [Sarah Hall Boardman Judson] appeared to be drawing near to the end of her pilgrimage." He says that he stayed with

really too soon for such *business* as this. I do not think he would have entered into it so soon, but his own observation told him that I would in all probability be lost to him if he delayed.[174] Don't tell anybody out of the house—Mr. Corey,[175] Horace Hawley,[176] nor anybody.

I cannot thank you enough, dear Miss C., for your sympathetic kindness in this matter, especially to mother[177] and Kate.[178] I will remember it when I am at the other side of the earth, my feet pointing towards yours. I should not have thought to ask you to write them, but it was just the thing and has I know been a great comfort to them. You must not forget them when I am gone. Kate takes it much better than I expected, but I am a good deal afraid of the effect on mother. Father[179] is perfectly willing that I sh'd go—the dear good old man! He will feel it the more severely that he cannot talk about it—no one ever understands his feelings. For myself I have got over that whirl of excitement—laughing and crying alternately and together and begin to understand something of my own feelings. Now, with the doctor gone, the decision made, and my mind at rest, I am perfectly happy in my prospects. I shall be obliged to sacrifice a great deal—to deny myself of

her throughout the night, they had some conversation early the next morning [September 1], she asked for one last kiss which they shared, and then "another hour passed, life continued to recede, and she ceased to breathe."

[174] This is a very important statement by Emily E. Chubbuck. Here, she was saying that Adoniram Judson acted precipitously in cementing their relationship, perhaps even before decorum would have allowed it, but he did so because he knew that in the delay he would lose her. This is likely a reference to her relationship with N. P. Willis and his imminent return from England. Certainly, N. P. Willis believed that he and Emily would be married upon his return.

[175] Mr. Corey was the pastor of the Bleecker Street Baptist Church near the Utica Female Academy, and Miss Sheldon and many of the girls from the academy attended worship there. (Cynthis Sheldon, Alma Anable, Deacon Asa and Isabell Sheldon, Edward Bright, and Horace Hawley had been charter members of the church in 1838.) In April 1844, he wrote to Emily expressing dismay that at a school program one of the girls had read a composition justifying dancing as exercise; he spoke of this as a roadblock to the salvation of many. Then, on March 10, 1846, Emily indicated in a letter to Anna Maria that Mr. Corey had been critical of her relationship and impending marriage to Adoniram Judson. Miss Cynthia Sheldon wrote a number of times expressing Mr. Corey's regret and support, and in 1847, there were letters of reconciliation between Emily and Mr. Corey. In spring 1848, letters reveal that Mr. Corey's wife had died of consumption, her condition exacerbated by recent child-birth. She had left behind four children. In July 1849, Anna Maria Anable wrote of his impending marriage to Jane Backus, a good choice for this "rising man." Mr. Corey remained popular with the Sheldon-Anable families even after their move to Philadelphia in 1848. A March 2, 1852, letter from Charles B. Stout told of Mr. Corey's call to the Stanton Street Church in New York City, which Mr. Corey did not accept. Finally, in 1854, there was a pastoral letter from Mr. Corey to Emily on her illness and her possible death. He preached at the Bleecker Street Church as late as January 1867.

[176] Mr. Horace H. Hawley enjoyed a family relationship with the Sheldons; with them he had been in 1838 one of the charter members of the Bleecker Street Baptist Church in Utica. A letter Emily wrote on May 7, 1841 reveals that he was to marry a niece of Misses Cynthia and Urania Sheldon and Mrs. Alma Sheldon Anable, the daughter of their brother John Sheldon. Through the help of Miss Cynthia Sheldon, he was introduced into the life of Emily Chubbuck. A member of a publishing firm, he also worked with Alexander Beebee in publishing the *Baptist Register*. Beginning in 1841 with the publication of *Charles Linn*, Mr. Hawley was enormously helpful to Emily Chubbuck as she was publishing her early stories and books. There are numerous references to his help and his generosity.

[177] Emily's mother. See vol. 1, "Cast of Characters," s.v. "Chubbuck, Lavinia Richards."

[178] Sarah Catharine Chubbuck, "Kate," "Kit," or "Kitty" was Emily's older sister by ten months. Outside of the two terms at the Utica Female Academy, which Emily arranged for her, Catharine always lived at home with her parents in Hamilton, New York. The letters indicate opportunities for marriage, but she, for unknown reasons, remained single. She later helped to care for Henry and Edward Judson after their return from Burmah in fall 1851 when they moved into the Hamilton home with their "aunt" and "grandparents," and she was remembered by them as "dear old Aunt Kate—a dear friend."

[179] Emily's father. See vol. 1, "Cast of Characters," s.v. "Chubbuck, Charles."

luxuries and sometimes comforts, but I would not exchange situations (in prospect) with any person living. I have for the first time for years an approving conscience and I find it a greater comfort than I had imagined. I know that I hav'nt [sic] a single quality which a missionary's wife ought to have; but I will *try* to do my best, and that will be all that is required of me. Some say it will cost me my life—I don't believe it, but life is a short thing at best, and I would rather die there than here. If my health is good and I am free from domestic cares, I can do a great deal of good with my pen; but if I fail to do anything I believe God will regard the *attempt* approvingly. If I were only rich Lydia[180] sh'd go with me and then would'nt [sic] we make the world feel our united efforts? She has just what I lack.

I don't know what to do about returning home. Mr. Gratiot[181] don't [sic] go to Utica at present. I think I shall go to N.Y. in about a week, just as quick as I can get matters arranged here, and wait an opportunity. The doctor is greatly troubled about my going north this cold weather, as he thinks a very slight cold might be the death of me. As he is a bit of a physician I place some confidence in his opinion. But really I have no time to lose. Think of starting off in July and ten thousand things to look after. I am just now settling up with the magazine people, for I suppose I shall not write for them any more [sic]. I shall devote my leisure to preparing the memoir of Mrs. Judson as I wish to do enough of it before I go to secure the copyright and so receive the proceeds.

Written in the right margin of the address page: "The Doct. says he little dreamed when he was at Utica whose house it was, and how nearly his heart ought to grow to it, and he already loves you all very much—you and A.M.[182] especially[183]. And now I think of it I must write a word to A.M. Love to all grandpa, grandma,[184] Mrs. A.,[185] Julia,[186] Sarah Bell[187] and all—much, very *very* much love and gratitude to yourself for all your kindness from

---

[180] See vol. 1, "Cast of Characters," s.v. "Lillybridge, Miss Lydia." Also the timeline "Lydia Lillybridge Simons."

[181] See vol. 1, "Cast of Characters," s.v. "Gratiot, Charles."

[182] See vol. 1, "Cast of Characters," s.v. "Anable, Miss Anna Maria."

[183] Sometime earlier, probably in November after meetings in New York, Adoniram Judson passed through Utica and met with Miss Sheldon and others within the household and school.

[184] See vol. 1, "Cast of Characters," s.v. "Sheldon, Deacon Asa."

[185] Alma Sheldon Anable was the sister of Miss Cynthia Sheldon and Urania Sheldon Nott. Genealogy sources show that she married Joseph Hubbell Anable in Troy, New York on July 28, 1814, and that it was the second marriage for Mr. Anable. Born in 1773, he was forty-one at the time of the marriage, and Alma was likely considerably younger. He died in 1831, which explains why Alma Anable and her family lived and worked first at the Utica Female Seminary and then later at the Misses Anable's School in Philadelphia. Joseph and Alma Anable were the parents of nine children: Henry Sheldon Anable (b. June 21, 1815); William Stewart Anable (b. November 6, 1816); Anna Maria Stafford Anable (b. September 30, 1818), Cynthia Jane Anable (b. January 28, 1820); Samuel Low Anable (b. November 28, 1821); Harriet Isabella Anable, also known as Hatty or Hattie (b. December 18, 1823); Courtland Wilcox Anable (b. July 28, 1825); Frances Alma Anable, or Fanny (b. April 12, 1828); and Mary Juliet Anable (b. February 18, 1830).

[186] See vol. 1, "Cast of Characters," s.v. "Look, Julia."

[187] See vol. 1, "Cast of Characters," s.v. "Wheeler, Miss Sarah Bell."

"Yours most affectionately,

"Emily Chubbuck"

Source: Hanna family files.

Emily E. Chubbuck to Adoniram Judson[188] January 26, 1846

My very *very* dear friend,

The postman has just brought in a letter which must be re-mailed and I cannot resist the little temptation of saying one word to you. Your sweet note of farewell I held long to my lips, and the kiss I sent down into my heart and here it is snuggling in the warmest cradle that ever little fellow had. It was *so* kind of you to remember me just at that last moment! I wonder if you feel as lonely as I do, and if you think of me and love me as much as when you were here. I wonder if you pray for me *earnestly*—I am afraid that I shall lose even my slight inclination to "be good" now you are away. Pray God for me constantly, dearest.

I read some in Catherine Adorna[189] yesterday and find it very fascinating. But do you suppose persons can really attain to that state of grace which her biographer thinks she did?

I don't know what to say to you about going home. Miss Sheldon[190] says in a letter rec'd today that the thermometer ranges from six to sixteen below zero and she dare not have me come. I shall wait a little and be governed by the weather. In the meantime, I am very very lonely. I kiss first the dear little *hymn-book* that you gave me (your first present, dearest) and then the charmed watch and then to the book again. The watch stays next my heart[191] [*sic*] and I wish I could put the chain over your neck. I wouldn't care who looked in at the window—not I. It was a very naughty thing of you to stay and teach me to love you so much, and then go away away [*sic*] and leave me. Well, I will be revenged in some way yet—play F. F.[192] maybe and disgrace you. Oh, you should have taken Mrs. Jenkins—who believes in *unselfish* love—that is, if she can be quite sure that it don't [*sic*] interfere with her doctrine of atonement.

I think of you away off there among those strangers, and pity you most heartily—but even in the *midst* of my pity there comes up a vision of your *rueful*

---

[188] This is the first letter from Emily E. Chubbuck to Adoniram Judson in the period between their engagement in January 1846 and their marriage in June 1846. It is undated. Adoniram Judson answered this letter and a letter from January 28 on January 30. However, when Adoniram Judson responded on January 30, he spoke of it being written on Monday and mailed on Tuesday, so it apparently was written the same day as the letter to Miss Cynthia Sheldon and mailed with it on Tuesday.

[189] Catherine Adorna was a saint of the medieval church, and a number of biographies were written about her. Apparently, Emily has been reading such a biography, perhaps even at the suggestion of Adoniram Judson.

[190] See vol. 1, "Cast of Characters," s.v. "Sheldon, Miss Cynthia."

[191] See the letter of Adoniram Judson to Emily E. Chubbuck dated January 20, 1846.

[192] Emily Chubbuck as Fanny Forester. See vol. 1, "Cast of Characters," s.v. "Chubbuck, Emily," also "Forester, Fanny."

face when somebody who had heard of your mother's fiftieth cousin claims acquaintanceship and I must laugh. But I do wish that I could shield you by carrying you off into the *dining room*.

I should like to put my two arms over your neck or lay my head in your bosom, and feel the presence of your dear lips. It will be a long, long time and I shall forget how to love you. Just put on your sailor's gear and come back to Philadelphia for a minute. If you were only with me, dearest, I sh'd be happier than I have been in years. I dare not look at my future much more than at first, but I trust myself to my God and you—the heavenly Friend who is all powerful, and the earthly one who would not deceive me, who loves me I know most unselfishly—and I feel perfectly secure. I thank God for sending me your priceless affection. I cannot become worthy of it, but dear, dear doctor, you shall teach and guide me and I will do the best I can. I can love you at least, and will.

I kiss your eye-lids down darling, for it is late and you must sleep. If only I had your head in my lap. Heaven guard you—so prays your

Emily

Written in the top margin of page 1: "As I am anxious you shall get a wondrous high opinion of me I will enclose a notice of *Trippings* from the *Columbian Magazine*."[193]

Source: A. C. Kendrick, *The Life and Letters of Mrs. Emily C. Judson*, 151; Hanna family files.

Mr. James B. Colgate[194] to Emily E. Chubbuck, January 27, 1846— New York

Dear Miss Chubbuck—

I have the pleasure to acknowledge the receipt of your form of 26th inst. making inquiry as to Mary's whereabouts.

Sister Mary[195] left here about a month since for Norfolk, making some stay on her way there in [ ] [ ]. She is now in N. and is not expected to return before March. I know that she will most regret not having the pleasure of a visit from you.

Sister Sarah says though her acquaintance is but slight yet she will venture to extend to you a cordial visitation for you to tarry with them as good old Father Peck[196] says—if you can come [ ] [ ] [ ] [ ]—she will do all that lays in her power

---

[193] *Trippings in Author-land* was released by the publisher on November 22, 1845. This was a collection of her stories from the magazines for which Fanny Forester had written.

[194] James Colgate was the second of three sons born to William Colgate (of soap manufacturing fame) and Mary Gilbert Colgate.

[195] Mary Colgate is likely a daughter of William and Mary Colgate and a sister to James Colgate. Yet another sister, Sarah, is mentioned in the next paragraph.

to render your visit as interesting as circumstances will admit—Father is now in Norfolk—he expects to leave there [ ] evening and will be in Phila in the course of a day or so. Perhaps you could make it convenient to come on with him. He will [ ] first note hence; should he make any stay in Phil he will put up at Done's Hotel. At most any other time it would have given both wife and myself great pleasure to have had you make our house your home but circumstances are such now as to render such an idea out of our power.

We have been perusing this evening "Rug Raffles"[197]—and have found his acquaintance extremely interesting.—we were saying that it was fortunate this story fell into such good hands.

Wife is by my side and desires me to give her best love.[198] Elizabeth[199] returned a few minutes since, and wishes me to present hers also—in haste please accept the respects of your sincere friend

James Colgate

Source: American Baptist Historical Society, AJ 24, no. 1212.

Emily E. Chubbuck to Adoniram Judson, January 28, 1846

My dearest, dearest friend,

Oh, I am so, *so* miserable! At one moment I wish you here, and the next I am glad you are away, but in my own *reckless* unhappiness I sh'd *pain* you as I did once last week. Oh, it will prove a sad, sad thing to you ever to have loved me. I was

---

[196] The Reverend Doctor Solomon Peck was for twenty years the executive secretary of the American Baptist Missionary Union. Many believed him to be hard, stern, and judgmental, and from some of his comments, it is easy to understand that perception. Dr. Peck and Emily did not always have the easiest of relationships. She felt in him the judgment that came from many in the church at the announcement of her impending marriage to Adoniram; that judgment concerned her "secular" past and concern that she was not an appropriate companion for the venerable missionary. On July 18, 1849 Emily wrote a blistering letter of defense to Dr. Peck in response to a letter from him of February 20, 1849; her letter framed how she viewed his perception of her, and her response was meant to set the record straight. There are eleven letters in the collection from Solomon Peck to Emily.

[197] This is one of Fanny Forester's stories from the magazines. It later appeared in vol. 2 of *Alderbrook*. Its first paragraph reads:

Sovereigns of the olden time had their jesters; and the 'sovereign people' on this side the water have revived the fashion, with several other useful things dug up from the rubbish of the past. Every circle constituting a court, every individual of which is a king, has its 'queer genius;' and every little village has its privileged quizzer, its regularly installed jester. It is this important personage who goes about at night changing signs; leaving the barber's pole at the door of the merchant most renowned for shaving; putting 'turning' on the county Surrogate's office, and 'fancy goods' on the young ladies' seminary. The same enterprising gentleman pastes a little slip of white paper of the M, when the hand-bills announce that there is to be a *mass meeting*; sews up the top of his bed-fellow's hose; rings door-bells on his way home from a pleasant spree at midnight; and imitates most successfully the inarticulate language of every animal, from the tremulously vain crow of the novice cock, up to the roar of the infuriated bull! Oh, what a terror the humor-loving wight is to adventurous children and housemaids in search of recreation!

[198] James Colgate was married to S. Ellen Hoyt, and they had one son, William. Ellen Hoyt Colgate died a tragic death, which was mentioned in a letter from Miss Cynthia Sheldon to Emily C. Judson dated November 26, 1847.

[199] Ellen Hoyt Colgate had a sister, Elizabeth, who had been a favored student of Emily's ("one of my best") at the Utica Female Academy. Elizabeth died tragically in 1849 of the same disease that had claimed her sister Ellen Hoyt Colgate.

---

born for no good, I am sure. I do, dear doctor, the more I try not, I do make my friends very unhappy.

Your kind letter first written was last rec'd. Mr. Robarts[200] bro't one this morning, and about an hour ago the one I sh'd have rec'd long ago came accompanied by one from Gen. Morris[201] and two from Mr. Willis.[202] He is on his way home by this time—was to have sailed in a packet some time after the 18th accompanied by his little daughter and an uncle and aunt of hers. These letters, my dear friend, have pained me more than I can tell. You speak confidently of my "truthfulness," little knowing the cutting sarcasm there is in the word, so applied. I do love you with my whole heart—*You* have no right to accuse me of falsehood, but he has. His letters are in reply to a couple of mine and he says "while my life last I shall draw what sweetness you will permit from the *soul's well* within you. It is the assurance in your letter that this bountiful spring is open to me which made me last night so happy."[203] You may well believe, my excellent friend, that this was not written, and I faultless. Indeed I have given Mr. Willis every cause to believe that I loved him. I have said for a thousand times frankly as I would have said it to Anna Maria[204]— not weighing my words, and not caring what meaning was attached to them. The peculiar relation in which we stood to each other, the pride which he seemed to take in me, and the implicit confidence reposed in his nobleness of gesture, however perverted it might have been by circumstances, his generous conduct—everything combined made my words true when I told him that he was dearer to me than any other person on earth. There was a kind of poetical fascination thrown around our friendship, and he seemed to have won a right to a knowledge of all my thoughts by the interest he had taken in the development of what he is pleased to call my genius; and so I must confess to you that I have been more unguarded in my expressions than under other circumstances would have been consistent even with delicacy, I fear. I treated him coldly when I saw him in comparison with my treatment of you, *very coldly*,[205] but my letters are most objectionable things; and my respect for you, (to say nothing of a warmer feeling) my jealousy of your honour leads me to assure you that I never can be more to you than I am now while those letters are in existence.[206] Can you understand me? Can

[200] See vol. 1, "Cast of Characters," s.v. "Robarts, Mr. and Mrs. W. S."

[201] See vol. 1, "Cast of Characters," s.v. "Morris, General George."

[202] See vol. 1, "Cast of Characters," s.v. "Willis, Nathaniel Parker."

[203] See the letter of N. P. Willis to Emily E. Chubbuck dated December 17, 1845.

[204] See vol. 1, "Cast of Characters," s.v. "Anable, Miss Anna Maria."

[205] On May 15, 1845, N. P Willis wrote to Emily. "Your exterior is certainly far too cold, and had I met you without first knowing you as I do, I should have set you down for an unsympathising and unapproachable ascetic."

[206] Long before meeting Adoniram Judson, Emily had asked N. P. Willis to return the letters she had written to him. In a letter to Emily dated May 15, 1845, N. P. Willis acknowledged that she wanted her letters returned and said that he was not inclined to do so as they had been put aside for his daughter, a file of "my recognition of your genius and of your instant sympathy and friend-

you see how writing the most affectionate letters to Mr. W. while his wife was living and before I had seen him—addressing him as a spirit of good which I was bound to reverence, I was betrayed into keeping up the same tone afterwards? The only change was, tho, romance gave way to something like reality, though not like the sweet love I bear to you. While I live I shall have a peculiar interest in everything that relates to Mr. Willis—stronger probably than in any man living, except the one in whose heart I rest, but believe me, I never, never could think of being his wife. I did not think whether I could or not when I wrote him, and did not wait to consider the construction that must naturally be put upon my letters nor their probable tendency. My only thought was to express earnest heart-warm feelings, and make a desolate heart happy. I did not express more than I felt (for I recollect that the news of his being attacked by a brain-fever occasioned nearly a fortnight's illness) but—dear doctor, I wish I could throw open my heart to you and let you read it, for I cannot make the subject clear in words. Pity me, dearest, if you cannot comprehend. This thing makes me the more wretched that I can do nothing to extricate myself. If he were in London I might write—if he were in N. Y. I would go there, but I must wait patiently the movements of a slow-sailing packet; and I feel as tho I was wronging both of you every moment. My silence under these circum-stances is falsehood to him, and a species of dishonour to you. Don't you pity me? Or are you beginning to feel something like contempt? My head and heart are both aching terribly and I must get rest for one at least. Would you let me lean it against you if you are here?

I am not wearing the charmed watch today[207]—it seems a thing too holy. It has rested with those worthy of you and ought not to be in my hands. Dear doctor, let me say to you now what I have said before, if your judgement and affections do not both approve the choice you have made (made when you knew so very little of me) say it to me and be free. No one shall ever know the cause or know anything that has passed between us. And farther, I promise always to remember that you *have* loved me; and act accordingly. I will not go back to gay society, or do anything that could pain you if you sh'd know of it. Do you take it all back?

Take my letter, dearest of friends, to Him in whom you trust, your Guide in all things and lay it before him and do not retire until you are certain of his will. I have been there to ask wisdom, but even in time of trial I cannot pray. I am afraid

---

ship." Now, Emily feared that these letters contained information and expressions that could be misrepresented if made public, bringing significant harm to Emily and Adoniram's future together and casting a long shadow of judgment about Adoniram Judson's work and, indeed, the mission movement itself. In future letters, Emily asked for them again when Willis returned. At first, he refused her request, but apparently, he relented, for Emily sent Adoniram a letter not long before their departure for Burmah telling him that Mr. Willis had returned the correspondence. In 1860, when A. C. Kendrick asked N. P. Willis for the let-ters as he wrote *The Life and Letters of Mrs. Emily C. Judson*, Willis simply said that he could not locate them. Emily obviously had destroyed those letters, and they likely would have told us much more about her.

[207] See the letter of Adoniram Judson to Emily E. Chubbuck dated January 20, 1846. Also the letter of Emily Chubbuck to Adoniram Judson dated January 25, 1846.

that my religion does not come from the heart; and if not I cannot say from where—I am sure there is little of it in my words or actions. My character is a complete riddle to myself and the more I try to explain it to you, the darker I shall make it I fear. You must read for yourself, but dear, dear doctor, whatever you think in other respects, do not doubt the sincerity of my conduct towards you. I have tried to be sincere, I have *tried* to make you understand everything about me; and if you were too kind to do it,—it surely was not my fault. I do love you—a sweet confiding love which makes me very happy—not "passionately and overwhelmingly" as in the prophecy I showed you one day my capabilities are set forth—but I know it is a deeper truer love than I ever felt before.

I have just reread your dear, sweet, unsuspecting letter. Oh, I wish most heartily we were in that little cabin—"a dear little isle of our own" it would be to us.[208] I should feel more worthy of your affection there than here with all these surroundings. What will you do with me, my beloved one? Write as soon as you can and let me know, and even then, if you promise to be my guide, I shall not feel quite secure till I disentangle myself from this other affair. If I could see you but one half hour tonight it would be a relief to me. It seems to me that you would say something to take away this oppressive night-mare feeling—would you, darling?

I have written you a most comfortless letter. You will break the seal with a smile and then the chill that will fall upon your heart! I would have saved you the pain of knowing when I was unhappy, but I have been guided in what I have written by what I thought to be right. I do not ask you to pray for me—I know you will do it. Remember how much wisdom I need—how much faith—how much love to God—how much moral courage—how much of everything. Think kindly of me, dearest—best of men, and be assured of the unchanging affection of

Yours sincerely,

E. Chubbuck

Source: Hanna family files.

Mrs. Urania Sheldon Nott to Emily E. Chubbuck, January 29, 1846[209]

[Note: This is a letter fragment.] me. Our term closes in three weeks from Thursday last—and it is barely possible that the Doct.[210] will be obliged to go to New York—but I do not think he will—you will let me know if you intend to protract your stay so long—(which I do not think you will) and we will bring you

[208] See Adoniram Judson's first letter to Emily dated January 25, 1846.

[209] This is an undated letter fragment. Because it speaks of the matter of Emily's return from Philadelphia to Utica and Hamilton, we place it on January 29.

[210] See vol. 1, "Cast of Characters," s.v. "Nott, The Reverend Doctor Eliphalet."

up—there is however no reliance upon us—and I hope you will come up before. Write me when you decide, and we will meet you at the cars. Remember me affectionately to Mr. Gillette[211] and family.

And believe me ever yours,
Affectionally
Urania E. Nott

Source: American Baptist Historical Society, AJ 25, no. 1231.

Adoniram Judson to Emily E. Chubbuck,[212] January 30, 1846— Washington, DC

My sweetest Love,

What have I done to deserve such a kind, affectionate, loving letter from your dear hand and heart—date unknown (you careless girl) but Monday, I suppose, though not mailed till Tuesday.[213] I did expect another letter last evening, but the mails seem to be not well served in these parts.

And so you think "it was a very naughty thing"[214]—And was it you yourself, my darling, that could fancy it not a naughty, but a very good and wise and manly thing, for me to hold still, under the fascinations of your eyes and face and voice, like the simple bird under the spell of the rattlesnake, and not grapple with the foe and deal back spell for spell? No, no, I only wish that I had the naughty thing to do over again—and I will, if I live—there is any virtue left in the "black horse," and you will let me. And then will I not clasp your dear form in a closer hug, and glue my lips to yours in more commingling contact, and look into your eyes with more soul-absorption, that ever before? But O, I perceive that the charge of naughtiness lies chiefly in "and then go away and leave me." Sweet confession! Let me wrap it up in the inner folds of my heart, as some antidote to the pain of absence.

Thus far I had written, when your almost fatal letter of the 28th came in. But I clasp you to my bosom and my heart with warmer affection than ever. I say "almost fatal," on account of one sentence only:—"my respect for you (to say nothing of a warmer feeling) and my jealousy of your honor, lead me to assure you, *that I never*

---

[211] See vol. 1, "Cast of Characters," s.v. "Gillette, The Reverend Abram Dunn."

[212] For background information, see Emily's letters dated January 25, 1846, and January 28, 1846. The first section of this letter is in response to the former; he acknowledges that he had started the letter, then left off, and picked it up again with his receipt of the letter of January 28. This second half, considering what Emily was feeling and expressing, is a studied response in calm observance. It manifests the deep abiding faith of Adoniram Judson in application to every human situation and his loving, tender pastoral and personal response to her deep expression of angst.

[213] This is Emily's letter to Adoniram written January 26, 1846.

[214] Emily wrote, "It was a very naughty thing of you to stay and teach me to love you so much and then go away, away and leave me."

can be more to you than I am now, while those letters are in existence!" Cannot you take back that sentence dearest, by return of mail, (addressed to the "care Of Mr. Archibald Thomas Richmond, Va" etc.)? Cannot you say, dearest, that you will have me, *come what will?* As I am ready and do now and ever say concerning you.

I am too well versed in affairs of the heart in the case of both sexes, not to understand well all the windings of that affair, that you labored to make intelligible and yet fear will become darker from your very attempts to elucidate. Cannot you say to W[215] that you have loved with every feeling of gratitude, esteem and admiration, with indeed every sentiment of love, but one; that your expressions have been so unguarded, as to lead him, not unjustly, to infer that one also; that your only apology is, that you were not distinctly aware of the want of that sentiment, in your regard to him, because not well aware of its nature until you learnt it from a later acquaintance? But it is nonsense for me to attempt to aid female resource. And I make the suggestion above, chiefly to show you, that I understand the case. Did you not see how deeply I felt, when you showed me W's letter on Monday of the first week of love? From perusing that letter and learning that you had written him, since receiving it and hearing you say, that you would be unwilling to have me see your letters, I saw the whole at a single glance. There is indeed nothing new, nothing really heart-rendering in yours before me, but the one sentence quoted above. Do, dearest, take that back, and it is all well. "Contempt"? Don't pray write such a word. I see nothing in your intercourse with W, discreditable to your head or heart,—only as indication of a low state of religious feeling, in that you could have felt quite so kindly towards one of his moral character, was according to the most favorable construction you put upon it. "Take it all back"? [*sic*] Never, till reason is lost in insanity, or the heart's blood ceases to flow. "Would you let me lean"? etc.— Why, you ask such extraordinary questions, that I am almost tempted to think your love to me is but small, in that you judge my love by your own and that I could be with you by day and by night to hold your aching head and comfort your troubled heart.

In the present state of things, I resolve to go no further than Richmond. I would not even go there, but I have unfortunately committed myself by letter, to a series of meetings. And what is worse—the Baltimore ministers saying that I passed them by, came on yesterday, and induced a promise from me, that I would give them several meetings on my return from the south. How can I face the meetings in these two large cities, with the "night-mare" on my soul? Perhaps, dearest, you

---

[215] This is a reference to Nathaniel Parker Willis, Emily's mentor, friend, advocate, and guide. As editor of the *New Mirror*, he had "discovered" Fanny Forester, and his advocacy had catapulted her to fame. Emily thought herself to be in love with him, and her letter dated January 28 is filled with guilt and self-recrimination over what she had felt and how she had expressed her feelings to Willis in her correspondence.

will drive it away in your next. I know you can. And I will daily pray God to assist in driving away that which oppresses you.

Will you allow me to preach a word—I said above—"indication of a low state"—you are a child of God. In that view, it was wrong, and your conscience told you so, to be on *such* terms with *such* a man as W. Regard your present trouble, as a kind chastisement from your heavenly Father, for having swerved a little from the straight path. Look up to him *penitently*, and you will not have to say "in time of trial I cannot pray." You will find the throne of grace accessible, he will help you to come out of this trouble with a grateful, joyful heart, and you shall shine brighter for it, to all eternity. Pray do not hesitate to view the "charmed watch."[216] Do wear it for my sake and believe me-your entirely devoted friend and lover—

A Judson

Source: Hanna family files.

Emily E. Chubbuck to Adoniram Judson, January 30, 1846[217]

I take another scrap of paper to tell you that I shall not go to N.Y. till I hear of the arrival of Mr. Willis,[218] as I wish to see him particularly so I can *say* things that I cannot write, and I don't fancy telling him any more [*sic*] than I find necessary.

I hope I have not made you unhappy by my letter.[219] If I could show you the two he sent me you wouldn't wonder that I feel some remorse of conscience. A flirtation may be consistent with the character of a Fanny Forester,[220] but not the chosen bride of *the* missionary; and however innocently, I have encouraged him to love me, I will not write any more [*sic*], but that you may better understand the whole, allow me to enclose to you the little letter which—ought I to share it—the pretty lock and all.[221] Well, not the signature then. Do you wonder that all this is distressing since you have loved me? My lips have not taken the kiss[222]—they could not. Please return the note when you write. Adieu.—

Source: Hanna family files.

---

[216] See the letter of Adoniram Judson to Emily E. Chubbuck dated January 20, 1846, and Emily's letter to Adoniram of January 25, 1846.

[217] This letter is undated. We place it on January 30, 1846, because it seems to be a follow-up to her letter of January 28, 1846 and because Adoniram Judson quoted a part of it in his reply of February 3.

[218] See vol. 1, "Cast of Characters," s.v. "Willis, Nathaniel Parker."

[219] See the letter of Emily E. Chubbuck to Adoniram Judson dated January 28, 1846. The arrival of two letters from N. P. Willis precipitated this letter filled with her guilt and angst over her actions and the relationship with Willis.

[220] Emily Chubbuck as Fanny Forester. See vol. 1, "Cast of Characters," s.v. "Chubbuck, Emily," also "Forester, Fanny."

[221] The enclosure is the letter of N. P. Willis to Emily E. Chubbuck dated December 31, 1845.

[222] N. P. Willis closed his letter of December 31, 1845 with the line: "I will bite a kiss where my signature should be."

Emily E. Chubbuck to Adoniram Judson,[223] January 31, 1846

My own best-beloved,

I was ill in bed all day yesterday or I should have written you; and in that *slight* illness my heart clung to you—oh, *so* fondly! Strange that I should think of you, a comparative stranger, in preference to those who have loved and cared for me for many years. Oh, doctor, dear, you *must* love me, whatever wise things that judgement of yours may say; for there is no poet that could very well be trusted to make a second version of "Love lies bleeding" after your favourite [*sic*].

Mrs. Gillette[224] had a party on Thursday evening at which I was, of course, bound to exert myself to shine a little; and having taken a walk in the wet before evening came on, I found myself on the sick list by the time the guests were gone. I have quite recovered, however, today; and made a vow to be more careful. I saw Doctor Lyon, Mrs. Jewell's brother, at the party for the first time; and he flourished more like the gay New Yorkers than anyone I have met before in this sober quaker [*sic*] city. He professed the greatest reverence for genius, and then turned and complimented me so violently that I was fain to beg him show his reverence in the usual way, as we new-world people wor-shipped less clamorously than the orientals [*sic*]. He is a queer genius and I hardly know what to make of him. I fancy *him* something of a scape-grace, notwithstanding the perfect confidence he seems to inspire other people with. I have troubled you with all this because he has offered to go and take me home.[225] He says his time hangs heavily on his hands, and it would be a pleasant trip for him. I don't know whether to accept the offer or not. Mr. G[226] thinks it would be perfectly right and proper, and I am so very anxious to go that sometimes it seems very foolish to hesitate. But on the other hand I don't

---

[223] There are two versions of this letter: the original as written by Emily E. Chubbuck and the edited version published by Dr. A. C. Kendrick in his biography, *The Life and Letters of Mrs. Emily C. Judson.* Additions made by Dr. Kendrick are in parentheses, and words in the original left out by Dr. Kendrick have been added in bold. There are significant changes and omissions. In a note in his book, Dr. Kendrick explained that interest, purpose and propriety sometimes led to these changes and exclusions, "I remark here that in giving Miss Chubbuck's letters, I do not always indicate unimportant omissions. Real letters must always contain much which should not meet the public eye; and Emily's were real letters, dashed off hastily amidst pressing cares and duties. Written also after the exhausting labors of the day, they by no means do uniform justice to her epistolary powers." He later added, "In giving a few extracts from his and Miss Chubbuck's correspondence at this time, I have no wish to minister to a prurient curiosity, nor to violate that principle which would generally place letters written during the period of an 'engagement' under the shelter of inviolate secrecy."

[224] See vol. 1, "Cast of Characters," s.v. "Gillette, Mrs. Hannah."

[225] With all of the preparations to be made by July 1 when they were to sail for Burmah, Emily was anxiously looking for ways to return to Utica and Hamilton, New York. Because of her frail health, she looked for someone with whom she could travel, and that is mentioned a number of times over the next several weeks before she left on February 17. In her January 26 letter to Adoniram Judson, Emily had quoted Miss Cynthia Sheldon that temperatures in Utica were six to sixteen below zero and that it would be folly for her to go back to such devastating cold.

[226] See vol. 1, "Cast of Characters," s.v. "Gillette, The Reverend Abram Dunn."

care to be indebted to a man that I have but little respect for, and I am very certain that Doct. Lyon has more kindness of heart than principle. He is to leave the country in so short a time, however, (two or three weeks) that he could not be a troublesome acquaintance; and I can't imagine how any harm can result from accepting his services. I submit the matter to your superior judgment. I have concluded not to stop in N. Y. as Mary Colgate is not to be home before March, and her brother's family where I usually visit are troubled just now with sickness.[227]

I wrote you, dear doctor, when very much excited a couple of days ago;[228] and I fear such a letter as I ought not to have written. Forgive everything, please do, that was inconsiderate about it—I didn't mean to pain you—I only tried to be sincere. It is a very unpleasant thing—the peculiar predicament in which I find myself—but I looked all on one side when I wrote you. I never should have considered myself bound in any way to Mr. W[229] if I had not met with you; and he might have brought home a wife without my dreaming of any wrong in it. I did love him, however; but it was at first (before I had seen him) as I would love an angel; and afterwards a mixture of pity, sympathy with his beautifully poetical nature, gratitude, admiration—"So handsome yet so sorrowful"—so full of a patronising sort of flattery (women don't dislike patronage)—such fascinating manners—so apparently proud of me—do you wonder? I called him "papa" as he bade me and "brother"—and never hesitated to say that I loved him with all my heart. Now do you see how perfectly consistent this is with another love? As much so as that I bear my—[Note: The sentence ends here.]

I have just stopped to read your dear, sweet, kind, beautiful letter. Oh, you are *so* good! If you were only here, dear dear doctor! But you mustn't come till you have accomplished everything you wish—not a day sooner on my account.[230] I will keep a warm heart for you and a cheerful one too, for I think I shall get through all these little difficulties very wisely. I cannot take back, quite, what I have said about the letters for I *must* get them. I am not afraid that *he* will use them to my disadvantage but his biographer might. The whole taken together I think would explain themselves, but they would never be used

---

[227] See the letter from James Colgate to Emily E. Chubbuck dated January 27, 1846.

[228] See the letter of Emily E. Chubbuck to Adoniram Judson dated January 28, 1846.

[229] See vol. 1, "Cast of Characters," s.v. "Willis, Nathaniel Parker."

[230] On January 30, 1846, Adoniram Judson wrote of his plans: "In the present state of things, I resolve to go no further than Richmond. I would not even go there, but I have unfortunately committed myself by letter, to a series of meetings. And what is worse—the Baltimore ministers saying that I passed them by, came on yesterday, and induced a promise from me, that I would give them several meetings on my return from the south. How can I face the meetings in these two large cities, with the 'night-mare' on my soul?"

so. I must have them at any rate, but I apprehend no little difficulty in getting them. Of course he values them.[231]

Mr. Willis writes in one of his last letters, "If you should ever be placed in circumstances to call it forth, the world will find that there is stuff for a heroine hidden behind your partial development by literature." I fancy he will think my playing the heroine sooner than he expected. That Burmah is a great bug-bear. Mr. Wallace[232] continues to be "alarmed." He wonders, if people will be missionaries, that they don't select "some decent place."

Let me banish the night-mare, dearest.[233] How can I do it? By telling you how entirely my heart rests on yours? How very sweet your expressions of affection are? And how love for you brightens up the strange future? Can I do it by telling you that I am *all* your own, to teach and guide and *pet* too (don't forget that). Then go into the meetings with a light heart; but don't let them wear you out. Be very careful, for recollect that you have added another to your *responsibilities*, more dependent than either of them—than even your children. I am longing to see you, but if you can do any good by just showing your face, I sh'd be very wicked indeed to try to prevent it. And it will be only a little while—the "Loggery" shall be all ready for you,[234] and then—but don't promise yourself too much. I shall be at liberty then to behave just as badly as I choose, for you will have gone too far to retract. Oh! Such a life as I will lead you!

Mr. Gillette saw a portrait of you painted by Pratt in Mr. Sully's studio a few days ago. Mr. Sartain[235] was engraving it. Mr. G says that it is a good likeness, except that it makes the face too thin; and Mr. S. will engrave it beautifully. They tried to sketch you at the meetings here, but your were so

---

[231] It is a great loss not to have any of Emily's correspondence with N. P. Willis. In some letters, there is only a glimpse of what she might have said because he quoted from her letters. At the time of her engagement to Adoniram Judson, Emily suffered enormous pangs of guilt and anxiety, and she asked Willis to return all of her letters, believing that material in them would be an embarrassment to the great missionary and his new wife if it ever saw the public light. Writing to Judson on February 6 she said, "Why sh'd I wish the letters returned if they were not inconsistent with my new relations? Did I not tell you that it was jealousy for your honour which induced me? What has your honor to do with a common friendship? I tell you 'honestly' (not for the first time I believe) that I have given Mr. W. cause to believe that I loved him, and quite honestly that *I never gave a thought to the construction that might be put upon my letters till I examined the subject with the eyes which love for you had given me.*" At first, Willis refused her request, but apparently, he relented, for Emily sent Adoniram a letter not long before their departure for Burmah telling him that Mr. Willis had returned the correspondence. In 1860, when A. C. Kendrick asked N. P. Willis for them as he wrote *The Life and Letters of Mrs. Emily C. Judson*, Willis simply said that he could not locate them. Emily obviously had destroyed those letters, and they likely would have told us much more about her.

[232] See vol. 1, "Cast of Characters," s.v. "Wallace, Mr."

[233] See the letter of Adoniram Judson to Emily E. Chubbuck dated January 30, 1846. In that letter, he wrote, "How can I face the meetings in these two large cities, with the 'night-mare' on my soul? Perhaps, dearest, you will drive it away in your next. I know you can. And I will daily pray God to assist in driving away that which oppresses you."

[234] The loggery was Emily's father's home. See Kendrick, *The Life and Letters of Mrs. Emily C. Judson*, 166. See also Adoniram Judson's letter to Emily of January 25, 1846, where he mentions his desire to be there with her.

[235] John Sartain was one of the most prominent engravers of the mid-nineteenth century. His works appeared in prominent magazines and books. In 1846, he created an engraving of Emily E. Chubbuck that was used as a plate for *Alderbrook*. The correspondence of spring 1846 reflects meetings with Mr. Sartain on changes thought to be needed. In 1849, Mr. Sartain was publishing a magazine because a letter makes a reference to one of Emily's poems being in it.

perverse as always to get in a bad light—please write by return mail and tell me that the "night-mare" is dissolved—whether I shall let Doct. Lyon take me home, and whatever else your wisdom or *lack of wisdom* may suggest. Most lovingly yours—

Emily

Written in the left and top margins[236] of page 1: **"My intercourse with W. did not 'bring about'** (It was not this which brought about) a low state of religious 'feeling'[237]—the declension in religion came first; and I believe, as I now look back, that it was occasioned by the wish to show people I was not the saint they supposed. You know I carry something of a serious face—I had written a little for the *Register*[238] and some of my books for children brought me credit for qualities that I did not possess. When I was a pupil in Miss Sheldon's school[239] I was nicknamed (affectionately of course) the 'little saint.' And—I found people thought I had so much religion I came to the conclusion that I had none at all; and so went about to convince others of it. I know it was wrong; but however agreeable flattery may be, it is painful to be praised for such things. You must watch over me now and not let me take the first step in wrong; and may God in Heaven watch over you, my dearest friend." (See Appendix for sample of original letter.)

Source: A. C. Kendrick, *The Life and Letters of Mrs. Emily C. Judson,* 151–52; Hanna family files.

Miss Julia Look to Emily E. Chubbuck, January 31, 1846[240]

My dear Miss Chubbuck

One more Friday has gone and if the day had not gone *forever* and made all our lives so much shorter—how bad I *should* be. But all composition classes are over for this term and shouldn't I like to hold a jubilee. You'll soon be with us again and then won't we all sit round in a ring and listen to stories coined at Philadelphia. "They say" your [sic] living in the City of "brotherly love"—but I *guess* little

[236] This next section in print is the only portion of this long letter that was used by A. C. Kendrick in *The Life and Letters of Mrs. Emily C. Judson.*

[237] This paragraph was written in response to Mr. Judson's comments at the end of his January 30, 1846 letter to Emily.

[238] The *Baptist Register* was a local Baptist paper in central New York that grew into regional prominence. Published by Alexander Beebee, it had significant influence in Baptist circles. The *Baptist Register* was a natural outlet for some of Emily's work as a budding writer. Later, in 1846 and the immediate time after her engagement and marriage to Adoniram Judson, there was conflict between Emily Judson and Mr. Beebee, who was less than enthusiastic about Emily's suitability for missionary service, reflecting the attitude of many in the wider Church. Emily was, after all, a secular, popular writer, and Adoniram Judson was the venerable missionary held in awesome respect. Eventually, Emily and Mr. Beebee were reconciled, and Mr. Beebee was often mentioned in letters from Miss Cynthia Sheldon as Emily's strongest supporter.

[239] See vol. 1, "Cast of Characters," s.v. "Sheldon, Miss Cynthia."

[240] This is a combined letter. Julia Look wrote a portion, and then Sarah Bell Wheeler added a note. See Sarah Bell Wheeler to Emily E. Chubbuck, January 31, 1846. Then, Julia added yet another note. We place these letters at the end of January 1846.

Cupid—the rascal!—has dared to get up something more than "brotherly" affection just for once.[241] The composition class and the young ladies who compose it are anxiously [ ] your return. I guess you'll mark the cheering—and I mean to get up a torchlight procession all by myself and escort you from the cars. They come in at two o'clock I believe—

We are to have a [ ] examination next week—consequently are all on qui bien—and Susy is coming to see us too, with Mr. Amy and "little Kitty." Did I tell you that Sarah B.[242] and I spent the holy days with Susy at her own nice home—and we had such a time among that "Old Bachelor Club"—and Sarah fascinated *all* of them by singing "LonNor"—But of all this nonsense when you come—in the mean time [*sic*] I know you have no heart for all these things just now.

We hope to see you as rosy and well as can be and as happy as well. I've promised Sarah part of this note or I should never stop. Love to Fanny[243]—and to yourself a *great* deal with a good night kiss from

Julia.

[Note: The letter from Sarah Bell Wheeler dated January 31, 1846, is between these two sections.]

Here I am again—for I can't bear to have this note go with a vacant corner—We felt as if a missionary spell had fallen on just about every one—and when we go down to Miss A.M.'s room—you should see how sober and good we try to *look*—and then some body says something funny and away we go to laughing as hard as we can scream—and then, somebody says "hush! Girls" and so we take to looking good again. Dear! dear! Isn't it queer—But if something had not happened to make us better the board would have been obliged to send a missionary to us—we were growing such heathens—but seems to me we are growing better now—It's all because we hear your D. D. is so good—couldn't you give him two kisses for each of us? Perhaps it would not be very disagreeable—Well, you [ ] if you *don't want* to—but we *wish* you would.

Julia

Source: American Baptist Historical Society, AJ 27, no. 1295.

Emily was in Philadelphia, and there are references in Julia's letter to "Cupid," in Sarah Bell's letter to the "Dear Dr.," and to the fact that Anna Maria Anable could not keep herself from telling them.

[241] The students and teachers at the Utica Female Academy were quite taken with the budding romance between their composition teacher, and Adoniram Judson, the great missionary.

[242] See vol. 1, "Cast of Characters," s.v. "Wheeler, Miss Sarah Bell."

[243] See vol. 1, "Cast of Characters," s.v. "Anable, Fanny."

Miss Sarah Bell Wheeler to Emily E. Chubbuck, January 31, 1846[244]

My dear Miss C.

Julia[245] has left a page for me so I've come up from prayers to finish this before the mail goes out. Nemmy[246] we can hardly wait for you to *come* home we want to see you so badly. Jule and I go to A.M.'s[247] room every day and *talk* and talk till we relieve ourselves a little.

That picture of yours is very natural and you don't know how much we love to look at it. Has anyone told you that Cousin Fanny B.[248]—has a *little son*? The *company* had a long letter from Miss Barber[249] yester. She is having fine times in Middlebury. Wish she'd catch a widower.[250] [ ] is [ ] and if you'd only come and spend the day in Ninny's[251] room we'd all visit you. We are all so anxious to see your "dear Dr." (Ninny couldn't help telling us.)[252]

Is Fanny[253] well? Give her much love for me. I am very anxious to hear her sing. Expect she will astonish the natives when she goes back. Come home my dear Nemmy. My love to Mr. and Mrs. [ ] [ ] [ ]. And any quantity for yourself from your affectionate

Sarah Bell

---

[244] See vol. 1, "Cast of Characters," s.v. "Wheeler, Sarah Bell."

[245] See vol. 1, "Cast of Characters," s.v. "Look, Julia."

[246] Emily Chubbuck. See vol. 1, "Cast of Characters," s.v. "Nemmy, Nem, or Nemmy Petty (Nemmie Pettie)." Also the chapter "Names of Endearment."

[247] See vol. 1, "Cast of Characters," s.v. "Anable, Miss Anna Maria."

[248] Fanny Buckingham was the daughter of Fred Sheldon. She would have been a niece of the Sheldon sisters and a cousin of Anna Maria Anable.

[249] Mary Barber was mentioned frequently in Emily Chubbuck Judson's letters; she was a student and then a teacher at the Utica Female Academy, There were ups and downs to that relationship; in fall 1845, apparently Mary had written to someone expressing what Anna Maria Anable called "ingratitude," and Mary had been banned from the academy until she made proper apologies to Miss Sheldon. A September 7, 1845 letter from Anna Maria shows that her remarks had been about Miss Cynthia Sheldon. In November 1847, Jane Kelly remarked that they had not heard from Mary in more than a year. In 1848, Mary Barber was back at the Utica Female Academy teaching with Jane Kelly. At this time, Miss Sheldon was living in Philadelphia, but Mary Barber had been able to reconcile with her, and in later years Mary was very close to the Sheldon-Anable families. Later, there was considerable consternation on Miss Cynthia Sheldon's part in her correspondence with Emily about Mary's health, the seriousness of it, and her impending death. These letters were written in April 1852. Miss Sheldon went to help transfer Mary to Albany in June 1852, where she would be better situated and perhaps have access to better doctors. On September 9, 1852, Anna Maria Anable wrote to Emily of Mary Barber's death.

[250] "The Widower" was a frequent reference in the letters of these unmarried friends. The reference was usually a suggestion of their availability and interest in marriage. As one example, see Emily Chubbuck's letter to her sister Catharine Chubbuck dated April 2, 1845, in which she mentions the Reverend Rufus Griswold. Emily referred to him as a clergyman who had called upon her when she arrived in Philadelphia and said, "He is a widower what's more and crazy to get married. Don't you think I shall accomplish something?"

[251] Anna Maria Anable. See vol. 1, "Cast of Characters," s.v. "Ninny."

[252] In her January 26 letter to Miss Cynthia Sheldon, Emily cautioned her not to release the information on her engagement to Dr. Judson. She mentioned that it had only been a short time since Sarah Hall Boardman Judson had died, and Adoniram Judson was sensitive to honoring her memory. At the same time, Emily said, Adoniram realized that if he did not act soon, Emily might be claimed by someone else, likely a reference to N. P. Willis.

[253] Anna Maria Anable. See vol. 1, "Cast of Characters," s.v. "Ninny."

[ ] does go [ ] [ ] [ ]. Don't you think she is growing good. We wonder if it doesn't come from rooming with Lydia.[254] It is too bad L.—can't go with you.[255]

Source: American Baptist Historical Society, AJ 27, no. 1295.

---

[254] See vol. 1, "Cast of Characters," s.v. "Lillybridge, Miss Lydia." Also the timeline "Lydia Lillybridge Simons."

[255] This is an ironic comment, for Lydia did indeed end up going to Burmah with Adoniram and Emily.

LETTERS

—⚡—

FEBRUARY-MARCH 1846

Mr. John P. Sheldon[1] to Emily E. Chubbuck, February 1, 1846— Washington, DC

Dear Miss C.

I received yours of the 29th ult. yesterday. It relieved me from no little anxiety—for, from the moment Charles[2] told me that you seemed "troubled" and that he feared your book or writings had been roughly treated by some villainous newspaper [ ], I had thought of you only as a sensitive and ill used girl, and forthwith determined like an ancient and tough knight of the olden time to set my lance in rest and ride down the miscreant.

But your favor of yesterday has relieved me, and in return for your kindness, I will give you the satisfaction of knowing that that Neuralgia [*sic*] has "let me be" for a time—would it were for "a time a time and half a time."

You admit, however, that you were "troubled" when Charles called on you; and that you were "balancing pros and cons" launching "a very important matter," of which you will "perhaps" tell me "hereafter." Now, I cannot imagine of but *one* "very important matter" that Miss Emily C. can be "troubled" about; and if it be *that*, and she *is*, or *was*, "balancing the pros and cons" to determine whether she will or will not—surrender—why, I can't venture to *prescribe*, without a full knowledge of the entire case. I can, however, *suggest*—that if the "pros and cons," when balanced, will settle the fate of Mr. X or Mr. Y, you would do well to hold the scales a long time, for your ultimate decision may make one of them very miserable, perhaps *make away* with himself.

Do you not perceive that I have no *ralgia* this evening—neither new nor old? Indeed I feel so free from ailments that I propose to myself to leave the focus of factions tomorrow or the day after, and go to Philadelphia to see you. If my health is spared, and no untoward accident intervenes you may look for me—and when I am with you I think I can persuade you to come back to the political Gotham with me, if it be only for the purpose of listening a few days to our Senators and representatives.

I think that "Fanny Forester"[3] would be able to find, among the mortals who congregate here, some characters for her pencil.

---

[1] On May 7, 1845, Anna Maria Anable referred to a "Cousin John Sheldon," who had seen Emily's brother, J. Walker Chubbuck, in Wisconsin. This is likely the son of John Sheldon. There are also two letters from him in the correspondence: this one dated February 1, 1846 in which he speaks of coming from Washington, DC, to Philadelphia to see Emily and a second on February 7 in which he apologized for having to leave without properly saying "good-bye" to her.

[2] Charles Gratiot grew up in St Louis, where his father was an army engineer responsible for developing the Port of St. Louis. He married Ann Sheldon, who was a cousin of Miss Cynthia Sheldon, Mrs. Urania Sheldon Nott, and Alma Sheldon Anable. Together, Charles and Ann Gratiot had six children. Because they often lived with the Sheldon family, their letters contain a great deal of him. Letters in 1847 speak of his religious awakening; those of 1849 speak of his leaving for the California gold fields. In 1853, Charles Gratiot applied for a grant of 400 acres in Illinois, and he already owned 148 acres.

[3] Emily Chubbuck wrote under the *nom de plume* Fanny Forester. Asked about it once, she said, "Would anyone buy a book written by Emily E. Chubbuck?"

Yours truly

Jn P. Sheldon

Charles left Washington for Baltimore six or seven days since, and he must have gone thence to Boston, for I have not heard from him. He told me he intended to bring Ann[4] to Washington as soon as winter broke.

Source: American Baptist Historical Society, AJ 26, no. 1260.

Adoniram Judson to Emily E. Chubbuck, February 3, 1846—Richmond VA

So dearest, after all that has passed between us, it appears, for you have distinctly stated it in one letter and confirmed it in your last,[5] that if you cannot get the letters from W,[6] we must part, and yet you can write lightly and even jocosely, and yet most affectionately and confidingly. All this is puzzling and distressing to me. And you say "I never should have considered myself bound to W, if I had not met with you."[7] From this I cannot help inferring, that your letters to him are of such a kind, as, though [Note: "They were" was written and crossed out.] not intended to bind yourself to him absolutely, are inconsistent with any other union. If this is the case, had you not better say so plainly [Note: "And honestly" is written and crossed out.]! And then tell me what, as a wise man, I ought to do—Whether I had better go on plunging deeper and deeper in love and without a reasonable hope that every plunge will not but aggravate the pain of final parting. You say "Let me banish the night-mare"—and then without having touched a hair of his hide, you say, at the close, "Please write by return mail, and tell me, that the night-mare is dissolved!"[8] In your former letter, you say that you shall not go to New York till

---

[4] Ann Sheldon was a younger cousin of Miss Cynthia Sheldon, Mrs. Alma Sheldon Anable, and Mrs. Urania Sheldon Nott. She married Charles Gratiot, the son of a prominent army officer and engineer who opened the port of St. Louis. Because Charles and Ann Gratiot often lived with the Sheldon-Anable families, both at Utica and in Philadelphia after 1848, they were often mentioned in the correspondence. They had six children, one of whom was born very close to the birth of Emily Frances Judson. The letters reveal how Ann coped in her husband's absence when he went west during the gold rush to seek his fortune.

[5] On January 28, 1846 Emily wrote, "I never can be more to you than I am now while those letters are in existence."

[6] Nathaniel Parker Willis was the editor, with General George Morris, of the *New Mirror*, a prominent literary magazine in New York. His "discovery" of Emily in the June 8, 1844 edition of the *New Mirror* catapulted her into literary fame and enabled her to command the highest prices for her articles and stories from the major magazines of that period. It began a new and glorious chapter in her life. Over the next two years, he became her friend, mentor, and confidant. His black-bordered letter of March 21, 1846, made it abundantly clear that her engagement to Adoniram Judson had come as a "death blow" and that he had expected to marry Emily upon his return that month from England. He returned several letters to Emily to demonstrate to her, lest she had forgotten, why he had felt right in that expectation. In vol. 1, there is a timeline that presents in some detail the substance of their developing relationship, all from the letters Willis had written to Emily. When she received her letters back from Willis, she destroyed them, feeling that they would cast a negative shadow on her life and, because of that, the life and ministry of Adoniram Judson.

[7] See Emily's letter of January 31, 1846.

[8] See the letter of Emily E. Chubbuck to Adoniram Judson dated January 31, 1846.

you have seen W.[9] and that for weighty reasons, and now without alluding to that, you ask my advice about allowing Dr. Lyon[10] to take you home! Truly, I find myself thoroughly mystified or mesmerized and quite incompetent to advise you or myself. So far as Dr. Lyon is concerned—I should think that Mr. Gillette[11] would be able to give safe advice. But I thought that Miss Sheldon[12] strongly objected to your coming home on account of the cold,[13] and that you felt the force of the objections. Ever since your former letter, I have been planning to slip through the country incognito from Richmond to Philadela [*sic*], and after seeing you two or three days, turning back to Baltimore, to fulfill my engagement there.[14] But now, I know not whether I should find you in Philadela [*sic*] even if I should be able to carry out my plans, which I much doubt.

You speak of the good times we will have in the "loggery"[15] etc.,—"for you will have gone too far to retreat!" Good gracious! Have I not said—"*come what will?*"— I thought that was the *ne plus ultra*. No higher pledge than that, is there? A pledge that you decline giving—Nor can I have any claim on you for such a pledge. I only wonder at my impudence in suggesting it. I only wonder that you can receive my overtures with so much kindness and express yourself so affectionately as you do to such a one as I am—

[9] See the opening paragraph of the letter of Emily E. Chubbuck to Adoniram Judson dated January 30, 1846.

[10] See Emily's letter of January 31, 1846. Dr. Lyon was related to an acquaintance. An internationalist, he had time on his hands while in Philadelphia and offered to accompany Emily back to Utica. Emily felt him to be a bit unscrupulous and wondered at the propriety of it. In the end, she turned him down.

[11] Following several successful pastorates, the Reverend A. D. Gillette was the founding pastor of the flourishing Eleventh Baptist Church in Philadelphia in 1839. With his wife Hannah and several children (they would eventually have six), they graciously opened their home to Emily Chubbuck when she came to Philadelphia at the end of March 1845 for her health. The connection had been made through Miss Cynthia Sheldon, a family friend of Mr. Gillette and his parents. A prominent Baptist, Mr. Gillette journeyed to Boston in December 1845 to accompany Adoniram Judson to Philadelphia for meetings, and on Christmas Day, he introduced Dr. Judson to Emily Chubbuck with the hope that Fanny Forester could be persuaded to write the memoir of Sarah Hall Boardman Judson. A. D. Gillette and his wife Hannah remained valued and trusted friends, not only with Emily, but with the Sheldon and Anable families. He moved from Philadelphia to New York in 1852.

[12] Miss Cynthia Sheldon was in charge of the administrative and financial departments of the Utica Female Academy. Miss Sheldon and her sister Urania, who was literary principal, gave Emily Chubbuck a place at the academy in October 1840. They had deferred any cost to a future time when Emily could afford to reimburse them. Upon Miss Urania Sheldon's marriage in the late summer 1842 to the Reverend Doctor Eliphalet Nott, the president of Union College, and her subsequent move to Schenectady, Miss Cynthia Sheldon assumed a larger leadership role at the academy. Active and well-known in Baptist circles, Miss Cynthia was to become an important mentor, advisor, and friend to Emily until the time of Emily's death in 1854. She was the aunt of Emily's best friend, Anna Maria Anable, and was addressed by most as "Aunt Cynthia." In 1848, Miss Sheldon moved to Philadelphia to help Miss Anable with the startup of the Misses Anable's School.

[13] Emily quoted Miss Sheldon on temperatures in Utica between six and sixteen degrees below zero in her letter of January 26, 1846.

[14] On January 30, 1846, Adoniram said of his travels, "In the present state of things, I resolve to go no further than Richmond. I would not even go there, but I have unfortunately committed myself by letter, to a series of meetings. And what is worse—the Baltimore ministers saying that I passed them by, came on yesterday, and induced a promise from me, that I would give them several meetings on my return from the south."

[15] From A. C. Kendrick, *The Life and Letters of Mrs. Emily C. Judson* (New York: Sheldon and Company, 1831): "Emily reached home—'the loggery,' as she playfully styled her father's humble but very comfortable dwelling—the first week in March" (166).

The night-mare presses on me more heavily than before. Pray write by the return of mail and tell me what I shall do.

Perhaps I have taken a wrong view of this whole matter—If so, I beg your pardon. When I re-peruse the first part of your last, it seems as if you fully intended to be mine—Is it not so? And then there is a most precious paragraph in the middle of the last page—When you say, "I am all, *all* your own to teach and guide and pet too"[16]—But how can that be, if W keeps the letters? But I suppose, that you understand all the windings of this matter, dearest. And I feel the transparency of your character and the sincerity of your emotions—I cling to the dear hope and belief that you are mine and will be mine, come what will—And in that hope and belief I will try to bear up under the night-mare, as long as you please—

A Judson

Source: Hanna family files.

Adoniram Judson to Emily E. Chubbuck, February 4, 1846—Richmond VA

I wrote you yesterday, dearest, and thought I should not write again from this place; but the first sentence of your last is *so delicious*,[17] and then you seem to be so sincere in your intended efforts to get disentangled from W,[18] that I wonder the night-mare[19] will stay. But where was the necessity of your trying again to explain the reasonableness and innocence of your love for W? Had I not said enough on that subject? And how *do* you explain it? "So handsome, yet so sorrowful." "Such fascinating manners." "Hesitated not to say, that I loved him with all my heart."[20] Pretty expressions to drive away my night-mare! I have no doubt you are now sincere. But art thou sure of all the future turnings of thy little mischievous heart! Thou hast seen it in one view only. When thou seest him at thy feet, offering his heart and hand, poetic genius, for a fashionable life, and the dear hope of bene-

[16] See the letter of Emily E. Judson to Adoniram Judson dated January 31, 1846.

[17] On January 31, Emily had opened her letter with "my own best-beloved, I was ill in bed all day yesterday or I should have written you; and in that slight illness my heart clung to you—oh, *so* fondly!"

[18] See vol. 1, "Cast of Characters," s.v. "Willis, Nathaniel Parker."

[19] Speaking of Emily's angst, her worry over her letters to N. P. Willis, what future release of them might mean, and her question as to whether or not she can follow through on her commitment to Adoniram Judson while all of this is swirling around in her heart, Judson says on January 30, 1846: "How can I face the meetings in these two large cities, with the 'night-mare' on my soul? Perhaps, dearest, you will drive it away in your next. I know you can. And I will daily pray God to assist in driving away that which oppresses you." On January 31, Emily wrote, "Let me banish the night-mare, dearest. How can I do it? By telling you how entirely my heart rests on yours." On February 3, Judson responded: "You say 'Let me banish the night-mare'—and then without having touched a hair of his hide, you say, at the close, 'Please write by return mail, and tell me, that the night-mare is dissolved!"

[20] For a full explanation as to what is behind Emily Chubbuck's thoughts here, refer to her letter to Adoniram Judson dated January 31, 1846.

fiting the "fascinating" creature,—an old haggard missionary, a grim Burmah to repel, and a high spiritual life and a bright heaven too remote and indistinct to counteract the other drawing, what wilt thou think and feel? Gettest thou a peep at my night-mare! However, young woman, don't think that you are the only being in the world that is worshipped and run after. I can assure you there are lots of "handsome," "fascinating" creatures (other darlings) all the way from Boston to this blessed city, who are longing to pitch themselves head foremost, "come what will," into the arms of one of the most finished creatures about town.[21] So don't imagine that he will go hang himself through fear of dying of a broken heart. That my friend, the night-mare, just gives me a slight squeeze, that such strain is too playful for the occasion—quite unbefitting his august, hairy presence. Peace, genius of night, dread alley of despair and death, and as I just recollect part of a stanza to thy praise, let me venture to preface it and present on bended knee before thy sable shrine—

> Close on my bosom and greatt'st [*sic*] thou, goblin ape,
> Toad-like and swelling up thy bloated shape;
> "Roll'st in their marble orbs thy gorgon eyes,
> And drink'st with leathern ears my gasping sighs.

I have been obliged to lay by this letter so many times—lock up my portfolio and go down to the parlor to see company, that you must not wonder that it hangs together so inharmoniously. I am laying my plans and preparing the way, with infinite difficulty and opposition, to get free of this city next Monday or at farthest Tuesday—and I shall be guided in my next movements by your answer to mine of yesterday which I shall hope to get on Saturday. Don't trouble yourself to write again to this place.

"Oh! Such a life as I will lead you!" Do, dearest dear—I am only afraid, that you will take it into your head not to lead me any life at all. But after the sweet interchange of affection that we have enjoyed, and sweet assurance that your every letter contains, ought I to be "afraid" [*sic*]? Is not my apprehension now an offence against your constancy and truth? Yes, I will believe so till I see you, and then extract a confirmation of such faith out of your sweet lips. You will let me, will you not, dearest? Will you not let me do the naughty things over again, and banish the night-mare forever to his native pit? I think of you constantly and pray for you more than for myself—How it will be my greatest happiness to lead you to the enjoyment of higher religion, and to more extensive usefulness in the cause of

[21] See vol. 1, "Cast of Characters," s.v. "Rhees, Miss Rebecca." Miss Rhees would be one such example of what Adoniram said in this instance to Emily. Her three letters to Emily Judson and her five letters to Adoniram Judson are included in these volumes. The first of these letters was dated February 19, 1846.

Christ, than I have ever obtained myself. Pray take care of your health and ever remember me in your affection and prayers that you—[Note: The rest of letter is missing.]

Source: Hanna family files.

Emily E. Chubbuck to Adoniram Judson, February 6, 1846

God help me now, for I have no other help. I have been looking *so* eagerly for this letter of yours. Can it be possible that you know what a chilling thing it is? Mrs. Robarts is right. She says I am not the one for you, and she "shudders when she thinks etc."[22] Do you wonder that I am anxious to get away from Philadelphia. I am constantly receiving such things as the note enclosed—do you wonder that I am longing to be among my friends and let them see for themselves that I am happy in my—I had almost said my prospects, but I have no prospects now. All are kind but there is not a person on earth to say the word I need—even your affection has a severity in it that makes me shrink from you and long to lay my poor head in my Mother's[23] bosom as it first rested. I do try to act as near "right" as I can—believe that, I beg—but I am not sure that I know what right is. I will not attempt to defend any of my positions; but, dear doctor, if you could only read the heart![24]

"From this I cannot help inferring that your letters to him are of such a kind, as, though not intended to bind yourself to him absolutely are inconsistent with another union. If this is the case had you not better say so plainly and honestly?"[25] Why, what have I been doing from the very first? Why sh'd I wish the letters returned if they were not inconsistent with my new relations? Did I not tell you that it was jealousy for your honour [sic] which induced me? What has your honour [sic] to do with a common friendship? I tell you "honestly" (not for the first time I believe) that I have given Mr. W. cause to believe that I loved him, and quite honestly that I *never gave a thought to the construction that might be put upon my letters till I examined the subject with the eyes which love for you had given me.*[26]

It is as I fear and almost expected. You are beginning to distrust me, to misunderstand my feelings and misinterpret my words. I think however that we both of us gave a promise that no serious difference sh'd be created by letter-writing. You

---

[22] See Emily Chubbuck's letters of February 6 to Adoniram Judson (the second letter, written in the evening) and her letter of February 9 to Anna Maria Anable, for more on Mrs. Robarts and her comments. Adoniram Judson stayed with Mr. and Mrs. Robarts while he was in Philadelphia. See vol. 1, "Cast of Characters," s.v. "Robarts, Mr. and Mrs. W. S."

[23] Emily's mother, Lavinia Richards Chubbuck, was born June 1, 1785, at Goffstown, New Hampshire, the eldest of thirteen children. She married Charles Chubbuck on November 17, 1805, at Goffstown, New Hampshire. Four of her children were born at Goffstown, and moved with Charles and Lavinia Chubbuck to Eaton, New York in September 1816; they were Lavinia, Benjamin, Harriet, and John Walker. Sarah Catharine, Emily, and Wallace were all born in Eaton.

[24] This is Emily's emotional response to the letters which Adoniram Judson had written on February 3 and 4, 1846.

[25] This is from Adoniram Judson's letter of February 3, 1846.

[26] This is one of Emily's clearest explanations on why she felt it so important to receive the letters she had written to N. P. Willis.

must believe that I *try* to tell you everything "plainly and honestly" until we meet. If you wish me to do it after telling you the nature of this letter and take back what I have said about recovering them; but at the same time let me say that I *must* have them, for I foresee that we never can be perfectly happy until I make you acquainted with their contents. I take back what *I* said, but I will not accept your pledge, until you can give it with entire confidence. Do not tell me that you do that now—your letter gives a different interpretation. I have nothing, dear doctor, to bring you but a truthful character, and an affectionate heart—let them at least be free from incumbrances and draw-backs.

I had a great many things to tell you, but I cannot speak of them now. I write with a very heavy heart. Col. Gratiot[27] from Washington is to take me home next week; but if you write immediately I can receive one more letter from you. If the assurances I have when my heart was clinging to you with the most entire confidence and affection had no power over the "nightmare" you speak of, it is a thing beyond my skill. The shadow had gone from my heart when I wrote you and in the sudden gush of sunny feeling, I might have seemed to trifle a little, but—I do not think that I was very "jocose." If so, forgive me. I feel serious enough now. Oh do not, do not, think unkindly of me. You have my whole heart unreserved and I sh'd be made happy by thinking I could make you so.

Affectionately

E.

I dare not look over my letter lest a second tho't sh'd disapprove of it. If it does not go now it will be too late for the mail.—Your love for me is love now—some of those tho'ts which haunted you at night when you first began to teach me the love-lesson have intruded between us—I know they have. You would not be unkind but your confidence is waning. Dear, dear doctor, my own best beloved one—sit beside me a moment in that little dining-room—have my arms no power? Cannot I kiss the mist away? I lay my head again upon your bosom—do not put me away. I am indeed yours to teach and guide if you will have it so, but oh, *so* much guiding as I need.

I take this from the wrapper to add yet one more word. "Yours come what will" from any source but yourself. One kiss darling—one!

Source: Hanna family files.

---

[27] Colonel Gratiot was a brother to Charles Gratiot. Both were sons of General Charles Gratiot, a military engineer who had done much of the engineering work on the port of St. Louis as the Mississippi was opened to traffic. Colonel Gratiot, also an engineer, saw distinguished service in the Civil War. He is mentioned in the letters of February, 1846; he was able to accompany Emily from New York City to Albany as she returned home to make preparations for her marriage to Adoniram Judson.

Emily E. Chubbuck to Adoniram Judson, February 6, 1846[28]— Philadelphia

My dearest friend,

Mr. Sheldon[29] came from Washington this morning determined to make me return with him,[30] which I of course could not do. He had been here about a half hour when your letter came and I excused myself to read it. First I wept over it— then I prayed over it—and then without re-reading (which I ought to have done) I sat down to answer it.[31] When I came down with my letter Mr. S. had gone, leaving word that he was off for Washington in the evening train. Of course, I feel sorry for having treated him so carelessly; but this is nothing when I think of the trouble I am in with you.[32] I have been thinking this difficulty over seriously and perhaps the fault is entirely my own. It is five weeks today since we first met.[33] You had never heard of me before, and you have seen me under unfavourable circumstances here. You know but very, very little of me, and what you do know is not calculated to give you confidence. A little while ago I tho't I would not have you see my letters to W.[34] for the world—now, if I could spread them all before you and say "decide as you will have it" I would do it without a moment's delay. I have told you "plainly and honestly"[35] (those words so used, were *almost* unkind, dearest) all that I could tell. I have confessed to thoughtlessness, inconsistency—everything, it seems to me that I have been guilty of—and I have said that I never could become his wife, and never thought of such a relation. I have labored to be perfectly sincere with you and I suspect it is this very sincerity which has puzzled you. If I had told you less about myself and my affairs, you need never to have known that I had

---

[28] This is the second letter Emily wrote to Adoniram Judson on February 6, 1846. See the earlier letter dated "February 6 A.M."

[29] See the letters dated February 1 and February 7, 1846 from Mr. Sheldon. This was John Sheldon, a nephew of Miss Cynthia Sheldon, Mrs. Alma Sheldon Anable, and Mrs. Urania Sheldon Nott. He was a cousin of Anna Maria Anable.

[30] Emily had been looking for a way to return to the Utica Female Academy in Utica, New York, after having been in Philadelphia for a couple of months. Although she planned to stay for the winter, her engagement to Adoniram Judson made her return imperative because there was much that needed to be done before their marriage and voyage to Burmah.

[31] See the earlier letter that Emily wrote to Adoniram Judson dated "February 6 A.M." The handwriting and content indicates that it was emotionally written in haste.

[32] The correspondence tells us that Emily became despondent as she thought of the letters and expressions of commitment and affection that she had written to N. P. Willis. She thought that if ever he released them, it would be problematic to the image of the venerable Dr. Judson and to the image that would be projected to the church and the general public. She was expressing these sentiments and her self-doubts in her letters to Adoniram Judson.

[33] Adoniram Judson and Emily Chubbuck first met on Christmas Day 1845. The meeting had been arranged by the Reverend A. D. Gillette at the request of Adoniram Judson, who hoped to have her write the memoir of his late wife, Sarah Hall Boardman Judson.

[34] See vol. 1, "Cast of Characters," s.v. "Willis, Nathaniel Parker."

[35] See the letter of Adoniram Judson to Emily Chubbuck dated February 3, 1846.

acted imprudently.[36] It was not in my nature however to do differently—I never sh'd have had a moment of peace while there were concealments, even of innocent things, on my conscience. The fault may be still farther mine in this unhappy difference of ours. I may have been foolishly fastidious with regard to his letters. I still feel as though it would be doing you a wrong to give the pledge your affection asked, which notwithstanding your disclaimer, you *had a right* to ask, if you wished it; but, if it be not too late now, you shall direct me—I will do whatever you bid me. "The night-mare presses on me more heavily than before."[37] I do not feel quite at liberty to use the "come what will," so I will vary it—*advise as you will, it is my law.* Does that dispel the night-mare, dearest? And now will you take me back to your heart, and speak kind words to me? I have been thinking when I have nobody to love me but you, what a dreadful thing it will be to displease you. You must learn to practice forgiveness, dearest, for you will have enough to forgive. When I really set out to do what I suppose to be right, from principle, I am always sure to go the widest from it. I mean one of these days to dispense with the trouble of thinking for myself and let you take the responsibility of all my doings. Will you do it, dear?

I thought when I wrote you the letter containing W's[38] that I *must* see him,[39] but after deliberating a little I concluded that I might write saying that I have found a yet dearer friend than himself, without mentioning you or telling any particulars, and let him come to Utica if he wished to know more. It is not the most expeditious way of being at peace, but I am *so* anxious to be with those that love me! Mrs. Robarts[40] makes a great many unkind remarks and Mrs. J. and Mrs. G.[41] with the best intentions in the world are foolish enough to repeat them to me. I am

[36] Beginning with her letter of January 28, 1846, Emily spoke of the letters she wrote to N. P. Willis and how her words could easily be misconstrued if ever released to the public. Upon his return in March and his learning of the engagement between Adoniram Judson and Emily Chubbuck, Willis sent Emily a letter edged in black (March 21), saying that her letter about her situation came as a death blow to him. Then, writing on April 6, he spoke of looking through her letters to him and said, "I found the passage (in one which I enclose to you marked with red pencil) which gave shape and voice to a secret feeling I had not dared to acknowledge—and from the moment of reading it, I felt myself coming home to be your husband." Emily is feeling guilt over her actions, and comes back again and again in this section of the correspondence to pressing the issue with Adoniram Judson.

[37] In addition to Emily's angst over her letters to N. P. Willis and what future release of them might mean, she wondered whether or not she could follow through on her commitment to Adoniram Judson while all of this was swirling around in her heart. On January 30, 1846, Judson said, "How can I face the meetings in these two large cities, with the 'night-mare' on my soul? Perhaps, dearest, you will drive it away in your next. I know you can. And I will daily pray God to assist in driving away that which oppresses you." On January 31, Emily wrote, "Let me banish the night-mare, dearest. How can I do it? By telling you how entirely my heart rests on yours." On February 3, Judson responded: "You say 'Let me banish the night-mare'—and then without having touched a hair of his hide, you say, at the close, 'Please write by return mail, and tell me, that the night-mare is dissolved!'"

[38] See vol. 1, "Cast of Characters," s.v. "Willis, Nathaniel Parker."

[39] See the letter of Emily E. Chubbuck to Adoniram Judson dated January 30, 1846. In that, she said, "I shall not go to N.Y. till I hear of the arrival of Mr. Willis, as I wish to see him particularly so I can say things that I cannot write, and I don't fancy telling him any more than I find necessary."

[40] See vol. 1, "Cast of Characters," s.v. "Robarts, Mr. and Mrs. W. S."

[41] Mrs. Jewell and Mrs. Hannah Gillette. Emily was staying with the Reverend Mr. and Mrs. Gillette while in Philadelphia. Mrs. Jewell is mentioned as a part of Emily's Philadelphia social circle.

invited to spend the day with Mrs. R. tomorrow, but I shall not go. Perhaps you will recollect that I told you of going into a public ball for about an hour and a half one evening. Well, she is making the most of it, and yet this week while sighing over my wickedness in the morning, she has attended at evening one private ball and one dancing party—of course not to dance herself. I mention it, not to excuse myself thro her, but to show her inconsistency! They are very dear kind friends here in the house, but not like those at Utica. Miss Sheldon[42] told me not to come while it was so cold, but I cannot obey her. Both Anna Maria[43] and my sister Kate[44] send me very doleful letters (the scrap that I enclosed to you was from A.M.) and I cannot help their casting something of a shadow. If I could once see them I could make them feel differently. You seem to forget, dearest, how many things I have to trouble me—you must not wonder at some display of irresolution. The more I see of Dr. Lyon[45] the less I like him; and just as I had decided not to accept his escort Col. Gratiot,[46] a friend of Miss Sheldon's, called to say he would accompany me to Utica next week. I sh'd be very *very* much delighted to see you, but I shouldn't like to have you do the imprudent thing you proposed to yourself before the receipt of my last letter. Why, all Philadelphia would be acquainted with the fact, and poor Mrs. Robarts would be a great sufferer. Perhaps we shall *have* a *right* to be together sometime and then dearest—then—will you learn to have more patience with me? I cannot help anticipating frequent misunderstandings and such things make the heart cold. You will require a new outlay of love everyday and then I am afraid it will never cover my multitude of sins.

You do not tell me a word of the meetings in Richmond, nor how you are situated, whether seeing pleasant people or bored with stupid ones, nor how they lionize you. Are you well? Do you sleep at night? I am tempted to believe, when I remember how warm my heart was at the time I wrote you last week and from that infer that my letter must have partaken a little of that warmth of feeling that you

---

[42] See vol. 1, "Cast of Characters," s.v. "Sheldon, Miss Cynthia."

[43] Anna Maria Anable was the niece of the Misses Urania and Cynthia Sheldon and the daughter of Joseph and Alma Sheldon Anable. Emily first met Anna Maria in fall 1840 when she went as a student to the Utica Female Academy; both Emily and Anna Maria became members of the faculty there. In these years, Anna Maria became Emily's dearest friend, and the extensive correspondence between the two reflects sensitive, flirtatious spirits and a deep intimacy. Emily was "Nemmy" to Anna Maria's "Ninny." In 1848, Anna Maria Anable, with the help of her extended family, moved to Philadelphia and started the Misses Anable's School in Philadelphia. At Emily's death in 1854, Anna Maria was given guardianship of Emily Frances Judson, daughter of Emily and Adoniram Judson.

[44] Sarah Catharine Chubbuck, "Kate," "Kit," or "Kitty" was Emily's older sister by ten months. Outside of the two terms at the Utica Female Academy, which Emily arranged for her, Catherine always lived at home with her parents in Hamilton, New York. The letters indicate opportunities for marriage, but she, for unknown reasons, remained single. She later helped to care for Henry and Edward Judson after their return from Burmah in fall 1851 when they moved into the Hamilton home with their "aunt" and "grandparents," and she was remembered by them as "dear old Aunt Kate—a dear friend."

[45] Dr. Lyon was a relative of Mrs. Jewell. He was planning to go back overseas, but he had time to accompany Emily on her trip to Utica if she needed someone to travel with her. In her letter to Adoniram of January 31, 1846, Emily has a great deal to say about Dr. Lyon and his character, or rather his lack of it in her estimation.

[46] See vol. 1, "Cast of Characters," s.v. "Gratiot, Charles."

were worn out and sick when you penned the reply. Was it so, darling? No, you mean it all—that first severe page and all;[47] and I must not try to evade it by thinking otherwise. Oh, why why did you come and try so hard to make me love you, when you must have known all the time that I was [Note: "Incapable of" is written and crossed out.] not qualified for the place you would give me, and you were endangering the happiness of both of us? Perhaps though you will make me different after awhile. I have been among worldly people and you among Christian, and I don't know but it is strange that we have any tho'ts, darling, or opinions in common. A few years' training may make all right—at least I will hope so.

I wish I could see you tonight—just one sweet minute, dearest—and then we would not go to rest with a cloud on either heart. Would we?—I see you now, there in your quiet room in slippers and dressing-gown—open your arms to me dearest.

Thine forever,

Written along the left and top margins of page 1: "Mr. Hoanukin has offered $150 for the temperance story book; and if I could govern my tho'ts would do it. As it is I don't know whether to accept it or not.

"When you come to Philada.again you must not stay. Make some excuse and be off to Utica for it seems as tho' I never could feel quite happy, quite sure that you had not lost some of your love for me till I heard your own lips say it. Tell the people here that you will try to come back—or something that will free you. There would be no harm in your coming the *first* of March.

"Please write by return mail and I shall get it before I leave.

"*Au soin de Dieu*—angels guard you dear. Good night."

Source: Hanna family files.

Emily E. Chubbuck to Adoniram Judson, February 7, 1846— Philadelphia

"But art thou sure of all the future turnings"[48] etc. No, dearest friend of mine, not entirely sure, for it is a very mysterious thing; but I do *know* that W.[49] with all his "fascinations" will never have a larger share of it than now. Why, you seem to think that admiration is love itself—I sh'd never think of fixing a *green eye* on you because you told me of a pretty girl. This is all foolish, dear, all, and we will just put it aside. If I had never tried these fascinations which make you so distrustful of me your apprehensions would be a little more reasonable; but I suppose I have seen

[47] This is likely a reference to Adoniram Judson's letter to Emily Chubbuck of February 3, 1846.

[48] This quote is from Adoniram Judson's February 4, 1846 letter to Emily.

[49] See vol. 1, "Cast of Characters," s.v. "Willis, Nathaniel Parker."

the very brightest or rather the most attractive side of "gay and fashionable life." I have seen it softened down, with its most beautiful features on, nothing to startle or shock—seen it in its poetical dress. You know this has failed to gain my entire heart, and so I think you need not fear the glitter for me. What have you seen in me that could lead you to suppose for one moment that the parade of fashionable life would be agreeable to me—that it would not be annoying. Here I have refused three invitations today—two to dinner, one with one of the most fashionable families in the city—and one to a dashing party made expressly for me. Very fond of gayety [*sic*], am not I? I know it is the general impression that I like gay society—an impression that I have taken some pleasure *in heightening rather than correcting*, but I tho't you knew my tastes better.

With (not boastingly, but for truth's sake, do I write it) a very wide powered choice, much more extensive than would generally be supposed a woman in my position—poor and without high connections—could have. I have voluntarily and with but a single condition founded on regard for you, said "all, all your own" [*sic*]; and yet you stumble on little expressions of admiration, making me a model of falsehood. So dear, once for all, be assured that I understand something of my own heart; and believe me when I say that you alone have power to effect a change in its feelings with regard to yourself. Is it such a very light thing to adopt an entirely new course of life, new in feelings, thoughts, associations—everything—is it such a very light thing to do that I can take it all back tomorrow as I would undo a riband I had knotted? The future certainly looks very dark to me, but with my hand in yours, if you will only clasp it close, and the certainty of a place in your heart, I can look upon it courageously. Dear doctor, only love me, do not see too many faults, censure gently, lead me "to the enjoyment of higher religion and to more extensive usefulness," *trust me*, and no place on earth is one half so pleasant as "grim Burmah." I shut my eyes on all you tell about it, because I know that all my conceptions must be very imperfect, and *you* can make gloom or sunshine for me. The *place* is not what constitutes my home—it is your presence. Will you give me the home in the heart so very very dear?

What made you write me such a queer letter on the third?[50] You seem to be entirely unconscious about it, and write sweetly and lovingly now, as though I had not been so unfortunate as to offend you. Were you offended? Or were you only tired and was I so foolish as to take what you said for more than it meant? "Forgive and forget" and we will begin again all anew.

I am longing to see you, but if you can have any kind of peace and comfort pray go on south. You will be glad hereafter that you have done it. Don't engage yourself to meetings any more, for I am afraid they will wear you out, but go as far

---

[50] See the letter of Adoniram Judson to Emily E. Chubbuck dated February 3, 1846.

as you can without injuring your health. The meeting when you come will be all the sweeter. Don't come back to P. now if you can be comfortable and happy elsewhere; but when you do at last come, make a very short stay indeed. I shall grudge every moment that you are here.

So they are, are they? Those "darlings" all the way from Boston southward?[51] That *men* sh'd be vain! Why, they only mean—Shall I tell you what? No, I will reserve that until I see you. But some old ladies from Sansom St. church told Mrs. Robarts[52] yesterday, in strict confidence, that Miss Hug (one g or two?) was the honoured one. Mrs. R is particularly kind to me again today.[53] [Note: Several words are written and crossed out.]

I write you this hoping it will reach you before you leave Richmond, and prevent any consideration for me from influencing your movements. Go on just as you would if you had never met me—you will feel better satisfied afterwards. In the meantime be fully assured that your absence does not diminish my affection for you, and that just such as you left me will you find me again. Fickleness is not among my very [Note: Written in the right margin of the address page.] numerous faults. What I wrote you about certain letters[54]—the mischievous determination which has caused so much trouble, was not, as you seemed to suppose, indicative of changeableness or of little love. Perhaps it cost me quite as much as you but I resolved as I tho't I ought to act. It might be an error of judgment and as such I yield it to your opinion, whatever that may be.

Written in the left margin of the address page: "Thanking you for your sweet letter—thinking of you always—longing to see you—and praying most earnestly that our Father above may have you under his especial protection, I remain as ever"

Yours entirely,

Emily

Source: A. C. Kendrick, *The Life and Letters of Mrs. Emily C. Judson*, 152–53, has the first portion of this letter; Hanna family files.

---

[51] Speaking of those men who were interested in Emily, in his February 4, 1846 letter, Judson wrote about all of the women who were attracted to him and said, likely with a smile, that should Emily move out of his life, there would be many others who would be glad to enter into it.

[52] See vol. 1, "Cast of Characters," s.v. "Robarts, Mr. and Mrs. W. S."

[53] See the second letter of Emily E. Chubbuck to Adoniram Judson dated February 6, 1846 in which she outlined the situation with Mrs. Robarts.

[54] See Emily's letters beginning January 28, 1846, regarding her angst over the letters she sent to N. P. Willis.

Mr. John Sheldon[55] to Emily E. Chubbuck, February 7, 1846— Washington, DC

My dear Fan. Forester, [56]

How very sensitive, imaginative, and apprehensive all *we* scribblers are!— While I was suffering grievously from the apprehension that my *sans ceremonie* [sic] departure from Mr. Gillette[57] would make me appear [ ] an unamiable attitude in the eyes of Fanny Forester, that dear good hearted girl was herself suffering from the supposition that her strict attention to her own duties had caused her to neglect her visitor!

I did intend to call again; but having fallen into the company of some old political friends, I lost an hour or two in chatting; after which I was obliged to transact business with some printers—all which detained me until I was too late to return to the G's. I left Philadelphia without seeing my niece, Rosa.

You will not see Charles[58] until Thursday—he will be detained in Baltimore by business. This is as you would wish—and you may say to your [ ] that he need not hasten that representation of Fanny Forester but make it as perfect as possible.

Yours truly

Jn P. Sheldon

When you can find nothing better to do—write to me.

Source: American Baptist Historical Society, AJ 26, no. 1259.

Emily E. Chubbuck to Anna Maria Anable, February 9, 1846

Well, Ninny,[59] I wonder if you really intend ever to write me. I suspect not. I had a most miserable time last week for I have had letters from my poor dear papa[60] saying he is on his way home. He is desperately in love with me I know, and is just as certain of getting me as he is of living. He brings Imogen[61] back with him. He enclosed me a lock of hair and there are the prints of his cunning little white teeth at the close where he bit in a kiss by way of signature.[62] Shan't I have a time out, and don't you pity me? You know I have given him reason to be so confident.

---

[55] See vol. 1, "Cast of Characters," s.v. "Sheldon, Cousin John."

[56] Emily Chubbuck as Fanny Forester. See vol. 1, "Cast of Characters," s.v. "Chubbuck, Emily," and "Forester, Fanny."

[57] See vol. 1, "Cast of Characters," s.v. "Gillette, The Reverend Abram Dunn."

[58] See vol. 1, "Cast of Characters," s.v. "Gratiot, Charles."

[59] "Ninny" was a name of endearment given to Anna Maria Anable by her most intimate friends at the Utica Female Academy. Emily was "Nemmy."

[60] Emily and Anna Maria often referred to N. P. Willis as "papa."

[61] Imogen Willis, the daughter of N. P. Willis.

[62] See the letter of N. P. Willis to Emily E. Chubbuck dated December 31, 1845.

He is in wretchedly low spirits, but hopes to be happier when we meet. My conscience gave me a kick at every word I read. He says he knows me thoroughly, poor fellow! He will change his mind when he finds that I have proved traitorous. I sent the letter to my good noble doctor with proper explanations and he wrote me such a kind sweet reply—blaming me so gently. His censure is better than any other man's praise Ninny.[63] I am longing to have you see him. I begin to think it a very pleasant thing after all to go to Burmah under such auspices—Why, I would go to the palace of the gnomes with him! But how he came to pick me out to fall in love with is the greatest mystery. How it ever entered his cranium that I of all human beings could possibly be trained into becoming a missionary's wife is more than I can tell. He acknowledges himself that he don't [sic] think I am good for anything but to love. He was quite astonished when I showed him my new silk dress; and could'nt [sic] be convinced that I made it. He thinks I can't do anything. By the way, I made the biggest baulk in that dress that ever was. It is schockingly short-waisted. When I get home I must have the defect remedied for it spoils the whole. But for that it would be perfectly elegant. Such quantities of scalloped trimming as I made you don't see ever done.

I don't know yet when or how I shall get home. There is a magnificent fellow here from New South Wales, a brother of Mrs. Doct. Jewell[64]—a sort of Willisy-Byronical chap—and he thinks the privilege of escorting Fanny Forester[65] from here to Utica is a very daring thing to aspire to. He sh'd consider himself too much blessed, too highly honoured [sic]. I don't know whether I shall so honour [sic] him or not, and have written for the doctor's opinion. If I come so I will drop you a line before hand as I want you to be prepared to receive my beau in state. He was educated here by Doct. Staughton[66]—went to England and flourished awhile in gay society—knew Mrs. Norton (thru Miss Sheridan) very well—met Lady Blessington and all that sort of people—fought like a tiger on the side of the *sans culottes* during the terrible three days in Paris—was on terms of intimacy with La Fayette—turned soldier in the Russian service for a few years (he is a physician by profession) and then put off for the land of the orientals. There he plays the shepherd. I should think him about as old as Willis.[67] What I have told you of his history I have gath-

---

[63] See the letters of Adoniram Judson to Emily E. Chubbuck dated February 3 and February 4, 1846.

[64] Mrs. Jewell was a part of Emily's social circle in Philadelphia. See Emily's letter to Adoniram of January 31, 1846 for her introductory remarks on Dr. Lyon and the possibility of him escorting her to Utica.

[65] Emily Chubbuck as Fanny Forester. See vol. 1, "Cast of Characters," s.v. "Chubbuck, Emily." Also "Forester, Fanny."

[66] William Staughton emigrated from England to the United States in 1793; over the course of his life, he became known as a beloved pastor, a gifted preacher, an educator of excellence, a friend of missions, a transformational leader. Among his pastorates was the Sansom Street Church in Philadelphia. He was the president of Columbian College in Washington, DC, and of Georgetown College in Kentucky. Dr. Staughton was the first corresponding secretary of the American Baptist Board of Foreign Missions.

[67] See vol. 1, "Cast of Characters," s.v. "Willis, Nathaniel Parker."

ered accidentally—I presume there is *enough sight* that I don't know. He is an accomplished gentleman, but full of blarney; and I am not sure that he is precisely the proper person to choose for a traveling companion. These chaps that have seen the worst side of the world are mighty fascinating, but they are not apt to be over scrupulous in the minor matter of morals. I sh'd like to bring Doct. Lyon to you though for he is quite a show.

Your note has come in Ninny since I wrote the above. Your questions about "relentings," "misgivings" etc. are partially answered on the first page. Of course I have some sad, *very* sad moments; but I know that as far as any man on earth has power to make me happy doct. Judson will do it. And I can't conceive of any situation in which I could be happier. You know I never had much taste for general society, and was always contented to be loved and petted by one. I think too that it would be easy for me to practice one kind of self-denial; for you know I was born to poverty. Then I have a way of being interested in whatever I am engaged in etc. etc. A forlorn hope you will say; but Ninny darling, let me just remind you that I shall have one sure solid comfort. When I pledge my heart and hand to my good doctor, I also take upon myself *another vow* which has been before taken, but not kept. The small remnant of my life shall be devoted to doing good; and if everything else sh'd be dark, it will only make the lamp within the brighter. I know that I have not been influenced in my decision by religious enthusiasm, but of course I have not taken this step with no thoughts beyond my own immediate gratification. I am in the way of folly—God sends a good man and I believe the only man on earth who could have done it to lead me into "the more excellent way" and I do not think I shall have more trouble than is for my good. If you could only go with me! Oh Ninny, what would'nt [*sic*] I give? I think we (you and I) would be happier in our little barn (the doctor says it is a barn) on the other side [of] the world than we have ever been in our lives. The only thing about it that really makes my heart ache is parting with my friends—*parting with them for life*. I know I never shall come back again.

The doctor has given me some dear little presents; and Mrs. Daniel Gillette gave me last week $20, in money. She has been visiting here. Mr. Gillette[68] seems very anxious that my outfit sh'd be made here; but the doctor (for reasons concerning Mrs. Robarts which I can better explain when I see you)[69] told me to let those do it who loved me best.

Written in the right margin of the address page: "I told him that I tho't I was better loved at Utica than anywhere else; but that I doubted whether it could be done as well there. He then advised me to keep still, express no preference, and let

[68] See vol. 1, "Cast of Characters," s.v. "Gillette, The Reverend Abram Dunn."
[69] See vol. 1, "Cast of Characters," s.v. "Robarts, Mr. and Mrs. W. S."

Aunt C.[70] and Mr. G. do as they tho't proper. Whatever I might lack could be obtained when I got to Boston[71] etc. So there the matter rests. I did hope to keep the engagement still until the doctor's visit but I am afraid that Prof. Raymond[72] can't keep such a formidable secret. I regret more than I can tell his knowing it. It will do Mother[73] and Kate[74] no good at all to have comparative strangers to talk to them about it—it is a kind of sympathy [Note: Written in the left margin of the address page.] which they cannot appreciate; and they care no more for Prof. R than for twenty others at Hamilton. It would annoy Doct. J. very much if he knew it. I am sorry; but what is done can't be remedied. Only don't for pity's sake let it go any farther before he is ready to have it known. If it is not known before the last of March there will be plenty time to get ready in—three months. I want to have a nice quiet peaceable time for a while with you too. I don't expect to have much peace after the matter becomes public. There will be all sorts of speculations afloat and many an unkind remark, I dare say. If I can get my head in your bosom tho' I shan't care. I will keep it there till I put it in his. Lovingly, Nem"

Written in the bottom margin of the address page: "In order that you may have the same opportunity to know something of him that you have of others I enclose to you my blessed doctor's last letter.[75] What I have told you in the beginning will explain it. I tho't it my duty to make known to him the whole W. affair."[76]

Written in the left and top margins of page 1: "You may let A. Crafts[77] know if you have a proper opportunity that I have decided against Willis. It may serve to quiet her when farther developments are made. I think Wallace[78] is serious in his intentions, but I ceased flirting with him six weeks ago and he hardly knows how to

[70] See vol. 1, "Cast of Characters," s.v. "Sheldon, Miss Cynthia."

[71] Adoniram and Emily were to sail from Boston around the tenth of July, and were in Boston for some days before they left.

[72] In 1846, Dr. John Howard Raymond was a professor of rhetoric and English language at Madison University. Apparently, Miss Cynthia Sheldon told him very early of the budding relationship and impending engagement of Emily Chubbuck and Adoniram Judson, and Mr. Raymond is frequently mentioned as a source of the information getting into the community, much to the consternation of Emily and Adoniram, who wanted to keep the matter a "secret" for as long as possible.

[73] Emily's mother. See vol. 1, "Cast of Characters," s.v. "Chubbuck, Lavinia Richards."

[74] See vol. 1, "Cast of Characters," s.v. "Chubbuck, Miss Sarah Catharine."

[75] This is likely one of the letters of February 3 or 4.

[76] See the letters of Emily E. Chubbuck to Adoniram Judson beginning January 28, 1846, and including her early February letters.

[77] Augusta Crafts is mentioned frequently in the letters written from the Utica Female Academy. A number of references chronicle her very strong opinions; many of these were spoken against N. P. Willis and Emily's relationship to him (Mrs. Crafts did not approve of either). In an April 30, 1845 letter Anna Maria Anable said, "The Dr. is not engaged nor isn't going to be to Mary Spencer I imagine, and tho' Mrs. Crafts intimated very strongly that there was *some one* he had his eye upon, he denied it to me strongly and scolded about Mrs. Crafts gossiping tongue."

[78] Mr. Wallace was the nephew of Horace Binney Wallace. An attorney, whom Emily called aristocratic and privileged, he called on her regularly during winter 1845 when she was in Philadelphia, and then after her engagement to Adoniram, he became a trusted friend and advisor.

take my rather dignified seriousness. Neal[79] is a very warm friend but not a lover. I know he suspects that I am going home to get ready to be married, but of course don't [sic] dream to whom. I just rec'd a present of a pretty China ink-stand from Mrs. Tyndale[80] and a set of tablets from Mrs. Mitchell."[81]

Written in the left and top margins of page 2: "I hope I shall get an answer to my last letter tomorrow. You ought to have had it long before the date of yours. The books I sent were for Kate. The Daguerre you may keep as long as you can but the Doct. has set down his foot against everything of the kind. He says they are horrible caricatures and ought to be rubbed out. He sees me of course with partial eyes and I suppose would be difficult to please."

Written in the left and top margins of page 3: "I don't expect to stop in N. Y. or I would see about the cameos. Mr. G will see about the head by Sully,[82] but it can't be done for a trifle. The Doct. won't sit for a Daguerre anyhow he hates them so; but they are getting out some 'fine engravings' of him and I will bring you one of those. I hav'nt [sic] seen them yet. I hope to be with you before I can get an answer to this, but I am still a good deal afraid. I shall wait I think for Mrs. Delivan."

Source: Hanna family files.

[79] Joseph Neal was a prominent member of the literary establishment in Philadelphia and became a part of Emily Chubbuck's circle of friends when she was there. Neal was well known and respected as a writer and editor; one of his best known works was the *Charcoal Sketches*. In 1842, he founded the *Saturday Gazette*, a successful publication that contained a great deal of humorous satire. Anna Maria Anable frequently referred to Neal as a beau for Emily. Mr. Neal married Alice Bradley in 1846; he died in 1847.

[80] Sarah Tyndale was the mother of Mrs. Mitchell of Philadelphia. A successful businesswoman, she ran a large store in Philadelphia that specialized in china. She lived with her daughter and her family. In fall 1845, as Emily went to Philadelphia for her health, the Mitchells were active in inviting her to stay with them. They offered her a room, as much privacy or company as she desired, and all of the benefits of their extended household. On February 9, 1846, Emily recorded the gift of a china ink-stand from Mrs. Tyndale. There is one letter in the correspondence from Sarah Tyndale, dated April 19, 1846.

[81] Mr. and Mrs. Mitchell lived in Philadelphia; Mrs. Tyndale, Mrs. Mitchell's mother and the owner of a prosperous china shop in downtown Philadelphia, lived with them. In November 1845, as Emily was thinking of prolonging her stay in the city to last through the winter, the Mitchells generously offered to open their home to her, promising that they would do everything in their power to take good care of her: her own room, solitude or company as desired, the ability to write, and all of the comforts they could provide. Emily did express appreciation, saying that many of her friends told her what wonderful people they were and how sensitive they were to the needs of an invalid such as Emily was at that time. Her one serious reservation was that they were Unitarians. In the end Emily decided that she would stay with the Reverend and Mrs. Gillette, knowing from her past experience that she would be more than comfortable with them.

[82] On January 31, Emily wrote to Adoniram Judson, "Mr. Gillette saw a portrait of you painted by Pratt in Mr. Sully's studio a few days ago. Mr. Sartain was engraving it. Mr. G. says that it is a good likeness, except that it makes the face too thin; and Mr. S. will engrave it beautifully.

Miss Cynthia Sheldon to Emily E. Chubbuck, February 12, 1846

My dear Emily,

Your letter to Anna[83] was put in Henry's box and we did not get it till tea time—you may know my girl we had the horrors about your being sick for not getting the letter in the morning. But dear Emily how little did I dream of your new trials, and I cannot even now bring myself to the belief that they are real in the degree you seem to think.[84]

It truly was a great blunder in Mr. Corey[85] to cast a shade on the picture. I was not aware that he was anything but a comforter—he said the family felt very sad indeed about it—he pitied them from the heart. This was all he said in relation to his call there. I do hope dear E.—you will waive the sentence that he is not your friend until you can have an opportunity to talk with him freely.

It is as you say my girl passing strange that all your religious friends do not rejoice in this crowning act of goodness on your part—but do place it in all such cares where I think it really stands, to their ignorance of your former feelings—also of your incentives to action—this will give way to a sober rational view of the subject—you will have the prayers, the sympathies, the "God speed you" from every Christian heart before you go out. If any are hanging back none [sic]—they will I trust come fully to the work—and the more heartily for having misapprehended you. We live in a strange world—and pity it is that Christians act strangely on many occasions—but we must be very careful not to have our faith shaken in the pure word of prophecy, "That our God has a people to serve Him in this world." To be Christ like is a great calling. I have ever felt the Missionary life was of all situations the most propitious for carrying out the principles of the Gospel.

I have been called away—heaven bless you all—

Your friend C.

---

[83] See vol. 1, "Cast of Characters," s.v. "Anable, Miss Anna Maria."

[84] In this letter of February 9, 1846, Emily spoke of trying to explain her relationship with N. P. Willis, the matter of getting her letters to him returned to her, the utter despair that it might not happen, and the importance that it does happen. She had made expressions of love to him, but her new experience of love showed her that she did not mean what she said in the way he had interpreted it.

[85] Mr. Corey was the pastor of the Bleecker Street Baptist Church near the Utica Female Academy, and Miss Sheldon and many of the girls from the academy attended worship there. (Cynthis Sheldon, Alma Anable, Deacon Asa and Isabell Sheldon, Edward Bright, and Horace Hawley had been charter members of the church in 1838.) In April 1844, he wrote to Emily expressing dismay that at a school program one of the girls had read a composition justifying dancing as exercise; he spoke of this as a roadblock to the salvation of many. Then, on March 10, 1846, Emily indicated in a letter to Anna Maria that Mr. Corey had been critical of her relationship and impending marriage to Adoniram Judson. Miss Cynthia Sheldon wrote a number of times expressing Mr. Corey's regret and support, and in 1847, there were letters of reconciliation between Emily and Mr. Corey. In spring 1848, letters reveal that Mr. Corey's wife had died of consumption, her condition exacerbated by recent child-birth. She had left behind four children. In July 1849, Anna Maria Anable wrote of his impending marriage to Jane Backus, a good choice for this "rising man." Mr. Corey remained popular with the Sheldon-Anable families even after their move to Philadelphia in 1848. A March 2, 1852, letter from Charles B. Stout told of Mr. Corey's call to the Stanton Street Church in New York City, which Mr. Corey did not accept. Finally, in 1854, there was a pastoral letter from Mr. Corey to Emily on her illness and her possible death. He preached at the Bleecker Street Church as late as January 1867.

If the Dr. comes we will not detain him if these Moonlight people have not passed by—

Source: American Baptist Historical Society, AJ 26, no. 1265.

Anna Maria Anable to Emily E. Chubbuck, February 12, 1846[86]

Dearest Nemmy[87]

Did you have the blues so badly? and did not the Dr's[88] good letter come and drive them all away? Your letter almost unfitted me for the wedding-party but after commenting and giving out a piece of my mind about Mr. Corey[89] I marched up stairs [sic] and made (on dit [sic]) a most exquisite toilet! (The letter went in Henry's box and I didn't get it till tea-time). I had *a talk* with Jimmy[90] and Judge Bacon[91] and Mrs. Kirkland[92] and they all I suspect are dying with curiosity to see the man who could fascinate Miss Chubbuck with doing so foolish a thing. Mrs. K. says she didn't think the difference in ages is anything—she has seen enough sight more agreeable old men than young. Jimmy says "Well women will do such things when they get in love."

You must [ ] the Dr. up out at Hamilton for every body [sic] has the impression that he is a complete bump of infirmity that only expects to get back and finish the dictionary before he dies and what under the sun he wants to carry you off to die too for they can't imagine. Tell the Dr. he must leave off playing venerable to the people now.

[86] This letter is undated. It is dated by Miss Cynthia Sheldon's letter of February 12, as they often wrote at the same time.

[87] "Nem" and "Nemmy" were names of endearment given to Emily by a small group of her intimate friends at the Utica Female Academy. Anna Maria Anable was "Ninny."

[88] Dr. Adoniram Judson.

[89] See vol. 1, "Cast of Characters," s.v. "Corey, The Reverend D. G."

[90] Jimmy Williams was often mentioned in Anna Maria Anable's letters, mostly simply as Jimmy. He was around the Utica Female Academy, and she spoke of their conversations, what he was doing, and his interests. She often referenced him as being with "Helen." Writing to Emily on April 29, 1845, Anna Maria had some interesting comments to make. In a paragraph of gossip she spoke of Jimmy and Helen and a recent party. All of the "flowers of Utica Society" were there in contrast to "poor dowdy looking little Helen," who in Anna Maria's estimation would never make the kind of wife who could help Jimmy in his future life. Yet he loved her, and the comment was made that "the one hundred thousand will make up for some deficiencies or ought to."

Then on November 14, 1845, Anna Maria said to Emily: "Do you know Jimmy is really engaged to Helen M? He hasn't been to see me yet, and he came home last Sat. Oh, love! love! Even a seven year friendship must fade before thy potent spell. Little did I think tho' that Jimmy would be faithless."

[91] Early into her relationship with Adoniram Judson, Judge Bacon sent Emily a poem about the publication of *Trippings in Authorland* and about her relationship with the venerable missionary. We have dated it as March 17, 1846. From comments about him in the correspondence, we gather that the judge was a prominent member of the Bleecker Street Baptist Church in Utica, of which Mr. Corey was the pastor.

[92] Mrs. Charles Kirkland lived in Utica, New York. She and her husband had at least two daughters, Julia and Amelia, who are mentioned in a letter from Anna Maria Anable to Emily dated April 21, 1845. On September 7, 1844, N. P. Willis wrote, "Give my kindest remembrance to our common friend, Mrs. Kirkland, when you return to Utica." On November 30, 1844, he said of his college days, "Mrs. C. Kirkland, was a kind of good-natured aunt to us."

After every body [*sic*] has had his say I think he'll come around and be quite reasonable.

Oh Nemmy! ducky darlin' here's your little note of yesterday. Oh how I wish I had your poor head right on my arm or right in my lap.[93] How *did* you get such a color? Do take care of yourself or I shall have to come and see to you.

I am provoked that the Dr. is not coming along—this fine weather. So Mr. Raymond[94] behaves beautifully. I thought he would—I guess Aunt C.[95] will put a plea in Mr. Corey's ear that will scare him—She is pretty much provoked at him, and she is mortified that the Baptists should distress themselves so much—[ ] of *my* getting in that clique! O, I should read Taylor with renewed unction. I *do* want to see you so badly I can't bear to wait till you have made your visit. Aunt U.[96] wants us to make our visit there before the 6th of April as their term closes then. She wants you and me to stay ten days or a fortnight at least. She cautions me not to cheat her.

Now Nem don't let that confounded Abbott[97] worry you a bit—and what do you think? Mr. Gillette[98] wrote to Aunt C. that he thought I was *just the one* for Mr. Dean,[99] who is only second to Dr. Judson!!! Hasn't that man gone *daft*—on the subject of missionaries' wives? When I marry miss (as we have the reputation of liking old men pretty well here) I shall take a boy of eighteen *to bring up*, and so

---

[93] In her letter of February 9, 1846 to Anna Maria Anable, Emily said, "If I can get my head in your bosom tho' I shan't care. I will keep it there till I put it in his."

[94] See vol. 1, "Cast of Characters," s.v. "Raymond, Dr. John Howard."

[95] See vol. 1, "Cast of Characters," s.v. "Sheldon, Miss Cynthia."

[96] Urania Sheldon had been the literary principal of the Utica Female Academy in fall 1840 when Emily Chubbuck came to study there. Emily was able to afford this wonderful education through the generous offer of Miss Sheldon and her sister Cynthia, the executive and financial head of the academy, to defer tuition. Urania Sheldon left in late summer 1842 upon her marriage to the Reverend Doctor Eliphalet Nott, the president of Union College in Schenectady, New York. Because of the distance separating them, Emily's relationship with Urania Sheldon Nott did not develop the intimacy that grew between Emily and Miss Cynthia Sheldon. Urania Sheldon Nott remained a mentor, advisor, and friend to Emily in the years of her writing, her missionary endeavors, and upon her return to America in 1851. She was also the aunt of Anna Maria Anable.

[97] Elisha Abbott was born October 23, 1809 in Cazenovia, New York. He graduated from the Hamilton Theological Institute and was ordained August 25, 1835. His wife was Ann P. Gardner, and they were married April 2, 1837. Though they were appointed for work in Telagus, India, that changed upon their arrival, and they went to Maulmain in April 1837. They continued on to Rangoon shortly after that. In March 1840, they established the station at Sandoway. Mrs. Abbott died in Sandoway on January 27, 1845. Mr. Abbott left for the United States in November 1845, returning in August 1847. At one point in the correspondence, Mr. Abbott was mentioned as a possible husband for Lydia Lillybridge.

[98] See vol. 1, "Cast of Characters," s.v. "Gillette, The Reverend Abram Dunn."

[99] The Reverend Doctor William Dean was a distinguished missionary to Hong Kong for more than fifty years. As the pastor of the local church in Morrisville, he baptized Emily Chubbuck when she was seventeen. There are nine letters in the correspondence from Mr. Dean, beginning after Emily's appointment to missionary service. After the death of Adoniram Judson, it was speculated, and not without reasonable support, that William Dean had an interest in taking Judson's place in Emily's life and affections. The later correspondence between Emily and Anna Maria Anable shows that Dr. Dean was often the butt of their ridicule, so something had happened to challenge that relationship. In 1854, when William Dean was courting Mrs. Maria Brown in New York City, Abby Ann Judson was working for Mrs. Brown as an in-house teacher for her children. For the complete story of William Dean's life and the many ways he touched the mission movement and the life of Emily Chubbuck Judson, see vol. 1, "Cast of Characters," s.v. "Dean, William."

give a new term to people's ideas—We shall be very anxious till we hear your cold is better.

I enclose this letter—Lydia[100] has copied all but the last two pages. Give a great deal of love to your mother[101] and Kate[102] and don't forget poor Ninny who hasn't got nothing to do but suck her thumb and feel bad from this afternoon till Monday when she'll have to begin to teach again.

Source: American Baptist Historical Society, AJ 23, no. 1146.

Emily E. Chubbuck to Adoniram Judson,[103] February 15, 1846

I saw the engraving yesterday made from Harding's picture of you. It is a horrible thing, too vile for even a caricature. It required only a dirk in place of the bible [sic] to make a very excellent representation of some desperate ruffian. If the board get [sic] out such a thing as that I am glad they can't have the monopoly. Pratt's portrait of you[104] is here in the hands of Mr. Sartain,[105] one of the finest engravers in the country. I called this morning to see it and find it a very excellent likeness. I don't like his colouring, but that of course will not affect the engraving. I think he has not given you quite breadth enough of forehead and he has pinched up your nose a little too much. Mr. Sartain says he will have an eye to those defects when he makes the engraving.

---

[100] Lydia Lillybridge was one of Emily's closest friends at the Utica Female Academy. When Emily made the decision to go to Burmah as the wife of Adoniram Judson and as a missionary, Lydia wanted to go with them. Emily spoke to Adoniram Judson of Lydia's extraordinary abilities, and Adoniram advocated her appointment before Dr. Solomon Peck and the Board of the American Baptist Missionary Union. Lydia was commissioned to go with them, in spite of the fact that she remained single. Always independent, outspoken, and unafraid to cause ripples in the missionary community, Lydia served on the mission field for twenty-eight years. She married missionary Thomas Simons in May 1851. See the timeline on the life and service of Lydia Lillybridge Simons in vol. 1.

[101] Emily's mother. See vol. 1, "Cast of Characters," s.v. "Chubbuck, Lavinia Richards."

[102] See vol. 1, "Cast of Characters," s.v. "Chubbuck, Miss Sarah Catharine."

[103] Beginning with her letter of January 28, when Emily reacted to the letters she had received from N. P. Willis, there are about two and a half weeks of letters filled with her personal pain and guilt, her worry about the existence of her letters to Willis, and what their future revelation could mean to her and to Adoniram Judson. Judson's responses are pastoral and affirming, yet obtuse at times to fully understanding her feelings. In her letter on February 15, the tone changes to a warmer and gentler Emily, and this continues. As March picks up, their letters take on the character of two teenagers who are positively giddy with the love that they share for each other. In an earlier letter Judson had spoken of changing his travel schedule to return to Philadelphia to see Emily; it is obvious that this return visit did happen, and that it resolved all of Emily's issues.

[104] On January 31, Emily wrote to Adoniram Judson, "Mr. Gillette saw a portrait of you painted by Pratt in Mr. Sully's studio a few days ago. Mr. Sartain was engraving it. Mr. G. says that it is a good likeness, except that it makes the face too thin; and Mr. S. will engrave it beautifully."

[105] John Sartain was one of the most prominent engravers of the mid-nineteenth century. His works appeared in prominent magazines and books. In 1846, he created an engraving of Emily E. Chubbuck that was used as a plate for *Alderbrook*. The correspondence of spring 1846 reflects meetings with Mr. Sartain on changes thought to be needed. In 1849, Mr. Sartain was publishing a magazine because a letter makes a reference to one of Emily's poems being in it.

I called on Mr. Rothermel,[106] a very excellent artist, this morning; and he is to make a sketch of me for Anna Maria.[107] He cannot quite finish it, and I shall leave it to trouble you with when you come to Utica. A tho't occurred to me today that it might be well to get out an engraving just before I leave the country—what would you think of it? My going will create something of a sensation among all classes and rouse a great deal of curiosity. I am Fanny Forester,[108] it will be known that I am, and I can not [*sic*] escape it. I cannot of course come out publicly and give my reasons for the step or can say that I am in any way changed. How would you like me to get the engraving out with an autograph at the bottom reading thus,

"Henceforth to loftier purposes, I pledge myself"

Fanny Forester

and just below it the dear name that you will give me printed? It is the tho't of today and perhaps not a wise one.

Mr. Wallace[109] called this evening and, as usual, inquired for you the first thing. We had quite a little talk about you and now that his alarm in my case is subsiding he talks as I sh'd like to hear more of those high church men (and) he has decided that you are the greatest man of the age because you imitate the Saviour and go about doing good. Goodness he considers the very highest kind of greatness. Pretty well for a talented young lawyer, rich and aristocratic—isn't it?

Please, dear doctor, make the best of anything I may chance to write you. My heart is really and truly all yours; and you must regard all my vagaries as you would those of a child. I am to be your pet you know—your baby—and really, my darling, must not expect too much of me. I will not so pressure upon your kind indulgences as to do wrong willfully [*sic*]; but we must either never meet again and strive to forget as soon as possible—or I must endeavour [*sic*] more to consult your judgement [*sic*] and wishes, and you must have more [Note: consideration is marked out!] patience with me. Cannot the love that I know we bear to each other (notwithstanding a horrible misgiving that came over me when I read your letter today)[110] cover all differences, dissipate all clouds, and inspire a happy trust which will make us certain that the fountain is pure, whatever bubbles may rise to the surface. Will you not trust me? I am turning from old dear things, and there are

---

[106] P. F. Rothermel was a well-known portrait painter in the Philadelphia area. In a letter of February 15, 1846, Emily said that she had been to see Mr. Rothermel and that he was painting a portrait of her for Anna Maria Anable. On December 25, 1851, Anna Maria wrote, "Mr. Rothermel has repainted you entirely and we think he has got a good likeness." In a February 2, 1852 letter, Miss Sheldon makes the comment that "the painting was greatly improved by Mr. Rothermel."

[107] See vol. 1, "Cast of Characters," s.v. "Anable, Miss Anna Maria."

[108] Emily Chubbuck as Fanny Forester. See vol. 1, "Cast of Characters," s.v. "Chubbuck, Emily," also "Forester, Fanny."

[109] See vol. 1, "Cast of Characters," s.v. "Wallace, Mr."

[110] The last in the correspondence from Adoniram Judson is February 4, which is eleven days prior to when Emily is writing this letter. Because of the personal angst Emily was feeling over her letters to N. P. Willis, reflected in her letters beginning January 28, Adoniram Judson changed his travel schedule to return to Philadelphia for several days so that they could be together. This visit brought some healing to Emily, and the relationship as expressed in their correspondence became much stronger.

little annoyances meeting me at every turn—thousands of which you would scarce be able to understand. They are none the less annoyances that they are foolish ones, and though I do not mean to have them influence me I cannot help it sometimes. Among some of these today your letter was the drop too much and if I had not first consulted my Heavenly Friend I fear I sh'd have taken a fatal step. I sat down pen and paper before me to hew words which would have made me afterwards wretched; when I remembered Him I had forgotten to consult, I wrote you a cold letter I doubt not, for at first I conceived myself deeply injured, but my heart grew soft before I had finished it—and now that I have told you all, will you forgive and love me? May I rest again in your heart my *own beloved*?

[Note: This is the end of the page, and the letter is not signed. Perhaps a page is missing.]

Source: Hanna family files.

Emily E. Chubbuck to Adoniram Judson,[111] February 18, 1846— New York[112]

My own dear "home,

I carried a sad heart with me in the cars yesterday notwithstanding I was on my way to old friends. The disappearance of Philadelphia seemed like the dissolving of a dream; and I could not make myself believe that my relation to you, my prospects or even my own feelings were real. How I longed to have you with me! I reached here about two o'clock, my brain half-muddled with thinking and half disposed to wish for drowning, and found Col. (G.) **Gratiot**[113] waiting for me. We proceeded here forthwith (to the Colgates)[114] where I met an old school-mate that I had almost forotten. Col. (G.) **Gratiot** leaves for Albany tomorrow morning so I hope to reach Utica Friday afternoon. I find myself very well this morning, but think I shall not go out today.

I told you I was troubled yesterday. There is something so unreal (sometimes) in the position in which I find myself that reflection becomes absolutely painful; and I am half-tempted to doubt my own identity. But like the old woman of the nursery rhyme I hope home will dissipate the mist.

---

[111] There are two versions of this letter: the original as written by Emily E. Chubbuck and the edited version published by Dr. A. C. Kendrick in his biography, *The Life and Letters of Mrs. Emily C. Judson*. Additions made by Dr. Kendrick are in parentheses, and words in the original left out by Dr. Kendrick have been added in bold. There are significant changes and omissions. In a note in his book, Dr. Kendrick explained that interest, purpose and propriety sometimes led to these changes and exclusions, "I remark here that in giving Miss Chubbuck's letters, I do not always indicate unimportant omissions. Real letters must always contain much which should not meet the public eye; and Emily's were real letters, dashed off hastily amidst pressing cares and duties. Written also after the exhausting labors of the day, they by no means do uniform justice to her epistolary powers."

[112] Emily left Philadelphia on February 17, traveled to New York, and reached Utica on February 20.

[113] Colonel Gratiot was a brother to Charles Gratiot.

[114] See the letter of James Colgate to Emily E. Chubbuck dated January 27, 1846. This was the family of William Colgate of soap-manufacturing fame.

> **"If I is I as I do hope to be**
> **I've got a little dog at home—he'll know me."**

They will make it all real when I get to Utica, for they seem to think it a very nice thing for (me) **Fanny Forester**[115] to turn missionary. I (thought) **tho't** it a very nice thing too when I went to my room last night and at last laid my head upon the pillow perfectly happy. Things were reversed—the bug-bears haunted me in the day-time and at night they fled. I seemed to feel that you had been praying for me, and (thought) **tho't** there was a double guard of angels set for me. Oh, I thank God constantly for the sweet way in which he has chidden my follies and pointed out a better path for me to walk in. I have been (and am still) a great world-lover; and he might have sent severe punishment—might have led me on to find pain and sorrow in the things I valued. But instead of that he has made the new way *so* attractive! He has sent you, dearest, to love and care for, to guide and strengthen me. I believe what you have so often said, that God delights in the happiness of his creatures; and I know that Burmah will be a happier place for me than any palace on earth. (Shall I not have your own arm) **Shan't' I have your own bosom** there to lean upon and your own wisdom to guide me. Mr. Hoffman[116] remarked when in (Philadelphia) **P.** that the reason literary women were so universally unhappy was that they married men who (can) **could** not appreciate them. He said they needed cherishing and guidance more than any other class—their husbands at first (thought) **tho't** them **but** little less than goddesses; but looking for equality of excellence, a well-balanced character, and discovering striking defects, weaknesses and eccentricities, they soon came to think them little better than fools. So (dear) **deary,** pray (do not) **don't** [*sic*] think me a *goddess*, for I must **be your pet, baby—** have you to think and act for me. But woe be to the day (when) you, for that, (you) call me *fool*. Then just to show you that I am not a fool, I shall set up for myself and *such* a house as we shall have!

[115] Emily Chubbuck as Fanny Forester. See vol. 1, "Cast of Characters," s.v. "Chubbuck, Emily," also "Forester, Fanny."

[116] Charles Fenno Hoffman was a prominent literary figure in Philadelphia and New York, who was well known as an adventurer, an editor, a poet, and a writer of exceptional talent. In fall 1843, he wrote three letters to Emily Chubbuck addressed to "Laura Linden," for Emily had written to him under that name, asking his advice about love, fame, and fortune. Only one of these letters is in the correspondence. Hoffman was not to learn of Emily's identity until spring 1845; in a letter dated approximately April 7, 1845, he spoke of Laura having taken off her mask and revealing herself to him. There were four letters from Hoffman in April when Emily was in Philadelphia. There were another three in December 1845 when Emily again was in Philadelphia. See vol. 1, Cast of Characters:, Hoffman, Charles Fenno, and vol. 1, Places and Events, Laura Letters. Anna Maria Anable frequently intimated in her letters that Emily was interested in "Hoffy" as a beau.

I send you fifty kisses which you may get somebody to deliver, or shut your eyes and get imagination to play upon your lips. Get away from Baltimore as soon as you can and come soon to the loggery[117] and your pet

Nemmy[118]

Source: A. C. Kendrick, *The Life and Letters of Mrs. Emily C. Judson,* 155–56; Hanna family files.

Paine and Burgess to Emily E. Chubbuck,[119] February 18, 1846—New York

Trippings in Author-Land

No copies published	1986	
No copies given away	108	
	1878	
Copies in book sellers' hands	741	
On hand in store	630	1171
		707 copies sold

Miss Emily E. Chubbuck

In a/o with Paine and Burgess, 6 J 1846

Jany 31 By Copyright on 707 copies *Trippings in Author-Land* sold to Jany/6h @ 4 1/4 $46.19

Miss Chubbuck

I have your due on account of the copies printed and sold of *Trippings* to Jany 1/46 showing due you $46.19 for which you are at liberty to draw for at one days sight or we will remit you a check if you prefer.

Respectfully yours
Paine and Burgess

Source: American Baptist Historical Society, AJ 25, no. 1221.

---

[117] The loggery was Emily's father's home. See Kendrick, *The Life and Letters of Mrs. Emily C. Judson,* 166. See also vol. 1, "Places, Events, Organizations, and Magazines," s.v. "The Loggery."

[118] See vol. 1, "Cast of Characters," s.v. "Nemmy, Nem, or Nemmy Petty (Nemmie Pettie)." See also the chapter "Names of Endearment."

[119] This is a statement to Emily from her publisher on the sales and her royalty for the initial offering of *Trippings in Author-Land.* The book had been on sale just about three months at this time. To gain perspective on financial income, Emily had purchased a home for her parents for $400, payable at $100 a year for four years. At the same time, she received $45 for a 9-page story published in one of the magazines.

Miss Rebecca Ann Rhees to Adoniram Judson,[120] February 19, 1846

Forgive what you may deem the forwardness which offers such a trifle as the enclosed to one so free from earthly feelings as yourself. Believe me, I am not so weak as to imagine that you can attach any value to so worthless an offering, but there are moments when the heart's feelings refuse control, and in this way only can find expression.

You can scarcely realize how we feel at meeting one whose name has been for years, familiar as a household word, yet whom we scarcely hoped to see and know on earth. To *you we* are *strangers*, but you seem to *us* like one long known and loved—one, whose toils and trials we have read of and wept over, till we seemed almost identified with them. This visit, which is to *you* but an episode in your existence, will be to *us*, an era from which many a precious memory will date.

Accept this slight expression of feeling, and if at any future period, it should meet your eye, let it recall for an instant, one, who, last evening, was privileged to linger for an hour by your side, and who will never forget the moment when she stood alone with you in the gallery of the old church where first she learned to worship. If you ever think of me, let it be as of one who loved you with a daughter's deep affection, and for once at least, remember me in your prayers.

Affectionately and Respectfully Yours

R. A. Rhees

Rev. A. Judson.

"The Lord bless thee and keep thee. The Lord make his face to shine upon thee, and be gracious unto thee.

The Lord lift up the light of his countenance upon thee and give thee peace."

---

[120] Miss Rebecca Ann Rhees, who wrote this and four other letters to Adoniram Judson, also wrote three letters to Emily C. Judson beginning in September 1850 with the death of Adoniram. Miss Rhees met Adoniram, she said, while he was traveling on deputation in 1846 and transcribed several of his sermons and remarks for publication.

On March 6, 1846, Adoniram wrote to Emily about a letter he had received from a woman he thought interested in him and said he would share it with her; then, he added, "And that also of R. A. Rhees, one of the few flames I have had since you left."

In her first letter to Emily, she spoke of her grief at Adoniram Judson's death as inconsolable. A second letter followed in December 1851 in which she commented on meeting Emily briefly at Miss Sheldon's in Philadelphia, probably when Emily traveled there after her return to America. This letter was in response to Emily's request for materials for the Judson memoir. Here, Miss Rhees implored that she be allowed to address her as "Emily," and she obviously was hoping to establish a relationship. Apparently, she was unsuccessful, for in the third letter, she said, "I will not ask you again to write to me." It appears that she had sent something to Emily, who had returned it to her, for after saying the above, she went on to ask Emily to excuse her for sending it along. In not getting what she hoped for from Emily, a hard edge emerges, suggesting that there was more to the request than what was seen on the surface.

The letters of Rebecca A. Rhees ("Bessie") to Adoniram are included in the correspondence to fill in some background information. Their dates are February 19, 1846; May 8 and 10, 1846; October 1, 1848; and November 25, 1849. There are currents emerging that are expressed in a multitude of ways; it seems evident that Miss Rhees would today be called a "groupie" with a strong need for attachment to a famous figure. There is an unfolding story of unrequited love that forms an interesting subchapter to the life of Adoniram and Emily.

Addressed to A. Judson

We may not tell thee what we feel,
For words are powerless to reveal
    Love deep as ours to thee,—
Love which no stain of earth partakes,
Love pure and holy for his sake,
    Whose image lives in thee.

We may not *praise* thee, who could gaze
One instant on the calm sad face,
    Nor feel that praise were vain?
Nor ours thy deeds of love to tell,
The tale a brighter song shall reveal,
    Amid the angel train.

When taught by thee the way to heaven,
These for whose sake thy life was given
    Gather from Burmah's shore
Thy name shall mingle with the song
Rising from that immortal throng
    Loved and to sin no more.

We may not comfort, though for years,
Our sympathy, our prayers, our tears
    Have known no ebbing tide;
Though oft we deemed our love had power
To cheer thee in thy bitter hour
    Were we but by thy side.

Now we are near thee. On thy head
Again affliction's hand is laid
    Can we console thee now?
Alas! Words would but mock the grief
Too deep to find on earth relief
    Which shades thy placid brow.

We may not *praise*; we dare not tell
The love with which our bosoms swell
    Nor can we cheer thy heart;
But with a power unfelt till now,

We would call down upon thy brow,
    A blessing ere we part.

We *bless* thee. Feelings long repressed,
Emotions ne'er before expressed,
    Break from their long control.
We *bless* thee with no uttered word,
But heaven the voiceless prayer has heard,
    The language of the soul.

We bless thee for the living light,
Poured upon Burmah's starless night
    Bidding its darkness flee;
Let heathen converts tell the rest:
They bless thee and thou shall be blest
    Through all eternity.

Farewell! We may not call thee ours,
Beloved from childhood's early memory
    Thy home is far away.
Thou art not of us, and thy heart,
Even now is longing to depart,
    We may not bid thee stay.

Yet, yet 'tis hard to let thee go,
Feeling that never more below,
    Thou in our midst may'st dwell
How will our spirits cling to thee
Though we no more thy face may see;
    We will not say—Farewell.

We will go with thee. Seas may roll
Between our homes, love the free soul
    Across their waves shall glide
God grant us, when this life is over
To meet thee on a happier shore
    And still be by thy side.

Feb. 18th 1846 R. A. Rhees

Source: American Baptist Historical Society, A.J. 7, No. 148.

Adoniram Judson to Emily E. Chubbuck, February 19, 1846—Philadelphia

My dearest Love,

Not a single word yet from you. I longed for a letter last night to relieve me from my anxiety. My imagination conjures up some illness or disaster which may have befallen you on the way to New York. But I commend you in my prayers to the kind care of our heavenly friend. I think of you incessantly—O that the love of Jesus blended with all my thoughts, as the love of you does. Think of me, dearest, but think of the Savior more.

I *suggest* that in the sentence,—"but that same day a man knelt in prayer." the word *person* be substituted for *man?* I beg you to erase the word *honestly* in my phrase—*plainly* and *honestly.* It had no meaning, but was hitched on to the other word, as we sometimes do, in a current common-place phrase. The offensive implication was never in my mind, even at the dark time when I wrote that letter. Believe me, love, that I only meant to say, "tell me plainly," And as the word "honestly" does injustice to us both, I beg that it may be effectively erased from the letter.[121]

Since writing the above, I have been so miserable. Hour after hour passed away and brought no letter from you, though several came all day from other quarters. The Gillettes[122] also became much concerned. I fancied you sick and friendless in New York—unable to write[123]—and another night-mare, (not the Washington and Richmond *familiar*[124]) came to the squatting place, and under that load, I was called at 5 o'clock to face Mr. Gillette's meeting house, quite full of ladies, and was obliged to speak for full fifteen minutes, so as to be heard. This is the third day that I have had to attend such female meetings. Well, I got home and sent Mr. Robarts[125] for the third time to the post office, and at 7 o'clock he put your dear letter into my hand. The beast fled after his elder brother. Thank God you are well and are probably now in Albany. I wish I could know how you have borne the

---

[121] This is a reference to the letter of Adoniram Judson to Emily E. Chubbuck dated February 3, 1846. He had written about how he interpreted what she had said in her letters to Willis: "If this is the case, had you not better say so plainly [Note: "and honestly" is written and crossed out]!"

[122] See vol. 1, "Cast of Characters," s.v. "Gillette, The Reverend Abram Dunn."

[123] Emily left Philadelphia on February 17 and traveled to New York City for an overnight at the William Colgate home. Col. John Gratiot accompanied her to Albany, and he made sure that she was on transportation to Utica, which she reached on February 20.

[124] See the letters between Adoniram Judson and Emily Chubbuck beginning January 28, 1846, as they discussed the "nightmares" they were creating for each other during what seemed to be a time of indecision, discovery, and seemingly questioning their commitment to each other. Most of the issue centered on her guilt and angst over her letters to N. P. Willis and her desire to have them returned to save future embarrassment to them all. Adoniram Judson was eloquently pastoral in his responses, though at times Emily would pick up what she thought was a sharp edge to his words, and then she would fire off another salvo in an ongoing uncomfortable discussion.

[125] See vol. 1, "Cast of Characters," s.v. "Robarts, Mr. and Mrs. W. S."

fatigue of this day. I hope well, and that tomorrow you will find yourself safe in the bosom of your friends. But you will find none among them that loves you as I do. Nor will you find one (how proud and happy I am to think so) that you can love as you love me—Dearest dear, love me with all my unloveliness and faults, and I will love you with all your excellencies. Faults indeed you have before God—great faults—We are both, I fear, low in religion,—in all things coming short of the glory of God. But we must bear with and help one another, and become blessings to each other's souls. I shall leave this for Baltimore tomorrow morning. Please to direct my letters to "W. S. Robarts Esq. Philadelphia"—Mr. R. says, give my love to Cousin Emily. In your autograph just sent for Mr. Sartain,[126] you write "holier purposes." In mentioning the subject to me at Richmond, you wrote "loftier" etc. so varying from the original. Was this accidental?[127]—or have you any preference? When you write me, please to ascertain, as soon as you can, whether the stage-coach travels from Utica to Hamilton every day, and whether before or after, and how long after the train from Albany comes in. If you should have gone to Hamilton, would there be time for me to make a private call on Miss Sheldon[128] and Cousin 'Bel'?[129] And could this be done so that no one besides should know that I have arrived at Utica? Please to advise and direct me in all these matters.

My life, I love thee. [Note: Here there is a line written in Biblical Greek.] In Burmese thus [Note: Here there is a line written in Burmese characters.]—that is, Ngah athet thengo ngah kyeet-the. When shall I again throw my arms around you and fastening my lips to yours, feel that I have indeed two lives in one. Think of me kindly, dearest, while far away. Change of scene and friends will perhaps direct your thoughts from me and divide your affections. But you will not forget me. You will not forget, when lying in Anne Maria's[130] arms and nestling in her bosom, that there are other arms and another bosom, that loves you for a stronger, dearer claim. Thine are those arms and bosom and all I am and have—and how thankful and joyful do I ever feel, that your kind, sweet love allows me this precious privilege of saying that I am thine. Heaven will be brighter to me for thy presence.

---

[126] John Sartain was an engraver who brought to the publishing world the art of mezzotint engraving. On January 31, Emily wrote to Adoniram Judson, "Mr. Gillette saw a portrait of you painted by Pratt in Mr. Sully's studio a few days ago. Mr. Sartain was engraving it. Mr. G. says that it is a good likeness, except that it makes the face too thin; and Mr. S. will engrave it beautifully." Mr. Sartain, within a few months, would be doing a magnificent engraving of Emily for the publication of *Alderbrook*.

[127] See the letter of Emily E. Chubbuck to Adoniram Judson of February 15, 1846. She suggested the possibility of having an engraving of herself published as she left for Burmah with the caption: "Henceforth to loftier purposes, I pledge myself [signed] Fanny Forester."

[128] See vol. 1, "Cast of Characters," s.v. "Sheldon, Miss Cynthia."

[129] "Cousin 'Bel'" was Anna Maria Anable and the "character" from Emily's letter to the *New Mirror*, which was published on June 8, 1844 and catapulted Emily to literary fame. The letter concerned Emily and Cousin 'Bel's visit to New York and their lack of money to enjoy the wares of the many shops they passed. She asked if the editor of the *New Mirror* would like to help them out.

[130] See vol. 1, "Cast of Characters," s.v. "Anable, Miss Anna Maria."

Those will be with Ann[131] and Sarah[132]—We shall join in the same song of love and praise.[133] And how happy we shall be in beholding one another's faces glow with heavenly rapture, as we drink in the life-giving, joy-inspiring smiles of Him, whom we shall all feel to love above all.

Thine in life and forever

A Judson

Source: Hanna family files.

Charles Chubbuck[134] to J. Walker Chubbuck, February 21, 1846—Hamilton NY

Dear Walker,

As important events are about taking place in our family, I feel it my duty and privilege to write to you. I shall make no apology for not writing before, but proceed to give a sketch of our affairs. My health is as good as can be expected for a man of my age and feeble constitution, I carry the mail 2 1/2 days a week and do my chores, but am not able to work much. Your mother's[135] health is very feeble, she has a very bad cough, bleeds considerably at the lungs, and has other complaints. She was under the doctor's care a good part of last summer and at times since, and is better on some accounts than she was last Summer, but very feeble yet. Catharine's[136] health has been better the past year than it was some years ago, but for a few days she has not been as well as usual. Wallace[137] took a school in this town about five miles from home, for three months, closed in on the 13th instant, and on the 17th went to Madison to teach one month and a half, where they had turned away their teacher, his health is not very good. He thinks of making a busi-

---

[131] Ann Hasseltine Judson, the first wife of Adoniram Judson. They were married in 1812, and she died in 1826.

[132] Sarah Hall Boardman Judson, the second wife of Adoniram Judson. They were married in 1834, and she died in 1845.

[133] Emily wrote of Ann Hasseltine Judson and Sarah Hall Boardman Judson: "For death but lays his mystic spell / Upon affection's earthliness; / I know that though thou lov'st me well, / Thou lov'st thy sainted none the less."

[134] Emily's father, Charles Chubbuck, was born at Bedford, New Hampshire on March 3, 1780; he was married to Lavinia Richards in Goffstown, New Hampshire on November 17, 1805. They were to have seven children. Though he held varying jobs over the years, he failed at many of them, and Emily was the main support of the family after she purchased a home for her family in fall 1842.

[135] Emily's mother. See vol. 1, "Cast of Characters," s.v. "Chubbuck, Lavinia Richards."

[136] See vol. 1, "Cast of Characters," s.v. "Chubbuck, Miss Sarah Catharine."

[137] Born January 1, 1824, William Wallace Chubbuck was six years younger than Emily. During these years of Emily's correspondence, Wallace lived at or near home and worked at different occupations including printing, office work, and teaching. Emily wrote of him as capable in many areas, but seeming to lack ambition at times. He proved to be a strong support for the Chubbuck family over these years, and at the time of her death in 1854, Wallace had become one of Emily's primary caregivers. After February 1854, she dictated all her letters to him because of her failing strength. Wallace was active in newspaper and political activities; he also worked with at least one of the legislative committees in Albany. He was married in July of 1854; he died in August of 1861.

ness of teaching, and intends to get a school next summer if he can. Benjamin[138] is in Michigan at Dea. Holland's this winter, his health was very poor when we heard from him last, probably he never will do much, his wife and children are at her father's in Morrisville.

But the most important news is about Emily. You know she has become one of the most popular female writers in America, well, would you believe it? She is going to be married to the Rev. Adoniram Judson D. D., Missionary to Burmah, who is on a visit to this country after an absence of thirty-three years in Burmah. Emily went to Philadelphia in the fall, intending to make a visit and return to Utica, but was urged and accepted an invitation to spend the winter there at the Rev. A. D. Gillette's.[139] After she had been there sometime, Doctor Judson visited the city, became acquainted with her, and the agreement was formally concluded between them in January. They will probably be married about the last of June, and sail for Burmah soon after.

Doctor J. is 57 years old, is one of the best and most noted of men, and I believe he and Emily think all the world of each other. Will it not be consistent for you to make us a visit in the spring? We all want to see you very much, and Emily says you will never see her unless you come then and she is very anxious to see you.

Write as soon as you receive this and let us know how you are and what you think about coming home though I hope you will conclude to come. Our friends are generally in usual health.

When you write, let us know about your circumstances, what business you follow etc. I cannot think of any thing further that would be very interesting to you.

Things generally go on about as usual. We have had first rate Sleighing from the first of December to the 15th of February without interruption, just snow enough to make Sleighing. On the 15th the snow fell over two feet deep, we have had another storm since, and the snow now over three feet deep, and roads considerably blocked up. But I must conclude my letter. Don't fail to write immediately.

Yours most affectionately
Charles Chubbuck

Source: Jerome Walker Chubbuck Collection, Wisconsin Historical Society Archives, Madison WI.

---

[138] Emily's older brother Benjamin or "Ben" was born March 25, 1809. In a biography of her life that she wrote for Adoniram Judson after their marriage, Emily told of how Ben, as a young boy, had sustained some kind of brain inflammation, which seriously impaired his judgment and behavior. See Emily's letter of February 18, 1838 for some sharp comments on Ben. Then, on April 2, 1839, Emily wrote to her brother Walker that Ben had been sent to state prison for stealing a horse, blanket, and saddle. Later correspondence had litanies of such problems—stealing a cow, difficulties holding jobs, problems with his marriage, and situations exacerbated by character flaws. He died in September, 1846, shortly after Emily had left for Burmah. Ben had married Ann Fleming of Morrisville in 1837, and he was the father of two children.

[139] See vol. 1, "Cast of Characters," s.v. "Gillette, The Reverend Abram Dunn."

Mrs. Eliza C. Allen to Emily E. Chubbuck, February 21, 1846[140]— New York

My Dear Miss Chubbuck

I have many reasons for being anxious to write to you, and also for mortification and apprehension in doing so; and I shall proceed to allude to some of both, without specifying a distinction, which your own ingenuity will discover. I must promise, however, that I addressed a letter to you at Utica after I last received anything from you, but cannot recollect at what period. A considerable time afterward I heard that you had been in Phila, but did not learn whether you are still there. Again, last fall I learned that you had been in this city, and had gone to Phila, and would return at a certain time to Mr. Colgate's,[141] when I called to see you, but without success. From that time, when I relinquished the hope of seeing you here for the present, I have been purposing to write to you. You will, I trust, do me the justice to recollect that most of the time previous to that, for a year or more, I was ignorant of your residence, and that my last letter was unanswered—probably never recd by you.

I have very much feared that nothing like justice was ever recd from me by you. I instructed B. B. & H.[142] of Utica to furnish you the *Mother's Journal* regularly, and begged you to let me know if they did not, as I would have it sent by mail; and the only reason why I did not do so, irrespective of them was, to save you postage. I am ignorant, however, how that is—Of course, you have not rec'd it for a year or more, for I have not known how to get it into your hands. I should be happy to send the work to you, if it will interest you at all; and shall request our agents to furnish it to you in Phila.

I also repeatedly *instructed* B. B. & H. to pay you whatever was due from me for your contributions, after the work came into our hands at the commencement of 1844; and *reminded* them to do the same on their own account for former years— respecting this last, I could not dictate. I also sent you an order upon the firm, and requested you to receive pay't from them. I do not know whether you ever recd this, or are aware of the efforts I have made that you should do so.

---

[140] This letter was sent to Emily in Philadelphia and forwarded to her at "Miss Sheldon's Female Academy, Utica."

[141] See the letter from James B. Colgate to Emily E. Chubbuck dated January 27, 1846.

[142] The publishing house of Bennett, Backus, and Hawley. Mr. Horace H. Hawley enjoyed a family relationship with the Sheldon family. Emily's letter of May 7, 1841 said that he was to marry a niece of Misses Cynthia and Urania Sheldon and Mrs. Alma Sheldon Anable, the daughter of their brother John Sheldon. Through the help of Miss Cynthia Sheldon, he was introduced into the life of Emily Chubbuck. A member of a publishing firm, he also worked with Alexander Beebee in publishing the *Baptist Register*. Beginning in 1841 with the publication of *Charles Linn*, Mr. Hawley was enormously helpful to Emily Chubbuck as she was publishing her early stories and books. There are numerous references to his help and generosity. With Cynthia Sheldon, her parents and her sister Alma Anable, Mr. Hawley had been a charter member of the Bleecker Street Baptist Church in Utica in 1838.

Allow me to send to you by the first opportunity the vols. of the Jour. for /44 and /45 bound in one, as a slight token that I have not forgotten my obligations to you.

I send with this the first 3 nos. for the present year. In the first I have a little *notice* of your volume published in this city.[143] I should have sent you the No. when it came out, but that I wished to write at the same time; and I have been looking for leisure ever since. But this is a word which I have almost ceased to use in regard to myself. My time is occupied to the utmost, as I believe I could convince you by a little sketch of my engagements. However, I have resolved to take time to give myself the pleasure of writing, if I could not find the leisure.

And now let me beg to hear from you at an early day. And will you not still show some favor to my unpretending publication. I shall be very sorry to lose you, altho' I may not, perhaps, be able to hold out all the inducements to attract your pen, that some other works do. But will not the prospect of usefulness be a consideration in addition to any more material that I would suggest?

I hope there is nothing in the *notice* to which I have referred, which convicts me of playing the monitor too far. But indeed, my dear Miss C., I am a little jealous for you. Do not bestow all your fine talent upon the fashionable, light magazines. Let the children have some more of those capital books. We want just such a pen as yours in Christian literature. We have prosy didactic writers enough, but we cannot spare you.

I hope your health is confirmed by a Phila sojourn, and that we shall soon have the pleasure of seeing you in New York. Please write me how you are, and when you propose to be in the city; and be sure you inform me how [ ] [ ] [ ] [ ] stands. Direct to me, B[ ] P.O.—no number.

My own health is tolerable good. It was improved by a three month's Journey to the west last year of which, by the way, you may see some slight sketches in the July, Aug., and Sept. Nos. of the Journal.

Affectionately yours

Eliza C. Allen

Source: American Baptist Historical Society, AJ 22, no. 1087.

---

[143] On November 22, 1845, *Trippings in Author-land*, a collection of stories Emily had written for various magazines, was released by the publishers.

Emily E. Chubbuck to Adoniram Judson, February 22, 1846— Utica NY

My Dearest friend,

I cannot tell you how disappointed I was when the mail came in to-night without bringing me a letter from you. I suppose the neglect must be owing to the late storm and the state of the roads, and I would not fret myself about it, but for your sake. I fancy that you may be anxious to hear from your pet not knowing but she may have been lost in a snow drift. (Oh, such snows as we have! I had quite forgotten that they could be so deep.) I should have written you immediately on my arrival, but I reached here the very day (Friday) on which you were to leave P. and I have no sure address. I hope this will reach you.

I had an excessively tedious day on Thursday—left New York at six and reached Albany at 10 1/2 o'clock so fatigued that I could scarce drag myself to my room. Col. Gratiot[144] was the kindest and most careful of escorts—pitied me, and got me all the nice things that he could, but I missed your two arms sadly. Mrs. Nott[145] expected me to stay in Schenectady[146] until Monday but it was storming so that I was afraid the roads might be blocked up by that time and so I came on. Reached here about three o'clock, and oh, such an uproar as we had! Was'nt [sic] I happy, though? Oh, dear, dear doctor, you cannot imagine how I love all these darling people. It seems harder to go to Burmah than ever, but yet I know that you will make it easy for me—I love these, but you are far dearer.

I have been thinking almost constantly of Willis[147] for a few days past. He has many noble traits of character and has been a true generous friend to me; and I sh'd like to make some return. I am anxious to do him good and it seems as though I might. If he would only become a truly pious man and turn his singular talents to good—if he would, dear doctor! Will you help me pray for him? You will not mistake my interest, I am sure; and I hope you will not consider his case a desperate one. Mr. Hoffman[148] told me that this step of mine would affect some of my friends powerfully. If it would only be blest to W. Will you help me pray for it darling "Home."[149] I shall write when he returns and I find a kind of confidence in the result that I have not felt before. If I could only see him a humble Christian man, and in the slightest degree through my means I sh'd feel as tho' I had accomplished the work of a life-time.

---

[144] See vol. 1, "Cast of Characters," s.v. "Gratior, Colonel John."

[145] See vol. 1, "Cast of Characters," s.v. "Nott, Urania Sheldon."

[146] See the letter of Mrs. Urania Sheldon Nott to Emily E. Chubbuck dated January 29, 1846.

[147] See vol. 1, "Cast of Characters," s.v. "Willis, Nathaniel Parker."

[148] See vol. 1, "Cast of Characters," s.v. "Hoffman, Charles Fenno."

[149] In a letter from Emily E. Chubbuck to Adoniram Judson dated February 18, 1846, Emily addressed Judson as "my own dear 'home.'"

Anna Maria[150] is very jealous of you and threatens to give you a severe scolding, so you may as well be prepared. You will have to suffer terribly when you get here. By the way, there is a rumour [*sic*] of our engagement at Hamilton, though it is not credited. Some Miss Trevors, formerly of Philadelphia have [*sic*] rec'd letters from P. full of suspicions.

Lydia Lillybridge[151] is not only willing, but quite anxious to go with us (she says from mere love to me, but if her self-sacrificing spirit is not a missionary one, I am not a judge of those things) and she promises to make herself very useful. I don't know whether she would be of much use, but if she could it would make me perfectly happy to take her. She is a singular creature. I do not believe there is another person in the wide world with her education and prospects who would consent to leave friends and country and take upon herself the duties of a servant. She insists that she could do a great deal in the way of sewing, ironing, dusting and putting to rights all about and that she could save a servant. Then—But I am filling my letter with this because we have just been talking it over—no other reason.

Oh, how I do want to see you, dearest! I shall make my way to the "loggery"[152] soon, and then we will have just the sweetest pleasantest time when you come. I am quite enchanted with the prospect. You don't know what a darling little bird's nest of a loggery it is. Then on our return they are planning to give us a quiet pleasant time here. Anna Maria says you shall sit in our room and she is in school all day. It will be delightful.

I must not write any more [*sic*]. Don't forget to love me and think of me, and pray for me, and believe yourself always close in the heart of

Yours forever,

Emily

Source: Special Collections, Colgate University, Hamilton NY.

Emily E. Chubbuck to Mr. Horace Binney Wallace, February 23, 1846 —Utica NY

My Very Excellent Friend,—

I regret exceedingly the *malapropos* illness which prevented me from seeing you again before I took my final leave of Philadelphia, particularly as I wished to have a good, cozy, confidential *talk* with you, which, for reasons that you will understand and appreciate, I deferred till a good-bye meeting.

---

[150] See vol. 1, "Cast of Characters," s.v. "Anable, Miss Anna Maria."

[151] See vol. 1, "Cast of Characters," s.v. "Lillybridge, Miss Lydia," also the timeline on "Lydia Lillybridge Simons."

[152] The loggery was Emily's father's home. See Kendrick, *The Life and Letters of Mrs. Emily C. Judson*, 166. See also vol. 1, "Places, Events, Organizations, and Magazines," s.v. "Loggery, The."

What induced you to suspect that I was going to Burmah? Did you see any thing [sic] missionary-like in Fanny Forester?[153] You don't know how your suspicion pleased and encouraged me; for I expected that the first thought of my friends would be a lunatic asylum and straight jacket. You were right. I expect to sail about the first of July, and under the protection of Dr. Judson. I am a great admirer of greatness—real, genuine greatness; and goodness has an influence which I have not the power to resist. I believe the reason that I have never loved before (for I think that I have a somewhat loving nature) is, that I never saw the two so beautifully combined in one person. My good Doctor's hair is as black as the raven's wing yet; but if it were not, if he were many years older, it would be all the same: I would go with him the world over. There is a noble structure within, singularly combining delicacy and strength, which will afford me protection and shelter in this world—a place where my own weak nature may rest itself securely—a thing that never will grow old, and that I shall love in eternity. So you see that, in going to Burmah, I make no sacrifices; for the things that I resign, though more showy, are not half as dear to me as those which I gain. I believe that you know women well enough, and know this one woman well enough, to see clearly how that can be.

What I have told you is, perhaps, enough to make you understand that I would not object to Siberia, or Patagonia, or Burmah, since my heart-home goes with me; but will you believe me when I tell you that I find actual pleasure in the thought of going? Did you ever feel as though all the things that you were engaged in were so trivial, so aimless, that you fairly sickened of them, and longed to do something more worthy of your origin and destiny? I can not [sic] describe the feeling entirely; but it has haunted me for the last six months, sleeping and waking—in the crowd and in solitude—till, from being the most contented of humans, I have been growing dissatisfied with every thing [sic]. True, I had the power to amuse, and make some people momentarily happy. I tried to weave some little moral into all I wrote; and while doing so, endeavored to persuade myself that this was sufficient. But, though I seemed to convince myself, I was not convinced nor satisfied. Now it is different. I shall really have an opportunity of spending my short life in the way which would make me most happy—in doing real, permanent good. Here, there are so many others better and more influential than myself, that what little influence I now and then find myself capable of exerting, seems entirely lost—is like one leaf on the tree which shelters you from the sun—of some worth as part of a great mass, but comparatively useless. There, every word and act will have a very important bearing. The consciousness of this will make me more watchful of myself, more careful to be governed by the very highest of principles and motives; and so a double good will result. It is the same with my pen. With all the wise

[153] Emily Chubbuck as Fanny Forester. See vol. 1, "Cast of Characters," s.v. "Chubbuck, Emily," also "Forester, Fanny."

heads in the country plotting a literary inundation, what can the brain of poor, simple Fanny Forester effect? *There* is a great nation on whose future character every pen-stroke will have a bearing. Doctor Judson has given them the entire Scriptures, written several small books in the Burmese, and has nearly completed a dictionary of the language. He will be the founder of a national literature, give its tone (a pure and holy influence he exerts) to the character of a mighty people; and I must own that I feel rather inclined to thrust in my own little finger. Do you wonder? Do you think that I am carried away by a foolish enthusiasm—a false zeal? or do you think that I have made a sober, common-sense estimate of things, and decided wisely? As to my way of living there, I shall be obliged to deny myself many luxuries and elegancies which I know I shall miss very much at first, for the salary of a missionary is small; but I shall try to make every thing as tasteful and home-like as possible, and then accommodate myself to circumstances.

I will promise you not to write a journal, for I have no greater fancy for holding up a heart-thermometer before the world than you; and I don't think that I shall be any "wiser," or any more in love with wisdom than ever. I confidently expect, however, to be very, very happy; and to make a dear, little home, which, if you ever "go to the Indies to make your fortune," you shall not think it a very great bore to visit. And hereby, Mr. Wallace, consider yourself invited to Maulmain. When may we expert to see you?

Please keep my secret for me until it becomes public; and let me know that I have your earnest and hearty God-speed. The approbation of my friends will make the painful parting from them and the home which I love, oh, so dearly! much easier. Probably I never shall see you again; but whether I do or not, I shall think of you, and the kind interest you have shown in me, often; and shall always be your most sincere friend,

Emily Chubbuck.

Source: A. C. Kendrick, *The Life and Letters of Mrs. Emily C. Judson*, 158–60.

Adoniram Judson to Emily E. Chubbuck,[154] February 23, 1846— Baltimore

My dearest Love, A storm prevented my leaving Phil. on Friday as I intended, so that I did not reach this city till Saturday afternoon. Yesterday I was exhibited, as usual, at the three principal churches here. I intend to leave this, on Thursday the 26th, spend a day or two at Wilmington; the next sabbath, that is, the 1st of March, and a day two more at Philada., thence to New York—a day or two there;

[154] There is an addendum to this letter dated February 24, 1846.

thence to Hartford, and spend the second sabbath in March there;—and thence to Hamilton incognito, as I traveled from Richmond to Philad—for I shall not reach the loggery[155] in all March, if I proceed in the usual way. There is a special reason, why I should take Hartford in my way now, as I should go up the North river at once, as I suppose it will be open by that time. The above is the course I shall take, if nothing unforseen prevents, so that if you will write me once, after receiving this and direct to the care of I. Newton Esq. New York;[156] it is all the letter I can calculate on receiving from you, till I see you face to face, or rather clasp you heart to heart, in an embrace which this long absence will make to me—O so sweet—so you anticipate the same, dearest!

Source: Hanna family files.

Adoniram Judson to Emily E. Chubbuck, February 24, 1846[157]

I have risen this morning before light and made a fire that I might get a little time to write you before company comes in. All the forenoon it will be incessant. I am to dine out—and then a tea party—and later in the evening, a musical concert. O for a lodge—or a loggery,[158] which is a far better thing than ever poor Cowper dreamt of. How could he? He was never in love. Not that I could intimate being myself in that category—But I must say, that I am anxious to get your first letter from your new position.[159] I must own that I am a little afraid (now don't make up a face) that being in new circumstances, a change may come over the spirit of your dreams—that those "misgivings" that Cousin 'Bel'[160] spoke of, may come to haunt you in the day time. May they never venture near the pillow that your sweet cheek presses, or if they do, let me in imagination lay my face close to yours and kiss them all away. I wish I had pressed the subject of a private marriage—Tremlett and Isny—Frere—I fancy you did listen some. If I ever get you in cue again—at the log-

---

[155] The loggery was Emily's father's home. See Kendrick, *The Life and Letters of Mrs. Emily C. Judson,* 166. See also vol. 1, "Places, Events, Organizations, and Magazines," s.v. "Loggery, The."

[156] There are seven letters in this correspondence from Mr. and Mrs. Isaac Newton of New York City. In a June 1846 letter, Mrs. Newton indicated that they are "new friends," certainly of Emily. They obviously had considerable wealth, which they shared generously with Adoniram and Emily through packages and, upon Adoniram's death, an immediate check to Emily of $500. Mr. Newton called Adoniram his "friend." One of the letters invited Emily to stay with them in New York upon her return, and a later letter indicated that she had indeed done that. On May 15, 1846, Adoniram Judson inscribed a dedication to Mrs. H. H. Newton on the fly-leaf of a volume of Burmese hymns that had been compiled by Mrs. Sarah B. Judson: "Mrs. H. H. Newton From A. Judson/ The wings [ ] [ ] / [ ] are folded in St. Helena—New York—May 15th, 1846."

[157] This letter is an addendum to Adoniram Judson's letter of February 23, 1846.

[158] The loggery was Emily's father's home. See Kendrick, *The Life and Letters of Mrs. Emily C. Judson,* 166. See also vol. 1, "Places, Events, Organizations, and Magazines," s.v. "Loggery, The."

[159] Emily had left Philadelphia on February 17, and arrived in Utica, New York, on the 20th.

[160] "Cousin 'Bel" was Anna Maria Anable.

gery—Raymond,[161] who is already in the secret, can be sworn to further secrecy over a Bowie, you know—wouldn't it be a nice thing, when near embarking—old folks begin to look grave and intimate the propriety of being married, to be able to stare them out of [ ]ntinance, with—why, we were married long ago! Do pray let us continue to get a little romance into the thing and not plod along in the old humdrum fashion. However, have it all your own way, darling, I am sure your way will be the best. Yes, my own dear pet, you shall be petted—But I want to know, whether you are to be always in the passive participle and never in the active. What if I should want to be petted just now and then only.—Don't you think you could shake off your passivity upon a pinch?

I shall seal this letter with your wafer and as I put it to my lips, shall remember where it has been before. You will find a lot of kisses stored away under it. Suppose you send them to auction. You might turn a handsome penny, or especially if some of my flames should be within sound of the hammer—"That men should be vain." So I will not tell you how many times my virtue has been endangered since you left [Note: Written in the right margin of the address page.] me. But as my vanity can afford to bear a slight blow I will just tell you, that my Richmond flame, the belle of Virginia, has just sent me $50 and *no lock*![162] O sad—

My dearest love, Don't forget me—I think of you incessantly. O that the love of Jesus blended with all my thoughts, as the love of you—

Written in the left margin of the address page: "Endeavour [*sic*], dearest, to commit yourself to God for all the future, in some peculiar act of strong faith and certain conscience, whh [which] you may be sure will secure to you the divine protection, and advance your soul in the divine life."

Ever entirely thine

A. Judson

Source: Hanna family files, Adoniram to Emily.

Emily E. Chubbuck to Adoniram Judson,[163] February 25, 1846

My best, dearest friend,

Your sweet letter came yesterday[164] and I have bestowed on it all of the kisses which your lips should have rec'd. You are right—none of these friends,

---

[161] See vol. 1, "Cast of Characters," s.v. "Raymond, Dr. John Howard."

[162] This is an allusion to the letter from N. P. Willis to Emily Chubbuck dated December 31, 1846, in which he enclosed a lock of his hair. Emily then sent it on to Adoniram in her letter of January 30, 1846.

[163] For an understanding of the comparison on an original letter with the letter actually printed by Dr. A. C. Kendrick in *The Life and Letters of Mrs. Emily C. Judson*, see the first footnote for the letter of Emily to Adoniram dated January 31, 1846.

[164] See the letter of Adoniram Judson to Emily E. Chubbuck dated February 19, 1846.

very very dear though they are, can I love as I love you.[165] And I am so anxious to see you. Please write the minute you get this and let me know when to expect you—the very day. The stage for Hamilton leaves about twenty minutes after the cars come in.[166] You can give your trunk to a porter to take to the stage-office and go with him or perhaps send by him to order them to call for you at Miss Sheldon's Seminary.[167] Then come up Genesee St. (I believe the stage office is on your way—the lefthand side a few doors below the bridge— that is before you reach the bridge) and stop at a large straw-coloured [sic] brick building on the corner of Washington and Genesee and call for Miss Sheldon[168] and Miss Anable.[169] They say you shall see no one else. Perhaps you had better send your name on a card, as they might otherwise be in less haste to meet you. It would be perfectly safe—the servant would deliver it to none but them. And don't dear, pray don't stop at N.Y. or Albany or anywhere; I long so much to see you.

I must own to you, dearest, now that I am away from you, misgivings will trouble me. I believe that you love me with the whole of your noble heart; but I am afraid, when the whole storm of wonderment bursts upon us, you will—perhaps you will not doubt your having acted wisely—but I am afraid you will be very much troubled. I know that there will be a great deal said—a great many unpleasant things—and should I not feel badly to see you made sad for a single moment by having taken such an unworthy creature to your heart? I can not [sic] make-believe good when I am not; but I pray God daily to make me better and wiser, to fit me for the future, and make me a blessing instead of a curse to you who have loved me with all my follies. I will try to be all to you that I can, and to do all the good that I can, but I feel that it would be wicked cant in me to sit down and talk in the canting way that the multitude expect. **Don't tell me that I am wrong, darling; what might be wise and pardonable in another would be hypocrisy in me. I have been led into this by a conversation that I had with Miss Sheldon this morning.**

[165] Closing his letter to Emily dated February 19, 1846, Adoniram Judson said:

> When shall I again throw my arms around you and fastening my lips to yours, feel that I have indeed two lives in one. Think of me kindly, dearest, while far away. Change of scene and friends will perhaps direct your thoughts from me and divide your affections. But you will not forget me. You will not forget, when lying in Anne Maria's arms and nestling in her bosom, that there are other arms and another bosom, that loves you for a stronger, dearer claim. Thine are those arms and bosom and all I am and have—and how thankful and joyful do I ever feel, that your kind, sweet love allows me this precious privilege of saying that I am thine.

[166] In his letter of February 19, Adoniram asked Emily to provide him with this information on catching the coach. He also hoped to catch a quick visit with Anna Maria Anable and Miss Cynthia Sheldon.

[167] This is the Utica Female Academy where Miss Sheldon was in charge of the financial and administration departments.

[168] See vol. 1, "Cast of Characters," s.v. "Sheldon, Miss Cynthia."

[169] See vol. 1, "Cast of Characters," s.v. "Anable, Anna Maria. See vol. 1, "Cast of Characters," s.v. "Anable, Anna Maria."

[170] See vol. 1, "Cast of Characters," s.v. "Chubbuck, Miss Sarah Catharine."

Did I tell you that the news of our engagement was all over Hamilton. I had a letter from Kate[170] saying that a Philadelphia lady had written the news to a friend in H. Kate still professes great ignorance. If you can slip into our house quietly, you may remain several days before it is discovered that you are there. You can have it quiet here too—up in this dear little room where nobody ever comes. Mrs. Nott[171] has been here and is just as kind as she can be. She is very anxious to have you pay them a visit and I have promised to use all my influence to induce you to stop there on your return to Albany. Anna Maria and I will go to Schenectady with you, and stay after you are gone a week or two. By that means I shall escape the storm of surprise which I expect will overwhelm the city. The current report here is that I am engaged to Mr. Wallace,[172] and people are throwing up their hands and eyes in astonishment for they tho't the affair with Mr. Willis[173] was as good as in print. What will they say to you? Will you love me just as much, dear, when all the wise men in the country are thinking of a straight-jacket for you? I shall feel more secure when your two arms are folding me close and my head rests on its dear living pillow. Come soon then, dearest, just as soon as you can, and make your pet happy.—My thoughts are not for one moment away from you; but I think too too [sic] little of my Saviour. I do desire to love Him better, but I have a dull eye for the invisible. Still, pray for me, my beloved guide—pray for faith, spirituality, and all the good things that I need. I still think more of earth than heaven, "for I am frail;" but I find some pleasure in the contemplation of higher things; and a heaven with you, dearest! That is the *visible* link, my love for you. I am not afraid of loving you too much, for that love is closely connected with all my better feelings. You freed me from a glittering coil which was growing irksome to me, and you are to be my spiritual teacher. God will lead us both, but my hand will be in yours. It is His own work: He sent you, and I shall not displease Him by clinging to you with all the affection He has blessed my heart with. And you will not disappoint me when I have none but you; I am sure you will not. It is a long way to Burmah, and I have a great many friends to leave.

I intended the autograph as in the original and the word as first written was a mistake.[174] Shall I have the engravings in my books if they are published by Paine and Burgess, and if so shall I merely have Fanny Forester[175] printed at

[171] See vol. 1, "Cast of Characters," s.v. "Nott, Urania Sheldon."

[172] See vol. 1, "Cast of Characters," s.v. "Wallace, Mr."

[173] See vol. 1, "Cast of Characters," s.v. "Willis, Nathaniel Parker."

[174] On February 15, 1846, Emily wrote to Adoniram Judson and asked his opinion on having an engraving done for her public before they sailed. It was to be signed, "Henceforth to loftier purposes, I pledge myself [signed] Fanny Forester." Judson wrote on February 19, saying that she had written "holier purposes," and which did she mean.

[175] Emily Chubbuck as Fanny Forester. See vol. 1, "Cast of Characters," s.v. "Chubbuck, Emily." Also "Forester, Fanny."

the bottom, or how? Mr. Hawley[176] (B. B. and H) who has my three books insists on having them come out in the name of "F. F." and says he doubts whether he can sell an edition without it.[177] Now I cannot for various reasons consent to this and besides I sh'd like it amazingly if the books were in my own hands. I shall let the matter rest and perhaps you will talk with him about it when you come.

The word you wish crossed from the letter does no harm. Your lips cropped it effectually from my heart and effaced the shadow with it on the afternoon of your return from Richmond.[178] Indeed, instead of remembering that one word I am very proud of the confidence you repose in me, meeting me as you have under such circumstances. And now may I tell W. when I write him that instead of losing a friend he has gained another and that both of us take and will take a peculiar interest in his welfare. My conscience troubles me very much about him, for I know that I have not done quite right. I dread having him return, and have a thousand vague apprehensions of some evil. If I escape with his friendship and my own self-respect—I shall have cause for gratitude all my life long; and if I make an enemy of him it will not change my feelings of kindness, for indeed I have made a poor return for all his generous interest. Will you assist me in trying to return good for good instead of the evil I had prepared for my [ ] best friend.

Do dearest love me with all my faults—don't let the opinion of others concerning our relations turn your heart from me and believe me now and ever thine entirely

Thine own loving

Emily

Written along the left and top margins of page 1: "**Your letter did not reach me till yesterday—the mails are provokingly slow. Please give love to the**

---

[176] See vol. 1, "Cast of Characters," s.v. "Hawley, Mr. Horace H."

[177] At this time Emily was thinking of a publication much like *Trippings in Author-land*. "*Alderbrook: A Collection of Fanny Forester's Village Sketches, Poems, etc.* by Miss Emily Chubbuck." eventually came out in 1847. It was an anthology of her writings after *Trippings*, but eight of her pieces from *Trippings* were included in it.

[178] On February 3, 1846, Adoniram Judson wrote to Emily Chubbuck in response to her tortured letters, which began with her January 28, 1846 letter. He said that he wanted to leave Richmond and go "incognito" to Philadelphia before fulfilling his obligations in Baltimore so that he could try to resolve some of the issues that were coming between them. Emily wrote to Adoniram, Judson on February 5, 6, and 7. Her next letter was written on February 15, 1846, and its tone had changed completely. The dearth of letters, and her comment in this letter—"the afternoon of your return from Richmond"—all indicate that Adoniram Judson was able to spend several days in Philadelphia with Emily in this period between February 7 and February 15.

[179] See vol. 1, "Cast of Characters," s.v. "Robarts, Mr. and Mrs. W. S."

[180] See vol. 1, "Cast of Characters," s.v. "Gillette, The Reverend Abram Dunn."

Robarts[179] and Gillettes.[180] I do hope you will have no more female meetings[181] to attend; and you must not let them lionize you to your harm when you return to P. Come away as quickly as you can for I am very, very anxious to see you. I send ever and ever so many kisses—there—there—there. Heaven guard you! Good-night."

Source: Hanna family files. There is a fragment of this letter in A. C. Kendrick, *The Life and Letters of Mrs. Emily C. Judson*, 163–64.

Adoniram Judson to Emily E. Chubbuck, February 25, 1846[182]— Baltimore

I just take my pen to say good morning, my dearest love. O that I could lay my arms over you and press a good morning into your sweet lips. I am so anxious to hear that you arrived safe and well at Utica and that changing scenes have not effaced from your mind any the "love lesson"—not that I taught you—but that we taught one another. I reached home at 10 o'clock last evening, and found a letter from Maulmain Nov. 18th, mentioning the expected death of Mrs. Ingalls.[183] "Her last days were days of pleasantness and peace to herself and of instruction to us all. Her exhortations were soul-stirring, but marked with deep humility and the peculiar emotions of one just entering eternity." "Your little ones are well and doing well."[184]

Have you seen the notices of *Trippings*[185] in the Jan. number of the *Mother's Journal*?[186] I never saw it till just now and I am most gratified and delighted with it. For the *Mother's Journal* exerts a powerful influence throughout the religious world—my friends—not yours? Shall I ever forget my extraordinary proposal to run away incognito and be married in England, because I was so ashamed of you! And so afraid of breaking the hearts of all the friends and patrons of the mission! And then your naive reply—that you thought you could not be able to get out of the country without your friends knowing it! Friends, thought I, what friends has the actress got except the very scum of the yellow world, who have no business to

---

[181] On February 19, 1846, in his letter to Emily, Adoniram Judson said, "I was called at 5 o'clock to face Mr. Gillette's meeting house, quite full of ladies, and was obliged to speak for full fifteen minutes, so as to be heard. This is the third day that I have had to attend such female meetings."

[182] There are addendums to this letter dated February 27, February 28, and March 1, and they appear under those dates.

[183] Lovell and Marcia Dawes Ingalls were appointed missionaries to Burmah, arriving at Amherst on February 20, 1836. In 1838 they moved to Mergui and in May 1845 to Maulmain. Marcia Dawes Ingalls died in Maulmain on November 9, 1845. The mother of three children, her youngest, Sarah, had died in 1844.

[184] When Adoniram and Sarah Hall Boardman Judson had left Burmah because of Sarah's health, with them were Abigail (Abby Ann), Adoniram ("Pwen" or "Addy") and Elnathan ("Elly"). Because of their young age and frail health, they left behind Henry, Charles, and Edward. Charles died shortly after they left, and in fact, his death preceded that of Sarah on September 1, 1845.

[185] *Trippings in Author-land*, a collection of Emily's stories written for the magazines, was published in November 1845.

know anything about my bride elect!! O did that scamp Cupid ever go to work more recklessly and do his work more effectually, than when he lately took me in hand. But thank God "there's a sweet little cherub aloft, that kept up a watch for poor Jack." And when he was surrounded by what might have been rocks and breakers, and he half expecting the danger, still gave his canvass to the gale; they turned out to be buoy, marking out the channel of safety—guiding him to—to—the loggery[187]!

Source: Hanna family files.

Adoniram Judson to Emily E. Chubbuck, February 27, 1846[188]— Philadelphia

Just arrived and find no letter from you![189]—yet you left this ten days ago! A letter to Fanny[190] from her sister,[191] however, assures me of your safe arrival at Utica.[192] Perhaps you was [sic] taken ill immediately, from the fatigue of the journey, and have been unable to write.

Source: Hanna family files.

Adoniram Judson to Emily E. Chubbuck, February 28, 1846[193]

No letter yet.[194] Something must have happened, and I am always fearing the worst. But perhaps the cars are impeded by the snow. I have been reading over all your letters, but I am too anxious now to get another to make any comments.

---

[186] Emily wrote for the *Mother's Journal*, and there are several letters in the correspondence from its editor, Mrs. Eliza Allen. Mrs. Allen wrote on February 21, 1846 to Emily about some compensation matters and told her that there would be a piece about *Trippings in Author-land* in the next number.

[187] The loggery was Emily's father's home. See Kendrick, *The Life and Letters of Mrs. Emily C. Judson*, 166. See also vol. 1, "Places, Events, Organizations, and Magazines," s.v. "Loggery, The."

[188] This letter is an addendum to a letter begun February 25, 1846. There are also addenda dated February 28 and March 1, 1846.

[189] Emily had written on February 22, 1846.

[190] Fanny Anable was one of nine children born to Joseph and Alma Anable and was a niece of Miss Cynthia Sheldon and Mrs. Urania Sheldon Nott. The correspondence indicates that in April 1845 she was away from home studying and taking music lessons. These spring letters indicate that she was in Philadelphia, working in the home of and with the family of the Reverend A. D. Gillette. See Miss Sheldon's letter to Emily of November 30, 1845, in which she spoke of all that Fanny was doing to improve herself in the field of music, but also her concern for Fanny's interest in the party life and the "vanitie" which surround her." A March 30, 1847 letter from Anna Maria Anable told of Fanny's conversion following her grandmother's death. In September 1847, she was listed as one of the teachers at the Utica Female Academy. Fanny became a teacher with her sisters in the Misses Anable's School in Philadelphia.

[191] See vol. 1, "Cast of Characters," s.v. "Anable, Miss Anna Maria."

[192] Emily left Philadelphia on February 17, 1846. She had stayed overnight in New York City with the Colgate family, and then accompanied by Col. John Gratiot, she had made her way to Albany, where she picked up transportation to Utica. She arrived in Utica on February 20.

[193] This letter was an addendum to one started February 25, with another addition on February 27 and yet another on March 1, 1846.

[194] Emily wrote to Adoniram Judson on February 22, 1846.

Late in the evening and no letter nor has Mr. Gillette[195] or any body [*sic*] else heard a word from you, since the day you reached Utica, and that was a week yesterday![196] If I could get one line only, saying that you are well and happy, I should go to bed with a happy heart. But not now—So closes another month—six months since the death of Sarah[197]—What further misery is impending, God knows.

Source: Hanna family files.

Emily E. Chubbuck to Adoniram Judson,[198] February 28, 1846— Utica NY

So you really expect petting of me![199] *Me!* And after I have told you that I don't know how to do anything. Babies never pet back again and I am your baby you know, so hold your arms and I will spring into them and then—well maybe I will love back a little, just a little bit. My arms are not very strong you know and I can't love so hard as you.[200]

"I fancy you did listen some!" Oh, the strange fancies of some people! Didn't I tell you that I had concluded not to be married at all just to save myself from the whipping (Old father Peck![201] I always tho't there was something sinister about him.) I don't think it at all worth while to be married; since I have returned to our pleasant nunnery I have returned to my old notions too. Wouldn't it be a very nice thing for you to take Miss H., Miss Grice, Fanny Forester[202] and few others that I might drum up for you under your paternal wing to go back to Burmah. I can fancy

---

[195] See vol. 1, "Cast of Characters," s.v. "Gillette, The Reverend Abram Dunn."

[196] Emily left Philadelphia on February 17, 1846. She had stayed overnight in New York City with the Colgate family, and then accompanied by Col. John Gratiot, she had made her way to Albany, where she picked up transportation to Utica. She arrived in Utica on February 20.

[197] Sarah Hall Boardman Judson died September 1, 1845, at the Isle of St. Helena as the Judson family was coming back to America because of her health.

[198] Beginning January 28, 1846, there were two weeks of letters filled with pain and angst over her letters she had written to N. P. Willis. Then, a shift to a gentler Emily takes place around February 15, following an unexpected return visit by Adoniram, a visit which obviously settled Emily's feelings.

[199] On February 24, Adoniram Judson wrote: "Yes, my own dear pet, you shall be petted—But I want to know, whether you are to be always in the passive participle and never in the active. What if I should want to be petted just now and then only.—Don't you think you could shake off your passivity upon a pinch?"

[200] See Adoniram Judson's letters to Emily E. Chubbuck dated February 23 and 24, 1846.

[201] The Reverend Doctor Solomon Peck was for twenty years the executive secretary of the American Baptist Missionary Union. Many believed him to be hard, stern, and judgmental, and from some of his comments, it is easy to understand that perception. Dr. Peck and Emily did not always have the easiest of relationships. She felt in him the judgment that came from many in the church at the announcement of her impending marriage to Adoniram; that judgment concerned her "secular" past and concern that she was not an appropriate companion for the venerable missionary. On July 18, 1849 Emily wrote a blistering letter of defense to Dr. Peck in response to a letter from him of February 20, 1849; her letter framed how she viewed his perception of her, and her response was meant to set the record straight. There are eleven letters in the collection from Solomon Peck to Emily.

[202] Emily Chubbuck as Fanny Forester. See vol. 1, "Cast of Characters," s.v. "Chubbuck, Emily," and "Forester, Fanny."

with what pride you would head the troop; but poor Fanny! She would have to march in the rear. Alas for the unuseful!

So I may expect you about the tenth. Bless your dear heart! I do want to see you so badly. If you stop in Hartford I hope you will call on Mrs. Sigourney;[203] and you may as well tell her all about this affair of ours. It is known pretty extensively now. Mr. Abbott[204] told it a few weeks ago at Woodstock, a little village in Madison Co. Mr. Gillette's brother made a confidant of one of his church members who has a sister residing in Hamilton, so the Hamiltonians are all on the *qui vive*. You will leave this place in the after part of the day and so I suppose will not reach H. before 10 o'clock in the evening. Poor dear doctor! How forlorn it will be. I wish I could be with you and kiss your lips warm at last. The weather is dreadfully cold and the snow on the ground is over three feet deep. If you sh'd take cold and be ill I never sh'd forgive myself for letting you come. But we will try to make it as comfortable as we can for you. You will have a tedious cold ride from here to H., worse than all the rest of the journey, and you must be very, *very* careful when you leave the cars to wrap yourself up warm. If you think the day's journey from Albany will be too much for you, stay here with Miss Sheldon,[205] do. You can stay here and none in the city know of it, and now I think of it again I am afraid to have you leave the warm cars for the stage-coach. If you sh'd take cold! If you *should*! Please, darling, do take care of yourself, do if you love your Nemmy.[206] I would rather than have you come at all than it sh'd injure you.

Please write me, a line at least, from Hartford, addressed Charles Chubbuck,[207] Hamilton, to let me be sure of the day; for if you sh'd arrive in the evening I sh'd want some intimation of it before-hand. The stage will bring you to our door. Make them find out for you where we live to set you down there without any trouble on your part. You shall find warm heart, and some warm kisses. We do keep both of these commodities at the loggery;—[208]and I will take your head into my lap and put

---

[203] Lydia Huntley Sigourney was one of the first American women to succeed at a literary career. She wrote more than forty volumes of prose and verse between 1825 and 1850. She was a strong supporter of the mission movement both at home and abroad.

The following poem, written by Mrs. Sigourney, was found in the Hanna family files, written in the handwriting of Emily E. Chubbuck. Apparently, Emily had liked it enough to copy it, and keep it for future reference and/or enjoyment:

> The spring with tardy step appears,
> Chill is her eye, and dim with tears,
> Still are the founts in fetters bound,
> The flower-germs shrink within the ground,
> Where are the warblers of the sky?
> I ask—and angry blasts reply.

[204] See vol. 1, "Cast of Characters," s.v. "Abbott, The Reverend Elisha."

[205] See vol. 1, "Cast of Characters," s.v. "Sheldon, Miss Cynthia."

[206] See vol. 1, "Cast of Characters," s.v. "Nemmy, Nem, or Nemmy Petty (Nemmie Pettie)." Also the chapter "Names of Endearment."

[207] Emily's father. See vol. 1, "Cast of Characters," s.v. "Chubbuck, Charles."

[208] The loggery was Emily's father's home. See Kendrick, *The Life and Letters of Mrs. Emily C. Judson,* 166. See also vol. 1, "Places, Events, Organizations, and Magazines," s.v. "Loggery, The."

you asleep and then you may make-believe sick and I will watch with you all through the night. I am in very, very great haste for the time to come. "Do I anticipate etc.—?" Don't I though! I do not have "misgivings" except on my own account. When I think of my own utter uselessness—my unfitness for any thing except to write stories, I can not [sic] help being sad; and. when I look away over to Burmah, and see you in your study, and me engaged in things that have never interested me and that I do not know how to do, spending day after day *alone*, my very heart retreats in utter consternation. I do not know how I shall get along with it. But the Heavenly Friend who I believe has directed all this, will be still a better friend than any one on earth; and you, dearest, will be considerate and patient—I know you will. You don't expect me to be very good or very sensible; but I shall take no advantage of that. I will be as good and wise as I can. God in heaven help me![209]

I must close lest I sh'd be too late for the mail. All blessings attend thee, my truly dearest best friend. Do not let the people tire you out. Kiss cousin 'Bel'[210] when you see her and hurry from the academy as soon as it is safe—to the blessed little loggery. Mr. Raymond[211] shall not be sworn on the Bowie;[212] but when we get back to Doct. Nott's,[213] just the morning you leave—maybe—I can't say. Kiss your pet (never mind the wise ones there in N.Y.) and make room in your bosom for your loving,

Sister Peakedchin[214]

Source: Hanna family files; A. C. Kendrick, *The Life and Letters of Mrs. Emily C. Judson*, 165.

---

[209] In *The Life and Letters of Mrs. Emily C. Judson*, A. C. Kendrick quotes these nine lines, beginning with "I do not have 'misgivings'" (165).

[210] "Cousin 'Bel'" was Anna Maria Anable.

[211] See vol. 1, "Cast of Characters," s.v. "Raymond, Dr. John Howard."

[212] In Adoniram Judson's letter of February 23, 1846, he said, "If I ever get you in cue again—at the loggery—Raymond, who is already in the secret, can be sworn to further secrecy over a Bowie, you know."

[213] The Reverend Doctor Eliphalet Nott was the president of Union College in Schenectady, New York. An ordained Presbyterian minister, he was married to Urania Sheldon Nott, the sister of Miss Cynthia Sheldon and Mrs. Alma Anable and the aunt of Anna Maria Anable.

[214] Emily E. Chubbuck used a number of different names over the course of her life and career. She wrote often under the name Fanny Forester, her argument being "who would buy a book authored by Emily Chubbuck?" At other times, she used Amy Scribbleton (July 6, 1841); Amy S. (September 28, 1841); Nem or Nemmy (Emily was always Nem or Nemmy to Anna Maria Anable who was Ninny); Pithy to Anna Maria (April 29, 1845); Peaked chin (See Anna Maria Anable, November 12, 1845); Sister Peakedchin (See Emily Chubbuck, February 28, 1846); Miss Peakedchin (Adoniram Judson, March 7, 1846); Miss Nemmy Petty (Adoniram Judson, March 7, 1846); Petty (April 13, 1846).

Emily E. Chubbuck to Urania Sheldon Nott, February 28, 1846— Utica Female Seminary

My Very Dear Friend,—

I received a letter from my good doctor on Saturday, and shall expect him in Hamilton about the middle of next week. I think of going myself on Thursday. Kate[215] advises me not to come so soon, as she fears it will become known that I am there; but I am anxious to see my mother.[216] We shall manage to pay you the proposed visit, if possible. If you will only see him as I do! I am not afraid but that you will like him; every body [sic] likes him. But it is not the wonder, the lion that I care to have you see; it is the refined, generous, high-souled, strong-minded, true-hearted man, and the humble, devoted, unostentatious Christian. I fancy that you will be pretty sure that no common man could have made a missionary of me; and no common man would have had the independence to choose me. I will endeavor to behave as well as I can; but I must own that I have been twice surprised—at seeing the tear in the eye of the careless worldling, and receiving the God-speed from his lips, and at seeing those from whom I had a right to expect encouragement looking askance and doubtful. I have resolved, however, not to see any of the latter things, and I hope they will not be forced on my attention.

I must close my letter, or Mary will be gone. Please remember me always kindly, and drop me a line when you have time. I shall try hard to return to those who need it most all the kindness which you have shown to me; and however lightly I may speak sometimes, believe me, if God spares my health, I will do good. I know I can. I have always felt that I had unappropriated energies, and, however wild the notion may seem, I think my whole life has had a tendency to prepare me for this very thing. I can see it from the very beginning to this present winter, which I commenced so gayly in P. It has been, you know, a peculiar training, and had I but more religion! Give me your prayers, and God help me!

Ever yours affectionately,
Emily

Source: A. C. Kendrick, *The Life and Letters of Mrs. Emily C. Judson*, 157–58.

Adoniram Judson to Emily E. Chubbuck, March 1, 1846[217]

No letter to be got from the post-office today because it is Sunday—May God preserve and bless you dearest

---

[215] See vol. 1, "Cast of Characters," s.v. "Chubbuck, Miss Sarah Catharine."

[216] Emily's mother. See vol. 1, "Cast of Characters," s.v. "Chubbuck, Lavinia Richards."

[217] This letter is an addendum to a letter started February 25, 1846, with additions made on February 27 and February 28.

Written in the upper margin of page 1: "Don't write me again till further advice. I fear that your letter will pass me on the way. Fanny[218] is nearly or quite well and quite contented to remain here—" Source: Hanna family files.

Mr. Horace B. Wallace to Emily E. Chubbuck,[219] March 1, 1846[220]— Philadelphia

I have rcd [*sic*] your beautiful letter, dearest Lady, with deep interest, and the liveliest gratification. If anything could have given increased enthusiasm to the perfect respect with which I have regarded the pure and exquisite nature that was revealed to my admiration when I had the happiness to become acquainted with you,[221] it would be such new evidences of goodness and high principle and noble sentiment as are implied in the intelligence which your letter communicates. So faithful a picture of a refined and elevated and generous heart must touch and charm the feelings of every one [*sic*] who has any sensitivity to excellence or any perception of what is honourable [*sic*] and great. I beg you to permit the warmest congratulations, and most earnest good wishes of one who loves you as a brother, or feels, in all that concerns your welfare the concern of a devoted friend.

Your choice is worthy of you. It commends itself to my highest sympathy and admiration. You always seemed to me to be too exalted and heaven-like for the mere affection of ordinary persons; and not to be waited upon by them with any feelings but such as so blended with something of worship. You may recollect that I said to you, at a time when I could not be suspected of a design to flatter, that Dr. Judson was one of my *heroes*; that goodness such as his, was the highest type of greatness,—far surpassing all such ambition as is founded on views that are limited by this world, and beating down the rivalry of such fame as has in it any admixture of vanity. It produces no wonder, in me, but the utmost interest and delight, to know that your spirit is so finely sensitive to the lofty attractions that belong to a character and career so disinterested—so sublime. That which at first engaged my regards and curiosity in relation to you, was the fascinating delicacy of thought and feeling which your writings displayed. What struck me most in approaching more nearly, and placed my respect upon a higher and surer basis, was, the superiority

---

[218] See vol. 1, "Cast of Characters," s.v. "Anable, Fanny."

[219] This letter was written in response to Emily's letter to Mr. Wallace of February 23, 1846.

[220] This letter was also published in A. C. Kendrick's *The Life and Letters of Mrs. Emily C. Judson.* It was printed with very little editing and is virtually identical to the original.

[221] Emily met Horace Binney Wallace on her first stay in Philadelphia in spring 1845. A member of high Philadelphia Society and a literary critic, he was a part of an intimate circle of friends when Emily was in Philadelphia. He was both Emily's mentor in her literary pursuits and a strong friend, as evidenced by the correspondence between them. Emily also established a friendship with the nephew of H. B. Wallace, an attorney, whom she called aristocratic and privileged. He seemed to have a deep interest in Emily.

which your nature insensibly always displayed to the interests and excitement of literary reputation. That "pettiness of fame" which is the glory of so many, seemed to excite your aversion; and what in other cases is the coveted result of authorship seemed to be to you the only annoying and painful part of it. These traits and evidence of the lofty and noble nature, I appreciated thoroughly, and understood. That your feelings, unsusceptible to all that addresses that portion of our being which is earthly and transitory, should respond so freely to that which appealed to those great sentiments of duty and goodness, which partake of the eternal and bring us into union with what is permanent and changeless, shows me that I had not mistaken my gentle friend; but that she whom I had valued so highly, "deserved to be dearest of all."

You may acknowledge that I possess some discernment; since, from the moment in which I first heard the name of this eminent and honoured [*sic*] person pronounced by your lips, I saw and predicted the result. The purest streams are the most transparent; and it seems to me that I can read your feelings and their operations, with great distinctness. I hope that this will be a tie of friendship between us; or, at least, that you will suffer me always to indulge those sentiments of proud and tender interest in your welfare, which perhaps I express more strongly than you will approve, but which are inseparable from my recollection of you.

You speak of the probability of my not seeing you again. I shall surely see you, before you take your leave of shore where your name will long flourish with added honours [*sic*] and new distinction. I shall come to mingle my best and brightest omens with "the might of the whole world's good wishes," that will attend your going. You will not be separated wholly from me, in seeking the realities of that *Burmah*, which I prophesied would be your destiny; for my constant thought and earnest interest will accompany you; and, even if your remembrance should never visit me, will deprive you of the power to escape from me entirely.

I feel highly honored by the confidence which you repose in me; and you may rely upon the secret being faithfully kept, while it suits your convenience to become known.

May all your hopes be realized! May all of kind and good that you intend for others, be fulfilled on them and on you. May you be happy!—"a wish—that came,—but it hath passed into a prayer."

H. B. Wallace

Source: A. C. Kendrick, *The Life and Letters of Mrs. Emily C. Judson,* 161–63; American Baptist Historical Society, AJ 27, no. 1303.

Adoniram Judson to Emily E. Chubbuck, March 1, 1846[222]

Evening—O I am so miserable. I attended Mr. Gillette's[223] communion this afternoon and made an address to the church—and afterwards I took my pay by making Gillette depart from the usages of religious people here and send to the post-office. But alas, there is no letter—I am afraid you are ill and dangerously ill, therefore it is, that none of us get any letter from you, or from your friends about you. O I am learning by sad experience how much I love you. But I have no heart to go on writing. May God help me this once—

Source: Hanna family files.

Adoniram Judson to Emily E. Chubbuck,[224] March 2, 1846[225]

Your dear precious letter of the 25th last has just come in. O what a load is removed from my heart—Thanks be to God. But I know not when I shall reach Utica or Hamilton. I took a very severe cold on my way from Baltimore, and it has left the worst cough I have had since arriving in the country. The weather is dreadfully cold and it is snowing here to the terror of the Philadelphians. And all say, that it is infinitely worse at the north and the delay of the mails shows that the roads must be blocked up with the snow. I intended to have left today, as I think I mentioned in my last, but it is out of the question. I may get to New York day after tomorrow, if the roads are open. There I shall hope to get another letter from you and then I shall write you again. Don't think however, that I am ill. The cough is merely the result of a common cold—is much better today—and will, I doubt not, with proper care, be removed in a few days. I am only unwilling for your sake, to plunge into too great exposure and get it settled in my lungs. I shall be able to reach New York without much exposure, and I am sure of a warm house at Mr. Newton's.[226] Do dearest **darling, O** most dear from every letter and every recollection, do erase that word "misgivings"[227] from the vocabulary of your heart. "Storm

---

[222] This letter has an addendum dated March 2, 1846.

[223] See vol. 1, "Cast of Characters," s.v. "Gillette, The Reverend Abram Dunn."

[224] For an understanding of the comparison on an original letter with the letter actually printed by Dr. A. C. Kendrick in *The Life and Letters of Mrs. Emily C. Judson*, see the first footnote for the letter of Emily to Adoniram dated January 31, 1846.

[225] This letter is an addendum to a letter started the evening before, March 1, 1846.

[226] There are six letters in the correspondence from Mr. and Mrs. Newton of New York City.

[227] This is from the letter of Emily E. Chubbuck to Adoniram Judson dated February 28, 1846, where she said, "I do have 'misgivings" except on my own account."

of wonderment."[228] I shall only exult in it. "A great many unpleasant things."[229] My love would not be worthy of your accepting if it could be affected by such things. I have some confidence in my love for you, because I began at the bottom of this ladder. I loved you, not as a goddess, but as a very wicked creature, wickeder than myself. Now I have discovered my mistake and can I love you less. **Nor did I love you because grandmother[230] and Uncle Peck[231] told me to be a good boy and do so, nor shall I ever think of paying the least deference to their opinions, or of asking leave of them or of any body [sic] else, but your own dear self.**

I esteem W.[232] for his many excellent qualities and have every friendly feeling towards him for your sake; but I am sorry to hear, that he fought a duel in England, and gave out publicly that he was ready to fight another in similar circumstances.

Mr. E and Mr. Sartain[233] think that the engraving will be done much better in a larger size—a large octavo, and I am inclined to the same opinion. Mr. E. suggests to have Graham[234] pay for a large number to be inserted in his magazine. But more of these things hereafter—

My eyes ache to see you, my lips to kiss you, my ears to hear the music of your voice and my arms and heart to clasp you in an indissoluble embrace.

Entirely and ever thine

A. Judson

Source: Hanna family files; A. C. Kendrick, *The Life and Letters of Mrs. Emily C. Judson*, 164–65.

---

[228] From the letter of Emily E. Chubbuck to Adoniram Judson dated February 25, 1846:

I must own to you, dearest, now that I am away from you, misgivings will trouble me. I believe that you love me with the whole of your noble heart; but I am afraid, when the whole **storm of wonderment** bursts upon us, you will—perhaps you will not doubt your having acted wisely—but I am afraid you will be very much troubled. I know that there will be a great deal said—a great many unpleasant things—and should I not feel badly to see you made sad for a single moment by having taken such an unworthy creature to your heart?

[229] In a January 21 letter from Emily E. Chubbuck to Anna Maria Anable, Emily wrote, "The doct. has not deceived me—he has told me the bright side and the dark, and there will be **a great many unpleasant things**, but, in some shape or other, they will come in all situations of life. I would rather live in a barn with the doctor and have him love me as I am confident he will, than in a palace with Willis and be sometimes petted and sometimes neglected."

[230] This would be a reference to Emily's friend, Anna Maria Anable, who was often called "mother," "mother-in-law," and, here, "grandmother."

[231] See vol. 1, "Cast of Characters," s.v. "Peck, The Reverend Doctor Solomon."

[232] See vol. 1, "Cast of Characters," s.v. "Willis, Nathaniel Parker."

[233] See vol. 1, "Cast of Characters," s.v. "Sartain, John."

[234] George Graham was the editor of *Graham's Magazine*, one of the preeminent literary magazines of Emily's time. He took an interest in Emily Chubbuck as Fanny Forester; he mentored her and published every piece of writing that she could submit to him, and for it all, he remunerated her with the astounding sum of five dollars a page. In April 1845, when Emily was staying in Philadelphia with the Reverend and Mrs. A. D. Gillette, Mr. and Mrs. Graham were frequent visitors, often inviting Emily to tour parts of the city with them in their elegant carriage. That relationship picked up again when Emily returned to Philadelphia in fall 1845.

Mr. Robert A. West to Emily E. Chubbuck, March 3, 1846[235]— South Brooklyn

My dear friend,

I scarcely dare open your last note because I feared that it would contain a severe demand for what you will probably have attributed to neglect; such seeming neglect has not [been] voluntary I assure you. Day after day I have [intended] to write you, and as often something has occurred [to] prevent the fulfillment of my purposes. Now however this duty *must* be performed and therefore I set about [it].

I fully and cordially agree with you as to [the] intrinsic value of the poems herewith. Your friend writes true poetry[236] with however an occasional [ ]ness of rhythm. But we were obliged to look at [the] matter as a business—a profit and loss question. [ ] dollars for a short poem by a debutante. Poets [of] established and good reputation do not demand such except in one or two instances, whereto the use [of] the poet's name as a contributor to the magazine is part of the return for the outlay. Admiring very much in all sincerity as I do the poetry by your friend I was precluded pressing its acceptance upon the proprietor because I felt that losing sight even of the price asked for it, the magazine would in fact derive [ ] advantage from its publication than would the [ ] seeing that she would thereby enter upon an avenue to that temple which as yet she has not reached, but where I feel sure her name will one day, be suitable if she continue to write such poetry. I should [presume] that few, if any, or our popular poets received remuneration for their early productions. Poetry is not valued and not intrinsically so marketable as prose. You would think me a very cool, calculating, practical [ ]—I had almost expressed a wish that such mar my character—but in this matter the proprietor has to be considered.

And now as to your good self—[I am] about to make *proposals to you*—don't be offended [ ] the sentence will be less objectionable when it is published—[ ] of a literary character, on the part of the proprietor of the *Columbian*. I regret I did see you when you last flitted through this city. Your note did not reach me until too late. [ ] [ ] assigned for your departure, and by the messenger who brought it from the office. I dispatched a hurried note of apology for my inability to wait upon you. In calling at the *Columbian* office afterward I learned that he could not find the number, (61 I think) to which it was addressed.

---

[235] The copy of the original letter cut off the end of the lines on each of the two pages, accounting for the larger than usual amount of omissions.

[236] On many occasions, Emily was asked by her friends and acquaintances if she would provide access to publishers for their poetry, stories, or creative writing.

Your letter from Philadelphia explained [your] plans and intentions for the picture[237] and there [was] an implied, or half expressed farewell to the *Columbian* which I feel unwilling to believe will come to pass.[238] You say you purpose to write only a very limited number of articles during the year, publishing them under your nom de plume, your terms for each of which will be $50. Would you object to furnishing them on those terms exclusively for the *Columbian*? If the proposal will not clash with your interests or preconcerted [sic] arrangements the proprietor would gladly secure [your] aid on those terms. Please let me know your views on the subject. I would just say that you may safely rely with perfect confidence on the stability of the magazine and the ability of the proprietor to meet any engagement with you he may enter. This entre nous, for your guidance should you entertain the proposal.

Most cordially do I assure you, my dear friend, that whether the pleasure of my editorial acquaintance with you be perpetrated or otherwise the past will be remembered with pleasure and in all the future most happy sh[ould] I be if I can in any way serve you. The frankn[ess] and kindness that have emboldened me to write with similar freedom, have also, permit me to say, constituted a bond of esteem and friendship that I hope this cessation of professional interchanges will not entir[ely] sever, and greatly shall I rejoice if my misgivings that you propose withdrawing from the *Columbian* are not to be confirmed.

Believe me, my dear friend

At all times and sincerely yours,

Robert A. West

Written in the lower right hand corner of page 2: "[ ]ndo your quiz about my notice [ ] your *Trippings*—but [ ] could [ ] do wish [Note: Rest of line is lost.]"

Source: American Baptist Historical Society, AJ 27, no. 1299.

---

[237] Emily had been speaking with John Sartain, the prominent engraver of his time, about having an engraving to be published by one of the magazines with the caption: "Henceforth to loftier purposes I pledge myself. Fanny Forester." It was to have been released for her public just before her sailing for Burmah. In the end, Sartain did an engraving that was used in the publication of *Alderbrook*. He was also doing an engraving of Adoniram Judson.

[238] At this time, Mr. West was likely unaware that Emily was engaged to Adoniram Judson and that she would no longer be writing because she would be in Burmah. Later in this paragraph, he revisited the financial stability of the *Columbian*, as if this might be the question behind her giving up writing for them. There had been rumors that the financial stability of the *Columbian* was in question, and Mr. West had addressed this issue in his letter of August 22, 1845. Contrast this letter and its content with Mr. West's letter of April 28, 1846, after he had learned of her engagement and pending departure.

Mrs. Urania Sheldon Nott to Emily E. Chubbuck, March 4, 1846— Union College

My dear Emily,

Your precious letter by Mary[239] made me very, very sad—indeed I am quite a child when I think how soon, how very soon I shall think of you as a dream that has vanished forever—dear girl—how can we give you up.

9 o'clock

I could not write further—but am now more myself—and shall endeavor to behave more courageously in future—you need not, and must not think of what people say, or will say about your affairs and I trust you will be sustained by His arm that is strong to share—I had intended a longer letter—but Miss Prescott is going and company has prevented my writing before—I hope to hear from you at Hamilton—and to see you before long.

Ever yours most affectionately,

U. E. Nott

"Our pleasures are born but to die
They are linked to our hearts, but to sever,
And like stars shooting down in dark sky,
Their loveliest when flitting forever."

Source: American Baptist Historical Society, AJ 25, no. 1229.

Adoniram Judson to Emily E. Chubbuck, March 5, 1846[240]— Philadelphia

My dearest love,

Here I am sorry to say I still am. I took a violent cold at Wilmington, on return from Baltimore, which brought on the most tearing painful cough I have known for years past. I have been going several days—fully intended to have gone today but last evening being very bad, I thought I would have recourse to some of the old methods of treating a cold, and today I am vastly better. I think one more night and day will quite restore me, and it is my present intention to go next Saturday, the 7th to New York—spend Sunday and Monday there, on Tuesday go to Hartford, in which case I don't know whether I shall reach Hamilton in all the week that closes with the 14th. It must depend on the state of the roads, the weather and my health. If the north river should be open, when I leave New York,

[239] See the letter of Emily E. Chubbuck to Mrs. Urania Sheldon Nott dated February 28, 1846.

[240] There is an addendum to this letter dated March 6, 1846.

I should come up directly, but of this there is no prospect. You may be sure I pass my time most unpleasantly. I have a warm house and the most kind attentions, but am dying to get away. I hope to get a letter from you at New York and will write you again from that place. On one account I am glad to be detained. While you are at Utica, you have a warm house and every comfort, but I fear that you, not to say myself, will be too much exposed this inclement season, in the house at Hamilton, will you not?

Source: Hanna family files.

Adoniram Judson to Emily E. Chubbuck, March 6, 1846[241]

Something interrupted me as I finished the last sentence.[242] I had a very good night and am much better this morning.[243] Shall most certainly go to New York tomorrow—but will send on this letter before me. I have just been to take leave of the Gillettes.[244] A day or two ago, I sent them a dozen very nice teaspoons—$22, marked A. J. to A. D. G. and I learn from Mr. Robarts[245] that they are delighted with the present—I asked leave of Fanny[246] to go into your chamber and look about, which she allowed after making me wait ten minutes to put it in order, as she said. And then I stood and looked at the table, the window, the stove, the bed etc.—O thou mischievous one! Thou disturber of the peace of honest men! However, I am proud to plead guilty to the charge of attempting to deserve similar epithets. I have no idea of adopting the following lines, or of confessing any sympathy with the poet:

> "Keep if thou wilt, thy maiden peace, still calm and fancy free,
> For God forbid thy gladsome heart should grow less glad for me.
> Yet while that heart is still unwon, oh bid not mine to rove,
> But let it muse in humble faith and uncomplaining love (fool)
> If these, preserved for patient years at last avail me not,
> Forget me then, but ne'r believe that thou canst be forgot."[247]

---

[241] This letter is an addendum to Adoniram Judson's letter to Emily of March 5, 1846.

[242] See the abrupt stop in his letter to Emily of March 5, 1846.

[243] In his letters to Emily dated March 2 and March 5, 1846, Adoniram Judson spoke of catching a severe cold which had with it an uncomfortable cough.

[244] See vol. 1, "Cast of Characters," s.v. "Gillette, The Reverend Abram Dunn."

[245] See vol. 1, "Cast of Characters," s.v. "Robarts, Mr. and Mrs. W. S."

[246] See vol. 1, "Cast of Characters," s.v. "Anable, Fanny."

[247] This is a poem by John Moultrie, "Forget Thee?" This is the third of three stanzas.

It is nine days since the date of your last. I hope to get another tomorrow. May I hear, that you are well and happy, and that your prospect of the future seems bright, and that you remember me and love me, though indeed I deserve it not.

But if love for you deserve a return, I can urge a strong claim—and think of you, dearest, by day and by night, alone and in company, wherever I am. I don't know, but I wrong my poor dear children, whom I have watched over from their birth, who cling to me so fondly, but who are almost forgotten in my love for you. Is not this passing strange? I must beg you to try to make up for my deficiency, when you see them, grant them a share of your warm love—grant them a place in your kind heart, that they may not be left children orphans indeed. Will you not spend some time with them at Worcester[248] and Bradford?[249] And when we arrive in Burmah, will you not take up poor little abandoned Henry and Edward[250] and love them for my sake and their own? Burmah! Will that ever be? Shall we ever get away even from this country—in our own little cabin and in one another's arms, forgetting all the world beside! And I will keep school and teach you Burmese—no kissing, mind, in school hours, and if you spell b-a-g-baker, I shall have to do something to you. Dean[251] passed me, on his way from Baltimore, so I have not seen him. He got no hint of matters and things, until he reached Boston! Chance he wrote to Mr. Gillette—tell Bro. Judson to take care how he trespasses on my sheepfold!! He spoke of you, while here, in the highest terms and wanted to know all about your spiritual state and your prospects. He is, by this time, on his way to England, to visit the relatives of his late wife. It is doubtful whether Miss Hugg[252]

---

[248] Elnathan and Adoniram Judson were living in Worcester, Massachusetts, with Dr. and Mrs. Calvin Newton. They remained there until Emily returned home in October 1851. George Boardman was with Dr. and Mrs. Newton as well.

[249] Bradford was the home of Ann Hasseltine Judson, Adoniram's first wife. Abby Ann Judson, his daughter with Sarah Hall Boardman Judson, began attending Bradford Academy in April 1846. She had been living with Adoniram's eccentric sister, Abigail Brown Judson, in Plymouth, Massachusetts.

[250] Henry and Edward were the youngest surviving sons of Adoniram and Sarah Boardman Judson. Later correspondence has all of the children fondly addressing Emily as "Mother" or "Mamma." In 1849, Emily wrote a poem, "The Two Mammas," explaining to Edward and Henry how she had become their "new Mamma."

> He told me of his darling boys,
>> Poor orphans far away,
> With no Mamma to kiss their lips,
>> Or teach them how to pray.
>
> And would I be their new Mamma,
>> And join the little band
> Of those who for the Saviour's sake
>> Dwell in a heathen land.

[251] See vol. 1, "Cast of Characters," s.v. "Dean, William."

[252] In her February 7, 1846, letter to Adoniram, Emily said that Philadelphia gossip had Miss Hugg as Adoniram's intended bride.

will get an appointment. Kincaid[253] is in Boston[254] and doing all he can to prevent it, being of the opinion, that no single woman ought to be sent.[255] Dr. Lincoln writes me from Washington, again delicately hinting at one of his nieces, so he has heard nothing. But Mrs. Allen[256] has found it all out,[257] and begs for the sake of mercy, that I will not refuse her an interview, while in New York. She speaks of you most highly but the news had evidently astounded her. I will show you the correspondence if we ever meet, and that also of R. A. Rhees[258] one of the few flames I have had since you left. Another—is Sydney Gill and there is Hannah Shephard. How can I get away from this drear place! O my heart—The Gillettes say that they have had very quiet times since you took your departure. "The country beaux and city cousins, lovers no more—flew off by dozens." I flatter myself that Philada. will be a dull place when we are both gone! The frolic loves must perch on other pinnacles than those. Can't you get brother Wallace[259] to erect a pole at the gable end

---

[253] Born in 1797, educated at the seminary in Hamilton, New York, and ordained in 1822, the Reverend Eugenio Kincaid served several churches before being appointed as a missionary to Burmah in February 1830. His first wife died soon after their arrival. His second wife was Barbara McBain, and they were married in 1833. In these years, they served in Rangoon, Ava, Saduja, and Akyab. The Reverend and Mrs. Kincaid returned to the United States in 1843; because of her persistent health problems, they were not reappointed in 1846. While in the United States, Rev. Kincaid became instrumental in the establishment of the University of Lewisberg (later Bucknell University). Upon Mrs. Kincaid's restoration, they returned to Burmah, arriving in February 1851 just as Emily Judson was embarking for her return voyage. With his knowledge of the language and customs, Rev. Kincaid was able to establish himself in work with the Burmese government at Ava. With one more trip home (in 1857, on an official mission for the King of Burmah to President Buchanan of the United States), they retired to Gerard, Kansas, in 1866. Of Rev. Kincaid, the correspondence indicates a man of convictions and occasional independent action.

[254] The offices of the American Baptist Missionary Union were housed in Boston.

[255] This seemed to be the prevailing notion of the time, although some single women were occasionally appointed. This "rule" was about to be tested with the appointment of Miss Lydia Lillybridge to accompany Emily and Adoniram Judson to Burmah.

[256] Mrs. Eliza Allen was the editor of the *Mother's Journal* and included material by Emily as early as 1843. Their correspondence went through spring 1846. In December 1848, Emily received a letter from Mrs. Allen's husband, the Reverend Ira Allen, describing in some detail the death of Eliza Allen. The *Mother's Journal* continued, and in an 1849 letter Anna Maria Anable informs Emily that a piece that she had written had appeared in the publication. In a letter to Emily during their courtship, Adoniram mentioned that he had met Mrs. Allen and went on to say that the *Mothers' Journal* was considered to be a prestigious publication for the church. On May 27, 1846, after a meeting with her, Judson wrote: "I am afraid I shall get to dislike her. She is a woman that I could make some use of. She has a sharp, strong intellect—is a good critic in the rough, but not in the nice. No heart—no amiability—very severe and what is worse, glaringly envious."

[257] Previous letters from Emily had asked her friends to keep secret the knowledge of Emily's engagement to Adoniram. They wanted to do this as they realized it would create quite a stir; they were also sensitive to the fact that Sarah Hall Boardman Judson had died only the previous September,

[258] This reference is to Miss Rebecca Ann Rhees ("call me 'Bessie'"). She sent three letters to Emily Judson at the time of Adoniram Judson's death (September 15, 1850, December 8, 1851, and January 1, 1852). Her loss as expressed in the correspondence was inconsolable, and from her letters, there was the intimation that the relationship between Miss Rhees and Dr. Judson had been special indeed, from the time of their first meeting in Philadelphia in 1846. Apparently, Emily had said something in a return letter to Miss Rhees, returning a gift she had sent, for Miss Rhees' final letter to Emily was judgmental and let Emily know that she would not be hearing from her again, which is probably what Emily desired. With this in mind, it was of significant interest when Adoniram mentioned a letter from Miss Rhees, joking to Emily that she was one of his many new "beaux." There were five letters in the archives of the American Baptist Historical Society to Adoniram Judson from Rebecca Rhees; because of their significance and because of this reference, all five of her letters to him are in the correspondence (February 19, 1846; May 8 and 10, 1846; October 1, 1848; and November 25, 1849). Perhaps, these letters to Adoniram later turned Emily "off" Miss Rhees.

[259] See vol. 1, "Cast of Characters," s.v. "Chubbuck, William Wallace."

of the loggery?[260] O thou ultramontane personification of flight. Three hundred miles lie between us at the present moment. Tomorrow I will reduce it by a third. And next week, if it be the will of God, but I cannot now say any thing [sic] near what day. Twenty minutes between the cars and the stage coach [sic] will not afford time sufficient for any thing [sic] like a call and I am afraid too of being recognized by some one.[261] But perhaps you will not have gone on to Hamilton. Wherever you are, I cannot rest until I find you and see your dear, dear face, and throw my arms around your dear, dear form. But how soon we shall have to part again. Dearest love—farewell.

Thine with my whole heart—

A Judson

Source: Hanna family files.

Adoniram Judson to Emily E. Chubbuck, March 7, 1846[262]— New York

My dearest love, on my arriving here just now, instead of finding a letter from you, which I had longed for and thought of all the way from Philada—I find one from one Miss Peakedchin,[263] to be sure, of Utica. Who can it be? I have a slight recollection of a young lady who affected some longitude of the southern organ of the face, (though people generally thought it was mere affectation in her) and with whom I once had a dethperate [sic] flirtation, but the thing has gone by—so don't be jealous, it does not become you, dear. I suppose it must be one of your yellow acquaintances in Utica, so to save postage, I will just answer her on this sheet and trouble you to communicate at leisure.

My ever sweet charming little Peakedchin, you began your last full of fun and frolic, thinking to escape the whipping, I see, but at the close, you grew a little sedate and tame, when thinking of Dr. Nott[264] and "maybe maybe—I can't say." Yes, you began then to apprehend that you should catch it after all. And you may be sure you shall, unless you spring right away into my arms, my dear darling pet. Here they are, wide open and I will hug you and pet you, nor ever hand you up to "old Peck";[265] I would die first. But don't tell me about spreading my paternal wing

---

[260] The loggery was Emily's father's home. See Kendrick, *The Life and Letters of Mrs. Emily C. Judson*, 166. See also vol. 1, "Places, Events, Organizations, and Magazines," s.v. "Loggery, The."

[261] Emily hoped that Adoniram could make a quick call on Anna Maria Anable and Miss Cynthia Sheldon at the Utica Female Seminary and gave him directions from the cars. The stage office was on the way, and she told Judson to ask the stage-driver to pick him up at the academy. See her letter of February 25, 1846.

[262] This letter has an addendum dated March 8, 1846.

[263] Emily signed her letter of February 28, 1846 "Sister Peakedchin."

[264] See vol. 1, "Cast of Characters," s.v. "Nott, The Reverend Doctor Eliphalet."

[265] See vol. 1, "Cast of Characters," s.v. "Peck, The Reverend Doctor Solomon."

and heading the troop. My vanity has flashed in the pan. I can't get a single recruit, unless you go yourself, sweet Peakedchin. Do, darling, think of it and not leave me to go alone. By the way, who is that Fanny Forester[266] you speak of, as obliged "to follow in the rear." Is it the same that "I am" has immortalized in the following sonnet, that appeared in Neal's[267] last, prefaced with—"we are pleased that I am shares with us in admiration of Fanny Forester, who is all that he imagines her to be, and who, in her retirement at *Alderbrook*, for she left Philada. not long since, will hear this pleasant voice and correct appreciation of one whose merit qualify him to judge of hers—"

> "O fair and fanciful Fan Forester!
> I wish I knew her, honestly I do!
> A brotherly regard have I for her,
> She is so natural, sisterly and true—
> There is no cant in her—her feelings rise
> From nature's fountain, like a crystal stream
> Upspringing from the depths, love's sunny beam
> Reflected there—and glistening in our eyes,
> As if pure diamonds over beds of gold
> In liquid torrents beautifully roll'd.
> Would it were mine to leave the world's confusion,
> And live in love, in some hill-hidden nook
> Like Fanny's green, romantic Alderbrook,
> And sing, like her, life-long in my seclusion. I am."

As to Schenectady proposal, in which I see that you indulge a strong squint at the shrine of Hymen,[268] I am sorry to have to break your heart, dear, but as I have only one heart to spare, I beg you will try to excuse me to yourself and Fanny and all the rest you mention, and tell them that I have plighted my faith and troth to Miss Nemmy Petty[269] of your city or town, as the case may be, the very flower of the forest, that I feel very grateful to Bishop Gillette[270] of Phila. for helping me pull

---

[266] Emily Chubbuck as Fanny Forester. See vol. 1, "Cast of Characters," s.v. "Chubbuck, Emily." Also "Forester, Fanny."

[267] See vol. 1, "Cast of Characters," s.v. "Neal, Joseph."

[268] Hymen, or Hymenaeus, was the god of marriage and the marriage feast or song. He is often depicted with a marriage feast torch in his hand. He was the son of *Aphrodite* by *Dionysus* and, therefore, the full brother of Priapus. His attributes are referred to in the opening sections of Homer's *Iliad* as well as playing a part in Virgil's *Aeneid*. From www.pantheon.org *Encyclopedia Mythica: Greek Mythology*.

[269] See vol. 1, "Cast of Characters," s.v. "Nemmy, Nem, or Nemmy Petty (Nemmie Pettie)"; also the chapter "Names of Endearment," 333.

[270] See vol. 1, "Cast of Characters," s.v. "Gillette, The Reverend Abram Dunn."

the said flower, and I intend, with Petty's leave, to get the old president[271] just to tie a silk string about it, that it may not stray into any body else's bosom. So farewell, and believe me was thine to serve—Hilarion Johnson.[272]

Source: Hanna family files.

Adoniram Judson to Emily E. Chubbuck, March 8, 1846[273]

My cold and cough are nearly removed but I am staying in the house today and tomorrow. Intend to start on Tuesday for Albany, the next day for Utica and the next day, that is Thursday, for Hamilton, by a private conveyance—for I eschew an evening ride in a stage coach [sic].[274] But it is possible that if I am very well, and the weather quite moderate, I shall go through on Wednesday but I don't expect it. It is more probable that I shall not get through on Thursday, in consequence of a fresh fall of snow, which may impede the cars, and be discouraging to an invalid, for in that category, I am half inclined to class myself just at present.

If I ever get to the loggery,[275] it will be enough for me to sit and look at you, across the table (you have a table, haven't you?) for the first half hour. It will be too sweet to kiss you at once. I must come to it gradually—A thousand things to say, but no paper or time.

Yours ever and ever,
A Judson

Source: Hanna family files.

Emily E. Chubbuck to Anna Maria Anable, March 10, 1846—Hamilton NY

Dear darling, blessed Ninny[276]—So it is, little dear. If you were only here! It is *so* cozy and nice. 'Tis almost letter time and I am wondering if I have got one. You may imagine how I worried about the poor Doct. during my tedious ride yesterday.

---

[271] This is likely tied to the statement about the "Schenectady Proposal"; there was some talk of asking the Reverend Doctor Eliphalet Nott, the president of Union College in Schenectady, to officiate at their wedding ceremony.

[272] Adoniram Judson signed this March 7, 1846 letter to Emily as "Hilarion Johnson." He also used this again, or variations on it, such as "The Hon. Captain Johnson," on April 20, May 8 and May 14, 1846.

[273] This is an addendum to Judson's letter of March 7, 1846.

[274] See the letter of Emily E. Chubbuck to Adoniram Judson dated February 28, 1846. In this letter, Emily speaks of the rigors of the journey from Utica to Hamilton, approximately a twenty-four-mile journey by stagecoach.

[275] The loggery was Emily's father's home. See Kendrick, *The Life and Letters of Mrs. Emily C. Judson,* 166. See also vol. 1, "Places, Events, Organizations, and Magazines," s.v. "Loggery, The."

[276] Anna Maria Anable. See vol. 1, "Cast of Characters," s.v. "Ninny."

The sleighing was miserable and yet I reached home about eleven. Today am "as well as could be expected," tho' how well that is I would'nt [sic] like to say.

I suppose my name is pretty current in Utica today; and am glad to be even at this little distance. Our folks discovered by Mr. Corey's[277] manner that he was not pleased. I shall not say anything to the Doctor about the marrying business; for, whatever I might have thot when I first came home, of course, I should'nt [sic] have Mr. Corey's now. It was no place for him to show his one-sidedness here; and, if he was too frank to conceal it, he better not have called. Those who love us are sharp-sighted always and can see when a cold, criticizing fault-finding eye is turned upon anything which their own heart-ache teaches them to estimate properly. God forgive those who set-themselves up as judge of holiness for questioning his own doings!

Tell Aunt C.[278] that mother[279] thanks her a thousand times for the oysters—we are saving them for better and dearer lips—dearer now than ever, for I am wanting him to come and teach me not to care for all this unkindness. I was fully prepared for all sorts of ridicule and could sit with perfect patience under a whole newspaper full of Judge Bacon's[280] poetry, but these things—Do you know Ninny I never in all my life had anything occur so to shake my faith in the purity of the professedly religious portion of community—one part of it at least—as the course they have adopted towards me. I used the talent God had given (the talent that in me comes nearer to perfection than any other) for good. I certainly used the money for good purposes and I wrote simple innocent stories that I know have exerted a good influence (else how do men like Hoffman,[281] Wallace[282] etc. gain such an opinion of me?) Good people censured me for them, as though I had'nt [sic] a right to work at my trade as well as the mechanic or merchant. Well after awhile I became tired of my trade—I was half-[ ] in it and my mind craved a higher and holier employment. [ ] [ ] the better thing came in my way, I made one tremendous sacrifice, cast everything from me that I had ever lo[ved] and entered upon the good. And now forsooth those same good people turn about and censure me for acting [ ]. I

---

277 See vol. 1, "Cast of Characters," s.v. "Corey, the Reverend D. G."

278 See vol. 1, "Cast of Characters," s.v. "Sheldon, Miss Cynthia."

279 Emily's mother. See vol. 1, "Cast of Characters," s.v. "Chubbuck, Lavinia Richards."

280 See the poem by Judge Bacon dated March 17, 1846.

281 See vol. 1, "Cast of Characters," s.v. "Hoffman, Charles Fenno."

282 Horace Binney Wallace was a member of high Philadelphia Society. A literary critic, he was a part of an intimate circle of friends when Emily was in Philadelphia in the winters of 1845 and 1845–1846. He was both Emily's mentor in her literary pursuits and a strong friend, as evidenced by the correspondence between them. His letters of March 1 and June 28, 1846, are especially instructive. Of him Kendrick wrote in the *Life and Letters of Mrs. Emily C. Judson*, "His polished and gentlemanly bearing, his broad culture and sound judgment, his ripened knowledge of the world, his taste at once enthusiastic and discriminating, made a profound impression on her fresh and susceptible intellect, while he in turn perceived all the delicate beauty, and as yet half-latent capacities of her opening genius" (136). Kendrick also quotes an analysis of "Fanny Forester" taken from Mr. Wallace's "Literary Criticisms." For more on Mr. Wallace, see A. C. Kendrick, *The Life and Letters of Emily C. Judson*, 135–38.

might have supposed they were desirous of having [ ] act. I am not to be allowed to follow the dictates of my own conscience and engage in a course of life indisputably good because my hands are not holy. They are not—there are thousands on thousands more fit; but the commission has come to me and I dare not cast it aside. God is able to prepare me. But do you know that I think the greatest stick with people is—that we love each other. They think we are very wicked because we are not to [ ] our love.

Written along the left and top margins of page 1: "I did'nt [sic] mean to write so much about my own botherations but the subject had got into my head and I could'nt [sic] get it out.—Kitty[283] had got the room fixed up *so* nicely and as soon as I am a little better I am going to give it some little touches myself. The lamp is real cunning and mother dances round it like a little girl. She thinks Anna Maria[284] is the blessedest creature in the world to remember her. We are to light up the lamp this evening. We *will* have a cozy little corner for the doctor if he ever comes. But it almost seems as though [ ] would I have got horribly blue today. I wish your darling little arm were here now. A whole shower of kisses there—there—there. Good bye."

Nathaniel Parker Willis to Emily E. Chubbuck, March 13, 1846—Astor[285]

My dear Emily

I arrived last night and am in a confusion which permits me only to send you this word of greeting and to beg for a word from you by return of mail. I was certain to find a letter from you waiting for me, and was disappointed. When shall I see you. I probably pass thro Philadelphia[286] to Washington in two or three weeks, but shall I not see you before?

God bless you
Yours affectionately
N. P. Willis

Source: Hanna family files.

---

[283] See vol. 1, "Cast of Characters," s.v. "Chubbuck, Miss Sarah Catharine."

[284] See vol. 1, "Cast of Characters," s.v. "Anable, Miss Anna Maria."

[285] The Astor Hotel in New York City, where N. P. Willlis resided.

[286] N. P. Willis was obviously unaware that Emily had left Philadelphia for Utica, which also means that he knows nothing at this time about her relationship with Adoniram Judson.

Reverend Abram Dunn Gillette to Emily E. Chubbuck, March 14, 1846—Philadelphia

Dear Friend

We received a line from Miss Cynthia[287] this morning, which quite relieved our anxieties. We had no news from you direct or otherwise, except by way of two letters from Anna Maria[288] to Fanny.[289]

We knew you were altogether taken up by getting home and seeing the Many at the Seminary. Miss Cynthia says you are now home—and I hope ere this reaches you One dear to us all, but dearer to you than all is with you and that you have fine times at the Loggery[290]—dear little Cottage—how I should love to peep in once in a while, and chat, as old times have allowed us to do. Shall we ever again—gracious Heaven direct us.

All about town the topic is now *the* engagement, and for your consolation let me say not one person here has as yet to my knowledge questioned the propriety of it—one did think the disparity of age too great but he has never known one hour of conjugal bliss—tho married twenty or more years. Of course the idea of marrying in any shape brings twinges of no small sharpness and agony to him in his sensitive state—So much for one weak mortal's doubts about a matter that concerns not him—more than his marriage concerns others.

Well I suppose all Hamilton is in a buzz—and professors and all—let them buzz—and if some of them should thrust out the sting, let it not my dear girl enter your too sensitive soul—Sorry is a child of Hell and it will nestle and [ ] in some bosoms where one would fain hope grace had entered and triumphed—perhaps it is so permitted in order to compel us all to be vigilant against our own foes, and [ ] lenient towards others—Envy has as yet a strong influence over human hearts—the person alluded to would never have thought of an objection even on the rose of age—if the fair covered one had chanced to have been selected from among the lambs of his fold.

Poor humanity is weak pity it is so but so it is—Do not in one case out of forty (if so many should utter their *grave* reasons why you should not become the wife of Dr. Judson) believe that the objection has any higher or holier origin then *envy-dressing.*

But enough of this. Only think we have not heard direct from the good Dr. J. since he left us—we hope he is well and safe by the side of his Pet ere this—the

---

[287] See vol. 1, "Cast of Characters," s.v. "Sheldon, Miss Cynthia."

[288] See vol. 1, "Cast of Characters," s.v. "Anable, Miss Anna Maria."

[289] See vol. 1, "Cast of Characters," s.v. "Anable, Fanny."

[290] The loggery was Emily's father's home. See Kendrick, *The Life and Letters of Mrs. Emily C. Judson,* 166. See also vol. 1, "Places, Events, Organizations, and Magazines," s.v. "Loggery, The."

cold morn is all gone—it is now raining warm and sweetly—how we wish you were here to enjoy it all with us. O [ ] times—the [ ] I doubt not await you—it is a lovely country—you have for good reasons been shown the worst side of it.

The Snyniring [*sic*] by Sartain[291] is begun and in one or two weeks more will be done *well* I doubt not. Daniels is *perfect*, it is just out—more life like [*sic*] by far than the painting—all who see your Portrait pronounce it excellent, it is improved even by *finishing*—Soon as I get a proof from Sartain[292] I will send it you [*sic*]—If you see Miss Trevor remember us to them—especially to Sister Kate[293] to whom I introduced myself over the gate last year.

Written in the right margin of the address page: "As N. P. W.[294] has arrived I enclose a line which from the hand I take to be his. I have thought best to write him a note saying where you were and have done so today. Mrs. R.[295] is now loud and laudatory of you."

Written in the right margin of the address page: "Mrs. G. joins me—I write in haste—Mother Fanny up and all well and happy but Miss our [ ] Emily—you are four fold dearer to us than ever. The Lord bless you."

Yours

A. D. Gillette

Written in the bottom margin of the address page: "Let me hear soon [ ] the Dr.'s outfit goes on swimmingly. Mrs. G. has future and you in mind for a few comforts at least, *as you are an important part* of Dr. outfits."[296]

Source: American Baptist Historical Society, AJ24, no.1197.

[291] See vol. 1, "Cast of Characters," s.v. "Sartain, John."

[292] Emily spoke previously of having an engraving done. Beginning in her letter of February 15, 1846, she spoke of a portrait to be engraved with the caption: "Henceforth to loftier purposes, I pledge myself [signed] Fanny Forester." It was to be published in one of the magazines, either the *Columbian* or *Graham's Magazine*. An engraving of Emily by Sartain was eventually used in *Alderbrook*.

[293] See vol. 1, "Cast of Characters," s.v. "Chubbuck, Miss Sarah Catharine."

[294] See vol. 1, "Cast of Characters," s.v. "Willis, Nathaniel Parker."

[295] See vol. 1, "Cast of Characters," s.v. "Robarts, Mr. and Mrs. W. S."

[296] Emily asked Mrs. Hannah Gillette and Miss Sheldon to take on a major share of helping them get ready for the trip to Burmah and the years they would be there.

Nathaniel Parker Willis to Emily E. Chubbuck, March 15, 1846—Astor[297]

My dear Emily

This is the 3rd day after my return and no letter from you. Every body [sic] whom I see says you are in Philadelphia, and I wrote to you the morning after my arrival addressing my letter there. Can you be ill? You must have seen by the papers that I was here, and if not ill would have written to me. I feel uncomfortable and apprehensive—too much so to write with confidence—but I will send this to Utica for the chance that you are there, and your friends will answer it if you are ill. Pray God you are not.

I remain here till the first of April, and then go to Washington for a month— then return to live in New York. Are you to be always at letter-length off from me? But I will not write till I hear from you.

May God bless you, my dear Emily

Yours affectionately

N. P. Willis

Source: Hanna family files.

Judge Bacon[298] to Emily E. Chubbuck, March 17, 1846[299]

To a fair 'tripping Forester'

We have witnessed the "Trippings"
And inhaled the rich sippings
Of your own sweetly sketched "Author-land,"
But there still are *some things*
Which a view of it brings
That we cannot well understand.

In truth fair Miss Fanny[300]
You're so *au-fait* and canny
In all *the deep mysteries of love*
That when bent upon wooing

---

[297] The Astor Hotel in New York City, where N. P. Willis resided.

[298] Judge Bacon was one of the leading members of the Utica Bleecker Street Baptist Church where D. G. Corey was pastor, and where many from the Utica Female Academy were involved.

[299] This poem is undated. We place it in the middle of March because *Trippings in Author-land* had been published, the relationship with Adoniram Judson had been made public, and Emily had returned home to Hamilton.

[300] Emily Chubbuck as Fanny Forester. See vol. 1, "Cast of Characters," s.v. "Chubbuck, Emily," and "Forester, Fanny."

You sit "billing and cooing"
Like unto some sweet turtle dove.

You so well *theorize*
It would not much surprise
Your friends, who have witnessed your art
If in treading the way
In which *Cupid* doth stray
You had heedlessly *lost your own heart.*

Pray, who is the swain
Who in following your train
Has had the good fortune to find it?
For whatever his [ ]
Our advice to him is
With *Hymen's* fast cord quick to bind it.

Since whatever we find
It is well "sure to bind"
Lest haply it may be found slipping
From out of our hand
In that bright Foreign land
Where you're ever wont to be "tripping."

A Saucy Querist

Source: American Baptist Historical Society, AJ 23, no. 1156.

Anna Maria Anable to Emily E. Chubbuck, March 18, 1846[301]

Now Nemmy[302] dear I am going to protest against you two lovers being so exclusive any longer. Won't you have enough of that sort of thing for the whole rest of your lives—oh, think of the time when you can see no one *but* him—and give the rest of us some till then. O, I am so jealous of that man every time I think of him that I could cry from very vexation. Do you know Nemmy I have a presentiment that we shall not like each other—wouldn't it be [ ] winding up of our

---

[301] This letter is undated. It is placed on March 18 because of the comment in the letter that Mrs. Nott would be leaving for New York in a fortnight.

[302] See vol. 1, "Cast of Characters," s.v. "Nemmy, Nem, or Nemmy Petty (Nemmie Pettie)," also the chapter "Names of Endearment."

friendship for you to go and marry a man who would be always wondering what you could see in me to like. I expect it will be so, and then very soon you would begin to wonder too—Ah! Me! I feel in the anticipatory mood like the poor girl who took a peep into the future over the kitchen fire. Seriously when are you coming back? Aunt U.[303] is in a great taking to know when we are coming down. She is going to N. Y. the 3rd of April that is, in a fortnight, and she wants us to visit her next week or put it off till May when she thinks we can make her a longer visit and she can make it pleasanter for us—If you stay over Sunday in H. I suppose we shall have to give up our little trip to S. By the way you may as well let folks in S. know the Dr. is there before he leaves for they will find it out. Some folks here know it and are expecting him to be here on the coming Sabbath. I like his keeping so quiet there. There's *wisdom* in it. It's natural and proper that he should give your friends an opportunity of knowing intimately the man who is to take away their darling and be hereafter her all-in-all.

I had a very affectionate note from Aunt U. this morning. She thinks I'll "come back to her one of these days like a bird to her nest." Will I? Or rather have I ever been away? Did she not rather leave me just as you are doing.

There, I feel horrid blue tonight.

I am in a frightfully unamiable mood, and just careless enough of what you think to tell you all sorts of disagreeable things.

I expect you will have a shockingly disagreeable time here. In the first place there is our great [ ] of a house which the moment the door opens into the [ ] [ ] makes one think of a town—then there will be lots of people pouring in all the time to see you and the Dr.—and you *must* see them—and then you can't bring his lordship up into our room because there's that forlorn little library with its outlandish looking books covered with dust close by the parlors so that you can be called in a moment when company comes—and there's no reason why you shouldn't sit *there*. And then when visitors are not here, they'll be a set of forlorn old maid teachers with me at the head wanting to know something about the man that's a-going to carry off Emily. Don't you feel comfortable already? Thought you would.

Now Nemmy dear if you don't come this week won't you write me one sweet little letter? please! for I can't bear to feel as I do tonight that you don't care a straw for me! Give my love to every body [*sic*] in the 'loggery'[304] and for yourself darling I'd take you to my bosom and hold you so tight nobody could get you away—if I could, *if you'd let me.*

Ninny

Source: American Baptist Historical Society, AJ 23, no. 1139G.

[303] See vol. 1, "Cast of Characters," s.v. "Nott, Urania Sheldon."

[304] The loggery was Emily's father's home. See Kendrick, *The Life and Letters of Mrs. Emily C. Judson,* 166. See also vol. 1, "Places, Events, Organizations, and Magazines," s.v. "Loggery, The."

Anna Maria Anable to Emily E. Chubbuck, March 21, 1846[305]

So, "little darling." The Dr. is there and has performed this wonderful event! The sly old fellow! How dared he go through without stopping to get *mama's*[306] consent? I shall look very frowningly upon him for this disrespect when he comes I assure you. Do you think "it will make any difference if my opinion should happen not to coincide with his"? Ah, Nem![307] Nem! What [ ] did the Dr. use to blind you so entirely? or to open your eyes perhaps he'd say.

I must confess I admire him for stepping in so opportunely and carrying you off from all your young "beaux" with such a sober, earnest air defying grave and gay. He's a grand old fellow (that ever I should be left [ ] [ ] disrespectfully of that "perfect man"!) and you *may* love him just as much as you please and nobody *should* prevent it. As I have often told you tho', it's all owing to his Presbyterian education. He's no more a Baptist by nature than you or I. How the brethren would be grieved and "tried" if they thought he had any other motive in selecting you than that you were the most capable lady he had seen to write the History of the Burman Mission.

From [ ] I can hear I think there is revolution taking place in the minds of the Brethren, and by the time you get back here I expect you'll be in their estimation the proper goddess for the god. Other people seem to think it's a regular love affair, for nothing else under the sun would induce you to go or him to ask you. Now that the first burst of astonishment is over folks are beginning to be sensible and reasonable. When are you coming back? Come soon for I am crazy to see you and him too—[ ] [ ] you [ ] him tho'—for I don't [ ] [ ] towards him yet for taking you from us forever? Ah! I must not think of that. I should blubber like a baby if I do.

Matilda Berthoud[308] came yesterday and is making us a nice little visit. She is a sweet charming girl and a lovely Christian. She is getting over her reclusive notions and is a right sensible girl. She will write you soon. Now should n't [sic] there be a nice one for me to fall in love with after you have really deserted me. I'll be faithful to you till the last moment of your single life miss, but then—I wonder

---

[305] This letter is undated. We place it on March 21, 1846, which was a Saturday. In previous letters, Adoniram Judson had spoken of getting to Hamilton soon, and in this letter, he is there with Emily.

[306] Anna Maria Anable often referred to herself as "mother-in-law," "mother," or as here, "mama."

[307] Emily Chubbuck. See vol. 1, "Cast of Characters," s.v. "Nemmy, Nem, or Nemmy Petty (Nemmie Pettie)." Also the chapter "Names of Endearment."

[308] Matilda Berthoud was a friend of Anna Maria Anable and probably of Emily as well, for Anna Maria's and Miss Sheldon's letters refer to her. In one letter, Miss Sheldon tells how Anna Maria had gone to visit Matilda, and while there, Matilda's brother had taken Anna Maria for a buggy ride. Somehow the horse got frightened, and Anna Maria and her host were taken on a wild ride, which they survived by the heroic actions of the brother, the undaunted courage of Anna Maria, and the providence of God. In a letter shortly after their move to Philadelphia in 1848, Miss Sheldon says that Matilda is everything to them. She is perfectly happy being with them, and she adds that she is a "host in French." When Henry and Edward went to Hamilton to live with Emily's parents and sister, Matilda was one of the individuals considered to be employed to help with work around the house and with the care of the family.

if men are more constant than women! If only one with the least pastille of attractiveness would fall in my way how I believe I'd try him. They are so mortal flat and insipid (begging your pardon and making no allusion to the *elders* of course) that I am afraid I should get sick of my bargain.

What do you think Nem? Lydia[309] has been closeted with Mr. Corey[310] all the evening and she has been sounding him about going on a mission! If she would get appointed by the board would she go etc. etc. Now Aunt C.[311] happened to have heard thro' cousin Ann[312] and [ ] Hawley[313] that some missionary had been sending a message to Lydia. Put the two together and what do you think will come next? If Abbott[314] only would propose to Lydia and get rejected wouldn't it be rich? [Note: The last page of the letter has two inkblots that obscure the text; there are also six lines on the left side of the page written perpendicularly to the main text of the letter and making transcription difficult.] But—that isn't his plan if it is him that's making the inquiries; Lydia is to go out single and he will get the [ ] of practicing the wonderful self-doubt of going out without a wife but being thrown into each other's society on the passage the delinquency of falling in love will be excused—especially as the board are so anxious he should marry. Poor Lydia. She is frightened to death that any body [*sic*] should tamper with her name and reputation in this manner. If she had imagined anybody had been speaking about her [ ] she would have said decidedly that she *never would go*. I am glad she didn't. I expect to have some fun out of this yet.

Miss Crafts[315] has just been in—she sends her love to you but thinks it highly unusual of you to have the Dr. there [ ] [ ]. Come back soon Nemmy dear. [ ] [ ] [ ] Wednesday so as to [ ] [ ] [ ] company Thursday eve'g. I want to see you badly! And I am so provoked that I do, for I know you don't care a straw for me as long as you have the Dr.

I don't feel exactly right towards that

Written across the text in the left margin: "[ ] I know. I am somewhat in the mood that" [Note: The last five lines are vague. The following phrases are legible: "about it"—"kiss good night notwithstanding"—"I won't" "it would not be proper

---

[309] See vol. 1, "Cast of Characters," s.v. "Lillybridge, Miss Lydia." Also the chapter "Lydia Lillybridge Simons."

[310] See vol. 1, "Cast of Characters," s.v. "Corey, the Reverend D. G."

[311] See vol. 1, "Cast of Characters," s.v. "Sheldon, Miss Cynthia."

[312] See vol. 1, "Cast of Characters," s.v. "Sheldon, Ann."

[313] See vol. 1, "Cast of Characters," s.v. "Hawley, Mr. Horace H."

[314] See vol. 1, "Cast of Characters," s.v. "Abbott, The Reverend Elisha."

[315] Speaking of Miss Crafts in November 1845, Anna Maria Anable reflected, "What a blessing to society it is, that she was never married. What a shame it would have been for *her* to have settled down into a mere *me* and *my husband* and *my children*! I wonder if I should ever make such a good old maid!"

would it"—"I'll warrant"—"be glad of an excuse"—"your little man"—"affectionately to your mother[316] and Kate![317]]

    Ninny

Source: American Baptist Historical Society, AJ 23, no. 1158.

Nathaniel Parker Willis to Emily E. Chubbuck,[318] March 21, 1846[319]

The news you send me, is, to me, another death—stunning like the last.[320] I
cannot write to you. I shall see you perhaps before you sail. You are doubtless right,
and God is right, as He has been before, and must be ever. But I did not look for
another calamity so soon.

My child is well. I am on the look-out for a house, or part of one, in which,
with her, I can make something like a home. The link between me and her is the
only one now that is not dead past restoring. Pardon this brief letter. I write as I
finish reading yours. May God, who has taken you from me and to Himself, bless
you and your husband.

Source: Hanna family files.

Miss Cynthia Sheldon to Emily E. Chubbuck, March 21, 1846

Dear Emily

    Notwithstanding it is such a provoking disappointment to be cheated out of a
call[321]—we have roared in my room loud enough to raise the roof. Your Dr. should
have the palm for management, and I am right glad he is with you—have my girl
for the return visit—do let it be as early as Thursday.

    I have sundry plans to give you quiet and yet see the good folks here. Urania[322]
writes importuningly [*sic*] for your visit as early as the week after on account of
their arrangements to leave home the following week. She is so much afraid of
being disappointed—I shall write to her tonight of the fair prospect.

---

[316] Emily's mother. See vol. 1, "Cast of Characters," s.v. "Chubbuck, Lavinia Richards."

[317] See vol. 1, "Cast of Characters," s.v. "Chubbuck, Miss Sarah Catharine."

[318] This letter was written on stationary that had a black border around it.

[319] This letter is undated. It is postmarked March 21, 1846.

[320] The wife of N. P. Willis died a year previously. Emily learned of it on March 27 as she arrived in New York on her way to
Philadelphia.

[321] Adoniram Judson had planned a quick call at the Utica Female Academy on his way to Hamilton to visit Emily. See the letter
of Emily E. Chubbuck to Adoniram Judson dated February 25, 1846.

[322] See vol. 1, "Cast of Characters," s.v. "Nott, Urania Sheldon."

The Dr—letter came from the office this morning—had we not anticipated his call when the card came it would have been forwarded. I shall put a wrapper on it to protect my doings from being the tell tale of his whereabouts.

I had some talk with Mr. Corey[323] about his course at Hamilton, I found he was misapprehended as I had supposed—do not my *girl* charge him with a want of interest in your welfare—he feels it will be the highest privilege he could ask to have the Dr. spend one Sabbath with us in our own chh—we will earnestly pray great good may come to our house, our church, and the blessed cause in the earth.

How little did we think at the time of Dr. Judson's short call here[324]—that we should have the privilege of becoming personally acquainted with him. I shall not be ambitious to show off you *know*—but I expect to be half crazy on the great occasion.

Mother[325] is very weak yet, but Dr. James[326] thinks she is decidedly better—my cough remains about the same. Another Sabbath to be spent at home—heaven grant we may all meet with renewed health and spirits—Much love to each and every one of your dear circle—dear. They will ever be to your truly attached

C. Sheldon

Source: American Baptist Historical Society, AJ 26, no. 1265.

Dr. John Howard Raymond[327] to Emily E. Chubbuck, March 23, 1846—Hamilton NY

My dear Miss C.

Your note was put into my hands on my return from meeting last Saturday night. I had been listening to "Confessions" all the week, but really this last was the most startling of all. Forever henceforth am I a believer in Animal Magnetism—for, though I did not notice the waring [sic] to which you allude, I certainly did *feel* that there was *something in the air*—which (if you will pardon the prop()tion[sic]) seemed *an air of mystery*—some invisible presence or proximity, the nature of which I could not divine, but the influence of which I could not but feel. It oper-

[323] See vol. 1, "Cast of Characters," s.v. "Corey, the Reverend D. G."

[324] In November, Doctor Judson made a quick call at the Utica Female Academy as he passed through Utica. All of them were unaware of the events soon to unfold.

[325] Mrs. Sheldon and her husband lived with their daughters Cynthia Sheldon and Alma Sheldon Anable at the Utica Female Academy.

[326] Dr. James was a trusted physician, who attended the students and faculty of the Utica Female Academy. He is mentioned frequently in the correspondence as having been consulted for varying medical complaints, and his advice was always welcomed and highly regarded.

[327] Dr. John Howard Raymond was to have a brilliant career as a college professor, linguist, and college president. At this time he was on the faculty of Hamilton College. He was to move in 1849 when the University of Rochester was created from dissidents at Hamilton College (now Madison University). In 1856 he would found the Collegiate and Polytechnic Institute of Brooklyn, and in 1865 become the founding president of Vassar College.

ated as a sort of spell on my faculties—a constraint—an embarrassment, which I wondered at somewhat, but could not throw off. Now Mesmerism [sic] goes to the heart of the difficulty at once—and solves the mystery. It was the presence of a great spirit, spiritually revealed to a mind possessing (of course, for so my theory demands) congenial, or at the very least corresponding, sensibilities. That is, I felt a low degree of what Eliphaz experienced, when in thoughts from the visions of the night, a spirit passes before his face, and the hair of his flesh stood up. It stood still, but I could not discern the form thereof—an image (a phantasm, a formless sub-stanceless, shadowless specter) was before me—there was silence, etc."—And do you know I was on the point, more than once, of asking you whether Dr. Judson was not in the house? How would you have "evaded" that? Eliza Gilman, being a person of more spiritual discernments was absolutely certain of his being there, and (as I learn) expressed her strong conviction at my house. I am not sure indeed, but the impression was made on her mind two or three days before his arrival. That only establishes the connection which some knowing ones have already suspected, between the magnetic fluid and the spirit of prophecy! We have the testimony, you know, of one Scotch gentleman of very distinguished mesmeric susceptibilities—indeed a *clairvoyant*, or *seer* (as they want to be called)—that "*coming* events cast their *shadows* before." And so we need not be surprised, since the Dr. is most unde-niable an "event," that his *shadow* anticipated his own arrival by a day or two. And now I must tell you, that I have become the depository of another of your secrets—at least, "the thing was secretly brought to me, and my ear received a little thereof." It pertains to nothing less than the manner of your departure, and embraces the whole contrivance and execution thereof: and it proves that the Dr.'s body has a shadow (may it never be less!) as well as his sone [sic], and that old Argus (the public) has an eye out on every body and every body's [sic] concerns. In this case I am informed it was a *pair* of eyes, by what fortunate individual proposed I do not know—one who knew a thing or two, however, in advance, was on the look out and saw the matter clear through from the beginning to the end. So, as there's no help for it, prepare another confession.—And pray tell me one thing. What do folks tell you secrets for? When a man (or lady) comes to you with sparkling eyes and an intensely [sic] significant air of exuberant caution—looking as though they (i.e. he or she—now mind the pronoun) were swelling—full of a good thing, which they ask the privilege of communicating to you through the smallest conceivable aperture, and having done so, charge you to keep *all to yourself*—do they mean to have you do as they say, or do as they *do*? In my simplicity, I have always thought that a promise of this kind was like other promises, a thing to be kept—and I even find myself harboring an old-fashioned notion, that there is something more than a mere tonal similarity between a *secret* and a *sacred* thing?

Now is this only my verdancy [*sic*]? Is there some conventional understanding about this matter, which I have overlooked? Did Miss Cynthia[328] when she committed that sacred deposit to my keeping some weeks ago, do it with a quiet expectation (like Gen. Jackson's, when he transferred the public deposits to the pet banks) that it would steal into general circulation *pro bono publico*? For myself, I seem to be getting into luck in this way—and it's high time I should know what is expected of me. I have been wont to fancy, that my mind had a very small *inlet* for secrets, and no *outlet* at all—but I am willing to go to some expense for the general good—and if these things are poured in for the very purpose of having them run out, if "to do good" is inseparable from "to communicate," if I am expected, having freely received, freely to impart, why, I must e'en knock a hole through my receiver, put in a sieve-bottom, and become leaky with the rest. Do resolve me my doubts.—

On which condition (to return to the confession) I will freely forgive you. I say *forgive*—because, you see, the duty of confession on your part implies the [ ] of forgiveness on mine—an advantage which in the present case I value too highly to use lightly. Meanwhile believe me, with assurances to the Dr. of highest consideration (despite his monstrous irreverence of our national deity, Public Opinion)—

Very truly yours,

J. H. Raymond

P.S. You will be pleased to hear that our school continues in a highly interesting state of religious feeling. Others from among the impenitent have, we trust, been brought to a knowledge of the truth, and are rejoicing in the hope of immortality. What sight more delightful, or more rich in suggestions of lofty interest, than that of youth revolving with becoming solemnity the highest question in the range of thought, the most momentous in the science of life—prostrated before the Supreme under a just consciousness of their vileness and guilt—slowly admitting to their understanding, and then into their hearts, the great theory of salvation by grace through the suffering Christ—joyfully resting on the pious foundation—intelligently consecrating their all to the service of the King of kings! This sight it has been one to look upon until the joys of our own spiritual infancy return, and we join voice and heart with the young converts in singing "the new song, even praise unto our God!" And again, say, by His name be praised.

Source: American Baptist Historical Society, AJ 26, no. 1287.

---

[328] See vol. 1, "Cast of Characters," s.v. "Sheldon, Miss Cynthia." Miss Sheldon had revealed to Dr. Raymond early on the relationship between Emily Chubbuck and Adoniram Judson, and he had kept the secret in the same way that she had, to the consternation of Emil and Adoniram.

Newark Daily Advertiser,[329] March 24, 1846

Fanny Forester (Miss Chubbuck,) the popular magazine writer, it is said in a Phila. letter to the *Journal of Commerce*, is to be married to the Rev. Mr. Judson, and will accompany him on his missionary labors in India. She will carry with her, it is added, the high devotion which a former one of the name exhibited, who followed the missionary fortunes of her husband in the East.

Adoniram Judson to Emily E. Chubbuck, March 28, 1846— Albany NY

I hope there is no harm, dear love, in writing you a short line, though at so early date, since leaving you. At any rate there is no great cause for apprehension, for I have but a short time before breakfast and getting off in the cars. I am writing in the chamber of Mr. Wilder's, which I occupied the early part of last November, when I had my dear children with me,[330] going and returning, when I had never had so much as a thought of Fanny Forester,[331] and was ever pouring out my griefs and my tears at the tomb of St. Helena.[332] What strange changes take place in outward things and in the inner heart! And what greater changes are just at hand, when we shall tread the untrodden path and look for the first time, into the unknown world! Let those that have wives be as though they had none. And they that weep, do. *For the fashion of this world passeth away.* Here is true wisdom communicated by the light of inspiration to guide man in his passage through this dark and dangerous world. I wish, not that I had kissed you less, but that I had preached to you more and you to me. Dearest love, we *must* be blessings to one another. We must *so* love and *so* live, that we shall love the more and live the happier through endless ages. If we truly love, what greater desire can we have, than to brighten up each other's eternal crown? We can and shall exert a greater influence on one another, than all the world beside. *O let it be of the best kind!* We cannot be too good. O let us *be* good and *appear* good, avoiding even the appearance of evil.

I went last evening incognito with the Wilders, to hear Mr. Knapp but was most disappointed. He had neither the strength of mind, nor the power of oratory which I had expected. They say, however, that he was quite worn out with previous labors, and did not give a fair specimen.

---

[329] *Newark Daily Advertiser* (Newark, NJ) March 24, 1846. See page 2, column 5.

[330] Adoniram, Elnathan, and Abby Ann Judson. Adoniram and Elnathan went on to Worcester, Massachusetts, to live with Dr. and Mrs. Calvin Newton. Abby Ann went to Plymouth to stay with Judson's eccentric sister Abigail Brown Judson.

[331] Emily Chubbuck as Fanny Forester. See vol. 1, "Cast of Characters," s.v. "Chubbuck, Emily." Also "Forester, Fanny."

[332] On their return trip to America, the ailing Sarah Hall Boardman Judson died on September 1, 1845 at the Isle of St. Helena.

The breakfast bell is speaking—so farewell, dearest sweetest one. I hug you in my heart. I have got your lips there, and I will kiss them as much as I like. [Note: Two lines are marked through.]

Love to Anna Maria[333] and tell her, that if she does not mend her ways and appear as good as she is, I shall tell her mother[334] of her next time.

Thine ever

A Judson

My best regards to Dr. and Mrs. Nott

Source: A. C. Kendrick, *The Life and Letters of Mrs. Emily C. Judson*, 173–74; Hanna family files.

Adoniram Judson to Emily E. Chubbuck, March 28, 1846[335]—Worcester

My dearest Love,

It is late in the evening, and I am so tired, that I can hardly think, but I must just say—goodnight, and add a line tomorrow morning—which if sent off immediately, will reach you at Skenactady. [*sic*]—I reached here just at dark, and found George Boardman[336] and the two dear boys, Adoniram and Elnathan[337] waiting at the depot. They have both grown some and appear to be in excellent health. And how glad we all were to meet and what hugging and kissing ensued! I am sure you will love them when you see what dear nice fellows they are. And all testify that they behave well in the house and at school, and are better scholars than any of their age.

I wrote you a line from Albany this morning—I believe they know nothing here of our affair, but I shall send George to the post office with this letter, and that will probably give him an idea. Goodnight darling dear. May all blessings cluster around your pillow, and the protection and presence of God be granted in answer to your prayers.

Source: Hanna family files.

---

[333] See vol. 1, "Cast of Characters," s.v. "Anable, Miss Anna Maria."

[334] Anna Maria often referred to herself as Emily's "mother" or "mother-in-law." Here, this is likely applied to Emily as Anna Maria's "mother."

[335] There is an addendum to this letter dated March 29, 1846.

[336] George Dana Boardman, the son of George Dana Boardman and Sarah Hall Boardman, was born August 18, 1828, in Tavoy, Burmah. George returned to the United States in 1844 at the age of six and lived with Dr. and Mrs. Calvin Newton in Worcester, Massachusetts. He never saw his mother again. He attended Brown University in Providence, Rhode Island, graduating after taking a few years off for travel in the West. He went on to attend Newton Theological Institute, and in 1855, he married Miss Ella Covell. He served two churches before settling into the First Baptist Church of Philadelphia, where he served with distinction for thirty years. He formed a close relationship with Emily upon her return in 1851; when she gave him a copy of *An Olio of Domestic Verses*, she addressed it "Georgie—from Mamma."

[337] Adoniram and Elnathan Judson were the sons of Adoniram and Sarah Hall Boardman Judson. They too were living in Worcester, Massachusetts, with Dr. and Mrs. Calvin Newton; they stayed there until Emily returned from Burmah in October 1851.

Adoniram Judson to Emily E. Chubbuck, March 29, 1846[338]

Sunday morning. Whatever be the theory of "square mouths," the theory of square characters proceeding from stiff fingers in a cold New England chamber, is exceedingly clear. I saw in my dream last night, and behold a lady, face not recognized, came up to me and asked, "Where did you learn to kiss Miss Chubbuck so gracefully"?!! Was not this excessively kind and complimentary? So much so, that I thought it deserved a place among the materials I am collecting for an autobiography. Don't you wish you knew what I replied? So do I—I ought to have replied—Read Nora Maylie[339]—But a shadow came over my dream. And my reply is to be found only in that world of non-entities, where existence still sleeps in the wide abyss of possibility. But I ought to collect my better thoughts if I can find any, not only because it is Monday morning, but because the two Baptist ministers were here last evening, and informed me, that they are going to exhibit me today, and see if they cannot extract something out of that other world of non-entities, that has grown out of the end of my neck, the greatest humbug ever.

Farewell, dear, dear, Emily Chubbuck, Fanny Forester, Nemmie Pettie[340] or whatever name thou art known by. I hope that we shall both learn to live near to God, and be prepared for the great work before us. The longer I stay in this country, the more formidable it seems to leave all again and go to the heathen world. And much more for you. May heaven help you dearest love, is the fervent prayer of

Your ever devoted friend and lover,

A Judson

Source: Hanna family files.

---

[338] This is an addendum to Adoniram's letter of March 28, 1846.

[339] This is one of Emily's popular stories from the magazine. It appeared also in vol. 2 of *Alderbrook*. The first page reads:

"Do!"

Tell more of Nora Maylie? Ah yes! With pleasure; I love dearly to think of her.

Please vacate that ottoman, 'Bel, and betake yourself to the sofa. My first sketch was written on that, and I have a kind of fondness for it; "by the same token," as an Irish woman would say, that we love the haunts of our childhood. Besides, it is just the right height; allowing head, neck and a very small portion of the shoulder to rise above the table. That will oblige me to sit straight.

High shouldered? Oh no! see how easily the thing is done, and without the possibility of lounging.

[340] See vol. 1., "Cast of Characters," s.v. "Nemmy, Nem, or Nemmy Petty (Nemmie Pettie)"; also the chapter "Names of Endearment," 333.

Adoniram Judson to Emily E. Chubbuck, March 30, 1846[341]—Boston

My dearest Love,

Having written the preceding page, I proceed to observe (you perceive that I am writing in the land of steady habits), that I arrived here about noon, with the two boys,[342] whom I immediately sent on to Plymouth,[343] intending to go thither in two or three days. Miss Hugg's application has been expressly and finally declined, on the grounds of unfavorable testimonies from the physicians.[344] Mr. Peck[345] speaks favorably of Miss Lillybridge,[346] but says that nothing can be done, unless I and my wife take the entire charge and responsibility on ourselves. As to the other matter about which I wrote to Mr. Peck, it seems there are wonderful difficulties[347] in the way, so that he has not ventured to bring it before the Board, and so nothing is yet settled. As to the *Woodside*, I hunted up the owner and found that her destination has been changed to Bombay! All my friends here might have known, if they had taken the least interest in the matter. So I have got to hunt up another ship which I shall set about tomorrow. Neither Kincaid[348] nor Abbott[349] will probably go at present, nor any body else except one Harris and wife[350] to join the Karen department in Maulmain. Most probably we shall go by the way of Calcutta. Haven't you got yourself into a pretty scrape, my poor darling? Well, here is one

---

[341] There is an addendum to this letter dated March 31, 1846.

[342] Adoniram and Elnathan Judson, the two oldest sons of Adoniram Judson and Sarah Hall Boardman Judson. There were living in Worcester, Massachusetts, with Dr. and Mrs. Calvin Newton.

[343] Plymouth was the home of Abigail Brown Judson, the sister of Adoniram Judson.

[344] A previous letter from Adoniram Judson said that Mr. Kincaid was voicing opposition to her appointment because she was single. On March 6, 1846, he wrote, "Kincaid is in Boston and doing all he can to prevent it, being of the opinion, that no single woman ought to be sent."

[345] See vol. 1, "Cast of Characters," s.v. "Peck, The Reverend Doctor Solomon."

[346] See vol. 1, "Cast of Characters," s.v. "Lillybridge, Miss Lydia." Also the chapter "Lydia Lillybridge Simons."

[347] See the reference to "wonderful difficulties" in Emily's letter to Adoniram Judson dated April 1, 1846. She refers to the board as "their strictnisses" and makes the comment "I will go and support myself." We are not sure of the issue. At the present the indication is it is with Dr. Peck who has yet to address it with the board. It could have to do with the fact that Emily hoped to write, and the board policy that missionaries could not receive independent income from their writing. Or it could involve her hope to write the memoir of Sarah Hall Boardman Judson. Or it could be something else.

[348] See vol. 1, "Cast of Characters," s.v. "Kincaid, The Reverend Eugenio."

[349] See vol. 1, "Cast of Characters," s.v. "Abbott, The Reverend Elisha."

[350] Norman Harris was born February 19, 1813 in Becket, Massachusetts. He attended Columbia College and Hamilton Literary and Theological School, graduating in 1844. Olive Celina Wadsworth was also born in Becket, Mass July 6, 1814. They were married on August 9, 1844, and were appointed to missionary service on October 28, 1844. In July 1846, they sailed to Burmah with the newly married Adoniram and Emily Judson. Olive Harris died in childbirth on November 23, 1853, in Shwegyin, Burma. In 1856, Norman Harris married for the second time; Miranda Harris died of fever in September that very same year. Norman Harris left the mission field shortly after the death of his wife Miranda and returned to the United States. There, in June 1858, he married for the third time; his third wife was Julia Wadsworth Chapman, the sister of his first wife, Olive Celina Wadsworth. Norman and Julia Harris returned to Burmah in 1858, though not under the auspices of the American Baptist Missionary Union; they were reappointed as missionaries in 1861. Norman Harris died March 1, 1884 in Hamilton, New York. Julia Harris died in September 1905.

warm heart, that you shall always have to rest your head upon, and two faithful arms to protect and pet you withal—Just 12 o'clock—goodnight.

Source: Hanna family files.

Marie Dawson Bates[351] to Emily E. Chubbuck, March 30, 1846—Cazenovia

My dearest Emilie

It has been a long time since I have availed myself of the pleasure of writing to you, though I have many times thought of so doing, but the uncertainty I was under as to your whereabouts has as often deterred me—and now shall I tell you dear E. what induces me to write this evening. Frankly then, a *certain rumor* reached me some weeks since, and to-day has been renewed from pretty good authority—which if true will soon deprive me of the privilege of consorting with you even in this unsatisfactory manner. Tell me dear E. is it true that you are soon to leave your native land, your *home* and *home friends* for Burmah? Is it also true that you go as the chosen companion of the noble, devoted, exalted Christian Mr. Judson? If this be so—Ah, my dearest Emily, I know not how to express the feelings of my heart. I could not add a pang to your many—and I know it will cost you many struggles to leave your parents—those kind and loving ones, who have cherished you so tenderly, that dear sister, and brothers who have returned your love so fervently—yes it will be hard to leave them all—yet if duty dictates, you cannot do otherwise than submit. But this must be confirmed by Emily before I can give full credence to the report, and I must see you too, pray tell me when it will be most convenient to see us at Hamilton—and when we may expect you here.

I often think of you, as I last saw you—on a bed of sickness—and then I fear, that delicate frame will not be able to endure the hardships of missionary life. Would that I could see you dear E. and could enjoy a visit with you such as we used to have when seated in some snug corner, locked in each other's arms, we unfolded all our plans for the future, and every thought and feeling was confidentially whispered!

And now I am going to tell you about our family circle—it is comprised of Emilius and myself and our two little sons. You will be surprised at this—you

---

[351] Marie Dawson Bates was a childhood friend of Emily Chubbuck. The first letter in this correspondence, dated May 2, 1834, was sent by Emily to Marie. It was a personal letter about her religious awakening and how this was going to set the course of her life. Marie and Emily visited over the years, but this is the last letter in the correspondence from Mrs. Bates. The next to last letter in this correspondence from Marie Dawson Bates was written in January 1845, and they had not seen each other in that time, so they were likely already growing apart. After this letter, it would seem that their lives continued to move in different directions, and they lost contact with each other.

remember "Eddy" do you not? We have also a little Willie—a bright, laughing, joyous little fellow 9 months old. Come and see him dear E. won't you? My mother has lived with us the last year and adds much to our enjoyment by her presence. Our social intercourse is very pleasant.

Sister Maryanne is now at Sackett Harbor where she has been engaged in teaching more than a year.

Please remember me affectionately to your father[352] and mother,[353] also to Katie[354]—and now my dear Emily write to me soon—will you not? Anything related to yourself and friends will be interesting—may the God of peace sanctify you wholly—and bless you in all things, my friend and sister.

Ever yours truly,
Marie L. Bates

Miss E. E. Chubbuck.

Written along the right margin of page 2: "Your friend Mr. Bates wishes to be remembered with much love. Be assured of his best wishes in all your undertakings. He unites with me in requesting a visit and letter from you. M."

Source: American Baptist Historical Society, AJ 23, no. 1147.

Adoniram Judson to Emily E. Chubbuck, March 31, 1846[355]

I will finish this letter, without being able to give you any more [sic] information, and send it to the post office, that it may go on today. I suppose it will find you in Utica. I should be glad to be in its place. Think of me kindly, love, though far away and going farther, and involved in business and company which strive to drive you from my constant thoughts, but cannot. There are some, I see, who will regard our affair with coldness and suspicion, but shall we not love one another the more? I feel that I shall. And I feel sure, that, come what will, you will not be disposed to "take it all back." Yet I sometimes think it possible and my heart dies within me.

I hope to get a letter from you today—you know how to direct—"Bapt Mission Rooms, 17 Joy's Building, Boston." I will write you tomorrow, if I can learn any thing [sic] more definitely and must now close, fearing I shall be too late for the mail. I ever hug you in my heart and kiss you there, my dearest love

A Judson

Source: Hanna family files.

[352] Emily's father. See vol. 1, "Cast of Characters," s.v. "Chubbuck, Charles."

[353] Emily's mother. See vol. 1, "Cast of Characters," s.v. "Chubbuck, Lavinia Richards."

[354] See vol. 1, "Cast of Characters," s.v. "Chubbuck, Miss Sarah Catharine."

[355] This is an addendum to Judson's letter of March 30, 1846.

Mr. Morven M. Jones to Emily E. Chubbuck, March 31, 1846—Utica NY

Dear Madam

I am glad you have resolved to become a missionary, to devote your life and talents to the high and holy object of aiding in throwing the influences of the Gospel of Christ around the souls of the dying heathen. Our mortality shrinks from the sacrifice, from leaving for time, relatives, friends, home, country, from cutting those ties which bind us to a civilized and Christian land, but the soul plants itself upon the Rock of Ages and looks upward, onward to the end, to the glory of God. As soon as Mary told me the secret, I was glad although somewhat surprised. You will go out under peculiar circumstances. By your literary labors you have acquired such a reputation that we shall expect more of you than is ordinarily expected of female missionaries. You can do much to arouse the American Churches to a sense of the condition and wants of the heathen world, after you have seen that condition and those wants. Your delineations of heathen character, your portraitures of the condition of heathen society, your pictures of the degradation, the soul debasing influences, the wretchedness and woe of those who know not God but who worship things, when written as well as you may write them cannot fail of increasing the zeal and efforts of those you leave.

The station of that great and good man whom you love, respect and revere also lends importance and peculiarity to your enterprise. The world will expect more than is ordinarily expected and I am one who believes what with your trust in God and with His aid that expectation will not be disappointed. When you take your place before the whole world by the side of Dr. J. I confess you attain to an almost giddy heighth, a heighth at which caution and prudence will be requisite for you will recollect that the gaze of a great number of both friends and enemies of the cause of Christ will be upon you.

If some old father in Israel had written the foregoing prosey sermon I conclude you will think it would have been altogether more appropriate than for me, a young man. But the fit came on and I have written it and if it has wearied your patience or aroused your disgust, this part will never be read. Well burn it.

The missionary life never had any terrors for me. Do not let any thing [*sic*] depress your spirits. Look forward, upward, onward.

When you get to India I wish you would write to Mary and me often, familiarly and particularly. If this letter is not burned upon its receipt I wish you would take it to India to act as a remembrance for a person hereafter to be named. I never write a letter without thinking of autographs.[356]

---

[356] See the letter of Morven Jones to Emily E. Chubbuck dated October 17, 1845. In this letter, he sought autographs and explained his passion for collecting autographs.

I wish you would make me your residency legatee and give me all the scraps of your own hand writing [*sic*] which you would burn or not give to any one [*sic*] else, with your signature written somewhere on each piece. A hundred or a thousand such scraps of all shapes and sizes would be considered each a great favor. When you get to India I want you to send me all the autographs you can possibly lay your hands on such as Carey and Boardman, Mrs. Judson, Dr. Judson's and others, missionaries, officers, natives etc. etc. etc. I would not put you to any trouble to do all this, and will do any thing [*sic*] which would be proper to reciprocate the favor. I will send you the *Bapt. Register*[357] and other newspapers and books unless you advise me not to do so.

I hope this familiar epistle will be pardoned and if its familiarity and plainness are offensive, I am sorry for it. Nothing was further from my thoughts when it was written than the wish to do or write any thing not acceptable.

Mary and I hope to have the pleasure of Dr. J. and yourself to tea before the Mission Ship sails, and we hope you will call more than once or twice yourself.

With True Regard, Truly Yours,

M. M. Jones

Miss Chubbuck

Source: American Baptist Historical Society, AJ 24, no. 1174.

Emily E. Chubbuck to Adoniram Judson,[358] March 31, 1846—Utica NY

"Call me pet names, dearest—call me thy bird,
   That flies to thy breast at one cherishing word
   That folds its wild wings there in loving delight"[359]

Is there room for thy birdie, darling, now that its poor little wings are folded, and the time is so very very near, when there will be no other bosom for it to nestle in? It makes me sad to see *all* my friends, and think how soon their kind looks and loving words will be for other eyes and other ears, and yet you are more to me than

---

[357] The *Baptist Register* was a local Baptist paper in central New York that grew into regional prominence. Published by Alexander Beebee, it had significant influence in Baptist circles. The *Baptist Register* was a natural outlet for some of Emily's work as a budding writer. Later, in 1846 and the immediate time after her engagement and marriage to Adoniram Judson, there was conflict between Emily Judson and Mr. Beebee, who was less than enthusiastic about Emily's suitability for missionary service, reflecting the attitude of many in the wider Church. Emily was, after all, a secular, popular writer, and Adoniram Judson was the venerable missionary held in awesome respect. Eventually, Emily and Mr. Beebee were reconciled, and Mr. Beebee was often mentioned in letters from Miss Cynthia Sheldon as Emily's strongest supporter.

[358] Anna Maria has added a note at the end of this letter. It appears separately following it.

[359] These lines are an adaptation of the poem "A Song" by Frances S. Osgood (See vol. 1, "Cast of Characters," s.v. "Osgood, Frances S."

all of them. "Room for me in thy heart-place, dearest, in thy prayers." We returned from Schenectady—date! date! When!

Utica March 31 (Tuesday) 1846

We came in the cars about an hour ago and I found the letter from Mr. Peck[360] which was rec'd on Sat. I can't feel much sorry for Miss Hugg,[361] the probabilities are so much in Lydia's[362] favour [sic]. By this time you have seen Mr. Peck and know something about it.[363] You have had no other letters. Thanks for your kind remembrance of me on Sat. morning. Your letter was all the sweeter for being unexpected. Did you miss a pair of lips there? And did the little boys (dear little fellows!) make up the deficiency at Worcester?[364] Mr. Gillespie[365] will see something about getting Fanny Forester[366] a publisher. How would you like to have me dedicate the book to Mrs. Nott?[367] With two such names (that and my new one) for bladders, I think poor Fanny may swim. I am in utter consternation at this (our affairs) getting into the papers and I am afraid some of those Bostonians will make you feel troubled about it. This is a hard world to live in—and it is a great deal harder to do right than wrong! I find it so. I somehow do not feel secure when I am away from you—I dread the coming of something that may separate us or make us less happy in each other or—*something*. (I just stopped and begged A. M.[368] to finish my letter, as I am dreadfully tired and cross, and didn't like to inflict my stupidity on you. O how I wish I could just lay my head in your bosom—it is the only place in the world for me now. I can't write any more [sic], but love me, pray for me, and try to make me good, and I will repay you at least by loving, if I fail in all

[360] See vol. 1, "Cast of Characters," s.v. "Peck, The Reverend Doctor Solomon."

[361] According to Adoniram Judson's letter of March 30, 1846, Miss Hugg had applied for missionary service and been rejected because of reports from the medical evaluations.

[362] See vol. 1, "Cast of Characters," s.v. "Lillybridge, Miss Lydia." Also the timeline on Lydia Lillybridge Simons.

[363] See the letter of Adoniram Judson to Emily E. Chubbuck dated March 30, 1846.

[364] Adoniram Judson traveled to Worcester, Massachusetts; picked up Adoniram and Elnathan, his two oldest sons by Sarah Hall Boardman Judson; traveled to Boston with them; and sent them to his sister Abigail Brown Judson's home in Plymouth, Massachusetts, where he planned to join them in several days.

[365] William Gillespie was a professor of civil engineering at Union College in Schenectady, New York. He wrote two long letters to Emily, dated August 15 and September 11, 1845. His second letter originated from Union College where Dr. Nott (husband of Urania Sheldon Nott) was the president, and he noted that Mrs. Urania Sheldon Nott was "his special friend." In his first letter, he asked Emily if a certain poem had appeared in the New York *Mirror*, and if it had, he had identified the writer (if it was Emily) early on as one of great promise. In a time when Emily was considering a trip to the continent, he spoke to her of weather conditions in certain of the European countries. His second letter was filled with literary allusions, a long story to prove the point that "widows are dangerous," and a reflection on some of her writings. Mr. Gillespie was mentioned in Urania Sheldon Nott's June 11, 1845 letter to Emily; he had given Mrs. Nott the latest issue of the *Columbian Magazine*, which contained the first installment of Emily's story "Grace Linden." Then, on July 9, 1845, Emily mentioned Mr. Gillespie in a letter to her sister Catharine. Emily was speaking of going to Schenectady for the commencement of Union College, and she says, "A man there has fallen love with me—Mr. Gillespie, author of 'Rome as seen by a New Yorker.'"

[366] Emily Chubbuck as Fanny Forester. See vol. 1, "Cast of Characters," s.v. "Chubbuck, Emily" and "Forester, Fanny."

[367] See vol. 1, "Cast of Characters," s.v. "Nott, Urania Sheldon."

[368] See vol. 1, "Cast of Characters," s.v. "Anable, Miss Anna Maria."

other respects. Kiss your Abby[369] for me and tell her that I love her very much for your sake and expect when I see to add to the love for her own sake. I am growing *bluer* and bluer every moment "so no more at present." God help us both!

From your own Emily

Mr. Corey[370] has been distorting the conversation that you had with him once in the library and says that you disapprove of my course; but people are liable to err and if they repent etc. Did you make the remark or did Mr. Corey? I understood you that it came from him. These things going about are rather humiliating to me. My impression has been that you, considering all the circumstances of the case, tho't I had done right, tho' the publication of the few letters might not have been wise. Do I lack your strong arm now when I need it most. [Note: "Is the weight of your censure" is written and crossed out.] Have you really made admissions which must lower me to please the multitudes? I never sh'd have embarked in this strange enterprise but for the entire *certainty* of your support. I have done what I believe to be right and *do not repent*. If you thought there was any occasion for it—if you intended to throw your own opinion onto the scale which was already too heavy, I ought to have known it earlier. I do not believe that you did but the story annoys me.

Written in the right margin of the address page: "Darling—my dearest, *dearest* friend, do not mistake me. I am perfectly willing to be censored by you; and I will love you the more for every word you say to me. But let it be *to me*, only to *me*, love. If you think I have done wrong in any one thing, please do not express an opinion upon the subject, do not lower *us both* by confessing to men who are watching your life for a word that they may entail to excuse their own first impressions. Throw your arms about me, darling—can you kiss away the trouble?"

Written in the left margin of the address page: "What horrible *gawk* has been addressing a letter to me? Why Fanny Forester, my dear sir, the celebrated F. F. that is her autograph on the outside."

Source: Hanna family files.

---

[369] Abby Ann Judson, the first daughter and oldest child of Adoniram and Sarah Hall Boardman Judson, was born September 26, 1835. She saw her mother die on the Isle of St. Helena as they returned to the United States from Burmah. Just before leaving for Burmah with Emily, Adoniram Judson placed Abby Ann at Bradford Academy for her education. The family of Ann Hasseltine Judson was generous to Abby Ann and supportive of her interests and her future. On October 15, 1851, Abby Ann started a course of study at the Misses Anable's School in Philadelphia, and in fall 1853, she moved to New York City to take a teaching position in the home of Mrs. Maria Brown, a former missionary to Siam. She enjoyed a warm relationship with Emily, and her letters show that the two could speak freely with each other.

[370] See vol. 1, "Cast of Characters," s.v. "Corey, the Reverend D. G."

Anna Maria Anable to Adoniram Judson, March 31, 1846[371]

Do dear doctor write Nemmy[372] one consoling word, for she has got the "blues" horribly and I can do nothing to dispel them—she seems disjointed with the whole world. I wish she would let me read half way [*sic*] down the other page that I might follow out her train of thought. When she is in a little better humour [*sic*], I shall let her take the pen again as I see her fingers are uneasy as mine in enclosing it so long.

Source: Hanna family files.

---

[371] This letter was written as an addendum to Emily's letter from Utica of March 31, 1846.

[372] Emily Chubbuck. See vol. 1, "Cast of Characters," s.v. "Nemmy, Nem, or Nemmy Petty (Nemmie Pettie)." Also the chapter "Names of Endearment."

LETTERS

—⁂—

APRIL 1846

Adoniram Judson to Emily E. Chubbuck, April 1, 1846

My dearest love,

I have conversed with some of the leading members of the Board about Miss Lillybridge,[1] and her case will be brought forward at a special meeting of the Board which takes place the 12th inst. Before that meeting, four documents must be placed in the hands of Mr. Peck,[2] viz. 1. A pledge that we will take the charge of the said person, considering her a member of our family, though probably resident elsewhere. 2. A written application from herself to be appointed as an instant missionary in the Maulmain mission, to be employed in such service as shall appear requisite and desirable, after arrival. This will, perhaps, be better than to be limited to any particular department. 3. A letter from Miss Sheldon,[3] giving some statements concerning the health of Miss L. and her qualifications for a missionary life, particularly in the department of school teaching. 4. A line from her pastor, Mr. Corey,[4] saying that she is a member of his church (or of some other Baptist church

---

[1] Lydia Lillybridge was one of Emily's closest friends at the Utica Female Academy. When Emily made the decision to go to Burmah as the wife of Adoniram Judson and as a missionary, Lydia wanted to go with them. Emily spoke to Adoniram Judson of Lydia's extraordinary abilities, and Adoniram advocated her appointment before Dr. Solomon Peck and the Board of the American Baptist Missionary Union. Lydia was commissioned to go with them, in spite of the fact that she remained single. Always independent, outspoken, and unafraid to cause ripples in the missionary community, Lydia served on the mission field for twenty-eight years. She married missionary Thomas Simons in May 1851. See the timeline on the life and service of Lydia Lillybridge Simons in vol. 1.

[2] The Reverend Doctor Solomon Peck was for twenty years the executive secretary of the American Baptist Missionary Union. Many believed him to be hard, stern, and judgmental, and from some of his comments, it is easy to understand that perception. Dr. Peck and Emily did not always have the easiest of relationships. She felt in him the judgment that came from many in the church at the announcement of her impending marriage to Adoniram; that judgment concerned her "secular" past and concern that she was not an appropriate companion for the venerable missionary. On July 18, 1849 Emily wrote a blistering letter of defense to Dr. Peck in response to a letter from him of February 20, 1849; her letter framed how she viewed his perception of her, and her response was meant to set the record straight. There are eleven letters in the collection from Solomon Peck to Emily.

[3] Miss Cynthia Sheldon was in charge of the administrative and financial departments of the Utica Female Academy. Miss Sheldon and her sister Urania, who was literary principal, gave Emily Chubbuck a place at the academy in October 1840. They had deferred any cost to a future time when Emily could afford to reimburse them. Upon Miss Urania Sheldon's marriage in the late summer 1842 to the Reverend Doctor Eliphalet Nott, the president of Union College, and her subsequent move to Schenectady, Miss Cynthia Sheldon assumed a larger leadership role at the academy. Active and well-known in Baptist circles, Miss Cynthia was to become an important mentor, advisor, and friend to Emily until the time of Emily's death in 1854. She was the aunt of Emily's best friend, Anna Maria Anable, and was addressed by most as "Aunt Cynthia." In 1848, Miss Sheldon moved to Philadelphia to help Miss Anable with the startup of the Misses Anable's School.

[4] Mr. Corey was the pastor of the Bleecker Street Baptist Church near the Utica Female Academy, and Miss Sheldon and many of the girls from the academy attended worship there. (Cynthis Sheldon, Alma Anable, Deacon Asa and Isabell Sheldon, Edward Bright, and Horace Hawley had been charter members of the church in 1838.) In April 1844, he wrote to Emily expressing dismay that at a school program one of the girls had read a composition justifying dancing as exercise; he spoke of this as a roadblock to the salvation of many. Then, on March 10, 1846, Emily indicated in a letter to Anna Maria that Mr. Corey had been critical of her relationship and impending marriage to Adoniram Judson. Miss Cynthia Sheldon wrote a number of times expressing Mr. Corey's regret and support, and in 1847, there were letters of reconciliation between Emily and Mr. Corey. In spring 1848, letters reveal that Mr. Corey's wife had died of consumption, her condition exacerbated by recent child-birth. She had left behind four children. In July 1849, Anna Maria Anable wrote of his impending marriage to Jane Backus, a good choice for this "rising man." Mr. Corey remained popular with the Sheldon-Anable families even after their move to Philadelphia in 1848. A March 2, 1852, letter from Charles B. Stout told of Mr. Corey's call to the Stanton Street Church in New York City, which Mr. Corey did not accept. Finally, in 1854, there was a pastoral letter from Mr. Corey to Emily on her illness and her possible death. He preached at the Bleecker Street Church as late as January 1867.

of like communion), and adding whatever he may think proper in regard to her religious character. The first document, I shall furnish. The three others you will please to procure as soon as convenient, and forward under cover to me, "Care of Rev. S. Peck, Boston, Mass. before the 10th inst.—as I expect to go east on that day. But my stay will be short, so that I shall be able to forward you the result of the meeting, within two or three days after it takes place.

Mr. Peck thinks that the Board will be glad to have you prepare a memoir of Sarah,[5] and allow the avails indefinitely to be appropriated to a certain purpose, but that is all that the rules of the mission will admit. He intends to bring the matter before the Board at some future meeting, probably on the 17th.

Mr. Beecher[6] has been appointed to the Karen department in Arracan, and he and Mr. Harris[7] will probably go out in the same ship with us. As, in that case, there will be seven passengers, it is probable that a ship bound to Calcutta would be induced to land us at Maulmain. We know yet of no ship in particular, but through the months of May, June and July, there will be many ships sailing for those parts. It is the prevailing idea, that we shall all be ready to embark the latter part of June. If Miss L. be appointed, 150 or 200 dollars will be appropriated for her outfit, if it be desired.

I intended to have written you last evening, but after being on the run all day, I crept into bed from a party at Roxbury, to oblige the Colby's,[8] between 11 and 12 o'clock, half dead—and this morning I must be out early and in the afternoon, go to Plymouth.[9] So no time for love letters, but plenty for love, for the heart will take time for that in the house and by the way—If fondest "fancy blending thee with all my future lot—If this thou call'st forgetting, then indeed thou art forgot." I feel

---

[5] Adoniram Judson's second wife, Sarah Hall Boardman Judson, died September 1, 1845 as they returned from Burmah to America. Emily wrote the memoir of Sarah Judson. It was for this purpose that Adoniram Judson first met Fanny Forester on Christmas Day 1845; he read *Trippings in Author-land*, and when he found out that the authoress was staying with Reverend and Mrs. A. D. Gillette, he asked for an introduction.

[6] John Sydney Beecher sailed to Burmah with Adoniram and Emily Judson; he served there from 1846 to 1866.

[7] Norman Harris was born February 19, 1813 in Becket, Massachusetts. He attended Columbia College and Hamilton Literary and Theological School, graduating in 1844. Olive Celina Wadsworth was also born in Becket, Mass July 6, 1814. They were married on August 9, 1844, and were appointed to missionary service on October 28, 1844. In July 1846, they sailed to Burmah with the newly married Adoniram and Emily Judson. Olive Harris died in childbirth on November 23, 1853, in Shwegyin, Burma. In 1856, Norman Harris married for the second time; Miranda Harris died of fever in September that very same year. Norman Harris left the mission field shortly after the death of his wife Miranda and returned to the United States. There, in June 1858, he married for the third time; his third wife was Julia Wadsworth Chapman, the sister of his first wife, Olive Celina Wadsworth. Norman and Julia Harris returned to Burmah in 1858, though not under the auspices of the American Baptist Missionary Union; they were reappointed as missionaries in 1861. Norman Harris died March 1, 1884 in Hamilton, New York. Julia Harris died in September 1905.

[8] A prominent businessman, Gardner Colby and his family lived in Pemberton Square in Boston before moving "to the country," Newton Centre, Massachusetts. Mr. Colby was a member of the Board of the American Baptist Missionary Union and an avid supporter of the missionary movement. In a letter after they sailed from Boston to Burmah, Emily mentions the extravagant hospitality extended to them in early July as they waited for the *Faneuil Hall* to embark. Adoniram and Emily stayed with the Colby family frequently.

[9] Adoniram and Elnathan, Judson's two oldest sons with Sarah Hall Boardman Judson, were staying in Plymouth with Judson's sister, Abigail Brown Judson.

thee in my arms, the last evening at Dr. Nott's.[10] I see thy face at the window as I drove away.

May God preserve us both and bring us safely together to the same dwelling place, where we may find a bright oasis, though it may be but for a time, in the barren wilderness of this world. But the bright world above and a heaven together and with all those we love, and with our Incarnate Lord of Love.

Yours ever

A Judson

I want to add a thousand things. I want to give you a thousand kisses, but it is a cold way to do it by letter. Think of me, darling, and pray for me—

Source: Hanna family files.

Emily E. Chubbuck to Adoniram Judson, April 1, 1846—Utica NY

My head bows to *the warm* heart, dearest. I am folded in the protecting arms—to the heart noble as I know it is, be the arms faithful and nothing can trouble me. Thine, my beloved, and His who can protect us both. Dark forebodings *will* come, I cannot help it—they are much darker when you are away; and sometimes I am almost tempted to wish I had never lived. But I am fast learning the lesson of trustfulness; I have no doubt but God approves the step—a singularly great one for a person so timid as I am—and I believe he will care for me, for both of us. Take me to thy true heart, dearest, and I will try to charm away all trouble.

You will understand the inconveniences of going by way of Calcutta[11] much better than I can. The lack of company will be to me a very pleasant thing, and I dare say, you will arrange everything for the best. Let me beg you, however, not to lay your plans to hurry off too soon. Much as I wish myself off—fairly off—it is like death to think of going, and besides there are other reasons for some delay.

I don't quite understand what you mean by "entire charge and responsibility"[12] in the case of Lydia.[13] If to look after her, give her home, protection, etc. I think

---

[10] The Reverend Doctor Eliphalet Nott was the president of Union College in Schenectady, New York. An ordained Presbyterian minister, he was married to Urania Sheldon Nott, the sister of Miss Cynthia Sheldon and Mrs. Alma Anable and the aunt of Anna Maria Anable.

[11] See the letter of Adoniram Judson to Emily E. Chubbuck dated March 30, 1846. On April 1, he said that if they found a ship going to Calcutta, they might be able to have the captain stop in Maulmain on the way.

[12] See the letter of Adoniram Judson to Emily E. Chubbuck dated March 30, 1846. He said, "Mr. Peck speaks favorably of Miss Lillybridge, but says that nothing can be done, unless I and my wife take the entire charge and responsibility on ourselves." He addressed this again in his letter of April 1, 1846.

[13] See vol. 1, "Cast of Characters," s.v. "Lillybridge, Miss Lydia." See also the timeline on "Lydia Lillybridge Simons."

you would find the charge easy and pleasant. For my part, I sh'd like to have her belong to us. But if Mr. Peck[14] means anything more of course we couldn't do it.

So in my case there are "wonderful difficulties"[15]—well, deary, just say to their *strictnisses* [sic] that they needn't do anything about it—I will go and support myself. You would have to lend me the passage money, but I could replace it in a little while. I foresee difficulties, but with a little energy they can be met. I have accomplished much wilder and more difficult schemes and I know that I can do it. Now you think I am looking only at the present, but you are mistaken—I see much farther than you imagine. Just please tell Mr. Peck that I have resolved to go with you and support myself. I have done much more than that in this country.

I am sorry that I didn't, while you were here, learn more of your plans with regard to George Boardman.[16] Mrs. Nott[17] made a great many inquiries about him which I was ashamed not to be able to answer. She told me after consulting the doctor that if you wished to give him a classical education they would be glad to have him come there—*free of expense*, she first said, but, she added that the *other* expenses would be but a very small thing. I have since inquired and learn that board in respectable families may be obtained for ten or twelve shillings per week, but yet I have doubted some whether the "other expenses" are not the greatest. The terms are three in a year of eleven weeks each, intentionally arranged so that those students who desire to do so may go out to teach. If you and George wished it he might—I sh'd think, defray his own expenses, except perhaps in the matter of clothing. If he were off in vacations his expenses would certainly be very light; but the wages of a teacher in the kinds of school that he must necessarily take are low. I believe Courtland Anable[18] gets from $12 to $16 per month. I don't know of

---

[14] See vol. 1, "Cast of Characters," s.v. "Peck, The Reverend Doctor Solomon."

[15] See the letter of Adoniram Judson to Emily E. Chubbuck dated March 30, 1846: "As to the other matter about which I wrote to Mr. Peck, it seems there are wonderful difficulties in the way, so that he has not ventured to bring it before the Board, and so nothing is yet settled."

[16] George Dana Boardman, the son of George Dana Boardmanand Sarah Hall Boardman, was born August 18, 1828, in Tavoy, Burmah. George returned to the United States in 1844 at the age of six and lived with Dr. and Mrs. Calvin Newton in Worcester, Massachusetts. He never saw his mother again. He attended Brown University in Providence, Rhode Island, graduating after taking a few years off for travel in the West. He went on to attend Newton Theological Institute, and in 1855, he married Miss Ella Covell. He served two churches before settling into the First Baptist Church of Philadelphia, where he served with distinction for thirty years. He formed a close relationship with Emily upon her return in 1851; when she gave him a copy of *An Olio of Domestic Verses*, she addressed it "Georgie—from Mamma."

[17] Urania Sheldon had been the literary principal of the Utica Female Academy in fall 1840 when Emily Chubbuck came to study there. Emily was able to afford this wonderful education through the generous offer of Miss Sheldon and her sister Cynthia, the executive and financial head of the academy, to defer tuition. Urania Sheldon left in late summer 1842 upon her marriage to the Reverend Doctor Eliphalet Nott, the president of Union College in Schenectady, New York. Because of the distance separating them, Emily's relationship with Urania Sheldon Nott did not develop the intimacy that grew between Emily and Miss Cynthia Sheldon. Urania Sheldon Nott remained a mentor, advisor, and friend to Emily in the years of her writing, her missionary endeavors, and upon her return to America in 1851. She was also the aunt of Anna Maria Anable.

[18] Courtland Anable was a younger brother of Anna Maria Anable. He held several positions over the years, and he studied at Hamilton College while he boarded for a time with Emily's parents. In 1853, he returned to Philadelphia where he preached his first sermon at the Eleventh Baptist Church. He was "Uncle Court" to Emily Frances Judson. In 1880, Courtland Anable was listed in the Massachusetts Census as an ordained minister serving in a church.

course, not knowing George, how much you wish to throw him on his own responsibility; and have not the least inkling of your plans or expectations with regard to him. I have often heard Doct. Nott remark that his students who had been obliged to look out for themselves made the strongest and ablest men; and I am rather favourable [*sic*] to the plan in general, tho I have a troublesome share of sympathy where it comes to individuals.

How good you were, darling, to write me a letter every day—from Albany, from Worcester, and from Boston. Love the dear little fellows! To be sure I will, with all my heart.[19] I only wish that I were with them and their papa this evening, with Abby[20] and aunty,[21] a snug little party, at Plymouth.[22] Wouldn't we have a nice time? And wouldn't the very fairies envy us? If they (the children not the fairies) happened to learn of my existence you must kiss them all around for me, at least every night and morning. And you must make Abby kiss you for me.

You must not think me neglectful for not writing from Schenectady[23]—it was utterly impossible. People were calling all the time, and what with that, listening to Mrs. Nott's sermons, and frolicking with the doctor, you may imagine me pretty busy. I tho't of you none the less [*sic*]—tho't of you all the time.

I have consulted Miss Sheldon[24] about the little favour [*sic*] you proposed asking of Doct. Nott; and she decides that if we are married *here*, Mr. Corey[25] ought to do it. Now I can't bear to have Mr. C.—I like him well enough for some things; that is I respect his piety, etc. etc. but I must tell you he is very disagreeable to me. An unreasonable prejudice, you will probably think and possibly it may be so; but I have tried to look into the matter, and I am pretty confident that I am not

[19] Writing on March 6, 1846, Judson had said: "I don't know, but I wrong my poor dear children, whom I have watched over from their birth, who cling to me so fondly, but who are almost forgotten in my love for you. Is not this passing strange? I must beg you to try to make up for my deficiency, when you see them, grant them a share of your warm love—grant them a place in your kind heart, that they may not be left children orphans indeed. Will you not spend some time with them at Worcester and Bradford? And when we arrive in Burmah, will you not take up poor little abandoned Henry and Edward and love them for my sake and their own?"

[20] Abby Ann Judson, the first daughter and oldest child of Adoniram and Sarah Hall Boardman Judson, was born September 26, 1835. She saw her mother die on the Isle of St. Helena as they returned to the United States from Burmah. Just before leaving for Burmah with Emily, Adoniram Judson placed Abby Ann at Bradford Academy for her education. The family of Ann Hasseltine Judson was generous to Abby Ann and supportive of her interests and her future. On October 15, 1851, Abby Ann started a course of study at the Misses Anable's School in Philadelphia, and in fall 1853, she moved to New York City to take a teaching position in the home of Mrs. Maria Brown, a former missionary to Siam. She enjoyed a warm relationship with Emily, and her letters show that the two could speak freely with each other.

[21] Abigail Brown Judson, the sister of Adoniram Judson, lived in Plymouth, Massachusetts. A spinster of eccentric character and behavior, she was a beneficiary of her parents' considerable wealth. She took a strong interest in Adoniram's children and offered them considerable support—though not often without complaint or comment—for their clothing and education in the years to come.

[22] At this time Adoniram was in Plymouth, Massachusetts, at the home of his sister Abigail Brown Judson, which had also been the home of Adoniram Judson's youth. Abby Ann Judson had been staying there with her Aunt Abby, and Adoniram and Elnathan, two of her younger brothers, had been visiting for several days.

[23] Emily and Anna Maria Anable had left Utica on March 24, and as Adoniram went on to Worcester and Boston, Anna Maria and Emily visited with Dr. Eliphalet and Mrs. Urania Sheldon Nott.

[24] See vol. 1, "Cast of Characters," s.v. "Sheldon, Miss Cynthia."

wrong. I am on terms of friendship with Mr. C and would'nt [*sic*] like to say much about the personal dislike; but you see how unpleasant it would be to employ him. There is only one way of getting around the difficulty and that way pleases me. How would you like to go to Hamilton, have a quiet little affair of it (nobody invited or a few of the professors' families as you sh'd prefer) stay there a little while, or take leave the next day for Mrs. Yates'. How would you like it? Mrs. Yates' place is about 22 miles from Hamilton and that is all the extra travelling we sh'd have. Miss Cynthia would like to have the affair take place here, but readily yields to my mother's[26] claims; and all of our people have felt rather badly about the first arrangement. It would be certainly quite as respectable, if not a little more so, to go to my own home on such an occasion. Anna M.[27] would of course go with us, and she is a regularly trained fairy at transformation. You have no idea of the rose's nest we sh'd turn the loggery[28] into. (Birds nest among roses, I mean, of course) After the stop at Mrs. Yates' we would come and make a little visit here at Utica and then go on. I sh'd hope Doct. Kendrick[29] would be well enough to "do the needful" for us, but if not, there are enough others there. How would you like the arrangements? We could not have it done quietly here. I find by talking with Miss C. that some *must* be invited—at H we could have our own way entirely.

I have made out a long letter and there is but little in it. I shall hope to hear from you tomorrow. Dream of me again, and in your sleep, "Call me sweet names, darling, call me thy flower." Thy flower nestles bird-like in thy bosom and "fluttering its fresh lips together" whispers "thine forever."

---

[25] See vol. 1, "Cast of Characters," s.v. "Corey, the Reverend D. G."

[26] Emily's mother, Lavinia Richards Chubbuck, was born June 1, 1785, at Goffstown, New Hampshire, the eldest of thirteen children. She married Charles Chubbuck on November 17, 1805, at Goffstown, New Hampshire. Four of her children were born at Goffstown, and moved with Charles and Lavinia Chubbuck to Eaton, New York in September 1816; they were Lavinia, Benjamin, Harriet, and John Walker. Sarah Catharine, Emily, and Wallace were all born in Eaton.

[27] Anna Maria Anable was the niece of the Misses Urania and Cynthia Sheldon and the daughter of Joseph and Alma Sheldon Anable. Emily first met Anna Maria in fall 1840 when she went as a student to the Utica Female Academy; both Emily and Anna Maria became members of the faculty there. In these years, Anna Maria became Emily's dearest friend, and the extensive correspondence between the two reflects sensitive, flirtatious spirits and a deep intimacy. Emily was "Nemmy" to Anna Maria's "Ninny." In 1848, Anna Maria Anable, with the help of her extended family, moved to Philadelphia and started the Misses Anable's School there. At Emily's death in 1854, Anna Maria was given guardianship of Emily Frances Judson, daughter of Emily and Adoniram Judson.

[28] The loggery was Emily's father's home. See Kendrick, *The Life and Letters of Mrs. Emily C. Judson*, 166. See also vol. 1, "Places, Events, Organizations, and Magazines," s.v. "Loggery, The."

[29] When Emily Chubbuck was in her teens, Dr. Nathaniel Kendrick was the pastor of the Baptist church in Eaton and also a professor in a local theological school; he eventually became the president of the Hamilton Literary and Theological Institution. At that time in her life, Emily spoke with him about becoming a missionary. Dr. Kendrick gave her the wise counsel of discernment, patience, and waiting. Adoniram and Emily turned to Dr. Kendrick to officiate at their marriage. He married Adoniram and Emily on June 2, 1846. A. C. Kendrick, in *the Life and Letters of Mrs. Emily C. Judson*, says that the marriage of Emily and Adoniram Judson was the last service for which Dr. Kendrick was able to leave his home. Other correspondents mention his continued frailty. He died on September 11, 1848.

Forever thine,
Nemmy Petty[30]

Source: Hanna family files.

Nathaniel Parker Willis to Emily E. Chubbuck, April 2, 1846—Astor House

My dear Emily

I should be very unworthy of the constant tenor of my feeling toward you, if I did not do all in my power to lighten the "trials" of which you speak and to heighten if possible the "happiness" you balance against them. I will do so to the utmost of my ability. You shall not "lose one true friend," nor will I "lose sight of you till one of us is hidden by the grave."[31] All that concerns you must, of course, interest me more than all other news. But you must forgive my abrupt letter written last,[32] and you must forgive some change in the tone of what I write now and hereafter, for you were the nearest link to my heart in this world's chain, and you have broken it to place a dearer link between us. Coming home as I did with distrust of every other and reliance only on you, this sudden remove—with an exile too, that divides you from me forever—was news of a *death*. And it does not soften grief that the one who is gone is made happier by the removal.

I do wrong, perhaps, to write on this feeling at all. You are another's now, and his is the privilege of writing to you without a guard upon the pen. But I have not only the apology to make for my *rude* reception of the news of your coming marriage, but reason to give for the hesitation which you refer to, in my promise to see you before you sail for India. After what I have said you will understand this. I loved you too tenderly dear Emily, to be resigned in a moment to losing you forever—I may say too exclusively—for you were all alone in your nearness to me. And if you can think what the death of the most beloved would be if repeated by re-visitation, you can comprehend my unwillingness to see you in your happiness before your departure. I say only "willingness"—for if you wish'd much to see me, your request would, in anything, overrule all reluctance.

And now to answer your questions—I am preparing to establish my residence in New York. I have an engagement with a London paper as a correspondent which gives me, for the trifling labor of two letters a month, a sufficient income. If

---

[30] Emily E. Chubbuck used a number of different names over the course of her life and career. She wrote often under the name Fanny Forester, her argument being "who would buy a book authored by Emily Chubbuck?" At other times, she used Amy Scribbleton (July 6, 1841); Amy S. (September 28, 1841); Nem or Nemmy (Emily was always Nem or Nemmy to Anna Maria Anable who was Ninny); Pithy to Anna Maria (April 29, 1845); Peaked chin (See Anna Maria Anable, November 12, 1845); Sister Peakedchin (See Emily Chubbuck, February 28, 1846); Miss Peakedchin (Adoniram Judson, March 7, 1846); Miss Nemmy Petty (Adoniram Judson, March 7, 1846); Petty (April 13, 1846).

[31] These quotes were likely taken from the letter Emily had written to him.

[32] This was his letter of March 21, 1846, a letter that was edged in black.

we have a war I shall take a commission in the army. My child would be well cared for if I were not here, and my life is worthless. I propose at present, no engagement with any American paper, but my leisure may be spent on such *vent* to my heart as I can find in poetry. Imogen is well and growing hourly more beautiful and attaching. In her presence I feel fenced in from the world and may God spare her to me.

Mr. and Mrs. Dennett came over with us. They are gone to Boston.

Any thing [*sic*] you send to me at the Astor will reach me tho', if, as I conjecture, the "little package" is my letters and what I enclosed to you just before I sailed, burn them and spare me the repossession.[33] With endurance as much tried as mine has been, trifles startle.

May God guard your life on your dangerous road to happiness, dear Emily, and bless you in your husband.

Yours affectionately always

W

Gratify me by burning this explanatory letter. I had look'd forward to writing you my first unfetter'd one, at this close of the year now just completed, but I did not think it would need this apology for its freedom. Let it be for your eye only.

Source: Hanna family files.

Adoniram Judson to Emily E. Chubbuck,[34] April 2, 1846[35]—Plymouth

How I wish, my dearest love, that you were here. I arrived last night and found my sister[36] and three children[37] and this is the last visit, in all probability, which we shall all enjoy together in this world. I shall stay here three days more, and then we

---

[33] The letters of N. P. Willis to Emily were retained, and Emily did not follow his instructions. Because of her strong feelings of shame about having written them, she evidently destroyed the letters she had sent to him. See her letters that begin January 28, 1846, expressing her pain and anguish

[34] There are two versions of this letter: the original as written by Emily E. Chubbuck and the edited version published by Dr. A. C. Kendrick in his biography, *The Life and Letters of Mrs. Emily C. Judson.* Additions made by Dr. Kendrick are in parentheses, and words in the original left out by Dr. Kendrick have been added in bold. There are significant changes and omissions. In a note in his book, Dr. Kendrick explained that interest, purpose and propriety sometimes led to these changes and exclusions, "I remark here that in giving Miss Chubbuck's letters, I do not always indicate unimportant omissions. Real letters must always contain much which should not meet the public eye; and Emily's were real letters, dashed off hastily amidst pressing cares and duties. Written also after the exhausting labors of the day, they by no means do uniform justice to her epistolary powers." He later added, "In giving a few extracts from his and Miss Chubbuck's correspondence at this time, I have no wish to minister to a prurient curiosity, nor to violate that principle which would generally place letters written during the period of an 'engagement' under the shelter of inviolate secrecy."

[35] This letter has an addendum dated April 3, and a second addendum dated April 4, 1846.

[36] See vol. 1, "Cast of Characters," s.v. "Judson, Abigail Brown."

[37] These were Abby Ann Judson, Adoniram Judson, and Elnathan Judson, his three oldest children with Sarah Hall Boardman Judson.

shall be all scattered again. I have not yet received a line from you, nor shall I now, until I get back to Boston, for I have not directed letters to be sent on, lest they should pass me on the way. The children are mightily amused at their papa's marrying Emily Chubbuck. Abby Ann[38] had found out from some of the neighbours [*sic*], that it was Fanny Forester,[39] but she is quite sure that Fanny Forester must be very good, since she wrote *Effie Maurice*, one of her favorite books. Our affair, I find, has been not the town talk but the country talk for a fortnight or month past. The Philada. announcement, that marriage was intended between the Rev. and "the dear delightful Fanny Forester, *as Willis*[40] *calls her*" opened people's eyes a bit. Even that slow deliberative Mr. Peck[41] committed it to memory and was able to repeat it verbatim, which I made him do. He did not know, not he, but that I had found a jewel but timidly inquired whether you would be arrayed in other jewels and finery and evidently fearing that you would come dancing through the country like other Fannies—the style laid down in Isaiah chapter iii. I replied, from considerable acquaintance, I was satisfied you enjoyed a tolerable modicum of common sense. How astonished they will be, when they see you and become a little acquainted with you. **But that is a privilege very few of them will catch, for I have no idea of having you exhibited, as I have been served myself. Well, what if we should give it up—"Take it all back!" Do let me, darling dear—you see what a pucker I am in. And yourself too, sweet Fanny. O I am so happy to feel sure that you will not let me, no never.** The truth is, it is not strange, that there should be a great wonderment. We calculated on it. But we need not care for it. We can both, perhaps, afford to be pretty independent of it. And we know it will soon pass away and still more, that a reaction will probably take place. We feel that God has directed us in this affair, and we may hope that he will grant his rich blessing. And if he blesses us we shall be blessed indeed.

Source: Hanna family files; A. C. Kendrick, *The Life and Letters of Mrs. Emily C. Judson*, 174–75.

---

[38] See vol. 1, "Cast of Characters," s.v. "Judson, Abby Ann."

[39] Emily Chubbuck wrote under the *nom de plume* Fanny Forester. Asked about it once, she said, "Would anyone buy a book written by Emily E. Chubbuck?"

[40] Nathaniel Parker Willis was the editor, with General George Morris, of the *New Mirror*, a prominent literary magazine in New York. His "discovery" of Emily in the June 8, 1844 edition of the *New Mirror* catapulted her into literary fame and enabled her to command the highest prices for her articles and stories from the major magazines of that period. It began a new and glorious chapter in her life. Over the next two years, he became her friend, mentor, and confidant. His black-bordered letter of March 21, 1846, made it abundantly clear that her engagement to Adoniram Judson had come as a "death blow" and that he had expected to marry Emily upon his return that month from England. He returned several letters to Emily to demonstrate to her, lest she had forgotten, why he had felt right in that expectation. In vol. 1, there is a timeline that presents in some detail the substance of their developing relationship, all from the letters Willis had written to Emily. When she received her letters back from Willis, she destroyed them, feeling that they would cast a negative shadow on her life and, because of that, the life and ministry of Adoniram Judson.

[41] See vol. 1, "Cast of Characters," s.v. "Peck, The Reverend Doctor Solomon."

Adoniram Judson to Emily E. Chubbuck,[42] April 3, 1846[43]

Tell me in your next whether I shall send your "Young Novel Reader" inserted in the *Mothers' Journal* to the Editor of the *Christian Watchman*, adding "By the author of *Effie Maurice, Anna Bailey,* and *The Great Secret.*"[44] Where are you now and what are you doing? It is a week today since we parted. I have almost forgotten how you look—let me consider—But you have such a Protean face, that it is impossible to fix you—There is Kitty Colman's[45] mischievous face, full of fun and frolic. Catch her, catch her if you can. **And hold her by the hair—(otherwise) she'll slip your fingers through. In a twinkling gone for [ ]. And the doctor he will have to trudge a solitary way**—And then there is the philosophic or poetic development—pen in hand—form bending—upper lip full of thought "a fair and fanciful Fan Forester."[46] Or is it Jeane Marie Guion[47]—

> "ye who know my heavenly fire,
> Softly speak and soon retire."[48]

[42] This is the first addendum to a letter started April 2, 1846. There is a second addendum written April 4, 1846.

[43] For an understanding of the comparison on an original letter with the letter actually printed by Dr. A. C. Kendrick in *The Life and Letters of Mrs. Emily C. Judson,* see the first footnote for the letter of Adoniram to Emily dated April 2, 1846.

[44] These were three books written by Emily Chubbuck—*Effie Maurice* in 1842, *Anna Bailey* in 1844, *The Great Secret* in June 1842.

[45] "Kitty Coleman" was a story by Fanny Forester and printed in the revised edition of vol. 1 of *Alderbrook.* The first page of this story read:

An arrant piece of mischief was that Kitty Coleman, with her winsome ways and wicked little heart! Those large, bewildering eyes! How they poured out their strange eloquence, looking as innocent all the while as though they had peeped from their amber-fringed curtains quite by mistake, or only to join in a quadrille with the sunlight! And then those warm, ripe lips! The veritable "rosy bed, That a bee would choose to dream in." That is, a well-bred bee, which cared to pillow his head on pearls white as snow, on the heaven-side of our earthly atmosphere, and sip the honey of Hybla from the balmy air fanning his slumbers. And so wild and unmanageable was she! Oh! it was shocking to "*proper* people!" Why, she actually laughed aloud—Kitty Coleman did! I say Kitty, because in her hours of frolicking, she was very like a juvenile puss, particularly given to fun-loving: and moreover, because everybody called her Kitty, but aunt Martha. She was a well-bred woman, who disapproved of loud laughing, romping, and nicknaming, as she did of other crimes; so she always said, Miss Catherine. People always have their trials in this world, and Kitty Coleman (so she firmly believed) would have been perfectly happy but for aunt Martha. She thought, even, that Miss Catherine's hair—those long, golden locks, like rays of floating sunshine wandering about her shoulders, should be gathered up into a comb; and once the little lady was so obliging as to make a trial of the scheme; but, at the first bound she made after Rover, the burnished cloud broke from its ignoble bondage, and the little silver comb nestled down in the long grass forever more. Kitty *was* a sad romp.

[46] Emily Chubbuck as Fanny Forester. See vol. 1, "Cast of Characters," s.v. "Chubbuck, Emily," and "Forester, Fanny."

[47] Jeane Marie Guion was a Christian mystic, born in the middle of the seventeenth century.

[48] This is from one of the poems of Jeane Marie Guion: "Repose in God."

> Blest! Who in thy bosom seeks
> Rest that nothing earthly breaks,
> Dead to self and worldly things,
> Lost in thee, thou King of kings!
> **Ye that know my secret fire,**
> **Softly speak and soon retire;**
> Favour my divine repose,
> Spare the sleep a God bestows.

Pass on, ye fair, fascinating, fantasies. What comes next? O I see—I fell—This the face of love, not hidden in the hands—upturned—beaming, glowing, in the sympathetic mesmerism of commingling spirits—And must this face ever become settled, cold, lifeless, like those other faces that I once feasted on? And must I again press down the stiffening eyelids over the extinguished orbs of love!

> "Are hope and love and beauty's bloom,
> But blossoms for the tomb,
> And nothing bright but heaven?"

Well, be it so, for heaven is in full prospect, and immortal life and love and joy.

Source: Hanna family files; A. C. Kendrick, *The Life and Letters of Mrs. Emily C. Judson*, 174–75.

Emily E. Chubbuck to Adoniram Judson, April 3, 1846—Utica NY

I am distressed to death with the thousand things which I am called to endure, and I cannot help letting you know it. I wonder if men—Christian or infidels, have any human feeling about them, that they sh'd think their pillows made of stone. I carefully kept my name from the public eye, addressed a *nomme de plume* for the sake of privacy and now every fool that can pen a clumsy paragraph must needs drag it before the public, and make his senseless comments, something after the fashion of a turkey strutting in a barn-yard. I don't care whether they praise or censure me—of the two perhaps the praise is most provoking. I wish they would just let me alone; give me some place [*sic*] to be quiet in, if it be only a hovel, and I will be grateful. I am heart-sick now, and, if the feeling be not wicked, would rather die than live. It is not enough that I have resolved on a step which is almost death— forgive me, dearest, I am troubled and do not consider what I write. I shall be happy with you, I know; but now I am most miserable. It seems that all New York is alive about the affair. It is the common subject of conversation on steamboat and in hotel, in parlour [*sic*] and in grog-shop. Miss Anable[49] who has just returned from N. Y. says there is no place, no circle where my name is not heard. There is even talk of preventing (very likely by the same kind of "active measures" Mr. Backus[50] had in his mind) such an insane proceeding as F. F.'s[51] "throwing herself away." They say such a senseless sacrifice is unparalleled.

[49] See vol. 1, "Cast of Characters," s.v. "Anable, Miss Anna Maria."

[50] This was probably Mr. Backus of the publishing firm of Bennett, Backus, and Hawley.

[51] Emily Chubbuck as Fanny Forester. See vol. 1, "Cast of Characters," s.v. "Chubbuck, Emily," and "Forester, Fanny."

I am glad to learn by your letter rec'd tonight,[52] that there is strong hope of Lydia's[53] being appointed. I will get the papers and send them as soon as possible. She will need the appropriation for outfit.[54]

Accompanying your letters was one from Mr. W.[55] in which he speaks freely of what had been his intentions, promises continued friendship etc.[56] Sometimes it seems to me that I was born to create unhappiness; and in that last I feel more and more as though I had been reckless, if not heartless. If you knew how much occasion I had given him to believe that when this explanation came it would be favourably [sic] rec'd I am afraid you would not love me. And yet it was done thoughtlessly—I always wrote from the impulse of the moment, and I could not but express myself warmly to one so kind.

Don't darling, let them drive you about to parties and all such places and keep you up late at night.[57] To be sure "Nemmy Petty"[58] kept you up, but that was a different thing. Were not her kisses as good as a nap? I don't believe it is so hard to entertain *one*, even if she sh'd be so heavy and make your arms ache, as a room full. Take good care of yourself, at any rate, for you will soon be where you will have more *partifying* [sic] to do. The way I shall train you about Hamilton next time you come! Oh, but would'nt [sic] I give a nice little sum to lay my head in your bosom tonight, and hear sweet words from your lips, for, darling, I need kind words said to me, soothing words—something to make me better. This is a severe school for me and I am afraid I shall become irritable and resentful. I must try not to be so bad as to make you unhappy.

I regret Mr. Peck's[59] decision[60] and am very much disappointed. Mrs. Nott,[61] Miss Sheldon[62] and Anna Maria all seem to think there is an impropriety in my writing the memoir[63] since the engagement has been made public. I had the same

[52] See Adoniram Judson's letter of April 1, 1846, in which he sent a list of documents needed to be presented by Miss Lydia Lillybridge to the Board of the American Baptist Missionary Union.

[53] See vol. 1, "Cast of Characters," s.v. "Lillybridge, Miss Lydia." Also the timeline on "Lydia Lillybridge Simons."

[54] See Adoniram Judson's letter of April 1, 1846, in which he said that the board would appropriate $150 or $200 for Lydia's outfit if she were appointed.

[55] See vol. 1, "Cast of Characters," s.v. "Willis, Nathaniel Parker."

[56] See the letter from Nathaniel Parker Willis to Emily E. Chubbuck dated April 2, 1846.

[57] On April 1, 1846, Adoniram Judson wrote, "I intended to have written you last evening, but after being on the run all day, I crept into bed from a party at Roxbury, to oblige the Colby's, between 11 and 12 o'clock, half dead."

[58] See vol. 1, "Cast of Characters," s.v. "Nemmy, Nem, or Nemmy Petty (Nemmie Pettie)"; also the chapter "Names of Endearment," 333.

[59] See vol. 1, "Cast of Characters," s.v. "Peck, The Reverend Doctor Solomon."

[60] On April 1, 1846, Adoniram Judson wrote, "Mr. Peck thinks that the Board will be glad to have you prepare a memoir of Sarah, and allow the avails indefinitely to be appropriated to a certain purpose, but that is all that the rules of the mission will admit. He intends to bring the matter before the Board at some future meeting, probably on the 17th."

[61] See vol. 1, "Cast of Characters," s.v. "Nott, Urania Sheldon."

[62] See vol. 1, "Cast of Characters," s.v. "Sheldon, Miss Cynthia."

[63] There was conversation about Emily writing the memoir of Sarah Hall Boardman Judson; this discussion brought Emily and Adoniram together on Christmas Day 1845.

feeling myself, but I did not know but it was one of my queer notions, and so did not like to speak about it. Besides I am afraid the materials would fail; so that I could do neither the subject nor myself justice. You can say to Mr. Peck that when I proposed doing it I hoped to arrange the matter before a change of names took place. Why not allow me something else? If my twenty pages per year will not do, why not let me write your biography? (would you dare trust me?) or a history of the mission? I have resolved the plan of self support, and don't believe it at all impracticable.[64] I could make at times large sums, much more than I needed, and then lay by the surplus and add now and then a little to it for time of need. Don't you think I could do it? Well, don't get worried, darling; I am a little provoked at this (as it necessarily seems to me) narrowness, but we won't fret ourselves about it. They cannot take your love from me and that makes me richer than all the wealth I might have inherited as "princess of Ophir,"[65] joined with the approbation of the universe. By the way, I ought to tell you what a wondrous temptation I have resisted. Only think of my having the purse of Fortunatus[66] offered me with the little proviso that I wouldn't go to Burmah. A gentleman had promised to keep my purse full to the brim, allowing me to scatter the contents as freely as I choose. Only think! By staying at home I might establish some entirely new mission.

New York Express, March 28, 1846

"Fanny Forester"

"The Boston Transcript in announcing the marriage of this lady with the Rev. Mr. Judson, and her intention of going with him to Burmah says: 'This is another instance of infatuation which would almost seem to be for an untimely death. We really think there should be a law against the wholesale sacrifice of life which is continually chronicled amongst those who imagine they are called to labour in unhealthy climes as the wives of missionaries. How any man can answer to his conscience for beguiling any woman to become his wife, with almost sure death in the face of such an undertaking we know not. Our remarks may seem uncalled for, but from observing the numerous sacrifices of life attending these missionary marriages, we feel justified in a sort of admonitory warning.' The *Transcript* is quite right. The notice of the sailing of missionaries is too often and speedily followed by the account of their early death, and it is time a word of caution is spoken at least to females. The devotion of missionaries cannot be too highly commended, but there

[64] In response to a comment from Adoniram Judson about "wonderful difficulties" in her April 1, 1846 letter to Adoniram, Emily raised the possibility of supporting herself in Burmah by writing. This would remove all difficulties that they might have with the American Baptist Missionary Union.

[65] One of the enduring tales to come out of the reign of Sultan Mansur Shah is the legend of the Fairy Princess of Mount Ophir.

[66] Fortunatus was a Christian poet of the mid-sixth century.

is a point beyond which it may be carried too far. Where the chances of life to Europeans are so small as they are known to be in some parts of India, it is criminal to trifle with human life."

There, Mr. Judson, don't you catch it as well as this from little Nemmy?[67] Aren't you no better than a naughty blue-beard carrying off this silly child for the tiger to eat up? That is an offset to some of the nice things you will pick up in Maine.[68] Don't imagine you are an angel, dear; because some of the newspaper people have discovered that you are a vile deluder.

I mustn't fill this wee bit of a corner with this trash. These changes within are very queer. I began my letter crying and I finish laughing. I have a great, great deal to annoy and trouble me, but I know that if I look to God he will care for me. I am longing for the time to come when I can be with you again. I could scarce live through this all alone. Anna Maria is worth all the world to me—all the world but one. Pray for me, love me, think kindly of me, darling. I send you a shower of kisses. Balm be on your eyelids, sleep sweetly, and dream of your own tired bird.

Written upside down to the text on page 1 in the top margin: "I cut from the *N.Y. Recorder*, a religious paper, of April 2, an article which shows what a pass you have arrived at—actress and all. Poor doctor! But we couldn't have run away to England. F. F. couldn't have got out of the country without all newspapers down at her heels."[69]

Source: Hanna family files.

---

[67] Emily Chubbuck as Fanny Forester. See vol. 1, "Cast of Characters," s.v. "Chubbuck, Emily," and "Forester, Fanny."

[68] Adoniram Judson would soon be traveling to Maine to meet with the extended family of George Dana Boardman. He succeeded in obtaining from them sufficient pledges to cover the cost of Boardman's education at Brown University.

[69] In his letter to Emily of February 25, 1846, Adoniram speaks of having suggested they travel incognito to England to be married, to which Emily replied that they could not get out of the country without her friends knowing it.

Adoniram Judson to Emily E. Chubbuck,[70] April 4, 1846[71]

I think I told you, that Mr. Beebee[72] mentioned in terms of high commenda-tion, a piece which you wrote on Prayer published in the *Register*,[73] some four years ago. Could you promise to send me a copy? And suppose I should repub-lish it in the *Watchman* or *Reflector*, "By the author of *Effie Maurice*,"[74]—"Clinging to Earth"[75] is too good a thing to be lost. Suppose you should, sometime, when you have nothing else to do, write a counterpart. "Aspiring to Heaven"[76] or the like and let them stand together.

A change comes o'er my dream. Did not I scold Anna Maria[77] for not appearing as good as she is? The fact is, that you two girls have been trying with all your might, for some years past, to spoil one another. And I must con-fess you have succeeded to a charm. You are so afraid of spirit, not pride or hypocrisy or some such bugbear, that you have learnt to act just as bad as you dare, without being actually read out of church. If your ministers only have the moiety, you may depend you would catch such an overhauling. And I am not sure how long my conscience will let me remain without informing against you. And then what serious godly young candidate for the ministry (and I hope

---

[70] This is the second addendum to a letter started April 2, 1846. The first addendum was added April 3.

[71] For an understanding of the comparison on an original letter with the letter actually printed by Dr. A. C. Kendrick in *The Life and Letters of Mrs. Emily C. Judson*, see the first footnote for the letter of Adoniram to Emily dated April 2, 1846.

[72] Alexander Beebee was trained as a lawyer, but after experiencing strong religious convictions after the death of his first child, he became active in a Baptist church near Skaneateles, New York. In 1824, he observed that the Baptist denomination had only a few credible newspapers in the United States, none of them being in New York. In 1825, he became the editor of the *Baptist Register*, and over the next thirty years, it became a strong foundation for the rapidly growing Baptist churches of Central New York. During the course of Emily's engagement to Adoniram, Mr. Beebee must have said something reflecting the religious wisdom or judgment strongly expressed by many about the marriage of Adoniram Judson and Emily Chubbuck. Many of Emily's letters reflect the antagonism she felt for him. In July 1849, she wrote him a confrontational letter about something he had said. Morven Jones and Miss Sheldon, through continued efforts, did bring about a truce. Morven said that Emily had "no better sup-porter" than Mr. Beebee.

[73] The *Baptist Register* was a local Baptist paper in New York that grew into regional prominence. Published by Alexander Beebee, it had significant influence in Baptist circles. Emily wrote for it on occasion, though less often as her stories appealed to the more popular literary magazines.

[74] *Effie Maurice* was one of Emily's earlier books published in 1842.

[75] This was a continuing discussion and disagreement. On April 4, Adoniram wrote to Emily to say, "'Clinging to earth' is too good a thing to be lost. Suppose you should, sometime, when you have nothing else to do, write a counter part, 'Aspiring to Heaven' or the like and let them stand together." On April 8, Emily wrote, "I gave 'Clinging to earth' to Neal for his paper a few days ago. I am sorry if you didn't like to have it come out alone. Maybe I will write a counterpart to it." Then, on April 10, Judson wrote, "I am dismayed at your sending 'Clinging to Earth,' to Mr. Neal 'a few days ago.' I know not with what face I can put the other pieces in the Boston papers, if that appears in a Phila. paper, *at such a late* date. That piece, though beautiful poetry, is so much at variance with your present views and prospects and our fondest hopes!" On April 11, he had written a letter of apology for his "ill tempered" remarks, but she would not have received it at the time she was writing this letter. On April 13, she wrote, "When I read your letter last night, I dropped one little tear for the 'dismay' which I had caused you; and then, as a naughty child should, sat down to repair the wrong as I best might. I wrote 'Aspiring to Heaven'; and it is on its way to Philadelphia now. Lest, however, the first should be in press so that they cannot come out together. I will enclose a copy of both which you may get published if you think proper."

[76] The two poems "Clinging to Earth" and "Aspiring to Heaven" appear as the next two pieces in this volume.

[77] See vol. 1, "Cast of Characters," s.v. "Anable, Miss Anna Maria."

---

you are not so far lost as to think of any thing [*sic*] below the cloth) will ever look at either of you the second time? Depend on it, you will have to lead apes somewhere. I pity you, 'pon my honor, I do. So much so, that I have a good mind to take one of you! Now isn't that kind? Couldn't you hug me for it? Well, let me see, which shall it be? Emily—I think, for she is the worst off, having almost worked herself into an actress. And if I take her, it may lay a streak of whitewash on the other and I may venture to recommend her to my noble-minded friend Mr. Weed, who has lost his lady love. Think of these things, girls, put your sweet little hand (I must own that) into your left bosoms, and feel and see, whether you have any hearts left, or whether they have evaporated and flown up to Milton's Fools' Paradise. And when I come out with old Father Peck[78] and Father Bennett, we will see. But it is an awful sacrifice on my part. Perhaps I cannot come to the scratch. So don't set your hearts on it too much, for I would fain not break any more, having too much in that line to answer for already!! Thine to serve, (Thine ever)

A Judson

Written across the top margin of page 1: **"I have a writing case for you, similar to mine, which I mention, lest you should see another in Utica and be tempted to buy it—"**

Source: Hanna family files; A. C. Kendrick, *The Life and Letters of Mrs. Emily C. Judson*, 174–75.

Emily E. Chubbuck to Joseph Neal for Publication

Clinging to Earth[79]

O do not let me die! the earth is bright,
And I am earthly, so I love it well;
Though heaven is holier, all replete with light,
Yet I am frail, and with frail things would dwell.

I cannot die! the flowers of earthly love
Shed their rich fragrance on a kindred heart;
There may be purer, brighter flowers above,
But yet with these 't would be too hard to part.

[78] See vol. 1, "Cast of Characters," s.v. "Peck, The Reverend Doctor Solomon."

[79] For the complete story on this poem, see the letter of Adoniram Judson to Emily E. Chubbuck dated April 4, 1846. See also the footnote in that letter to "Aspiring to Heaven."

I dream of heaven, and well I love these dreams,
They scatter sunlight on my varying way;
But 'mid the clouds of earth are priceless gleams
Of brightness, and on earth O let me stay.

It is not that my lot is void of gloom,
That sadness never circles round my heart;
Nor that I fear the darkness of the tomb,
That I would never from the earth depart.

'T is that I love the world—its cares, its sorrows,
Its bounding hopes, its feelings fresh and warm,
Each cloud it wears, and every light it borrows,
Loves, wishes, fears, the sunshine and the storm;

I love them all: but closer still the loving
Twine with my being's cords and make my life;
And while within this sunlight I am moving,
I well can bide the storms of worldly strife.

Then do not let me die! for earth is bright,
And I am earthly, so I love it well,
Heaven is a land of holiness and light,
But I am frail, and with the frail would dwell.

Source: Fanny Forester, *Alderbrook*, 10th ed. (Boston: Ticknor, Reed and Fields, 1851) 1:73.

Emily E. Chubbuck to Adoniram Judson

Aspiring to Heaven[80]

Yes, let me die! Am I of spirit-birth,
And shall I linger here where spirits fell,
Loving the stain they cast on all of earth?
O make me pure, with pure ones e'er to dwell!

'Tis sweet to die! The flowers of earthly love,
(Fair, frail, spring blossoms) early droop and die

---

[80] For the complete story on this poem, see the letter of Adoniram Judson to Emily E. Chubbuck dated April 4, 1846. See also the footnote in that letter to "Aspiring to Heaven." This was written as a counterpoint to "Clinging to Earth" at the request of Adoniram Judson.

But all their fragrance is exhaled above,
Upon our spirits evermore to lie.

Life is a dream, a bright but fleeting dream,
I can but love; but then my soul awakes,
And from the mist of earthliness a gleam
Of heavenly light, of truth immortal, breaks.

I shrink not from the shadows sorrow flings
Across my pathway; nor from cares that rise
In every foot-print; for each shadow brings
Sunshine and rainbow as it glooms and flies.

But heaven is dearer. There I have my treasure,
There angels fold in love their snowy wings;
There sainted lips chant in celestial measure,
And spirit fingers stray o'er heav'n-wrought strings.

There loving eyes are to the portals straying;
There arms extend, a wonderer to fold;
There waits a dearer, holier One, arraying
His own in spotless robes and crowns of gold.

Then let me die. My spirit longs for heaven,
In that pure bosom evermore to rest;
But, if to labor longer here be given,
"Father, thy will be done!" and I am blest.

Source: Fanny Forester, *Alderbrook*, 1:74.

Emily E. Chubbuck to Adoniram Judson[81] April 5, 1846—Utica NY

Why didn't you write your Petty[82] a letter for tonight darling? Why did not you? Did not you know she had been expecting it all day? And didn't you know how she went down to Aunt C's[83] room to wait for the mail, and clapped her hands with delight when the boy came in? That everybody else sh'd have a letter and poor Nemmy[84] none—*your* Nemmy. There, I have had my murmuring out,

[81] There is an addendum to this letter dated April 6, 1846.

[82] See vol. 1, "Cast of Characters," s.v. "Nemmy, Nem, or Nemmy Petty (Nemmie Pettie)"; also the chapter "Names of Endearment," 333.

[83] See vol. 1, "Cast of Characters," s.v. "Sheldon, Miss Cynthia."

[84] "Nem" or "Nemmy" were names of endearment given to Emily by a small group of her intimate friends at the Utica Female Academy. Anna Maria Anable was "Ninny."

and now I will have the grace to thank you for having been so very, *very* kind in writing so often. I sh'd not have been so exacting, but that your attentive goodness has taught me to expect a great deal. Then I am worried, in a constant state of excitement, so nervous that the slightest thing startles and alarms me. I am not afraid you will cast me off; but sometimes I fear that you will almost wish that you could do it; and the wish would be equivalent to the act. Does the wish ever creep into your mind? Is it unjust in me even to think of it? I suppose it is; but if you could only be in my place for a little while, this strange, terrible position,—you wouldn't wonder that I have a dread of things indefinable. That poor I should be set up in a pillory! Please write me a little, (*just* a *very* little, if you sh'd chance to be busy) everyday, and put down all your thoughts and feelings. Let me have a piece of your heart, a word from away down where it is warmest, every day; and then I will try to be as happy as I can till you come.

I will get you the papers[85] about Miss Lillybridge[86] tomorrow, and I hope you will receive them before you leave. You didn't tell me where you were going. To Maine?[87] I hope not to attend meetings. I hope the vessel which takes us will not sail before July; altho' I am truly anxious to be away. I presume I shall repent this feeling hereafter as unkind to those who love me and whom I so truly love; but now it seems to me that I sh'd be perfectly happy out of this terrible bustle and excitement—"anywhere, anywhere, out of the world." The vessel, good or bad, will be "some dear little isle of our own," and I am sure we shall be happy in it. You shall teach me to say "kyeu-the," and I will *put up my lips*, just as often! I would put them up *now* if it would do any good, but you would'nt [sic] touch them. You are talking with some stupid old fellow that I sh'd like to shut the door against, and you won't look this way at all. Well, I will revenge myself by kissing A. M.[88] Ah, you repent? Your two arms are about me. My head lies in your bosom. Good-night, darling; I will just take a little short nap there. Good-night—good-night. You do love your Nemmy, don't you, *bestest*?

Source: Hanna family files.

---

[85] See the letter of Adoniram Judson to Emily E. Chubbuck dated April 1, 1846 about the documents that the Board of the American Baptist Missionary Union will need to consider the application of Lydia Lillybridge to go with Adoniram and Emily to Burmah as a missionary.

[86] See vol. 1, "Cast of Characters," s.v. "Lillybridge, Miss Lydia." Also the timeline on "Lydia Lillybridge Simons."

[87] Adoniram Judson would soon be traveling to Maine to meet with the extended family of George Dana Boardman. He succeeded in obtaining from them sufficient pledges to cover the cost of Boardman's education at Brown University.

[88] See vol. 1, "Cast of Characters," s.v. "Anable, Miss Anna Maria."

Emily E. Chubbuck to Adoniram Judson,[89] April 6, 1846

Another mail, and no letter. Are you sick, darling? Or are you sick of Nemmy?[90] Perhaps you have gone to Plymouth[91] and so have not rec'd my first letters. I cannot bear to believe that you think of me less than when you first went away and wrote me every day. Well I have nothing to do but hope till tomorrow's mail comes in.

When I returned from Schenectady I found a very amusing note from Prof. Raymond[92] relative to your stealthy visit to Hamilton; and today I had a letter from Kate[93] in which she says, "Father called on Doct. Kendrick[94] a few days after you left; he was pleased with Dr. J's note and thought he did perfectly right." I hope we shall be able to require the good Doctor's services before the summer closes.[95] Next after Dr. Nott[96] I should like him best. What kind of talk did you have with Mr. Gillette[97] before you came away? I am afraid there is some misunderstanding, for Fanny[98] wrote home a few days ago, "Mr. G. is afraid that Emily is offended at

---

[89] This is an addendum to Emily's letter dated April 5, 1846.

[90] Emily Chubbuck. See vol. 1, "Cast of Characters," s.v. "Nemmy, Nem, or Nemmy Petty (Nemmie Pettie)." Also the chapter "Names of Endearment," 333.

[91] Adoniram had been in Plymouth, Massachusetts, visiting with his sister Abigail Brown Judson. Also there were the three oldest children by Sarah Hall Boardman Judson—Abby Ann Judson, Adoniram Judson, and Elnathan Judson.

[92] In 1846, Dr. John Howard Raymond was a professor of rhetoric and English language at Madison University. Apparently, Miss Cynthia Sheldon told him very early of the budding relationship and impending engagement of Emily Chubbuck and Adoniram Judson, and Mr. Raymond is frequently mentioned as a source of the information getting into the community, much to the consternation of Emily and Adoniram, who wanted to keep the matter a "secret" for as long as possible. This warning to Miss Sheldon came too late. See the letter of John Howard Raymond to Emily E. Chubbuck dated March 23, 1846.

[93] Sarah Catharine Chubbuck, "Kate," "Kit," or "Kitty" was Emily's older sister by ten months. Outside of the two terms at the Utica Female Academy, which Emily arranged for her, Catharine always lived at home with her parents in Hamilton, New York. The letters indicate opportunities for marriage, but she, for unknown reasons, remained single. She later helped to care for Henry and Edward Judson after their return from Burmah in fall 1851 when they moved into the Hamilton home with their "aunt" and "grandparents," and she was remembered by them as "dear old Aunt Kate—a dear friend."

[94] See vol. 1, "Cast of Characters," s.v. "Chubbuck, Miss Sarah Catharine."

[95] These lines are a discussion as to who will officiate at their marriage ceremony.

[96] See vol. 1, "Cast of Characters," s.v. "Nott, The Reverend Doctor Eliphalet."

[97] Following several successful pastorates, the Reverend A. D. Gillette was the founding pastor of the flourishing Eleventh Baptist Church in Philadelphia in 1839. With his wife Hannah and several children (they would eventually have six), he graciously opened their home to Emily Chubbuck when she came to Philadelphia at the end of March 1845 for her health. The connection had been made through Miss Cynthia Sheldon, a family friend of Mr. Gillette and his parents. A prominent Baptist, Mr. Gillette journeyed to Boston in December 1845 to accompany Adoniram Judson to Philadelphia for meetings, and on Christmas Day, he introduced Dr. Judson to Emily Chubbuck with the hope that Fanny Forester could be persuaded to write the memoir of Sarah Hall Boardman Judson. A. D. Gillette and his wife Hannah remained valued and trusted friends, not only with Emily, but with the Sheldon and Anable families. He moved from Philadelphia to New York in 1852.

[98] Fanny Anable was one of nine children born to Joseph and Alma Anable and was a niece of Miss Cynthia Sheldon and Mrs. Urania Sheldon Nott. The correspondence indicates that in April 1845 she was away from home studying and taking music lessons. These spring letters indicate that she was in Philadelphia, working in the home of and with the family of the Reverend A. D. Gillette. See Miss Sheldon's letter to Emily of November 30, 1845, in which she spoke of all that Fanny was doing to improve herself in the field of music, but also her concern for Fanny's interest in the party life and the "vanitie" which surround her." A March 30, 1847 letter from Anna Maria Anable told of Fanny's conversion following her grandmother's death. In September 1847, she was listed as one of the teachers at the Utica Female Academy. Fanny became a teacher with her sisters in the Misses Anable's School in Philadelphia.

---

something the reason she doesn't write; and has perhaps given up the idea of having him come on next summer." I wrote them last week, and made some slight allusion to it as though I was sorry, but supposed it all settled.

Lydia[99] has gone home. She will return tomorrow morning; but then her application to the board might be too late.[100] I will write tomorrow and address the envelope to you, to be opened by Mr. Peck[101] in case you have left. The other papers I can send now. We have thought as Miss Kelly[102] is principal it would be well to have her recommendation in addition to Miss Sheldon's[103] which I will also inclose [sic]. Mr. Corey[104] has just sent in his letter addressed to Mr. Peck and *sealed*. There would of course be no use in my inclosing [sic] it to you and so I will send it by itself and make your letter thinner. Mr. Corey is a great donkey—beg his pardon!

Darling, I am getting into the worst wickedest faultfinding mood. It don't agree with my mental or rather moral constitution to occupy such a conspicuous position. I grow unamiable every day and shall be a perfect Zantippe by the time we get to *heathendom*. Don't you pity yourself? Seriously, pray for me, dearest; I never felt in so much danger of turning to the world as at this very time when I sh'd be all for Jesus. I find so much among Christians which they call religion and which if just antipodes that they grow disagreeable to me; and there is so much in the world (particularly the refined poetical part of the world which perhaps has too much of my sympathy) like the purest religion that it attracts me in spite of myself. I know it is to Jesus Christ alone that I should look, and, dearest, my truest best friend—my all in this world—pray for me and help me in every way, that I may not be a hindrance to you; that I may do all I can to make the autumn of your days brighter than their summer has been, that their winter may be glorious. Pray for me constantly, dearest, for I am exposed to severe temptations and I am very weak. The God we both love watch over you and bring us again together in love and happiness. How kind of him to make us capable of loving each other! Do not forget me; and believe, my best-beloved darling one, that you are ever in the heart of

Your affectionate

Emily

Source: Hanna family files.

---

[99] See vol. 1, "Cast of Characters," s.v. "Lillybridge, Miss Lydia." Also the timeline on "Lydia Lillybridge Simons."

[100] See the letter of Adoniram Judson to Emily E. Chubbuck dated April 1, 1846, about the documents needed by the board of the American Baptist Missionary Union for consideration of Lydia's application to go to Burmah as a missionary with Emily and Adoniram.

[101] See vol. 1, "Cast of Characters," s.v. "Peck, The Reverend Doctor Solomon."

[102] Miss Jane Kelly was Emily Chubbuck's friend at the Utica Female Academy, and then she became a teacher with Emily at that institution. Miss Kelly became the literary principal in 1844 with the retirement of Mr. and Mrs. James Nichols from that position. During a period of Miss Kelly's illness in 1844, Emily filled in the position for her. Then, in 1848, when Miss Cynthia Sheldon moved to Philadelphia to help start the Misses Anable's School, Miss Kelly became the "headmistress" of the academy and successfully brought it into the future, though not without some initial disparagement from the Sheldon-Anable families.

[103] See vol. 1, "Cast of Characters," s.v. "Sheldon, Miss Cynthia."

[104] See vol. 1, "Cast of Characters," s.v. "Corey, the Reverend D. G."

Nathaniel Parker Willis to Emily E. Chubbuck, April 6, 1846—Astor House

My dear Emily,

Your calm letter, with its sincere rejoicing in your new prospects, removes much of my tremulousness of hand and heart in writing to you, for I see that you are to be happier than I could have made you, and any evidence that my letter may give of emotion will be looked upon from your tranquil sphere, tranquilly and kindly. I will bring you all your letters as you request. In looking them over this morning, however, I found the passage (in one which I enclose to you marked with red pencil) which gave shape and voice to a secret feeling I had not dared to acknowledge,—and from the moment of reading it, I felt myself coming home to be your husband. In my love for you, however, there was no more "of earth" than in your own. We have not seen enough of each other to do more (on my part) than simply satisfy the soul that its tender yearning and abandonment were not misplaced. I knew you, spiritually, as well as your guardian angel knows you—and personally enough to be sure that you could make me happy as my wife. Your expression of a desire to "be all" to me seemed to me as far as maiden delicacy could go in the assurance that you loved me with both heart and soul, and I gave you my heart and hand solemnly from that instant. Your other letters, (I will enclose you one or two of them) will show you, if you read them with this light, how naturally I believed that, by so resolving, I not only secured my own happiness but yours. Now that you have shown that your love, when we met, did not, like mine, take in what more was thus added to our knowledge of each other, you will see how easily I ran into the error, and how unconsciously your letters foster'd it. But for a propriety which you understand, I should have written at once, and thus been spared the endearing of a hope by months of secret nurture—but my letters, I still thought, *must* reveal to you that my love for you was not *all* brotherly. I supposed you would feel *true* that I was coming home to marry you. I talked freely of you as my future wife, to my sister in England, thus relieving much of her anxiety about Imogen.

I wish, for once, to tell you all this dear Emily, for the recognition of your spirit in this world has been to me one of the most soul-awaking and full events of my life. I am not willing to let you go from me to see me no more here, without informing you how complete was my love for you—how much more complete than your own for me—and how capable you are, of out-valuing, in the eyes of one who knows the world, all other women, even those whom you thought more attractive. Your nature has a fullness, a delicacy, an inward excessive beauty, that make you rare. You will not wonder—you must not—at the abrupt manner in which I acknowledged the news that I had irrevocably lost you.

You wish me to see you before you sail and I will. Write me when you are to be married, and where you are to be till then. I may wish to go to Washington first. When I see you, too, it must be alone. When I know these things, I can arrange my visit.

I enjoin upon you to burn my two last letters and this.[105] Men are not willing to have such secrets in danger. Many thanks for the slippers. But I shall seal them up like memorials of one dead. I must. May God bless you in your husband.

Ever yours affectionately

N. P. W.

Source: Hanna family files.

Adoniram Judson to Emily E. Chubbuck,[106] April 7, 1846—Boston

My dearest love,

I have just been having a good cry, here alone in Mr. Colby's[107] chamber, about my poor dear children. I left the two boys[108] yesterday, crying, as they set off in the cars for Worcester. Abby-ann[109] [sic] I took on to Bradford; and this morning I left her crying at the Hasseltines.[110] And thoughts of the children lead my mind to their departed mother, and I review the scenes on board the *Sophie Walker* and at St. Helena.[111] And then I stretch away to my two little forsaken orphans[112] in Burmah. And then I turn to you, whom I love above all though but a recent acquaintance. What a strange thing is the human heart! O if all our severe trials and our sweet enjoyments are but sanctified to us, it will be well. All my children

[105] These were his letters of March 21 and April 2, 1846. While there are fifty-one letters in the Correspondence from N. P. Willis to Emily E. Chubbuck, there are no letters written by Emily to Mr. Willis. When Emily made the commitment to marry Adoniram Judson and go with him to Burmah, she asked N. P. Willis to return all of her letters, believing that some of what she had written to him over two years might not reflect well on the wife of the great Dr. Judson and the missionary cause or might be misinterpreted by her Fanny Forester readers and by the church that Adoniram and Emily now served together in Burmah. At first, Mr. Willis refused, but then in this April 6 letter he agreed to return them, pausing again to quote from several to remind her of how he had gained confidence of her love. Jubilantly on April 9 Emily wrote to Adoniram letters of Willis' acquiescence. In *The Life and Letters of Mrs. Emily C. Judson*, Dr. Kendrick says that he had written to Mr. Willis to ask if he might use letters he had received from Miss Chubbuck; Mr. Willis said that he would look for them, but later reported that only one or two could be found, and those would shed no light for the purpose of the biography (109-10).

[106] For an understanding of the comparison on an original letter with the letter actually printed by Dr. A. C. Kendrick in *The Life and Letters of Mrs. Emily C. Judson*, see the first footnote for the letter of Adoniram to Emily dated April 2, 1846.

[107] See vol. 1, "Cast of Characters," s.v. "Colby, Gardner."

[108] These were Adoniram and Elnathan, the two oldest boys of Adoniram and Sarah Hall Boardman Judson. They lived with Dr. and Mrs. Calvin Newton in Worcester, Massachusetts.

[109] See vol. 1, "Cast of Characters," s.v. "Judson, Abby Ann."

[110] This was the family of Ann Hasseltine Judson, Adoniram Judson's first wife.

[111] Sarah Hall Boardman Judson died September 1, 1845, on the trip home from Burmah to the United States and was buried on the Isle of St. Helena.

[112] Henry Hall Judson and Edward Judson, the two youngest surviving boys, sons of Adoniram and Sarah Hall Boardman Judson. Another son, Charles, had also been left in Burmah, and he died in August 1845.

are now settled for the present. As to George Boardman,[113] he will enter Providence College next fall. I shall probably succeed in raising enough for his education before I embark, so that he will be off our hands. My other pecuniary arrangements are such, that we shall have an ample sufficiency for all our purposes, and enough to furnish your parents with what you may think necessary,[114] without your contributing a single cent. So that you can write just as much or little as you choose and if you take any remuneration, you can have the pleasure of presenting it through the mission treasury as an expression of gratitude of Him, who gave his life for you and is now laboring to prepare your seat and your crown. This is the course I have taken myself, and I am more and more convinced, that it is the best, the most excellent course.[115] You thought so at once, when we first conversed on these matters, and it was I that proposed another course and have been trying to ascertain whether it is consistent, and practicable. But I rather think that it is neither. The Rules of the Board which some consider too rigid, I made myself, when I viewed the subject impartially and consulted the general and the ultimate good; I sent them home to the Board; they were adopted without even a verbal alteration, and have been acted on ever since.

In regard to yourself you say, "My impression has been that you, considering all the circumstances of the case, thought I had done right, though the publication of a few letters might not have been wise."[116] Your impression is perfectly correct. That is just my sentiment. But you know I always thought that you have not been, for a year or two, in *the most excellent way*, and that it was exceedingly desirable, that you should henceforth pledge yourself and [vows] to holier purposes.[117] And this was the aim of my first plain and rather ungallant exhortations. And I shall always think, that your own sense and love of right initially aided me in my adventurous attempt on your heart. But by whatever means it was affected, it is the joy of my life, that I have secured a little lodgment in that dear, dear heart. Don't, darling, turn me out, because Mr. Corey[118] distorts what I said[119]—you know how a

[113] See vol. 1, "Cast of Characters," s.v. "Boardman, George Dana."

[114] Adoniram Judson promised this to Emily when he proposed to her. See the letters of Emily E. Chubbuck to Catharine Chubbuck and Anna Maria Anable dated January 6, 1846.

[115] In a March 30 letter, Adoniram wrote to Emily that some "wonderful difficulties" had presented themselves. Emily responded on April 1 and again on April 3 that she would support herself with her writing; that the "wonderful difficulty" likely had to do with the terms of her appointment as a missionary. Here, Adoniram closes the door to her need to raise any of her own support.

[116] This is quoted from the letter of Emily E. Chubbuck to Adoniram Judson dated March 31, 1846.

[117] On February 15, 1846, Emily suggested that an engraving be made of her likeness, and that the magazines for which she was writing publish it with the caption: "Henceforth to loftier purposes, I pledge myself [signed] Fanny Forester."

[118] See vol. 1, "Cast of Characters," s.v. "Corey, the Reverend D. G."

[119] On March 31, 1846, Emily wrote, "Mr. Corey has been distorting the conversation that you had with him once in the library and says that you disapprove of my course; but people are liable to err and if they repent etc. Did you make the remark or did Mr. Corey? I understood you that it came from him. These things going about are rather humiliating to me. My impression has been that you, considering all the circumstances of the case, tho't I had done right, tho' the publication of the few letters might not have been wise."

thing can be almost honestly misrepresented by being repeated and re-repeated—I don't recollect what I said to him but certainly not what is imputed to me. **At any rate, Mr. C has evidently not done well, and I must withdraw from him that cordiality that I began to feel. No—he shall never marry us**. As to *who* shall marry us, and the time and place etc.—have it all in your own way, dear, only give me this root *marry*, and you may vary it by any inflection and conjugate it in any mode or time you please.

I dread the coming of something that may separate us, or make us less happy in each other or *something*. I wonder whether you think that I divide my heart between you and all my friends here in Boston and elsewhere. And whether you think that any thing [*sic*] I hear or can hear will ever make me regret the blessed providence that carried me to Delaware (the) 12th—or feel ungrateful for your kind love, which allowed me to take you in my arms and draw the sweetest happiness I have ever enjoyed from your own lips—that love which has allowed my spirit to mingle with yours in a union which neither time nor death can ever dissolve—

As to what the newspapers and public say, can you not, darling, receive it with that cool quiet composure which best becomes you, nor let anyone, but me, know that it disturbs you. In fact be not disturbed. There is nothing that ought to disturb one of your pure and high purpose—Before God, we are indeed full of sin, but we may still feel that the path we are treading is one all the common public have neither capacity to investigate nor right to judge. The opinion of one such man as President Wayland[120] is worth that of ten thousand of this mass, for it is the opinion of such men, that finally sways the rest, and here it is—under Mch 26th. "I know not where you are, but hear you are tripping in author land, under the guidance of a fair Forester.[121] I am pleased to hear of your engagement, as far as I know of it. Miss C. is every where [*sic*] spoken of, as a pious, sensible, cultivated and engaging person. I pray God it may prove a great and mutual blessing. I write, at a venture, to say that our house is at your service, whenever you will come and occupy it. Should you bring anyone with you, both will be equally welcome." Would you like to have—the "Dissatisfied Spirit"[122] put into a Boston paper? And will you alter the last sentence or let it remain as it is?

Source: Hanna family files; A. C. Kendrick, *The Life and Letters of Mrs. Emily C. Judson*, 177–78.

---

[120] Dr. Francis Wayland, a prominent Baptist, was the president of Providence College, later to become Brown University. In 1853, he and Emily wrote write the memoir of Adoniram Judson.

[121] This is a play on Emily's book *Trippings in Author-land* and Fanny Forester, her *nom de plume*.

[122] This is an article or a story written by Emily, and evidently the ending was not satisfactory to Adoniram Judson. On April 11, Emily wrote to Adoniram, "Do whatever you please with the 'Dissatisfied Spirit.' Mr. Beebee has my copy. He is to publish it in the *Register* next week. He has found the article entitled 'Prayer' and is to publish that also. (Note: See Adoniram Judson's letter of April 4, 1846, in which he asked about this article previously published.) I did not make the alteration at the end of the 'Dis. Spirit' for it does not read quite as smoothly, and I do not care to help people in making a personal application."

Editor's Note

In the summer of 2010, as this volume was being edited, David Hanna, who is the great-great-grandson of Adoniram and Emily Judson, found a treasure trove of papers as he went through some storage boxes recently obtained from his father, Stanley Hanna. This remarkable discovery opened up close to several hundred pages of material all in Emily Chubbuck's handwriting, and among them was a copy of "The Dissatisfied Spirit."

We first hear of this story in a letter Adoniram sent to Emily on April 7, 1846. He mentions the story, asks Emily what she is going to do with it, and then asks her if she is going to alter the closing sentence or allow it to stay as it is. He fears that the way that it ended does not reflect Emily in terms of all that she was becoming as she committed herself to marriage and missionary service; leaving it would simply reinforce some of the opinion within the Church that Emily was a more secular author, and not one who would be a fit companion for the venerable missionary. There were other such instances; the reader would find a similar discussion around her poem "Clinging to Earth" with Judson feeling the same about that, eventually bringing Emily to write "Aspiring to Heaven."[123]

Emily responds on April 11, 1846 saying that she had given a copy to Mr. Beebee of the *Baptist Register*, and that she had not made any alternations to it. She stated that the alteration does not read as smoothly and that personally, "I do not care to help people in making a personal application.

In many ways this editor feels that this is an extraordinary story, "extraordinary" because it is so personally Emily.

In short, a created spirit takes the form of a butterfly, and then a songbird, and in both manifestations brings great joy to numerous people because of the beauty of appearance and the magic of song which they are able to bring. But in both instances the butterfly and the songbird are dissatisfied, hearing some deep inner voice that there is much more to life than what they are experiencing. The spirit begins to think of other possibilities. It "heard of a nobler mission it had yet dared to contemplate." Looking at life it had seen a terrifying and difficult path, yet that path had been made holy having been "trodden by a Holy One who had linked it to heaven." The bird and the butterfly realized that as such they would perish, but the "'living soul' born of the breath of the Almighty could not so perish."

Emily had achieved great success in life with her writing, and she was aware of her gifts and her competency. Yet she was realizing that it was not bringing her the

---

[123] These two poems with explanatory footnotes are found in this volume following Adoniram Judson's letter to Emily dated April 4, 1846.

satisfaction for which she deeply yearned, feelings she so often expressed in her correspondence.

We note that the poem within us is a reflection of this struggle. Tellingly, we find in the poem a line we have seen before: "Henceforth to loftier purposes I pledge myself." Early on in her relationship she had written to Adoniram Judson about the possibility of having a portrait done of her—of Fanny Forester—and attaching to it those very lines: "Henceforth to loftier purposes I pledge myself."[124] At one point there was discussion that it should be "holier" rather than "loftier," though "loftier" won out in the end.

"The Dissatisfied Spirit" is in fact a personal allegory reflecting the very inner process which was taking place in the innermost crucible of her being. For this reason this editor finds the story compelling, and with these notes, we include it for your own discernment.

What do you think? Does this allegory call for a stronger ending?

George Tooze
Indianapolis, Indiana
November, 2010

THE DISSATISFIED SPIRIT
An Allegory

God bowed the heavens and came down and breathed upon the earth, and a "living soul" was born. It was not an angel to watch over the destinies of man, and interpose its white wing between him and evil; but it was a thing as lovely; and so it looked about to find itself a fitting dwelling-place. While it paused in doubt there came fluttering by a gay beautiful creature, its bright wings woven in the loom from which the Iris sprung; all glittering in gold and crimson, now bathing in the dew, and now in the sunlight, brilliant, and blithesome, and light as the air on which it balanced. The spirit grew glad at the pretty sight; and as the tiny wonder again swept past, it thought within itself "What a delightful thing to be a butterfly!"

Instantly a pair of gorgeous wings sprouted from the thought; and the embodied spirit flew exultingly up and down the earth, careering in the light and glorying in its new-found beauties. Sometimes it paused to jump into the hearts of the young flowers, and sipped daintily the sweets which dwelt on their fresh lips, and fanned them when they drooped and bathed in their perfume; and at night it folded up its wing and made its couch where the moon-beam lay most lovingly. That was a breath from heaven stirring those gorgeous wings; the "living soul"

---

[124] See the letter of Emily Chubbuck to Adoniram Judson dated February 15, 1846.

within swelling and struggling, conscious that it was not performing its mission. There could not be a brighter nor gayer life, and surely the innocent little butterfly was not guilty of doing harm; but there was a chiding voice came up from within and the dissatisfied spirit could not sleep. Finally, it grew sorrowful even in the midst of its light companions, as they poised and reeled and strove to balance themselves in the sunlight, intoxicated with the mere bliss of living. And every day it grew more and more sorrowful and its wings heavier till at last it cried out in sharp anguish. Beautiful and innocent was the life of the gay insect, but the God-born spirit was not created to waste itself on a sunbeam or a flower; and those magnificent wings were leaden fetters to it. A bird was caroling on the tree above; and, as the saddened spirit looked up, it thought of the happy hearts the little song-ster made and how it praised God in its light joyousness, and then exclaimed pantingly, "What a sweet beautiful thing to be a bird!"

A little child found a dead butterfly at the foot of the red maple-tree that morning; and as she stooped to pick it up there came such a gush of melody from the green above that she started back in pleased astonishment; and then, clapping her soft hands together, she raised her infantile voice in clear ringing tones fraught with the music of a mirthful heart. On the instant there came a rustling sound from the heavy masses of foliage; a pair of beautiful wings broke thence and bal-anced for a moment above, then descended, hovering for a moment about the head of the child, as though bestowing some wordless blessing; and finally spread themselves for flight. The bird paused where the labourer [sic] rested at noontide, and the eye of the strong man brightened as he wiped the sweat away, and leaned against the rugged bark of the meadow-tree, yielding himself up to the delicious influence of its music. Then it flew to the casement of the invalid, and thence to the roof-tree of the colter [sic]; and thence it still pursued its way kindly and lov-ingly, pausing to warble a moment even by the iron-barred windows of the criminal. For many a day the bird-embodied spirit was happy and contented and believed itself sent upon the earth but for the purpose of winning men by such small sweet efforts from sorrow. But, as it nestled one night in the foliage of the forest-tree, there came a sad misgiving to trouble it. It had heard of a nobler mis-sion than it had yet dared to contemplate—it had looked into a path toilsome and difficult to walk in, strewn with thorns and beset with dangers; but yet glorious in that it had been trodden by a Holy One who had linked it to heaven. The timid spirit trembled as it thought, and folded its soft pinions over its breast, and strove to recollect all the good it had done that day: —how it had softened the nature of the sinful and dropped balm into the bosom of the sorrowing; but it could not shut down the high aspirations which were swelling within it. It knew well that the spirit of the little bird was not, like itself, an emanation from the Deity. When the song was hushed and the plumage drooped it would "go downward to the earth;" but the "living soul" born of the breath of the Almighty could not so perish. Should it fling aside its loftier gifts, and take upon itself the mission (sweet and beautiful though that mission might be) of the soulless bird? "Ah no!" thought the pretty warbler, while its wings seemed swelling to eagle's pinions, "the air is full of birds—the world is ringing with melody—it is delightful to swell the care-free chorus—but there is a higher nobler mission still." As its breast heaved with these new emotions, a soft sound, as of a lute stole up from a neighbouring (sic) grove and an exquisitely modulated voice, with deep earnestness clothed its secret thoughts in words.

> "I waste no more in idle dreams, my life, my soul away;
> I wake to know my better self —I wake to watch and pray.
> Tho't, feeling, time on idols vain, I've lavished all too long;
> Henceforth to holier purposes I pledge myself, my song!
> Oh, still within the inner veil, upon the Spirit shines,
> Still unprofaned by evil, burns the one pure spark divine,
> Which God has kindled in us all, and bid him to tend
> Henceforth with vestal tho't and care, the light that lamp may lead.
> I shut mine eyes in grief and shame upon the dreary past,
> My heart, my soul poured recklessly, on dreams that could not last;
> My bark has drifted down the stream, at will of wind or wave,
> An idle light and fragile thing, that few had cared to save.
> Henceforth the bitter truth shall hold, and [ ] as low science tells,
> And I will brave the storms of fate, tho' wild the ocean swells.
> I know my soul is strong and high if once I give it sway;
> I feel a glorious power within, tho' light it seems and gay.
> O laggard soul! unclose thine eyes. No more in luxury soft
> Of joy ideal waste thyself! awake and soar aloft!
> Unfurl this hour those falcon wings which thou dost fold too long;
> Raise to the skies thy lightening gaze, and sin the loftiest song."

The song ceased and the struggling, God-born spirit looked down on the cold earth; and, not forgetting toil, and suffering, and weariness—not forgetting the degradation of sin, and the constant wrestling of the higher with the baser nature, exclaimed, with deep enthusiasm, "What a sublime thing to be a man!"

A songster was missed from the woodland; and that same day a man knelt in prayer, and then, humble but strong and happier far than butterfly or bird, went cheerfully forth on man's great mission —**to do good**.

Adoniram Judson to Emily E. Chubbuck,[125] April 8, 1846

I have received three letters from Utica—thank you darling. The last contained this extract from the *N. Y. Express*. That surely does not trouble you. Another article in the *Recorder* is not bad, though clumsily got up. True, it is unpleasant to have one's private affair before the public. But after all, it is a small matter. Let us rest in one another's love, but chiefly in the love of Jesus, and in the consoling consciousness that we are endeavoring to serve him, and that he will forgive all our follies and sins—send forth judgment unto victory. I have been so cried down at different passages of my life, especially when I became a Baptist and lost all, all but Ann,[126] that I suppose I am a little hardened, but I feel for you, for it is your first field. Come to my arms, darling dear, whatever of strength or shield is mine as I can draw down from heaven, is yours. Thine with my whole heart A Judson

Source: Hanna family files; A. C. Kendrick, *The Life and Letters of Mrs. Emily C. Judson*, 177–78.

Emily E. Chubbuck to Adoniram Judson, April 8, 1846

Wednesday morning, 10 o'clock

"Zoe mon"—dearest, blessed one—best-beloved—There don't "take any pride at" that line. It is only because I can't sleep that I get up to nick-name you. I have been tossing and tumbling and groaning for about three hours (for you must know that I have been really ill today—or rather yesterday)—and can't get one wink of sleep.

Your sweet, sweet letter from Plymouth![127] It did the soul of me good, I can assure you. What makes you so kind and good to me, darling? How hard I shall have to try to be good so as to deserve it! Perhaps that is what you mean to do— *kiss away the bad*. Oh, I mean to put on bracelets and anklets[128] both when I see Mr. Peck![129] When I can ask him ever so innocently if he isn't fond of waltzing, how he liked the last Italian opera, and which he considers the best danseuse Ellsler or Faglioni! Would'nt [*sic*] it be charming?

[125] This letter is an addendum to Adoniram Judson's letter of April 7, 1846.

[126] Ann Hasseltine Judson, Adoniram Judson's first wife. The reference is to their sailing in 1812 under the auspices of the Congregational church and being convicted of baptism by immersion on their journey. With that decision, they lost all of their financial support, and Luther Rice, one of the other missionaries, returned to America to bring the Baptist churches together for the support of missions. This work in support of Adoniram and Ann Judson was the genesis of the Triennial Convention which first met in 1814, and the subsequent Baptist denominations which emerged from it. This would include The American Baptist Churches, USA, The Southern Convention, and the Cooperative Baptist Convention.

[127] Written over three days, these are the letters dated April 2, 3, and 4, 1846.

[128] Adoniram Judson wrote, "He did not know, not he, but that I had found a jewel but timidly inquired whether you would be arrayed in other jewels and finery and evidently fearing that you would come dancing through the country like other Fannies—the style laid down in Isaiah chapter iii."

[129] See vol. 1, "Cast of Characters," s.v. "Peck, The Reverend Doctor Solomon."

I do wish I could make one in your dear little circle at Plymouth[130]—very dear is it to me, my beloved. I am longing to see the children and shall regret not seeing them together. The little weazels! Did you pinch their cheeks for me? Well then, I shall be mighty savage when I see them if they laugh at my beautiful name.[131] I went to the bookstore before you left to get some of my books for Abby;[132] but they had none but "Allen Lucas"[133] and that in a very ugly binding. Please give the little boys your copy of "Charles Linn."[134] It is much better calculated to be useful to children than any of the S.S. books. I will enclose a little scrap which please hand to Abby with a kiss from me. You will see that there is not much poetry in it, and she may be less critical.

Anna Maria[135] is just waking and I shall get a lecture; so good-night—one more—now—now—sleep darling and dream of Nemmy.[136]

Wednesday morning 8 o'clock

I am feeling pretty badly this morning—nervous, and weak enough. The excitement has been killing me, but I am learning to bear it better now. I partly expected it, and yet not altogether so much—not quite so much indelicate mudding on the part of newspaper editors.

Mr. Beebee[137] called last night for the article you mentioned on Prayer.[138] I have no copy, but I happened to have the date down in a book and so I think he will find it. Do with that and the "Young Novel Reader" or anything else whatever you think proper. I gave "Clinging to Earth"[139] to Neal[140] for his paper a few days ago. I am sorry if you didn't like to have it come out alone. Maybe I will write a counterpart to it.[141]

---

[130] Staying with his sister, Abigail Brown Judson, Adoniram Judson was with his oldest three children by Sarah Hall Boardman Judson—Abby Ann Judson, Adoniram Judson, and Elnathan Judson.

[131] Adoniram Judson said, "The children are mightily amused at their papa's marrying Emily Chubbuck."

[132] See vol. 1, "Cast of Characters," s.v. "Judson, Abby Ann." Adoniram Judson said, "Abby Ann had found out from some of the neighbors, that it was Fanny Forester, but she is quite sure that Fanny Forester must be very good, since she wrote *Effie Maurice*, one of her favorite books."

[133] One of Emily's books, published just before Christmas in 1843.

[134] Another of Emily's books, published in 1842.

[135] See vol. 1, "Cast of Characters," s.v. "Anable, Miss Anna Maria."

[136] Emily Chubbuck. See vol. 1, "Cast of Characters," s.v. "Nemmy, Nem, or Nemmy Petty (Nemmie Pettie)."

[137] See vol. 1, "Cast of Characters," s.v. "Beebee, Alexander."

[138] See the letter of Adoniram Judson to Emily E. Chubbuck dated April 4, 1846. Judson asked her about the article on "Prayer."

[139] Regarding this continuing discussion on "Clinging to Earth" and "Aspiring to Heaven," see the footnotes to these two poems, both of which appear in this volume following the letter of Adoniram to Emily dated April 4, 1846.

[140] Joseph Neal was a prominent member of the literary establishment in Philadelphia and became a part of Emily Chubbuck's circle of friends when she was there. Neal was well known and respected as a writer and editor; one of his best known works was the *Charcoal Sketches*. In 1842, he founded the *Saturday Gazette*, a successful publication that contained a great deal of humorous satire. Anna Maria Anable frequently referred to Neal as a beau for Emily. Mr. Neal married Alice Bradley in 1846; he died in 1847.

[141] For the complete discussion on "Clinging to Earth" and "Aspiring to Heaven," see the footnotes to these two poems, both of which appear in this volume following the letter of Adoniram to Emily dated April 4, 1846.

I intend to make an assault on Mrs. Allen's[142] heart the next thing I do. I have been drumming up a couple of contributors for her—two girls for whom I feel a great deal of solicitude—pupils of mine, over whom I have unbounded influence, without knowing just how to exert it. One of them will I am confident become a popular writer yet; and I have been for six months past trembling for her. If the religious part of the world will not appreciate and pay for talent, how can they expect it to stay with them. People of genius are never rich enough in this world's goods to afford to work for nothing; and even if they were what right has any body [sic] to expect them to do it? My brain is as much my own as my hands; God has a right to the labour [sic] of both—one as much as the other; but I am no more bound to write without receiving a liberal remuneration than I am to teach or sew gratis for the good of community. I believe when I get time I will write Mrs. Allen an article on the subject for her journal, hoping it may go the rounds. I went into the lighter magazines deliberately—with my eyes open—understanding my ground so well that it was less likely to do me harm; but in the case of a young girl, I do not know what to do.[143]

It is time for the mail to go out and I must close. I will send in the envelope Lydia's[144] application and Miss Kelly's[145] recommendation.

Love to the darlings; I think of them always.

All thine own

Emily

Source: Hanna family files.

Emily E. Chubbuck to Adoniram Judson, April 9, 1846—Utica NY

Well, deary, who think you has been here today? who?—who?—Why old Father Peck[146] sure—he of wife whipping memory. Now you suppose I went snickering down to see him, and when he asked me to "relate my exercises" played up

---

[142] Mrs. Eliza Allen was the editor of the *Mother's Journal* and included material by Emily as early as 1843. Their correspondence went through spring 1846. In December 1848, Emily received a letter from Mrs. Allen's husband, the Reverend Ira Allen, describing in some detail the death of Eliza Allen. The *Mother's Journal* continued, and in an 1849 letter Anna Maria Anable informs Emily that a piece that she had written had appeared in the publication. In a letter to Emily during their courtship, Adoniram mentioned that he had met Mrs. Allen and went on to say that the *Mothers' Journal* was considered to be a prestigious publication for the church. On May 27, 1846, after a meeting with her, Judson wrote: "I am afraid I shall get to dislike her. She is a woman that I could make some use of. She has a sharp, strong intellect—is a good critic in the rough, but not in the nice. No heart—no amiability—very severe and what is worse, glaringly envious."

[143] Emily had an ongoing discussion with Eliza Allen of the *Mother's Journal* on remuneration for writers. Emily had demanded and received the highest level of compensation from the magazine publishers. Mrs. Allen advocated that religious writers must sacrifice financially for the betterment of the church, and the necessity for the gospel to be proclaimed.

[144] See vol. 1, "Cast of Characters," s.v. "Lillybridge, Lydia." See also the timeline on Lydia Lillybridge.

[145] See vol. 1, "Cast of Characters," s.v. "Kelly, Miss Jane."

[146] See vol. 1, "Cast of Characters," s.v. "Peck, The Reverend Doctor Solomon."

Kitty Coleman[147] like a little sarpens [*sic*]. Just so much you know—I did no such thing. I did you credit sir—credit; and the old gentleman thinks I am a remarkably sensible young woman, I have no doubt. Even Aunt C.[148] with whom I usually stand quite well (considering) was all taken aback by seeing me behave so beautifully. What did I do? Why, I said "yes sir," and "no sir" and "of course you are right sir," and insinuated a little bit of flattery about the kind friends that I should make through you (of course he considered himself one of them) and then watched the charm work—the eyes brighten, the muscles of the mouth relax—oh, it was grand! What a pity that he has a wife because if you should at last find the "sacrifice" too great I might take him.

I have just rec'd a letter from Mr. Gillette.[149] He is terribly disappointed, indeed almost heart-broken about the marriage affair.[150] My letter, in which I alluded to it incidentally, was the first intimation he had ever rec'd of the state of affairs. I understood by you that it would be inconvenient for him to come but—I will enclose the letter.

What do you think, darling, I have been about today? There is in the city a Mr. Edson, a famous teacher of sacred music, and I have been seeing him today about giving me singing lessons. He is coming tomorrow to give me a trial and then will decide whether I can learn or not. If there is a bare possibility in the case I will do my best. It is the only way in which I think you will be able to turn "the unuseful" to account.

Poor W.![151] he is in a terrible scrape, but he behaved beautifully. Sometimes I cry for him and sometimes I laugh at his simplicity. He is actually the most simple-minded man that I ever knew.[152] I would give my two ears (notwithstanding they are yours) to help him in some way. He will return all my letters.[153]

[147] "Kitty Coleman" was the title of and character in one of Emily's stories. It was also published in vol. 1 of *Alderbrook*. In his April 3, 1846 letter, Adoniram had written, characterizing Emily as having "such a Protean face." Then, he added as commentary, "there is Kitty Coleman's mischievous face, full of fun and frolic."

[148] See vol. 1, "Cast of Characters," s.v. "Sheldon, Miss Cynthia."

[149] See vol. 1, "Cast of Characters," s.v. "Gillette, The Reverend Abram Dunn."

[150] The Reverend Mr. Gillette had hoped to be asked to officiate at the marriage of Adoniram and Emily. At some point Adoniram said something about it being "inconvenient" for Mr. Gillette, and Emily wrote him with that assumption, only later to realize that they seemed to have misread the situation. Emily's first choice of officiant was Dr. Eliphalet Nott, the president of Union College in Schenectady, New York, and the husband of Urania Sheldon Nott; then, when they decided to move the ceremony to her home in Hamilton, they turned to Dr. Nathanial Kendrick, a pastor from Emily's childhood with whom she had discussed as a young lady the possibility of her becoming a missionary.

[151] See vol. 1, "Cast of Characters," s.v. "Willis, Nathaniel Parker."

[152] See the two letters from N. P. Willis dated April 2 and 6, 1846.

[153] While there are fifty-one letters in the Correspondence from N. P. Willis to Emily E. Chubbuck, there are no letters written by Emily to Mr. Willis. When Emily made the commitment to marry Adoniram Judson and go with him to Burmah, she asked N. P. Willis to return all of her letters, believing that some of what she had written to him over two years might not reflect well on the wife of the great Dr. Judson and the missionary cause or might be misinterpreted by her Fanny Forester readers and by the church that Adoniram and Emily now served together in Burmah. At first, Mr. Willis refused, but later, on April 9, 1846, Emily told Adoniram that Mr. Willis had a change of heart, (see his letter of April 6, 1846) and there was a simple line, "He will return all my letters." In *The Life and Letters of Mrs. Emily C. Judson*, Dr. Kendrick says that he had written to Mr. Willis to ask if he

I wish I could know just where you are and what you are doing tonight. I am disappointed at not receiving a reply to some of my letters. You must have been in Boston long enough to answer. Tomorrow you leave for—where? Bradford?[154] Or Maine?[155] I mean to be mesmerized and to know what you are about. Do you know I think it schockingly hard-hearted in you, to get me into this scrape, set the whole world to talking about me, and then go and leave me to bear it all alone? Oh, by the way, Anna Maria[156] says if she isn't an actress she is a dancer; but if you don't think that bad enough why she can do something worse. She will try to be bad enough to suit you, for she rather prefers you on the whole to Mr. Weed.[157] I think myself you and A. M. particularly suited to each other; and there are plenty of more fellows who would take me. I don't much fancy *the cloth*.[158]

How long will it be, dearest, before you will be here again? It seemed an age since we parted. I am longing to hear your kind voice once more. What would you say to me tonight? Sweet words? Would you "call me pet names?" People say you never will appreciate me, and then others again say that I cannot appreciate you— how little they know about appreciation! As though there were nothing about us but a little piece of intellect—nothing deep down in the heart which we can see and they cannot. If our hearts grow together that is appreciation, and I am sure they will. Have you been annoyed by anything in the papers? I got so worried about that and some other things that I was quite ill, but I don't care so much now what is said. The report that you had sanctioned some of the fault-finding was the worst;[159] but I know that was false.

I do not know when my letter will reach you for you will leave Boston tomorrow and return I don't know when. I hope there is no doubt of Lydia's[160] appointment, for she considers herself "as good as gone." She will need the appropriation for outfit.[161] I think her going is just the nicest thing! People say she is "missionary to the back-bone." She and I stand, side by side, in beautiful contrast.

might use letters he had received from Miss Chubbuck; Mr. Willis said that he would look for them, but later reported that only one or two could be found, and those would shed no light for the purpose of the biography (109–10).

[154] Abby Ann Judson had recently been settled into Bradford Academy at Bradford, Massachusetts.

[155] Adoniram Judson was to travel to Maine to meet with the extended family of George Dana Boardman, in the hope that he could encourage them to cover the costs of Boardman's education at Providence College (later Brown University).

[156] See vol. 1, "Cast of Characters," s.v. "Anable, Miss Anna Maria."

[157] On April 4, 1846, Adoniram Judson wrote that he was trying to decide whether he would marry Emily or Anna Maria, both of them acting "just as bad as you dare, without being actually read out of church." Then, he ponders, "Well, let me see, which it shall be? Emily—I think, for she is the worse off, having almost worked herself into an actress. And if I take her, it may lay a streak of whitewash on the other and I may venture to recommend her to my noble-minded friend Mr. Weed."

[158] In a letter to Emily written April 4, 1846, Adoniram playfully spoke of the possibility that he would reject both Emily and Anna Maria as a suitable wife for him. To this he added: "And then what serious godly young candidate for the ministry (and I hope you are not so far lost as to think of anything [sic] below the cloth) will ever look at you the second time."

[159] In her March 31, 1846, letter, Emily recounted a rumor that Adoniram said something to the Reverend Mr. Corey that encouraged his negative observations on the marriage of Emily and Adoniram. Adoniram responded in his letter of April 7, 1846, unequivocally denying having intimated anything negative at all to Mr. Corey.

[160] See vol. 1, "Cast of Characters," s.v. "Lillybridge, Miss Lydia." See also the timeline on "Lydia Lillybridge Simons."

I do not think a better one could have been found in the whole country. Lydia has never done a naughty thing in her whole life. I have no heart to write any more [sic] for it seems as though my letter would never reach you. A long, long kiss and good-night.—Emily

Source: Hanna family files.

Emily E. Chubbuck to Adoniram Judson,[162] April 10, 1846—Utica NY

Thanks, darling, for your beautiful letter;[163] you do take all the trouble away so sweetly! I don't know why you should be so good and kind to me when I get out of patience **so much**. Yes, I do know that you will never repent the step you have taken; though the entire world sh'd disapprove of it; and with full faith in that, I will not be disturbed by trifles. I know these are all trifles—things that I shall laugh at when I get away from them, but sometimes they seem terrible now. They shall not any more though; I will rest in thy love, dearest; and in a holier....

Source: Hanna family files; A. C. Kendrick, *The Life and Letters of Mrs. Emily C. Judson*, 180–81.

Adoniram Judson to Emily E. Chubbuck,[164] April 10, 1846—Boston

I seize a little time, early this morning, for I am so driven with business and company through the day and evening that I have scarcely time to write, though I do now and then think of you. "Does the wish ever creep into your mind" that you could get rid of me?[165] Suppose it did. Doesn't Mr. Cutting[166] say that "now the name of the one is seldom separated from that of the other." Why, we are as good as married. I don't see how I can help myself now, whatever my wishes may be. I could not discard you without incurring universal execration; and that would be

---

[161] On April 1, writing to ask Emily for Lydia's application for missionary service and other supporting documents to be presented to the Board of the American Baptist Mission Union, Judson had said that the board would give her $150 or $200 for her to be outfitted for the mission field.

[162] This letter has an addendum dated April 11, 1846. This letter appears in *The Life and Letters of Mrs. Emily C. Judson*; the two words in bold are the only omissions made from the original.

[163] The reference is to Adoniram Judson's letter of April 7, 1846.

[164] For an understanding of the comparison on an original letter with the letter actually printed by Dr. A. C. Kendrick in *The Life and Letters of Mrs. Emily C. Judson*, see the first footnote for the letter of Adoniram to Emily dated April 2, 1846.

[165] This is a question that was asked in Emily's letter of April 5, 1846.

[166] Dr. Sewell Cutting was educated at Waterville College in Maine; ill health prevented him from going on for a theological education. He assumed the pastorate of a small church in West Boylston, Massachusetts and later followed the missionary Dr. Binney in Southbridge. In 1845, he went to New York to edit the *Baptist Advocate*, which name he changed to the *New York Recorder*. He immediately sold the magazine to Lewis Colby from New York who had published several of Emily Judson's books. For several years, he was the corresponding secretary of the American and Foreign Bible Society and "took a prominent part in the discussions between the two societies." (*The Baptist Encyclopedia*, ed. William Cathcart. Philadelphia: Louis H. Everts, 1881).

worse than the other alternative even. But there is one way—you can discard me, and I can tell you how to do it, so as rather to rise than fall in public estimation. But I won't, though—and what is more, I am sure you don't want to know. No **darling, dear Cutting** says that our *names* are *seldom* separated; our *hearts* are *never*; and may the time soon come when our *persons* shall be never separated. But that wish is linked to another thought, that a separation, a dread separation, must finally come. And that will be the more bitter, the longer we live together and the more we love. Nothing can temper that bitterness, but the assurance of an eternal reunion. Let us so live, that we shall have this full assurance. I must confess that, with you, I am disgusted with much I see in the religious world, and am sometimes pleased, too much pleased, with what I see in the irreligious.[167] But this I ascribe to my lowness in religion; for we ought to love the Saviour so entirely as to be unable to find pleasure in any thing [sic] which does not accord with his mind. But I have not the most distant desire of "turning to the world," nor ever have had since I first entertained a hope in Christ. Nor do I understand you to say that you have, though you feel exposed to danger. I know no other way than to make up one's own mind in regard to the right course, and then to pursue it steadily, always pressing to the right side and keeping as far as possible from the wrong, whatever our own secret inclinations; and thus, with the divine blessing, habits of virtue will be formed, and our inclination may be, at first wavering, will become co-incident with the Saviour. We shall love what he loves, and hate what he hates. Do not the late circumstances of your life, ordered of God, unsought by you, call on you, as with a voice from heaven, to become a devoted, holy missionary!—to love not the world, nor the things of the world?—to set your affections on things above? Pray turn away your ear from the censure and the commendation you may hear. Remember that the eye of Christ is especially observing you, and that your whole future life will take its coloring from the manner in which you now consecrate yourself to God.

I received your letter yesterday, inclosing [sic] Miss Sheldon's[168] note to Mr. Peck.[169] I hope that Lydia's[170] letter will come to-day—I shall leave this afternoon for Maine,[171] and be absent a week or more. The probability is, that we must be ready to embark by the middle of June. "Do not forget me,"[172] you say. "Forget thee!

---

[167] See the letter of Emily E. Chubbuck to Adoniram Judson dated April 3, 1846.

[168] See vol. 1, "Cast of Characters," s.v. "Sheldon, Miss Cynthia."

[169] See vol. 1, "Cast of Characters," s.v. "Peck, The Reverend Doctor Solomon."

[170] See vol. 1, "Cast of Characters," s.v. "Lillybridge, Miss Lydia." Also the timeline on "Lydia Lillybridge Simons."

[171] Adoniram Judson was planning to meet the extended family of George Dana Boardman, in the hope that they would be responsive to helping meet the costs of his education at Providence College (later Brown University).

[172] This was Emily's concluding request to Adoniram in a letter dated April 6, 1846.

If to dream by night and muse on thee by day;
If all the homage pure and deep a lover's heart can pay;
If prayers in absence breathed for thee to heaven's propitious power.
If winged thoughts that flit to thee, a thousand in an hour,
If busy fancy, blending thee with all my future lot—
If this thou call'st forgetting, then indeed thou art forgot."[173]

Though I am not the author of these beautiful lines, they express my very thoughts and feelings toward you, dearest.

Since writing the above, I have received yours of Wed. morn[174]—and given the papers you inclosed [sic] to Mr. Peck. I am dismayed at your sending "Clinging to Earth," to Mr. Neal[175] "a few days ago." I know not with what face I can put the other pieces in the Boston papers, if that appears in a Phila. paper, *at such a late date*. That piece, though beautiful poetry, is so much at variance with your present views and prospects and our fondest hopes![176]

Darling dear, what shall I say? Let us love one another entirely and with ever growing affection, but let us love the Saviour more, and let us cling to Him and to Paradise, not to Earth.

I am just going to Maine—shall take a steam-boat to Hallowell or Augusta and visit a very few places where Boardman relatives reside. Shall probably be here again by the 15th or 16th so please, dear, write me a letter which shall reach by that time, for I shall go straight to the Mission Rooms on first arriving in search of it. But don't be angry with me if I do not write you very often, for sometimes I do not get an hour to myself all day. Dearest love, the thought of going further from you, makes me turn to you with desperate longing. "My spirit clings to thine, love." Please look a little into Catherine Adorner or Kempis' Imitation of Christ—Live near the throne of grace, and pray for me that I may be more deserving of your precious love.

Entirely and forever thine,

A Judson

Source: A. C. Kendrick, *The Life and Letters of Mrs. Emily C. Judson*. 181–83; Hanna family files.

---

[173] This is the first of three stanzas of the poem "Forget Thee" by John Moultrie, though Judson does not quote it exactly.

[174] See the letter of Emily E. Chubbuck to Adoniram Judson dated April 8, 1846.

[175] See vol. 1, "Cast of Characters," s.v. "Neal, Joseph."

[176] For a complete discussion on "Clinging to Earth" and "Aspiring to Heaven," see the footnotes to these two poems, both of which appear in this volume following the letter of Adoniram to Emily dated April 4, 1846.

Nathaniel Parker Willis to Emily C. Chubbuck,[177] April 10, 1846

Dearest Emily

It was the farthest thing possible from my thoughts, to give you the least pain by what I sent you marked.[178] I merely wished to show you that I had *some* ground to build a hope upon, and I had the farther wish of proving to you how responsive I was to every call you made on me, from the first letter you ever wrote, to the last. I balanced your natural regret at leading me into an error, against the pleasure you will feel hereafter when you remember the complete enthralment of my nature by your own—a memory that need not be qualified, I assure you, by any suspicion that it was a "poetical fancy" on my part. That you are to be married to another man is no trifling pang to me, but it is no diminution of my instinctive conviction of your worth, and I may venture, without indelicacy, to still assure you that you have a personal quality as well as a mind, of rare richness and loveableness, and that my love for you was confirmed by my actual knowledge of the world and comparison of you with others.

You are going as far off as Death would take you, but you will still have hours of memory and I wish to tell you *all*,—that I may live, at least, second in your remembrance. And—do not give yourself troubled thoughts about me. I am reconciled, now, to your loving another better than me. I hear he is worthy of it—worthier of you than I could be—and I have mentally resigned you, with a blessing on your future love for another. I will come to you during next week, and we will have at least one hour's concourse before we are separated forever. I will write you the day before.

God bless you, my incomparably sweet and gifted Emily.

Ever yours affectionately

N. P. W.

Write to me Your letters are a great [Note: Material is missing.] between *us*" [Note: The rest of the letter has been torn away.]

Source: Hanna family files.

There was a similar discussion between Emily and Adoniram about a piece, "Dissatisfied Spirit," to be printed in the *Baptist Register*. On April 7, Adoniram asked her to change the ending; on April 11, she said that she did not make the change as "it does not read quite as smoothly." We have a good reflection of Adoniram wanting to monitor and perhaps control how the public perceived Emily.

[177] The last portion of this letter is torn away. Someone has made the notation on the letter: "The rest of this page is torn away and lost forever!! I would surmise that NPW had some very tender and caring words for EC that she didn't want to share with posterity!"

[178] In his letter of April 6, 1846, N. P. Willis enclosed some letters he had received from Emily, marking them to show her why he felt he had every right to believe that they would be married upon his return to the United States.

Emily E. Chubbuck to Adoniram Judson,[179] April 11, 1846[180]

I have just been in another pet, deary—just a little bit of a one. I wrote a little note to Mr. Hawley[181] a few days ago enclosing the paper you left with me, and have just rec'd the answer. I will enclose it. Please find out if you can who really owns the copyright, and if it is convenient—make inquiries about publishers.[182] I have dispatched a note telling Mr. H. how I understand the copyright matter; and intimating that I don't see the propriety of talking about "equity" after his letting the books be out of print so long. The more I think of it the more I think the copyright my own; for it is placing an author too much at the mercy of the published to have it otherwise. Mr. Gillespie[183] too told me that the agreement amounted to nothing more than permission from an author to publisher while the author may think proper for a stipulated consideration—10 or 12 1/2 per cent, as the matter may be.

I wish I could have kissed off your tears when you were crying for the (Would that I could have charmed away the tears for your) children[184]—poor **little** things! **If we could only take them back with us! I cannot do any thing [*sic*] for them though I love them already without seeing them; but won't I play mama to the others at a great rate? Can't you imagine how dignified I will be?** I am

---

[179] For an understanding of the comparison on an original letter with the letter actually printed by Dr. A. C. Kendrick in *The Life and Letters of Mrs. Emily C. Judson*, see the first footnote for the letter of Adoniram to Emily dated April 2, 1846.

[180] This letter is an addendum to Emily's letter of April 10, 1846.

[181] Mr. Horace H. Hawley enjoyed a family relationship with the Sheldon family. Emily's letter on May 7, 1841, indicates that he was to marry a niece of Misses Cynthia and Urania Sheldon and Mrs. Alma Sheldon Anable, the daughter of their brother John Sheldon. Through the help of Miss Cynthia Sheldon, he was introduced into the life of Emily Chubbuck. A member of a publishing firm, he also worked with Alexander Beebee in publishing the *Baptist Register*. Beginning in 1841 with the publication of *Charles Linn*, Mr. Hawley was enormously helpful to Emily Chubbuck as she published her early stories and books. There are numerous references to his help and his generosity. With Cynthia Sheldon, her parents and her sister Alma Anable, Mr. Hawley had been a charter member of the Bleecker Street Baptist Church in Utica in 1838.

[182] Emily was looking for a publisher for what eventually would be released as *Alderbrook*. She was also making sure about the copyrights of previously published material, for much of the material in *Alderbrook* came from what she had written for the popular literary magazines.

[183] William Gillespie was a professor of civil engineering at Union College in Schenectady, New York. He wrote two long letters to Emily, dated August 15 and September 11, 1845. His second letter originated from Union College where Dr. Nott (husband of Urania Sheldon Nott) was the president, and he noted that Mrs. Urania Sheldon Nott was "his special friend." In his first letter, he asked Emily if a certain poem had appeared in the New York *Mirror*, and if it had, he had identified the writer (if it was Emily) early on as one of great promise. In a time when Emily was considering a trip to the continent, he spoke to her of weather conditions in certain of the European countries. His second letter was filled with literary allusions, a long story to prove the point that "widows are dangerous," and a reflection on some of her writings. Mr. Gillespie was mentioned in Urania Sheldon Nott's June 11, 1845 letter to Emily; he had given Mrs. Nott the latest issue of the *Columbian Magazine*, which contained the first installment of Emily's story "Grace Linden." Then, on July 9, 1845, Emily mentioned Mr. Gillespie in a letter to her sister Catharine. Emily was speaking of going to Schenectady for the commencement of Union College, and she says, "A man there has fallen love with me—Mr. Gillespie, author of 'Rome as seen by a New Yorker.'"

[184] See the letter of Adoniram Judson to Emily E. Chubbuck dated April 7, 1846, which begins, "I have just been having a good cry, here alone in Mr. Colby's chamber, about my poor dear children. I left the two boys yesterday, crying, as they set off in the cars for Worcester. Abby Ann I took on to Bradford; and this morning I left her crying at the Hasseltine's. And thoughts of the children lead my mind to their departed mother, and I review the scenes on board the Sophie Walker and at St. Helena. And then I stretch away to my two little forsaken orphans in Burmah."

longing to see the little darlings; and dearest, my own dearest best friend, God helping me they shall never feel the loss of the sainted one.[185] Do not call them "orphans" <u>any more</u> [*sic*]; I will love them and watch over them,[186] and when I fail in anything you will point out the fault and teach me better. Won't you dearest? Oh, we will have a happy little home[187]—thankful that God allows us to care for some of the beloved ones, and leaving the others to him, who can do it much better than we can.

I hope I have not troubled you by anything that I have written you about the strict rules of the Board.[188] I don't like to be a burden to you who have already too much on your hands; and then I suppose that I have a little woman's pride in the matter. It is quite enough for you to have the care of *me*. But I know that you will do the best for me that you can, and whatever you do will be right. If they cannot vary the rule in our favour, why we must trust more to God and less to ourselves. If we give ourselves *all* to Him, he will care for us and those whom we love.

Do whatever you please with the "Dissatisfied Spirit."[189] Mr. Beebee[190] has my copy. He is to publish it in the *Register*[191] next week. He has found the article entitled "Prayer" and is to publish that also.[192] I did not make the alteration at the end

[185] The death of Sarah Hall Boardman Judson in September 1, 1845, at the Isle of St. Helena, as the Judson family returned from Burmah to the United States. Sarah was the mother of Abby Ann, Adoniram, Elnathan, Henry, and Edward.

[186] Abby Ann, Adoniram and Elnathan were the older Judson children; Henry and Edward were the youngest surviving sons of Adoniram and Sarah Boardman Judson. Later correspondence has all of the children fondly addressing Emily as "Mother" or "Mamma." Emily did shower love and care upon the children; she was never able, however, to give them a stable home where they could all be together. Her work on the Judson memoir and her increasingly frail health did not allow that to happen. In 1849, Emily wrote "The Two Mammas," a poem in which she spoke of the death of Sarah Hall Boardman Judson and of Emily becoming their "new mamma."

[187] In a letter written to Dr. Solomon Peck on September 22, 1850, Emily said that it was Adoniram Judson's wish that, if he were to die, she would return to the United States, "collect his scattered family, and assume the guardianship of his children." As early as February 1851, as she began her trip to the United States, Emily Judson spoke of a time and a place when all of the Judson children could be together. Indeed, she purchased a home in Hamilton, New York, where her parents, her sister Kate, and the six children could live as one family.

This was something for which each of the children hoped, and there are a number of references and pleadings in their correspondence to indicate this as their heartfelt desire. Nowhere was this expressed more eloquently than in Abby Ann Judson's letter to Emily dated April 24, 1851. This letter was both beautifully expressed and poignantly painful.

This dream never came to fruition. Upon Emily's return to the United States, she was physically unable to care for the Judson children. Then, she began work on the memoir of Dr. Judson. She lived in Providence for most of six months, and this delayed the possibility. Later, Emily's chronic ill health forced her to the realization that she had neither the strength nor the energy for such an arrangement. The six-week period in summer 1852 and 1853 were the only times the family came together.

[188] In a March 30, 1846 letter, Adoniram wrote to Emily that some "wonderful difficulties" had presented themselves. Emily responded on April 1 and again on April 3 that she would support herself with her writing. On April 7, 1846, Adoniram Judson wrote to close that door.

[189] On April 7, 1846, Adoniram Judson wrote, "Will you alter the last sentence, or let it remain as it is?" Once again, he was trying to create a public image that was favorable, and he strongly felt that the ending Emily had created would lead to readers capturing a wrong idea about her life and thoughts.

[190] See vol. 1, "Cast of Characters," s.v. "Beebee, Alexander."

[191] See vol. 1, "Places, Events, Organizations, and Magazines," s.v. "*Baptist Register*."

[192] On April 4, Judson had written, "Mr. Beebee mentioned in terms of high commendation, a piece which you wrote on Prayer published in the *Register*—Could you promise to send me a copy? And suppose I should republish it in the Watchman or Reflector, 'By the author of Effie Maurice'"

of the "Dis. Spirit" for it does not read quite as smoothly, and I do not care to help people in making a personal application.

I must stop without filling my sheet or doing justice to my heart. **It is brimming over for you, dearest. I spring into your arms and—your bosom is such a blessed pillow—and your lips—mine grow together. No, I will not say goodnight—here stay I and you cannot shake off**

Your loving
Nemmy[193]

Source: Hanna family files; A. C. Kendrick, *The Life and Letters of Mrs. Emily C. Judson*, 180–81.

Adoniram Judson to Emily E. Chubbuck[194] April 11, 1846— Augusta, Maine

I seize a moment to write you, while waiting for the stage-coach to take me to Waterville, where I shall spend the Sabbath. I thought of you all the way in the steam-boat from Boston, but could not write, because my writing case was stowed away. I am so miserable ever since I sent off my last, fearing that my expressions were too strong and would make you feel sad. I wrote in a hurry, just at the moment I read your word about sending off a certain piece to Neal's *Gazette*, and think I expressed myself much stronger than the occasion required.[195]

Waterville—April 11th—Late in the evening. The driver called me away as I wrote the last sentence, and from 12 till 7 o'clock I was in the coach, coming 20 miles, the roads being even worse than we found between Hamilton and Utica, so that I am dreadfully fatigued and almost sick. But I cannot go to bed without writing you a little, though I have ascertained that no mail will leave this place till Monday morning. I did hope and intend, that not more than one day should pass between your receiving my last and this. Your last left you ill, and you have trouble enough on my account, without having it aggravated by my inconsiderate fault-finding remarks. Do, darling dear, bear with me a little. You know how much I love you, and when I was devising ways and means to present you before the christian [*sic*] public in these parts, in your real character, your mention of what you had done in another direction, seemed to come so directly across my path, that, at the moment, I thought more of it than I should. I presume that you have done right and that it is all right. Think kindly of me, dearest. Don't think of me as unkind

---

[193] Emily Chubbuck. See vol. 1, "Cast of Characters," s.v. "Nemmy, Nem, or Nemmy Petty (Nemmie Pettie)." Also the chapter "Names of Endearment."

[194] There is an addendum to this letter dated April 11, 1846.

[195] For the complete discussion on "Clinging to Earth" and "Aspiring to Heaven," see the footnotes to these two poems, both of which appear in this volume following the letter of Adoniram to Emily dated April 4, 1846.

and severe. You know that things sometimes appear different in a hasty letter for want of additional explanation—but we once agreed that no difficulty should ever be allowed to spring out of letter writing. Let every apparent difficulty be referred to a personal meeting, when the lips, in more than one way, can dispatch it expeditiously to the heaven of the Boodhists. So let me kiss you good night, darling of my soul, and I will fold you in my arms and go to sleep happy.

Source: Hanna family files.

Adoniram Judson to Emily E. Chubbuck,[196] April 12, 1846

I am living at President Sheldon's. Have got through with another Sabbath, without much trouble, except having to address the assembled faculty and students of the Waterville College. This is the place where Boardman[197] was educated. Tomorrow I am going into the interior to visit his mother and near relatives. Then wheel about to Augusta—thence to Portland—thence to Bradford—and spend the next Sabbath there with my daughter—thence to Boston—get things ready for sailing—touch at Worcester one night—on to Albany for the next Sabbath, the 26th (don't mention this) and on the next Monday to visit my old flame Miss Peakedchin[198]—give my best love to her, and tell her, that as you are going to cut me adrift, I shall have to fall back upon her, for I must say I love her more than any body [*sic*] else about.

But, darling dear, you will love me still, and when I get to Utica, you will let me take you in my arms and try to get some amends for this long absence. But when I feel about for your lips, take care I don't bite you. I am so hungry. No kissing in these cold regions, nor any lady to kiss.

Please to tell Miss Sheldon[199] and Lydia,[200] that we must be ready to embark by the middle of June—For we know not what day a favorable opportunity may occur, which it would be a pity to lose, by not being ready. I shall write Mr. Peck[201] to let Lydia know at once of her appointment, if it be made tomorrow and not wait for me to reach Boston, so that she may lose no time in getting ready—

It is so late and so cold in this chamber without a fire, that I must leave some blank paper and cover myself up in the bedclothes. I hope your illness did not con-

---

[196] This is an addendum to a letter started April 11, 1846.

[197] George Dana Boardman, the first husband of Sarah Hall Boardman Judson; Boardman died in Burmah of tuberculosis on a jungle trip to witness the baptism of some of his beloved Karens. He was the father of George Dana Boardman, who was known as "the younger."

[198] Emily E. Chubbuck names. See vol. 1, the chapter on "Names of Endearment."

[199] See vol. 1, "Cast of Characters," s.v. "Sheldon, Miss Cynthia."

[200] See vol. 1, "Cast of Characters," s.v. "Lillybridge, Miss Lydia." Also the timeline on "Lydia Lillybridge Simons."

[201] See vol. 1, "Cast of Characters," s.v. "Peck, The Reverend Doctor Solomon."

tinue but I cannot hear, till I get to Boston. Perhaps I shall get there earlier than mentioned above,—and in that case earlier to Utica, but I fear not. I shall have dreadful travelling [*sic*] for three days, and make slow progress.

There is no use in wishing you were here or bewailing the great distance between us, which tomorrow I must make greater, and "drag at each remove a lengthening chain." May God preserve you, darling dear, from sickness and death. May he bring us together "in love and happiness" is my most ardent prayer. Give my love to Anna Maria,[202] Miss Sheldon, Miss Kelly[203] and all the rest and take for your own share, if you will, the whole heart of your devoted—

A Judson

Source: Hanna family files.

Emily E. Chubbuck to Adoniram Judson,[204] April 13, 1846—Utica NY

My blessed one! God make me grateful to him for sending you to love me, to teach and guide me, **(as well as to you)**—make me more and more grateful; for I am very much so now. Your letter rec'd last evening shows that I have worried you by my murmurings. Forgive me, **darling, and** I will try not to give way to such feelings again. I know it is wrong—I know it is the very height of ingratitude; for I am really happier in your love and in the consciousness of doing right, than when my praises were sounded from one end of the country to the other. Yet sometimes this does seem a severe ordeal. My health has not been quite as good and loss of sleep and appetite together may have made me a little more excitable. Pray for me, dearest, God help me and I will try to consecrate myself to him entirely. I do love his cause more than anything else; and I am happy in the thought of being permitted to do some good; but I need your constant unremitting prayers. I do not know how far I am influenced in this important step by love to you, nor how far by love to God; the two seem pointing so precisely the same way, and he has made it so sweet to do right. Of one thing I am sure, I cannot love you too much: pray, darling, for me, that I may love the blessed Saviour more.

I have already sent two letters to Boston which you will not receive till your return;[205] but I cannot forbear writing this. When will you be back to

[202] See vol. 1, "Cast of Characters," s.v. "Anable, Miss Anna Maria."

[203] See vol. 1, "Cast of Characters," s.v. "Kelly, Miss Jane."

[204] For an understanding of the comparison on an original letter with the letter actually printed by Dr. A. C. Kendrick in *The Life and Letters of Mrs. Emily C. Judson*, see the first footnote for the letter of Adoniram to Emily dated April 2, 1846.

[205] Adoniram Judson was in Maine visiting the relatives of George Dana Boardman; he hoped that they would give financial support to Boardman's education at Providence College (Later Brown University). His mail was being held in Boston at the Mission Offices until his return.

Boston? In one place you say in "a week or more," in another you say on the 15 or 16, which would be less than a week.

I do have the queerest things to go though. Since writing the other page Mr. Corey[206] has been here to have a private conversation with me. If we hadn't chanced to be pretty amiable people we sh'd have quarreled, for neither of us made any concessions. Please, darling, when you come here don't mention my name to Mr. Corey, or allow him to say anything to you about me. He is surely a gossip and (from a kind of pre-conceived notion which acts as a mental lens rather than from want of understanding) a great blunderer. You cannot talk with him without his telling it; and whatever you say he will misconstrue.[207] He told me his feelings were very much injured by hearing that some person from out of town was coming to marry us, and mentioned Mr. Gillette.[208] How he heard anything about it I can't imagine. I told him that he might be perfectly easy on that score, for I should not be married in Utica. Then in talking of the step I was taking, he said he had not disapproved of it on account of any personal feeling (he was perfectly satisfied) but because he knew the religious public would disapprove;[209] which gave me an opportunity to ask him which he preferred having me consult, my own sense of right, my conscience, and my God, or public opinion. Darling, how can I help paying too much regard to the opinions so freely expressed when I have them constantly thrust in my face. Good people even would convince me that the opinion of the world (they say "religious community,"—but they fear their Judge Bacons[210] more) was paramount to religious obligation. Pardon me for troubling you with this again. I intended to keep clear of it in this letter.

---

[206] See vol. 1, "Cast of Characters," s.v. "Corey, the Reverend D. G."

[207] On March 31, 1846, Emily wrote to Adoniram, "Mr. Corey has been distorting the conversation that you had with him once in the library and says that you disapprove of my course; but people are liable to err and if they repent etc. Did you make the remark or did Mr. Corey? I understood you that it came from him. These things going about are rather humiliating to me. My impression has been that you, considering all the circumstances of the case, tho't I had done right, tho' the publication of the few letters might not have been wise." On April 7, Adoniram replied, "Don't, darling, turn me out, because Mr. Corey distorts what I said—you know how a thing can be almost honestly mispresnted by being repeated and re-repeated—I don't recollect what I said to him but certainly not what is imputed to me. At any rate, Mr. C has evidently not done well, and I must withdraw from him that cordiality that I began to feel."

[208] See vol. 1, "Cast of Characters," s.v. "Gillette, The Reverend Abram Dunn." In fact, Mr. Gillette also expressed deep disappointment that he would not be asked to officiate at their wedding.

[209] Emily wrote on several occasions about Mr. Corey saying negative things about her engagement to Adoniram Judson. On March 10, just after arriving home in Hamilton, she tells Anna Maria Anable that "it was no place for him to show his one-sidedness here; and, if he was too frank to conceal it, he better not have called." Emily also spoke in several of her letters about the way she and Adoniram were being treated in the public press and by the Christian public. See, for example, her letter to Adoniram Judson dated April 3, 1846.

[210] Early into her relationship with Adoniram Judson, Judge Bacon sent Emily a poem (March 17, 1846) about the publications of *Trippings in Author-land* and about her relationship with the venerable missionary. From comments about him in the correspondence, the judge was likely a prominent member of the Bleecker Street Baptist Church in Utica, of which Mr. Corey was the pastor.

When I read your letter last night, I dropped one little tear for the "dismay" which I had caused you;[211] and then, as a naughty child should, sat down to repair the wrong as I best might. I wrote "Aspiring to Heaven"; and it is on its way to Philadelphia now. Lest, however, the first should be in press so that they cannot come out together I will enclose a copy of both which you may get published if you think proper.[212]

Oh how entirely I must belong to you—you whom four months ago I had never seen. Now all my hopes for this life cluster around you—all my earthly interests are bound up in yours, all my other feelings are but air balanced against my love for you—my thoughts, wishes and sentiments are under your control—your wish is my law, your smile my happiness, and your frown my misery. **What right have you, Mr. Judson, to make such a slave of Fanny Forester?**[213] **Can you answer that? Do you expect her to submit to all this? To let you put such degrading chains about her—the free, merry-hearted Fanny? Do you expect it?** Ah, well then, open your arms—there is something so sweet about this *heart*-slavery! I creep into your dear bosom, *so* blest! Take the hand, love, I place upon your lips, and lead your remorseful one through life up to heaven—**Fanny the trifler—Nemmy,**[214] **the helpless baby-pet**. Thine through life, thine in death, thine when **(God helping us)** we shall both awake in our blessed Savior's image. **We will "love one another entirely and with ever-growing affection"; and we will love the Saviour more."** We cannot help it, he is so good to us. His blessed care be over you darling,

Yours lovingly,

Emily

Monday 10 o'clock p.m.

Again—what now think you, dear? Would you believe that I have been in a great fret, and actually sent for a lawyer? Some rascally fellows have been collecting my F. F. stories and publishing them in the cheap style. I saw the book which was bro't to town today a few hours ago and sent for Mr. Williams. He says I could prosecute them for invasion of copy-right on account of a story they have taken from *Trippings*;[215] but it would occasion a great stir and place me in a very unpleasant predicament. I have written to Paine and Burgess[216]

---

[211] See the letter of Adoniram Judson to Emily E. Chubbuck dated April 10, 1846.

[212] Regarding this continuing discussion on "Clinging to Earth" and "Aspiring to Heaven," see vol. 1. These two poems appear in this volume following the April 4, 1846 letter.

[213] Emily Chubbuck as Fanny Forester. See vol. 1, "Cast of Characters," s.v. "Chubbuck, Emily," and "Forester, Fanny."

[214] Emily Chubbuck. See vol. 1, "Cast of Characters," s.v. "Nemmy, Nem, or Nemmy Petty (Nemmie Pettie)." Also the chapter on "Names of Endearment."

[215] *Trippings in Author-land*, a collection of Emily's stories from the magazines, had been published in November 1845.

[216] Paine and Burgess was the publisher of *Trippings in Author-land*.

asking them to do what they can quietly, to get the book suppressed and also to Graham.[217] *Graham's Magazine* copyright covers part of the things. I consulted Mr. Williams about the B. B. and H.[218] affair. He says he don't [*sic*] know how a court of justice would regard the matter; but he thinks booksellers would decide in my favour [sic]. He advises me to get a writing of Mr. Hawley,[219] stating his understanding of the agreement, that I may have the affair in some tangible shape.

Do you really think, darling, that we shall sail as soon as the middle of June?[220] It is very, very soon! I am anxious to wait till the first of July unless it would be much better to go sooner. However, arrange it in your own way. You will get sick enough of your bargain I can assure you. How often I shall detect you thinking of Miss Martha and Co.

When shall I see you again? Next week? Would you come next week? Nemmy Petty[221] wants the strong arm and the dear pillow—a real live pillow— with a heart in it. It may be an extravagant freak, but no other pillow takes away the headache like that. Bring it home, love. Thine forever and ever.

Written in the left margin of page 1: "I have succeeded in getting some medicine at last from Doct. James[222] which I hope will do me good. I have scarce eaten a meal since my return from Schenectady."[223]

Written in the left margin of page 3: "I have taken my third singing lesson and Mr. Edson[224] speaks quite encouragingly. The singing is all for you, so if I sometimes make your ears ache you can't find fault."

Source: Hanna family files; A. C. Kendrick, *The Life and Letters of Mrs. Emily C. Judson*, 183–84.

[217] George Graham was the editor of *Graham's Magazine*, one of the preeminent literary magazines of Emily's time. He took an interest in Emily Chubbuck as Fanny Forester; he mentored her and published every piece of writing that she could submit to him, and for it all, he remunerated her with the astounding sum of five dollars a page. In April 1845, when Emily was staying in Philadelphia with the Reverend and Mrs. A. D. Gillette, Mr. and Mrs. Graham were frequent visitors, often inviting Emily to tour parts of the city with them in their elegant carriage. That relationship picked up again when Emily returned to Philadelphia in fall 1845.

[218] Bennett, Backus and Hawley printed several of Emily's earlier books. She was having a discussion with them over the copyrights. See Emily's letter of April 11, 1846.

[219] See vol. 1, "Cast of Characters," s.v. "Hawley, Mr. Horace H."

[220] Obviously, Adoniram Judson and Emily had been talking of this departure date. He said again on April 12, 1846 in his letter to her, "Please tell Miss Sheldon and Lydia, that we must be ready to embark by the middle of June—For we know not what day a favorable opportunity may occur, which it would be a pity to lose, by not being ready. In fact, they sailed on July 11, 1846."

[221] Emily E. Chubbuck names. See vol. 1. Also the chapter "Names of Endearment."

[222] Dr. James was a trusted physician, who attended the students and faculty of the Utica Female Academy. He is mentioned frequently in the correspondence as having been consulted for varying medical complaints, and his advice was always welcomed and highly regarded.

[223] Emily was back in Utica by March 31, 1846, when she wrote to Adoniram, so she is talking about approximately a two-week period when she has eaten so little.

[224] On April 9, Emily wrote, "What do you think, darling, I have been about today? There is in the city a Mr. Edson, a famous teacher of sacred music, and I have been seeing him today about giving me singing lessons. He is coming tomorrow to give me a trial and then will decide whether I can learn or not. If there is a bare possibility in the case I will do my best. It is the only way in which I think you will be able to turn 'the unuseful' to account."

Emily E. Chubbuck to Miss Catharine Chubbuck, April 13, 1846— Utica NY

Dear Kit,

I write in great haste to say nothing. Mrs. Eaton[225] told me you were expecting us this week. The doctor is in Maine now, and I don't know when he will be back, probably sometime next week. I shall not come home till I come with him 'cause why of my singing lessons. If you can get some fine, very fine strong doubled and twisted woollen [sic] yarn and get Nancy to knit it I shall be glad. Why don't you send out the hair I wrote for? If any of the old farmer people say anything about doing for me say flannel shirts, flannel petticoats, or anything they choose. We are to sail I expect about the middle of June. I shall be married *at home* about a fortnight before. I will enclose the thing from Mr. G.—do as you think best about having it published—it seems to me rather flat.—Have you seen one of my gold pens since I came away? I have lost one. Have things out of the way, for when I come home I shall bring some fine night-gowns and such things for you to do for me. Don't get worried about my coming home, for you may be assured that I shall be with you as much as possible. I have everything on my hands though, and so am obliged to do differently from what I should like. Love to all

From your loving
Nemmy[226]

Source: Hanna family files.

[225] The Reverend Doctor George W. Eaton was a distinguished professor and future president of Madison University and the Hamilton Theological Institution. He had a warm relationship with the Sheldon-Anable families, especially while they were at the Utica Female Academy. Mrs. Eaton was his wife.

[226] Emily Chubbuck. See vol. 1, "Cast of Characters," s.v. "Nemmy, Nem, or Nemmy Petty (Nemmie Pettie)." Also the chapter "Names of Endearment."

The Reverend A. D. Gillette to Emily E. Chubbuck, April 13, 1846

Monday, April, 1846

Dear Emily

Your kind letter to my poet wife, received this morning made me sorry, and I repent having said a word in my last on the subject of marriage.[227] I explain—

When I wrote[228] I supposed some of the Prof's at Hamilton were to do the deed—as I supposed good Dr. Kendrick[229] was too ill, indeed I have been looking for news of his death daily.

Miss Cynthia[230] says he is to do the deed of love not [ ]ying—this alters the case—Now do not take one inch of pains to make it different from your plans. I am your servant and friend. I love you and the Dr. too well to take any offence or to be hurt, certainly too well to suppose for a moment, that you would have it otherwise, than what in your united judgment was wisest and best. I presume the Dr. misunderstood me about the affair—do not trouble him with it.

Should matters so turn out as that my services were needed you have only to command and I come as if by telegraphic dispatch.

I admire your spunk expressed in yours to Mrs. G.—"If it is among the number of possibilities shall be indebted to no body [*sic*] for the not [Note: This is likely meant to be "knot."] tying, but your good husband"—Now that is enough.

We know that we never doubted your feelings, and now I beg you do not feel unhappy about it one moment.

You need all your time, strength and unpained affections for present duties, and future emergencies. Would heaven only [ ] with you to help you—dear little wife would go on to Utica if she could do you any good—command her if you need, or can use her to better purpose there than here—do—do yet and know your dear friends there are too kind not to do all they can.[231]

Do not stop to be sick, do not—no [ ] keep up and Heaven sustain and bless you.

---

[227] There has been an on-going discussion in the correspondence as to who would officiate at the marriage of Adoniram Judson and Emily Chubbuck.

[228] Emily had written to Adoniram on April 6, 1846, saying that she had received a letter from Fanny Anable, who was living with the Gillettes, indicating that there was some kind of misunderstanding on Mr. Gillette's part regarding his possible participation as officiant at their wedding, and Emily asked Adoniram what he might have said to him. On April 9, Emily reported that she had just received a letter from Mr. Gillette, and that he was terribly disappointed that he was not to receive an invitation.

[229] When Emily attended as a young woman, Dr. Nathaniel Kendrick was the pastor of the Baptist church in Eaton and a professor in a local theological school; He officiated the marriage Adoniram and Emily on June 2, 1846. He died on September 11, 1848.

[230] See vol. 1, "Cast of Characters," s.v. "Sheldon, Miss Cynthia."

[231] Emily asked Miss Sheldon and Mrs. Gillette to take major roles in pulling together all that she would need for living in Burmah.

Mrs. and Dr. Nott[232] arrived Saturday—Fanny[233] starts probably tomorrow or next day with Rose Guise.

We are all well—boys noisy—wife [ ], and sleeps as usual soundly and serenely—I as usual have some fidgets—not many more than when you were here.—O how we miss you—can we not have you and Dr. one week before sailing—O can we not? Why—why—do tell him to rest here quiet all of one week none shall intrude.

Mrs. G. is attending to the mullers you want—Dr. Potter speaks exultingly of the enterprise and is confident of your future better health. We all hope and pray for it.

If you can give me one paragraph of recollections of [ ] B. do so please. I must have you in my pretty book—it is indeed I think interesting and will be useful—I shall send you one soon as out.

I write this to heal all where I have wounded. Believe me yours forever, A. D. Gillette

Written in the left margin of the address page: "O what a luxury one of these days to receive a letter all the way from Burmah. How quiet [ ], and [ ] by the [ ] [ ] world you will be in that little Missionary Home."

Written in the left margin of the address page: "Dr. Nott was too unwell to preach or he would have given me one service. I regretted it. Poor Abbott[234]—I pity him. I wish I could see him here again."

Written in the bottom margin of the address page: "Dr. Judson wrote to me of going to see Dr. [ ] who I see is deceased by the last *Register*[235]—he also said he should 'visit Alderbrook' which I guess [ ] [ ] yet."

Written in the bottom margin of the address page: "I had a letter from Dr. Judson while at Plymouth [ ]."

Source: American Baptist Historical Society, AJ 24, no. 1196.

---

[232] See vol. 1, "Cast of Characters," s.v. "Nott, Urania Sheldon."

[233] See vol. 1, "Cast of Characters," s.v. "Anable, Fanny."

[234] Elisha Abbott was born October 23, 1809 in Cazenovia, New York. He graduated from the Hamilton Theological Institute and was ordained August 25, 1835. He wife was Ann P. Gardner, and they were married April 2, 1837. Though they were appointed for work in Telagus, India, that changed upon their arrival, and they went to Maulmain in April 1837. They continued on to Rangoon shortly after that. In March 1840, they established the station at Sandoway. Mrs. Abbott died in Sandoway on January 27, 1845. Mr. Abbott left for the United States in November 1845, returning in August 1847. At one point in the correspondence, Mr. Abbott was mentioned as a possible husband for Lydia Lillybridge.

[235] See vol. 1, "Places, Events, Organizations, and Magazines," s.v. "*Baptist Register*."

Mrs. Hannah J. Gillette to Emily E. Chubbuck, April 14, 1846—Philadelphia

My dear Emily,

The long looked for letter arrived at last, and whether I forgive you or not for what "seemed like past forgetfulness" I must excuse all future appearances—but in truth dear E. I did feel a "little cut" and altho' I did want to write to you for many *reasons* yet I stoically forbore to do so standing as I do some times [*sic*] on my dignity as Mrs. G says—but you will own that I was in rather a mortifying situation when by *all hands* I was asked "when I had heard from my dear Friend Miss C." Of course I said *not lately* but I will excuse [ ] now—and say no more about it. The necklace I obtained and hope it will please you—the price four dollars—much cheaper than expected—it is as simple could [ ] be but I think it chaste and beautiful.

Now I have been interrupted in the writing of this and consequently must hasten to business, as I am intending to leave for New York in the morning, and have yet to pack my trunk and it is now ten o'clock.

I am anxious dear Emily to do what I can as Mrs. Robarts[236] is enlisted on behalf of the Dr. I would be mindful of your necessities—I want to make up a *few presents* and send them on to you when the opportunity may offer—I shall not probably see you before [ ] leave the whole probable course of events seems to be changed—and so far as regards my intended visit there is not much hope that I can leave home this summer—I do regret the disappointment of not seeing you for I did not think for a moment nor realize at our parting that I should *never* see you again but I *will* not dwell on the sad reality.—May Heaven bless you and yours will be my prayer.

Will you my dear girl please send me [ ] a *list* of little *luxuries* if you please—or give me a sort of an idea as to what you both probably *lack* in the outfit—you knew there are many things which you would like but which would not come with that kind of *outfit*—for *instance* the *riding cap* I can get it for you (a handsome velvet cap) and [Note: The next line is lost because it is out of focus.] can get something

---

[236] Mr. and Mrs. W. S. Robarts were active in Philadelphia Baptist circles. They were frequent visitors to the home of the Reverend and Mrs. A. D. Gillette and later to the Misses Anable's School, which Anna Maria Anable and her extended family had started in Philadelphia in 1848. In his biography of his father, Edward Judson mentioned that Adoniram Judson stayed at the Robarts's home when he came to Philadelphia in December 1845 when he met Emily Chubbuck. A. C. Kendrick said, "(Mr. Gillette and Dr. Judson) arrived in (or out of) due time in Philadelphia, and Dr. Judson was welcomed to the house of Mr. and Mrs. W. S. Robarts, who became warm personal friends, as they were already active friends of the mission cause." In 1846, with the engagement of Adoniram Judson and Emily Chubbuck, the correspondence indicates some hard feelings toward Mrs. Robarts for comments disparaging the coming marriage and missionary service. This is found in Emily's letter to Adoniram dated February 6, 1846; Mrs. Robarts seemed to be accusing Emily of worldliness when all the time, Emily was quick to say, Mrs. Robarts was engaging in the same activity of which she was accused. The correspondence also indicates a satisfactory healing of the relationship. In January 1849, Miss Sheldon told Emily that Mrs. Robarts had placed their daughter Mary in the Misses Anable's School.

---

else—or use the money—I thought but to write to you on this subject and [ ] hope for an answer as soon as possible—I was pleased with the prospect there is of your having Miss Lillybridge[237] in company—we dare not breathe it here, as *Miss Hugg*[238] might call it a slight.

Now I must close this as I must pack the trunk now in earnest—I shall remain in New York about a week, and then look for a letter soon upon my return—

May heaven's richest blessings rest on you and your undertaking and grant you health to perform your work of love—is the prayer of

Your ever affectionate friend

Hannah J. Gillette

Miss E. Chubbuck

Source: American Baptist Historical Society, AJ 24, no. 1195.

Adoniram Judson to Emily E. Chubbuck, April 15, 1846[239]

My dearest Love, Since I wrote you from Waterville,[240] I have been to New Sharon and visited Boardman's relatives and stirred up their sympathy for George, so that they have pledged themselves to contribute $200 towards his collegiate education, which, added to $500 which I had got pledged in Boston and elsewhere, leaves $100 only of the sum required to carry him through, and that I shall pick up somewhere, so that though I must be ready to fulfill any pledge that may fail, I hope I shall be able to keep the whole $800, which I had laid aside for him, to buy you a wedding ring, or for some dearer object, if by searching and ransacking the country, I should succeed in finding one. I did overhear of a giddy, hair-brained gipsy [*sic*], who squandered away all her earnings for the support of her parents.[241] Do you think that by advertising the newspapers, I would find her out? They say she is already figuring in the public prints, under some fantastic name—Fanny[242] something. Could you give me a clue? And they do say, that she is going out to some Hottentot country to teach the fair darkies to wear clothes! Now I must say, that I have a sort of fellow-feeling for the poor crazy girl, for "Kate is crazed"[243]

---

[237] See vol. 1, "Cast of Characters," s.v. "Lillybridge, Miss Lydia." Also the timeline on "Lydia Lillybridge Simons."

[238] Miss Hugg had applied for missionary service, and on March 30, 1846, Adoniram wrote that the board had not supported her application because she did not successfully pass her medical examinations.

[239] This letter has an addendum dated April 16, 1846.

[240] See the letter of Adoniram Judson to Emily E. Chubbuck dated April 12, 1846.

[241] In summer 1842, Emily purchased a home for her family in Hamilton, New York, at a cost of $400, pledging to pay $100 a year. There were many occasions in the correspondence when she mentioned this debt and the pressure it placed upon her.

[242] Emily Chubbuck as Fanny Forester. See vol. 1, "Cast of Characters," s.v. "Chubbuck, Emily," also "Forester, Fanny."

[243] See the letter of Adoniram Judson to Emily E. Chubbuck dated April 16, 1846. "Kate is crazed" is from a poem, "The Task," by William Cowper.

most evidently. Look her up, darling dear, and send her to me. I will put my arms around her neck and lay her poor head on my bosom, and press my lips to hers, and try to kiss the mad away. But, perhaps, she will become more crazy for my kissing her. Well, to tell the truth, that is just what I intend. And then I will shut her up in a madhouse and have her all to myself. Wouldn't that be charming? O that I had her here, in this nice chamber this evening, by this nice fire, if I wouldn't drive her raving distracted.

I am here in a chamber of what they call the Hallowell House, after having been shaken all day in a stage coach [*sic*], from Farmington, 20 miles. O what a comfort it is to be at a hotel, free from all company and the annoyances of friends. But tomorrow I must turn out and proceed to Bath and the next day to Portland and the next to Bradford.

Source: Hanna family files.

Adoniram Judson to Emily E. Chubbuck, April 16, 1846[244]

My right thumb is so lame from an accident yesterday, that it is rather painful to write or I should not have broken off so abruptly last night. Was not I saying something about crazy girls? Cowper understood when he wrote:

> "She begs an idle *pin* of all she meets,
> And hoards them on her sleeve, but needful food,
> Though pinched with hunger off or comelier clothes
> Asks never: Kate is crazed."[245]

What girl was that that said—her pen should be her *pin* money? It seemed that *she* wanted *pins*. That is a sure mark. Now if you are that crazy girl what wants pins, don't tell her that when I get her into my clutches, I don't intend to give her any. But I don't, for I suspect that crazy girls want pins for as to prick their lovers with. I suspect, and intend to ask Cowper next time.

Dear darling Emily, I thought of you all last night, except when I was asleep, which occupied the time between 9 and 6 this morning, for I thought I would wipe out all the old scores of Bedford Sommes, as the beautiful sun came blazing into my window, making a very different morning from that of yesterday, when I set out in a downright snowstorm, in an uncovered wagon.

---

[244] This letter is an addendum to a letter dated April 15, 1846.
[245] This is from "The Task" by William Cowper.

Oh, this living apart from those we love is miserable work. Three times we have parted. Once, in the entry of Mr. Gillette's[246] house, when I left for Washington,—once in the cars, when you left for Utica, and once at Dr. Nott's[247] window. Each parting was worse to me than the last. When shall we part again? After a sweet meeting of several days, I trust, and I have to leave you to go down the river to New York to attend the great meeting on the 20th of May. "What are meetings here but partings?" Any novice can answer that. For meetings, with those we love, when continued at least for awhile, are the balm of existence. Religion is indeed the philosophy, but love is the delicious poetry of life. Religion may be the roast beef, most nutritious, but love claims to be the cake and the pie. Don't you think I am turning to the transcendental?[248] However that may be, I never felt a more desperate longing to be in a certain place, with a certain person in my arms— O my! O my! My what? Nothing—all vacuity in this chamber. Let me pitch this letter into the post office and look out for the steam-boat. Dear, dear Nemmy.[249] I hug you ever in my heart of hearts—A Judson

Source: Hanna family files.

Nathaniel Parker Willis to Emily E. Chubbuck, April 16, 1846

My dear Emily,

I find myself obliged to go to Philadelphia and Washington before going to Utica.[250] This is only a line written in the whirl of hurried departure to say this much. If you will write to me at Washington (I stay there probably a week) you will make me very happy. God bless you.

Ever yours affectionately
N. P. W.

Source: Hanna family files.

---

[246] This parting had been toward the end of January, about a month after they had first met on Christmas Day 1845. See vol. 1, "Cast of Characters," s.v. "Gillette, The Reverend Abram Dunn."

[247] This parting had been towards the end of March 1846; Emily, Anna Maria Anable, and Adoniram Judson had traveled to Schenectady to visit with Dr. and Mrs. Eliphalet Nott, and then Judson had moved on to see his sons in Worcester and then went on to Boston and Plymouth, where Abby Ann was staying with her Adoniram Judson's eccentric sister.

[248] On December 30, 1845, Anna Maria Anable wrote to Emily, "Some folks here think you are getting transcendentalist. What do they mean do you suppose? I guess it's because you say 'God-gifted' and 'inner light.' If a body advances an original idea now-a-days one is transcendentalist." On January 2, 1846, Emily responded, "So Ninny darling, I have had quite a 'set down' up there at Utica, hav'nt [sic] I? Anything but a 'gospel' way of doing things that. But never mind, it was quite refreshing—I have been praised till it makes me sick at the stomach. Doct. Judson says the paragraph is 'brutal'—the dear, *dear* doctor!"

[249] Emily Chubbuck. See vol. 1, "Cast of Characters," s.v. "Nemmy, Nem, or Nemmy Petty (Nemmie Pettie)." Also the chapter "Names of Endearment."

[250] Emily Chubbuck asked N. P. Willis if she could see him before she left for Burmah. On April 10, 1846, N. P. Willis wrote, "I will come to you during next week, and we will have at least one hour's concourse before we are separated forever."

Emily E. Chubbuck to Adoniram Judson,[251] April 17, 1846—Utica NY

Shall I send another letter to Boston, **darling**? There will be three or four awaiting you, but perhaps you will like something of a later date. Yours from **Waterville**[252] (Boston) was rec'd last evening—it *does* take letters a long time to come!

Pray don't make arrangements for sailing the middle of June[253] if you can help it—don't. It is so, *so* soon! I have been through with a terrible scene today. I was induced to go into the school-room for an hour, and such sobbings! I haven't got the tears out of my eyes yet. Oh, it is hard to have these dear little creatures, who love me so much and over whom I have so much influence. Do you wonder that I doubt whether I can ever do as much good elsewhere? Have you ever thought that teaching in this School has been my *business*; and that I have incurred censure because I have employed my *leisure* hours in the way that I considered the most useful? My writing time was made up of the stray hours which I saved from society etc. Yet everybody looks upon the writer and forgets the teacher entirely—everybody out of the house. They forget too that what they call my better sort of writing (I don't think it so) balances the other, in quantity, fully; and seize upon the innocent doings of lighter moments as though these things had been the business of life. I believe nobody ever lisped a word against my usefulness as a teacher. **People (my friends) are becoming quite reconciled to my going, and are doing everything for me that they can; but the Baptists who seem to think it a very nice time to show resentment for my having chanced to fall into a different kind of society when I came here, do not exhibit any kind of interest except what appears very much like an unfriendly one. Do not answer this fair statement of things, darling; there are not more pious people in the Baptist church than Mrs. Martin, Mrs. Kirkland, the Trays, the Seymours, and ever so many others I might mention, and I am confident that religion has nothing to do with the peculiar conduct of the Baptists here. Anna Maria**[254] **has become quite vexed; and I am afraid her disgust will warp her conscience. By the way, our friend Mrs. Yates**[255] **has been having a bit of trouble. She went forward to communion a week or two since, and Mr. Switzer walked up the aisle and told her she was quite out of place. She answered that she tho't not, but if he did not wish it she**

---

[251] For an understanding of the comparison on an original letter with the letter actually printed by Dr. A. C. Kendrick in *The Life and Letters of Mrs. Emily C. Judson*, see the first footnote for the letter of Adoniram to Emily dated April 2, 1846.

[252] See the letter from Adoniram Judson to Emily Chubbuck dated April 11 and 12, 1846.

[253] Adoniram Judson mentioned the middle of June, saying that they had to be prepared if a ship was sailing that early, as they would not want to miss such an opportunity. As it turned out, they did not sail until July 11, 1846.

[254] See vol. 1, "Cast of Characters," s.v. "Anable, Miss Anna Maria."

[255] On April 1, 1846, Emily wrote to Adoniram about their wedding plans, suggesting that they be married in Hamilton and then travel the next day to stay with Mrs. Yates, a journey of about twenty-two miles.

would not partake. Mr. Switzer was not satisfied with this, but came back to her and insisted on her leaving the seat which she had taken and going to her own pew. Mrs. Yates has a great many friends, and so it has created quite a sensation in Chittenango.

I have been expecting Willis[256] here this week,[257] but he was obliged to go to Washington and now I doubt whether I see him at all. I wonder whether I was born to act such a singular part in this world or whether I cross my own destiny. I certainly never did anything in my life that was expected, and have done nothing but keep people staring all my days. I have tried to make those about me happy too, but I have seldom accomplished it. Are you not afraid to undertake me? W. was one of the kindest friends that I ever had—think how I have repaid him. I shall not, of course, bring the same kind of pain upon you, but—don't you feel any misgiving. Oh, these vixenish authoresses!

It is a week today since I commenced taking singing lessons of Mr. Edson.[258] He says I have improved very fast,—but I can't sing a tune through yet. I learn more slowly because I can't practice much—it is too great exertion. Mr. Edson says that singing much in the present state of my health would be dangerous. My health has improved since I wrote you last—indeed, for two days I have been quite well.

I had a letter from dominie [sic] Gillette[259] last night.[260] He is quite reconciled to giving way to Doct. Kendrick[261] in a certain nice little affair and regrets writing the letter that I sent you.[262] Doct.-Mrs. Nott[263] are in Philadelphia—the doctor not very well. Bishop Potter is delighted with our engagement; and speaks of my prospective doings as a "most glorious enterprise." I have some personal acquaintance with him you know, and you called on him in Phil. I am glad you did.

[256] See vol. 1, "Cast of Characters," s.v. "Willis, Nathaniel Parker."

[257] See the letters of April 10 and 16, 1846, from N. P. Willis to Emily E. Chubbuck.

[258] On April 9, 1846, in a letter to Adoniram Judson, Emily wrote, "What do you think, darling, I have been about today? There is in the city a Mr. Edson, a famous teacher of sacred music, and I have been seeing him today about giving me singing lessons. He is coming tomorrow to give me a trial and then will decide whether I can learn or not. If there is a bare possibility in the case I will do my best. It is the only way in which I think you will be able to turn 'the unuseful' to account." Then, on April 13, 1846, she wrote, "I have taken my third singing lesson and Mr. Edson speaks quite encouragingly. The singing is all for you, so if I sometimes make your ears ache you can't find fault."

[259] See vol. 1, "Cast of Characters," s.v. "Gillette, The Reverend Abram Dunn."

[260] See the letter from the Reverend A. D. Gillette to Emily E. Chubbuck dated April 13, 1846.

[261] See vol. 1, "Cast of Characters," s.v. "Kendrick, Dr. Nathaniel."

[262] On April 9, 1846, Emily wrote to Adoniram, saying that she had just received a letter from Mr. Gillette and that he was terribly disappointed. Apparently, from something that Adoniram Judson had said to him, he had come to believe that he would be asked to officiate at their marriage ceremony.

[263] See vol. 1, "Cast of Characters," s.v. "Nott, Urania Sheldon."

Courtland Anable[264] has just left college, and is half crazy to go to India with us. If he could get employment (especially teaching) for a few years I think it would be a very excellent thing for him. He is certainly dependent on his own resources, and is the very fellow that some travel would benefit. Please advise about the matter. He is a fine young man and decidedly pious—a member of Mr. Corey's[265] church.

You did not say anything unkind about the poetry that I sent to Neal.[266] It was a very careless thing for me to do. I was making a little arrangement with him and wished to give him a piece of poetry. That was prettier than anything I had, and I sent it, supposing that no one would ever think whether it was published of late or not. I ought to have considered that it might trouble you at any rate, and perhaps do others harm.[267]

Evening 8 o'clock

What a dull statistical letter I have written you, **dearest**. The truth is I was fatigued into utter stupidity this afternoon, and am but very little better now. I fancy that I am nearly as much thronged with company as you are; having been away so long *all* my friends come now to see me, and it is tiresome and exciting. Oh, if I could only have your kind bosom for my head tonight! And your lips to speak gentle words to me. My precious guide and teacher! God keep me humble that your instructions may always be dear to me—your kind censure severe. Do I seem to lack the proper degree of meekness when I try to defend myself from what seems to me undeserved blame? I know, darling, that God sees a very wicked heart in me; I know that you and other intimate friends must be aware of faults, and I love you better for telling me of them; but the censure that I receive just now is unjust. Perhaps I ought to take it just as patiently, though. Pray for me, darling, that I may have a right spirit, and that I may have wisdom to guide me through all difficulties.

A paper has just been bro't me with Gen'l Morris'[268] notice of our engagement. He says in allusion to the article in the *Boston Transcript*,[269] "It is an old

---

[264] See vol. 1, "Cast of Characters," s.v. "Anable, Courtland."

[265] See vol. 1, "Cast of Characters," s.v. "Corey, the Reverend D. G."

[266] See vol. 1, "Cast of Characters," s.v. "Neal, Joseph."

[267] For the complete discussion on "Clinging to Earth" and "Aspiring to Heaven," see the footnotes to these two poems, both of which appear in this volume following the letter of Adoniram to Emily dated April 4, 1846.

[268] General George P. Morris was a partner with N. P. Willis at the *New Mirror* and a prominent literary figure in New York and Philadelphia. The original founder of the *New York Mirror* in 1823, beginning in 1843 with the *New Mirror*, he entered into a succession of publication enterprises with N. P. Willis. A writer, poet, and songwriter, Morris published a number of anthologies of both prose and poetry. When Willis went to Europe in 1845 after the death of his wife, he asked General Morris to guide Emily in her literary endeavors. Known universally as General Morris, his title came from his rank as a brigadier-general in the New York Militia.

[269] See Emily's letter of April 3, 1846, in which she enclosed a column from the *Boston Transcript* that spoke harshly about missionaries taking their wives to the mission field. Laboring in "unhealthy climes," it said, is almost an invitation to death.

---

maxim that 'those things which concern us least are the very ones to throw us into the highest fever. He will venture to say that a lady who writes so well and so feelingly as 'Fanny Forester'[270] will make a wise selection of a 'partner for life.'"

I am very, very tired; so, my dear "wise selection," just spread open your arms to me while I say good-night—good-night, good-night. Heaven watch over thee, darling.

Ever thine, Emily

Source: Hanna Family files; A. C. Kendrick, *The Life and Letters of Mrs. Emily C. Judson*, 184–86.

Adoniram Judson to Emily E. Chubbuck,[271] April 18, 1846— Bradford MA

Here I am, dearest, in the chamber where I spent so many hours and days with Ann.[272] She passed away years ago, and her place in my heart was filled by another;[273] she too had passed away and now my heart turns as fondly to you, dear, dear Emily. From Hallowell, I wrote Mr. Peck[274] to have my letters from Utica forwarded to this place, but the mail this evening brought me nothing, and I must wait till I arrive in Boston, Monday forenoon. I spent one night in Bath and one in Portland, and arrived here today noon. Found Abby-ann[275] [*sic*] well and happy. She repeated your lines and thought them very beautiful.[276] But she begins to anticipate, with bitter feelings, the parting which is drawing near, and clings to me frequently with tears.[277]

I wonder whether you love me as *ardently* and *entirely* as I love you—and whether desertion on my part would crush you, or desertion on your part would crush me. Love me, darling, though it be only from pity. Leave me not to return alone, so much more miserable than if I had never seen you. But why do I write so?

---

[270] Emily Chubbuck as Fanny Forester. See vol. 1, "Cast of Characters," s.v. "Chubbuck, Emily," and "Forester, Fanny."

[271] This is the first part of a letter written over three days. An addendum appears as an April 19, 1846 letter, and one as an April 20 letter.

[272] Ann Hasseltine Judson was from Bradford, Massachusetts. Adoniram Judson and Ann Hasseltine were married in 1812 just before their departure for the mission field. Ann died in 1826.

[273] Sarah Hall Boardman Judson married Adoniram Judson in 1834.

[274] See vol. 1, "Cast of Characters," s.v. "Peck, The Reverend Doctor Solomon."

[275] See vol. 1, "Cast of Characters," s.v. "Judson, Abby Ann."

[276] On April 8, Emily enclosed a poem for Abby Ann in her letter to Adoniram: "I will enclose a little scrap which please hand to Abby with a kiss from me. You will see that there is not much poetry in it, and she may be less critical."

[277] Later in life, Abby Ann Judson and her brother Adoniram became quite vocal about the practice of separating missionary families. George Boardman was sent back to the United States when he was six years old, never to see his mother again. After Adoniram and Emily left for Burmah in July, Abby Ann, Adoniram, and Elnathan would never see him again.

Is it that I have a kind of presentiment that your next letter will be—I know not what?

Source: Hanna family files.

Adoniram Judson to Emily E. Chubbuck,[278] April 19, 1846

I have passed another pleasant Sabbath, sitting in pews like other people and allowed to join in worship unmolested. And after spending the evening with the family, have now retired to the old chamber to hold a moment's communion with you, dear dear "Cousin Emily." I shall be in Boston tomorrow forenoon, and hope to find letters from you and also from Maulmain as I hear that the Unicorn has at last arrived. My last date from you is the 8th, eleven days ago! The world has turned over several times in eleven days. And you too? Not your heart, I trust. But your last left you ill. And what may have happened I know not. May God watch over you and preserve you, and bring us together again "in love and happiness."

I heartily approve of having the good deed performed in Hamilton[279] under the auspices of Dr. Kendrick,[280] though I think it would be quite as well done by Mr. Sheldon, your parents' pastor. That would preclude all remark and give offence to no one. But it shall be as you say. What is the necessity of going to Mrs. Yates[281] if it be done at your father's? Could we not stay a few days there?

Goodnight, my best beloved. I hope I shall not have to hear bad news tomorrow.

Source: Hanna family files.

[278] This is an addendum to a letter of April 18, 1846. Adoniram wrote from Bradford Academy in Bradford, Massachusetts, where he was visiting Abby Ann Judson, his oldest surviving child and daughter with Sarah Hall Boardman Judson. There is a second addendum placed as April 20, 1846.

[279] This is a reference to their impending marriage ceremony. Emily spoke of having the service in Utica, and then, she decided on Hamilton because of the politics of who would officiate at the ceremony. Mr. Gillette was in turmoil because he had not been asked, Mr. Corey said that he thought it should be offered to him, and Dr. Eliphalet Nott was being considered. In the end, the simplicity of Hamilton and the presence of Dr. Kendrick, Emily's pastoral friend from many years past, informed the decision.

[280] See vol. 1, "Cast of Characters," s.v. "Kendrick, Dr. Nathaniel."

[281] On April 1, Emily spoke of the possibility of their being married in Hamilton and then visiting with Mrs. Yates, who lived far enough away to give them some privacy, but not far enough so as to force an extended journey. On April 17, Emily spoke of some problems Mrs. Yates was having within her church, having been asked not to take communion. Then, in a letter approximately dated April 23, Emily said that she had heard some things about Mrs. Yates and thought they best not go there.

Mrs. Sarah Tyndale[282] to Emily E. Chubbuck,[283] April 19, 1846— Philadelphia

Why did you not my Dear Emily send me your *attempts* to write—they would at least have saved me from the mortification of thinking myself forgotten, and it would also have flattered my vanity exceedingly to tell the talking public that I was your confident [*sic*] and knew from your own lips of your intended alliance before they did. You should not have shrunk from giving me your confidence as in one important point at least we agree in differing from almost every body [*sic*], that spirits never grow old. *You* will not accuse me of selfishness in the sentiment nor think that I wish to defraud time of his honours [*sic*]. Your choice has proven that the sentiment is yours also. I feel no reluctance at the thought of having lived more than half a century in the world, but I should feel miserable indeed at the thought of living so long under the withering influence of worldly persuits [*sic*] that I could not enjoy the peace and ever fresh feelings of [ ] spiritual life.

Knowing my loquacious propensity you will not be surprised at my frequent mention of you to many of my friends, in one instance I fear you will think the result has imposed a task on you. A friend (Mrs. Capt Page) in speaking of you, told me very seriously that she was convinced you were a New Church woman by reading Ida Ravelin [*sic*],[284] and begged me to send you three pamphlets written by professor of the New Jerusalem Church, and as she is a most excellent woman I could not refuse her request. I am quite ignorant of their content, as I seldom or I may say never read any thing [*sic*] upon the doctrine of religion. We Quakers have a very short way of getting at the result of religion. We believe that Christ is within us, is our spiritual guide, our hope of glory, and will teach us by the still small voice (if we will listen in spirit and in truth to its inward teachings), all that is necessary

---

[282] Sarah Tyndale was the mother of Mrs. Mitchell of Philadelphia. A successful businesswoman, she ran a large store in Philadelphia specializing in china. She lived with her daughter and her family. In fall 1845, as Emily went to Philadelphia for her health, the Mitchells were active in inviting her to stay with them. They offered her a room, as much privacy or company as she desired, and all of the benefits of their extended household. On February 9, 1846, Emily recorded the gift of a china ink-stand from Mrs. Tyndale.

[283] There is an addendum to this letter dated April 20, 1846.

[284] We know of three stories at least that span the life of Ida Ravelin. "Bending the Twig" is the first. The second is "Another Era in the Life of Ida Ravelin," which appeared in the December 1845 issue of *Graham's Magazine*, and the third is "The Last Page in a Heart's Book," which appeared in the March 1846 issue of *Graham's Magazine*. The opening of "Bending the Twig reads:

"I see nothing peculiar about her."

Very coolly and complacently dropped the above words from lips which seemed to be totally unaware of the deed of death they were doing; crushing the rare fancies of love's weaving, with the same indifference that your horse dyes his coarse hoofs in prairie-blossoms, or the followers of the Prophet treat an inconvenient beauty to a coral pillow and a silver coverlet. A heart-swell, deeper than a sigh, a quick flushing over of the cheeks and forehead, then a closing of the slightly parted lips, a drooping of the lids, and a tenderly caressing movement of the hands, followed this confession of short-sightedness. Oh! what cold, blind, unappreciative being fathers are! As though genius never hid itself under-cap!

"I see nothing peculiar about her."

for our salvation, and that without this inward teaching we know not the things that are of God.

That light and knowledge resulting from the love of God is rapidly spreading in the world is very evident to any one who is at all acquainted with the history of the world. Oh how happy the thought that the world will one day be governed by love.

You did not expect to hear a sermon from me—but it is Sunday and I feel a little like preaching.

I had written a letter to you before I received yours, but had not sent it, and to show you what my thoughts then were, I will copy it on this and hope you are not very busey [*sic*] or weary.

March 20

My Dear Emily

I received your kind message (and as yet unfulfilled promise) through our friend Mr. Neal,[285] which was indeed very pleasant to us all. I acknowledge my motive in wishing to occupy your time in reading my unasked for letter is a selfish one. I can not [*sic*] indeed feel satisfied that you should go away so far from your native clime, without making an effort to keep alive a little feeling of sympathy which I flattered myself existed between us, and now (if rumor speaks true) that you are about to leave us, I feel self-condemned for not having used more exertion to make your visit to Phil'a more cheerful and agreeable to you for although in years I must be classed out of reach almost of youthfull sympathy, I feel that spirits do not get old, and in the mission to which you feel yourself called my Dear Young Friend you no doubt have something of the same feeling. May you in every emergency, be clothed with spiritual strength and wisdom, discerning all sectarian feeling. Stand forth a champion for the spirit of truth, feeling the constant influence of a risen Christ whose radiance enlightens the whole moral world, callusing all who evince their love to him, by the love they exercise to their fellow beings to "rejoice with joy unspeakable and full of glory."

Source: American Baptist Historical Society, AJ 26, no. 1256.

[285] See vol. 1, "Cast of Characters," s.v. "Neal, Joseph."

Mrs. Sarah Tyndale to Emily E. Chubbuck,[286] April 20, 1846

Monday. I should have finished my first letter to you very soon after the above *attempt* was written but my daughter Mrs. Millegin was taken alarmingly ill, which put every thing [*sic*] else out of my head for the time. She is now recovering very rapidly. She presented us with a fine little boy on the first of the month. Mr. and Mrs. Mitchell[287] and the boys are quite well. Hector and Julia are also well. Hector is so great a rambler that it is quite possible he may yet enjoy a Tiger [Note: Written in the right margin of the address page.] hunt on your plantation, but there seems to be so great an aversion in the most of [ ] children to the serpent species, that the Cobra de Capella might be allowed to enjoy his life for its natural term. Clara is well and as joyous as ever, [Note: Written in the left margin of the address page.] every one of them join me in sending their warmest love to you. If you can spare time will you not write to Mrs. Mitchell and myself before you leave? Or perhaps you may visit us, but in any event we earnestly desire to be sometimes remembered by you in your new and happy home, and if when there you should think us worthy of a correspondence, how happy you [Note: Written in the bottom margin of the address page.] would make us. Your name is now as familiar in our house as any of our old friends.

Mr. and Mrs. Neal[288] are well and desire to be kindly remembered to you. Wishing you all health and happiness, I am your Friend Sarah Tyndale.

Source: American Baptist Historical Society, AJ 26, no. 1256.

Adoniram Judson to Emily E. Chubbuck,[289] April 19, 1846

April 19th. Just arrived in Boston. Three precious letters from you—three![290] How kind you are, dearest of all creatures. And your letters so full of precious thought

---

[286] This letter is an addendum to Sarah Tyndale's letter of April 19, 1846.

[287] Mr. and Mrs. Mitchell lived in Philadelphia; Mrs. Tyndale, Mrs. Mitchell's mother and the owner of a prosperous china shop in downtown Philadelphia, lived with them. In November 1845, as Emily was thinking of prolonging her stay in the city to last through the winter, the Mitchells generously offered to open their home to her, promising that they would do everything in their power to take good care of her: her own room, solitude or company as desired, the ability to write, and all of the comforts they could provide. Emily did express appreciation, saying that many of her friends told her what wonderful people they were and how sensitive they were to the needs of an invalid such as Emily was at that time. Her one serious reservation was that they were Unitarians. In the end Emily decided that she would stay with the Reverend and Mrs. Gillette, knowing from her past experience that she would be more than comfortable with them.

[288] See vol. 1, "Cast of Characters," s.v. "Neal, Joseph."

[289] This is a second addendum to a letter of April 18, 1846. In his letter of April 18, Adoniram was writing from Bradford, where he was visiting Abby Ann Judson, his oldest child and daughter with Sarah Hall Boardman Judson. He clearly closed that portion of the letter with a "good-night," and then this letter picks up on the next morning as he has arrived in Boston. He was to write yet another letter on the evening of the April 20.

[290] These were her three-part letter of April 9, which we have as April 9, 10 and 11; her letter of April 13; and finally her letter of April 17.

and affectionate feeling. I wish I could write such good letters as you do, if it were only by way of making some suitable return. But dear, I love you with all my heart. I know I do. I hope you received my confession and that it wiped away the "little tear" dropped for the "dismay." O how I thank you and love you for writing "Aspiring" so promptly and so beautifully done.[291] No—no—I agree with some of your friends who say that I shall never appreciate you. Yes, they are quite right, but I will love you, dearest, and much more I guess, than they fancy or can comprehend. And then—you are trying to sing, just to please me. No—no—your friends are right—and I agree with them. I have some indistinct views, no appreciation. And have they?

As to Hawley's[292] affair, don't trouble yourself about it any more.[293] I doubt now I shall be able to arrange it amicably when I come to Utica. As I said before, I shall, Providence permitting, be in Albany next Sabbath. But don't mention this, if you have not already, for I don't want Dr. Welch to know it and make a great row beforehand. I have not yet seen Mr. Peck[294] and know not what was decided in the case of Miss Lillybridge,[295] but I shall know this afternoon and will write again by next mail.

I feel for poor Mr. Gillette,[296] but he need not act so childishly.[297] He certainly appeared to me very indifferent about it and gave me to understand that it would be rather inconvenient for him to visit the North so early as we should require.

Don't talk to me about "Miss Martha and—"[298] I know no such people, except in the way of playful speaking. The "real live pillow with a heart in it"[299] is all ready—all your own and ever as long as its pulsation continues—your dear, dear,

[291] For the complete discussion on "Clinging to Earth" and "Aspiring to Heaven," see the footnotes to these two poems, both of which appear in this volume following the letter of Adoniram to Emily dated April 4, 1846.

[292] See vol. 1, "Cast of Characters," s.v. "Hawley, Mr. Horace H."

[293] See Emily's letters of April 11 and 13, 1846. She had been having a discussion with Mr. Hawley about the copyright ownership of some of her previous writings. She hoped to publish them as a sequel to *Trippings in Author-land*. While Mr. Hawley maintained that they continued to be owned by his firm, which had initially published the volumes, Emily couldn't understand why that copyright remained, for they had been derelict in publishing additional printings as Emily thought they were needed.

[294] See vol. 1, "Cast of Characters," s.v. "Peck, The Reverend Doctor Solomon."

[295] See vol. 1, "Cast of Characters," s.v. "Lillybridge, Miss Lydia." Also the timeline on "Lydia Lillybridge Simons."

[296] See vol. 1, "Cast of Characters," s.v. "Gillette, The Reverend Abram Dunn."

[297] The Reverend Mr. Gillette had hoped to be asked to officiate the marriage of Adoniram and Emily. At some point, Adoniram said something about it being "inconvenient" for Mr. Gillette, and Emily wrote Gillette with that assumption, only later to realize that they seemed to have misread the situation. Emily's first choice was Dr. Eliphalet Nott, the president of Union College in Schenectady, New York, and the husband of Urania Sheldon Nott. When they decided to move the ceremony to her home in Hamilton, they turned to Dr. Nathanial Kendrick, a pastor from Emily's childhood with whom she had discussed as a young lady the possibility of her becoming a missionary. On April 8, 1846, Mr. Gillette wrote to Emily to tell her how "terribly disappointed" he was to be excluded from officiating their wedding. Apparently, his interpretation of his conversation with Adoniram was that Dr. Judson had given him an indication that they wanted him to take on that duty. Mr. Gillette was much more positive and reconciling in his letter to Emily of April 13, 1846.

[298] On April 13, Emily wrote, "Do you really think, darling, that we shall sail as soon as the middle of June? It is very, very soon! I am anxious to wait till the first of July unless it would be much better to go sooner. However, arrange it in your own way. You will get sick enough of your bargain I can assure you. How often I shall detect you thinking of Miss Martha and Co."

most dear head has a heart to rest upon it. And I will carry it home next Monday, if possible.

Your own—

A Judson

Written in the top margin of page 1: "No letters yet from Maulmain."

Source: Hanna family files.

Adoniram Judson to Emily E. Chubbuck, April 20, 1846—Boston

Away with Anna Maria[300] up into the attic or some other hiding place—quick—and any other of your community who has such a wicked face and is addicted to such carryings on—Be quick, or he will be upon you. And put on a quan[tity] suf[ficient] of longitude of face yourself and pitch all the "bracelets and anklets"[301] into the oven; and don't think of Fanny Elsler[302] or any thing [sic] bad. As to Lydia,[303] tell her to get ready. However, *she* is a good girl, and requires no getting ready—and whitewashing like some of you. And all put on your best bibs and tuckers, and tell those wild boys not to be poking fun at Miss Look[304]—and tell Aunt Cynthia[305] to get the strangers [sic] room ready for he is coming—he is coming—father Peck—not *old* father Peck—but the great hideous, the Corresponding Sec. of the A.B.B.F.M.—which means the American Baptist Board of Foreign Missions, even the Rev. Solomon Peck[306]—he is coming—not the subdued, meek man that lately visited you[307] and bore so much without complaining—no—no—but Solomon Peck, the organ of the Board, a man to take

---

[299] On April 13, 1846, Emily E. Chubbuck wrote to Adoniram Judson, "Nemmy Petty wants the strong arm and the dear pillow—a real live pillow-with a heart in it. It may be an extravagant freak, but no other pillow takes away the headache like that. Bring it home, love."

[300] See vol. 1, "Cast of Characters," s.v. "Anable, Miss Anna Maria."

[301] On April 2, 1846 Adoniram wrote that Dr. Peck had "timidly inquired whether you would be arrayed in other jewels and finery and evidently fearing that you would come dancing through the country like other Fannies—the style laid down in Isaiah chapter iii."

[302] Fanny Esler was one of the great Austrian ballet divas of the mid-nineteenth century.

[303] See vol. 1, "Cast of Characters," s.v. "Lillybridge, Miss Lydia." Also the timeline on "Lydia Lillybridge Simons."

[304] Julia Look was a student of Emily's at the Utica Female Academy and later a fellow teacher. A November 22, 1845 letter from Anna Maria encouraged Emily to stay in Philadelphia for the winter for her health and remarked that Julia had the hardest part because she was teaching Emily's composition class, and the students kept asking for Emily. In a September, 1847 letter, she was listed as one of the teachers at the Utica Female Academy. On September 23, 1849, Anna Maria wrote that Julia and Albert B. Casswell were married and came to visit with her. In one 1849 letter Julia spoke of another teacher who was teaching "our composition class." On October 27, 1850, Anna Maria Anable noted that she had had a son. She was one of a small number of people who addressed Emily as "Emily" and as "Nemmy" in her letters.

[305] See vol. 1, "Cast of Characters," s.v. "Sheldon, Miss Cynthia."

[306] See vol. 1, "Cast of Characters," s.v. "Peck, The Reverend Doctor Solomon."

[307] See Emily's letter of April 9, 1846, about her visit with Dr. Peck in Utica at the Utica Female Academy.

the shins off of you, before you can get your stockings mended and the great Alexander Beebee[308] Esq. who have been voted and appointed, at a special meeting of the Board holden last Monday, a committee to proceed forthwith to the Female Academy at Utica and there to summon into their presence Lydia Lillybridge spinster, in order to inspect and investigate her corporeal and mental qualifications and report thereon to the Board. The reverend inquistor will bestride the black horse tomorrow afternoon and I am writing with all my might to get this letter into the post office this evening so that it may go off early in the morning and have several hours start of Solomon, so that you will have timely notice to get your faces washed and all things put in apple pie order. This, I take it, is very kind in me and I am sure you will give me some sweet kisses when I meet you—will you not, darling dear? I am sure you will. I can almost feel them now. O that I could annihilate the space between us just for this evening and I would have my pay in cash down—no credit allowed in this chamber—my own chambers at Mr. Gardner Colby's[309] 12 Pemberton Square.

Mr. Peck said to me rather interestingly, that as he was going out to see Miss Lillybridge, he should be very glad to have an interview with the other lady. I said,—I supposed the Board would be pleased to have him do so. He replied—Not at all—her case was not even mentioned before the Board. (I had ascertained the same in private communication with Mr. Colby, who is also a member of the Board.) And so I said, you would be most happy to see him. Well, where was she to be found? Why, of course, at the same place with Miss Lillybridge, at the Female Academy where they both have rooms as assistant teachers. His eyes opened considerably and his countenance lightened up most luminously. He seemed to be surprised that [Note: Written and crossed out is "such a person as."] Fanny Forester[310] was a person of such character and was allowed to burrow in such a reputable hole. Perhaps, however, he was only pleased that he should find you together, and thus hit two birdies with one pebble. He further observed that the Board was quite satisfied with Miss Lillybridge and she would no doubt, be appointed; but that it had long been a rule of the Board to have an interview with

[308] See vol. 1, "Cast of Characters," s.v. "Beebee, Alexander."

[309] See vol. 1, "Cast of Characters," s.v. "Colby, Gardner."

[310] Emily Chubbuck as Fanny Forester. See vol. 1, "Cast of Characters," s.v. "Chubbuck, Emily," also "Forester, Fanny."

those they appointed, either in their presence or by a Committee—that the thing was little more than a formality in the present case.[311]

I have had letters from Maulmain of the 20th of Jan. Henry[312] and Edward[313] were well and happy. Not a word of Mrs. Howard.[314] They had not heard long of Sarah's[315] death, and were all lamenting the loss. Henry was able to say, on being asked where his mamma was—My mamma dead in the ship—My little Edward is not dead. Poor little fellows and yet not poor, when you feel so kindly towards them.[316] What greater favor could I do them, than get your dear heart interested for them? Thanks be to God. I must close this letter forthwith.

You must be in a miserable state of health to have such a poor appetite. And I am afraid you will suffer a great deal from sea sickness. May God preserve my dearest love. Do take care of yourself. Don't be worried at the little things that are said about us. They are even now passing away, and the affair is assuming in these parts a most favorable aspect. No use in sending kisses. They won't go—Yours—

A Judson

Source: Hanna family files.

[311] In a notebook belonging to Emily Chubbuck, there is a news clipping pasted with the heading "Another Assistant for Burmah." The articles reads: "Last week on Thursday, Br. S. Peck, the Corresponding Secretary of our Foreign Mission Board, was in Utica as a member of the committee appointed to make the usual and necessary inquiries of Miss Lydia Lillybridge, one of the teachers in the Utica Female Seminary, in regard to her views and feelings touching missionary labor at Maulmain, for which she had offered herself. The result of the examination was highly satisfactory, and great expectations are indulged respecting her, should the Lord vouchsafe his blessing. Miss L. is a much esteemed member of the Bleecker Street Baptist church, and in her departure from Utica both the church and institution will experience the loss of a superior young lady. With her valuable mental and moral qualities she has a fine constitution. It may wilt to be sure, under that hot climate, as quickly as one less robust, but it is very desirable to have missionaries go out in good health. She will go in company with Dr. Judson, and reside in his family. Her services will be mostly devoted to the school at Maulmain, where her previous influence will give her a great advantage" (notebook 4, p. 24).

[312] Henry Hall Judson, born July 8, 1842, was the son of Adoniram and Sarah Hall Boardman Judson. Henry was the sixth of their eight children, the fourth of five who survived. He remained in Burmah in 1845 when Adoniram and Sarah returned to the United States with the three older children. He returned with Emily in 1851 and went to live with her family in Hamilton, New York. Henry attended Brown University and Williams Collage; he enlisted in the army at the time of the Civil War in January 1864. Later that year, he experienced a debilitating accident attributed either to sunstroke or a horse kicking him in the head. He was married once—unhappily according to his own correspondence—and he eventually died in a veteran's home in 1918, the last of his siblings to die. Of this, the chaplain noted, "The end was a genuine example of Christian fortitude." See Rosalie Hall Hunt, *Bless God and Take Courage, The Judson Legacy*, 291 (Valley Forge PA: Judson Press, 2005).

[313] Edward Judson, born December 27, 1844, in Maulmain, Burmah, was the eighth child of Adoniram and Sarah Hall Boardman Judson and the fifth of their children to survive. Only a few months old when Sarah and Adoniram returned to America, Edward's life was saved by the nurture and care he received from Elizabeth Stevens. He loved Emily as the only "Mama" he had ever known and returned with her to the United States in October 1851. Edward, who was Eddy to his family, became a minister; he did mission work with the immigrants in New York City, and with the aid of the Rockefeller Family, he built the Judson Memorial Baptist Church in what is now Washington Park.

[314] Hosea and Theresa Howard were in Maulmain as missionaries with Adoniram Judson. Mr. Howard's responsibility was to run one of the schools that the mission maintained. Mrs. Howard was involved in that work as well. In one letter, he claims that they worked there with Adoniram Judson longer than any other missionaries.

[315] Sarah Hall Boardman Judson died September 1, 1845, at the Isle of St Helena.

[316] For the time that she had them, Emily established a great relationship with the Judson children, and they lovingly called her "Mamma" in their letters to her.

Emily E. Chubbuck to her Critics, Spring 1846

From the *National Press*[317]

"Does she deem that stern duty calls her to resign the home and friends of her heart—the fame which she has so gloriously won, nay, perhaps, even life itself, for the far-off heathen? Methinks, the 'orphans of the heart' are gathered in crowds about our very doors."

A Reply by Emily E. Chubbuck (Fanny Forester)

Stern Duty

"Stern duty?" Why rest on the breast of thy mother?
Why follow in joy the proud steps of thy brother?
Why flutters thy heart at the voice of that other
  Who calls thee from mother and brother away?
When the lip clings to thine, why so fondly dost press it?
When the loved arm encircles, why smile and caress it?
That eye's gentle glancing—why doth thy heart bless it?
  Why love, trust, or labor for loved ones, I pray?

There's a Dearer than mother, whose heart is my pillow,
A Truer than brother's foot guides o'er the billow
There's a Voice I shall hear at the grave-guarding willow
  When they leave me to sleep in my turf-covered bed;
There's a lip with soft love-words forever o'er flowing,
An eye in which love-thoughts forever are glowing,
A hand never weary of guarding, bestowing,
  A heart which for me has in agony bled.

"Stern duty?" No; love is my ready foot winging;
On duty's straight path love her roses is flinging;
In love to the FRIEND of my heart I am clinging;
  My "home" is His smile—my "far-off" His frown.
He shaped the frail goblet which Death waits to shiver,
He casts every sun-ray on life's gloomy river,
They're safest when guarded by Maker and Giver-
  My laurels and life at His feet I lay down.

---

[317] Of this inquiry of the National Press, A. C. Kendrick commented in *The Life and Letters of Mrs. Emily C. Judson*: "She responded in a strain of noble eloquence, which needs but the revision of a few harsh lines to place it among her finest pieces" 171.

"Stern duty?" Come death to thy door a prey-seeker,
Markedst thou the eye glazing, the pulse growing weaker,
And clasped in thy hand were a life brimming beaker,
    In duty, "stern duty," the draught wouldst thou bring?
Sawest thou a rich crown to thy brother's brow bending,
At his feet a black pit, its death-vapors upsending,
As thou sprangst to his side, thy voice, eye, and hand lending,
    Is it only "stern duty" thy footsteps would wing?

Away to my brother, the orphaned of heaven!
Away, with the life-draught my Saviour has given!
Away, till the web time is weaving be riven!
    Then my wings, and my harp, and my crown evermore!
But back this one prayer my full spirit is throwing,-
By these warm gushing tears that I leave thee in going,
By all that thou lov'st, by thy hopes ever glowing,
    Cheer *thou* the "heart-orphans" that throng at thy door!

Source: A. C. Kendrick, *The Life and Letters of Mrs. Emily C. Judson*, 171–72; Emily Judson, *An Olio of Domestic Verse*, 133–37.

Adoniram Judson to Emily E. Chubbuck, April 21, 1846[318]—Boston

Have just received yours of the 17th, my dearest love. So glad that you are better. Pray give up singing, if you think it hurts you in the least.[319] Pray do your health is of more importance that any thing [*sic*] else. I don't see why you get worried and excited and lose your appetite[320]—Surely you have nothing to do, but to eat and sleep and get ready to go by the middle of June! Not that I think it probable we shall go so soon, or that I wish to go so soon any more than you; but there may be a good opportunity then, which, if neglected, may leave us in the predicament of herding with several families, in the same cabin, which is commonly the fate of passengers on board American ships. I see but little chance of having a cabin to ourselves unless we take passage in a vessel which carries no other passengers. The Americans are far behind the English in the interior arrange-

---

[318] This letter has an addendum dated April 23, 1846.

[319] Emily had been quite excited about taking singing lessons from Mr. Edson, a well-known vocal coach, and this excitement is evident in several of her previous letters. However, on the April 17, Emily said, "I learn more slowly because I can't practice much—it is too great exertion. Mr. Edson says that singing much in the present state of my health would be dangerous."

[320] On April 13, 1846, Emily wrote to Adoniram: "My health has not been quite as good and loss of sleep and appetite together may have made me a little more excitable. Pray for me, dearest."

ments of the ships. I am doing all I can, but the prospect of a comfortable passage is rather dark.

Source: Hanna family files.

Adoniram Judson to Emily E. Chubbuck, April 23, 1846[321]

Not a word with you since day before yesterday! I have been so busy shopping and calling and writing letters for the next steamer, that I have not had time to write you or think of you, only now and then, just "a little bit." The thought of your sweet face and provoking lips would ever and anon creep through my hair and dive away down to some far recess about the center of gravity and finding old friends there, would make such an uproar. But I soon succeeded in dragging out the intruder (too welcome wretchs) and pitching him among the air lights and the saddles—Last evening, I wrote a small letter to my dear sisters Osgood,[322] Stevens[323] and Haswell,[324] the three who took charge of my younger children, and told them that I had found a phenomenon, but that their regards might be chastened and concili-ated. I gave them two or three extracts—one in which you set yourself off, as the unuseful,[325] and another in which you speak so kindly of the children. The latter would please them particularly, for I suppose they love the children as their own.

[321] This letter is an addendum to a letter dated April 21, 1846.

[322] Rev. Sewall Osgood was a missionary in Maulmain who worked with and lived by Adoniram Judson. Judson and Osgood occupied two of the four homes in the mission compound and lived so close that it "allowed me the pleasure and profit of almost hourly intercourse." He arrived in Burmah in 1834. His first wife Elhira Brown Osgood died on October 5, 1837, in Maulmain. On July 8, 1838, he married Sarah Thomas, the widow of the Reverend Jacob Thomas, with Adoniram Judson officiating at the wedding. He spoke in the letters to Emily, of which there are five between July 1850 and April 1852, of Adoniram Judson as his "most intimate friend." He never personally met Emily, as he had returned from the field prior to 1846. At the time of his letters, he was working with the American Baptist Missionary Union as a district secretary. In 1845, just as they were leaving for the United States, Sarah and Adoniram Judson gave care of Charley, too young to make the trip, to Mr. and Mrs. Osgood. Charley died not long after their departure. Mr. Osgood visted Adoniram, Elnathan, and Abby Ann in the United States. His third wife was Caroline Wait; they were married December 30, 1850 at Saratoga, New York. With all of his suggestions of "intimacy" and "his most intimate friend," Mr. Osgood stated that his life was so busy that he simply did not have the time to look through his papers for anything that would be helpful in writing the Judson memoir.

[323] Elizabeth Stevens arrived in Maulmain in February 1838; her husband was Edward Stevens. Elizabeth Stevens took six-month-old Edward Judson into her home when Sarah and Adoniram had to leave for the United States in 1845, and her care and nurture saved his life. She served forty-eight years in Burmah. She had extensive correspondence with Emily Judson, and her letters spoke of everyday life among the missionaries. When Emily returned to the United States, the letters from Mrs. Stevens brought news of friends and colleagues. Mrs. Stevens had a sister, Sarah Haven, in Massachusetts, who wrote a number of letters to Emily asking for information on the Stevens family.

[324] Jane Haswell sailed for Burmah in 1835, arriving in February 1836 to work with the Talaings. Her husband was James Haswell. She served as a missionary for more than forty years. Mrs. Haswell took in Henry Hall Judson when Adoniram and Sarah sailed for the United States in spring 1845. The correspondence between Emily and Jane Haswell reflects a warm relation-ship between the two.

[325] There is an early story written by Emily named "The Unuseful"; it was also published in *Trippings in Author-land*. It is a reoc-curring theme in her letters as she describes herself. The opening lines are as follows:

Man is born equestrian; and from the time when mother Eve fixed her anxious heart on improving her condition, and crushed a world at a single bound, to this present writing, he has never lacked a hobby whereon to exercise to his heart's con-tent. And it is no tame, gentle exercise; for, whatever the hobby may be, and whether well-mounted or otherwise, he not only rides tantivy, but hesitates not to "run through a troop and leap over a wall." We have innumerable hobbies now-a-days; and many of them (to our credit be it said) are of an excellent character. But, poor things! They are ridden down most savagely.

You ask whether the newspapers give me any uneasiness. It is, perhaps, not much to say, by one who has seen some fields, not the slightest, scarcely a thought, except that I fear they may disturb you and for this reason and for the fun of it, I *should* like to have our marriage so managed and kept secret for a little time, that the whole pack would be thrown off the chase and find themselves completely at fault.

As to the coldness of the Baptists—you must remember that they had set me up as a sort of model apostle, and that I should take F .F.[326] the author of *Trippings*,[327] was such an astounder, how ever [sic] much they might be pleased with her in herself, and so silenced them before gainsayers, that if they are only cold towards us, we may think ourselves extremely fortunate. The best way is look beyond the praise or censure of men of all parties, love them and be moderately desirous of conciliating other good opinion, but *rest* in the consciousness of pleasing God—and feel grateful to him that he allows us to be sure of each other's esteem and love. We know something of our own faults and failings, and that it becomes us to be humble and walk softly before God. If we are praised, let us remember that we deserve it not—if we are censored, let it make us cling to the Saviour, who will forgive all.

Since writing the above I have been aboard several ships with Mr. Colby[328] and Mr. Shaw, to show them and give them a definite idea of what I consider comfortable accommodations at sea. They are heartily disposed to make every effort to meet my wishes, but there are many difficulties in the way.

I have about done up my little business in this city—expect this evening to meet the ladies of the Federal Street Church in what is called a sewing circle, and tomorrow afternoon, shall joyfully set my face towards that blessed place where you live. I hope to get a letter from you before I leave, but if not I feel no disposition to complain. You have been too kind and good in that respect. I regret the delay in Albany, but it is unavoidable. I have several times passed through that place without attending any meeting—Monday afternoon, I hope, I hope to see you once more. Cannot we meet in the library, or the room opposite, or some place alone? I am afraid I shall bite you, and when you go mad, folks will know what dog did it. May we meet in *love* and *happiness* and feel more thankful to God for the great mercy than I at least have been. Darling dear, love me, when we meet. It seems so strange that you should continue to love such a one as I am, that I am always fearing that a change will come over the spirit of your dream. O if you should wake up and find it was but a dream, and I should find that I have lost you! But this cannot be. Death alone can part us. Is it not so my Emily—dearest Emily? My unuseful baby pet—my bird on the finger? "Ah me." Say yes, and let me ever be

---

[326] Emily Chubbuck as Fanny Forester. See vol. 1, "Cast of Characters," s.v. "Chubbuck, Emily," and "Forester, Fanny."

[327] *Trippings in Author-land* was a collection of Emily's stories written and printed in the popular literary magazines of her time.

[328] See vol. 1, "Cast of Characters," s.v. "Colby, Gardner."

Yours

A Judson

Written in the right margin of the address page: "I want to know—Do tell—as they say in this country—when you wrote that article on Genius[329] in the May *Columbian*. And are you never going to mind me, truant, songtress [*sic*] of the forest? And [ ] your wings and lie quiet in my bosom? Though not a [ ] nest for a bird of such pinions and such [Note: Written in the left margin of the address page.] plumage? Or must I send for neighbour Dominic the blacksmith, and cross a pair of long, sharp shears? No rather, I fancy I hear you say—let it be the black-smith of Gretna Green. No thank you—Not this week or fortnight. After that 'maybe, maybe! Can't say.' But it must be shears or the fetters, one of the two—or you will burn out and I shall have nothing but cinders to carry to sea."

Source: Hanna family files.

Emily E. Chubbuck to Adoniram Judson, April 23, 1846[330]—Utica NY

I must write you a word before they go to the office, darling, though I can tell you no good news. I am fairly on the invalid's list today—though whether Doct. James[331] has frightened me into being ill or whether I am really so, is a serious question with me. I wish I could see you and know just how you are and kiss the lame thumb[332]—and maybe the lips, just a little bit. Have you been in the meetings all day and are you tired and ill? Don't you wish you had Nemmy Petty[333] to put you to sleep?

I have just been hearing something about Mrs. Yates[334] which makes me not care one cent to visit her—nothing regarding you or me, but exhibiting a trait of character that I don't like. And on the whole, if you like the arrangement, I think it would be pleasanter for us not to go there. We shall not have too much time at H

[329] "Genius" also appeared in vol. 2 of Alderbrook.

[330] This letter is undated. Her mention of Dr. James and the injury to Adoniram's thumb places it in this time period—and April 23 is the closest Monday.

[331] Dr. James was a trusted physician, who attended the students and faculty of the Utica Female Academy. He is mentioned frequently in the correspondence as having been consulted for varying medical complaints, and his advice was always welcomed and highly regarded.

[332] See the letter of Adoniram Judson to Emily E. Chubbuck dated April 16, 1846.

[333] See vol. 1, "Cast of Characters," s.v. "Nemmy, Nem, or Nemmy Petty (Nemmie Pettie)." See also the chapter "Names of Endearment."

[334] There was dialogue over the month about Mrs. Yates. On April 1, Emily spoke of the possibility of their being married in Hamilton and then visiting with Mrs. Yates, who lived far enough away to give them some privacy, but not far enough so as to force an extended journey. On April 17 Emily spoke of some problems Mrs. Yates was having within her church, having been asked not to take communion. Then, in this letter of April 23, Emily said that she heard some things about Mrs. Yates and thought they best not go there. In his April 19 letter Adoniram asked Emily why they wouldn't just stay in Hamilton with her parents if that is where they were to be married.

and here. And they are so very very kind to me here and always have been, that I am anxious to do everything in my power to oblige them and to be with them as much as possible. How would you like to spend the Sabbath here and baptize Anna Maria?[335] I sh'd like to have you do it if you would—provided it met with Mr. Corey's[336] approbation. Being married in Hamilton we couldn't have Mrs. Yates at the wedding you know, as we sh'd have done here, and the change in that respect is a sufficient excuse for the other.

Poor A. M. cries almost all the time and I have got a silly notion today of helping her. Everything seems very forlorn. Please write me a little very often; and pray don't let the big wigs down there tell you that it is wicked to carry a bird on the finger. What would some poor birdies do if there were no strong nice finger for them?

Spread open your arms, dearest—I kiss your lips, your eyes, your forehead, and snuggle down in your bosom—Good-night. Don't move or you will wake me— Good-night, my blessed one.

Thy loving Emily

Source: Hanna family files.

The Reverend Doctor Benjamin H. Hill[337] to Emily E. Chubbuck, April 24, 1846—New York

Dear Friend,

Allow me as an introduction, to remind you of a short but to me very pleasant acquaintance last Autumn, at the home of our good friend and brother A. D. Gillette[338] in Phil. and to say that I claim by [ ] of the foregoing as my youngest "pet." I enclose her declarations of enjoyment in reading the articles from your pen, and regret on account of the probable discontinuance of them. I would add that, as I have sometimes found time to listen as she runs over your "charming immaginationy [sic]" I sincerely share in her regret.

Please accept my congratulations, also for all the prospects of usefulness and happiness before you.

May our heavenly Father guide and support and bless you in their enjoyment.

Yours with Christian regard,

Benj. H. Hill

[335] See vol. 1, "Cast of Characters," s.v. "Anable, Miss Anna Maria."

[336] See vol. 1, "Cast of Characters," s.v. "Corey, the Reverend D. G."

[337] Dr. Benjamin Hill was the secretary of the American Baptist Home Mission Society

[338] See vol. 1, "Cast of Characters," s.v. "Gillette, The Reverend Abram Dunn."

[Note: There is a four line post script that is very difficult to read because of the copy. The following is legible: "which my little girl's letter," and "It was whole when it came from her hands but was accidentally torn since; and as we are about moving [ ] she will immediately after go into the country she will not be able to copy it."]

Source: American Baptist Historical Society, AJ 24, no. 1184.

The Reverend John M. Peck to Emily E. Chubbuck, April 24, 1846—Philadelphia

Miss Emily Chubbuck, My dear sister, your letter proposing certain books, to our Society for publication, of the 11th inst, came to my office during my absence to Boston and Providence. As our rules require all books proposed for publication to be examined and approved by our committee on Publication it will be necessary to have a copy of each before we can act. I have made inquiry and can find no copies of the works proposed.

Bro. Gillette[339] gave his copy to Dr. Judson.[340] He speaks well of the works and I presume they will be approved. Presuming you have copies in Utica, will you please forward a copy of each by mail immediately. For this purpose it will be necessary to tear off the covers so as to convert each book into a pamphlet. In this form, each may be done up in a separate wrapper and addressed to our office 31 North 6th Street. If approved by the Publishing Committee, and I doubt not will be done, I apprehend no difficulty about the percentage in your case.

As I shall retire from the office next week, I will leave the business so that my successor will understand it and have our Committee act promptly.

I hear you are preparing a memoir of the second Mrs. Judson. May I hope our Society will have the publishing of that work on the same terms?[341] When we publish on percentage, the usage is to estimate sales each six months, and credit the author accordingly. For works that will continue to be issued from year to year as yours will, it is better to the author than one payment for copy right. It provides an annuity, that continues so long as the work sells—

I am very respectfully yours

J. M. Peck, Cor. Secy

[339] See vol. 1, "Cast of Characters," s.v. "Gillette, The Reverend Abram Dunn."

[340] As Reverend Gillette and Dr. Judson returned to Philadelphia from Boston, the train ran into some difficulties and was delayed. To help him pass the time, Mr. Gillette gave Dr. Judson a copy of *Trippings in Author-land* to read. Judson became enthralled with the writing style and, finding that the author was both a Christian and a Baptist, resolved to speak to her about the possibility of writing the memoir of Sarah Hall Boardman Judson. They met for the first time on Christmas Day 1845.

[341] The memoir of Sarah Hall Boardman Judson was later published by L. Colby and Company of New York.

P.S. Owing to the press being crowded we have not been able to get "Walter Lowry" out yet. I hope it will be out by May 10th.

J. M. P.

Source: American Baptist Historical Society, AJ 22, no. 1075.

Eliza C. Allen to Emily E. Chubbuck,[342] April 25, 1846[343]—New York

My Dear Miss Chubbuck

I am aware of having treated you very ill, in not answering either of your obliging letters earlier. I was condemning myself for not having replied to the first before the reception of the second. Since that period I have been suffering from a severe cold, and have with great difficulty performed my indispensable labors.

I wish to say so much to you upon the subject of your last letter, mentioned also in your first, that I know not where to begin, or how to express myself as briefly as I must, without danger of being misunderstood.

But first allow me a word in relation to the leading article in the May No. of the *Journal*.[344] You may think that I reflect too severely upon a large class of writers, including yourself. If it will be any amends, I would say, it is my intention to pursue another branch of the subject in the following No., and speak of the accountability of those who *support* such a vast amount of trifling literature.

You will observe that in the article already published I do not base the [ ]ality of light writing upon the ground that it is wrong to write or read *any* light matter, nor shall I use such an argument with the purchase of these trifling words. It is the fact of the already over whelming amount of such matter, and of the existing bia[ ] the reading masses, in a very disproportioned and injurious degree, towards such reading, which in my view, renders it wrong for a Christian to swell the amount of brilliant nothings, or throw additional attractions into the path of light reading, already too seductive.

Will you, dear Miss C., permit me to speak [ ]. You may say I have no right to do so. Personally I have none, I am well aware. But, the function in which I am

[342] In a previous letter of February 21, 1846, Mrs. Allen told Emily that she could not understand why Emily had not been compensated for her work used in the *Mother's Journal*, for she had told her publishers to pay Emily. In the end, Mrs. Allen might have thought that writers should be satisfied to write for her journal because of its high moral ground and that taking care of her writers was not a high priority. Part of her thinking is that in the Christian cause a price is to be paid by everyone, publisher, editor, and writer alike. This view is quite different from Emily's experience with George Graham and John Inman, both of who paid her premium prices because of her name, experience, and excellence as she wrote for *Graham's Magazine*, the *Columbian Magazine*, and the *Knickerbocker Magazine*. Obviously, the writing that Emily did for the public press sold magazines. From the text of this letter, Emily may have pushed Mrs. Allen on the matter of compensation and gave her reasons why she needed the money. She also likely spoke of the high moral tone of what she was writing.

[343] This letter is dated April 25, 1846. At the end of it, Mrs. Allen says that as she finished it, it was May 1, so we understand the letter to be written on and off over the course of seven days. It was postmarked May 4.

[344] Mrs. Allen was the editor of the *Mothers' Journal*, a prominent Christian publication.

placed, the anxiety which the line of my duties and observations has naturally achieved in my mind, upon subjects connected with the training of the young, will perhaps create an apology, and save me from the charge of presuming. It is not, of course, with a view to any practical leaning upon yourself, that I wrote otherwise that as you have it in your power, and will still have, to influence the literary cause of others.

It seems to me that in view of writing for the public, the question is not, at least for a Christian, what will assure the largest compensation, but what will be justifiable, in view of the circumstances of the public, and of the legitimate influence of any given discipline of writing? The use to be made of money does not determine the morality of the deed by which it is obtained. I must think that a pupil debating how to employ her abilities so as to "pay her education bills," "educate her younger sister," or "support herself and her widowed mother"[345] ought first to settle the question, what is right and what is wrong, viewing society and the supply of reading as they are. God will take care of those who do right. In sincerity and industriously following a Christian course, we may safely trust Providence. We are not required to do good with more money than we can get in a Christian manner. Christian labor of any kind is seldom immediately profitable in a pecuniary sense. [Note: The next line is inserted.] My remarks respect those inquirers after their proper field of labor, who are professing Christians. I would not include those who lack religion to put on its semblance, in writing; although, to be *useful* in whatever calling they adopt, should be forced as a duty upon all.

The word "useful" just written, suggests to me thoughts which I have had in reference to your piece entitled "The Unuseful."[346] And as I have begun to "unburthen [*sic*] my mind" I will venture to proceed. Promising that I have no fault to find with the charming Nora,[347] and that I readily admit that [ ] such characters might contribute to swell the sum of human happiness, and that one would rather be like her than [ ] busy sister, allow me to ask, do our girls generally, do our mothers *need* to have industry and usefulness, as qualities in women, made to appear ridiculous? On the other hand, is there not urgent occasion to improve upon mothers and doing [ ] of the present day the *religious* duty of being useful? It may be the mission of none to be useful by soothing, charming, elevating, refining, those around them. But I fear that while our Savior's sentence of condemnation against the *unprofitable* servant stands as an admonition, very many of our females have cause to inquire how *they* will stand before *Him*. Considering the present

---

345 These are likely the quotations from the letter Emily sent to Mrs. Allen that prompted this long and defensive response.

346 The "Unuseful" was written for one of the magazines; it appeared subsequently in *Trippings in Author-land*, vol. 2 of *Alderbrook*, vol. 2 of the revised *Alderbrook*, and *Tales for All Seasons*.

347 The main character in "The Unuseful" was Nora Maylie; there was also a subsequent story with the title "Nora Maylie." Both of these stories appeared in *Trippings in Author-land* and vol. 2 of *Alderbrook*.

habits and notions of large portions of our sex, whatever tends to confirm them in the conceit that it is very pretty to be "unuseful," and very unlovely to be useful, or to be deplored. Women may be useful, and men [ ]ally industrious, without being sordid or mercenary busy bodies [sic]. Some of our best female writers, ladies of great refinement, too, have strongly urged that in a family of daughters the arts of making various kinds of clothing shall be taught—both to the affluent, as a resource in case of reverses, and to those of more limited means, constituting the larger class, and the most likely to look upon the requisition of a "trade" as a disparagement to be practised [sic] in their own homes as a matter of economy. How much will such [ ] effect against the influence of—shall I say it? [ ] the article I have named? And yet, aside from the fact that [ ] existing circumstances, we have crying need for influence, [ ] a directly opposite character, I have not a particle of objection to the price or prices. For somewhat similar reasons I have questioned whether it must not have been wise to introduce a character that *could be loved* of a medium [ ] between "Our Mag" and "Miss Mag"—a character not so sh[ ] [ ]ish and exclusive as that of the latter, yet seeming [ ]mon congruous as the companion of a Minister of Heaven, than that of the former? Not that in "Our Mag" there is any thing [sic] *bad*—but that the tendency of the piece is to turn the scale, in the minds of giddy girls, in favor of trifling—a tendency which is already too strong.— Since I commenced this letter, my eye has fallen upon a piece of yours copied into some newspaper entitled "The Rose-bud." Is it in accordance with evangelical views to represent "Lilian" (I think that is the name) as a "[ ]," an "angel" going to her "sister angels" without the least allusion to religious influence, and when the gay girl went from the "midnight dance" to the grave?

Pardon me again I say—It is an up hill [sic] task that I [ ], or any one who seeks to give mind and habits, at the present day, bias towards the solid and useful; and when Christian writers throw absolutes in the way, altho' they may be loads of beautiful and fragrant flowers, it is painfully disheartening. You are ready to pronounce me cold, soulless, lacking mosicial [sic], austere, destitute of an appreciation of the beautiful or playful, and therefore unwilling to grant their engagement to others. Ask those who know me best, how I am constituted, and what are my views and deportment.—I must not begin to express my sins and the overflowing bounty with which the Creator has given us sources and capabilities of refined enjoyment, and delights in our appropriating and multiplying them. I shall exceed your patience and my own sense of propriety in the length of my letter unless I had written something more agreeable than I can [ ] that this will be. Your remarks in reference to what [ ] considered to be the character of your pieces have been in part the occasion of my writing this. My own anxiety regarding the education of the young, and convictions respecting the requirements of the present age upon Christians have impelled me. If I offend, I shall constitute as [ ] mediator *one* who should have great influence with you and who, I believe, will not be unwilling to use it in my behalf. Do let me know how I stand on your tablet [ ] [ ] early day; and be as candid as I have been.

In answer to your inquiry respecting the two young ladies mentioned, I scarcely know what to say.[348] We have nearly doubled the expense of the *Journal* this year. My husband can give it no attention, to save expense or further its circulation. I am uncertain whether any compensation will remain for me from its receipts. I am supplied by friends of the work, casual contributions, with mother in abundance of certain descriptions. I have three regular paid contributors who furnish me with very pleasant articles, and very good, to whom I give the compensation which works like mine usually give. Not that these are the only paid writers I have—these have written for me from my first engagement. Another such died last year. Others have written more or less.

I do not feel prepared to promise extra compensation to inexperienced, unknown writers much as I should like to hold out inducements to them to enter upon a course of endeavoring to do good. I should like to see some of these pieces, and then I could judge what I could do, and leave it optional with them to accept my terms or not.—It seems to me that the work of [ ] in our literature must be effected by the joint efforts and sacrifices of writers, publishers, and readers. A publisher cannot incur all the risk. And we are not in circumstances to justify an unusual outlay in the expense of publishing.—I am mortified at having been so long in concluding this letter (May 1) but illness is my apology.

Affectionately Yours

Elisa C. Allen

Written in the right margin of the address page: "I find that thro' my illness and consequent delays and temptations in writing this, I have neglected to refer to your proposal to write for the *Journal* an article upon the encouragement of genius, or the lack of this, by the religious community.[349] Do this, I beg of you. There is need of connecting influence somewhere."

Written in the left margin of the address page: "I do not think that Christian people of the same grade in intellect and cultivation with others who do appreciate genius are specially deficient in this respect. But many Christians think genius an un[ ] thing, when not associated with an intrinsically good production. But genius

---

[348] Emily was trying to promote some members of her composition class at the Utica Female Academy. She felt that they had talent and that they could fill in some of the gaps that she was creating with her departure to Burmah. See also the March 3, 1846, letter from Robert West.

[349] Emily offered the *Mother's Journal* an article on "Genius," and she is instructed to send it. It is unclear whether this was ever done for Mrs. Allen, but the *Columbian Magazine* published an article titled "Genius" by Emily Chubbuck in 1846, and this piece was later included in *Alderbrook* and *Tales For All Seasons*.

as a handmaid to Christianity will commend itself to Christians as well as others. Still, this same defect somewhere, they do not sufficiently encourage its ministrations in their own publications. They do in lighter ones."

Source: American Baptist Historical Society, AJ 22, no. 1086.

Mr. Robert A. West to Emily E. Chubbuck, April 28, 1846—South Brooklyn

My dear friend

Is it possible that your last kind letter is dated April 4? And yet it even readeth so, and I must be an incorrigible fellow, for I thought I was going to be something like punctual in replying to said letter. If it were not that I never like to despair where my own amendment is concerned, I should certainly renounce all hope of ever becoming a man of punctual habit. As apology implies something like justification or palliation, and I wish to make an open honest confession that I have not done the thing I ought to have done, I shall ask nothing more than that you will in your goodness *forgive me this time*.

O but I am a worse sinner than I [ ] of for there is your book which you wish to publish "before you *leave*"[350]—I don't like the word "at all, at all"—My conscience will indeed be burdened if I have burdened you in that matter. If you have not done anything in it the following information may be of service to you. Wiley and Patnamus would be a likely house, if you only want a publisher, not intending to dispose of your copy-right, but I happen to know that they have resolved not to publish at their own risk any collection that may have appeared in other channels—to confine themselves to originals in fact. Harpers would give you the best chance of a wide circulation, and Mr. Inman[351] could serve you in that quarter, better than any man I know. Appleton I should think a likely house for the publication of a handsome volume. These three appear to me the best suited for your purpose and next to them, Saxton and Miles. These, supposing you intend to publish in New York—if in Boston or elsewhere I can give you no information except that Ticknor of Boston turns out some well printed books.

---

[350] Emily was looking to publish a second collection of her magazine stories, a sequel to *Trippings in Author-land*. *Alderbrook* was published after she had left for Burmah. Copies of it were sent to Catharine Chubbuck on December 9, 1846. (See letter from Mr. Ticknor December 9, 1846).

[351] John Inman was the editor of the *Commercial Advertiser* and the *Columbian Magazine*, responsibilities that failing health forced him to give up early in 1845. He was Emily Chubbuck's initial contact with the *Columbian Magazine*, which began to publish some of her stories early in 1844. He strongly encouraged Emily in her writing, said that they would publish everything they could get from her, hoped that she would consider writing exclusively for them, and when she asked for it, gave her the unheard of rate of five dollars a page for her articles. When he did that, he candidly stated that with this, they would not consider it fair if she continued to write for N. P. Willis and the *New Mirror* without charge.

If you have no friends here who can do you better service, and wish to open a negotiation with any house and will give me sufficient instructions, most cheerfully will I do anything in my power for you, and will do it without twelve hours delay and communicate at once with you on the subject.

As to the *Columbian*—is the following the correct understanding? That you will write for no other magazines of its class under any signature—that *as Fanny Forester*[352] you will write exclusively for the *Columbian*—and that with these restrictions, you will furnish three or four (your former letter says two or three) articles, during the year at fifty dollars each. If this be understood, we shall be glad to consider it as settled and agreed to. If I misinterpret please inform me—if I do not misinterpret then that business is disposed of.[353]

But again—the Editor of the *New York Recorder* Rev. S. S. Cutting,[354] a personal friend of mine, with whom I have talked about you more than once. I shall not offend your modesty by telling you what we have said about you. Suffice it to say that from him, some time [sic] before it appeared (when it had no business to appear) in the public points, I heard of your probable destination. He wishes to negotiate with you about writing occasionally for his paper. I think he would offer fair terms. I see he has once to [ ] up cudgels in your behalf, though I think it was a work of supererogation. I know however that it was well meant. If you wish it I will desire him to write you a note on the subject.

And now my dear friend, most sincerely do I wish you all happiness in your future path. May God bless you and make you a blessing—may his grace sustain you and his providence encircle you, so that you shall pass unhurt amidst perils by water and by land and ever enjoy in all its length and breadth, its fullness, depth and continuity that perfect peace which passeth mere natural understanding. I knew not until recently that my valued correspondent was one whose heart was turned to serve the Lord and for [ ] hour an inscrutable but ever wise providence has prepared for so inconvenient a station, so desting [sic]

Written perpendicular to and across the text of page 1: "[ ] a part in the operations which by his Church on earth He is so gloriously carrying on."

For the kind and confidential manner in which you communicate what you intended should be news, accept my sincere thoughts, and believe me not a little was I pleased to find that the impertinences perpetuated by a certain Boston

---

[352] Emily Chubbuck as Fanny Forester. See vol. 1, "Cast of Characters," s.v. "Chubbuck, Emily." Also "Forester, Fanny."

[353] See Robert West's letter to Emily of March 3, 1846; this is the exact proposal he made there. *The Columbian*—and the other magazines as well—all had tried to get Emily to write exclusively for them. Compare the fifty dollars for each story or article to the fact that Emily received approximately forty-six dollars for one of her earlier books. Writing for the magazines was far more profitable.

[354] On April 10, 1846, Adoniram quoted Mr. Cutting in a letter to Emily: "Doesn't Mr. Cutting say that 'now the name of the one is seldom separated from that of the other.'" See vol. 1, "Cast of Characters," s.v. "Cutting, Sewell."

paper[355]—the editor of which by the way is an [ ] lady and a perhaps excusable—you understand, tho it would be [ ] [ ] for me for this to explain—that those impertinences have only [ ] your playful sarcasm and gentle piety.

Permit me now that I know a little more about you, to give *you* a short passage of autobiography. I too am a member of a Christian Church—the Methodist Episcopal—a licensed [Note: Text continues perpendicular to and across the text of page 2.] lay preacher in that denomination (though at present "on the shelf" on account of a slight muscular affection or [ ] of the chest) and moreover the son of an English Wesleyan Minister and the brother of another. More-ever if that does not entitle me to a *share* of the "succession" my dear little wife is the daughter of another and the sister has another brother a missionary in New Zealand and a sister the wife of a missionary in the Island of Ceylon. Can you doubt that as your [ ] friend, I feel a lively interest in your future career. To tell you the truth one reason why I have delayed writing you was to have a longish talk with you out of my heart though pressure of business after all compels to write in a hurry and in a scrawl you will scarcely be able to read. I had the pleasure [Note: Text continues perpendicular to and across the text of page 3.] of seeing Dr. Judson during my attendance at the session of the Baptist Convention in this city. Shall it be taking too great a liberty in obtaining an introduction to him through my friend Mr. Cutting at the coming convention. And shall *you* be *there* during that convention? When I saw you last I had been up all night with a sick friend and had not been home to dress and my strong desire to see you alone influenced me to forget all that. But however I should like to see you once more, at least before you leave, and if you do not visit New York do not be surprised if I visit Utica before you "leave." Whether I do or not be assured of this that no one of your friends will watch with more kindly interest your future career or more sincerely [Note: Text continues perpendicular to and across the text of page 4.] offer up to our common Father the giver of all consolation unceasing prayer, that all the blessings both of the upper and the nether springs will be abundantly bestowed upon you and him who [ ] will ere long be your earthly support, whose wisdom shall be your earthly [ ] and with whom you will [ ] long share in sweetest sympathy your hopes and fears, your joys and sorrows. May God bless your union my friend, may God bless you ever.

Yours very sincerely and truly

Robert A. West

Source: American Baptist Historical Society, AJ 27, no. 1298.

[355] On April 3, Emily sent Adoniram a copy of a *Boston Transcript* article that had appeared in the *New York Express*. It spoke against missionaries who exposed their wives to untold hardships in foreign lands, leading to certain death.

Ms Martha Russell to Emily E. Chubbuck April 28, 1846—Port Drumford

Dear Miss Chubbuck,—no, no, Dear Fanny Forester[356] for under that name I have learned to love you. As a stranger I should not venture to address you, but they tell me that you are going to the golden Orient where "Eden's Pleasance was" and I cannot let you go without expressing to you my heartfelt thanks for the pleasures which I have experienced in reading your tales,—and, not for the pleasure only, but for the kind, gentle and truthful lessons,—for the deep, earnest and beautiful thoughts which they contain.

I feel assured that you will pardon this liberty, when I remind you of that intense yearning, which we feel after reading the productions of those gifted souls, whose beautiful and truthful words cast light on the dim pathway of life, to go to them and express our deep and sincere gratitude, to tell them that, to one human soul, at least,—

> "Earth seems more sweet to live again;
> More full of love because of them."

It must be sweet to anyone, whatever be their position in life, to know that they have raised within one heart promptings of a higher and better life, that they have strengthened the weary and care worn, or made [ ] and beauty more holy— more attractive to the thoughtless head of youth, and I know you will not refuse the thanks, of a village girl like me.

Permit me to say that you are no stranger at my mother's cottage and to one who can heartily sympathize with sweet "Rosa Vaughan"[357] in her admiration of pink [ ], and has followed her with a healing heart to its miserable dwelling of poor "Ellen," and wept with her over their desolation and distress;—who has turned with a glad heart from the glowing factory with little, highhanded "Gracy Linden" [sic] and sat by her side while she shaped the apron for her beaux protector, "Harry Russel,"—who has followed her with intense interest through those painful trials that brought out her noble qualities and made her what she was—a high souled, conscious woman; one who has mineralized and botanized with dear, good "Uncle Hilling" and lain on the sunny bank with beautiful "Ida Ravelin" and watched the flitting clouds, while the solemn shadow of Ideal Beauty stole over the green earth and consecrated it anew unto God,—to me, who has *lived* all this, you can never be a stranger.

---

[356] Emily Chubbuck as Fanny Forester. See vol. 1, "Cast of Characters," s.v. "Chubbuck, Emily"; and "Forester, Fanny."

[357] All of the characters mentioned in this paragraph are from the stories by Fanny Forester.

It is selfish of me I suppose to regret that you are about to leave the country, but if your heart bids you go, dear lady, may God bless you on your way and forever bless both you and yours.

Respectly and affect yours

Martha Russell

"Miss Fanny Forester"[358]

P.S. As I am ignorant of your address this will reach you through the hands of our excellent friends, Messer's Inman and West.[359]

Yours M. Russell

Source: American Baptist Historical Society, AJ 26, no. 1281.

The Reverend Doctor Solomon Peck to Emily E. Chubbuck, April 30, 1846—Boston

My dear Miss Chubbuck,

I seldom begin a letter with more embarrassment than now. If I understand my motives, they are right, honorable, kind, disinterested. And they are all but compulsory. I cannot forbear addressing you, without doing violence both to my feelings and judgment. Yet how far I may presume on our brief acquaintance, though exceedingly frank and generous on your part, and how far, if at all, I may be allowed from my public official relations to speak *unofficially* as a friend and Christian brother—and in what words to convey to your mind *just* what I mean and *no more*, this is, in part, my problem. The truth is, I feel too deeply on the subject, and too variously, to speak at all if I could help it. I pray you that whatever I do say, may not harm you.

The simple thought that has filled my mind and which I wish to convey to you, is the *one thing* mentioned by Paul—Forgetting the things *that are behind and reaching forth to the things that are before.*—I believe you have a right to do this—to count but *loss* what was *gain* to you; to *act on the principle* embodied by our Savior in the words *Let the dead bury the dead.* Oh what emotions, how many, how varied, how weighty, constrain to this—in *your* case above any I have ever known—your past history, your present relations, and those about to be formed—the excited interest, yet exceedingly diverse, in the social and Christian worlds—the new field

---

[358] Emily Chubbuck as Fanny Forester. See vol. 1, "Cast of Characters," s.v. "Chubbuck, Emily," and "Forester, Fanny."

[359] John Inman and Robert West were editors of the *Columbian Magazine*. Mr. West took responsibility as Mr. Inman had to limit his activities because of health concerns. Both had been strong supporters of Emily as she wrote for the *Columbian*, offering her compensation at the highest level.

for exertion opening upon you—the [ ], *and* consequences of failing to make full proof of your opportunities.

I cannot allude to these things in detail. I can express to *no* human being *all* I think and feel in regard to them. And I would not express what I do to *you* by way of alarm, or even of warning, but except to indicate the height of your calling and to lead you to the feet of your Redeemer and Lord—and especially to illustrate the preciousness of your privilege, and your *right to improve it*,—to give yourself to *prayer*. The Lord Jesus *only* can help you. And *He can* make all grace abound unto you, so that you shall have *all sufficiency in all things*.

In reviewing what I have written I am a little apprehensive that my words may seem to imply an inaccurate distrust. This is not my meaning. I choose for the future *the bright side*. I am full of hope. I say most emphatically—the goal is before you. I only wish *one* impression to be made, and to be cherished by you, that you must "so run, not as uncertainly;" and that you above most others are exposed to the temptation, or rather to the embarrassment, of former engagements. But there is a remedy—a safeguard—and it is in your own favour [*sic*]. You *can*, God helping you, cast the bonds asunder that bind you to the past, not consenting ever to *look* back.

The sentiments I have expressed have of course an influence with me in regard to the republication of the book which you put into my hands on leaving you.[360] I read it with interest and pleasure; yet you will pardon me for saying there would be a feeling of incongruity if I should be active, in my present position in bringing it before the public; and more especially I should fear that, in so doing, I should help to defeat the very object which has focused so heavily upon my mind, and in view of which I have contrived to form this letter. And I see *no necessity* for burdening your mind with these matters. Surely you have enough to occupy your mind and heart the few weeks you are to remain in this country. And are you not authorized—invited, in the circumstances as Providence has arranged them—to cast your care as on God, and to *believe*, with a childlike simplicity of faith, that if you will do His work and leave yours to Him, *He will abide faithful*.

Respectfully and sincerely
Your friend and brother
Solomon Peck

Source: American Baptist Historical Society, AJ 25, no. 1224.

---

[360] From her letter of May 8, 1846, we learn that the book to which Dr. Peck is referring is *Allen Lucas*. Apparently, it did not meet the high theological, moralistic, biblical standards of Dr. Peck. His feelings about it no doubt prompted the letter.

LETTERS

—⁓—

MAY-JUNE 1846

Anna Maria Anable to Emily E. Chubbuck May 3, 1846—Utica

Miss Nemmy[1] Chub

I should like to know what's going on there at Hamilton that all the time from Tuesday to Sunday should pass by without my *getting* a single line. [ ] a day! how these people have changed. Time *was* when a letter came every day—but now—hang the Dr.! I wish he'd make you behave. We shall expect you on Tuesday and I'll try and restrain my curiosity till then tho' if there don't [*sic*] come a letter from you tomorrow Miss—I shall tell the Dr. to "do something to you."

I am dying to know what sort of a time you have had and particularly what all this raft of letters is about; especially do I want to know what brother Solomon[2] says. Your letter was enclosed in one to Amelia in which he says he read every book she gave him before he got to Boston,[3] and he cried over little Mollie White.[4] Think of that Master Brooke! The sec. of the A. B. B. F. M. crying over a story of Fanny Forester.[5]

Tell it not in Gath! (which means Bethel) nor let it reach the ears of Mr. Corey[6] or else.—Mr. Peck will certainly have to be removed from his responsible station, which would be a dreadful trying circumstance to you and the Dr. I know. He is so considerate and friendly to you. Why he can't do enough for brother and

---

[1] "Nem" or "Nemmy" was a name of endearment given to Emily by a small group of her intimate friends at the Utica Female Academy. Anna Maria Anable was "Ninny."

[2] The Reverend Doctor Solomon Peck was for twenty years the executive secretary of the American Baptist Missionary Union. Many believed him to be hard, stern, and judgmental, and from some of his comments, it is easy to understand that perception. Dr. Peck and Emily did not always have the easiest of relationships. She felt in him the judgment that came from many in the church at the announcement of her impending marriage to Adoniram; that judgment concerned her "secular" past and concern that she was not an appropriate companion for the venerable missionary. On July 18, 1849 Emily wrote a blistering letter of defense to Dr. Peck in response to a letter from him of February 20, 1849; her letter framed how she viewed his perception of her, and her response was meant to set the record straight. There are eleven letters in the collection from Solomon Peck to Emily.

[3] Solomon Peck visited the Utica Female Academy toward the end of April to meet with Lydia Lillybridge as a candidate for the mission field. Adoniram Judson wrote on April 20 to say that he was coming and that they should be prepared. While there, he also planned to meet with Emily.

[4] A story written by Emily as Fanny Forester. It was to appear in vol. 1 of *Alderbrook*.

[5] Emily Chubbuck wrote under the *nom de plume* Fanny Forester. Asked about it once, she said, "Would anyone buy a book written by Emily E. Chubbuck?" While Dr. Peck is favorable to Emily's fiction in these comments by Anna Maria, in his letter of April 30, 1846, to Emily, he expresses regret about one of her books and does not feel that the Mission Board could release it. On May 8, 1846, we learn from Emily that this was a reference to *Allen Lucas*.

[6] Mr. Corey was the pastor of the Bleecker Street Baptist Church near the Utica Female Academy, and Miss Sheldon and many of the girls from the academy attended worship there. (Cynthis Sheldon, Alma Anable, Deacon Asa and Isabell Sheldon, Edward Bright, and Horace Hawley had been charter members of the church in 1838.) In April 1844, he wrote to Emily expressing dismay that at a school program one of the girls had read a composition justifying dancing as exercise; he spoke of this as a roadblock to the salvation of many. Then, on March 10, 1846, Emily indicated in a letter to Anna Maria that Mr. Corey had been critical of her relationship and impending marriage to Adoniram Judson. Miss Cynthia Sheldon wrote a number of times expressing Mr. Corey's regret and support, and in 1847, there were letters of reconciliation between Emily and Mr. Corey. In spring 1848, letters reveal that Mr. Corey's wife had died of consumption, her condition exacerbated by recent child-birth. She had left behind four children. In July 1849, Anna Maria Anable wrote of his impending marriage to Jane Backus, a good choice for this "rising man." Mr. Corey remained popular with the Sheldon-Anable families even after their move to Philadelphia in 1848. A March 2, 1852, letter from Charles B. Stout told of Mr. Corey's call to the Stanton Street Church in New York City, which Mr. Corey did not accept. Finally, in 1854, there was a pastoral letter from Mr. Corey to Emily on her illness and her possible death. He preached at the Bleecker Street Church as late as January 1867.

sister (?) [Note: The inserted question mark is original to the letter.] Judson—just now can he?

Nem I have been so good all day that I feel a little inclined to be wicked tonight. We had in our church a most delightful missionary prayer meeting this evening. There was a sailor there who had just come from the S[ ]thain islands—a good pious man and he gave us a great deal of information about the mission there and then the deacons prayed—so feelingly. O, I never can leave all those good folks and go among such a set of heathen as they are at Bethel.

Think of it. They haven't had a monthly concert in two years. And if they should have one think of such men as Hawley[7] and Backus[8] or the "poor [ ]" to lead your devotions. I have been reading Madam Adams and think strongly of becoming a Catholic. All those books that I like best were written by Catholics and if forms are of so much consequence I may as well have enough of them. Nem I have always had a great fancy for the Quakers who reject all forms, and believe in a real spiritual religion. If Madame Adams had not been in the way I should have read your Swedenborgine [sic] tracts today. What do you suppose all this hubbub that's raised on my little [ ] will end in? Smoke, I dare say. I wish you would come home, Lydia[9] has gone and you have gone, and I am left all alone, the "lost leaf." I wander from one room to the other and over to Lydia's and then back again. All, everything is [ ]. Eugenia[10] has gone to spend a week with Mary Spencer.[11] L[ ] Avery and her sister Kitty came Friday. She has not come up into our room yet. We

---

[7] Mr. Horace H. Hawley enjoyed a family relationship with the Sheldon family. Emily's letter on May 7, 1841, indicates that he was to marry a niece of Misses Cynthia and Urania Sheldon and Mrs. Alma Sheldon Anable, the daughter of their brother John Sheldon. Through the help of Miss Cynthia Sheldon, he was introduced into the life of Emily Chubbuck. A member of a publishing firm, he also worked with Alexander Beebee in publishing the *Baptist Register*. Beginning in 1841 with the publication of *Charles Linn*, Mr. Hawley was enormously helpful to Emily Chubbuck as she published her early stories and books. There are numerous references to his help and his generosity.

[8] Bennett, Backus, and Hawley had published some of Emily's earlier books.

[9] Lydia Lillybridge was one of Emily's closest friends at the Utica Female Academy. When Emily made the decision to go to Burmah as the wife of Adoniram Judson and as a missionary, Lydia wanted to go with them. Emily spoke to Adoniram Judson of Lydia's extraordinary abilities, and Adoniram advocated her appointment before Dr. Solomon Peck and the Board of the American Baptist Missionary Union. Lydia was commissioned to go with them, in spite of the fact that she remained single. Always independent, outspoken, and unafraid to cause ripples in the missionary community, Lydia served on the mission field for twenty-eight years. She married missionary Thomas Simons in May 1851. See the timeline on the life and service of Lydia Lillybridge Simons in vol. 1.

[10] Eugenia Damaux was part of Emily's intimate circle of friends at the Utica Female Academy. Living in New York City, Eugenia suffered from some kind of eye problem that at times made life difficult for her; this was a matter of comment in many of the letters exchanged between the girls themselves and with Miss Cynthia Sheldon. In 1848, Eugenia was in New York living "at Mrs. Brown's—the same warm-hearted French girl as ever." In 1849, she married Johnny Edmonds, described as rich and pious, and they lived in Utica.

[11] On February 28, 1848, Anna Maria Anable wrote to Emily, saying, "Mary Spencer has just returned from Albany. It is said she is engaged to John James, a handsome young widower with three children, and two or three hundred thousand $'s."

---

have been cleaning house in the upper region. I had a nice letter from E. Joselyn[12] yesterday.

Do come as soon as you can, for I am terribly lonely, and besides we shall have no visit from the Dr. if you don't come soon. Give love to all your folks. What with stopping to look into the future a little bit and to "give [ ] my feelings" it has got to be the [ ] of night. Adieu.

Ninny[13]

Source: American Baptist Historical Society, AJ 23, no. 1157.

Paine and Burgess to Emily E. Chubbuck May 3, 1846—New York

Miss Emily Chubbuck

Dear Madam

Your favor of the 26th ult. we have recd—We can date our check on the Bank of the State of N. York payable to your order for Forty-four 19/100 Doll being [ ] due you for copyright to the 1st May inst per statement already rendered.[14]

In reply to your proposition for further publication of your writings, we have to say we are disinclined to increase our Miscellaneous publications. We prefer to reduce them and confine our selves [sic] to what has been our chief business—School Books.

Under these circumstances we cannot make arrangements with you for the notes you propose.[15]

When you find a publisher for those you have in hand we will sell them the plates of *Trippings* at a fair price—We may find a publisher ourselves. If so will advise you.

---

[12] Mrs. Josslyn was associated with Emily at the Academy in Utica. Her letters are filled with references to people they both knew. At the time of the second letter, she was living in Michigan. Her husband had just sold their farm, and they were thinking of moving into town. They were uncertain about the future, but Mr. Josslyn had a business of making buggy whips. Though this letter was written in January, Mrs. Josslyn did not have any idea that Emily had been in Philadelphia for the previous two months for her health.

[13] "Ninny" was a name of endearment given to Anna Maria Anable by her most intimate friends at the Utica Female Academy. Emily was "Nemmy."

[14] The first statement was rendered on February 18, 1846, in the amount of $46.19, which means that through this point Emily would have received $90.38 for *Trippings in Author-land*. In the meantime, she was negotiating with the magazines—and the *Columbian* agreed to meet her requirements—that she would receive fifty dollars for any of her articles published. See the letter from Robert West dated March 3, 1846. Writing for the magazines was much more remunerative to Emily than publishing books, and this again was a reinforcement of what she had learned in 1844 when she first began writing so seriously for the magazines.

[15] Apparently, after the publication of *Trippings in Author-Land*, Emily was looking ahead to what eventually was published as *Alderbrook*, which Paine and Burgess did not want to handle. There is a letter from Robert West of the *Columbian Magazine* (April 28, 1846) that gave her some suggestions for publishers, including the Boston firm of Ticknor, which eventually did publish the volumes.

We hope your *Trippings* to another country may be both pleasant and profitable,[16] and that your real name may be so strongly linked to the fictitious, as to add to the popularity of your already popular writings.

We shall be glad to hear from you, at any time, especially if you find a publisher who wants to have your writings uniform.

We hope to sell the balance of the Edition of *Trippings in Author-Land* before the 1st July next. I shall then make you a further statement.

Respectfully Your Obt Sevt

Paine and Burgess

Source: American Baptist Historical Society, AJ 25, no. 1222.

The Reverend Abram Dunn Gillette to Emily E. Chubbuck, May 5, 1846[17]—Philadelphia

Very dear friend Emily

I forward enclosed in a newspaper a proof of yourself, and I trust you will pronounce it good.

Sartain[18] will make any alternations you suggest. I intend to tell him to give the right side of the neck a little more curve—indeed it is now straight as you perceive.

Shall I offer to arrange with Graham[19] or Godey,[20] or the *Columbian*[21] for its insertion with a brief sketch of yourself[22]—better than any that has as yet appeared—not excepting the *New York Recorder*—by the way I offered him what I

[16] They are obviously aware that Emily will be leaving the country shortly to go to Burmah as a missionary.

[17] An addendum to this letter by Mrs. Hannah Gillette appears as the next letter in the correspondence.

[18] John Sartain was one of the most prominent engravers of the mid-nineteenth century. His works appeared in elegant magazines and books. In 1846, he created an engraving of Emily E. Chubbuck that was used as a plate for *Alderbrook*. The correspondence of spring 1846 reflects meetings with Mr. Sartain on changes thought to be needed. In 1849, Mr. Sartain was publishing a magazine because a letter makes a reference to one of Emily's poems being in it.

[19] George Graham was the editor of *Graham's Magazine*, one of the preeminent literary magazines of Emily's time. He took an interest in Emily Chubbuck as Fanny Forester; he mentored her and published every piece of writing that she could submit to him, and for it all, he remunerated her with the astounding sum of five dollars a page. In April 1845, when Emily was staying in Philadelphia with the Reverend and Mrs. A. D. Gillette, Mr. and Mrs. Graham were frequent visitors, often inviting Emily to tour parts of the city with them in their elegant carriage. That relationship picked up again when Emily returned to Philadelphia in fall 1845.

[20] *Godey's Lady's Book* was one of the high end magazines of the mid-nineteenth century. It contained poetry and articles and always included lavish illustrations of fashion and landscape.

[21] *The Columbian Magazine*, under the leadership of John Inman and then Robert West, was one of Emily's earliest publishers. Early on, they agreed to pay Emily five dollars a page, and the other magazines fell into line at that rate. On several occasions, they asked her to write exclusively for them. On March 3, 1846, Robert West offered to publish the picture, but he hated to see it as a "farewell" because he could not deal with the fact that her leaving was "forever." He then offered her fifty dollars per article for any work that she would submit, asking for an exclusive in the future of anything she would produce.

[22] Emily had been talking of a "farewell" piece to be placed in one of the magazines. It would include a picture of herself and a caption. One suggestion was: "Henceforth to loftier purposes, I pledge myself [signed] Fanny Forester."

wrote [ ] published in the *North American* and Neal,[23] but he preferred his own—very natural.—Surely—

Well you will see in the *Courier* which I forward you, that I am indeed your own true knight and the [ ] also I mean to be—Miss Trevers are here [*sic*], speak in rapturous terms of the whole affair.

I hear good Dr. Kendrick[24] is ill again, I hope the venerable man will revive and recover—do give him my most respectful regards. Should Heaven remove the dear patriarch I shall be looking out for a call on a certain solemn and *holy* and happy occasion.[25]

How do you endure to see and hear all—O it must be a luxury to look by faith on the broad blue ocean and anticipate a release there from all the confusion, and vexation consequent upon a preparation, and then that dear little home in Maulmain. O shall I step in some time [*sic*] and take tea—? no palace on earth would so enchant me—your own little self at my *left* hand then, as you will have become another right hand Wo-man then—? [*sic*] Well we will think about it, because there is some innocent pleasure in that and why not have it—a [ ] is worth a great deal, if it be enjoyed with the right circle around us. We had a fine visit from Dr. and Mrs. Nott,[26] who with Bishop Dolter speak highly of the providential arrangement.

I do not know if I shall be able to get the Dr's Bible and his and your other books ready to take with me to New York but if I do not I shall either take them

---

[23] Joseph Neal was a prominent member of the literary establishment in Philadelphia and became a part of Emily Chubbuck's circle of friends when she was there. Neal was well known and respected as a writer and editor; one of his best known works was the *Charcoal Sketches*. In 1842, he founded the *Saturday Gazette*, a successful publication that contained a great deal of humorous satire. Anna Maria Anable frequently referred to Neal as a beau for Emily. Mr. Neal married Alice Bradley in 1846; he died in 1847.

[24] When Emily Chubbuck was in her teens, Dr. Nathaniel Kendrick was the pastor of the Baptist church in Eaton and also a professor in a local theological school; he eventually became the president of the Hamilton Literary and Theological Institution. At that time in her life, Emily spoke with him about becoming a missionary. Dr. Kendrick gave her the wise counsel of discernment, patience, and waiting. Adoniram and Emily turned to Dr. Kendrick to officiate at their marriage. He married Adoniram and Emily on June 2, 1846. A. C. Kendrick, in *the Life and Letters of Mrs. Emily C. Judson*, says that the marriage of Emily and Adoniram Judson was the last service for which Dr. Kendrick was able to leave his home. Other correspondents mention his continued frailty. He died on September 11, 1848.

[25] There had been some previous difficulty over the choice of who would officiate at the wedding of Adoniram Judson and Emily Chubbuck. Several, including the Reverend Gillette, thought they had an entitlement to the duty, and through a misunderstanding, some hard feelings were expressed. Adoniram said something to Emily about Mr. Gillette not being interested in being involved because of his schedule, and when Emily wrote and expressed this, it was obvious that Adoniram Judson misunderstood. It seems to have been straightened out, and the correspondence reflects that fact, but it is quite obvious that in this paragraph Reverend Gillette is again fishing for the opportunity.

[26] Urania Sheldon was the literary principal of the Utica Female Academy in fall 1840 when Emily Chubbuck came to study there. Emily was able to afford this wonderful education through the generous offer of Miss Sheldon and her sister Cynthia, the executive and financial head of the academy, to defer tuition. Urania Sheldon left in late summer 1842 upon her marriage to the Reverend Doctor Eliphalet Nott, the president of Union College in Schenectady, New York. Because of the distance separating them, Emily's relationship with Urania Sheldon Nott did not develop the intimacy that grew between Emily and Miss Cynthia Sheldon. Urania Sheldon Nott remained a mentor, advisor, and friend to Emily in the years of her writing, her missionary endeavors, and upon her return to America in 1851. She was also the aunt of Anna Maria Anable.

into Boston when you sail on send them then on some time before. Mrs. G.[27] is arranging and will speak for herself—I have talked with Lippincott but he hesitates—the Palm Society will give you and the Dr. twelve and a half percent for all for all the religious works you will furnish[28]—why not get a Book or your religious Scraps of poetry and prose for our Society[29]—do it—can be done easily—I will select and arrange them if I can have the papers or pieces—

As much love as ever, and ever increasing to you and yours the dear man of Burmah

A. D. Gillette

Source: American Baptist Historical Society, AJ 24, no. 1194.

Mrs. Hannah Gillette to Emily E. Chubbuck, May 5, 1846[30]

My dear Emily—Mr. G. has left me a small space to occupy on this sheet, and I am obliged as there are a few suggestions which I would like to make—I requested you in my letter to furnish us with a list of articles[31]—and you was [sic] kind enough to do so, but with a sort of hesitancy which I did not expect—I will certainly get all the articles you mention—but I am confidant you was [sic] not frank in suggesting *what you want*—*please do so* and write me soon.

[ ] [ ] [ ] [ ] [ ] [ ]

H. L. Gillette

Written in the right margin of the address page: "I dreamed out a nice cunning idea the other day when I was snoozing with Danny[32]—to get your loving and kind friend Mrs. Tyndale[33] to give you a pretty china tea set—tell me if you like the idea,

---

[27] Hannah Gillette was the wife of the Reverend A. D. Gillette, pastor of the Eleventh Baptist Church in Philadelphia. Emily stayed with them when she came to Philadelphia in spring 1845 for her health, and she returned in November. In the parlor of their home, she met Adoniram Judson on Christmas Day 1845. Mr. and Mrs. Gillette became strong friends and supporters; Mrs. Gillette played an important part in getting Emily's outfit together for her life in Burmah.

[28] Emily was searching for a publisher for a successor to *Trippings in Author-land*. It would contain all of the new material she had written since that time and eventually would come out as *Alderbrook*, published by Ticknor, Reed and Fields of Boston.

[29] Mr. Gillette served on the Board of the American Baptist Publication Society. He was helpful in working with Emily on the projected series on the Ten Commandments, only some of which were published. He later lobbied Emily intently—and unsuccessfully—for the right of the Publication Society to publish the memoir of Dr. Judson.

[30] This letter appeared as an addendum to a May 5, 1846 letter written by the Reverend A. D. Gillette.

[31] When Emily made her decision to accompany Adoniram Judson to Burmah, much of the task of pulling together her outfit was assigned to Miss Cynthia Sheldon and Mrs. Hannah Gillette.

[32] Daniel Gillette was the fourth of six children born to the Reverend and Mrs. Gillette

[33] Sarah Tyndale was the mother of Mrs. Mitchell of Philadelphia. A successful businesswoman, she ran a large store in Philadelphia that specialized in china. She lived with her daughter and her family. In fall 1845, as Emily went to Philadelphia for her health, the Mitchells were active in inviting her to stay with them. They offered her a room, as much privacy or company as she desired, and all of the benefits of their extended household. On February 9, 1846, Emily recorded the gift of a china inkstand from Mrs. Tyndale. There is one letter in the correspondence from Sarah Tyndale, dated April 19, 1846 with an April 20 addendum.

and there will be no difficulty in taking them—give much love to Fanny[34] and tell her I will answer her letter as soon as I can conveniently—[ ] is quite sick and I find my [Note: Written in the left margin of the address page.] hands quite full of business—give much love to the Dr. if he [ ] for it—but I presume your love is all he craves or is anxious to obtain—I am rejoicing on your account that Miss Lillybridge[35] is to accompany you—how nice that will be for you—just the thing—how I should long to see you in your new home in Burmah but this [ ] must be [ ] your [ ] [ ]."

H. L. Gillette

Source: American Baptist Historical Society, AJ 24, no. 1194.

Emily E. Chubbuck to Anna Maria Anable, May 6, 1846[36]

Dear Ninny,[37]

I have tried and tried and tried to get a minute to write you but I can't and you must'nt [sic] expect it.—The Doctor has concluded to stay here one Sunday more, for he must give a little time to Eaton and Morrisville. Father[38] and mother[39] were members of the Eaton church more than twenty years and Morrisville is the only *religious* home that I have ever had. I was baptized there and remained a member until I removed to Bethel about two years ago. The doctor is delighted with the Hamilton people and I must say that I never saw a set of folks behave so beautifully in my life. They are very kind and attentive, but don't annoy us one particle. Then he is very much pleased with the way they treat me—no fussing about it—

---

[34] Fanny Anable was one of nine children born to Joseph and Alma Anable and was a niece of Miss Cynthia Sheldon and Mrs. Urania Sheldon Nott. The correspondence indicates that in April 1845 she was away from home studying and taking music lessons. These spring letters indicate that she was in Philadelphia, working in the home of and with the family of the Reverend A. D. Gillette. See Miss Sheldon's letter to Emily of November 30, 1845, in which she spoke of all that Fanny was doing to improve herself in the field of music, but also her concern for Fanny's interest in the party life and the "vanitie" which surround her." A March 30, 1847 letter from Anna Maria Anable told of Fanny's conversion following her grandmother's death. In September 1847, she was listed as one of the teachers at the Utica Female Academy. Fanny became a teacher with her sisters in the Misses Anable's School in Philadelphia.

[35] See vol. 1, "Cast of Characters," s.v. "Lillybridge, Miss Lydia." Also the chapter "Lydia Lillybridge Simons."

[36] This letter is undated. By a process of elimination, and knowing that Adoniram Judson was away from Emily by at least May 17, this date fits best.

[37] Anna Maria Anable. See vol. 1, "Cast of Characters," s.v. "Ninny."

[38] Emily's father, Charles Chubbuck, was born at Bedford, New Hampshire on March 3, 1780; he was married to Lavinia Richards in Goffstown, New Hampshire on November 17, 1805. They were to have seven children. Though he held varying jobs over the years, he failed at many of them, and Emily was the main support of the family after she purchased a home for her family in fall 1842.

[39] Emily's mother, Lavinia Richards Chubbuck, was born June 1, 1785, at Goffstown, New Hampshire, the eldest of thirteen children. She married Charles Chubbuck on November 17, 1805, at Goffstown, New Hampshire. Four of her children were born at Goffstown, and moved with Charles and Lavinia Chubbuck to Eaton, New York in September 1816; they were Lavinia, Benjamin, Harriet, and John Walker. Sarah Catharine, Emily, and Wallace were all born in Eaton.

respectful and affectionate. Doctor Kendrick[40] is evidently delighted. The old man sits and laughs more heartily than I ever heard him before. He says he has always believed I would be a missionary.

We have some engagement every day, but are not otherwise troubled. To be sure people call frequently, but we have not had a single *long* call yet. Hurrah for Hamilton! I say! It beats all places yet for a very flattering sort of propriety.

Please tell Miss Guin that Miss Whiffur's waist is too short in the back. The skirt is also short and the cape I hav'nt [*sic*] been able to wear. Kate[41] is just making it over. I am sorry I did'nt [*sic*] bring my bettermost silk.

We shall be back in Utica on Monday and on Wednesday the doctor will leave for N.Y. Tell Mrs. Avery and Eugenia[42] to *hold on*. Perhaps Eugenia would be ready to go on Wed. and like a beau.

I am very sorry that we can't come back sooner but it is impossible. I have had a terrible time with my teeth since I came home, and they are aching very hard now. I have taken cold in them.

Please write—do; and believe me ever

Your loving

Nemmy[43]

The Doc. sends love to all A. M.[44] especially. We took dinner at my cousin's in Eaton yesterday and at Underhill[45] we tea'd it. Had a most delightful time. To-night we go to Prof. Maginnis' and I must [ ] and dress. I do wish you were here. It is just as dry as it can be.

Source: Hanna family files.

[40] See vol. 1, "Cast of Characters," s.v. "Kendrick, Dr. Nathaniel."

[41] Sarah Catharine Chubbuck, "Kate," "Kit," or "Kitty" was Emily's older sister by ten months. Outside of the two terms at the Utica Female Academy, which Emily arranged for her, Catharine always lived at home with her parents in Hamilton, New York. The letters indicate opportunities for marriage, but she, for unknown reasons, remained single. She later helped to care for Henry and Edward Judson after their return from Burmah in fall 1851 when they moved into the Hamilton home with their "aunt" and "grandparents," and she was remembered by them as "dear old Aunt Kate—a dear friend."

[42] See vol. 1, "Cast of Characters," s.v. "Damaux, Eugenia."

[43] Emily Chubbuck. See vol. 1, "Cast of Characters," s.v. "Nemmy, Nem, or Nemmy Petty (Nemmie Pettie)." Also the chapter "Names of Endearment."

[44] Anna Maria Anable was the niece of the Misses Urania and Cynthia Sheldon and the daughter of Joseph and Alma Sheldon Anable. Emily first met Anna Maria in fall 1840 when she went as a student to the Utica Female Academy; both Emily and Anna Maria became members of the faculty there. In these years, Anna Maria became Emily's dearest friend, and the extensive correspondence between the two reflects sensitive, flirtatious spirits and a deep intimacy. Emily was "Nemmy" to Anna Maria's "Ninny." In 1848, Anna Maria Anable, with the help of her extended family, moved to Philadelphia and started the Misses Anable's School in Philadelphia. At Emily's death in 1854, Anna Maria was given guardianship of Emily Frances Judson, daughter of Emily and Adoniram Judson.

[45] Underhill Cottage was an idealic setting near Hamilton and the little village of Alder-brook; it is a site that Emily immortal-ized in her piece "Underhill Cottage," which was printed in *Trippings in Author-land*.

[46] See the letter of the Reverend A. D. Gillette to Emily E. Chubbuck dated May 5, 1846.

Emily E. Chubbuck to The Reverend Abram Dunn Gillette, May 8, 1846—Hamilton

My Dear Mr. Gillette,—

I received yours,[46] together with the engraving[47] and newspaper, this morning. You are so very kind that I do not know how to thank you enough. I like your suggestion about curving the neck more. There is also too much of a dimple in the chin, though perhaps not more than in the painting. The nose, as I have often said before, is too pointed, a little too long, perhaps, at the tip, and, where it joins the face, a little bit too narrow. It gives the whole face a sharp look. Yet I do not know as it would be best to touch it. I wish, however, that something could be done to subdue and soften down the expression of the whole thing. It is quite too spirited—not so meek-looking as I fancy myself to be. The amount of the whole is, the picture is a grand one—beautifully painted and very beautifully engraved—but precious little, if at all, like me, except in the outline—not the least particle in expression. However, I do not care; it is as like, I suppose, as engravings usually are, and I would rather be flattered than caricatured, as Dr. J. is. Please have no name attached to it; neither my old true name, nor my intended new one. I have concluded not to have any loose engravings out (at least until I leave the country), but reserve the picture for my "Fanny Forester"[48] sketches. For the same reason I do not wish it to appear in any magazine.

I thank you for your warm, kind interest; but I am not troubled now by what people say. Indeed, I never in my life before was so perfectly indifferent to any thing relating to myself. I am very happy in my new prospects—though there are terrible sacrifices close at hand—and in my happiness I can afford to hear the wind blowing around me. It is all wind—"only that and nothing more." Do not be troubled for me. "If God be for us, who can be against us?" I feel in my very soul that I have the approbation of God in this step; and really the approval or disapproval of men, who are incapable of understanding or appreciating the matter, is an exceedingly small thing. Let it pass....

Yours sincerely,

E. C.

Source: A. C. Kendrick, *The Life and Letters of Mrs. Emily C. Judson*, 186–87.

---

[47] The engraving done by John Sartain, one of the nation's foremost pictorial engravers, was commissioned to go to one of the magazines for which she had written the previous two years. At the end of this paragraph, this idea was rejected in favor of using the portrait in the new book planned for her stories: *Alderbrook*.

[48] Emily Chubbuck as Fanny Forester. See vol. 1, "Cast of Characters," s.v. "Chubbuck, Emily," also "Forester, Fanny."

Emily E. Chubbuck to Anna Maria Anable, May 8, 1846—Hamilton

My dear Mother-in-law,[49]

A certain D. D. rec'd a note of inquiry concerning myself this morning which I take to be on the whole rather impertinent, considering that such characters have no right to interfere in my affairs. If you had applied to a respectable source, it is possible that your curiosity with regard to dear Hilarion[50] and myself might have been gratified; as it is, "perhaps—perhaps—Don't know—can't say."

We are going on here in a jog-trot way—Always busy—nothing important but no time to spare. I have had hosts of letters—all business affairs, however—nothing interesting. Mr. Peck[51]—"Solomon the hideous" has decided (by the way, don't talk about it much) that "Allen Lucas"[52] is one of the wicked books which must not be republished!!! I have had a letter from West[53] and he accedes to my terms; so I have sent him "Ally Fisher"[54] and the historical bit but concluded not to let him have the other. Do you know how the papers all over are abusing the doc? They call him a "wizzled up old widower" and some of them make a regular "Bluebeard" of him, asserting that he takes women out there for the sake of murdering them. They have no idea that I am *merely* the third.[55] Friend Gillette[56] has

---

[49] "Mother-in-law" was a term Anna Maria frequently used of herself in her letters to Emily, and here Emily uses it of her.

[50] Adoniram Judson signed his March 7, 1846 letter to Emily "Hilarion Johnson." He also uses this again, or variations on it (The Hon. Captain Johnson) on April 20; May 8; and May 14, 1846

[51] See vol. 1, "Cast of Characters," s.v. "Peck, The Reverend Doctor Solomon."

[52] *Allen Lucas* was one of Emily's earlier books, published in late 1842. She received the proofs in early November that year.

[53] Mr. West, at the age of thirty-five, took over the position of editor of the *Columbian Magazine* following the serious illness of John Inman. In an extensive letter written April 28, 1846, Mr. West revealed to Emily that he was a Methodist lay minister, sidelined for the present by illness. He went on to list all of the clergy in his family, including his father and his brother, and said that his wife was the daughter of missionaries to Ceylon. Wishing Emily many blessings and an abundance of God's grace, he said in part, "I knew not until recently that my valued correspondent was one whose heart was turned to serve the Lord and for [ ] hour an inscrutable but ever wise providence has prepared for so inconvenient a station." He said that he had met Adoniram Judson at a convention and hoped to meet him again and gain and introduction at a major convention in New York. See his letters to Emily E. Chubbuck of March 3, 1846, and April 28, 1846.

[54] "Ally Fisher" also appeared in vol. 1 of Alderbrook. Its opening lines read:

> Study, study, study!
> Trudge, trudge, trudge!
> Sew, sew, sew!

Oh, what a humdrum life was that of little Ally Fisher! Day in, day out, late and early, from week's end to week's end, it was all the same. Oh, how Ally's feet and head and hands ached! And sometimes her heart ached, too—poor child!

[55] On April 3, Emily sent Adoniram an article from the *Boston Transcript* that raised the question as to how any man who loved a woman could ask her to go to a foreign country as a missionary, exposing her to "sure death in the face of such an undertaking we know not."

[56] Following several successful pastorates, the Reverend A. D. Gillette was the founding pastor of the flourishing Eleventh Baptist Church in Philadelphia in 1839. With his wife Hannah and several children (they would eventually have six), he graciously opened their home to Emily Chubbuck when she came to Philadelphia at the end of March 1845 for her health. The connection had been made through Miss Cynthia Sheldon, a family friend of Mr. Gillette and his parents. A prominent Baptist, Mr. Gillette journeyed to Boston in December 1845 to accompany Adoniram Judson to Philadelphia for meetings, and on Christmas Day, he introduced Dr. Judson to Emily Chubbuck with the hope that Fanny Forester could be persuaded to write the memoir of Sarah Hall Boardman Judson. A. D. Gillette and his wife Hannah remained valued and trusted friends, not only with Emily, but with the Sheldon and Anable families. He moved from Philadelphia to New York in 1852.

---

taken up the cudgel in his behalf as well as mine. Don't [sic] the poor fellow have his hands full? One paper however says they may as well not fret themselves for probably Miss Fanny[57] is a true daughter of Eve and that "If she will she will you may depend on't and if she won't she won't so there's the card on't." Some papers are incredulous; and one asserts that we were married last winter in Philadelphia. They cut him up much worse than they ever did me. *N'importe*. We have both concluded that we don't care an apple-blossom for what people say; and I don't believe that the whole world combined could ever make me feel as badly as I have. It is all smoke, anyway. I had a letter from the Gillettes today.[58] Mrs. G. sends love to Fanny[59] and says she shall answer her letter soon. I also rec'd a letter from Willis[60] in which he invites himself to my wedding.[61] He is anxious to see the doc. Mr. Gillette sent me an impression of my phiz.[62] It is a fine thing resolute and spirited, but like any person in the world rather than me. However, I shall put it in the book. There's a "say what you dare, and I don't care" air to it which I rather like. I wish the portrait could be bro't on. I have arranged with Freeman to paint one and he wants that to look at. Sartain[63] has done with it now. I fancy that Freeman will make a pretty nice picture; and he has asked the privilege of doing it in consideration of my having said some nice things to him when he came here a stranger. The doc. wishes me to tell you that it is best to box up things as fast as a box full is made, for he says you have no idea of the hurrying there will be at the end. He is anxious that all the boxes sh'd leave Utica as soon as the middle of June.

I do hope that Eugenia[64] and Sue will not be gone before we get back to Utica. Don't let them go. We sh'd'nt [sic] stay so long but it really seems a matter of duty.

---

[57] Emily Chubbuck as Fanny Forester. See vol. 1, "Cast of Characters," s.v. "Chubbuck, Emily," also "Forester, Fanny."

[58] See the letters from A. D. Gillette and Hannah Gillette to Emily E. Chubbuck dated May 5, 1846.

[59] See vol. 1, "Cast of Characters," s.v. "Anable, Fanny."

[60] Nathaniel Parker Willis was the editor, with General George Morris, of the *New Mirror*, a prominent literary magazine in New York. His "discovery" of Emily in the June 8, 1844 edition of the *New Mirror* catapulted her into literary fame and enabled her to command the highest prices for her articles and stories from the major magazines of that period. It began a new and glorious chapter in her life. Over the next two years, he became her friend, mentor, and confidant. His black-bordered letter of March 21, 1846, made it abundantly clear that her engagement to Adoniram Judson had come as a "death blow" and that he had expected to marry Emily upon his return that month from England. He returned several letters to Emily to demonstrate to her, lest she had forgotten, why he had felt right in that expectation. In volume 1, there is a timeline that presents in some detail the substance of their developing relationship, all from the letters Willis had written to Emily. When she received her letters back from Willis, she destroyed them, feeling that they would cast a negative shadow on her life and, because of that, the life and ministry of Adoniram Judson.

[61] There may be a missing letter from N. P. Willis to Emily. In a May 9 letter, which was mailed May 11, he says, "I have received no letter from you in reply and write simply to beg you to write me by return of mail answering this query. I proposed to go to your wedding if you would like it." Emily would not have received this letter of May 9 when she wrote this letter dated May 8.

[62] See the letter from the Reverend Mr. Gillette to Emily E. Chubbuck dated May 5, 1846. The picture was an engraving by John Sartain, which eventually was to be the picture included in her second publication of her sketches, *Alderbrook*.

[63] See vol. 1, "Cast of Characters," s.v. "Sartain, John."

[64] See vol. 1, "Cast of Characters," s.v. "Damaux, Eugenia."

Oh Ninny,[65] you don't know how I like to be with the good doc, he makes me so much better. I go back to my first impression that he is the holiest man on earth. Be a little more serious—I mean have some serious talk with him when you see him. You know you have been in a gale nearly all the time.

The doc. has just bro't me a note for you.[66] Scamp! He won't let me see it. Father[67] says it is time to go to the office so I must close. Fifteen kisses, ducky and—who do you sleep with? Ah, don't you want Peaked-chin?[68] How can you sleep without Miss Snugglie? Well, get your bed-fellow to kiss you. Good-night-good night.

Nemmy Petty[69]

Source: Hanna family files.

Adoniram Judson[70] (Hilarion Johnson) to Anna Maria Anable, May 8, 1846[71]—Hamilton

Dearest Blidgy[72]—My heart is well nigh broken. Not by the unkind insinuations in your note to Dr. Judson, which came into my hands, not unfairly upon my honor—but that a far greater evil has come upon dear Petty[73] than any about which your polished solicitude (beg pardon) was exercised. She has disappeared it is true, but not with the Honorable Captain Johnson,[74] which would have been a most inevitable thing to her and her friends, notwithstanding your ill-mannered intimations (beg pardon)—most inevitable, considering what has happened—Get

[65] Anna Maria Anable. See vol. 1, "Cast of Characters," s.v. "Ninny."

[66] See the letter of May 8, 1846, next in the correspondence, from Adoniram Judson to Miss Anna Maria Anable.

[67] Emily's father. See vol. 1, "Cast of Characters," s.v. "Chubbuck, Charles."

[68] Emily E. Chubbuck used a number of different names over the course of her life and career. She wrote often under the name Fanny Forester, her argument being "who would buy a book authored by Emily Chubbuck?" At other times, she used Amy Scribbleton (July 6, 1841); Amy S. (September 28, 1841); Nem or Nemmy (Emily was always Nem or Nemmy to Anna Maria Anable who was Ninny); Pithy to Anna Maria (April 29, 1845); Peaked chin (See Anna Maria Anable, November 12, 1845); Sister Peakedchin (See Emily Chubbuck, February 28, 1846); Miss Peakedchin (Adoniram Judson, March 7, 1846); Miss Nemmy Petty (Adoniram Judson, March 7, 1846); Petty (April 13, 1846).

[69] See the above footnote on *noms de plume* used by Emily. See also vol. 1, the chapter "Names of Endearment."

[70] This letter to Anna Maria Anable is a wonderful picture of the lighter, fun-loving, side of Adoniram Judson, better known here as "Captain Hilarian Johnson."

[71] This letter was enclosed with Emily's letter to Anna Maria of May 8, 1846. At the end of her letter, she references this one. She says that the doctor has just given it to her to be enclosed and has forbidden her to read it.

[72] "Blidgims" and the variation "Blidgy" are used quite frequently and interchangeably as names of endearment for Anna Maria Anable. In April 1845, Anna Maria signed several of her letters "Ninny Blidgims." On May 8, 1846, Adoniram began a letter to Anna Maria "Dearest Blidgy," and on May 14, she addressed "Miss Ninny Blidgims." See vol. 1, "Cast of Characters," s.v. "Blidgims."

[73] "Nemmy Petty," "Nemmie Pettie," or "Petty" were all terms of endearment used of Emily by Adoniram Judson and Anna Maria Anable, and Emily used them of herself.

[74] Adoniram Judson uses "Hilarion Johnson" and/or "The Honorable Caption Johnson" as references to himself in other letters dated March 7; April 20; and May 16, 1846.

ready your cambric, dear, and tell your aunts and grannies to do the same, if they have any, for tears will have their course in the wide wicked world. The last that was seen of them—them!? yes, that reverend gray-whiskered scamp, to whom you addressed your confidential note, has—but it is too awful to speak on. It is supposed that he brought home with him from some [ ] nigger country, a quantity of *A-noo*, such as the late queen of the said country contrived, when a fishmonger's daughter to administer to the heir apparent and so bewitched him, that he subsequently raised her to the throne. Well, the last that was seen of them was on the way to Binghamton, mounted on that misshapen animal that he has been exhibiting about the country, and him lugging all the goodies. He was himself strapped to a huge portfolio, full of manuscripts, inscribed with [Note: The next word is written in Burmese script.] [ ] Polyglott, and she (only think of it) our dear Nemmy Petty, poor crazy Petty siting on a pillow behind him, one hand around the old fellow's waist and the other holding a bunch of goose quills. On the poor girl's head was a thick, yellow covered pamphlet, open and astride, tied on with one of her garters, in a knot under her chin, to whh [which] was suspended an old fashioned ink horn—large letters on the cover of the pamphlet—"*Trippings*[75] rectified and on the way to Nod." This is all the information I can give you about our poor lost Nemmy. Perhaps dear Willis[76] (how he must feel for the poor creature) can give us some further information.

Dearest Blidgy—Now my *only* beloved one—I am sure you will esteem it a great privilege to bind up my broken heart. You have a compassionate, loving heart Verbum and at. But if our Petty should ever come to her senses, you must not mention this. Love to all inquiring friends. Most affectionately—

Your devoted

H. Johnson

Source: Hanna family files.

---

[75] This is a reference to Emily's first collection of her sketches, *Trippings in Author-land*. This was released by the publisher on November 22, 1845.

[76] See vol. 1, "Cast of Characters," s.v. "Willis, Nathaniel Parker."

Miss Rebecca Ann "Bessie" Rhees to Adoniram Judson,[77] May 8, 1846 —Philadelphia

Will you accept and wear this little gift, as the work, and for the sake of those who dearly love you? I had intended that the work should be entirely my own, but my sister Alice pleaded so earnestly to share the pleasure, that I could not deny her. Many a warm wish and earnest prayer for your happiness has been twined amid the flowers, and if those prayers are heard and answered, far brighter blossoms than these, will deck your future path through life.

Alice, who since you were here has been reading frequently and attentively your letter to American Females on Dress,[78] expressed a fear that you may be disposed to censure us for the bright colors and gaiety of our work. I hope, however, that her fears may be groundless, and that you will not refuse to gratify us by accepting our offering, though of little value in itself for the sake of the Christian affection which presents it.

My fear is, that as we had no measure to guide us, the slippers may not fit you, but, if they do not, you can give them to some one [sic] you love. And then please send us your measure, and we will work another pair, and send them after you to Burmah, if we cannot complete them before you leave the country. Do not refuse us this request, dear brother, or you will disappoint us sadly, as we have set our hearts upon your having some remembrance of us with you in that distant land.

That the choicest blessings of a covenant-keeping God may rest ever upon you is the constant prayer of

Rev. A. Judson

R. A. Rhees

[77] Miss Rebecca Ann Rhees, who wrote this and four other letters to Adoniram Judson, also wrote three letters to Emily C. Judson beginning in September 1850 with the death of Adoniram. Miss Rhees met Adoniram, she said, while he was traveling on deputation in 1846 and transcribed several of his sermons and remarks for publication.

On March 6, 1846, Adoniram wrote to Emily about a letter he had received and said he would share it with her; then, he added, "And that also of R. A. Rhees, one of the few flames I have had since you left."

In her first letter to Emily, she spoke of her grief at Adoniram Judson's death as inconsolable. A second letter followed in December 1851 in which she commented on meeting Emily briefly at Miss Sheldon's in Philadelphia, probably when Emily traveled there after her return to America. This letter was in response to Emily's request for materials for the Judson memoir. Here, Miss Rhees implored that she be allowed to address her as "Emily," and she obviously was hoping to establish a relationship. Apparently, she was unsuccessful, for in the third letter, she said, "I will not ask you again to write to me." It appears that she had sent something to Emily, who had returned it to her, for after saying the above, she went on to ask Emily to excuse her for sending it along. In not getting what she hoped for from Emily, a hard edge emerges, suggesting that there was more to the request than what was seen on the surface.

The letters of Rebecca A. Rhees ("Bessie") to Adoniram are included in the correspondence to fill in some background information. Their dates are February 19, 1846; May 8 and 10, 1846; October 1, 1848; and November 25, 1849. There are currents emerging that are expressed in a multitude of ways; it seems evident that Miss Rhees would today be called a "groupie" with a strong need for attachment to a famous figure. There is an unfolding story of unrequited love that forms an interesting sub-chapter to the life of Adoniram and Emily.

[78] In October 1831, Adoniram Judson had written a letter "from Adoniram Judson, missionary in Burmah, to the female members of Christian Churches in the United States of America."

Nathaniel Parker Willis to Emily E. Chubbuck, May 9, 1846[79]— Boston

Dearest Emily,

Did you get my letter from Washington requesting you to write to me at New York telling me when you go to Hamilton etc? I have received no letter from you in reply and write simply to beg you to write me by return of mail answering this query. I proposed to go to your wedding if you would like it.[80] My niece was married here on the 6th—Maria Dwight.

Calling yesterday on a Baptist family I heard that I had come home from Europe to offer myself to you and was broken-hearted to find that Mr. Judson had anticipated me! The lady declared that it was most authentically stated. This magnetic Telegraph seems to be doing wonders!

I write in great haste and merely to ask news of your movements. God bless you and your husband, my dear Emily.

Ever yours affectionately

N. P. Willis

Source: Hanna family files.

Anna Maria Anable to Emily E. Chubbuck, May 10, 1846[81]

Sunday Eve—9—

Dear Nem[82]

I am so sleepy that I can only say that I received your very kind invitation yesterday to come out to your house this week and have my portrait painted by Freeman.

I had intended all along dear to visit you this week and I hope I shall not be *de trope*.

The fact that your brother Walker[83] had received my letter was somewhat astounding to me and the request that I should write him *again* perfectly over-

---

[79] This letter was mailed on May 11, 1846.

[80] There is no copy of this letter. This is the first mention of this proposal.

[81] This letter is undated. There is already a letter from Anna Maria written on May 3, and by May 17, Emily was back in Utica, so May 10 seems to fit best.

[82] Emily Chubbuck. See vol. 1, "Cast of Characters," s.v. "Nemmy, Nem, or Nemmy Petty (Nemmie Pettie)." Also the chapter "Names of Endearment."

[83] Born September 24, 1815, John Walker Chubbuck was twenty-three months older than Emily. When Emily first began corresponding with him in February 1838, Walker was living in the Wisconsin Territory. Having been trained as a youth in the printing and newspaper business, upon his arrival, he started a newspaper with a partner and had a career in that business. In 1855 he married Caroline Sanborn, and they were to have three children. In 1857 he established the Central Wisconsin newspaper in Wausau; in 1863 he became the Clerk of the Circuit Court. He died at the age of 72 on May 27, 1885. He was active in the Presbyterian Church, much to the chagrin of his sister Emily, who, though delighted with his conviction partly through correspondence with Adoniram Judson, tried to convict him of Baptist ways.

whelmed me. I just folded the letter and sent it on to my dear Hilarion[84] as another proof of your insanity, with the prediction that by next week you would be fit for the Lunatic Asylum here.

If you have any commissions for me to execute, write again dear for it will be some time before I shall get your letters.

How provoked I was that this was such a sensible letter. What a rare [ ] there would have been [ ] for me to have seen one of your genuine love letters. Why, there was nothing worse in this than what you write to me any day. Mr. Dean[85] preached tonight and we were all quite delighted with him but I am so sleepy I must go to bed. Write to me immediately won't you? Good night.

Ninny

I wrote to the Dr. this afternoon. I felt so forlorn I could not help it. I wanted his advice and I knew I should never talk with him if I did not write first.[86]

I hope he will not think me impertinent or obtrusive. You must not let him. Really I feel as if I had not a friend on earth to advise me what to do.

Source: American Baptist Historical Society, AJ 23, no. 1139E.

Miss Rebecca Ann Rhees to Adoniram Judson, May 10, 1846[87]— Philadelphia

Might I spend this Sabbath evening in communing with you, whom I never expect to see on earth again? I did not ask permission to write you, and I fear you will think me very forward to trouble you so often. But I wish very much to hold converse with you once more, and if you have not time to read my letter, or to *think* of me *now*, perhaps you will have, when upon the sea, if not before, and, when you read it, you will, I hope, excuse what I feel to be the liberty I take in addressing you.

You will recollect what you said to me about going to Burmah as a teacher, and my apparent unwillingness to do so. This must have seemed to you the more singular, as I had before told you by letter, that I would, if possible, gladly give my life

---

[84] On March 7, 1846 Adoniram Judson signed a letter "Hilarion Johnson." He also signed a letter to Anna Maria Anable on May 8, 1846 the same way.

[85] Dr. William Dean was an interim pastor at the Morrisville (New York) Baptist Church in spring 1834, and he baptized Emily Chubbuck. In July 1834, he left for missionary service in China and served as a veteran missionary for nearly fifty years. There are letters to Emily from Dr. Dean in the correspondence, and there is some speculation that Dr. William Dean took a matrimonial interest in Emily after the death of Adoniram Judson. In 1854, when William Dean was courting Mrs. Maria Brown, Abby Ann Judson was working for Mrs. Brown as an in-house teacher for her children. For the complete story of his life and the many ways he touched the mission movement and the life of Emily Chubbuck Judson, see vol. 1, "Cast of Characters," s.v. "Dean, William."

[86] This is no doubt the first conversation on Anna Maria's baptism by immersion that Dr. Judson performed just before he and Emily sailed from Boston to Burmah.

[87] See vol. 1, "Cast of Characters," s.v. "Rhees, Miss Rebecca Ann."

to the cause. And so, if I know my heart, I would; from my infancy familiar with the life of your first sainted wife, one of my earliest wishes was to be a missionary like her. And though for a time, perhaps, lost sight of, the idea, during the last year, had returned with more than its original force. Still, as I told you, I had never thought of going alone until you suggested it, and then it appeared to me a terrible, almost unwomanly undertaking, from which I shrank instinctively. This may account to you for the reluctance I evinced to the idea, so inconsistent with my previously expressed devotion to the cause. But after you spoke of it so seriously, and especially after the last interview I had with you, I could think of nothing else. I could not banish your words from my mind by day, and when I slept, it was only to dream of them, and to hear the Macedonian cry, "Come over and help us." I felt—I do think I felt willing to go in any capacity, even it if were my Master's will, to go alone into the wilds, like Miss Macomber,[88] and die, as she did, far from friends and home. But the obstacles of my parents' unwillingness, and my own unfitness were strong objections to my going, and at length, agitated by conflicting ideas and emotions, I became seriously ill. After attending me for some time, my brother told me, that unless I soon began to regain my strength, I would be beyond the reach of medicine, and that he believed I must effect [sic] my own cure, and that no one else could do it. I knew that he was right; that it was the excitement of my mind acting upon a frail and nervous constitution that had made and was keeping me ill, rendering me unable to perform my many duties. And feeling that I should be no better until I could decide what course I should take, I resolved to make that decision. I prayed. oh! how earnestly that I might have wisdom to see, and strength to do the will of my Master, let it lead me in what path it might. I asked only that He would direct me by his Spirit, and that I might have no will of my own in the matter. I thought of the claims of the heathen, and of the last imperative command of Christ, and on the other hand, of my duty to my parents, and to the little sisters, who look to me scarcely less than to our mother, for instruction and care, and I was made to feel, (shall I own in opposition to my own desire?) that, for the present at least, my most important, my most obvious duty is to the latter. Other, far more competent and worthy than myself, may be found to carry the Gospel to the heathen, but I know that none could take my place at home. I believe too that my mother would not long survive the event of my leaving her on what she thinks so dangerous a mission; I am her eldest, and, (if she knows a difference among us) her favourite [sic] child,—can it be my duty to break the heart that loves me so fondly, and bring down her gray hairs with sorrow to the grave?

[88] In December 1836, Miss Eleanor Macomber opened a school and church in the out-station of Dong-yahn. She died in April 1840, and at the time of her death, Adoniram Judson wrote a eulogy, which was included in the appendix of Dr. Wayland's memoir (Wayland, Francis. *A Memoir of the Life and Labors of the Rev. Adoniram Judson, D.D.* Boston: Phillips, Sampson, and Co., 1853) 2:495–97.

God, who reads my heart, knows that *I* dread no danger, no trial with which I might meet in Burmah; I feel that it would be only too high an honor—too exalted a privilege, to bear the name of Missionary, and to labor for Christ among the heathen. It seems to me, that though I might be exposed to greater privations there, I should have fewer temptations to worldliness, and forgetfulness of my high vocation, and I do indeed feel it the heaviest cross I can take up, to resign all hope of devoting my life to the work. Yet such seems to me now my line of duty, and I am striving to submit cheerfully.

Am I wrong in my conclusions, dear brother? Perhaps you will think I am, for you cannot know the various reasons which lead me to feel that I am so much needed at home, but you will, I hope, I think—you will believe me sincere in my love to the cause of Missions, and my wish to aid it. And aid it I will, to the utmost of my feeble ability, the Lord prospering me; if I cannot give myself to the cause abroad, I will devote myself to it at home. I have little to give now, but my prayers, but, if the Lord ever releases me, as I have firm trust he will, from the crushing influence of poverty, I pledge myself to devote all that I have and am, to this cause—the cause of Missions.

Forgive this long and sadly egotistical letter; you may ask, why I should trouble you with the tale of my thoughts and resolves? It requires apology, I confess, and what can I plead except the one I offered for my last call upon you in Phila—I could not help it! Will you admit this as sufficient? Or shall I tell you how often I have grieved over the thought, that, if you remembered me at all, you would think me insincere in the declaration, that "I would gladly give my life to Burmah," since I seemed to draw back, so soon as you pointed out a way for me to go? Do not think this, I entreat you; I do love the cause, better than I love my life—better, I trust, than I love *any-thing* save him, whose cause it is.

I have no hope, now of ever seeing you on earth again but I will try to live, so that I may meet you in "that bright world to which

Absence and Death can never [ ] their way."

God forever bless and be with you. Will you sometimes think of and pray for (may I call myself and will you think of me as)

Your Daughter

R. A. Rhees

Adoniram Judson to Emily E, Chubbuck,[89] May 14, 1846[90]

Poor Johnson[91] has requested me to communicate the above card being, it seems, interdicted, for his impudence from writing himself; and I have complied with his request from mere pity, though he is rather prone to call pet names. And now, darling, don't you think you cut a pretty figure on the cover of the book,[92] from which you extracted "the Dissatisfied Spirit?" That was the reason you was [*sic*] in such a "fret" and sent off for a lawyer! And you did not like to tell me, or let me see the picture, naughty, distrustful one! And did you think, that my heart's love would be ruffled by seeing the caricature of my bride elect by the side of Fanny Elsler[93] and The Fair Bandit and other demireps in the low bookstalls and on grogging counters through the country? And did you think that my courage would quail and that I should wish I could "back out" and "take it all back," though, alas, too late? Let us rather be glad, dearest and best, of your beautiful sketches, which can never be tainted or depreciated by any contact or association, may through the low artifice of the publisher, reach some dirty hand and tearless eye and hardcrusted heart, and soften and cleanse and prepare, it may be, for higher and more spiritual influences. **I fold you, dearest Emily, closer than ever in my heart of hearts, especially now, when my best friends are trembling and taking me aside and begging me to tell them truly and confidentially whether it is all right, and whether your religion is really such, as may encourage them to go forward and espouse our cause, without endangering the great cause. A privilege I esteem it to tell the truth to those who know not your real character.**

[89] There are two versions of this letter: the original as written by Emily E. Chubbuck and the edited version published by Dr. A. C. Kendrick in his biography, *The Life and Letters of Mrs. Emily C. Judson*. Additions made by Dr. Kendrick are in parentheses, and words in the original left out by Dr. Kendrick have been added in bold. There are significant changes and omissions. In a note in his book, Dr. Kendrick explained that interest, purpose and propriety sometimes led to these changes and exclusions, "I remark here that in giving Miss Chubbuck's letters, I do not always indicate unimportant omissions. Real letters must always contain much which should not meet the public eye; and Emily's were real letters, dashed off hastily amidst pressing cares and duties. Written also after the exhausting labors of the day, they by no means do uniform justice to her epistolary powers." He later added, "In giving a few extracts from his and Miss Chubbuck's correspondence at this time, I have no wish to minister to a prurient curiosity, nor to violate that principle which would generally place letters written during the period of an 'engagement' under the shelter of inviolate secrecy." 154.

[90] There is an addendum to this letter dated May 16, 1846. While in New York, Adoniram Judson likely stayed at the home of Mr. and Mrs. Isaac Newton, friends and prominent supports of the mission cause. On page 456 of Edward Judson's biography of his father (Judson, Edward, *The Life of Adoniram Judson* [Philadelphia: The American Baptist Publication Society, 1883]). There is a facsimile of an inscription Adoniram placed in a book of Burmese hymns that had been compiled by Sarah Hall Boardman Judson; the inscription was to Mrs. H. H. Newton. There are letters from both Mr. and Mrs. Newton in the correspondence.

      Included with this letter was a card Adoniram was sending to Anna Maria Anable. That letter is also dated May 14, 1846 and follows this letter in the correspondence.

[91] Adoniram Judson signed his March 7, 1846 letter to Emily "Hilarion Johnson." He also uses this again or variations on it (The Hon. Captain Johnson) on April 20; May 8; and May 14, 1846

[92] In his letter to Anna Maria dated May 14, 1846, Adoniram Judson tells of seeing an unauthorized publication of many of Emily's writings—"Lilias Fane and other Tales"—in a bookstore while he was walking in New York. It was gaudily done and obviously appealed to a mass market. See Emily's letter dated April 13 for more information on these unauthorized publications.

[93] Fanny Elsler was a famous dancer of the mid-nineteenth century. Judging by this comment from Adoniram Judson, Ms. Elsler's picture saw wide publication.

And whence is the strange influence that I wield? And what is the magic that has invested me with such credit, that a single word will put hosts of doubts and fear to flight?

Source: A. C. Kendrick, *The Life and Letters of Mrs. Emily C. Judson*, 193–94; Hanna family files.

Adoniram Judson[94] to Anna Maria Anable,[95] May 14, 1846

The Honorable Captain Johnson's[96] tenderest compliments to Miss Ninny[97] Blidgims,[98] and warmest congratulations that the health of her exquisitely interesting friend, Miss Nemmie Pettie,[99] the dear delightful Fanny Forester,[100] has not at all suffered from the equestrian jaunt "on the way to Binghamton," with the Rev. Dr. Wizzleface (the old scamp),[101] as is evident from the fair middy complection [*sic*] on the cover of "Lilias Fane and other Tales,"[102] taken, it is to be presumed, since her arrival in New York, and it blazed upon the delighted optics of the Hon. Capt. J—as he passed from Astor House, in search of his friend Willis,[103] and entered an adjoining bookstore; but the Hon. Capt. J wants to beg Miss Blidgims to intimate to her dear friend, as delicately and respectfully as possible—A little less rouge on the lips dear, *sil* [*sic*] *vous plait*.

Source: Hanna family files.

---

[94] As in the letter dated May 8 from Adoniram Judson to Anna Maria Anable, in this letter there is a lighter side to Adoniram Judson. There is no stern, formidable, stereotypical missionary persona here, not even a hint of one. Instead, we find him frolicking like a teenager newly in love.

[95] This card to Anna Maria Anable was included with a letter written by Adoniram Judson to Emily Chubbuck on May 14, 1846.

[96] Adoniram Judson signed his March 7, 1846 letter to Emily "Hilarion Johnson." He also uses this again, or variations on it (The Hon. Captain Johnson) on April 20 and May 8 and May 14, 1846

[97] Anna Maria Anable. See vol. 1, "Cast of Characters," s.v. "Ninny."

[98] See vol. 1, "Cast of Characters," s.v. "Blidgims."

[99] Emily E. Chubbuck names. See vol. 1, "Cast of Characters," s.v. "Nemmy, Nem, or Nemmy Pettie." Also the section "Names of Endearment."

[100] Emily Chubbuck as Fanny Forester. See vol. 1, "Cast of Characters," s.v. "Chubbuck, Emily," also "Forester, Fanny."

[101] See the letter of Adoniram Judson to Anna Maria Anable dated May 8, 1846.

[102] This was an unauthorized publication of some of Emily's earlier sketches and stories. Because of her impending missionary status, she had been advised not to take any action against the publishers. See Emily E. Chubbuck's letter to Adoniram Judson dated April 13, 1846 for more information on these unauthorized publications.

[103] See vol. 1, "Cast of Characters," s.v. "Willis, Nathaniel Parker."

Adoniram Judson to Emily E, Chubbuck,[104] May 16, 1846[105]

Such a stream of romping and meetings, and I must go out in half an hour to breakfast. Yesterday was the great meeting of the Am. and For. Bible Society and Dr. Cone[106] read my ill-digested remarks penned at Hamilton, with as much unction and pathos as if they were really something, and when he began to read, some called out in the assembly, to have me stand by his side, so that all might see me! Can anything be more ridiculous and humbuggerish? But I suppose, that some thought—Well, that is Fanny Forester's[107] "selection," at any rate; and so he must be a nice fellow. And after the affair, the pulpit was thronged and among the rest, one grave gentleman wanted to know, looking earnestly at my apex, whether I wore my own hair!!! I meekly assured him of the fact, and he seemed to go away edified. And here is Dean,[108] and a fine fellow he is throughout, but he avows that he will not look on women's affectations and folly. And where is Jones,[109] rather without, but an excellent man. And Kincaid[110]—a real, designing, live humbug, whereas I am only a paper one stuck up against my own will, by Uncle Jonathan. K. is not going out at present

[104] For an understanding of the comparison on an original letter with the letter actually printed by Dr. A. C. Kendrick in *The Life and Letters of Mrs. Emily C. Judson*, see the first footnote for the letter of Adoniram to Emily dated May 14, 1846.

[105] This is an addendum to a letter written on May 14, 1846.

[106] This was probably Spencer Houghton Cone, a distinguished Baptist pastor of the early and mid-nineteenth century. Of him, the *Baptist Encylcopaedia* said, "For many years Dr. Cone was the most active Baptist minister in the United States, and the most popular clergyman in America. He was known and venerated everywhere all over this broad land. In his own denomination he held every position of honor which his brethren could give him, and outside of it men loved to recognize his worth. He had quick perceptions, a ready address, a silvery voice, impassioned eloquence, and deep-toned piety; throngs attended his church, and multitudes lamented his death" (Cathcart, William. *The Baptist Encyclopedia* [Philadelphia: Louis H. Everts, 1881]): 262–3.

[107] Emily Chubbuck as Fanny Forester. See vol. 1, "Cast of Characters," s.v. "Chubbuck, Emily," also "Forester, Fanny."

[108] The Reverend Doctor William Dean was a distinguished missionary to Hong Kong for more than fifty years. As the pastor of the local church in Morrisville, he baptized Emily Chubbuck when she was seventeen. There are nine letters in the correspondence from Mr. Dean, beginning after Emily's appointment to missionary service. After the death of Adoniram Judson, it was speculated, and not without reasonable support, that William Dean had an interest in taking Judson's place in Emily's life and affections. The later correspondence between Emily and Anna Maria Anable shows that Dr. Dean was often the butt of their ridicule, so something had happened to challenge that relationship. In 1854, when William Dean was courting Mrs. Maria Brown in New York City, Abby Ann Judson was working for Mrs. Brown as an in-house teacher for her children. For the complete story of William Dean's life and the many ways he touched the mission movement and the life of Emily Chubbuck Judson, see vol. 1, "Cast of Characters," s.v. "Dean, William."

[109] This was J. Taylor Jones, fellow missionary, located in Bangkok, Siam.

[110] Born in 1797, educated at the seminary in Hamilton, New York, and ordained in 1822, the Reverend Eugenio Kincaid served several churches before being appointed as a missionary to Burmah in February 1830. His first wife died soon after their arrival. His second wife was Barbara McBain, and they were married in 1833. In these years, they served in Rangoon, Ava, Saduja, and Akyab. The Reverend and Mrs. Kincaid returned to the United States in 1843; because of her persistent health problems, they were not reappointed in 1846. While in the United States, Rev. Kincaid became instrumental in the establishment of the University of Lewisberg (later Bucknell University). Upon Mrs. Kincaid's restoration, they returned to Burmah, arriving in February 1851 just as Emily Judson was embarking for her return voyage. With his knowledge of the language and customs, Rev. Kincaid was able to establish himself in work with the Burmese government at Ava. With one more trip home (in 1857, on an official mission for the King of Burmah to President Buchanan of the United States), they retired to Gerard, Kansas, in 1866. Of Rev. Kincaid, the correspondence indicates a man of convictions and occasional independent action.

but he is dying to go! Abbott[111] has not come in. They say he is very ill. I have not yet seen any of your wicked friends and know not when I shall.

I think of you, dearest and best, "a little bit," once an hour or so. I hope I shall soon get through with this row, and find the way to Hamilton and to your arms and heart and bosom—love. May God preserve your health and life, and may the Holy Spirit so direct your thoughts and sanctify your mind, in view of the missionary life and mine also, that we shall be blessings to one another in time and in eternity. My hand is better, but I write in some haste.

Yours ever with increasing love and devotion

A Judson

Source A. C.: Kendrick, *The Life and Letters of Mrs. Emily C. Judson*, 193–94; Hanna family files.

Emily E. Chubbuck to Adoniram Judson,[112] May 17, 1846

My best friend,

I have been quite ill since you left; but am much better today; so much so that, since I can't go out to church, I am wickedly impatient. It will creep into my head now and then that I have a half year's work to do in a half-month and my naughty fingers ache to be busy. They have done everything for me here in the school possible in the way of outfit[113] and have the heart to do impossibilities; but they must not attempt more than they have now on hand. I find that I lack a great deal. Tomorrow, if I am well enough, I shall spend in shopping; and then put all into the hands of sewing-women on whom I can depend. It is the only sure way. I pity poor Aunt Cynthia[114] and Anna Maria[115]—they are quite too busy and anxious for me.

[111] Elisha Abbott was born October 23, 1809 in Cazenovia, New York. He graduated from the Hamilton Theological Institute and was ordained August 25, 1835. His wife was Ann P. Gardner, and they were married April 2, 1837. Though they were appointed for work in Telagus, India, that changed upon their arrival, and they went to Maulmain in April 1837. They continued on to Rangoon shortly after that. In March 1840, they established the station at Sandoway. Mrs. Abbott died in Sandoway on January 27, 1845. Mr. Abbott left for the United States in November 1845, returning in August 1847. At one point in the correspondence, Mr. Abbott was mentioned as a possible husband for Lydia Lillybridge.

[112] For an understanding of the comparison on an original letter with the letter actually printed by Dr. A. C. Kendrick in *The Life and Letters of Mrs. Emily C. Judson*, see the first footnote for the letter of Adoniram to Emily dated May 14, 1846.

[113] Emily gave the responsibility of outfitting her for Burmah to Miss Cynthia Sheldon and Mrs. Hannah Gillette, wife of the Reverend A. D. Gillette.

[114] Miss Cynthia Sheldon was in charge of the administrative and financial departments of the Utica Female Academy. Miss Sheldon and her sister Urania, who was literary principal, gave Emily Chubbuck a place at the academy in October 1840. They had deferred any cost to a future time when Emily could afford to reimburse them. Upon Miss Urania Sheldon's marriage in the late summer 1842 to the Reverend Doctor Eliphalet Nott, the president of Union College, and her subsequent move to Schenectady, Miss Cynthia Sheldon assumed a larger leadership role at the academy. Active and well-known in Baptist circles, Miss Cynthia was to become an important mentor, advisor, and friend to Emily until the time of Emily's death in 1854. She was the aunt of Emily's best friend, Anna Maria Anable, and was addressed by most as "Aunt Cynthia." In 1848, Miss Sheldon moved to Philadelphia to help Miss Anable with the startup of the Misses Anable's School.

[115] See vol. 1, "Cast of Characters," s.v. "Anable, Miss Anna Maria."

My aunt Catherine (mother's sister) arrived last Friday, in Hamilton; and I am in a great tease to go to her. I cannot, however, get away from here before Wednesday. Mrs. Conant[116] has been with us since Friday. I seldom see a more agreeable woman.

I hope you will like to baptize Anna Maria,[117] and I hope Mr. Corey[118] will ask you. Will you do it if he does? She is very anxious to have you. I think it would be nice to stay in Hamilton a few days (after you get to be Mr. Chubbuck) and then come here and spend the sabbath. The church don't [sic] deserve it, but I feel inclined to do the amiable as far as is proper—to act our part under all circumstances. Still it may not be for the best. You know all about these things.

Mr. and Mrs. Beecher[119] dined with us today and I did'nt [sic] feel a bit flat—not I. She is a very good match for Miss Pokey; and on the whole I think you may as well leave the miniature with Aunt Cynthia and take a daguerreotype of her face. She is'nt [sic] as pretty as Lydia;[120] but she is good and I have quite fallen in love with her. She seems to be a very sensible woman withal, and was without doubt made for a missionary. I hope Mrs. Harris[121] will have a little touch of beauty though, to keep the ship above water. Oh dear! The mention of the ship sends my heart down into my shoes. How nice to sleep a half year and awake at our own dear, dear home. That home is very dear to me already, darling; and the children I am longing to see. By the way, I have been seriously thinking of

[116] Anna Maria's negative comments about Mrs. Conant in her letter of July 31, 1848 are quite interesting, if not surprising. In a May 1846 letter, Emily said that she had found Mrs. Conant quite "agreeable." In spite of Anna Maria's feelings, Mrs. Conant was an accomplished scholar. She wrote a number of articles and books about the Bible and was considered competent in the biblical field. Earlier letters indicate that she called on Emily a number of times when she was in Hamilton, and the references are always cordial. When Emily returned to the United States, a warm letter from Mrs. Conant invited her to stay with her should she come to Rochester. After the publication of the Judson memoir, written by Francis Wayland in collaboration with Emily Judson, Emily planned to write an abridgement of those two volumes as a more popular offering. As Emily's health deteriorated in late 1853 and it became increasingly obvious that she would be unable to take on such a task, Mrs. Conant was asked to take the responsibility for that project, and eventually it was published as: *The Earnest Man: A Memoir of Adoniram Judson, DD, First Missionary to Burmah.*

[117] Anna Maria Anable had been struggling with the issue of her baptism. In an earlier letter , she spoke of writing to Adoniram Judson about the matter. See her letter to Emily dated May 10, 1846 for more information.

[118] See vol. 1, "Cast of Characters," s.v. "Corey, the Reverend D. G."

[119] Mr. and Mrs. John Sydney Beecher sailed to Burmah with Adoniram and Emily Judson in July 1846. They served there from 1846 to 1866.

[120] See vol. 1, "Cast of Characters," s.v. "Lillybridge, Miss Lydia," also the timeline on "Lydia Lillybridge Simons."

[121] Norman Harris was born February 19, 1813 in Becket, Massachusetts. He attended Columbia College and Hamilton Literary and Theological School, graduating in 1844. Olive Celina Wadsworth was also born in Becket, Mass July 6, 1814. They were married on August 9, 1844, and were appointed to missionary service on October 28, 1844. In July 1846, they sailed to Burmah with the newly married Adoniram and Emily Judson. Olive Harris died in childbirth on November 23, 1853, in Shwegyin, Burma. In 1856, Norman Harris married for the second time; Miranda Harris died of fever in September that very same year. Norman Harris left the mission field shortly after the death of his wife Miranda and returned to the United States. There, in June 1858, he married for the third time; his third wife was Julia Wadsworth Chapman, the sister of his first wife, Olive Celina Wadsworth. Norman and Julia Harris returned to Burmah in 1858, though not under the auspices of the American Baptist Missionary Union; they were reappointed as missionaries in 1861. Norman Harris died March 1, 1884 in Hamilton, New York. Julia Harris died in September 1905.

asking you to take Abby[122] back. She is your only daughter and you love her so much and it will be so hard for the poor little creature to stay behind. And, dearest, you may be assured that she shall not lack for any good which I am capable of exerting. I know and you know the point where I sh'd be most likely to fail; but I would pray most earnestly to exert a healthful religious influence. And how I should love to have the training of her active little mind. I would pursue a regular system of instruction—give daily book-lessons, besides the other lessons that we could extract from things about us. It would be something of a task I know, but a very agreeable one, and one which would have a tendency to make me better. Then think of having her with you, developing under your own eye—can you think of anything pleasanter, having been to this country, tho' only for a little time, will be an advantage to her; and, if it is best, I dare say she will have the opportunity of coming again at some future day. **Now don't you think it would be nice to take her back? Say yes; ah do! And though I will still be your unuseful[123] baby-pet when we are alone; I will play the mama—oh, so discreetly!** The truth is, I plead as much as half for my own sake; for I begin to feel that I shall be out of my proper element when I miss my accustomed employments. For more than eight years I have had almost constantly some young girl in whom I was more especially interested than others, under my eye; and I suppose that I have (partly from peculiar taste and partly from favorable circumstances) had more influence in the formation of individual character in our school than all the rest of the teachers put together. The interest that I feel in some of these young ladies is peculiarly strong—and their love and gratitude very dear. Don't you see why I am selfish in wanting Abby? Don't dare trust her with me—eh? Ah, you don't know how wise and dignified I can be when occasion signifies—not one of my pupils was surprised at the news of my turning missionary. Don't I plead my cause pretty well for a novice? Please think the matter over seriously, darling; and if there are not insuperable objections let your heart decide. She would grow dearer and more interesting to you every day and—perhaps you will accuse me of vanity, but I must out with it—I am afraid she will not (if she is like her papa) be understood and fully appreciated and trained accordingly. I am afraid her peculiarities will be curbed instead of cultivated, her warm impulses checked instead of directed. Do my fears smack of vanity? It is so natural for us to think we can manage some such things better than anybody else—and I have seen

[122] Abby Ann Judson, the first daughter and oldest child of Adoniram and Sarah Hall Boardman Judson, was born September 26, 1835. She saw her mother die on the Isle of St. Helena as they returned to the United States from Burmah. Just before leaving for Burmah with Emily, Adoniram Judson placed Abby Ann at Bradford Academy for her education. The family of Ann Hasseltine Judson was generous to Abby Ann and supportive of her interests and her future. On October 15, 1851, Abby Ann started a course of study at the Misses Anable's School in Philadelphia, and in fall 1853, she moved to New York City to take a teaching position in the home of Mrs. Maria Brown, a former missionary to Siam. She enjoyed a warm relationship with Emily, and her letters show that the two could speak freely with each other.

[123] Based on one of Fanny Forester's stories, "The Unuseful," Emily used the term often of herself. It was a concept that seemed to capture the inadequacies she felt about being the wife of Adoniram Judson and succeeding in her service on the mission field.

so many lamentable instances of bad training from mere misapprehension of character among wise, sensible, cultivated and pious people.

Written in the right margin of the address page: "I fully expected a letter from you last night, dear; if it sh'd fail tonight I sh'd be quite alarmed. You were not well when you went away. Write often love—not *long* but very often. It is strange how you have weaned my heart from those I have formerly loved better than myself. I think it is very naughty of you; but somehow—somehow I can't help being reconciled. Adieu"

Thine lovingly,
Emily

Written in the left margin of the address page: "I have been much alarmed since you went away about my side, because I was afraid of a liver-complaint, but I have quite recovered from that fear now. I have found an outward application which helps it and it is much better today. I dare say, I shall be able to get out tomorrow. I presume I took cold and it settled there."

Source: Hanna family files; A. C. Kendrick, *The Life and Letters of Mrs. Emily C. Judson*, 195–97.

Emily E. Chubbuck to Adoniram Judson,[124] May 17, 1846[125]

Sunday evening

No, my own best friend, I never was alarmed or afraid to have you learn all about me, the worst and the best. Otherwise I should have not been so happy in your precious love. If I had the shadow of a concealment on my conscience, I should be made miserable by your arms opening to me so trustingly.

If I had supposed the red picture[126] on the cover intended for me, I should, of course, have been much more mortified than I was, by having my sketches appear in such low company. But I tho't it a kind of gratuitous embellishment. Mr. Williams said when he was here that he wondered whether it was intended for F. F.[127] or Lilias Fane; but I did not suppose him in earnest. **Darling,** why are you so good to me? **Oh, I love you so much for your sweet kindnesses—so much! But I never shall be able to repay any portion of it except by love [to be expressed either by] too deep word or action.** Talk of sacrifices! **Why, nothing could be**

[124] For an understanding of the comparison on an original letter with the letter actually printed by Dr. A. C. Kendrick in *The Life and Letters of Mrs. Emily C. Judson*, see the first footnote for the letter of Adoniram to Emily dated May 14, 1846.

[125] There is an addendum to this letter dated May 18, 1846.

[126] This was written in response to Adoniram Judson's letter of May 14, 1846, partly to Emily and partly to Anna Maria Anable. In his letter to Anna Maria dated May 14, 1846, Adoniram Judson tells of seeing an unauthorized publication of many of Emily's writings—"Lilias Fane and other Tales"—in a bookstore while he was walking in New York. It was gaudily done, and obviously appealed to a mass market. See Emily's letter dated April 13, 1846 for more information on these unauthorized publications.

[127] Emily Chubbuck as Fanny Forester. See vol. 1, "Cast of Characters," s.v. "Chubbuck, Emily," also "Forester, Fanny."

accounted a sacrifice since you love me. There is nothing which I would not cheerfully resign—no place to which I would not willingly, gladly go. Yes, take me to your heart, darling, and fashion me entirely—**I will do or be whatever you wish—only let me hide in that dear bosom.** There is a blessing, a deep, sacred blessing even in the humiliating position which I now occupy. A year ago nobody could equal Fanny Forester; nobody so praised and petted by the public; now I bring disgrace where I would give the world to be able to give just a little honor. But it is *so* sweet to know how much love it requires to cover all this! **My own best beloved one! My all on earth! My heart's home!**

Did you love your poor unuseful[128] more that you pitied fate? How could you say such good things of me, speak so tenderly, even praise me, when I have bro't you so much trouble? God in heaven bless you, love; and turn even me into a blessing. I do believe that he will, for I pray for it most heartily. Once more spread open your arms to me! Good night—good-night—good-night.

Your Emily.

Source: Hanna family files; A. C. Kendrick, *The Life and Letters of Mrs. Emily C. Judson*, 194–95.

Emily E. Chubbuck to Adoniram Judson,[129] May 18, 1846[130]

Monday evening

I wrote so far, darling, after the receipt of yours last evening and intended to have said more today, but must dispense with the privilege pretty much. I have been out shopping this morning, and am too much fatigued to use my pen; but I am a great deal better in health today than I was yesterday. (Don't mind my crossing out—Mrs. Conant[131] is talking to me.) I shall be well enough to go home by Wednesday I am sure. I am ears deep in trading, and making, and the like confusion. I hope you will find it best to accept the money for outfit; for Madame Extravagance has made sad inroads on the $50 you left today; and she is afraid of getting so deeply in your debt that she can't pay you back! Ah me! That a wise man should run his head into such a noose!

I had a letter from Carey and Hart yesterday. They offer me 12 1/2 percent, on the retail price of my book, but object to republishing any thing [sic] in *Trippings*,

---

[128] Emily had once written a story titled "The Unuseful." (See *Trippings in Author-land*.) She often referred to herself in terms of her perceived inadequacies for married and missionary life.

[129] For an understanding of the comparison on an original letter with the letter actually printed by Dr. A. C. Kendrick in *The Life and Letters of Mrs. Emily C. Judson*, see the first footnote for the letter of Adoniram to Emily dated May 14, 1846.

[130] This is an addendum to a letter dated May 17, 1846.

[131] See vol. 1, "Cast of Characters," s.v. "Conant, H. C."

and to including the poetry.[132] They say that republished articles injure the sale of a book, and that poetry is a drug. I shall not, of course, make an imperfect collection, and so am again without a publisher. Will you try to make a bargain for me with Lippincott? Mr. Gillette[133] consulted him about an illustrated edition; but I think the one which I propose making far preferable. In truth, I don't care so much about making a good bargain as about having the book brought out for other reasons. It is unjust to myself to rest my literary reputation on the *Trippings*.

(I have been out all the day shopping, and am) too tired to write any more. **Keep loving me, darling, for I could not live without it now; and then I love you a little—"just a little bit," you know. And maybe** I think of you now and then between exclamations concerning pretty frocks, etc. **Maybe I do—so knowing for**—Oh, that is a charming blue! And that purple—how exquisite! You don't know what *absorbing* things new frocks are, for you, poor man, never had any; so I must not look for sympathy. Mrs. Quin, however, is in ecstasies; so adieu, that I may join her.

Yours (all that remains from the frock),

Nemmie Pettie

Mother-in-law[134] Blidgims[135] spoke of having a message for you this morning; but, as she is not in, I fear you will lose the favor.

Source: Hanna family files; A. C. Kendrick, *The Life and Letters of Mrs. Emily C. Judson*, 194–95.

Adoniram Judson to Emily E. Chubbuck,[136] May 19, 1846—New York

"Somehow—somehow"! Why it is because you love me, you wretch (pet name) and won't own it—won't look me in the face, and say, in all the fervid glow and delicious abandon of true passion, I love you more than tongue can tell or lips express—when so closely compressed by yours. Yes, little prudy, that is the reason why; and it is "somehow, somehow I can't help being reconciler." Can't eh? Better try—Do. I'll give you a lump of sugar if you will—I see no other way of getting out of this awful fix. Why, it is the town talk. The ladies are crazy with curiosity. Was it in the cars, that after reading a page in

[132] Emily was searching for a publisher for the sequel to *Trippings in Author-land* that would include additional sketches, stories, and poetry Emily had written in the interim. They settled on Ticknor, Reed and Fields in Boston, and *Alderbrook* was published in late 1846.

[133] See vol. 1, "Cast of Characters," s.v. "Gillette, The Reverend Abram Dunn."

[134] "Mother-in-law" was often used of Anna Maria Anable in her relationship with Emily Chubbuck. This was a self-reference and Emily used it of Anna Maria.

[135] See vol. 1, "Cast of Characters," s.v. "Blidgims."

[136] For an understanding of the comparison on an original letter with the letter actually printed by Dr. A. C. Kendrick in *The Life and Letters of Mrs. Emily C. Judson*, see the first footnote for the letter of Adoniram to Emily dated May 14, 1846.

Trippings,[137] he turned about and threw his arms around her and went off in an ecstasy of love at first sight? Or where was it? Do tell. And grave reverend men think between their speeches and prayers—O the ark! Here is the very champion of the best, this incarnate goliath of our side, this martyr double dyed in his own blood—hugging and kissing Fanny Forester,[138] with all the ardor of a boy of eighteen! Stop your ears, O Gath, for they will tell it. Now little Prue, if you can only just help being reconciler, the world would get set on its right side again, and all things would go on comfortably. What think of the sugar, darling? But to push on and marry F. F.—and then still worse, to baptize Cousin 'Bel'!![139] This would be, as Cromwell says, the crowning mercy with a vengeance. Hope would then stand tiptoe on the pinnacle of Corey's temple, and gather up her underdress, and poise her wings for a final flight—

Speaking of Corey[140]—I saw him last night and told him what was to be done at Utica,—and he said that he should be most happy to have me do it—and he added that it would be communion Sabbath and all come right.

So happy that you have got rid of the pain in your side and are better in health.[141] But you don't mention the tooth.[142] I found your dear letter of the 17th, on my return home last evening at 11 o'clock—but all day at Brooklyn—such crowds and shaking of hands and exclamations of congratulations—and frequent inquiries from old acquaintances / whether Miss Chubbuck was present and could be seen. In the evening, it came my turn to edify the assembly—which I did in a small speech—a dead one—but Stow[143] galvanized it. The missionary spirit is cer-

---

[137] Emily's first collection of sketches and stories was *Trippings in Author-land*. Because of a delay and looking for some way to entertain the great missionary, Mr. Gillette gave Adoniram Judson a copy as they journeyed from Boston to Philadelphia, and after reading it, Judson asked to be introduced to Fanny Forester, and he hoped that she might write the memoir of Sarah Hall Boardman Judson.

[138] Emily Chubbuck as Fanny Forester. See vol. 1, "Cast of Characters," s.v. "Chubbuck, Emily," also "Forester, Fanny."

[139] "Cousin 'Bel'" was Anna Maria Anable and the "character" from Emily's letter to the *New Mirror*, which was published on June 8, 1844 and catapulted Emily to literary fame. The letter concerned Emily and Cousin 'Bel's visit to New York and their lack of money to enjoy the wares of the many shops they passed. She asked if the editor of the *New Mirror* would like to help them out. Anna Maria had been exploring the possibility of Adoniram Judson baptizing her by immersion before he left for Burmah.

[140] See vol. 1, "Cast of Characters," s.v. "Corey, the Reverend D. G."

[141] See the letter of Emily E. Chubbuck to Adoniram Judson dated May 17, 1846.

[142] See the letter of Emily E. Chubbuck to Adoniram Judson dated May 6, 1846.

[143] Born in New Hampshire and educated in Washington, DC, Dr. Baron Stow returned to New Hampshire to become the pastor of the Baptist church in Portsmouth. In November 1832, he became the pastor of the Baldwin Place Church in Boston, where he led a significant revival. With changing social conditions in the North End of Boston and with significant erosion of his congregation as members moved to different areas of the city, Dr. Stowe resigned in 1848. Following a time of rest, he became the pastor of the Rowe Street Church and was there until 1867. The letters of Charles Gould speak of the revival events taking place under the ministry of Dr. Stow. In his letter of May 1, 1852, Mr. Gould relates, "The religious interest still continues with us. Dr. Stow baptized fourteen last Sabbath, and it was an occasion of deep interest. Hundreds went away unable to find a standing place in the Church." In reply to Emily's request for materials for the memoir, Dr. Stow wrote from Boston in December 1851, sending Emily for the memoir a copy of a manuscript written in 1810 by Adoniram Judson for the ministers' meeting at Bradford, New Hampshire. A second letter in January 1852 accompanies six volumes of early records and reports of the Missionary Union.

tainly very high, but well regulated. Prospects were never brighter. We all feel, that God is blessing us and will bless us more and more. All my intelligent friends say, that *our affair* will turn out well—that it is honorable to both parties—and that the more you are known, the better you will be loved, and the match approved. But I shall love you no better for that. "All thine own, 'mid gladness, love, fonder still, 'mid sadness, love." May we love one another well—but Christ better.

We will talk about Abby Ann[144] when we meet.[145] There are serious objections to your proposal—but after stating them all, I shall be inclined to leave the matter to your decision.

I will drop this in the post office, before I go on to Brooklyn. In some haste—

yours a little bit—

A Judson

Source: A. C. Kendrick, *The Life and Letters of Mrs. Emily C. Judson*, 198; Hanna family files.

Adoniram Judson to Emily E. Chubbuck May 22, 1846—New York

My dearest Love,

The meetings are over[146]—thanks be to God—I attended them all, except last evening, when being quite worn out (though I have not spoken in public at all) I obtained leave of absence. I was sorry, because it was a business meeting and taking leave of the missionaries—It is early, and I have not heard what was done, nor what officers were finally chosen, and consequently know not yet who is the Corresponding Secretary. I suppose that Mr. Peck[147] yet has the situation, because they would agree upon no other one that would be persuaded to take it. Dr. Williams and Mr. Stow[148] have both been solicited. I write in haste, just going off to Philada—

Dearest Love—out of the whirl in which I have been plunged—hundreds shaking hands from all parts of the country—and never alone—I look away to the loggery[149] with intense longing—you, dear, are my sweet comfort and joy. May God open you to me, though I know I am wholly unworthy of you.

[144] See vol. 1, "Cast of Characters," s.v. "Judson, Abby Ann."

[145] In her morning letter of May 17, 1846, Emily had suggested very strongly, with surprisingly perceptive reasons, that Abby Ann be taken to Burmah with them.

[146] Adoniram Judson had been attending the meetings of the American Baptist Missionary Union (the new name for the American Baptist Board of Foreign Missions.

[147] See vol. 1, "Cast of Characters," s.v. "Peck, The Reverend Doctor Solomon."

[148] See vol. 1, "Cast of Characters," s.v. "Stow, Dr. Baron."

[149] The loggery was Emily's father's home. See Kendrick, *The Life and Letters of Mrs. Emily C. Judson*, 166. See also vol. 1, "Places, Events, Organizations, and Magazines," s.v. "Loggery, The."

Mrs. Allen[150] thinks it will be very wise indeed for you, not now, but at some future time, to prepare the memoir of Sarah[151]—I have had a pleasant interview with Mr. West,[152] but no opportunity for particular conversation—called at his house but he was not at home.

Love me, darling, though I am in a hurry

A. Judson   Source: Hanna family files.

Emily C. Chubbuck to Adoniram Judson, May 22, 1846—Hamilton

My dearest friend,

I sh'd not send you this little line, but that I am unfit for writing, and I am afraid you will think me neglectful. I have been very well indeed, but probably by over-doing and over-excitement I bro't on a severe attack which makes me too weak to use my pen, altho' I know I shall be quite well tomorrow.

Mother[153] and Kate[154] are half-crazy to have Freeman[155] paint your portrait, and he promises that he will not take a copy nor allow one to be taken. If you *can* make arrangements I sh'd like to oblige them.

I must not write any more. Ten thousand kisses, darling—ten thousand, thousand heart kisses. Good-night, good-night, good-night.

Your Nemmy[156]

My aunt Catharine[157] from Michigan is here and she says you *must* come *next week*. We have had glorious news from my brother Walker.[158] He has become pious and united with the church since you wrote him. Please send him another letter. He would have written you, but was too bashful.

Source: Hanna family files.

---

[150] Mrs. Eliza Allen, the editor and publisher of *The Mother's Journal*.

[151] The memoir of Sarah Hall Boardman Judson. Adoniram originally approached Emily on Christmas Day 1845 with this in mind after reading *Trippings in Author-land*; after their engagement, however, there was some question as to the propriety of Adoniram Judson's new wife taking on the responsibility. Emily said that even Miss Cynthia Sheldon and Anna Maria Anable questioned the propriety of it. In the end, however, Emily created a beautiful memoir of the second Mrs. Judson.

[152] See vol. 1, "Cast of Characters," s.v. "West, Mr. Robert." In his letter of April 28, 1846, Mr. West mentioned that he hoped he would see Adoniram Judson at the convention.

[153] Emily's mother. See vol. 1, "Cast of Characters," s.v. "Chubbuck, Lavinia Richards."

[154] See vol. 1, "Cast of Characters," s.v. "Chubbuck, Miss Sarah Catharine."

[155] In prior letters of this period, there had been several references to the idea of Freeman painting a portrait with some ideas from the engraving being done by John Sartain. The engraving became the portrait for *Alderbrook* when it was published. Emily suggests that they would like a portrait of Judson at the same time.

[156] Emily Chubbuck. See vol. 1, "Cast of Characters," s.v. "Nemmy, Nem, or Nemmy Petty (Nemmie Pettie)." Also the chapter "Names of Endearment."

[157] See Emily's letter of May 17, 1846 for another reference to Aunt Catherine, who was her mother's sister.

[158] See vol. 1, "Cast of Characters," s.v. "Chubbuck, John Walker."

Emily E. Chubbuck to Anna Maria Anable, May 22, 1846[159]—Hamilton

"Dearest Blidgy,"[160]

I rec'd Aunt Cynthia's[161] kind letter last night together with one from the honourable [sic] Capt.[162] who is in good health and spirits. Mr. Corey[163] has spoken to him about baptizing you and so Ninny[164]—Ninny darlin'! Go and see Mr. Wiley; and don't mind Horace Hawley[165] nor anybody else. It is best to *do it right*, let the consequences be what they may; and these are small things which will not last. I should'nt [sic] wonder if that church sh'd wake up to its self-righteousness before long; and an entire revolution sh'd take place in it. At any rate, it is your duty to be baptized, and the ignorance and error there is in the church the more good you can effect. The doc. thinks he is getting into the Forester[166] family pretty deeply—marrying Fanny and baptizing cousin 'Bel.'[167]

Tell Aunt C. that the Troy man is a real nice fellow and ought to make Mr. Bailey blush. We must stay over night [sic] in Troy, if it is among the number of possibles and they can have us.

Oh, Ninny, it takes me. When I got home they were all gone. I set to work and unpacked and put all my things out of the way; then cut out my chemise and commenced working on one that evening. Kitty[168] was—Ah, Ninny I have done it. I have had a little piece of a cachinnation and so can't brag any more. I'll write again soon. Ten thousand kisses. Love to all—Aunt C. in particular, and yourself, darling, more, most, mostest especially. Your lovin'

Nemmie Pettie.[169]

Source: Hanna family files.

---

[159] This letter is undated. In her May 26 letter, Anna Maria says that she had spoken with Mr. Wiley; here Emily encourages Anna Maria to do that, so the letter is placed the Friday before.

[160] See vol. 1, "Cast of Characters," s.v. "Blidgims."

[161] See vol. 1, "Cast of Characters," s.v. "Sheldon, Miss Cynthia."

[162] This is a reference to Adoniram Judson. He signed his March 7, 1846 letter to Emily "Hilarion Johnson." He uses this again, or variations on it (The Hon. Captain Johnson), on April 20; May 8; and May 14, 1846

[163] See vol. 1, "Cast of Characters," s.v. "Corey, the Reverend D. G."

[164] Anna Maria Anable. See vol. 1, "Cast of Characters," s.v. "Ninny."

[165] See vol. 1, "Cast of Characters," s.v. "Hawley, Mr. Horace H."

[166] Emily Chubbuck as Fanny Forester. See vol. 1, "Cast of Characters," s.v. "Chubbuck, Emily," also "Forester, Fanny."

[167] "Cousin 'Bel" was Anna Maria Anable.

[168] See vol. 1, "Cast of Characters," s.v. "Chubbuck, Miss Sarah Catharine."

[169] See vol. 1, "Cast of Characters," s.v. "Nemmy, Nem, or Nemmy Petty (Nemmie Petie)." See also the chapter "Names of Endearment."

Anna Maria Anable to Adoniram Judson, May 23, 1846—Utica

My dearest friend, my Hilarion[170]

Dost think our poor Nemmy Petty[171] will *ever* come to her senses! The last I heard of her—she was still haunting the road to Binghampton[172] and this communication (received this afternoon) which I forward for your inspection—gives very little encouragement for her restoration.

To be sure a sane person *might* be desirous of having my portrait[173] for a friend, but under existing circumstances, it would have been more *sensible* as well as more flattering, had she requested it for herself. And then, think of her getting it into her foolish head that I had written to her brother Walker?[174] Absurd! Never believe it, my dear Hilarion! Ah me! By week after next I am sure we shall be obliged to place her in the state Lunatic Asylum.[175]

Dearest Hilarion, "now my *only* beloved one" tell me frankly your feelings on this subject. I hope you are not utterly inconsolable. Believe me then in one heart that feels for you—female delicacy forbids her to say more. Forbear [ ]

Your ever devoted and *constant*

Ninny[176] Blidgims[177]

Wasn't it most insane of her to think any body [*sic*] could receive so many kisses at one dose.

Source: Hanna family files.

---

[170] Adoniram Judson signed his March 7, 1846 letter to Emily "Hilarion Johnson." He uses this again, or variations on it (The Hon. Captain Johnson), on April 20; May 8; and May 14, 1846.

[171] Emily E. Chubbuck names. See vol. 1, "Cast of Characters," s.v. "Nemmy, Nem, Nemmy Petty." Also the section "Names of Endearment."

[172] See the letter of Adoniram Judson to Anna Maria Anable dated May 8, 1846.

[173] There has been some talk in the correspondence of Freeman painting a portrait of Emily Chubbuck, referenced by the engraving being done by John Sartain. On May 22, Emily wrote that her mother and Kate were anxious to have Freeman paint Adoniram Judson's portrait. In this instance, it seems that Adoniram, on Emily's behalf, asked if Anna Maria would allow her portrait to be painted.

[174] See vol. 1, "Cast of Characters," s.v. "Chubbuck, John Walker."

[175] The time period spoken of here was to be the time of the marriage between Adoniram Judson and Emily Chubbuck.

[176] Anna Maria Anable. See vol. 1, "Cast of Characters," s.v. "Ninny."

[177] See vol. 1, "Cast of Characters," s.v. "Blidgims." Also "A timeline Blidgims References."

Adoniram Judson to Emily E. Chubbuck,[178] May 23, 1846— Philadelphia

My dearest Love,

Here I am in my old chamber, at the Robarts,[179] where I first began to love you, you creature, who have given me so much trouble—O my! To think of it all! And so much exquisite delight—O my! To think of that too! And here you sat on an ottoman at my feet, and dropt a hair comb, and next morning, it was found on the carpet—a pretty tell tale. Will there ever be any more tell-tales? And what will they tell about! And I have been through Courting Alley and observed all the well known sign-boards and marks, which used to guide my sometimes anxious, sometimes joyful steps between this and Mr. Gillette's.[180] I have called on your friends Mr. and Mrs. Mitchell[181] and Mrs. Tyndale,[182] and tried to make myself amiable and interesting for your sake, and I guess I succeeded pretty well.

Eve'g We have had a meeting at Mr. Gillette's, by appointment—Mr. Sartain[183] and I—and we discussed the alterations you proposed in the engraving—He is to give me an amended proof, before I leave, which I shall forward to you—probably with this letter .

---

[178] This letter had two addendums dated May 24 and May 25.

[179] Mr. and Mrs. W. S. Robarts were active in Philadelphia Baptist circles. They were frequent visitors to the home of the Reverend and Mrs. A. D. Gillette, and later to the Misses Anable's School which Anna Maria Anable and her extended family had started in Philadelphia in 1848. In his biography of his father, Edward Judson mentioned that Adoniram Judson had stayed at the Robarts' home when he came to Philadelphia in December 1845, where and when he was to meet Emily Chubbuck. A. C. Kendrick said, "(Mr. Gillette and Dr. Judson) arrived in (or out of) due time in Philadelphia, and Dr. Judson was welcomed to the house of Mr. and Mrs. W. S. Robarts, who became warm personal friends, as they were already active friends of the mission cause." In 1846, with the engagement of Adoniram Judson and Emily Chubbuck, the Correspondence indicates some hard feelings towards Mrs. Robarts for comments that were made disparaging the coming marriage and missionary service. This is to be found in Emily's letter to Adoniram dated February 6, 1846; Mrs. Robarts seemed to be accusing Emily of worldliness—when all the time, Emily was quick to say, Mrs. Robarts was engaging in the same activity of which Emily was accused. The Correspondence also indicates a satisfactory healing of the relationship. In January 1849 Miss Sheldon told Emily that Mrs. Robarts had placed their daughter Mary in the Misses Anable's School.

[180] See vol. 1, "Cast of Characters," s.v. "Gillette, The Reverend Abram Dunn." He and his wife Hannah remained valued and trusted friends, not only with Emily, but with the Sheldon and Anable families.

[181] Mr. and Mrs. Mitchell lived in Philadelphia; Mrs. Tyndale, Mrs. Mitchell's mother and the owner of a prosperous china shop in downtown Philadelphia, lived with them. In November 1845, as Emily was thinking of prolonging her stay in the city to last through the winter, the Mitchells generously offered to open their home to her, promising that they would do everything in their power to take good care of her: her own room, solitude or company as desired, the ability to write, and all of the comforts they could provide. Emily did express appreciation, saying that many of her friends told her what wonderful people they were and how sensitive they were to the needs of an invalid such as Emily was at that time. Her one serious reservation was that they were Unitarians. In the end Emily decided that she would stay with the Reverend and Mrs. Gillette, knowing from her past experience that she would be more than comfortable with them.

[182] See vol. 1, "Cast of Characters," s.v. "Tyndale, Sarah."

[183] See vol. 1, "Cast of Characters," s.v. "Sartain, John."

Mr. Kennard and other grave members of the publications Committee[184] hesitate about publishing *Allen Lucas*,[185] because it is not a decidedly religious work, and I have taken all your three revised copies out of their hands, as I am here and can take them, whereas when I am away and you might wish to recover them, you might write and write in vain for them. There is no energy or promptness in this committee. But I have left them your letter and requested them to answer it forthwith, and according as they and you decide, the copies can be returned to them at any time.

Source: Hanna family files.

Mr. Joseph C. Neal to Emily E. Chubbuck, May 23, 1846—Philadelphia

My Dear Miss Fanny[186]

I fear that so far as the publishers of Philadelphia are concerned, the prospect in regard to your volume is not very promising.[187] I called on Carey and Hart yesterday who decline, for reasons which I believe have been discussed between you and them—the poetry and the reproduction articles.—I also went to Appleton, who also declined, being unwilling to publish anything that had appeared before and having just refused to undertake a work coming under that objection for Mrs. Sigourney.[188]

Lindsay and Blackiston were likewise similarly unpractical, the objection apparently being universal here against undertaking to publish one's "remains" no matter how meritorious, and I therefore proceeded no further in the search, not knowing, indeed, to whom else to apply, especially as this is the dull season when booksellers are torpid.

I attended to the Graham[189] affair, and had orders given to the clerk to forward the money to you as requested. Should it not arrive in a reasonable time please do let me know.

[184] The Reverend Mr. Gillette was associated with the American Baptist Publication Society, and apparently, there had been some discussion of reissuing some of Emily's writings. See Mr. Gillette's letter to Emily Chubbuck dated May 5, 1846.

[185] *Allen Lucas* was one of Emily's earlier books. On May 8, 1846 Emily wrote to Anna Maria Anable reporting that Dr. Solomon Peck, executive secretary of the American Baptist Missionary Union, had called it an "evil book," not fit for republication.

[186] Emily Chubbuck as Fanny Forester. See vol. 1, "Cast of Characters," s.v. "Chubbuck, Emily," also "Forester, Fanny."

[187] After *Trippings in Author-land*, Emily was looking for a publisher for further sketches, poetry, and stories; it would be published as *Alderbrook*. The correspondence indicates that Robert West, Adoniram Judson, and the Reverend A. D. Gillette were also making publication inquiries on her behalf.

[188] Lydia Huntley Sigourney was one of the first American women to succeed at a literary career. A teacher, she had moved to Hartford, Connecticut, at the invitation of Daniel Wadsworth to open a school for the daughters of his friends. In 1819, she married Charles Sigourney, and the resulting financial stability allowed her to devote herself full time to writing and publishing anonymously. She used the proceeds from her writings to fund a number of charities, among them the cause of missions at home and abroad. Her celebrity reached its height with the 1849 publication of her *Illustrated Poems* in a sumptuously bound, gilt-edged edition.

[189] See vol. 1, "Cast of Characters," s.v. "Graham, George."

Our friends are well and sorry, as usual. The letters were delivered.
With regrets that I have not been better able to serve you,
Believe me
Ever your friend,
Joseph C. Neal

Source: American Baptist Historical Society, AJ 25, no. 1244.

Adoniram Judson to Emily E. Chubbuck,[190] May 24, 1846

I have just made my farewell speech at Mr. Gillette's[191] meeting house. Several ministers were present and the house full. I have now done with Philada—and shall leave for New York by the afternoon train tomorrow. Sweet place it is, on some accounts, and associated with some of the sweetest recollections of my life.[192]

Source: Hanna family files.

Emily E. Chubbuck to Adoniram Judson,[193] May 24, 1846—Hamilton

I rec'd yours of the 18th last evening, darling together with one dated 22nd. **I didn't know that my first letter to you went by private hand—it was some of aunt C's doings.**[194] I am kept at home another Sabbath by illness although I am much better than when I wrote last. The jaunt in the stage made my *side* worse;[195] and I find that this is no place to recruit. My last days at home!—everything, every word, every look brings this to mind constantly; and although I am always cheerful, it wears from day to day upon health and spirits. Oh, it is a dreadful thing to *live*— a thing for a great many reasons more to be dreaded than death. And this new life on which I am about to enter—in every respect new and crowded with responsibilities. It is too heavy for me; all the future is shut away by heavy clouds that I cannot look beyond. How do I even know that you will continue to love me, except from habit, when you know me still better and the knowledge has been "an old story." And then can you imagine a more miserable creature? "As thy day is so shall thy strength be" is a glorious promise sometimes; and sometimes it seems to me to have (utterly no meaning) **no meaning at all**. Now my faith in it is so low,

---

[190] This was the first addendum to Adoniram Judson's letter of May 23, 1846. Another was added on May 25.

[191] See vol. 1, "Cast of Characters," s.v. "Gillette, The Reverend Abram Dunn."

[192] Adoniram Judson had met Emily Chubbuck at the home of the Reverend and Mrs. A. D. Gillette on Christmas Day, 1845.

[193] For an understanding of the comparison on an original letter with the letter actually printed by Dr. A. C. Kendrick in *The Life and Letters of Mrs. Emily C. Judson*, see the first footnote for the letter of Adoniram to Emily dated May 14, 1846.

[194] See vol. 1, "Cast of Characters," s.v. "Sheldon, Miss Cynthia."

and my dread of the future so great that I would beg God to let me die here, and be buried away from all this tumult, this jarring, these trials, these duties and cares, but for leaving you again alone. It is impossible that I shall ever be anything but a weight upon your hands and heart. Why has all this been suffered to come about, dearest? Doubtless for good but it is a good which is hidden. I was **(Mrs. Allen**[196] **and the like to the contrary notwithstanding)** making myself indirectly useful— improving the peculiar talent which God had given me—perhaps not always with judgment; but my judgment was improving. Now I have placed myself in a position to be canvassed and have the influence which I was exerting destroyed. You were a demigod, and I have bro't you down. That is a little the worst. Do you recollect the evening of our last arrival here? The same feeling comes back to me every time I go into the parlour, and then (forgive me; you know that I love you with all my heart and soul) I am sorry that we ever met. I know that that same regret *must* come over you sometimes. Indeed, though no clairvoyant, I sometimes am quite sure that I can feel it shaping itself in your mind among the strange people that you meet in N. Y. and Philada.

Evening—I dare not read over what I have written dearest, for in truth I am very unamiable today—heart aching. It is a little doubtful whether this meets you, I suppose; it certainly will not if you return to N. Y. tomorrow. Shall I tell you, deary, how you spoil, almost, your own sweet letters by introducing Mrs. Allen's name. There never was anything written but you can distort into something bad (even the Bible itself) and I do not think Mrs. Allen a competent critic. She is a shrewd, observing woman, but in matters of literature she is inferior, I think, to educated ladies in general. I have Mrs. Conant's[197] **opinion to uphold mine in this. I am very sorry that I have written so many letters to Mrs. A. "Dignified silence" in this case, I think would have been more becoming.**

I understand what you mean by exalting genius[198] too highly, and in looking over the articles will try to express myself more clearly. I do believe genius to be a peculiar gift from God, requiring great simplicity of character, purity and innocence

[195] On May 17, 1846, Emily wrote to Adoniram: "I have been much alarmed since you went away about my side, because I was afraid of a liver-complaint, but I have quite recovered from that fear now. I have found an outward application which helps it and it is much better today. I dare say, I shall able to get out tomorrow. I presume I took cold and it settled there."

[196] This reference is to Mrs. Eliza Allen, the editor of the prominent Christian publication *The Mother's Journal*. Emily did write for her, but the correspondence indicates that Mrs. Allen thought that Christian writers had, or should have, high and noble purposes and not seek the kind of compensation for their articles that would be harmful to the publications for which they were written. There are six letters in the correspondence from Mrs. Allen, beginning February 1844. See Emily's comment on Mrs. Allen in the above paragraph marked with bold type (because A. C. Kendrick omitted this paragraph from the portion of the letter he included in *The Life and Letters of Mrs. Emily C. Judson*.

[197] Anna Maria's negative comments about Mrs. Conant in her letter of July 31, 1848. See vol. 1, "Cast of Characters," s.v. "Conant, H. C."

[198] Emily had recently written an article on "Genius" to be published in the *Columbian Magazine*.

for its proper development. When this gift is desecrated, its possessor is rendered miserable in proportion to his superiority to other men and proportionately depraved. The angels that sinned and fell became devils. There is something in the inspiration of genius partaking of religion, a hallowing influence **in it**; but **from various causes** men possessing this gift are exposed to **peculiar** temptations **which other men are not** and frequently fall—perhaps not more frequently than others, but the fall is more obvious because the descent is greater. **Religious people are very apt to make sweeping charges against genius, pronouncing it an "unhallowed thing" from the fact that like all the other gifts with which we are endowed it is liable to desecration and when badly used it is a dangerous thing. Genius** (Yet) wherever you find it (even in Byron) has **always** some touches to show its origin; like Milton's fallen one, you **can** still see the angel in it. Otherwise it would be less dangerous. **But the religious world does not** (Christians do not) do well to eschew the aid of Genius—**it is needed.** Some of the inspired writers had this inspiration also; David, Isaiah and John of Patmos. **There! Haven't I delivered myself of quite an essay? Don't yawn, deary; I will not inflict any more of my stupidity upon you.**

I would give you kisses if you were here, but there is no use in putting them on the paper—no use at all. Our lips will soon meet—a heart-meeting, I trust. And then—and then—Darling, do love me always, just as you do now—love me when you are all that I have, for once sure of that I know I shall be happy. God in heaven guard you, and grant you every blessing!

Your affectionate Emily

A friend of Miss C's in Troy has sent us two [ ] to Boston.

Source: Hanna family files; A. C. Kendrick, *The Life and Letters of Mrs. Emily C. Judson*, 198–200.

Anna Maria Anable to Adoniram Judson,[199] May 24, 1846[200]—Utica

My dear friend

I trust you will not think I presume too much on your kindness to me, and on your interest in me as a friend of Emily's if I write you for advice on a subject of vital importance to me.

---

[199] This letter was written to Adoniram Judson in New York City in the care of "I Newton Esq." Adoniram stayed frequently with them, and there are a number of letters in the correspondence from them; they were wealthy, ardent supporters of missions. We know from the page following page 456 of Edward Judson's biography of his father, that Adoniram gave Mrs. Newton an inscribed book of Burmese hymns collected by Sarah Hall Boardman Judson. Judon, Edward. The Life of Adoniram Judson (Philadelphia: *The American Baptist Publication Society*, 1883).

[200] This letter has an addendum dated May 25, 1846.

I write, because I know not what perverse spirit possesses me when in your presence to behave always as if I never had a sober thought; for you are no sooner gone than I regret nothing so much as that I have sought no opportunity of conversing seriously with you. You are almost the only man I have ever seen in whom I felt spontaneously such trust as to wish to repose this sort of confidence in, and even now, when I know you are overwhelmed with cares and business so much more important than my little perplexities will seem very trivial things to trouble you with, I trust without fear to your forbearance and to your natural benevolence of heart.

Now that Emily has gone, and the time is so rapidly approaching when I shall see her no more, there is nothing that can [Note: "soften" is written and crossed out.] sooth the uncontrollable bursts of anguish that come over me at the thought of parting with her forever but the reflection that all of these things are ordered for our everlasting good by a higher power—the righteousness of whose decrees we must not dispute. I can even see now that it will be better for Emily—and in the desolateness of my little chamber, with no human eye that can understand a tithe of my grief, the assurance that my Saviour [sic] is at the helm and orders all things in love to our souls is an inexpressible comfort to me.

The important question with me now is, have I ever in any degree appreciated that love? Do I desire the favor and friendship of my Saviour [sic] above all human friendship—above every earthly good? I shall then not only be submissive under his decrees, but desire to do his will in all things. He has said "if ye love me"—if "ye are my friends" "keep my commandments." Through you, I have learned that there is one explicit command of the Saviour [sic] which I have never obeyed. Do you now perceive why I write to you? I have no Baptist friends who know exactly what to advise under existing circumstances, and my Pedo-baptist friends will of course think I am doing a very foolish thing.

Is it wrong for me to desire to receive the sacred ordinance of baptism at your hands above all others? I should esteem it a very great privilege. In performing this simple act of obedience to the commands of my Saviour [sic] I wish to be distracted by no unpleasant associations such as might arise at some future time—I wish to feel the full impact, the *beautiful significance* of the symbols as I now see it expressed in my Bible.

I desire to be "buried with Christ in baptism" and to rise from that burial to *newness of life*.

Source: American Baptist Historical Society, AJ 6, no. 77.

Emily E. Chubbuck to J. Walker Chubbuck, May 24, 1846—Hamilton

My very dear brother,

I am sorry, very sorry, that I must never see you again in this world; but I suppose there is no hope of it now. It is impossible for us to defer sailing till August as we sh'd have a bad voyage and arrive in an unpleasant season. We are to be married in a week from next Tuesday, remain here a few days, stop in Utica over the Sabbath where the doctor will baptize my most intimate friend, Miss Anable[201] (the cousin 'Bel'[202] of my sketches) and then go on to visit the children[203] etc. We sail about the first of July. My good doctor is the noblest, best, and kindest man in the world, full of sympathy, generosity and every good quality. More still he is a humble, devoted Christian, one who will guide me always in the paths of right. He is much older than I am, true, but not as much as people generally think. I am twenty-eight and he fifty-seven. His hair is black, his teeth perfect and his face young-looking. He has, however, quite a stoop in his shoulders. His health is perfectly good except an affection of the throat, and he is very likely to outlive me. Oh, I am so sorry that you can't see him for no description can do him justice—so good, so humble, and gentle.

I was delighted to hear such good news of you. This will be the beginning of a new life for you—new tho'ts, new wishes, new hopes, new objects of interest. May God bless you by his presence ever, and may you "grow in grace" continually.[204] Pray for Wallace[205] and Ben.[206] There is but little hope I suppose that B. will ever be better, but W.—I can scarce be reconciled to his wasting his life so.

[201] See vol. 1, "Cast of Characters," s.v. "Anable, Miss Anna Maria."

[202] "Cousin 'Bel'" was Anna Maria Anable.

[203] Abby Ann Judson at Bradford Academy in Bradford, Massachusetts; Adoniram Judson, and Elnathan Judson, both with Dr. and Mrs. Calvin Newton in Worcester, Massachusetts. Henry Hall Judson and Edward Judson were in Burmah, taken care of by missionary families.

[204] Emily is speaking of the religious awakening that her brother was beginning to experience. Adoniram Judson wrote to him on these matters. Apparently, this was a continuing journey. See Emily's letter dated May 22, 1846, for more information on her brother's awakening. On June 21, 1848, Emily wrote Walker a strongly evangelical letter, inviting his conversion. In a letter dated August 15, 1849, she told him that she is glad to hear of his conversion, although she wished that he had become a Baptist instead of a Presbyterian.

[205] Born January 1, 1824, William Wallace Chubbuck was six years younger than Emily. During these years of Emily's correspondence, Wallace lived at or near home and worked at different occupations including printing, office work, and teaching. Emily wrote of him as capable in many areas, but seeming to lack ambition at times. He proved to be a strong support for the Chubbuck family over these years, and at the time of her death in 1854, Wallace had become one of Emily's primary caregivers. After February 1854, she dictated all her letters to him because of her failing strength. Wallace was active in newspaper and political activities; he also worked with at least one of the legislative committees in Albany. He was married in July of 1854; he died in August of 1861.

[206] Emily's older brother Benjamin or "Ben," born March 25, 1809. In a biography of her life which she wrote for Adoniram Judson in 1846, Emily told of how Ben, as a young boy, had sustained some kind of brain inflammation, which was to seriously impair his judgment and behavior. See Emily's letter of February 18, 1838 for some very sharp comments on Ben. Then, on April 2, 1839, Emily wrote to her brother Walker that Ben had been sent to state prison for stealing a horse, blanket and saddle. Later correspondence had litanies of such problems—stealing a cow, difficulties holding jobs, problems with his marriage, situations exacerbated by character flaws. He died in September, 1846, shortly after Emily had left for Burmah. Ben had married Ann Fleming of Morrisville in 1837, and he was the father of two children.

By the doctor's help I shall be able to leave the family in very comfortable circumstances. I have succeeded in paying for my place here, have furnished the house quite handsomely, and supplied Katy[207] with clothing to last her a long time. The doctor had purchased in my name three acres of land, nearby, where father may pasture his horse, raise a few oats etc. However, if they sh'd be sick you must look after them some. I hope you will find it in your power to remit little sums of money to mother, now and then, if it be only a dollar at a time. I would still continue to help them, however distant I might be, but after I leave the country I cannot take money for my writings. The mission rules are against it. As for Wallace, he picks all our pockets instead of putting a penny in. I paid $700[208] for my place at first and have since built a shed and kitchen which cost upwards of $80. I am just now having the house painted. I don't think that I would take $1,000 for my handsome corner lot now.

Aunt Catharine[209] is here and will stay until I am married. She sends love to you. Ben lives with her. He behaves pretty well in the main, she says, tho' he will go to these mean, low dances and now and then he drinks enough to show it. I wish you would write him about it.

I was sorry that you did'nt [sic] write the doctor—answer his letter. I do not know what it was about for he did'nt [sic] show it to anybody, but I am sure that it must have been very good. I wish you would write him before we leave the country. Address "Rev. A. Judson D. D., Bap't Mission Rooms, 17 Joy's Buildings, Boston, Mass." Enclose a letter to me at the same time.

May the kind God whom we both love, my dear brother, watch over and guide and be ever present with you—May he make you useful in this world and happy in the next. May we, though a hemisphere be between us in this world, meet above where there are no partings. Pray for me, my beloved brother, and think of me often—very often.

Your most affectionate sister,

Emily Chubbuck

When you come home Kate will tell you about some splendid offers that I have had in the matrimonial line which will convince you that I knew what I was about when I accepted my good, high-souled old doctor.

Source: Jerome Walker Chubbuck Collection, Wisconsin Historical Society Archives, Madison WI.

---

[207] See vol. 1, "Cast of Characters," s.v. "Chubbuck, Miss Sarah Catharine."

[208] A. C. Kendrick, on page 76 of *The Life and Letters of Mrs. Emily C. Judson*, says that Emily purchased "the house and garden in the village for four hundred dollars, the debt to be discharged in four annual payments."

[209] "Aunt Catharine" was a sister of Lavinia Richards Chubbuck.

Anna Maria Anable to Adoniram Judson,[210] May 25, 1846[211]

Monday morning

Mr. Corey[212] has been here to breakfast and he tells me you saw him in Brooklyn.[213] How kind and considerate it was of you. How easy you make it for me to perform my duty.[214] May Heaven bless you for that good heart of yours.

I do not know now whether it is best for me to send this letter or not. I believe I will though. You must submit to the penalty imposed on all persons of your disposition—that is, listen to the confidences of every insignificant person that "has a tale to tell."

Very respectfully and affectionately
Anna M. Anable

The Rev. A. Judson D.D.

Source: American Baptist Historical Society, AJ 6, no. 77.

Adoniram Judson to Emily E. Chubbuck,[215] May 25, 1846

Next Monday morning, I shall probably be at Skaneateles, preparing to start for Hamilton.[216] Ah, wild Fanny[217] birdie! The time is near when thou canst no more fly about at liberty and sing thy songs from tree to tree, but will have to hop about, at the beck of the bird catchers, with a string tied to thy poor little leg. Doesn't want [sic] to escape before it is too late? Can't help thyself birdie. It is even now too late. The huntsman has a hook in thy poor little heart. And it is too late—so hold still and have the string put on. It won't hurt you. Don't be concerned. He is rather a kind old fellow and he has got a live nest in his bosom, lined with soft heart-skin for birdie to sleep in.

Query—Why is it that lovers so frequently become unhappy after marriage? Because they depend too much on the sweet interchange of lips and arms and bosom love and know not that those indulgencies, however sweet, will at length pall upon the senses, unless sustained by interchange of mind and cultivated intel-

---

[210] This letter was written to Adoniram Judson in New York City in the care of "I Newton Esq.," missions supporters and frequent hosts of Adoniram Judson.

[211] This letter is an addendum to a letter dated May 24, 1846.

[212] See vol. 1, "Cast of Characters," s.v. "Corey, the Reverend D. G."

[213] See the letter from Adoniram Judson to Emily E. Chubbuck dated May 19, 1846.

[214] Anna Maria Anable was baptized by Dr. Judson before they left for Burmah, on June 7 in Utica, New York.

[215] This is the second addendum to Adoniram Judson's letter, which he began May 23, 1846. The first addendum was dated May 24.

[216] Adoniram and Emily were married in Hamilton on June 2, 1846, by Dr. Nathaniel Kendrick.

[217] Emily Chubbuck as Fanny Forester. See vol. 1, "Cast of Characters," s.v. "Chubbuck, Emily," also "Forester, Fanny."

lects, refined tastes; hearts touched by divine grace need only an interchange of congenial sentiments and of gracious affections to become indissolubly attached and blended in one. My prospect of conjugal happiness was never so bright as at present. I am sure that I shall not be disappointed. O that you may not be! Come to my arms, darling of my soul. Let us exchange those vows which will unite us forever, and may they be crowned with the blessings of God! Amen and amen.

I am just going out to Gillette's[218] and Sartain's,[219] and will take this letter though unfinished, to deposit in the post office, if I pass that way. Otherwise, shall add more at a later date—

Yours ever

A Judson

Post office, 12 o'clock

I start at half past 4 for N. Y. Sartain is still working on the engraving and will give me a copy before I leave.

I shall probably spend Friday night in Utica—this is my present intention.

Source: Hanna family files.

Anna Maria Anable to Emily E. Chubbuck, May 25, 1846

Monday Night between 11 and 12

Dear Nemmy[220]

C'est le [ ] *pas qui conte*, and I have taken it. I have talked this evening with Mr. Bacon one of my elders upon the subject of my leaving the church and he was—oh, so kind! He perfectly approved of my wishes—that is feeling as I do. I then went down into Aunt Cynthia's[221] room and have been talking ever since with Mr. Corey.[222] He had come back from New York, feeling perfectly right about everything (I guess the folks there think the Dr. has done a [ ] thing). Mr. Dean[223] has been staying with him too, and I rather think he has had some influence in setting him right. Everybody here is carried away with Mr. Dean—excepting your humble servant—who by general consent should have been *most* carried away. I saw him but a moment—*shall* I feel in [ ] of him? Now Nemmy darling I do not believe I

[218] See vol. 1, "Cast of Characters," s.v. "Gillette, The Reverend Abram Dunn."

[219] See vol. 1, "Cast of Characters," s.v. "Sartain, John."

[220] Emily Chubbuck. See vol. 1, "Cast of Characters," s.v. "Nemmy, Nem, or Nemmy Petty (Nemmie Pettie)." Also the chapter "Names of Endearment."

[221] See vol. 1, "Cast of Characters," s.v. "Sheldon, Miss Cynthia."

[222] See vol. 1, "Cast of Characters," s.v. "Corey, the Reverend D. G."

[223] See vol. 1, "Cast of Characters," s.v. "Dean, William."

can come out to you before Saturday. I ought to see Mr. Wiley and have a *talk* with him, but he will not return before Friday or Saturday—I dread having a talk with him, for he is one of your enlightened pedo baptists—very strong—and he will want to convince me. Seems to me that I should like to try my new arguments on him, if he will give me a chance. I saw Mrs. Churchill today—there are six chemises and two cross barred night-gowns ready for you, besides the quilt. I think we shall get your things all in fine train—Write me and let me know if you have any [ ]. I will attend to them. How are you getting on with your things there? Are you worried and does [sic] you want Ninny[224] to come and help you?

Mr. Corey said the Dr. spoke to him in Brooklyn about me[225]—and he is very cordial in having him baptize me. Wasn't it kind of the Dr.? How easy he makes it for a body to do what is right. I love that man Emily and you need'nt say nothing [sic] to the contrary. I am now a little worried about what I should hear from Aunt Urania[226]—I am afraid she will veto the whole thing—and I have almost promised to do nothing at present unless she gives her consent. I presume her Dr.[227] will bring her around right [ ] [ ] has [ ] [ ].

Good Night
Ninny

Source: American Baptist Historical Society, AJ 23, no. 1136.

Marriage Announcement, *Roman Citizen*[228] May 25, 1846

Fanny Forester[229]—"Dear, delightful Fanny Forrester," as Willis[230] calls her, is to be married in June. Her future husband is the Rev. Mr. Judson, who has been for more than thirty years a missionary in Burmah. His first wife was the lamented Harriet Newell [sic].[231] His second wife died lately at St. Helena[232] on her way back to America. Mr. J. is to return to Burmah immediately after his marriage.

[224] Anna Maria Anable. See vol. 1, "Cast of Characters," s.v. "Ninny."

[225] See the letter of Adoniram Judson to Emily E. Chubbuck dated May 19, 1846.

[226] See vol. 1, "Cast of Characters," s.v. "Nott, Urania Sheldon."

[227] The Reverend Doctor Eliphalet Nott was the president of Union College in Schenectady, New York. An ordained Presbyterian minister, he was married to Urania Sheldon Nott, the sister of Miss Cynthia Sheldon and Mrs. Alma Anable and the aunt of Anna Maria Anable.

[228] This was found in the "Scraps and Facts" column of the *Roman Citizen* a few weeks before the marriage of Adoniram Judson and Emily E. Chubbuck.

[229] We note the misspelling of "Fanny Forester."

[230] See vol. 1, "Cast of Characters," s.v. "Willis, Nathaniel Parker."

[231] We note the error; Adoniram Judson's first wife was Ann Hasseltine Judson. Harriet Atwood was a childhood friend of Ann Hasseltine; she was to marry Samuel Newell, and together they would sail with Emily and Adoniram in 1812.

[232] Sarah Hall Boardman Judson died at St. Helena on September 1, 1845, as she was returning to the United States with Adoniram and three of their children.

Adoniram Judson to Emily E. Chubbuck,[233] May 26, 1846—New York

I send you, **darling**, a copy of the improved engraving with one of the old,[234] that you may see the difference—I think the improvements are very considerable.[235] **The sleeve was done last, as Sartain[236] waited for Rothermel[237] (who was not at home) to sketch it, before he would alter the engraving. How do you like it?** If you have any further alterations to suggest, write immediately to Sartain through Mr. Gillette.[238] I had an idea of a closer sleeve, more like what you wear, but that would probably not have been on good keeping with the rest of the costume—and perhaps not easily done, as you will perceive—he has made the new sleeve out of the old.

I got your letter of Sunday and Monday week ago, on my arriving here last night. This morning, I wrote to Lippincott through Mr. Gillette and may get an answer before I **leave** (send) this. I have also been to the Harpers[239]—shall have definite proposals from them tomorrow. But they talk of "8 or 10 percent" only and they wish to have the matter all clear with Paine and Burgess, before they can think of engaging. This, I suspect, was the real reason why Corey and Hart objected to include any parts of the *Trippings*. I then went to Paine and Burgess.[240] They are very gentlemanly fellows—but they say, that all they ever intended to decline publishing was a revised and enlarged edition, such an one as you proposed—they never thought of giving up the *Trippings*—how could they when they have paid $190 for the stereotype plates[241]—and they intend to proceed and publish another edition, as soon as the first is out. I then requested them to make out

---

[233] For an understanding of the comparison on an original letter with the letter actually printed by Dr. A. C. Kendrick in *The Life and Letters of Mrs. Emily C. Judson*, see the first footnote for the letter of Adoniram to Emily dated May 14, 1846.

[234] John Sartain had been working on an engraving of Emily. She first thought it might be published as a farewell in the magazines for which she had written with the inscription "Henceforth to loftier purposes, I pledge myself [signed] Fanny Forester." Eventually, it became the portrait plate for *Alderbrook*. In Judson's letter of May 25, 1846, he closes the letter while waiting for the final version of the engraving to be done. It was promised to him before he left.

[235] See the letter from the Reverend A. D. Gillette to Emily Chubbuck dated May 5, 1846, for more information on this engraving.

[236] See vol. 1, "Cast of Characters," s.v. "Sartain, John."

[237] P. F. Rothermel was a well-known portrait painter in the Philadelphia area. In a letter of February 15, 1846, Emily said that she had been to see Mr. Rothermel and that he was painting a portrait of her for Anna Maria Anable. On December 25, 1851, Anna Maria wrote, "Mr. Rothermel has repainted you entirely and we think he has got a good likeness." In a February 2, 1852 letter, Miss Sheldon makes the comment that "the painting was greatly improved by Mr. Rothermel." According to family records which surfaced in the summer of 2010, in 1896 this portrait was included in the estate of Anna Maria Anable and left to Emily Frances Judson. When Emily Frances Judson died in 1911, this was included in her estate.

[238] See vol. 1, "Cast of Characters," s.v. "Gillette, The Reverend Abram Dunn."

[239] Emily had all of her literary friends—Joseph Neal, Robert West, N. P. Willis—and also Adoniram Judson talking to publishers about the possibility of a sequel to *Trippings in Author-land*. It would contain the sketches, poems, and stories written since the publication of *Trippings*; many of the publishers wanted only brand new material, and as is suggested here, there was some question as to what ownership Paine and Burgess had with the copyrights.

[240] Paine and Burgess was the publisher of *Trippings in Author-land*.

[241] See the letter from Paine and Burgess dated May 3, 1846. They offer to help Emily in any way that they can, including selling the plates to *Trippings in Author-land* if that is what she wanted.

---

their bill and prepare to give me a quit claim tomorrow. All say that there is no other way in which we can suppress indefinite editions of that work—and it is really altogether reasonable. So don't be worried about—will get all those matters arranged before I leave these parts or see them in a fair way.

Don't you think, that if I had foreseen some things, I should never have put my foot into a certain puddle—and it is great forbearance and condescension, that I do not pull it out now? So, dear, think so with all your might, and perhaps you will love me more—and your dear precious love I value beyond all money **and honor. Just snuggle down in my bosom and love me and let me love you, and I am happy.** In great haste to reach the mail

Yours ever,

A. Judson

Source: Hanna family files; A. C. Kendrick, *The Life and Letters of Mrs. Emily C. Judson*, 201–202

Miss Cynthia Sheldon to Emily E. Chubbuck, May 26, 1846[242]

Tuesday Morn'g

Dear Emily,

I cannot refrain from telling you the manifest change in Mr. Corey's[243] feelings—in some way he has got rid of his great burthen [*sic*]—and now seems to have his face turned towards the high and holy calling of some of his members—I have had but little time with him—for he was engaged talking with Anna M.[244] in a very cordial manner until late last evening[245]—he is perfectly willing the Dr. should baptize her[246] and anxious to render the Sabbath exercises appropriate— our communion will be observed on that day—heaven grant an unction from the most high may rest on each and every one.

I have just found Anna M. has written to you after her conversation with Mr. C.—you will have her feelings too—your work is going on well—I hope all things will come out right—we find many asking for work now[247]—the last piece of

---

[242] This letter is undated. It is placed based on the reference to Anna Maria Anable's conversation with Mr. Corey the evening before. A letter of Anna Maria to Emily dated May 25, 1846, says that conversation took place that evening. This places this letter on the May 26.

[243] See vol. 1, "Cast of Characters," s.v. "Corey, the Reverend D. G."

[244] See vol. 1, "Cast of Characters," s.v. "Anable, Miss Anna Maria."

[245] See the letter of Anna Maria Anable to Emily C. Chubbuck dated May 25, 1846.

[246] Adoniram Judson baptized Anna Maria Anable on Sunday, June 7, 1846. Emily first asked Adoniram if this would be possible in her letter of April 23, 1846. Anna Maria also wrote her thoughts and reasons in a letter to Adoniram Judson dated May 24, 1846.

[247] Miss Sheldon and the members of the Utica Female Academy accepted major responsibility in helping Emily be outfitted for her life in Burmah.

Chemise will be done in that way—you have before this seen Mr. Dean[248]—and I hope had a good long chat with him—we are really exceedingly interested in him.—

12 o'clock. I have been interrupted and this must go—we are disappointed in not having a line from you this morning—Am sorry to learn Dr. Kendrick[249] is so very feeble—who will you have officiate. The Professors stand alike would probably present equal claims—do write how Dr. Kendrick is—and when Dr. Judson will go through Utica.

Yours in haste

C. S.

Source: American Baptist Historical Society, AJ 21, no. 1536.

Adoniram Judson to Emily E. Chubbuck,[250] May 26, 1846—New York

I wonder whether it would break your dear little heart, darling, to give up Abram Esterley. "O what a horrid tyrant of a would-be-husband you are! What will you be, when you become Mr. Chubbuck at full length?" Well, dear, follow your own judgment and inclination—and upon my honor, I won't say a word to old father Peck[251] about it. There now, is not that kind? I love to surprise by kindness. But if you should just tell Abram to look about for his hat, I don't think he would even be missed. "What! At it again? Can't you let poor Abram lone?" Well, I will try—goodnight, for the bell rings for prayers.

Source: Hanna family files.

Nathaniel Parker Willis to Emily E. Chubbuck, May 26, 1846[252]

My dear friend,—

I have delayed replying to your letter till I could make some further inquiries touching your book.[253] And, after all, I have no news to give, for the best reception I had was from a publisher who said that the news of you from India would give an

[248] See vol. 1, "Cast of Characters," s.v. "Dean, William."

[249] See vol. 1, "Cast of Characters," s.v. "Kendrick, Dr. Nathaniel."

[250] There are two addendums to this letter dated May 27 and May 28, 1846.

[251] See vol. 1, "Cast of Characters," s.v. "Peck, The Reverend Doctor Solomon."

[252] A. C. Kendrick dates this letter as May 26, 1846, in *The Life and Letters of Mrs. Emily C. Judson*. Though the letter itself is dated May 23, the date is not in the handwriting of N. P. Willis.

[253] Emily was trying to find a publisher for her collected stories, poems, and sketches written after *Trippings in Author-land*. Most publishers were turning from the project, feeling that previously published stories were not as marketable. It came out the end of 1846 under the title *Alderbrook*.

impetus to the curiosity about you that might make it advisable to publish the revised edition; but that the first edition was still in possession of the field.[254] Apropos of Field[255]—send for him and talk to him about it. He is the partner of Ticknor of Boston, and will be delighted to render any service to Fanny Forester.[256] He will do all that is possible. I am myself a wretched bargain-maker, though I have done my best.

I should have understood Dr. Judson by a single look at his face.[257] It is a physiognomy of great sensibility and enthusiasm, and natural moral elevation. He looks refined and very gentle-manlike, and I am sure is what the English call a "fine fellow." I am very sure, since I have seen him, that you are to be very happy.

I shall be in Boston the first of next week, and shall hope to find you there. God bless you.

Ever affectionately yours,

N. P. W.

Source: Hanna family files; A. C. Kendrick, *The Life and Letters of Mrs. Emily C. Judson*, 200–201.

Adoniram Judson to Emily E. Chubbuck,[258] May 27, 1846[259]

I have got the stereotype plates out of the hands of Paine and Burgess[260] and had them packed up and ordered to be sent and deposited at Lewis Colby's.[261] They cost $190. P and B have also paid me $70 for you, being the percentage on the whole editions, beside what they have already paid you. So that your business with them is closed. The $70 I will hand you and take a receipt, dear, to prevent all mistakes. The Harpers decline publishing "the proposed volume of miscellanies by Fanny Forester,[262] partly on account of the pressure of pre-engagements and also

---

[254] The copyrights to *Trippings in Author-land* were still owned by Paine and Burgess, who had published it. See Adoniram Judson's letters of May 26 and 27 in which he describes purchasing the plates and all rights from them.

[255] James T. Fields, publisher, editor and author was a partner in Ticknor, Reed and Fields. This firm published *Alderbrook* the end of 1846. The contract with them was signed literally as Adoniram and Emily boarded the ship in Boston in July to sail for Burmah.

[256] Emily Chubbuck as Fanny Forester. See vol. 1, "Cast of Characters," s.v. "Chubbuck, Emily," also "Forester, Fanny."

[257] There is a suggestion in Adoniram Judson's letter to Anna Maria Anable of May 14, 1846, that when he first arrived in New York, he visited N. P. Willis at the Astor House where Willis stayed while in the city.

[258] For an understanding of the comparison on an original letter with the letter actually printed by Dr. A. C. Kendrick in *The Life and Letters of Mrs. Emily C. Judson*, see the first footnote for the letter of Adoniram to Emily dated May 14, 1846.

[259] This is an addendum to a letter started May 26, 1846. There is a second addendum dated May 28, 1846.

[260] See the letter of Adoniram Judson to Emily E. Chubbuck dated May 26, 1846. The plates were to *Trippings in Author-land*, which Paine and Burgess had published. In this time, Emily was picking up all of the copyrights on her stories so that she would not be inhibited from a second collection, which was published by Ticknor, Reed and Fields as *Alderbrook*.

[261] Lewis Colby was a publisher in New York. In agreeing to publish the *Memoir of Sarah Hall Boardman Judson*, they had also agreed to republish some of Emily's earlier books. Lewis Colby also published *An Olio of Domestic Verse*.

[262] Emily Chubbuck as Fanny Forester. See vol. 1, "Cast of Characters," s.v. "Chubbuck, Emily," also "Forester, Fanny."

from the present inauspicious aspect of political affairs for all kinds of literary enterprise." Wiley and Putnam[263] ditto—with the additional remark that there has been a glut of light writing for a year or two past, and the reading public is satiated. I see no chance of finding a publisher in New York. Perhaps I shall hear something favorable from Philada. The Harpers say that next fall they may be induced to undertake, but cannot give any definite encouragement. I guess we will not indulge the spoilt public at present. **Deposit the engraving and copy, all arranged and revised with Mr. Gillette[264] or some other friend and let the public get hungry and cry bored to Nurse Fanny for pap. Is not that the best way to carry it off!** The truth is, that the present is a most unfavorable time for any literary speculation. Peoples' minds are full of the Mexican War and probable rupture with England and all the world—too much stern reality, to allow time for fiction—too close engagement with Mars to allow time to flirt with Venus and the Muses. You can arrange for the purchase of the additional lot, if you please, for $300,[265] before I come, and for the fence at $50—and I shall be able to let you have as much of the sum appropriated for your outfit that is $200[266] as you wish. The $200 for myself I have declined. **I have with me summery cloth for dresses and a package of stockings, sent you by friends in Philada.**

Is this not a beautiful letter, full of gold and pearls and costly array? Don't wear it in your hair. It will be contrary to scripture. How is it darling, that your last date to me is the 18th?!—not a line since you left Utica for Hamilton! Did you send a letter to me, misdirected to Anna Maria?[267] I guess you did, you careless hussy. Just a fortnight since we parted. When we meet again, darling dear, shall we live together and travel together and eat together and sleep together? Shall we? Or do you mean to cut me at last? Very well—very well— There are more than two girls, that love me most desperately. O how sweet they kiss, and how despairingly they hang upon me! "Is this the last time" said one of them, "that I shall feel your dear arm around me?" But alas for her, when I put my arm around her and tried to give her a sweet kiss for the last time, I was thinking, what would I not give, if it was only Fanny Forester.[268] So cut me, if you will. I have no shield left and my heart must lie bleeding under the blow. But darling dear, how safe I feel in your dear hands. I love to clasp

---

[263] As the names of prominent publishers are mentioned, it is clear that Emily was leaving no stone unturned to find someone to publish her next volume. Many did not feel collections of previously published material were viable sellers; in this letter, Adoniram Judson also raises the issue of the mood of the country and the economic conditions that would suggest prudence in waiting for a later date and more opportune circumstances.

[264] See vol. 1, "Cast of Characters," s.v. "Gillette, The Reverend Abram Dunn."

[265] In a letter to her brother J. Walker Chubbuck on May 24, 1846, Emily said that Dr. Judson would purchase a lot of about three acres for her family so that Charles Chubbuck would have a place for his horse and to raise a few crops.

[266] Each of the missionaries was allotted a sum of two hundred dollars for their outfit for the mission field.

[267] See vol. 1, "Cast of Characters," s.v. "Anable, Miss Anna Maria."

your love to my heart and revel in the assurance that you love me irrecoverably and as much as I love you. I ponder over your last precious letter. What have I said or done that you should lavish such deep heart love upon me! May God graciously bring us once more together in love and happiness.

At noon—I have had another interview with Mrs. Allen.[269] I am afraid I shall get to dislike her. She is a woman that I could make some use of. She has a sharp, strong intellect—is a good critic in the rough, but not in the nice. No heart—no amiability—very severe and what is worse, glaringly envious. She has a brother, Mr. Crosby, now here from Kentucky, who though very unlike her, is a rather exceptionable character. But Mrs. Crosby, sister of Mrs. Rachelles [sic] of Lynn, is a truly excellent woman, an intimate friend and bosom companion of Sarah.[270] I am rejoiced to find that though her husband is about returning to their home, she is going to Boston and vicinity. I hope you will get acquainted with her, for she can give you more information about Sarah than all the world beside.

Source: Hanna family files; A. C. Kendrick, *The Life and Letters of Mrs. Emily C. Judson*, 202–203.

Adoniram Judson to Emily E. Chubbuck,[271] May 28, 1846[272]

Your letters, the one misdirected to Anna Maria[273] and that of the 24th have come to my hand and heart. I feel thankful to God, that he has given us such congeniality of taste, that we like and dislike the same persons and things. I allude to what you say of Mrs. Allen.[274] I presume our sentiments and feelings in regard to her are just the same. Still it is best to cherish no strong prejudices, but to try to

[268] Emily Chubbuck wrote under the *nom de plume* Fanny Forester. Asked about it once, she said "Would anyone buy a book written by Emily E. Chubbuck?"

[269] Mrs. Allen was the editor of the *Mother's Journal* and included material by Emily as early as 1843. Their correspondence went through spring 1846. In December 1848, Emily received a letter from Mrs. Allen's husband, the Reverend Ira Allen, describing in some detail the death of Eliza Allen. The *Mother's Journal* continued, and in an 1849 letter Anna Maria Anable informs Emily that a piece that she had written had appeared in the publication. In a letter to Emily during their courtship, Adoniram mentioned that he had met Mrs. Allen and went on to say that the *Mothers' Journal* was considered to be a prestigious publication for the church. On May 24, 1846, responding to something Adoniram had said about Mrs. Allen, Emily said, "There never was anything written but you can distort into something bad (even the Bible itself) and I do not think Mrs. Allen a competent critic. She is a shrewd, observing woman, but in matters of literature she is inferior, I think, to educated ladies in general." On May 27, 1846, after a meeting with her, Judson wrote, "I am afraid I shall get to dislike her. She is a woman that I could make some use of. She has a sharp, strong intellect—is a good critic in the rough, but not in the nice. No heart—no amiability—very severe and what is worse, glaringly envious."

[270] Sarah Hall Boardman Judson, Adoniram Judson's second wife, died on her way back to the United States the previous September. Emily was committed to writing her memoir.

[271] For an understanding of the comparison on an original letter with the letter actually printed by Dr. A. C. Kendrick in *The Life and Letters of Mrs. Emily C. Judson*, see the first footnote for the letter of Adoniram to Emily dated May 14, 1846.

[272] This is a second addendum to a letter started May 26, 1846. There is a first addendum of May 27, 1846.

[273] See vol. 1, "Cast of Characters," s.v. "Anable, Miss Anna Maria."

[274] See vol. 1, "Cast of Characters," s.v. "Allen, Mrs. Eliza."

love all and be beloved of all. **It is quite impossible for me to sit to Freeman,**[275] **so please give no encouragement. Thanks be to God for the blessed news concerning your brother.**[276] **Was my letter at all blessed to him? I should be so happy to find that I had been instrumental of spiritual good to your brother— dear, dear Emily, the darling of my heart and my judgment. I have been to see Mrs. James Colgate**[277] **and her sister Miss Hoyt the younger—and a sweet visit I enjoyed. They praised you so nicely, that it was a rich treat to sit with them and join now and then a little bit. "Our lips will soon meet—a heart meeting— I trust and then and then." What then, darling? Do you know? Can you guess? Why, we will get Dr. K**[278] **to tie the knot and then we will kiss one another to sleep and we will sleep so sweetly in one another's arms.**

I have done with New York. Leave at 7 o'clock on the steamboat for Albany. Mr. Bright[279] **is with me. Tomorrow to Utica, next day to Skaneateles—spend the Sabbath there—and on Monday—where shall I go, do you think? Visit the falls of Niagara? I have never seen them. Or shall I go and see old father Wykoff and some other old fellow and get him to marry me to Miss Pokey and then I will subscribe myself**

Your affectionate A Judson

Source: Hanna family files; A. C. Kendrick, *The Life and Letters of Mrs. Emily C. Judson*, 202–203.

[275] Freeman was a portrait artist. On May 8, 1846, Emily wrote that she had arranged with him to paint her portrait. Then, on May 22, she told Adoniram that her mother and sister Kate were anxious to have Freeman paint a portrait of Adoniram Judson.

[276] In her May 22, 1846 letter, Emily told Adoniram that her brother Walker, who lived in Milwaukee, the Wisconsin Territory, and worked as a newspaper publisher, had "become pious and united with the church" in great part because of a letter that Adoniram Judson wrote to him.

[277] Ellen Colgate had a sister, Miss Elizabeth Hoyt. In 1844, James Colgate, the son of William (of soap manufacturing fame) and Mary Colgate, married S. Ellen Hoyt, and they had one son William. Emily Judson wrote in 1849 that, in 1845, she and Mrs. Ellen Colgate had a pleasant visit. Ellen Colgate sent Emily a copy of *Pilgrim's Progress* in 1846 just prior to her departure for Burmah. Mrs. Urania Sheldon Nott saw Ellen Colgate on the boat to or from Schenectady in the company of James Colgate. On November 26, 1847, Miss Sheldon mentioned that Mr. and Mrs. Alexander Beebee (of the *Baptist Register*) were in New York "mourning deeply" the death of their beloved Ellen Colgate. Elizabeth Hoyt, the sister of Ellen Hoyt Colgate, was a student of Emily's ("one of my best"), and Elizabeth Hoyt died of the same disease in 1849 that her sister had died of in 1847. In 1851, James Colgate remarried. His new wife was Susan Colby, and they had two children, James and Mary.

[278] See vol. 1, "Cast of Characters," s.v. "Kendrick, Dr. Nathaniel."

[279] Upon her return to America in 1851, Emily Judson had a close relationship with Dr. Edward Bright, the corresponding secretary of the American Baptist Missionary Union. They knew one another previously in New York, as he worked with the *Baptist Register*, a prominent regional newsletter, at the time of Adoniram and Emily's marriage. He was appointed corresponding secretary the end of May 1846, just prior to Adoniram and Emily's departure for Burmah. Dr. Bright helped Emily with many of her business affairs, he carried on the publishing details of the Judson memoir because of a serious illness in Dr. Wayland's family, and he and his wife took in Henry and Edward Judson for a year beginning in October 1851. He, with Dr. Edward Granger, was the executor of the estate of Emily Chubbuck Judson. In 1838, Edward Bright had been the founding pastor of the Bleecker Street Baptist Church in Utica; amongst the charter members were many names to be important in Emily's life—Asa and Isabell Sheldon, Cynthia Sheldon, Alma Sheldon Anable, and Horace Hawley.

Emily E. Chubbuck to Adoniram Judson, May 28, 1846—Hamilton

Your two letters rec'd last night. Yes, dearest, I *will* "snuggle down in your bosom" and love you with the little piece of heart I have got left after coquetting so many years. Can't be much to be sure, but then if I do my best, how can you blame me? To think of your having caught a broken-winged bird after all!

I intended to have written you a long letter, but have been detained by company until now, and now I must hurry or be too late for the mail. Paine and Burgesss[280] certainly ought to be paid for their plates, but darling—Have not you entered upon a mighty speculation. Not a "bird on the finger"[281] quite, such useless things don't make their nests of hundred dollar bills. I hope the books will bring enough to pay for themselves. What will you do with the small ones?

Darling, I am very much ashamed of the last letter[282] I sent you—so full of murmurings, distrust, and foreboding. Forgive me, and I will behave better. You *know* that I am perfectly happy in your priceless love.

Had a letter from Mr. Willis[283] last night—he is a noble fellow, and I do wish you knew him, you could do him so much good. If he only were a Christian![284]

What a ridiculous mistake—that of misdirecting my letters! Did you ever see two flatter things.

I am longing and yet almost dread to see you. Don't forget to love me, dearest, and pray for me for I need it. It seems too bad for you to be in Utica tomorrow night and I not see you. Please play the agreeable a little to Miss Kelly[285]—I have had a visit from Mr. Dean.[286] He is a very fine man.

Dream about me darling, especially when waking—love me a little bit—and above all place due value on this, your last note from
Emily Chubbuck

Source: Hanna family files.

---

[280] See Adoniram Judson's first letter of May 26, 1846, in which he speaks of negotiating with Paine and Burgess for the plates of *Trippings in Author-land*. Emily would not have yet received the next letter begun on the evening of May 26 and ended on May 28, the same day this was written; in that letter, he speaks of the transaction actually having taken place.

[281] See letter from Adoniram Judson dated May 25, 1846, for information on these bird references.

[282] This was Emily's letter to Adoniram Judson dated May 24, 1846.

[283] See vol. 1, "Cast of Characters," s.v. "Willis, Nathaniel Parker."

[284] On March 12, 1845, N. P. Willis wrote a revealing letter to Emily about himself and his religious beliefs. After making a general statement about the spirit world, heaven and hell, and prayer, he goes on to say that religion had been forced upon him in his school years and that he never was willing to write about it publicly. At the same time, he felt himself to be a believing Trinitarian Christian.

[285] Miss Jane Kelly was Emily Chubbuck's friend at the Utica Female Academy, and then she became a teacher with Emily at that institution. Miss Kelly became the literary principal in 1844 with the retirement of Mr. and Mrs. James Nichols from that position. During a period of Miss Kelly's illness in 1844, Emily filled in the position for her. Then, in 1848, when Miss Cynthia Sheldon moved to Philadelphia to help start the Misses Anable's School, Miss Kelly became the "headmistress" of the academy and successfully brought it into the future, though not without some initial disparagement from the Sheldon-Anable families.

[286] See vol. 1, "Cast of Characters," s.v. "Dean, William."

Emily E Chubbuck to her Father, May 28, 1846[287]

To My Father[288]

A welcome for thy child, father,
A welcome give to-day;
Although she may not come to thee
As when she went away;
Though never in her olden nest
Is she to fold her wing,
And live again the days when first
She learned to fly and sing.

Oh, happy were those days, father,
When gathering round thy knee,
Seven sons and daughters called thee sire—
We come again but three;[289]
The grave has claimed thy loveliest ones,
And sterner things than death
Have left a shadow on thy brow,
A sigh upon thy breath.

And one—one of the three, father,
Now comes to thee to claim
Thy blessing on another lot,
Upon another name.
Where tropic suns for ever burn,
Far over land and wave,
The child, whom thou hast loved, would make
Her hearth-stone and her grave.

---

[287] This is undated, but it was written just before her marriage on June 2, 1846 to Adoniram Judson.

[288] From A. C. Kendrick, *The Life and Letters of Mrs. Emily C. Judson*: "Emily was now in Hamilton, awaiting the coming of him who was to take her beyond the ocean. As she moved among her parents and relatives, conscious that it was 'the last time,' that her farewell was soon to be uttered, and an ocean to roll between her and all she had before loved, no wonder that her heart sometimes sunk within her, and it required even more than her all of faith to banish the gloom that rested upon her spirit. From her heart's fountain gushed forth the following lines:"

[289] We are not sure of the three remaining Chubbuck children mentioned here, for actually there were five, including Ben, Walker, Catharine, Emily, and Wallace. We assume that the three referenced are the three "at home." Walker was in the Wisconsin Territory and Ben was living out of state with his Aunt Catharine.

Thou'lt never wait again, father,
Thy daughter's coming tread;
She ne'er will see thy face on earth—
So count her with thy dead;
But in the land of life and love,
Not sorrowing as now,
She'll come to thee, and come, perchance,
With jewels on her brow.

Perchance;—I do not know, father,
If any part be given
My erring hand, among the guides,
Who point the way to heaven;
But it would be a joy untold
Some erring foot to stay;
Remember this, when, gathering round,
Ye for the exile pray.

Let nothing here be changed, father,
I would remember all,
Where every ray of sunshine rests,
And where the shadows fall.
And now I go; with faltering foot
I pass the threshhold o'er,
And gaze, through tears, on that dear roof,
My shelter nevermore.

Source: A. C. Kendrick, *The Life and Letters of Mrs. Emily C. Judson*, 205–206.

Adoniram Judson to Emily E. Chubbuck,[290] May 29, 1846—Utica

So, darling, you dread to see me, and have sent me your "last note,"—
going to cut me after all—and those nice evening tramps at Philada.—through
the ice and snow, cold enough to make a greenlander shiver, are to go for
nothing—are they?[291] Very well, very well, young woman. I will go directly, like

[290] For an understanding of the comparison on an original letter with the letter actually printed by Dr. A. C. Kendrick in *The Life and Letters of Mrs. Emily C. Judson*, see the first footnote for the letter of Adoniram to Emily dated May 14, 1846.

[291] Adoniram Judson met Emily Chubbuck for the first time on December 25, 1845. It was another month before he began his travels to major cities and public appearances. While there (Philadelphia), he was staying with Mr. and Mrs. Robarts, and Emily was staying with the Reverend and Mrs. A. D. Gillette.

Poopoo, to the falls of Niagara and pitch myself head foremost over the roaring cataract. And when you hear that my poor bones lie bleaching on the rocks beneath, will you not drop a tear of—O I see you are beginning to relent—your heart is not all adamant—well, well, I don't know, that I shall relent, after such treatment. But perhaps I will take a tour round by Oregon and Mexico, and touch at Hamilton on my way back. May be—may be—can't say with any degree of certainty.

Just before leaving New York last night I received a line from Lippincott, saying that "he accepts the propositions of publishing Fanny Forester's[292] works with pleasure, provided the volume contains enough new matter to protect it from being termed a reprint."[293] He says nothing about terms, but I mentioned 12% percent to Mr. Gillette[294] and I suppose that that is understood. I have also opened a correspondence with a house in Boston, on the same subject. Lewis Colby[295] of New York is strongly inclined to undertake the publishing of the three Utica works, partly encouraged by the hope of getting the memoir of 2nd Mrs. J.[296]

I arrived here at 2 o'clock—much disappointed in finding that Anna Maria[297] had gone. I should have answered her very interesting and excellent letter[298] which I received in NY but expected to see her in a day or two and talk over the matter. And that is my present expectation. I have seen her good, appropriate letter to Mr. Wiley,[299] and I have no doubt the whole affair will be arranged satisfactorily.

I have got a nice time this evening and tomorrow morning to bring up my arrears of correspondence, which I intend to do as soon as I have dispatched this letter—the last letter that I hope I shall ever be pestered to write to Emily Chubbuck[300]—what oceans of ink I have expended on that girl!

---

[292] Emily Chubbuck as Fanny Forester. See vol. 1, "Cast of Characters," s.v. "Chubbuck, Emily," also "Forester, Fanny."

[293] Adoniram Judson and Emily's literary friends (Joseph Neal, N. P. Willis) had been seeking a publisher for what would be a sequel to *Trippings in Author-land*. It would contain the stories, sketches, and poetry Emily had written since its publication; most, if not all of it, would already have appeared in the magazines for which Emily wrote, and the lack of new material was a problem to all of the publishers, as noted here.

[294] See vol. 1, "Cast of Characters," s.v. "Gillette, The Reverend Abram Dunn."

[295] Lewis Colby was a publisher in New York. In agreeing to publish the *Memoir of Sarah Hall Boardman Judson*, they had also agreed to republish some of Emily's earlier books. Lewis Colby also published *An Olio of Domestic Verse*.

[296] Adoniram Judson first met with Emily Chubbuck on December 25, 1845, in the hopes that she would consent to write the memoir of Sarah Hall Boardman Judson.

[297] See vol. 1, "Cast of Characters," s.v. "Anable, Miss Anna Maria."

[298] Anna Maria Anable wrote to Adoniram Judson on May 24, 1846, with statements concerning her faith and her desire to be baptized by immersion. Adoniram Judson talked with Mr. Corey of the Baptist church in Utica about the possibility of Judson performing the baptism at Anna Maria's request. That baptism took place on June 7, 1846.

[299] In her letter of May 25, 1846, to Emily Chubbuck, Anna Maria speaks of a need to meet with Mr. Wiley for conversations around the matter of her baptism.

[300] May 29, 1846 was a Friday. Adoniram Judson and Emily Chubbuck were married on June 2, 1846, the following Tuesday.

I inclose [*sic*] you a line from Mrs. Stevens,[301] the only one that I have lately received from Maulmain.

Notwithstanding the nonsense I am too prone to write you, I am full and overflowing with most serious, joyful thoughts—The past, the present and the future are before me. If I should attempt to write I should not know where to begin or to end. May we meet in love and happiness—May God crown our union with his blessing, that we may be blessings to one another through life and to all eternity!

I love you a little bit—but I have never loved you so much as you deserve.

Ever thine—**"with every wish to please"**

A Judson

Source: Hanna family files; A. C. Kendrick, *The Life and Letters of Mrs. Emily C. Judson*, 203–204.

Emily C. Judson to Miss Catharine Chubbuck, June 5, 1846

By Emily C. Judson to Aunt Kate, Hamilton, June 5, 1846

"The Lord watch between thee and me when we are absent one from
    another."
  Such my darling only sister is the earnest
  Prayer of your changelessly affectionate sister on
  Her last day beneath the paternal roof. God bless
  And guard and guide thee; and at last give us harps
  That we may together attune to his praise in heaven.

Source: Hanna family files.

[301] Elizabeth Stevens arrived in Maulmain in February 1838; her husband was Edward Stevens. Elizabeth Stevens took six-month-old Edward Judson into her home when Sarah and Adoniram had to leave for the United States in 1845, and her care and nurture saved his life. She served forty-eight years in Burmah. She had extensive correspondence with Emily Judson, and her letters spoke of everyday life among the missionaries. When Emily returned to the United States, the letters from Mrs. Stevens brought news of friends and colleagues. Mrs. Stevens had a sister, Sarah Haven, in Massachusetts, who wrote a number of letters to Emily asking for information on the Stevens family.

Adoniram Judson to Miss Catharine Chubbuck,[302] June 5, 1846[303]

Written by Adoniram Judson in an album given to Aunt Kate Chubbuck, by Grandmother, Hamilton, May 4, 1846.

—"earth's broken tie."
Where, where shall sisters love, if not on high!
Yes, there the "broken tie" shall re-unite,
And sisters' love shall be so pure and bright,
That heavenly forms shall turn aside to gaze,
And make that sight a subject for new praise.

Source: Hanna family files.

Marriage Announcement, *Roman Citizen* (Rome, Oneida County, NY), June 9, 1846

JUDSON—CHUBBUCK

In Hamilton, Madison Co., New York, on June 2, 1846, by the Rev. N. Kendrick,[304] D. D., Prof. in the Madison University, the Rev. A. JUDSON, D. D. of Maulmain, Burmah, to Miss Emily Chubbuck (Fanny Forrester) [*sic*] daughter of Mr. Charles CHUBBUCK of the former place.[305]

Nathaniel Parker Willis to Emily C. Judson, June 9, 1846—New York

Dearest Emily,

I do not know where you are, but I presume you have given orders to your friend Miss Anable[306] to forward your letters to you. Will you write to me when you receive this, and inform me, exactly as possible, what your movements are to be before you sail. I will leave my sincere congratulations unexpressed till I see you.

May God bless you.

Yours faithfully,

N. P. Willis

---

[302] This expression of Emily to her sister Catharine was found on a sheet, at the top of which was the background statement, likely written by Emily Frances Judson.

[303] This, according to a second notation, was written "by Emily C. Judson to Aunt Kate, Hamilton, June 5, 1846."

[304] See vol. 1, "Cast of Characters," s.v. "Kendrick, Dr. Nathaniel."

[305] This is the marriage announcement of Adoniram Judson and Emily Chubbuck that appeared in the *Roman Citizen* shortly after their marriage. Fanny Forester was misspelled.

[306] See vol. 1, "Cast of Characters," s.v. "Anable, Miss Anna Maria."

Give my kindest wishes and felicitations to Dr. Judson.

Source: Hanna family files.

Mrs. Ellen S. Colgate[307] to Emily C. Judson, June 12, 1846—New York

I have been thinking over and over again my dear Mrs. Judson, what I could find that would be an acceptable token of my regard for you—Had I not been afraid of burdening you with baggage I should have sent you a portable writing desk, but knowing that you have long been so much of a scribe, I know you must be self sufficient with all the paraphernalia thereof.

I know too, you will be all loaded with books from the literary world, poetry, and prose of every society—So what could I send you? I concluded that like the rest of us you had an old copy of Bunyan's Pilgrims' Progress so I send you a new copy to take the place of the old one.

We are all pilgrims on life's journey, sometimes when weary and faint by the way, old Bunyan serves as a sort of talisman for us, so peruse it now and then. It chases away the shades of [ ] and sadness and causes us to bask in sunshine—May we like good old Bunyan reach the same blessed haven of rest.

I have wanted much to see you still [ ], very dear Mrs. Judson, but I cannot have that rather painful pleasure—I say painful for I dread to say the word Goodbye.

I assure you I shall ever remember you very dear friend with the greatest affection.

And now to sum up all my wishes for you, I shall simply say "God bless you"— I need not tell you how often, often I shall think of you, and I shall hope now and then to have a letter from you—I shall write to you, after I hear of your arrival, should I not have had the pleasure of a missive before.

Goodbye my dear friend, once more let me add May God bless you.—

Ever your ardently

Attached friend

Ellen S. Colgate

P.S. My kindest regards to Dr. Judson.

Source: American Baptist Historical Society, AJ 15, no. 608.

---

[307] See vol. 1, "Cast of Characters," s.v. "Colgate, Ellen S."

Ms Fanny Ledlie to Emily C. Judson, June 13, 1846[308]—Utica

Though personally [ ] [ ] will you permit me dear Madam, to offer you a *small memento* of my esteem for your worth. I trust your voyage hence to a far distant land may be propitious and that all who love and take an interest in your welfare will ere many months elapse, be cheered with good tidings of your safe arrival at your destination. Allow me to assure you, I earnestly desire your happiness temporal and spiritual and with kind Christian regards.

I would subscribe myself

Yours in sincerity

Fanny Ledlie [*sic*]

Source: American Baptist Historical Society, AJ 17, no. 758.

Emily C. Judson to Anna Maria Anable,[309] June 14, 1846—Worcester

Think of me "dearest Blidgy"[310] here with a great fellow of seventeen[311] calling me "Mother" and two little woodchucks[312] trying which can say "Mama" oftenest!

We had a most tedious day yesterday coming from N. Y. and a tedious time at N.Y. for Mrs. Newton[313] kept open door. The house was crammed constantly—a perfect hive—and *didn't* I play the lioness beautifully! The doc. says I am a perfect Napoleon. At any rate, I managed to get tears at parting from some who came in on purpose to turn up their noses and Mrs. Newton says all N. Y. is in a state of glorification. Such are the fools that people would have had me fear—wisps of straw,

---

[308] This is undated. Because it was written to Emily in Utica before she left for Burmah, and because Emily was in Boston on June 16, this is placed on the Saturday June 13.

[309] This is a letter fragment. Only the first page is available.

[310] See vol. 1, "Cast of Characters," s.v. "Blidgims." Also "A Timeline for Blidgims References."

[311] George Dana Boardman, the son of George Dana Boardman and Sarah Hall Boardman, was born August 18, 1828, in Tavoy, Burmah. George returned to the United States in 1844 at the age of six and lived with Dr. and Mrs. Calvin Newton in Worcester, Massachusetts. He never saw his mother again. He attended Brown University in Providence, Rhode Island, graduating after taking a few years off for travel in the West. He went on to attend Newton Theological Institute, and in 1855, he married Miss Ella Covell. He served two churches before settling into the First Baptist Church of Philadelphia, where he served with distinction for thirty years. He formed a close relationship with Emily upon her return in 1851; when she gave him a copy of *An Olio of Domestic Verses*, she addressed it "Georgie—from Mamma."

[312] This would be Adoniram "Pwen" or "Addy" Judson, age 9, and Elnathan "Elly" Judson, age eight; they as well were staying, and were to stay in Worcester, Massachusetts with Dr. and Mrs. Calvin Newton.

[313] There are seven letters in this correspondence from Mr. and Mrs. Isaac Newton of New York City. In a June 1846 letter, Mrs. Newton indicated that they are "new friends," certainly of Emily. They obviously had considerable wealth, which they shared generously with Adoniram and Emily through packages and, upon Adoniram's death, an immediate check to Emily of $500. Mr. Newton called Adoniram his "friend." One of the letters invited Emily to stay with them in New York upon her return, and a later letter indicated that she had indeed done that. On May 15, 1846, Adoniram Judson inscribed a dedication to Mrs. H. H. Newton on the fly-leaf of a volume of Burmese hymns that had been compiled by Mrs. Sarah B. Judson: "Mrs. H. H. Newton From A. Judson/ The wings [ ] [ ] /[ ] are folded in St. Helena—New York—May 15th, 1846."

all of them. I called at Mr. Osgood's studio and got his wife's[314] address, but had no time to call on her. He recognized me at once and professed to be delighted. He said if his wife was able to get out he sh'd bring her down, but they did'nt [sic] come. Willis[315] called twice. The last day we had a private interview while more than a dozen people were waiting me [sic] in the other parlour. He is a noble fellow, and he and the Doct. are completely charmed with each other. I am glad of it for each deserves the other's good opinion.[316]   Source: Hanna family files.

Emily C. Judson to Anna Maria Anable, June 16, 1846—Boston

Darling Ninny,

I rec'd your sweet little note this morning and as people are giving me a minute's leisure I will reply to it. You must'nt [sic] let Aunt U.[317] worry you. She will come round right soon, I am sure;[318] and if she don't [sic] you will have the consolation of knowing that you have pleased a greater than she. Wait, and "watch, and pray;" for I believe most firmly that there is a destiny before you requiring careful stepping. And if so, you need not give yourself anxiety about it— you will be led into the path and sustained in it.

We reached Boston last evening. I like the Colby's[319] [sic] and I am sure it will be pleasant for you to come here. I have just been talking to Mrs. C. about you and

---

[314] Frances or "Fanny" Osgood presents an interesting counterpoint to Fanny Forester or Emily Chubbuck. Both writers achieved fame in the same period of time. Fanny Osgood was both a writer and poet, and in 1845, she wrote regularly for *Graham's Magazine*. Estranged from her husband, famed portrait painter Samuel S. Osgood, she began a relationship with Edgar Allen Poe, who became the editor and part owner of the *Broadway Journal* in March 1845. Poe had been helped to fame by N. P. Willis when the *New York Daily Mirror*, the paper that preceded the *New Mirror* and that made Fanny Forester famous, published "The Raven" in January. Fanny Osgood presented a poem to the *Broadway Journal* for publication, and Poe printed a poem in reply. This went back and forth for a number of months, and the two were soon involved in a relationship; it was commonly thought that Fanny Osgood's third child was fathered by Poe. All of this was being played out in the press in September 1845 when William Gillespie wrote his letter to Emily Chubbuck in which he referenced the "*other* Fanny." The relationship with Fanny Osgood made Poe a pariah in the literary circles of New York within the year. In January 1845, Mrs. Osgood accused George Graham of not writing to her because of all of his correspondence with Fanny Forester. In June, just before sailing to Burmah, Emily mentioned in a letter that while in New York she stopped at Mr. Osgood's studio, hoping to make arrangements to see Fanny Osgood, but the meeting did not take place as she was out of town.

[315] See vol. 1, "Cast of Characters," s.v. "Willis, Nathaniel Parker."

[316] Writing to Emily on May 23, Willis said of Adoniram Judson, "I should have understood Dr. Judson by a single look at his face. It is a physiognomy of great sensibility and enthusiasm, and natural moral elevation. He looks refined and very gentle-man-like, and I am sure is what the English call a 'fine fellow.' I am very sure, since I have seen him, that you are to be very happy."

[317] See vol. 1, "Cast of Characters," s.v. "Nott, Urania Sheldon."

[318] Emily wrote Mrs. Nott on July 7, 1846. She begins the letter by saying that she had read the letter Mrs. Nott sent to Anna Maria; Emily went on to defend Anna Maria's right, if not her responsibility, to respond to her feeling that God had called her to ask for baptism by immersion, moving her into the heart of Baptist life. It is evident that Mrs. Nott, married to a Presbyterian minister, had expressed doubts, if not disapproval.

[319] A prominent businessman, Gardner Colby and his family lived in Pemberton Square in Boston before moving "to the country," Newton Centre, Massachusetts. Mr. Colby was a member of the Board of the American Baptist Missionary Union and an avid supporter of the missionary movement. In a letter after they sailed from Boston to Burmah, Emily mentions the extravagant hospitality extended to them in early July as they waited for the *Faneuil Hall* to embark. Adoniram and Emily stayed with the Colby family frequently.

she is very much interested. At a proper time I will just give her a chance to invite you. She wants me to ask Lydia[320] here and if she comes you can have her for a bed-fellow. We are to sail in the "Faneuil Hall"—its second trip—first only to Liverpool. She is to sail on the first of July; but between our two selves and the Dr. she will not be off before the 7th. Please hasten the packing, however, for the Dr. will go into cat-fits if everything is not on hand (to it) long before it is needed. We have heard that Abby[321] is ill and are going to Bradford tomorrow. It would'nt [sic] be *very* strange if we sh'd take her out yet to keep Lydia company. If this climate sh'd seem not to agree with her, we sh'd certainly do it. Ah Ninny,[322] I wish you were going your own self. Just to think of getting an ocean between us!

Please don't forget among my contraptions a couple of those dust brushes at Barnun's, and again I tell you if your money fails write me for more.

Oh, Blidgy![323] you may just throw away your portrait. Flattered you call it, eh! flattered! flattered! Ah, if you could but see the Daguerre that George Boardman[324] has got! I had two taken in N. Y. but they were bad—skeletons. I had such an one taken first in Worcester, but George was dissatisfied and made me go to another man,—and didn't [sic] I get a beauty though? It is a perfect likeness and yet a most beautiful picture. Aunt Urania's is nothing to it. It makes me handsomer than anything that has been taken yet and is notwithstanding the most perfect likeness. There, I have done glorifying [sic]. Not a word from Lippincott.[325] Mr. Colby of N. Y. is to publish the small books.[326]

I am sorry enough that I missed seeing Hatty.[327] Give her ever and ever so much love.

---

[320] See vol. 1, "Cast of Characters," s.v. "Lillybridge, Miss," also the timeline on "Lydia Lillybridge Simons."

[321] See vol. 1, "Cast of Characters," s.v. "Judson, Abby Ann."

[322] Anna Maria Anable. See vol. 1, "Cast of Characters," s.v. "Ninny."

[323] See vol. 1, "Cast of Characters," s.v. "Blidgims." Also "A Timeline for Blidgims References."

[324] See vol. 1, "Cast of Characters," s.v. "Boardman, George Dana."

[325] On May 29, 1846, Adoniram wrote to Emily that Lippincott agreed to publish a compilation of her sketches, stories, and poems, which would be a sequel to *Trippings in Author-land*. Apparently, this did not come through, for *Alderbrook* was published by Ticknor, Reed and Fields. A contract was sent July 10, 1846, as they were just leaving Boston.

[326] In that May 29, 1846 letter, Adoniram Judson said that Lewis Colby of New York would publish the small books in hopes of having a chance to publish the memoir of Sarah Hall Boardman Judson that Emily was about to write. Colby published this volume in 1848. He later published Emily Judson's *Olio of Domestic Verses*.

[327] Harriet or "Hatty" or "Hattie" or "Hat" Anable was one of nine children born to Joseph and Alma Anable, and was a niece to Miss Cynthia Sheldon and Mrs. Urania Sheldon Nott. In 1841, she had added a note to a letter written by Miss Cynthia Sheldon to Emily. As early as November 1842 she was away, and a letter from Emily to Catharine Chubbuck said that "she (Miss Sheldon) expected that Hat would return as accomplished as Anna Maria." Her trips away were both educational and employment, as she worked as a private tutor in families that would bring her into their homes. In August 1843, she had just returned from Beonsen, in the vicinity of New Orleans, and was engaged to go again. A letter from Anna Maria on January 6, 1845 said that she would stay South for another year. About this time Miss Cynthia Sheldon mentioned her concern for Hatty's spiritual health. In May 1845 she was in New Orleans. She was home again in summer 1846, but a September 27 letter from Anna Maria said she had been asked by Mr. Roman with some urgency to return and she thought that she should. She was to return home from New Orleans in January 1849 after Anna Maria Anable had started the Misses Anable's School in Philadelphia in fall 1848. Harriet was fluent in French, having placed herself earlier in a French environment in New Orleans. Hatty died in 1858.

I take comfort I tell you in my plaid barige dress and am *real* sorry I did'nt [*sic*] get more bariges.

How long would you like to be here before we sail? You will like Mrs. Colby— she is ever and ever so sweet—lady-like, refined, and liberal-minded. The Baptists here are very superiour [*sic*] people. I saw Mr. Peck[328] and Dr. Sharp[329] and mercy may know who all, this morning. Give love to everybody; and keep, Ninny dear, ever and ever so much for your own private personal use if you think you could appropriate it. The Dr. sends love to all—especially yourself and Aunt C.[330] Mr. Peck inquired particularly after Jane.[331] He is sickishly [*sic*] loving—pah! Write me very soon—every day—and believe me just as much as ever

Your Nemmy[332]

Source: Hanna family files.

Elizabeth U. Mitchell[333] to Emily C. Judson, June 17, 1846— Philadelphia

My dear friend

Imagine me shaking hands with Mr. Judson, embracing yourself, and wishing you, with all my heart, a long life of health and happiness together, for this is exactly what I feel like doing this moment. Just one month since your dear little note was addressed to me, I feel flattered by affectionate farewell, and sat down the very hour I received it to answer, and did write *almost* a letter, when suddenly my Quaker spirit arrested the wish impulse, and [ ] "you are presuming upon your friend's kindness, don't be hasty, her time and attention must now be wholly engrossed by those so much nearer and dearer." I listened to the Quaker voice and

---

[328] See vol. 1, "Cast of Characters," s.v. "Peck, The Reverend Doctor Solomon."

[329] Dr. Daniel Sharp was born in England and immigrated to the United States in 1805. By 1812, he was pastoring the Charles Street Church in Boston and was in an eminent position to form and nurture the fledgling missionary movement. Hearing of the conversion of Adoniram Judson and Luther Rice to Baptist principles, Daniel Sharp was among those who founded the General Convention of the Baptist denomination in the United States in April 1814. With the formation of the American Baptist Missionary Union, he became its first president and later the first editor of the *American Baptist Magazine*. Rev. Mr. Sharp sent a letter to Emily in December 1851 in reply to her quest for material for the memoir of Adoniram Judson. Having worked from the beginning for the magazine of the Missionary Union, he spoke of how letters from missionaries were routinely published in that form. He also enclosed two sermons he had preached with some letters that were quoted in the sermons, giving her permission to use any of it.

[330] See vol. 1, "Cast of Characters," s.v. "Sheldon, Miss Cynthia."

[331] See vol. 1, "Cast of Characters," s.v. "Kelly, Miss Jane."

[332] Emily Chubbuck Judson. See vol. 1, "Cast of Characters," s.v. "Nemmy."

[333] See vol. 1, "Cast of Characters," s.v. "Mitchell, Elizabeth." Elizabeth Mitchell's mother, Sarah Tyndale, was a Quaker, and in this letter Mrs. Mitchell alludes to her own inner "Quaker spirit" and "Quaker voice," a testimony to her upbringing. We are aware that in 1846, when the Mitchells invited Emily to stay with them while she was in Philadelphia, Emily said that she chose to stay with the Gillete family because she was uncomfortable with the Mitchells adhering to Unitarian principles.

laid aside my letter. A few days after this Mr. Judson called[334] with whose visit I was so much gratified, that I felt the strongest desire to acquaint you with our admiration of your choice. I considered a second letter which was disposed of in like manner as the first. But now as you have bade adieu to all those who have strongest claims, I can restrain the impulse no longer. You must remember that your kindness in writing to me, and in thinking of me, at so bewilding a period has emboldened me to write. I do not ask an answer—but I know and feel you will not forget me. Does this sound like presumption? I feel it is not, for I depend not upon my own merit—but your affectionate memory; and upon this hope I build [ ] an expectation that after you will have arrived at your new home, and written to all the dearer ones, you will find time to send me a "long talk" direct from your heart.

You don't know how delighted we were to see Mr. J. We had made very large allowances for newspaper gossip, but found ourselves even then, agreeably surprised—we expected intellect—principle, feeling—all the solid, and higher, moral qualities—but found added to these the lighter grace of manner—his very tone of voice—but I will not expatiate upon this theme, altho' I know you will read this particular passage with exemplary patience. I will only say we anticipate much happiness in store for you, and sincerely rejoice in your prospects, although for our own sake we could have wished that your home might be in our midst.

Every body [sic] has told me something to say to Miss "Fanny Forester"[335] but I cannot be partial—so reject all except their love and best wishes to Mr. Judson and yourself. Mother[336] sent a little box of china for you to the care of Mr. Peck.[337] She sent what she thought would be useful, and hopes you will find them so.

My sister Clara saw an engraved likeness of your husband, and is [ ] to try to procure it for me. When yours comes out[338] in "Graham"[339] Edward is going to have you both *framed and hung in gold*" for me, where we can look upon you often, and always with pleasure.

How I wish I could see you once again ere we part, but it cannot be—may this silent messenger, convey to you a faint impression at least, of our heartfelt good wishes for you and yours. Now the *farewell* feeling comes creeping over me—how sad it is. May God guide us both that our farewell be not forever. May every earthly blessing attend you, and should we meet no more on earth I now claim your friendship, when we shall meet for the first time hereafter!! If good wishes could insure

---

[334] In his letter of May 23, 1846, Adoniram Judson spoke of this visit with the Mitchells and Mrs. Tyndale, Mrs. Mitchell's mother.

[335] Emily Chubbuck Judson as Fanny Forester. See vol. 1, "Cast of Characters," s.v. "Chubbuck, Emily" and "Forester, Fanny."

[336] See vol. 1, "Cast of Characters," s.v. "Tyndale, Sarah."

[337] See vol. 1, "Cast of Characters," s.v. "Peck, The Reverend Doctor Solomon."

[338] At one point, Emily thought of having an engraving made of herself and having the magazines for which she wrote run it with a good-bye inscription: "Henceforth to loftier purposes, I pledge myself [signed] Fanny Forester."

[339] See vol. 1, "Cast of Characters," s.v. "Graham, George."

happiness surely you must be happy, and of all who are now with you a pleasant voyage none are more sincere than your Philadelphia friends, among whom will you always remember

Elizabeth U. Mitchell: farewell

Source: American Baptist Historical Society, AJ 18, no. 873.

Emily C. Judson to Horace Binney Wallace, June 19, 1846—Boston

My Dear Mr. Wallace,—

I received your kind, *very* kind letter, in due time; and you may be assured that it was highly valued.[340] It is said that "blessings brighten as they take their flight;" and although such heart-blessings as are furnished us by social intercourse, were always very dear to me, I do not know but I must acknowledge that the poet has told truth. As the time for sailing draws near, and I am doing up my last work on this side of the globe, cords begin to tighten around me so closely that it seems almost death to dissever them. And yet I am cheerful and strangely happy. There is a great object before me—my hand is about to be *filled*, and so I shall not waste my time on follies. Do not think now that I am anticipating perfect happiness, or any thing [sic] perfect. I know something of the disappointments incident to life, and something of my own weakness and inefficiency. I am only better satisfied to have an object before me—a great one, which does not begin and end with this life.

I should not venture to ask you to come to Boston, but that you promised it; but it would afford me great satisfaction to see you here. We sail in the *Faneuil Hall* on the first day of July; if there should be any delay, you would probably learn it by the papers—though I presume there will not.

Now, God in heaven guide, guard, and bless you, my friend! I hope to meet you again; but if I do not, there is a shadow-less world where angels dwell; and I believe that the redeemed are furnished with their wings, and their harps, and their hearts of love. May we both be among the redeemed. Till then, adieu!

Emily C. Judson

Source: A. C. Kendrick, *The Life and Letters of Mrs. Emily C. Judson*, 210–11.

---

[340] The only earlier letter from Mr. Wallace to Emily to be found in the correspondence is dated March 1, 1846.

Ms Fanny Newton[341] to Emily C. Judson, June 19, 1846—New York

My dear Mrs. Judson –

I can't begin to tell you how much I was disappointed in not seeing you—and more particularly as I had originally intended to leave Albany on Wednesday but was persuaded to stay longer. I don't know even that disappointed is a strong enough word for a feeling that put all my equanimity and amiability to flight, and sent them on so long a journey, that they found some difficulty in returning. I did not hear until Thursday that you had gone to New York, and then told that you would leave the same day—I do greatly regret that I could not in person welcome you to my home—tell you how glad I was to see you—how warmly your new friends sympathized with you. As all this has been denied me, I have tried to content myself by making rapid acquaintance with your likeness—and have almost had "momentary dreams" that it was yourself. I fancy that I have always known you—I am certain that I know you in spirit—and on faith of the beauty of that spirit let me love you as a dear friend—As a bride accept my most sincere wishes for your happiness—you are leaving home, kindred, childhood scenes, the sweet home flowers that with their mute eloquent looks have grown up around you— truly leaving *all* according to the marriage commandment of old—I admire and respect the noble self-denial, the Christian faith and hope, that enables you to resign, all these joys, and attachments that in times past have made life pleasant to you—for the great work you have undertaken. May the love that now sheds so bright a light on your path gild the intrepid future, shine on you still the same when that future shall be numbered with the yesterdays—and at life's sunset, may its soft holy rays give a glorious presage of the bright day, and new life to come.

I beg your acceptance of the little needle book—hoping that my idle fingers have made something that may be useful to you, and which you must use for my sake.—Please give Dr. Judson the knife, which I have ventured to send in defiance, of the old adage concerning sharp-edged presents—instead of cutting friend-ships—it must only cut away all but agreeable remembrance of me.

[ ] think sometimes of your New York friends, and of the unknown friend who has here sent you a kind of pen and ink daguerreotype of her mind—rather con-fused picture abounding in shadow—and when sometimes your pen looks beseechingly at you for some dainty portion of your notice then answer its appeal by writing to

Fanny Newton

Source: American Baptist Historical Society, AJ 18, no. 858.

---

[341] It would be easy to confuse Fanny Newton with Mrs. H. H. Newton. On June 14, 1846, Emily wrote to Anna Maria of a wonderful reception that the Mr. and Mrs. Newton had held for her and Adoniram. Here Fanny Newton, at the end of the letter, says that she is "an unknown friend."

Emily C. Judson to Miss Cynthia Sheldon, June 20, 1846

Saturday evening

My dear Miss Cynthia,

I have just returned from Plymouth[342] and am a little disappointed in not finding any of my boxes. We do not sail till the 6th. but yet there is no time to lose for the Dr. says we shall be obligated to re-pack every thing [*sic*]. I hope Lydia[343] will be here on Tuesday as the missionaries are to be set apart that day. I shall look for her and A. M.[344] and perhaps—perhaps—may I?—for *you*, on Monday. I am crazy to see Anna Maria.

I wrote Mrs. Nott[345] a short letter some time ago but have rec'd no answer. Saw Mr. *Sam* C. Nott today. Mr. and Mrs. Harris[346] have just arrived. The Beechers[347] came last week. Lydia is the only one behind. My health has been miserable some time past; and I am afraid it will be no better unless the good people stop eating me up. Mrs. Tyndale[348] has sent me a nice China breakfast set from Philada. and we have had a couple of solar lamps from N. Y.—so much for housekeeping. The air-tights from Troy have not arrived yet. Things from *Roudout* came last week.

I have a great, great deal to say to you, but no time. Your school stands high <u>every where</u> [*sic*] —very high. You don't know how much I think of you all. Please give much love and may God in heaven bless you!

Affectionately yours

Emily Judson

The doctor sends much love to all.

---

[342] Plymouth, Massachusetts, was the home of Adoniram Judson's sister, Abigail Brown Judson.

[343] See vol. 1, "Cast of Characters," s.v. "Lillybridge, Miss," also the timeline on "Lydia Lillybridge Simons."

[344] See vol. 1, "Cast of Characters," s.v. "Anable, Miss Anna Maria."

[345] See vol. 1, "Cast of Characters," s.v. "Nott, Urania Sheldon."

[346] See vol. 1, "Cast of Characters," s.v. "Harris, Norman."

[347] Mr. and Mrs. Beecher were appointed missionaries, leaving for Burmah with Adoniram and Emily.

[348] Sarah Tyndale was the mother of Mrs. Mitchell of Philadelphia. A successful businesswoman, she ran a large store in Philadelphia that specialized in china. She lived with her daughter and her family. In fall 1845, as Emily went to Philadelphia for her health, the Mitchells were active in inviting her to stay with them. They offered her a room, as much privacy or company as she desired, and all of the benefits of their extended household. On February 9, 1846, Emily recorded the gift of a china inkstand from Mrs. Tyndale. There is one letter in the correspondence from Sarah Tyndale, dated April 19, 1846 with an April 20 addendum: On June 17, Elizabeth Mitchell had written: "Mother sent a little box of china for you to the care of Mr. Peck. She sent what she thought would be useful, and hopes you will find them so."

Nathaniel Parker Willis to Emily C. Judson, June 24, 1846—Washington

My dearest Emily

Your letter, enclosing the money for books I received only yesterday from Boston with two forwardings and today comes this—written as you left Utica. I re-enclose the money, for the books can be had without it. I spoke to Secretary Bowers, at a party last night, and he was of course proud of the opportunity to present you with his book, and so will be Prescott, and Longfellow—and Willis. I shall make you up a box of books from my own stores to take with you, and I shall be in Boston when you sail and see you, with a tearful God-speed, off the shore. Will you write me at what time precisely you will be in Boston, directing your letter here.

The more I think of your coming marriage, the more I think you are doing the best for your happiness. Your husband has a prodigal largeness of nature and the kindest and most affectionate of hearts and you required a trying and unusual destiny to fill the capabilities of which late years have seen the dangerous formation. Both for your heart and your peculiar mind, therefore, Providence has sent you the needful scope, and you will be happy. Dr. Judson's errand abroad will soon draw on your volcanic enthusiasm, and the vent will be healthful to soul and body. With love satisfied and talents employed, change of climate and improved health, you will bless God for a merciful direction of your destiny.

I have taken a horror of home, and the look of my pictures and furniture in New York crush me so that I cannot stay there. I went back for a day, but came off to Washington immediately, where I can feel like a traveller [sic] not yet arrived at his destination. Can you imagine so silly a cabinet of illusive hope affecting a grown up man's movements. I fear I am very weak.

God bless you, dearest Emily. Let me see you alone when I first see you in Boston for my tears of late are as unmanageable as a baby's.

Ever yours affectionately

N. P. Willis

Source: Hanna family files.

Horace Binney Wallace to Emily C. Judson, June 28, 1846—Philadelphia

I have rcd your delightful letter with great interest.[349] I have delayed answering it, under a hope that I might be able to relieve myself from the engagements which oppose this fulfillment of my strong wish to attend your progress in person as far as

---

[349] This was Emily's letter to Mr. Wallace dated June 19, 1846. Note the similarity of this opening line to the opening line of his letter dated March 1, 1846: "I have rcd your beautiful letter, dearest Lady, with deep interest."

the limits of the land would permit, and to follow it with my eye when companionship had ceased to be practicable. I had hoped that you might sail from New York; in which case I should have broken through every occupation and appointment, to greet your going with the expression of the warmest good wishes, and the most constant respect and attachment. If the sailing of the ship *Faneuil Hall*, should be delayed to a more advanced season in the month, I cherish the hope of still accomplishing the desire of my feelings. But should the appointment for the first of July take effect, I believe that I shall be compelled to content myself with wafting my adieus to you across the interval between Boston and Philadelphia, and sending a troop of bright auguries and glowing kindnesses to be my representatives, and to speak the blessings which if I were present, perhaps I could not utter.

I hope that I shall not be deemed presumptuous in claiming the privilege of a *friend*, to be employed during your absence for any service which can promote your convenience or advance your wishes. You may remember that we once discussed sundry schemes in the optative mood, in which I proposed to hold the office of interpreter between your designs and the execution of them: and though the fulfillment of that plan was disturbed by the intervention of another absorbing influence, it may be that at some future day or in some other manner, I may be able to give the aid which was then defined. To such or a similar tack I should bring a disposition to do everything in my power, and a resolution to perform that primary duty of a Privy Counsellor [*sic*]—of keeping the Queen's secret."

Will you do me the favour [*sic*] to present me with great kindness to Dr. Judson! I had the pleasure once of taking him by the hand,—with a prophetic feeling which has been strangely fulfilled. I must get some friend to give me his autograph to place before yours in my collection.

I do not write this letter for the purpose of taking leave of you. I do not agree that we are going to part. I have so intimate—I may say, intense—a sense of your character and presence, that I do not admit that you are absent, or that you will be absent when at the distance of some thousands of miles. I scarcely venture to imagine that your recollection of me will be strong enough to conquer and expel the tyranny of distance. To me—in thoughtful memories, in ardent friendship, in constant, earnest hopes—You always will be present.

H. B. Wallace

Source: American Baptist Historical Society, AJ 22, no. 1119.

Mrs. Urania E. Nott to Emily C. Judson, June 29, 1846— Union College

My dear Mrs. Judson

I have read your note of the 24th with the peculiar interest of a keepsake from a departing friend—To you new prospects and new duties are opening upon you. Every thing [*sic*] around you will soon be new—and strange—A new heaven will be spread over upon your heart—and new stars will look down upon you at night—the people around you, with their customs, prejudices and religion will be new—and new cares, and joys and sorrows will spring up in your daily path.

Your undertaking you will find involves great sacrifices, and will call for great firmness, but promises great rewards.

There is no nobler character, nor one that commends so much of my respect, as that of a *missionary*—to be instrumental of carrying the knowledge of a Saviour [*sic*] to a heathen world—There is in it something so rich to the giver, as well as the receiver, that one may well surrender ease and home, and friend for the sake of sharing in it.

May you be supported in all the suffering and duties that will devolve upon you in your *new* home and your labours [*sic*] be blest to yourself and those whom you go to serve. We who remain behind, will have lives of less intensity of interest and less change, but we shall all alike move onward to our last great change—what will soon come—and seen from the other world how different will appear the incidents of this life—how opinions will have changed—habits of thought and duty, mistakes corrected, injuries forgotten, and distractions obliterated. There Christians of all denominations, and from every nation will be collected—and all unite in the work of praise to God the common Father, and Jesus Christ the Redeemer of Mankind.

Till we meet in that world—we shall not probably meet again—God grant, that tho' oceans roll between us we may each perform well our part in the field allotted to us on earth, and meet in heaven to part no more.

Your sincere friend
Urania E. Nott

Source: American Baptist Historical Society, AJ 18, no. 852.

The Reverend Rufus W. Griswold[350] to Emily C. Judson, June 30, 1846 —Philadelphia

Dear Madam

I dare hardly believe that I am honored by being remembered as one of your friends, yet few will recall your name with more emotion or pray more earnestly for your success and happiness.

I was in Boston a few days ago, but I did not know that you were there or I should have called upon you.

In my room at Jones's is your picture; a proof impression which was given me by Mr. Sartain;[351] and around it hang portraits of many whom I have called my friends, few of whom will be seen again by me, for in Burmah you will not be more isolated from this America world than I myself shall be, with only these silent companions looking from the wall.

May the fulfillment of all your hopes make you very happy for many years, and may we meet in Heaven, we and all who in this life are dear to us.

Vale!

Rufus W. Griswold

Source: American Baptist Historical Society, AJ 16, no. 692.

---

[350] In the correspondence, Mr. Griswold originally appeared in a letter of April 2, 1845, that Emily wrote to her sister Catharine Chubbuck. Emily referred to him as a clergyman who had called upon her when she arrived in Philadelphia and said, "He is a widower what's more and crazy to get married. Don't you think I shall accomplish something?" Then, speaking of her days in Philadelphia, Emily wrote to her brother Walker and said, "I got to be quite a belle while I was gone—gallivanted about with Graham and R. W. Griswold in Philadelphia." The Reverend Griswold was, in addition to an ordained clergyman, a noted anthropologist, editor, and writer, one of the distinguished literary figures of this period; he seemed to be, at least in Anna Maria Anable's eyes, a suitor for the affections of Emily Chubbuck.

[351] See vol. 1, "Cast of Characters," s.v. "Sartain, John."

LETTERS

—◊—

JULY-DECEMBER 1846

Mrs. Catherine Mears to Emily C. Judson,[1] July 1, 1846[2]

My dear Mrs. Judson,

As you are about to take your departure from your native land and go to the poor benighed [sic] heathen I felt constrained to say to you how much I rejoice at the noble sacrifice you are about to make to your blessed Saviour [sic]. Oh! that I could accompany you to test my love and the desire I feel to obey his blessed commandments "go says the Saviour [sic] into all the world," most gladly would I say! go where I do [ ] as you are endowed with the telents [sic] you pessess [sic] use them dear sister to promote the blessed course in which you have embarked cast away all fear whilst floating on the bosem [sic] of the sea, for he [ ] [ ] [ ] will protect you from all harm and will I trust carry you to the place of your destination in peace [ ] my dear Mrs. Judson the hundred and seventh Psalm, this was a great comfort to me and fixed my determination to let my Daughter go a voyage my faith was strong in God and the [ ] in that blessed Psalm comforted my heart my God was there and he ever will be to those who put their trust in him.

And now dear sister as much depends on our health to be useful I beg and entreat of you to be very careful of that do not undertake to [sic] much, your beloved companion can do enough for you both. I shall [ ] remember you when far away you shine in my most fervent prayers and I have found God to be a prayer hearing and a prayer [ ] God. My [sic] his [ ] blessings decend [sic] and rest upon you (and the great apostle of the east. I can think of no appellation more appropriate) is the sincere wish of one who is happy to subscribe herself your friend.

Catherine M. Mears

P.S. Will you my Dear Mrs. Judson assign the accompany bag you may find it useful the net is one of my own manufacturing value it for the work.

Written across the top of a back page: "I make all Ministers wives a present of one and I have earned twenty five Dollars in making them when I sheuld [sic] have been asleed [sic] for Missions on [ ]."

Written on the back page in the upper right fold of the letter and perpendicular to the above: "I want to say many things about your *Dear Dear* companion but words and time fail me. God bless you both."

Source: American Baptist Historical Society, AJ 17, no. 730.

---

[1] The original copy of this letter—its spelling and punctuation (or its lack)—allows a weak transcription. These deficiencies cannot detract from the warm heart that sent it to Emily Judson.

[2] This letter is undated. It is obviously written after Emily's marriage to Adoniram Judson, but before their departure for Burmah.

Mrs. Catherine Mears to Emily C. Judson,[3] July 1846

The Cabbage Net

"Every one [*sic*] may do some thing to circulate the Bible" said a clergyman one evening when advocating the cause of that Society whose object is to spread far and near that pure and hallowed volume. "None so poor none so young, as to be able in the Divine presence to say, I approve of the object and would if I could do some thing [*sic*] to promote its design, but cannot truly, I cannot." This sentiment was heard by a poor little cripple boy who was supported by publick [*sic*] charity in an alms house, and from motives of curiosity had strolled into the meeting struck with what he heard, he paid undivided attention, but when the words "none so poor where uttered, now thought he, what can I do? I have no money no friends to give me any, and I am lame so that I can not earn any." I feel certain I can tell God I wish I wish [*sic*] I could do something, but tis [*sic*] impossible and a sigh escaped him; the meeting dismissed; the lad went home retired to his bed awoke in the morning with the words, "every one [*sic*] may do something" fresh in his mind, and it troubled him in the course of the Day, as he was limping about on his crutches, he passed the door of a poor woman who was busily engaged in making Cabbage Nets. "What are you doing, mother?" said the boy making cabbage nets to sell for a living was the reply [*sic*] —Will you show me the way to make nets? Said he. "O," replied the old woman. "Look on and you will soon learn." She laid an object before him, and soon learned the *art*; and after thanking the woman, and biding [*sic*] her good he returned delighted with his new acquired knowledge, and determined to try if he could not do something for the Bible cause. Whilst turning the matter over in his mind, a very great difficulty presented itself; he had no pack thread nor had he way to procure any. What could he do? He thought of one plan, then of another and was at last obliged to relinquish his idea of making Nets and I need not tell you how sorry he felt. Some time [*sic*] after a resident clergyman visited the alms-house and talked very kindly to all the inmates on the state of their souls and said how much better off they were than those persons who had no Bible and had never heard of the way of salvation. This recalled in the boy's mind his former desires to do something to circulate the Scripture. A thought came into his mind and he determined to make an instant trial. He went to the clergyman's house, asked to see him, and in a very respectful but careful manner, begged for a piece of pack-thread, telling him he wished for it for a very particular purpose. The clergyman smiled. Remembering the boy and knowing his good character, he reached a ball and was in the act of cutting him a piece, when the boy immediately said, "Don't cut it sir. I shall need it all!" "All," said the

---

[3] On July 1, 1846, Mrs. Catherine Mears sent Emily C. Judson a net bag as a gift. This is a story about such bags, and at the end is a note to Emily saying that the cabbage nets of the story are similar to the net bag that she was sending to her.

clergyman. "[ ] [ ] [ ] must want a long piece indeed; but as you seem so much in earnest you shall have it." "Thank you sir, thank you sir a thousand times," and he hastened home as fast as his feeble frame and his crutches would let him; and to work he went, and in a few hours returned to the clergyman, with a good cabbage net in his hand; "now sir, sir" said he "I want you to give me six pence for this which I have made from the pack-thread you gave me. Mn—said every body [ ] ago at the Bible meeting every body [sic] could do something for that society. I have been thinking what I could do and have now found a plan. If you will take my net I will lay by some of the money with the rest I will buy some [ ] [ ] some more, try to sell them and lay aside every cent for the [ ] cause. [ ] I say [ ] [ ] was the [ ] made. Conscience [ ] [ ] appearance at the [ ] [ ] [ ] circumstances and [ ] between seven and eight [ ] [ ] [ ] [ ] of his labors and [ ] for the [Note: The rest of a line is lost in the fold.] stimulated you to make some effort to [ ] in this [ ] [ ] [ ] what may be done if there be a [ ] mind. May God help [ ] [ ] [ ] consecrate [ ] to his service, and then if you will be happy and [ ] [ ] [ ] all your energies and [ ] means to promote his glory.

This is similar to my nets of which I

Send you dear Mrs. Judson [ ],

Excuse the handwriting and (many) mistakes.

Source: American Baptist Historical Society, AJ 17, no. 803.

Mrs. Cole Bell to Emily C. Judson,[4] July 1, 1846

My dear Mrs. Judson

I scarcely know what to say, since the little book which seemed so Scriptural and so [ ] to her does not commend itself to you; but I answer your objections as best I can. I do not suppose that any one [sic] denies that [ ] will [ ] in the clouds etc. etc. and the question is as to the hour, [ ] better at the commencement of the Millennium, but a large portion of believers ([ ]to have reckoned [ ] [ ]) do believe that *when* he comes, he will find the earth covered with righteousness and there-fore in a fit position to sing the Jubilee Hymn, or for what other time could [ ] [ ] have [ ]? You say [ ] makes no mention of Satan's being loosed a little season etc etc and brings no [ ] to prove his position as to redeem the [ ] he has thrown down. I think he brings many trials to [ ], what the state of the world will be, when [ ] comes, the two [ ] striking [ ] [ ] are [ ] [ ] [ ] prediction "as it was in the days of

[4] This letter is undated. It was obviously written between the time of Emily's marriage to Adoniram Judson and their departure for Burmah. The handwriting in this letters presented a difficult task for transcription. Mrs. Bell is advocating a dispensation-alist biblical position to Emily. The letter hints that there had been other correspondence or communication between Emily and Mrs. Bell.

Noah, *so* shall it be etc. etc. and O[ ] the [ ] was not converted then or as in the days of Lot when destruction came upon Sodom of course it is clear in the XX of Rev 7th verse the hour of Satan's beings let loose but the small book could not contain [ ] [ ] of, [ ] [ ] wishes to prove to us, the Pre-millenial [ ]. As to what man does, that *proves* nothing, for [ ] says, as [ ] as [ ] are of [ ], the thing is, what God says is it not? You have [ ] me in a [ ] for a larger and more detailed work for I read very *few books*, ([ ] [ ] [ ] the [ ] [ ] [ ] the Bible is the best expositor and I think nothing could induce him to read a bulky book, [ ] however we have had a few on the subject, but they are scattered now—I have a small pamphlet on the matter which we think invaluable as far as it goes—and which I will send you tomorrow, it has been so [ ], and so [ ] [ ] about, that it is not I am sorry to say, in the most [ ]

Written in the top margin of the first page: "[ ] [ ]"

Believe me very sin'ly and [ ] yours

[ ] Bell

Source: American Baptist Historical Society, AJ 12, no. 322.

Adoniram Judson to Miss Cynthia Sheldon, July 2, 1846—Boston

My dear Miss Sheldon,

The instant you get this, please to mail to my address "Baptist Mission Rooms, Joy's Buildings, Boston" the engraved likeness of Emily[5] whh [which] I left with you. I hear you have put it in a frame. Out with it. Shear off the white paper, leaving the autograph at the bottom, and the body of the picture will make a good sized letter. Ticknor and Field[6] of this city are about engaging to be her publishers, and they want to see the likeness, before closing the bargain, as they fear it will not suit a duodecimo volume, as they are resolved against octavos. And as we have not a day to lose, you see why we are in a hurry. I have written to Philada. but if Sartain[7] happens to be out of the way, we may fail of getting a copy from him in time.

---

[5] Emily asked widely known engraver John Sartain to do a likeness of her. Originally, there was thought that the picture would be used in the magazines for which she had written—*Graham's Magazine*, the *Columbian*—with the caption "Henceforth to loftier purposes I pledge myself [signed] Fanny Forester." At the end, it was decided that the engraving would be used with the publication of *Alderbrook*, if she could find a publisher willing to take on the project.

[6] The Boston publishing firm of Ticknor, Reed and Fields sent Adoniram Judson a contract for *Alderbrook* on July 10, 1846. It was published before the end of the year.

[7] John Sartain was one of the most well-known engravers of the mid-nineteenth century. His works appeared in prominent magazines and books. In 1846, he created an engraving of Emily E. Chubbuck that was used as a plate for *Alderbrook*. The correspondence of spring 1846 reflects meetings with Mr. Sartain on changes thought to be needed. In 1849, Mr. Sartain was publishing a magazine because a letter makes a reference to one of Emily's poems being in it.

The boxes arrived yesterday[8]—all eight and the air-tights have come to light. But *the keys of the two chests* are not to be found. There is no mention of keys in your letters, and the *girls* know nothing about them. I have been trying all the keys in Boston without success, and suppose we shall have to break open the chests, whh [which] I am very [ ] to do. The 9th or 10th is now the day fixed for sailing, but it will probably be the 10th, perhaps later.

On *second* thoughts,—if you have the keys by you, suppose you mail them at once and I will not break open the chests till the last thing.

In great haste

Yours ever most affectionately

A. Judson

Emily C. Judson to Miss Cynthia Sheldon, July 2, 1846

Thursday morning

Dear Miss Cynthia,

I rec'd your kind favour of last evening together with a letter from Mr. Willis[9] and two from the doctor. Willis is a noble fellow, and behaves just as no man but himself would. He will be at Boston when we sail. Secretary Bancroft is to present me with his History of U. S., Prescott with his History of Mexico, Longfellow with his English Poets, and Willis is to make up a box of choice books from his own library.[10] He is in Washington. One letter from the doctor was dated Philadelphia and the other N.Y. I sh'd'nt [*sic*] wonder if he sh'd spend Friday night with you on his way to Skaneateles and so I shall venture to enclose a letter for him. Please don't mention to him anything about the board money without he speaks first. He would be mortified if he knew that I had borrowed money from you.

---

[8] See the letter of Emily E. Chubbuck to Miss Cynthia Sheldon dated June 20, 1846. Miss Sheldon had taken the responsibility of putting together all that would be needed by Emily for her time in Burmah, helped by Mrs. Hannah Gillette, and the staff and students of the Utica Female Academy.

[9] Nathaniel Parker Willis was the editor, with General George Morris, of the *New Mirror*, a prominent literary magazine in New York. His "discovery" of Emily in the June 8, 1844 edition of the *New Mirror* catapulted her into literary fame and enabled her to command the highest prices for her articles and stories from the major magazines of that period. It began a new and glorious chapter in her life. Over the next two years, he became her friend, mentor, and confidant. His black-bordered letter of March 21, 1846, made it abundantly clear that her engagement to Adoniram Judson had come as a "death blow" and that he had expected to marry Emily upon his return that month from England. He returned several letters to Emily to demonstrate to her, lest she had forgotten, why he had felt right in that expectation. In volume 1, there is a timeline that presents in some detail the substance of their developing relationship, all from the letters Willis had written to Emily. When she received her letters back from Willis, she destroyed them, feeling that they would cast a negative shadow on her life and, because of that, the life and ministry of Adoniram Judson.

[10] N. P. Willis wrote this to Emily in a letter from Washington, DC, dated June 24, 1846.

Mrs. Nott[11] sent me the corsets by Mrs. Eaton but they are double jean—not at all the thing for my new climate. Mrs. Cook said they might be exchanged for the Orleans dimity, so if you have any chance please send again. The size is 21, or, if not obtainable, 22. I can return these when I go through Albany, and I don't care to have the others before you can bring them out. Mrs. Eaton invited you to her house but we expect you to come straight here.

I cannot quite appreciate the *change* you speak of, until I see it; but I shall of course be glad of anything of the kind, however tardy. I sh'd think by what the professors tell me that I had got the world pretty much on my side. The people here are very, very kind. My work is going on nicely and will be finished I think without difficulty.

I shall hope to see Anna M.[12] tomorrow. I am half crazy for her to get here, the darling! People are very much interested in her and she will find them very agreeable. I don't believe that the higher traits of the doctor's character are so well appreciated anywhere in the country as here. They are very sensible liberal men and women.

Please come as early as you can. Love to all, especially yourself from

Yours most affectionately

Emily

Source: Hanna family files.

[11] Urania Sheldon had been the literary principal of the Utica Female Academy in fall 1840 when Emily Chubbuck came to study there. Emily was able to afford this wonderful education through the generous offer of Miss Sheldon and her sister Cynthia, the executive and financial head of the academy, to defer tuition. Urania Sheldon left in late summer 1842 upon her marriage to the Reverend Doctor Eliphalet Nott, the president of Union College in Schenectady, New York. Because of the distance separating them, Emily's relationship with Urania Sheldon Nott did not develop the intimacy that grew between Emily and Miss Cynthia Sheldon. Urania Sheldon Nott remained a mentor, advisor, and friend to Emily in the years of her writing, her missionary endeavors, and upon her return to America in 1851. She was also the aunt of Anna Maria Anable.

[12] Anna Maria Anable was the niece of the Misses Urania and Cynthia Sheldon and the daughter of Joseph and Alma Sheldon Anable. Emily first met Anna Maria in fall 1840 when she went as a student to the Utica Female Academy; both Emily and Anna Maria became members of the faculty there. In these years, Anna Maria became Emily's dearest friend, and the extensive correspondence between the two reflects sensitive, flirtatious spirits and a deep intimacy. Emily was "Nemmy" to Anna Maria's "Ninny." In 1848, Anna Maria Anable, with the help of her extended family, moved to Philadelphia and started the Misses Anable's School in Philadelphia. At Emily's death in 1854, Anna Maria was given guardianship of Emily Frances Judson, daughter of Emily and Adoniram Judson.

The Reverend Doctor William Dean to Emily C. Judson,[13] July 3, 1846 —Ship "Calcutta"

Dear Sister Emily.

I had almost by mistake written "Fanny"[14] and perhaps I have committed an offence by not commencing with "*Mrs. Judson*"—but my chosen mode of address seems to me the most natural,[15] and if it prove objectionable to your good husband I must leave you to settle the difficulty with him.

I regretted much after leaving the hustle of home and getting an hour for quiet reflection on ship board, whh [which] I have scarcely enjoyed since I landed in A.M., that I had enjoyed so little time with you, and especially since you resolved to go eastward.[16] As some sort of compensation for any loss I have engaged lately a visit to "Underhill Cottage" and rambled all about "Alder Brook," and fancy I have seen many familiar faces and looked again upon the scenes of my childhood, and after these "Trippings" with you over "Author Land"[17] came home in imagination and then almost believed that I might sometime become an author myself since I fancy myself born in that land. But then I am met with a difficulty at the outset, for I can't find those "little messages racing like mad through *my* head" indeed after rising up what few thoughts are processable [*sic*] on ship board in writing home to my friends, I can not scarcely find material even for a friendly letter—This is about the time appointed for your embarkation—Twelve years ago yesterday I sailed from Boston—first to Burmah, then to Singapore—Siam—and China, and have since been a wandering pilgrim and have still "no abiding city."

I wish your party might have sailed in company with ours then we wld have had a strong force.—As it is we get on very well—Mr. Everett and his lady are very agreeable, then we have Mr. and Mrs. Jenks and Messrs Clopton and Piercy[18] with their wives, all very kind and friendly—the ladies a little sea-sick but all appear on deck after dinner—and again, I have a music box, melodeon, flute, and fiddle, and not being a friend to long faces I persuade some one [*sic*] to play when there are

---

[13] Dr. Dean wrote two brief addendums to this letter, which was written on board ship as he traveled from the United States to the mission field. They are dated, and placed accordingly, September 14, 1846, and October 24, 1846.

[14] Emily Chubbuck wrote under the *nom de plume* Fanny Forester. Asked about it once, she said, "Would anyone buy a book written by Emily E. Chubbuck?"

[15] In 1834, William Dean was an interim minister in Morrisville, New York, as he was preparing to first go to the mission field. He grew up in that area and knew Emily and her parents from living in the village. In spring that year he baptized Emily.

[16] The correspondence reflects one visit with Emily. On May 28, 1846, Emily wrote to Adoniram Judson, "I have had a visit from Mr. Dean. He is a very fine man."

[17] This is a play on Emily's book, *Trippings in Author-land*. "Underhill Cottage" is one of the sketches in the book, and it invites to reader to come to "Alder-brook." It would seem that Dr. Dean had taken Emily's book with him for reading pleasure on the long journey to the East.

[18] These people would all be appointed missionaries on their way to the mission field. Earlier, when talking of their passage, Adoniram Judson was deliberate in booking passage on a ship that would afford them more solitude and privacy, as opposed to traveling with a larger party.

discoverable symptoms of undue solemnity, and as the last resort I can play on the *music box* myself.—And when this will not do, I take the ladies to look at my rose-bush and strawberry vines, the objects of my daily care, and pluck them a flower—a rare thing at sea,—and thus, as you perceive I make myself a man of great importance on board. Moreover, I have a *cow* on board wh [which], after furnishing all the milk I wish for my mush and "jonny-cake," affords an ample supply for the whole party. Then, to break the monotony of sea-life, we effect some internal revolutions by turning any thing [*sic*] out of our staterooms, and after a very careful rearrangement, in the course of a fortnight, bring all things back again to their original order.—How do *you* manage on ship board! I suppose your poetic eyes can see upon the blue seas, fields of living green, with forests waving o'er the flood, as myriads of merry songsters make music for the ear—while Old Ocean is cradling *us*, poor dull folks, into the imbecility of childhood. If you knew how much your "little feather-tipped pen" had done to charm an otherwise lonely hour and drive away the nausea of the sea, you would not be in haste to wash off that "ink-mask" from your fingers. At least I hope I may be favored with an occasional epistle from the same pen. Do write—will you? And you shall hear from your old friend [ ] his masks are made with a metallic pen, which is not adapted to description or incident but can inscribe how sincerely

I remain

Your friend and Xn brother

William Dean

Kindest regards to Dr. Judson and associates and to your parents when you write to Hamilton.

Written on the bottom of the address page: "Since I have not at my elbow, 'Dr. Johnson's London Edition' nor 'Webster's Wondrous Quarto,' will you kindly give me the significance of *Trippings*—"

Source: American Baptist Historical Society, AJ 15, no. 595.

Emily C. Judson to her Churches, July 6, 1846—Boston

In dissevering the various ties which bind me to the land of my birth, I find one of peculiar strength and interest. It is not easy to say farewell, when father and mother, brother and sister, and those scarcely less dear, are left behind us at the word; it is not easy to break away from the sweet, simple attractions of social life, or the increasing fascinations of a world but too bright and beautiful; but there are other ties to break, other sorrowful farewells to be spoken. The parents and friends, brothers and sisters, whom Christ has given us, and who for His sake have loved us, occupy no remote corner of our hearts. Such friends of mine are, I trust, scattered over various parts of the country; those whose prayers are at this very moment strengthening both hand and heart. Oh, I know you have prayed for me, ye whose prayers "avail much"; for, casting away my broken reed, and trusting in God only, I have been made strong.

We do not always feel the deepest love for those with whom we are visibly connected; so, though the beloved church in the village of Hamilton has never been my home, the strongest tie binding me to it is not that the names of those to whom God first gave me, are enrolled among its members. I have often worshiped there; there a resolution, a consecration of self which cost—the Omniscient only knows how great an effort—received ready encouragement and sympathy; there prayers were offered, tears wept, and blessings spoken, which I shall bear upon my heart—a precious burden; and thither I shall turn for future prayers, future encouragement, and future sympathy. Oh, my eyes grow dim when I think of the loved ones, friends of Jesus, in my own dear home—the beautiful village of Hamilton.

There is another church with whom I have a more intimate connection—the one whose commendation I bear to a strange people in a strange land, but worshiping no strange God. There are to me no dearer ones on earth, than a little circle at Utica, with whom I have hoped and feared, rejoiced, and wept, and prayed. God grant that I may join that same circle above! that the tremulous voice which thousands of times has borne a confession of our sins and follies up to our Intercessor, I may hear again in songs of praise; that when the thin gray hairs are brightened, and the heavy foot made swift and light, I may return heavenly love for the counsels to which I have so often listened. I do not *ask* to be remembered there, for I know that parting in person can not mar the union of spirit; and when my hand is strong, and my heart light, when Christ confers upon me any peculiar blessing, I shall think that Deacon Sheldon[19] and those who love him and me, are praying for me.

There is another little church worshiping God quietly away in an obscure village; and with that church before all others, I claim my home. All the associations of childhood cluster there; and there still sparkle the bright waters where the

[19] Deacon Asa Sheldon was the father of Miss Cynthia Sheldon, Urania Sheldon Nott, and Alma Sheldon Anable. Deacon and Mrs. Sheldon lived with their daughters and grandchildren as a part of the Utica Female Academy community. Mrs. Sheldon died January 29, 1847. Deacon Sheldon continued to have a room at the Utica Female Academy, where he died in March 1848. For many years, he led mealtime prayers for the academy family, and Deacon and Mrs. Sheldon were popular with the students, who often looked in on him.

revered Chinese missionary,[20] now on his way back to the scene of his labors, administered the initiatory rite of the church, when she consented to receive the trembling, doubting child into her bosom. Oh, the church at Morrisville, the sober, prayerful ones who were my first Christian guides, must let my heart have a home among them still. There are my Christian fathers and mothers, my teachers in the Sabbath school, and those whom I have taught; the dearest, sweetest associations of my life cluster around the little missionary society, the evening Bible class, the prayer circle, in which I first mingled; and the little plans for doing good, in which I was allowed to participate, when I first loved my Saviour, are as fresh in memory as though formed yesterday.

Dear friends of Jesus at Morrisville, ye whose prayers first drew me to the protection of your church, whose prayers sustained me through the many years that I remained with you, whose prayers, I trust, have followed me during the little time that we have been separated, will you pray for me still? When dangers and difficulties are about me, will you plead earnestly, "God help her?" Will you pray for me, now that we are to see each other's faces no more in this world? Ah, I know you will; so let me ask the same for those among who I go to labor, those who know not Christ and His salvation, and yet, "are without excuse." Pray for them, and for me, that I may do them good.

Emily Judson

Source: A. C. Kendrick, *The Life and Letters of Mrs. Emily C. Judson*, 212–15.

Nathaniel Parker Willis to Emily C. Judson, July 6, 1846—New York

Dearest Emily,

I had intended to be in Boston during the last week of your stay, and to be present at your embarkation. A little closer approach to the scene that embarkation would probably be—with the number of Mr. Judson's friends and the enthusiasm felt for him—made me shrink from compelling you to reserve for me any of the attention which those friends will expect from you at the parting hour, and still more, to shrink from adding to the emotion of that troubled hour, the pain of parting with one who must be dear to you as the foster-father of your genius. I

---

[20] The Reverend Doctor William Dean was a distinguished missionary to Hong Kong for more than fifty years. As the pastor of the local church in Morrisville, he baptized Emily Chubbuck when she was seventeen. There are nine letters in the correspondence from Mr. Dean, beginning after Emily's appointment to missionary service. After the death of Adoniram Judson, it was speculated, and not without reasonable support, that William Dean had an interest in taking Judson's place in Emily's life and affections. The later correspondence between Emily and Anna Maria Anable shows that Dr. Dean was often the butt of their ridicule, so something had happened to challenge that relationship. In 1854, when William Dean was courting Mrs. Maria Brown in New York City, Abby Ann Judson was working for Mrs. Brown as an in-house teacher for her children. For the complete story of William Dean's life and the many ways he touched the mission movement and the life of Emily Chubbuck Judson, see vol. 1, "Cast of Characters," s.v. "Dean, William."

see that it is better that we exchange our farewells as we have exchanged all other feelings—on paper. You must not think hardly of me for this.

I had another intention which I have not matured, but that I can do after you are gone. I heard that Prescott was away from Boston, and I thought I would make up the parcel of books for you and send them by the next ship.[21] Will you leave word and let me leave them with Mr. Colby[22] to be forwarded.

Write me a word of farewell before you sail. Give my warmest remembrance and every possible kind wish to your husband. May God preserve and restore you to us. Write to me from India. Command me freely on all you wish me to do.

Farewell, dearest Emily.

Yours ever most faithfully

N. P. Willis

Source: Hanna family files.

Emily C. Judson to the Missionary Society, Utica Female Academy, July 7, 1846—Boston

My Very, Very Dear Friends,—

I have postponed writing you till the present moment, hoping that I should find at least one half hour of leisure. But my time is constantly occupied, so you must excuse the hand-work in consideration of the heart's still lingering with you. I have received many presents since I left Utica, both from societies and individuals; but the work done in that dear school-room has a peculiar charm to me, bearing, as it does, the traces of loved fingers.[23] May the kind interest you have exhibited in me awaken a yet deeper interest in those among whom my future lot is cast; and those of you who pray (do not *all* of you?) pray for the Burmese and for me.

Remember me when I am gone; speak of me sometimes kindly; forgive and forget my thousand faults and follies; *serve God truly*, and may He bless you ever!

Affectionately and gratefully,

Emily C. Judson

Source: A. C. Kendrick, *The Life and Letters of Mrs. Emily C. Judson*, 212.

---

[21] See the letter from N. P. Willis to Emily C. Judson dated June 24, 1846, where he speaks of a collection of books that he and others want to give to her before she leaves.

[22] This is likely Lewis Colby of the publishing firm L. Colby in New York. Colby was known to N. P. Willis, and it was known that Mr. Colby had agreed to republish several of Emily's small books and hoped to publish the memoir of Sarah Hall Boardman Judson when Emily finished it, which they did in 1848.

[23] Many of the girls at the Utica Female Academy helped to prepare all that Emily would need in her new life in Burmah; Miss Cynthia Sheldon marshaled every person at her disposal to carry out this monumental responsibility.

Emily C. Judson to Mrs. Urania Sheldon Nott, July 7, 1846—Boston

My dear Mrs. Nott,

Anna Maria[24] has just shown me a letter from you which I take the liberty to notice a little, relying entirely on your indulgence which I believe has seldom failed me. I will say nothing concerning your allusions to doctor Judson, since they all spring from your not knowing him. You *do* know *me* and that knowledge I think will lead you to a proper estimate of the course I have taken since I returned from Philadelphia and found A. M. a most decided Baptist. If it do not, [*sic*] it will be of no use to say anything.

As for Anna M, whether wisely or not, she has acted conscientiously, and as a conscientious one I think the act sh' d be respected.[25] Even if she had been unduly influenced, the fault would not be hers. More, if she was excited and incapable of judging, she believed herself calm. I know that conscientiousness will not excuse a wicked act, but will it not a merely imprudent one? A.M. believed that God required her to be baptized—was it "unnatural" or "unaccountable" for her to obey? Cannot you see that but for conscience' sake the step was hard and unpleasant? She has left a church which she loved for one that, except in the things of religion, cannot sympathize with her.

In a worldly point of view she has not gained but lost most decidedly; and I have the means of knowing that all those sacrifices were duly estimated. It is merely on Anna Maria's account that I write; because I love her as a sister—more I believe than I do my sister—and I think that under existing circumstances she sh'd be treated with peculiar tenderness. I sh'd have left her with a much lighter heart in her own church, but after she had decided that she ought to leave it, I did not dare recommend her to remain. We shall part in three days forever, and with much more sorrow on my part, than if she were going back as in former times, to you, who I always supposed loved us both (*her* especially) changelessly. Surely, you should not be afflicted so very much at anything short of a wicked or disgraceful act. There is no disrespect or unkindness to even our most intimate friends in doing what we believe God requires; and we *must* judge for ourselves in matters of right and wrong after we have arrived to mature years. Anna Maria is not a child; she cannot help having an opinion on subjects which relate to her own spiritual advancement; and she must be guided by those opinions. It is the only safe course. I hope that the

---

[24] See vol. 1, "Cast of Characters," s.v. "Anable, Miss Anna Maria."

[25] Beginning in early May 1846, Anna Maria suggested to Emily that she has some personal matters that she would like to address with Adoniram Judson. As the correspondence unfolds, Emily revealed to Adoniram that Anna Maria was thinking seriously of being baptized by immersion and that she would like to ask him to do it in Mr. Corey's church in Utica. On May 19, Adoniram wrote to Emily that he had spoken with Mr. Corey about the matter and he was agreeable. On May 24, Anna Maria wrote a wonderful letter to Adoniram describing her deepest feelings, her faith, and what was working in her toward making this decision. Adoniram Judson did baptize Anna Maria Anable before the congregation of the Utica Church on June 7, 1846. The baptism itself was probably in the Mohawk River.

opinions and the acts to which they had will be such as both God and those who love her on earth will approve—that she may "grow in grace" and be happy in "doing good." Oh, let these small differences be forgotten—do not think whether she be a Baptist or Presbyterian; but dear, dear *Aunt* Urania,[26] take her to your heart as one who loves the same Master and desires above all things to serve and please him. It is my last request on this side of the world, that you forget all that is passed, leave it to be accounted for in "the great day"; and taking her whom we both love, as formerly, by the hand, lead her up to that higher state of grace to which you have attained. I know that she has a strong desire to live as God approves and she needs peculiar sympathy. Please love her for your self and for me too.

I have written much more than I intended, but could not well say less. You will forgive me, I know. We shall never meet again on earth; but God grant that we may see each others' faces above, where you will see how entirely you have misconstrued one of the purest and best spirits that ever trod the earth—one who "looks to God in all his ways." Till then the Omnipotent Arm sustain and guide you! May you be blest and happy! Such is the constant prayer of

Your sincerely affectionate friend,

Emily Judson

Source: Hanna family files.

Emily C. Judson to Catharine Chubbuck, July 9, 1846

I meant to have written you before, but if you could know what a siege I have had! I have been crowded almost to death with company. Sometimes my hand has been so swollen with constant shaking that I have not been able to get on a glove, and I have been obliged to use my left hand.

Source: A. C. Kendrick, *The Life and Letters of Mrs. Emily C. Judson*, 215.

Mr. William Crowell to Emily C. Judson, July 10, 1846—Boston

Mrs. Judson

Dear Madam

I have been solicitous for some time past to engage your literary contributions for the volumes of the *Christian Watchman*. For this purpose I intended to have embraced an early opportunity to see you, but I have done the next thing to it, I have seen and conversed with your husband on the subject. After remarking that

[26] See vol. 1, "Cast of Characters," s.v. "Nott, Urania Sheldon."

is yet doubtful how far it will be in your power to continue writing after your removal in Burmah he further observed, that as the missionaries are under the control of the Board it would be necessary to have an understanding with them on the subject, advised me to converse with the Secretary. I have done so, and I find that according to their rules, missionaries can receive no compensation for any services they may perform. It is impossible therefore for me to make you any proposals involving pecuniary remuneration, or for you to entertain them, but he further informed me that he would lay my proposition of [ ] before the Ex. Com. [ ] [ ] to any special modification of the rules.

Whether it will be advisable for one to do so I am not certain, but I may say to you that some of the members of the Comm. have expressed to me their *strong* wish that the products of your pen might be secured to the *Watchman*. All I can say therefore dear Madam, is that I have done all the [ ] admit of, to prepare the way for some honorable proposal to you, and I leave the subject to your consideration with the earnest request that the *Watchman* may be [ ] from time to time with your written thoughts, with the assurance that I will be ready to make such returns as shall be satisfactory to all concerned.

My best wishes and prayers [ ] [ ] you and the scene of your missionary labors. I trust that you will increasingly feel that it is good to make any sacrifice for Christ's yoke.

How great and precious are his promises to those who forsake the dearest objects of [ ] affection for his sake. It may seem foolish to the fashionable [ ] of this world now, but by faith we are favorably assured of a time when the [ ] wisdom of this world will be turned into folly, [ ] [ ] is [ ] [ ] foolish will be [ ] of the true wisdom.

Your brother in Christ
Wm Crowell

Source: American Baptist Historical Society, AJ 15, no. 615.

Emily C. Judson to Miss Cynthia Sheldon, July 10, 1846—Boston

It is late, dear Miss C.,[27] and I am nearly worn out, so I cannot say what I would. God will reward you for all your kindness—I never can. Do not forget me when I am on the water and in that strange land; nor let the rest whom I love forget. All of you pray for me—grandfather[28] especially. Anna M.[29] will tell you everything, and kiss all around for me. The people here almost idolize her, and Lydia[30] is liked by everybody.

Before you receive this I shall be out of sight of land, not to see a green thing for four months. Farewell!

Affectionately and gratefully yours

Emily C. Judson

Source: Hanna family files.

Emily C. Judson—Impromptu Verses,[31] July 10, 1846

Impromptu Verses.

Our "Cradle" rocks upon the tide;—
My heart is rocking too;
And warm tears gather blindingly,
And shut the shore from view.

I scarcely know why I should weep;
But 'tis so strange to be
An exile from my native land,
Upon the stormy sea!

[27] Miss Cynthia Sheldon was in charge of the administrative and financial departments of the Utica Female Academy. Miss Sheldon and her sister Urania, who was literary principal, gave Emily Chubbuck a place at the academy in October 1840. They had deferred any cost to a future time when Emily could afford to reimburse them. Upon Miss Urania Sheldon's marriage in the late summer 1842 to the Reverend Doctor Eliphalet Nott, the president of Union College, and her subsequent move to Schenectady, Miss Cynthia Sheldon assumed a larger leadership role at the academy. Active and well-known in Baptist circles, Miss Cynthia was to become an important mentor, advisor, and friend to Emily until the time of Emily's death in 1854. She was the aunt of Emily's best friend, Anna Maria Anable, and was addressed by most as "Aunt Cynthia." In 1848, Miss Sheldon moved to Philadelphia to help Miss Anable with the startup of the Misses Anable's School.

[28] See vol. 1, "Cast of Characters," s.v. "Sheldon, Deacon Asa."

[29] See vol. 1, "Cast of Characters," s.v. "Anable, Miss Anna Maria."

[30] Lydia Lillybridge was one of Emily's closest friends at the Utica Female Academy. When Emily made the decision to go to Burmah as the wife of Adoniram Judson and as a missionary, Lydia wanted to go with them. Emily spoke to Adoniram Judson of Lydia's extraordinary abilities, and Adoniram advocated her appointment before Dr. Solomon Peck and the Board of the American Baptist Missionary Union. Lydia was commissioned to go with them, in spite of the fact that she remained single. Always independent, outspoken, and unafraid to cause ripples in the missionary community, Lydia served on the mission field for twenty-eight years. She married missionary Thomas Simons in May 1851. See the timeline on the life and service of Lydia Lillybridge Simons in vol. 1.

[31] These lines were written on board the ship *Faneuil Hall* the day before it embarked for the long trip to Burmah.

Not that I leave my home behind;
For wheresoe'er thou art,
I know forever more will be
The dear home of my heart.

But still I hear my father's voice;—
Bend to my mother's kiss;—
I never dreamed, in other days,
Of such a love as this!

And yet it looses no true tie,
Knit 'mid those dreams of yore;
I even seem in loving thee,
To love the whole world more.

But cheerfully I yield it all,
(Would it were more) for thee;—
So bear me, Love, on thy strong heart,
Far o'er the billowy sea.

Source: Emily Judson, *An Olio of Domestic Verse*, 138–39.

W. D. Ticknor and Company to Adoniram Judson,[32] July 10, 1846

Articles of Agreement, made and concluded this tenth day of July in the year of our Lord one thousand eight hundred and forty six, by and between Adoniram Judson of Maulmain, of the first part, and W. D. Ticknor, John Reed Sr., and J. L. T. Fields of Boston County of Suffolk and state of Massachusetts of the other part, book sellers and Copartners.

Whereas, the said Adoniram Judson has furnished so said Ticknor and Co. in manuscript and printed copy, a work entitled "Alderbrook," [sic] a collection of Fanny Forester's Village Sketches, Poems etc., by Miss Emily Chubbuck, now these articles witness that the said Judson in consideration of one dollar to him paid by said Ticknor, the receipt whereof is hereby acknowledged, and in further consider-

---

[32] In spring 1846, as they prepared to leave America for Burmah, Adoniram Judson took upon himself the responsibility for the foundational work that would result in the publication of *Alderbrook*, a collection of Emily Chubbuck/Fanny Forester's poems and sketches. There were many copyright issues with which to deal, and in the April–May correspondence, there is a great deal mentioned of the work with John Sartain on the portrait engraving which was to appear in the publication. The portrait went through a number of changes as late as a May 26 letter. The responsibility for providing such an engraving is mentioned in this contract. This is the actual contract outlining the conditions of the publisher and the duties and rewards of the author between what then was Ticknor, Reed and Fields and Adoniram Judson/Emily Judson. The contract is dated July 10, 1846, and Adoniram and Emily sailed on the *Faneuil Hall* on July 11, 1846.

ation of the covenants and agreements on the part of said Ticknor and Co. herein—after contained, hereby grant unto the said Ticknor and Co. their representatives and assigns, the sole and exclusive right of publishing said book during the term of the copy right and this grant is made upon the conditions that the said Ticknor their representatives and assigns shall well and truly perform their costmants [sic] hereinafter contained.

The said Ticknor Co. on their part for themselves, their representatives and assigns, in consideration of the promises hereby covenant and agree that will cause to be stereotyped and will publish in handsome style, said book and use all proper exertions to promote its sale, and further, they agree to pay to said Judson his representatives and assigns, annually *Ten per cent on the retail price of each and every copy sold during the year.*

Said Ticknor and Co. agree to furnish to said Judson, without charge, such number of copies as he may desire as presentation copies, not exceeding in all twenty five copies.

Said Judson on his part, further agrees to furnish to said Ticknor and Co. an engraved likeness of the author of said book, and they the said Ticknor Co. agree to cause the same to be well printed and bound with the said book.

W. D. Ticknor and Co.

A. Judson

Source: American Baptist Historical Society, AJ 22, no. 1107.

Emily C. Judson to Mrs. Lavinia Richards Chubbuck,[33] July 11, 1846[34]

Dear Mother,[35]

We have just said good-bye to thousands and are fairly off. The land is a small speck in the distance—all strange, strange! I have an opportunity to send back by the pilot, and I thought you would like to know how very, *very* well I am.

Not withstanding all my fatigues, I have not been nearly so well this spring. **And** the ship is beautiful and comfortable, **everything new and clean about her, a very nice place to spend four months in. We have everything for our comfort and convenience, even to a cow which the doctor bought yesterday. I think you would like amazingly to look in upon us.**

---

[33] There are two versions of this letter: the original as written by Emily E. Chubbuck and the edited version published by Dr. A. C. Kendrick in his biography, *The Life and Letters of Mrs. Emily C. Judson* (New York: Sheldon and Company, 1831). Additions made by Dr. Kendrick are in parentheses, and words in the original left out by Dr. Kendrick have been added in bold.

[34] Emily has this letter dated July 10, 1846, and A. C. Kendrick, in *The Life and Letters of Mrs. Emily C. Judson*, has placed it a day later. Saturday fell on July 11, so Emily is off a day as she wrote the date.

[35] See "To My Mother," which Emily Judson wrote at this time; it appears after the letters of July 10.

You must not have a single sad thought about me, for I am very happy indeed; and God is with us on the sea as on the land. **You must** pray for me often, for that is now your only **way** (means) **you have** of keeping harm from me, **and it is a very good way. The passengers are all very pleasant people, and the captain and officers seem pleasant too. Tell Kate**[36] **and Wallace**[37] **they must be good children and if we never meet again in this world, try, with me to meet in heaven. Good-by Mother! All good-bye! Kisses all round!**

Emily

Source: A. C. Kendrick, *The Life and Letters of Mrs. Emily C. Judson*, 215; Hanna family files.

Emily C. Judson to Mrs. Lavinia Richards Chubbuck, July 1846

To My Mother[38]

Give me my old seat, mother,
With my head upon thy knee;
I've passed through many a changing scene
Since thus I sat by thee,
Oh! let me look into thine eyes—
Their meek, soft, loving light,
Falls like a gleam of holiness
Upon my heart to-night.

I've not been long away, mother,
Few suns have rose and set,
Since last the tear-drop on thy cheek
My lips in kisses met;
'Tis but a little time, I know,
But very long it seems,

---

[36] Sarah Catharine Chubbuck, "Kate," "Kit," or "Kitty" was Emily's older sister by ten months. Outside of the two terms at the Utica Female Academy, which Emily arranged for her, Catherine always lived at home with her parents in Hamilton, New York. The letters indicate opportunities for marriage, but she, for unknown reasons, remained single. She later helped to care for Henry and Edward Judson after their return from Burmah in fall 1851 when they moved into the Hamilton home with their "aunt" and "grandparents," and she was remembered by them as "dear old Aunt Kate—a dear friend."

[37] Born January 1, 1824, William Wallace Chubbuck was six years younger than Emily. During these years of Emily's correspondence, Wallace lived at or near home and worked at different occupations including printing, office work, and teaching. Emily wrote of him as capable in many areas, but seeming to lack ambition at times. He proved to be a strong support for the Chubbuck family over these years, and at the time of her death in 1854, Wallace had become one of Emily's primary caregivers. After February 1854, she dictated all her letters to him because of her failing strength. Wallace was active in newspaper and political activities; he also worked with at least one of the legislative committees in Albany. He was married in July of 1854; he died in August of 1861.

[38] This poem to Emily's mother falls after her letter to her mother as the ship began its long journey to Burmah. It was sent back with the pilot.

Though every night I came to thee
Dear mother, in my dreams.

The world has kindly dealt, mother,
By the child thou lov'st so well;
Thy prayers have circled round her path,
And 't was their holy spell
Which made that path so dearly bright,
Which strewed the roses there;
Which gave the light, and cast the balm
On every breath of air.

I bear a happy heart, mother;
A happier never beat;
And even now new buds of hope
Are bursting at my feet,
Oh, mother! Life may be "a dream,"
But if such dreams are given,
While at the portal thus we stand,
What are the truths of heaven?

I bear a happy heart, mother;
Yet, when fond eyes I see,
And hear soft tones and winning words,
I ever think of thee.
And then, the tear my spirit weeps
Unbidden fills my eye;
And like a homeless dove, I long
Unto thy breast to fly.

Then I am very sad, mother,
I'm very sad and lone;
Oh! there's no heart, whose inmost fold
Opes to me like thine own!
Though sunny smiles wreathe blooming lips,
While love-tones meet my ear;
My mother, one fond glance of thine
Were a thousand times more dear.

Then, with a closer clasp, mother,
Now hold me to thy heart;
I'd feel it beating 'gainst my own

Once more before we part.
And, mother, to this love-lit spot,
When I am far away,
Come oft—too oft thou canst not come.—
And for thy darling pray.

Source: Fanny Forester, *Alderbrook*, 10th ed. (Boston: Ticknor, Reed and Fields, 1851) 1:275–76.

Miss Cynthia Sheldon to Emily C. Judson,[39] August 9, 1846[40]—Utica

My ever dear Emily,

Four weeks on the ocean wave I am sure you would like to know what has transpired on land during that—heaven only knows how much you all are on our hearts, from morn to night. You are now where we can form no opinion of the weather—calms or tempests alike can be controlled by our Heavenly Father—may He make the billows as solid earth to your tread—the breeze as the breath of heaven to steer your bark steadily onward to the desired havens of your toils is the burden of many hearts you have left behind.—

I well know your mind is often with us—you know it is vacation—dear Anna M.[41] came home in safety—she spent the night in Troy—next morning met the Doct. and Urania[42] in waiting for her where she passed a few hours without any uncomfortable allusions[43]—seven o'clock saw her safe at home—The Soiree came off with *éclat*—and all dispersed the next day, with all the variety of feelings would be manifested on such occasions.—Fanny Buckingham and beautiful bright Master Judson[44]—Mrs. Henry Sheldon and two babies all under the care of Fanny,[45] good

[39] This letter is addressed to "Mrs. Dr. A. Judson. Via overland mail. Maulmain, Burmah."

[40] This letter has an addendum written August 10, 1846.

[41] See vol. 1, "Cast of Characters," s.v. "Anable, Miss Anna Maria."

[42] See vol. 1, "Cast of Characters," s.v. "Nott, Urania Sheldon."

[43] Mrs. Nott was severe with Anna Maria when she asked Adoniram Judson to baptize her by immersion. The baptism took place in Utica, New York, on June 7, 1846. Emily's letter July 7, 1846, to Mrs. Nott is clear in her defense of Anna Maria, and it reveals some of what Mrs. Nott said.

[44] Fanny Buckingham was the daughter of Fred and Martha Sheldon. She was a niece to Miss Cynthia Sheldon and a cousin to Anna Maria Anable. She was married to Mr. Buckingham, the second in command of the ill-fated steamship *Swallow*, which went down on the river with the loss of a significant number of passengers. (See the letter of Miss Cynthia Sheldon to Emily E. Chubbuck dated April 11, 1845.) Fanny Buckingham was mentioned in Anna Maria's letters of December 28 and 29, 1847. She had a young son Judson, and she was visiting Anna Maria.

[45] Fanny Anable was one of nine children born to Joseph and Alma Anable and was a niece of Miss Cynthia Sheldon and Mrs. Urania Sheldon Nott. The correspondence indicates that in April 1845 she was away from home studying and taking music lessons. These spring letters indicate that she was in Philadelphia, working in the home of and with the family of the Reverend A. D. Gillette. See Miss Sheldon's letter to Emily of November 30, 1845, in which she spoke of all that Fanny was doing to improve herself in the field of music, but also her concern for Fanny's interest in the party life and the "vanitie" which surround her." A March 30, 1847 letter from Anna Maria Anable told of Fanny's conversion following her grandmother's death. In September 1847, she was listed as one of the teachers at the Utica Female Academy. Fanny became a teacher with her sisters in the Misses Anable's School in Philadelphia.

Jonas arrived here before the general scattering, we had a nice ten days visit from them. Henry came for the last few days and to help [ ] [ ] the boxes homeward—Fanny writes the children were [ ] [ ] for the Auntys [sic] three days afterwards—the girls were all home. [ ] [ ] Harriet[46] spent three days away at Commencement—Anna M. went the next day after they left us, to spend a few days with Matilda Berthoud.[47] There she created a fame for self possession not thought of before—she was in great peril. The horse took fright and ran with all speed perfectly unmanageable, for a half mile it was almost impossible to hold on to the buggy—when by the dint of great dexterity in young Berthoud—he reigned the horse on to a pile of stones which broke his speed sufficiently for both to clear themselves—the carriage was dashed to pieces a few moments afterwards—there were dozens of people in chase, expecting every moment one or both would be killed, and when they came to them high and dry on the stones, all exclaimed they never saw such presence of mind evinced by two persons before. The lad is only 17—he had tried in vain by turning against the fence some half dozen times to give Anna M. a chance to jump—he had told her, and she had made up her mind to it, to go over with the carriage, with out [sic] he could stop the horse for a moment. This course with the blessing of God saved them—poor Matilda fainted on seeing the horse comeing [sic] full speed without carriage and driver—all the horrors of our grief at home were before her, until she was relieved by the evidence of their wonderful preservation—thus we have perils by land when you are only looking to the ocean for disaster—Anna M. brought home flesh bruises from the pelting against the carriage—otherwise she had entirely recovered from the shock—the

[46] Harriet or "Hatty" or "Hattie" or "Hat" Anable was one of nine children born to Joseph and Alma Anable, and was a niece to Miss Cynthia Sheldon and Mrs. Urania Sheldon Nott. In 1841, she had added a note to a letter written by Miss Cynthia Sheldon to Emily. As early as November 1842 she was away, and a letter from Emily to Catharine Chubbuck said that "she (Miss Sheldon) expected that Hat would return as accomplished as Anna Maria." Her trips away were both educational and employment, as she worked as a private tutor in families that would bring her into their homes. In August 1843, she had just returned from Beonsen, in the vicinity of New Orleans, and was engaged to go again. A letter from Anna Maria on January 6, 1845 said that she would stay South for another year. About this time Miss Cynthia Sheldon mentioned her concern for Hatty's spiritual health. In May 1845 she was in New Orleans. She was home again in summer 1846, but a September 27 letter from Anna Maria said she had been asked by Mr. Roman with some urgency to return and she thought that she should. She was to return home from New Orleans in January 1849 after Anna Maria Anable had started the Misses Anable's School in Philadelphia in fall 1848. Harriet was fluent in French, having placed herself earlier in a French environment in New Orleans. Hatty died in 1858.

[47] Matilda was a friend of Anna Maria Anable and probably of Emily as well, for Anna Maria's and Miss Sheldon's letters refer to her. In this letter, Miss Sheldon tells how Anna Maria had gone to visit Matilda, and while there, Matilda's brother had taken Anna Maria for a buggy ride. Somehow the horse got frightened, and Anna Maria and her host were taken on a wild ride, which they survived by the heroic actions of the brother, the undaunted courage of Anna Maria, and the providence of God. In a letter shortly after their move to Philadelphia in 1848, Miss Sheldon says that Matilda is everything to them. She is perfectly happy being with them, and she adds that she is a "host in French." When Henry and Edward went to Hamilton to live with Emily's parents and sister, Matilda was one of the individuals considered to be employed to help with work around the house and with the care of the family.

next Tuesday she left with Harriet for Aurora—Mary[48] went home with Louisa Marble[49] when H. returned from Commencement and Fanny went with our girls to Syracuse where Mary had just arrived—They are to spend two weeks with Augusta,[50] and then home, we shall indeed look for all of them on Saturday, next—Anna M. really disliked to be absent from her Sunday School. She has engaged to take a Bible Class when she comes back—you can hardly conceive how much comfort this change in her gives us—and how much it astonishes the good people—Mr. Corey[51] is perfectly delighted with her willingness to take the Bible Class—

Mrs. Anable[52] went with Mrs. Gratiot[53] to Western and Remson last week—they had a fine visit—you are of course thinking, our house very desolate—not so to me however—and we have had Miss Wright from Galene and Miss Campfield from Sacketts Harbor abiding the vacation in good humour [sic]—The Belle Bennetts finished up their visit in two weeks and came hopping home as happy as tho' they had been gone two months—our table is spread for only ten now—Elsina

---

[48] Mary Juliet Anable was born February 18, 1830 in Bethlehem, Albany County, New York, one of nine children born to Alma and Joseph Anable. She went to New Orleans with Hatty in 1847, but she returned home early in March 1848, and by 1849, she was working with Anna Maria in the Misses Anable's School in Philadelphia. Writing in March 1849, Hatty said of Mary, "She paints and draws, speaks French, plays the piano, sings, dances and is our mathematician. What should we ever do without her? She laughs from morning till night, and it is really refreshing to be with her." On December 26, 1860, she was married to Pierre Jacques Darey, the officiating minister being the Rev. Dr. Eliphalet Nott, her uncle. Mary died at the age of sixty-eight on April 20, 1898 in Ottawa, Ontario, Canada.

[49] In 1843, Miss Marble was a recent graduate of the Utica Female Seminary and wrote to Emily upon her return to Port Byron. In an 1848 letter to Emily, she was at the academy as a teacher and was fully involved there. According to a letter written by Sarah Hinckley in 1849, Miss Marble married and moved to New York City. In Emily's February 19, 1850 letter, she was referred to as "Lou Marble Wright." Then, in April 1851, Anna Maria mentioned that Louisa Marble Wright was now a widow, back living in Utica with her sister.

[50] Augusta Crafts is mentioned frequently in the letters written from the Utica Female Academy. A number of references chronicle her very strong opinions; many of these were spoken against N. P. Willis and Emily's relationship to him (Mrs. Crafts did not approve of either). In an April 30, 1845 letter Anna Maria Anable said, "The Dr. is not engaged nor isn't going to be to Mary Spencer I imagine, and tho' Mrs. Crafts intimated very strongly that there was *some one* he had his eye upon, he denied it to me strongly and scolded about Mrs. Crafts gossiping tongue."

[51] Mr. Corey was the pastor of the Bleecker Street Baptist Church near the Utica Female Academy, and Miss Sheldon and many of the girls from the academy attended worship there. (Cynthis Sheldon, Alma Anable, Deacon Asa and Isabell Sheldon, Edward Bright, and Horace Hawley had been charter members of the church in 1838.) In April 1844, he wrote to Emily expressing dismay that at a school program one of the girls had read a composition justifying dancing as exercise; he spoke of this as a roadblock to the salvation of many. Then, on March 10, 1846, Emily indicated in a letter to Anna Maria that Mr. Corey had been critical of her relationship and impending marriage to Adoniram Judson. Miss Cynthia Sheldon wrote a number of times expressing Mr. Corey's regret and support, and in 1847, there were letters of reconciliation between Emily and Mr. Corey. In spring 1848, letters reveal that Mr. Corey's wife had died of consumption, her condition exacerbated by recent childbirth. She had left behind four children. In July 1849, Anna Maria Anable wrote of his impending marriage to Jane Backus, a good choice for this "rising man." Mr. Corey remained popular with the Sheldon-Anable families even after their move to Philadelphia in 1848. A March 2, 1852, letter from Charles B. Stout told of Mr. Corey's call to the Stanton Street Church in New York City, which Mr. Corey did not accept. Finally, in 1854, there was a pastoral letter from Mr. Corey to Emily on her illness and her possible death. He preached at the Bleecker Street Church as late as January 1867.

[52] See vol. 1, "Cast of Characters," s.v. "Anable, Alma Shelton."

[53] Ann Sheldon was a younger cousin of Miss Cynthia Sheldon, Mrs. Alma Sheldon Anable, and Mrs. Urania Sheldon Nott. She married Charles Gratiot, the son of a prominent army officer and engineer who opened the port of St. Louis. Because Charles and Ann Gratiot often lived with the Sheldon-Anable families, both at Utica and in Philadelphia after 1848, they were often mentioned in the correspondence. They had six children, one of whom was born very close to the birth of Emily Frances Judson. The letters reveal how Ann coped in her husband's absence when he went west during the gold rush to seek his fortune.

and Mary Bennett[54] came home with the girls—but owing to painting and house-cleaning operations here their visit has thus far been to their Uncle's—they are to commence a weeks visit with us tomorrow—I have spoken to Maria[55] about enclosing a note in this to her Mother[56]—supposing it will arrive in time to send on with the package—the girls go from here to Hamilton Commencement, and if our girls get home, and father and mother[57] are comfortable my heart is quite set on seeing your dear Mother[58] and all.[59] Then, do you think we shall do much else but talk about you—I learned they were quite well there last week—Anna M. [ ] [ ] [ ] [ ] [ ] [ ] next week, when you will get the many items forgotten by me— The anticipated marriage of Mr. Willis[60] "to the daughter of a Senator" in Mass. went the round of the papers last month—nothing more is known about it in this quarter—we have not yet heard from Julia Look[61]—I conclude she is more engrossed with Mr. Casswell [sic] than she expected to be when she promised to write me on her arrival.

Source: American Baptist Historical Society, AJ 21, no. 100

---

[54] Elsina and Mary Bennett were the two oldest daughters (eighteen and sixteen at this time) of Cephas and Stella Bennett, missionaries to Burmah who were appointed in 1828.

[55] Ann Maria Bennett, b. August 1, 1833.

[56] Stella Bennett was the wife of Cephas Bennett; they arrived in Burmah in January 1830. Mr. Bennett remained the superintendent of the Baptist Press there for more than fifty years. From the Utica area, they sent their children back, and the girls were educated at the Utica Female Academy. The girls included Elsina (April 1828), Mary (November 1829), Ann (August 1833), Ellen (June 1835), and Sarah (June 1837).

[57] See vol. 1, "Cast of Characters," s.v. "Sheldon, Deacon Asa."

[58] Emily's mother, Lavinia Richards Chubbuck, was born June 1, 1785, at Goffstown, New Hampshire, the eldest of thirteen children. She married Charles Chubbuck on November 17, 1805, at Goffstown, New Hampshire. Four of her children were born at Goffstown, and moved with Charles and Lavinia Chubbuck to Eaton, New York in September 1816; they were Lavinia, Benjamin, Harriet, and John Walker. Sarah Catharine, Emily, and Wallace were all born in Eaton.

[59] Hamilton was about a twenty-five mile journey from Utica by stagecoach. Adoniram and Emily spoke of how brutal a ride it was in the winter.

[60] See vol. 1, "Cast of Characters," s.v. "Willis, Nathaniel Parker."

[61] Julia Look was a student of Emily's at the Utica Female Academy and later a fellow teacher. A November 22, 1845 letter from Anna Maria encouraged Emily to stay in Philadelphia for the winter for her health and remarked that Julia had the hardest part because she was teaching Emily's composition class, and the students kept asking for Emily. In a September, 1847 letter, she was listed as one of the teachers at the Utica Female Academy. On September 23, 1849, Anna Maria wrote that Julia and Albert B. Casswell were married and came to visit with her. In one 1849 letter Julia spoke of another teacher who was teaching "our composition class." On October 27, 1850, Anna Maria Anable noted that she had had a son. She was one of a small number of people who addressed Emily as "Emily" and as "Nemmy" in her letters.

Miss Cynthia Sheldon to Emily C. Judson, August 10, 1846[62]

(Monday Morn'g). Yesterday was our communion, and a good day to many, although in consequence of rain the congregation was smaller than usual—an appointed prayer meeting in the evening—but a full house inspirited Mr. Corey[63] to sermonize in the use of our Saviour's [sic] lamentation over Jerusalem—he was very happy in the effort—very impressive too—I observed one young soldier waiting to speak with him—a recruiting officer is now stationed here—The present prospect for a pacific negotiation with Mexico at this time is very hopeful—Mr. Polk[64] is said to have made propositions which show a willingness to back out of the war—Henry[65] went West with Sarah Bell[66]—his last letter was dated Milwaukee—he is perfectly delighted with the country and there is little doubt but he will effect a settlement some where [sic] for one of them—probably William[67] will go this fall with his nice little wife—he is set on being married in Sep.[68]— Courtland[69] writes fine letters from the woods—as yet he cannot know how long he may stay—Mr. Gratiot[70] writes in good spirits he intends being here the first of next month—Cousin Ann[71] speaks of you with affection. That farewell letter of

---

[62] This letter is an addendum to Miss Sheldon's August 9, 1846 letter.

[63] See vol. 1, "Cast of Characters," s.v. "Corey, the Reverend D. G."

[64] James Knox Polk, president of the United States, elected in 1844.

[65] Henry Sheldon Anable was the oldest of the six children born to Joseph and Alma Sheldon Anable. He was born June 21, 1815. In August 1846, he was in the Milwaukee, Wisconsin, area and was thinking of settling there. In a September 27 letter, he said he might leave Utica to join William and Olivia in Sheboygan, Wisconsin. He was married to Rosanna Frick in Sheboygan, Wisconsin, on February 13, 1855, and died September 3, 1887, in Flushing, New York.

[66] Sarah Bell Wheeler was a teacher at the Utica Female Academy, an intimate of Emily Chubbuck, and one of the few who addressed Emily as Nemmy. In a September 1847 letter, she was listed as one of the teachers at the Utica Female Academy. There are a number of letters from Sarah Bell before and after her marriage to Charles Gould of Boston in October 1850. There are several letters clustered in the year or two after Emily left for Burmah and a number at the time of her return to America. Emily stayed with Charles and Sarah Bell Gould in October 1851 when she arrived in Boston after the long sea voyage from Burmah and then England. She stayed there a number of times following that. In 1851, Anna Maria Anable wrote of Sarah Bell: "Sarah is grown so lovely in person as well as character that she must assert a blessed influence on all with whom she comes in contact."

[67] Born on November 6, 1816, in Albany, New York, William Stewart Anable was the second child and the second son of Joseph and Alma Sheldon Anable. In an August 31, 1844 letter, Miss Cynthia Sheldon reported to Emily that William had returned home, having "doff'd his sailor garb for age." He married Olivia Williams on September 24, 1846, according to a letter written on September 27 by Anna Maria Anable. They moved to Sheboygan, Wisconsin, where Will opened a store. William died February 9, 1863 in Virginia, California.

[68] The wedding was September 24, 1846. See Anna Maria Anable's letter of September 27, 1847.

[69] Courtland Anable was a younger brother of Anna Maria Anable. He held several positions over the years, and he studied at Hamilton College while he boarded for a time with Emily's parents. In 1853, he returned to Philadelphia where he preached his first sermon at the Eleventh Baptist Church. He was "Uncle Court" to Emily Frances Judson. In 1880, Courtland Anable was listed in the Massachusetts Census as an ordained minister serving in a church.

[70] Charles Gratiot grew up in St Louis, where his father was an army engineer responsible for developing the Port of St. Louis. He married Ann Sheldon, who was a cousin of Miss Cynthia Sheldon, Mrs. Urania Sheldon Nott, and Alma Sheldon Anable. Together, Charles and Ann Gratiot had six children. Because they often lived with the Sheldon family, their letters contain a great deal of him. Letters in 1847 speak of his religious awakening; those of 1849 speak of his leaving for the California gold fields. In 1853, Charles Gratiot applied for a grant of 400 acres in Illinois, and he already owned 148 acres.

[71] See vol. 1, "Cast of Characters," s.v. "Sheldon, Ann."

yours dear E. has done much good, heaven be praised for it[72]—I am sure you will rejoice—I begin to fear we shall not have any letters from you—What would I not give to know how you got along from day to day [Note: Two thirds of this line is lost.] second month now [Note: Two thirds of this line is lost.] The last day of your voyage will be counted—I [Note: A third of this line is lost.] there in time to meet you—how gladly would I convey a skilful hand in it to help you settle—do let me know just how every thing [*sic*] looks to you—If we can once get inside of your own house by means of description there will be some pleasure in casting thought into the very precincts—I shall in truth have an itching to employ some clairvoyance aid if you are not very minute—by the by—there is an immense estate like to be recovered by an Englishman residing in Troy, through this magic means, he has found the important documents to prove his title—they had been lost for half a century—this is the present version, if he really gets possession I will inform you—the next wonder in the world is, Eli[ ] Barrett is making a pedestrian trip through England, teaching the Nabobs how to make Jonny Cake—he is really much courted, and makes Jonny Cake fare the condition of his acceptance of an invitation to every gentleman's house—often goes [Note: Written on the right margin of the address page.] into the larder to show the cook the whole process. The object in view is to bring the corn meal into common use on the tables of the Lords of the land, thereby settle the dislike to it among the poor, who consider it only feed for hogs—rather starve than eat it.—What a field for this philanthropic Yankee—he is already making a burr—Monday E'g—can you divine any good reason for the interruptions in this—I shall charge it all to painters, store-men and company—our front Hall Cloth is enlivened to the admiration of all—a light crab where the green was—all the front part is now habitable—stairs and cross hall painted to day—have just discovered some [Note: Written along the left margin of the address page.] half a doz. *green* tracks for my comfort—you will so soon have the comforts, and discomforts of housekeeping that a little of others experience may be interesting—The widowers[73] continue their innovations, last week our good old Elizabeth assented to the claims of a now "come-over" Welshman, thought to be a good man, with $1000 to begin with in this country—I shall want to know how you like the Burmese servants, if they prove extra, I may send a draft for half a dozen—I am determined to bring Lydia[74] in my debt to night, and it is already

---

[72] On July 6 and 7, Emily wrote farewell messages to the churches she had attended in the Hamilton area. These churches had nurtured her life and her faith. She also wrote a message to the Missionary Society at the Utica Female Academy.

[73] "The Widower" was a frequent reference in the letters of these unmarried friends. The reference was usually a suggestion of their availability and interest in marriage. As one example, see Emily Chubbuck's letter to her sister Catharine Chubbuck dated April 2, 1845, in which she mentions the Reverend Rufus Griswold. Emily referred to him as a clergyman who had called upon her when she arrived in Philadelphia, and she said of him, "He is a widower what's more and crazy to get married. Don't you think I shall accomplish something?"

[74] See vol. 1, "Cast of Characters," s.v. "Lillybridge, Miss." Also the chapter "Lydia Lillybridge Simons."

late—Your good Dr. has all the share in this he wishes—I cannot write anything for Divines you well know—To both of you is tendered the warmest love from my parents,[75] Mrs. Anable,[76] William, and the Bennetts[77]—Heavens best blessings are invoked for you each morning, and now by your attached

C. Sheldon

Written along the left margin of the address page: "Your 'Ally Fisher' is going the rounds in the Temperance papers—"

Source: American Baptist Historical Society, AJ 21, no. 1007.

Emily C. Judson—A Tribute to Sarah Hall Boardman Judson,[78] August, 1846

Lines Written off St. Helena

Blow softly, gales! a tender sigh
Is flung upon your wing;
Lose not the treasure as ye fly,
Bear it where love and beauty lie,
Silent and withering.

Flow gently, waves! a tear is laid
Upon your heaving breast;
Leave it within yon dark rock's shade
Or weave it in an iris braid,
To crown the Christian's rest.

---

[75] See vol. 1, "Cast of Characters," s.v. "Sheldon, Deacon Asa."

[76] Alma Sheldon Anable was the sister of Miss Cynthia Sheldon and Urania Sheldon Nott. Genealogy sources show that she married Joseph Hubbell Anable in Troy, New York on July 28, 1814, and that it was the second marriage for Mr. Anable. Born in 1773, he was forty-one at the time of the marriage, and Alma was likely considerably younger. He died in 1831, which explains why Alma Anable and her family lived and worked first at the Utica Female Seminary and then later at the Misses Anable's School in Philadelphia. Joseph and Alma Anable were the parents of nine children: Henry Sheldon Anable (b. June 21, 1815); William Stewart Anable (b. November 6, 1816); Anna Maria Stafford Anable (b. September 30, 1818), Cynthia Jane Anable (b. January 28, 1820); Samuel Low Anable (b. November 28, 1821); Harriet Isabella Anable, also known as Hatty or Hattie (b. December 18, 1823); Courtland Wilcox Anable (b. July 28, 1825); Frances Alma Anable, or Fanny (b. April 12, 1828); and Mary Juliet Anable (b. February 18, 1830).

[77] See the reference in the letter dated August 9, 1846 to the Bennett girls. Their parents, Stella and Cephas Bennett, had been appointed as missionaries to Burmah in 1828.

[78] This was written on the *Faneuil Hall* as it passed the Isle of St. Helena, where Sarah Boardman Judson was buried. She died there on September 1, 1845, as Adoniram and Sarah were returning to the United States with three of their children: Abby Ann, Adoniram, and Elnathan. This poem was in tribute to her.

Bloom, ocean isle, lone ocean isle!
Thou keep'st a jewel rare:
Let rugged rock, and dark defile,
Above the slumbering stranger smile
And deck her couch with care.

Weep, ye bereaved! a dearer head,
Ne'er left the pillowing breast;
The good, the pure, the lovely fled,
When mingling with the shadowy dead,
She meekly went to rest.

Mourn, Burmah, mourn! a bow which spanned
Thy cloud has passed away;
A flower has withered on thy sand,
A pitying spirit left thy strand,
A saint has ceased to pray.

Angels rejoice, another string
Has caught the strains above;
Rejoice! rejoice! a new-fledged wing,
Around the Throne is hovering,
In sweet, glad, wondering love.

Blow, blow, ye gales! Wild billows, roll!—
Fling out the canvas wide!
On! —where she labored lies our goal,
Weak, timid, frail, yet would my soul,
Fain be to hers allied.

Source: Arabella M. Wilson, *Lives of the Three Mrs. Judsons* (New York and Auburn: Miller, Orton, and Mulligan: 1856) 326–27; Emily Judson, *An Olio of Domestic Verse* (New York: Lewis Colby, 1852) 140–41.

Emily C. Judson, September 1846

The Winged Watcher[79]

PART I

Morning arose, and from their dreams
Awoke the slumbering flowers;
Red glowed the hill-tops in her beams,
Her crest lay glittering on the streams,
And on one cot her gayest gleams
Broke in warm, golden showers.

A pair of eyes had oped that morn,
Eyes soft, and sweet, and blue;
A poor, weak, helpless thing forlorn,
Beneath that humble roof was born,—
A shut bud from a blossoming thorn,
Save that a soul looked through.

And many a jocund laugh there rung,
Up from that cottage low;
And glad words sat on many a tongue,
And bliss upon fond bosoms hung,
For there a rill of life had sprung,
Which would forever flow.

One form unseen stood meekly nigh,
Yet drew the sunlight there;
An angel from beyond the sky,
With love and pity in his eye,
His radiance for a time flung by,
His forehead veiled in care.

[79] The Houghton Library at Harvard University has a James Fields collection. Mr. Fields was a partner in Ticknor, Reed and Fields, publishers of several of Emily Chubbuck Judson's books. Mr. Fields had a habit of keeping a portrait and a handwritten manuscript from many of the authors with whom he worked over his career, and he kept a file on Emily Judson. The portrait is from the front plate of *Alderbrook*, which Ticknor and Company first published, and then Ticknor, Reed and Fields. Also in the file is a handwritten copy of Emily's poem "The Winged Watcher." A section of it is missing. The copy of the poem is in Adoniram Judson's handwriting. He noted that the poem was written "Off the Cape of Good Hope, September, 1846." He also enclosed a note as follows: "My dear Mr. Fields, Mrs. Judson sends you the accompanying lines, thinking, that you may be glad to make use of them to remind the public of the existence of *Alderbrook* and facilitate the progress of that publication. Yours affect'ly A Judson"

Although a number of items were added to the future editions of *Alderbrook*, "The Winged Watcher" was not one of them.

Down from the palace of the King,
That morning had he hied;
The song was stayed upon the string,
The glory folded in the wing,
For dark must be his wandering,
By that poor mortal's side.

PART II

Years passed. The boy a man had grown,
And shadowy things of fear,
With nameless ills his path had strown,—
Foes trooping came, and friends had flown,
But one White Wing—to him unknown—
Kept ever hovering near.

It was a lovely sight to see,
By those who watched above,
That Spirit glorious, pure, and free,
In such an humble ministry,
Through sin and woe, unfalteringly,
Pursue his work of love.

When the worn youth lay down to rest,
The Angel stood beside;
And stole the burden from his breast,
And soothed his wearied sense to rest,
Fanned his hot brow, his cheek caressed,
And blissful dreams supplied.

Once on a mountain peak stood he,
A high and rugged steep;
Where many dangerous shapes there be,
And many things most fair to see;—
There shouting crowds bent low the knee,
And broke wild Echo's sleep.

Pride centred in his burning eye,
Pride mantled on his brow;—
"Who ever stood the clouds so nigh?"—
Ah ! he has climbed a step too high,

And giddily—bewilderingly,
His brain is whirling now.

But ever that pure Watcher bright,
Pleads softly in his ear,
Think, mortal, of the coming night!
Think of the mildew, and the blight!
Think of thy ransomed spirit's light—
Dimmed by thy dallying here."

He hears,-and lo! his pulses wild
Are hushed, and in his veins
The riot ebbs; things, which beguiled,
Seem heaps of mist about him piled;
He bends his knee, a little child,
And tears efface his stains.

PART III

The babe—the youth was bent and gray,
A feeble man and old;
Death stood beside him as he lay;
No mourner there his breath could stay,
Or guide him on his untrod way,
When lip and heart were cold.

He loved, he had served the God of Heaven;
But Death's a fearful thing;
And when the ties of earth are riven,
When back to dust the dust is given,
The soul, which long with sin has striven,
May shrink to meet the King.

He trusted, but still shivering clung,
Where long he had been a guest;
Meanwhile death-pangs his bosom wrung,—
The scared soul on the hushed lip hung,
Then lay, soft wings about it flung,
Upon the Angel's breast.

Source: Fanny Forester, *An Olio of Domestic Verse*, 11–16; James Fields Collection, Houghton Library, Harvard University.

The Reverend Doctor William Dean to Emily C. Judson,[80] September 14, 1846

We have today been drinking in the "Sabean Odors" from the islands of Java and Sumatra while passing the *Straits of Sunda*.

Source: American Baptist Historical Society, AJ 15, no. 595.

Emily C. Judson to Miss Jane E. Kelly,[81] September 25, 1846— Off Cape Good Hope

My Dear Jenny,—

We have been lying by for the last three days under nearly bare poles, a strong gale dead ahead, and we all the time drifting landward "willy-nilly." There is a deal of fun in a heavy gale like this during the first day, but it becomes a rack after a while. Why, all my joints are stretched and my bones aching, as though I had been pulled by wild horses and cudgeled to a jelly. I can not sleep o' nights for the fear of being tossed out of bed, which I most assuredly should be but for the board at the foreside of my *bunk*. But the gale has at length subsided, the canvas is out, and we are stretching off southward with rather precipitate haste, considering that the bosom of the sea is still swelling and heaving like that of a passionate child whose anger is subsiding into involuntary sobs. But we have reason for haste. This morning a peculiar tinge in the water, warning us of the vicinity of land, startled the captain somewhat, as he had not been able to "take his observations" during the gale; and he soon ascertained that we were within thirty miles of the latitude of the Cape. A most dangerous proximity I learn this to be, and we are now putting off with the utmost speed. This gale has probably been the grandest sight that we shall have the pleasure of beholding. The sea lashed into perfect fury, rising and sinking in strange contortions, wresting our little floating nut-shell from the hands of the crew, to leap, and plunge, and wrestle, as though born of the mad billows which bellow as they rise, and, bursting, cover it with their foam. The water is of inky blackness in the hollows; but each billow, as it bounds upward, becomes green and half transparent, and bursts at the summit, the long wreaths of foam curling over and over each other, tumbling to the bottom, and disappearing like immense piles of down, with which your weary bones would sympathize, were there not more safety in the hard mattress. The air is thick with spray, at first tossed to an incredible height, and then every foam-bead shattered into ten thousand frag-

---

[80] This is the first addendum to a letter Dr. Dean wrote on July 3, 1846, while on ship sailing from the United States to the mission field. The second was dated October 24, 1846. This was written on the right side of the address page.

[81] Emily wrote an addendum to this letter on November 14, 1846, and it appears on that date.

ments, each invisible of itself, but helping the general mistiness, and making itself felt in chilling dampness through cloak and shawl. And still we go on rearing and plunging, reeling and tumbling, as though the centre of gravity were surely lost, and our frail tea-saucer capsizing itself, and then pausing on the top of a billow, quivering in every spar before venturing another plunge, which it seems must be fatal. Last night I dreamt that I could see the centre of gravity, in the shape of a *bull's-eye*, slide sideward and dip to the water at every plunge, each time approaching within a hair's-breadth of the water-base of the ship. I watched every plunge with trembling breathlessness—a kind of night-mare feeling—a little more, just a little more, and we were lost for ever! At length it came. I bounded from my berth, staggered, and tumbled headlong, grazing my shins most beautifully. It was an immense billow bursting over the quarter-deck with a roar like the report of a cannon—no unusual thing, and exceedingly lucky just then, as I am no friend to the night-mare.

Now, I know I have made a ridiculous affair of my fine gale, and you can have no idea of the sublime grandeur of such a scene at sea. Indeed it is indescribable, and should I attempt a formal description, I should inevitably fail. We lack nothing but sunshine to make it glorious. The old monarch of the upper regions has muffled his face in clouds, or even now the swell of the sea might give our fancies fine picking. I should like to observe the effect of a brilliant sunlight upon the angry face of brave old Neptune. But I am tired, Jenny, dear, and so a kiss, and more chit-chat on a stiller day.

Source: A. C. Kendrick, *The Life and Letters of Mrs. Emily C. Judson*, 218–21.

Anna Maria Anable to Emily C. Judson, September 27, 1846—Utica

"Come haste to the wedding heighho! ho! ho!"

Married on the 24th inst by the Rev. Pierre H. Proull D. D. Mr. W. S. Anable[82] to Miss Olivia Williams etc. etc.

The bride looked bewitching, the bridegroom looked *bien* content, and all the people thought the wedding cake was very nice! Altogether Nemmy[83] it was a very pretty wedding and we had the young couple and all the brides friends here on Friday evening to have one last grand meeting. They leave tomorrow morning for Sheboygan, Wis. where Will is to open a new store this Fall and if he succeeds well Henry[84] breaks up here and goes on in the Spring. Hank came home from the West

[82] See vol. 1, "Cast of Characters," s.v. "Anable, William Steward."

[83] "Nem" or "Nemmy" was a name of endearment given to Emily by a small group of her intimate friends at the Utica Female Academy. Anna Maria Anable was "Ninny."

[84] Henry Sheldon Anable. See vol. 1, "Cast of Characters," s.v. "Anable Henry Sheldon."

thinking Sheboygan was now going to be the biggest place in all America. The great Oregon rail road [*sic*] is certain [ ] to [ ] there and that in two years. [ ] [ ] [ ] [ ] [ ] [ ] [ ] [ ] [ ]. By the way I would give not a little to know what you and the Dr. think of my last crazy sort of a letter. Do you recommend a straight-jacket [ ] [ ] come on and go heart and hand with you on all your [ ] plans for benefiting poor [ ]? I won't dare to tell you how seriously I think of it sometimes.[85] Why a week ago I wrote you three pages of missionary [ ] that that [*sic*] would have satisfied the Board[86] and Mr. Corey[87] and Mr. Bethel in the bargain. But it had a special call to go on a mission. I was coming next summer and going to work like a regular missionary, learning the language—preparing to teach school all the rest of my days. Now what do you suppose [ ] my sending it? Why Hatty[88] has received and [*sic*] urgent proposals [*sic*] from Mr. T. Roman for her to come South again. He will give her $600 a year and Molly can take the same situation she thought of in the Lyceum for $500. Hat thinks their insisting so on it means that she should go—and so she is about decided. Of course it is *my duty to stay by the ship*[89] yet,—but I don't give it up—I believe the Dr. *baptized me a missionary* and that some way or other I shall find my way over to you. In the mean time [*sic*] I hope to do some little good here. I am for the present important to Aunt Cynthia[90] and the family. I try to identify myself more and more with the church and with religious people and to do my duty as it comes up from day to day and from week to week. Whatever is ordained for me in the future I give myself no uneasiness about. God will always find work for his children to do if they have heart willing to do it; and my concern is to do now "whatever my hands [ ] to do." What shall I do about Hatty tho' this Winter? We have taken so much comfort together and now I shall be left again doubly deserted. I believe I must get this heart of mine weaned from every thing [*sic*] on earth before it will be right. Do write to me often and ask the Dr. (if he will not think me too presuming) to give me some good advice once in a while. Nobody interested much in my religious progress and I need sadly religious friends. Aunt

---

[85] For the next year to a year and a half, Anna Maria was to seriously entertain thoughts towards serving with Emily and Adoniram as a missionary to Burmah.

[86] The Board of the American Baptist Missionary Union.

[87] See vol. 1, "Cast of Characters," s.v. "Corey, the Reverend D. G."

[88] See vol. 1, "Cast of Characters," s.v. "Anable, Harriet."

[89] As Anna Maria struggled with her call to be a missionary, always in the background was her commitment to the Utica Female Academy, the way that her Aunt Cynthia depended on her, and her responsibilities within the family. A later letter from Miss Sheldon will state that she thought it utter foolishness for Anna Maria to think of missionary service. In the end the family moved to Philadelphia in the late summer 1848 to start the Misses Anable's School, with Anna Maria in charge—a responsibility of which she spoke in terms of her calling.

[90] See vol. 1, "Cast of Characters," s.v. "Sheldon, Miss Cynthia."

U.[91] was much pleasanter to me the last time[92] she was up—tho' she is yet far from cordial. She gave Fanny[93] a superb silk dress, a wiazarine [*sic*] sleeve and crimson charnelion [*sic*] [ ] silk. Fanny's chair you remember—Well we had it beautifully mounted and sent to the State Fair at Auburn where it took the highest prize given for fancy chairs. Aunt U. is very much pleased with it. Grand pa[94] continues quite feeble tho' he comes out to his meals regularly. He cannot lead in family prayers any longer and Jane Kelly[95] always prays unless there are visitors here. He and Grand ma are like two children together. It is somewhat sadder to visit their room than formerly but perhaps for that reason the more beneficial to us. Mother[96] is not very well she has an occasional lameness in her hip which troubles her a good deal. I am very much afraid her work is too much for her. Any way [*sic*] she must be relieved whether whether [*sic*] she will or [ ]. To make her old age comfortable and pleasant is the present project of her daughters. Nothing but that takes Hatty back South—for she cannot bear the Creoles. Courtland[97] has had a remarkably successful Summer—Mr. Gratiot[98] thinks every thing [*sic*] of him, and will do anything in his power promote his interests [*sic*]. He is going to spend the Winter with William at S.[99] and next Summer go up the Lake again as explorer or geologist. He writes home interesting [ ] letters, and Aunt U. is as proud now of his manliness as she used formerly to be ashamed of what she called his foppishness. She sends for his letters to read to the young men in her family and holds him up I suppose as a bright example for them. Queer woman is not she? Cards have come for Jimmy's[100] wedding next Wed. eve'y [*sic*]—it will be grand affair I suppose.

---

[91] See vol. 1, "Cast of Characters," s.v. "Nott, Urania Sheldon."

[92] Mrs. Nott had been very severe with Anna Maria when Anna Maria had asked Adoniram Judson to baptize her by immersion. The baptism had taken place in Utica, New York on June 7, 1846. Emily's letter of July 7, 1846 to Mrs. Nott is very clear in her defense of Anna Maria, and by implication we can gather some of what Mrs. Nott had said.

[93] See vol. 1, "Cast of Characters," s.v. "Anable, Fanny."

[94] Deacon Asa Sheldon. See vol. 1, "Cast of Characters," s.v. "Sheldon, Deacon Asa."

[95] Miss Jane Kelly was Emily Chubbuck's friend at the Utica Female Academy, and then she became a teacher with Emily at that institution. Miss Kelly became the literary principal in 1844 with the retirement of Mr. and Mrs. James Nichols from that position. During a period of Miss Kelly's illness in 1844, Emily filled in the position for her. Then, in 1848, when Miss Cynthia Sheldon moved to Philadelphia to help start the Misses Anable's School, Miss Kelly became the "headmistress" of the academy and successfully brought it into the future, though not without some initial disparagement from the Sheldon-Anable families.

[96] Mrs. Alma Sheldon Anable. See vol. 1, "Cast of Characters," s.v. "Anable, Alma Sheldon."

[97] See vol. 1, "Cast of Characters," s.v. "Anable, Courtland Anable."

[98] See vol. 1, "Cast of Characters," s.v. "Gratiot, Charles."

[99] Earlier in the letter, we learn that William and his new wife Olivia will be leaving the next day, moving to Sheboygan, Wisconsin, where William will be opening a store.

[100] Jimmy Williams was often mentioned in Anna Maria Anable's letters, mostly simply as "Jimmy." He was around the Utica Female Academy, and she spoke of their conversations, what he was doing, and his interests. She often referenced him as being with "Helen." Writing to Emily on April 29, 1845, Anna Maria had some interesting comments to make. In a paragraph of gossip she spoke of "Jimmy and Helen" and a recent party. All of the "flowers of Utica Society" were there in contrast to "poor dowdy looking little Helen," who in Anna Maria's estimation would never make the kind of wife who could help Jimmy in his future life. Yet he loved her, and the comment was made that "the one hundred thousand will make up for some deficiencies or ought to."

What think you Nemmy? I have made a dress for the occasion all by myself. Am I not grooming *smart*? Eugenia[101] is still at Brattleboro—nobody hears a word from Mary Barber[102]—Augusta[103] and I will be the only [ ] taken of Jimmy's flowers at the wedding. Would not it be fun to get them all here at that time and have a jubilee! I am so sleepy I must say good night. I wish I could give you one two three and twenty kisses—but the Dr. may do it for me unless he has got out of the habit of kissing by this time. They say matrimony does cure people of such propensities. Anna M

Written upside down in the top margin of page 1: "Give love to Lydia[104] and the Dr." [Note: The remainder of the three lines are so faint that only a few words can be read. Those words are: "this time instead of waiting"—"write long and often won't you."]

Source: American Baptist Historical Society, AJ 23, no. 1166.

Miss Cynthia Sheldon to Emily C. Judson and Lydia Lillybridge, September 29, 1846

My dear dear girls Emily and Lydia,[105]
Anna M.[106] is sending off this morning without having the full weight of letter paper—and although it is now the tumultuous time immediately after breakfast I must add the paper—Dear father[107] is so far recovered as to give us his presence uniformly in the dining room to invoke the blessing—but cannot take the lead in

---

[101] Eugenia Damaux was part of Emily's intimate circle of friends at the Utica Female Academy. Living in New York City, Eugenia suffered from some kind of eye problem that at times made life difficult for her; this was a matter of comment in many of the letters exchanged between the girls themselves and with Miss Cynthia Sheldon. In 1848, Eugenia was in New York living "at Mrs. Brown's—the same warm-hearted French girl as ever." In 1849, she married Johnny Edmonds, described as rich and pious, and they lived in Utica.

[102] Mary Barber was mentioned frequently in the Emily Chubbuck Judson letters; she was a student and then a teacher at the Utica Female Academy. There were ups and downs to that relationship; in fall 1845, apparently Mary had written to someone expressing what Anna Maria Anable called "ingratitude," and Mary had been banned from the Academy until she made proper apologies to Miss Sheldon. In a September 7, 1845 letter from Anna Maria, we learn that her remarks had been about Miss Cynthia Sheldon. In November 1847 Jane Kelly remarked that they had not heard from Mary in over a year. In 1848 Mary Barber was back at the Utica Female Seminary teaching with Jane Kelly. Though at this time Miss Sheldon had moved to Philadelphia, Mary Barber had been able to reconcile with her, and in later years we find Mary very close to the Sheldon—Anable families; later, there was considerable consternation on Miss Cynthia Sheldon's part in her correspondence with Emily about Mary's health, the seriousness of it, and Mary's impending death. These letters were written in April 1852. Miss Sheldon went to help transfer Mary to Albany in June 1852, where she would be better situated and perhaps have access to better doctors. On September 9, 1852, Anna Maria Anable wrote to Emily of Mary Barber's death.

[103] See vol. 1, "Cast of Characters," s.v. "Crafts, Augusta."

[104] See vol. 1, "Cast of Characters," s.v. "Lillybridge, Miss," also the timeline on "Lydia Lillybridge Simons."

[105] Ibid.

[106] See vol. 1, "Cast of Characters," s.v. "Anable, Miss Anna Maria."

[107] See vol. 1, "Cast of Characters," s.v. "Sheldon, Deacon Asa."

prayer. That part is feelingly done by Jane[108]—still it is a sad change. Dear Mother is uniformly about the same—that they may tarry on earth longer in the enjoyment of blessings, to bless others is ever the burden of my heart—I cannot get beyond that point in feeling—

We have the "Judson Offering" a beautiful book—I am proud to send every which way as a keep sake [*sic*]. The new edition of the sermon too is so fine that we can use it as an instrument to proselyte working its way like a polished diamond— not to be rejected. Our dear Laura Wheeler has expressed her wish to accommodate her husband in the same way Sarah Look has seen fit to do— remaining a Baptist in heart—I have sent the package by Wm to Mr. B. enjoining close investigation of the contents with prayerful hearts—I hope it goes in time for a blessing. Anna M. has of course told you every thing [*sic*] about William's[109] wed- ding[110]—we find his selection of a wife is every thing we could wish—and this going west promises well for them.

Elisa Gilman[111] is here now fixing off to take Eliza Bright's place in Virginia— Sarah Hinckley[112] is going to Harriet Weston's place—they leave on Thursday, in company, as far as Washington—Elisa is teaching near her fathers [*sic*]—Mrs. Yates is really married to Mr. Bainkerhoff [*sic*] of N. York. The word came last evening— I fear it is a hasty foolish affair—cannot say certain—Martha is a dear good girl—and my young niece Martha Wheeler arrived yesterday, to spend a year in school—Harriet Sheldon Helen's sister is to be here soon for the same purpose— Heaven grant we may long have the number good surrounding us—But dear Harriet[113] is talking strange of going back—if she does, our pet Mary[114] will go with her—what do you think of these changes—Shall I have any nerves left—Mary has a fine painting class, does well in every thing [*sic*] but on Harriet's account we will

---

[108] See vol. 1, "Cast of Characters," s.v. "Kelly, Miss Jane."

[109] See vol. 1, "Cast of Characters," s.v. "Anable, William Steward."

[110] See the introduction of Anna Maria's letter dated September 27, 1846.

[111] On August 26, 1844, Miss Cynthia Sheldon wrote to Emily Chubbuck to ask if she knew of someone who could come to Utica and work with a young student who needed a caregiver. The young student was seven years old, the daughter of Cephas and Stella Bennett, missionaries to Burmah. Emily wrote back on August 28 to speak of a Miss Gilman, a teacher she had known, as a candidate. On August 29, Emily wrote that Miss Gilman felt that she could not take the position for family reasons; at the end of the letter, Emily added a postscript, saying that Miss Gilman had changed her mind and would, in fact, accept the position if it were offered to her. Emily wrote more on September 2, 1845, and on September 3, 1845, Miss Sheldon wrote to Emily to say that she had decided in favor of Miss Gilman. Emily wrote a note to Miss Gilman on the letter she had received from Miss Sheldon and passed it on. In a letter written April 15, 1845, Anna Maria is talking of the girls dispersing as the term ended, and she noted that "the stage has come for Miss Gilman," and Miss Gilman was delivering a note to Emily's sister Catharine Chubbuck.

[112] Sarah Hinckley was one of Emily's students at the Utica Female Academy. In an 1849 letter, Miss Hinckley reminisces about that time and brings Emily up to date on many of those who were there with her. She also speaks of the sad farewell when Emily left for Boston and then Burmah. In April 1851, Anna Maria Anable mentions that Sarah is a successful music teacher and that she will be soon returning from Kentucky.

[113] See vol. 1, "Cast of Characters," s.v. "Anable, Harriet."

[114] See vol. 1, "Cast of Characters," s.v. "Anable, Miss Mary Juliet."

say go—and get Jenkins to take her class—Harriet thinks she can get $600 salary for Mary—they stay a year and a half by engagement if they go—so before you get this most probably they will have their French home not far from each other—The Bennetts[115] are doing finely. We saw but little of Mary and Elsina because father was so very sick while they were in Utica—will you let Mrs. B.[116] know this—she will wonder why I have not written about the girls visit—this must go to the office. Mrs. Anable[117] is full of weeping, and rejoicing, too in her children. All join in abundance of love.

The clouds and winds are still watched thinking of your progress across the Mighty deep—Our God has charge of you—we leave it—I had dispatched to yourselves and Mrs. Bennett the week previous to father's sickness—hope that will be in waiting your arrival—in three weeks from this we shall fancy you landed—give up all hope of a way letter now—Oh the long time to [ ]

Written on the bottom of the address page: "I cannot begin to tell you how much comfort we take with dear Anna Maria, and how much I feel on her account too—fear she will not be happy when Harriet is away—Fanny[118] is doing nicely—her chair is finished[119]—she got a premium from the fair—a new silk dress[120] from her Aunt Urania[121]—and it is now in the parlour [sic]."

Written at the top of the address page: "Mr. Corey[122] was here yesterday; every thing [sic] moving on as usual in the church—this must go—your good Dr. is always in mind with you whether in thinking about or writing to you—All must ever feel and know too—that all three are embraced in the affection of their old friend"

C. S.

Source: American Baptist Historical Society, AJ 20, no. 1008.

<hr>

[115] Cephas and Stella Bennett were missionaries to Burmah. They arrived in Burmah in January 1830, and Mr. Bennett remained the superintendent of the Baptist Press there for more than fifty years. From the Utica area, they sent their children back, and the girls were educated at the Utica Female Academy. The girls included Elsina (April 1828), Mary (November 1829) Ann (August 1833), Ellen (June,1835), and Sarah (June 1837).

[116] Ibid.

[117] See vol. 1, "Cast of Characters," s.v. "Anable, Alma Sheldon."

[118] See vol. 1, "Cast of Characters," s.v. "Anable, Fanny."

[119] See the letter of Anna Maria Anable to Emily C. Judson dated September 27, 1846.

[120] Ibid.

[121] See vol. 1, "Cast of Characters," s.v. "Nott, Urania Sheldon."

[122] See vol. 1, "Cast of Characters," s.v. "Corey, the Reverend D. G."

Reverend Doctor William Dean to Emily C. Judson,[123] October 24, 1846—Hong Kong

We landed at Macao on the 5th inst. after a pleasant passage of 105 days, and after visiting the friends at Canton I am now settled at my old house in Hong Kong. You may have heard before reading this that our much esteemed sister Denan, died at Canton, last Sunday the 18th of Dysentery. She died as she lived, like a Christian.—This is the *tenth* missionary's wife connected with the Chinese mission who has died since I moved to Hong Kong in 1842. With these repeated instances of mortality, I need not exhort you to care for your health.
W. D.

Source: American Baptist Historical Society, AJ 15, no. 595.

Emily C. Judson to Mrs. Urania Sheldon Nott, October 31, 1846—Faneuil Hall, Latitude 22 [degrees] south, Long.

My dear Mrs. Nott,

It seems scarce a week to me since our cable was loosed at Boston *harbour* [sic] and we swung away upon the tide, amid the waving of handkerchiefs and kissing of hands of those [ ] dear faces we shall never, never see again in this world. We have had a very slow passage thus far, and I cannot tell how it is that the time sh'd pass so rapidly. We scarce welcome the morning when lo! it is evening—we say the Sabbath is over, and another Sabbath follows so quick upon its track that the six intervening days seem crowded into one. I do not wonder that this time sh'd seem short when we look back upon it, for it has passed very monotonously, but the quick flight of the passing hours I think would stagger lord James himself. The ship is very nice and comfortable, the captain exceedingly kind and attentive to all our wants, and the steward anxious to serve us in every way he can because it is for his interest to do so. Our fare is as good as we could expect to have on such a long voyage, and those who are not squeamish seem to have as good appetites as ever, tho' for myself, I eat less in a week than I used to eat at home in a day. We have been out sixteen weeks today, and expect it will take us about four more to reach Maulmain. I rather dread than desire to reach our destination, however, for I have been so happy in this little cabin, that I dread a change. The care of a house and two little children in a place where servants cannot be trusted for a moment in anything is no small bugbear to one who is an utter stranger to such cares, and I am in no hurry at all to be greeted mistress of a family. However, "sufficient unto

[123] This is the second addendum to a letter Dr. Dean wrote on July 3, 1846, while on ship sailing from the United States to the mission field. The first was dated September 14, 1846. This was written on the top of the address page.

the day, etc." My dreaded sea-voyage that turned out such a pleasant affair, notwithstanding adverse winds and dead calms, that my hopes soar high for the future. God help me to *do* right and then all will *be* right.

We left albatrosses, cape hens, pigeons, stormy petrels etc. behind us nearly a week ago, and are fast wending our way towards the *sunny north*. The south wind is yet raw and cold, though softening every day, but the northern breezes are warm and balmy and very grateful after the severe cold weather off the Cape. You cannot imagine how odd it seems to be talking of the soft *north* wind and shivering with that from the south—it seems as though the world had turned round with us. But we shall soon be where the wind is always warm and sun hot enough to please even me. We are taking our leave of sweet Maia Placida's, brilliant Canopus, and the beautiful Southern cross and the stars that you see will soon be visible to us again though they will not occupy the same place in the heavens. Last night we had what the doctor called a real East Indian sunset. A sunset at sea is at any time [*sic*] a sin-gularly interesting sight. The sun seems in great haste as he nears his destination, descending with strange rapidity—suddenly he dips his lower disk in the water and then glides under, away to his ocean nest, as though he had flung his whole weight upon the wave and it had been unable to bear him up. But last night we had an Indian sunset—a yellow, lazy, sleeping sunset, as why should'nt [*sic*] we now we are in the Indian Ocean. It seemed that a lump of half melted gold had grazed the sky from the south around to the west, waving as it passed, not great daubs, but thin transparent and yet brightly burnished of itself, which lay bedded in the softest, purest, *translucent* blue that my eyes ever looked upon. When it reached the western horizon [ ] whole had melted there and circled around the sun—all yellow and glowing, and red, no purple, but a rich soft, slumbering yellow, dazzling to the eyes—the centre to be sure but shaded off into a golden fleeciness a soft beautiful haze over which one might dream forever without the least desire to wake. All around, to the north and east especially the sky was a hazy and slumberous aspect, but *so* luxurious! You cannot conceive of anything more delicious. Now, I know I have failed to give you anything like a [ ]tion of it, but it was so exceedingly beau-tiful that even Lydia[124] seemed to hold in her breath as she looked and remarked when it was over that she would give anything if she could "send home a specimen."

I should like to look in upon you now, though I know that you have turned day and night, and are fast asleep while the broad sun is shining upon us, as high as you ever see him. But you would wake up wouldn't you? And give a kind word and wel-coming smile to your old pupil, who, however much she may have displeased and

---

[124] See vol. 1, "Cast of Characters," s.v. "Lillybridge, Miss," also the timeline on "Lydia Lillybridge Simons."

troubled you, has always loved you with all her heart.[125] Well, that may not be—never again in this world shall we stand face to face, but may we not hope to join the same circle among the redeemed, and spend an eternity where time and space have neither existence nor name.

Since we left the country I have made my husband (whose wearied head was crammed so full of everything that he could properly appreciate nothing at home) comprehend your former kindness to me and the reasons which I have for gratitude and love. He is very grateful to you on my account, for he considers my past struggles much *severer* than I have been accustomed to thinking them myself, and loves everybody who has been kind to me—you and Aunt Cynthia[126] especially. I wish you could have seen him more, for now you can never know him and my [ ] will not count a [ ] weight. Women always think their own husbands "the one man in the world," and so I will not tell you of his patience, gentleness, unvarying cheerfulness, unselfishness, humble fervent and devoted piety, nor tell you how he sits and teaches me, poor ignoramus that I am. Yet all the time as though he were the favoured one and person taught. I can never be thankful enough to my Heavenly Father for giving me so bright a destiny; I can only pray that he will make me grateful and prepare me for everything that lies before me—make me a blessing to my precious friend and earthly guide, true mother to his little orphans, and a light be it ever so feeble and flickering to benighted Burmah. I have learned a very little of the language, but have not been able to study much. It is very difficult to study at sea.

Please give my love to your dear doctor.[127] I believe mine intends to write him. Also remember me kindly to Mr. and Mrs. Pearson, C. Potter and Mr. Gillespie[128] if

---

[125] In this section and in the next paragraph of this letter, Emily extends a hand of friendship to her former mentor Mrs. Nott. Emily sent her a sharp letter on July 7, 1846, concerning a letter Mrs. Nott had written to Anna Maria Anable about her decision to seek baptism by immersion, forsaking the Presbyterian church for the Baptist. Now, she begins to rebuild the bridges, recognizing that Urania Sheldon Nott could be difficult at times; yet she had given Emily an opportunity for an education at the Utica Female Academy in fall 1840, and her life had been forever changed by the opportunities offered to her there because of Mrs. Nott and her sister, Miss Cynthia Sheldon.

[126] See vol. 1, "Cast of Characters," s.v. "Sheldon, Miss Cynthia."

[127] The Reverend Doctor Eliphalet Nott was the president of Union College in Schenectady, New York. An ordained Presbyterian minister, he was married to Urania Sheldon Nott, the sister of Miss Cynthia Sheldon and Mrs. Alma Anable and the aunt of Anna Maria Anable.

[128] William Gillespie was a professor of civil engineering at Union College in Schenectady, New York. He wrote two long letters to Emily, dated August 15 and September 11, 1845. His second letter originated from Union College where Dr. Nott (husband of Urania Sheldon Nott) was the president, and he noted that Mrs. Urania Sheldon Nott was "his special friend." In his first letter, he asked Emily if a certain poem had appeared in the New York *Mirror*, and if it had, he had identified the writer (if it was Emily) early on as one of great promise. In a time when Emily was considering a trip to the continent, he spoke to her of weather conditions in certain of the European countries. His second letter was filled with literary allusions, a long story to prove the point that "widows are dangerous," and a reflection on some of her writings. Mr. Gillespie was mentioned in Urania Sheldon Nott's June 11, 1845 letter to Emily; he had given Mrs. Nott the latest issue of the *Columbian Magazine*, which contained the first installment of Emily's story "Grace Linden." Then, on July 9, 1845, Emily mentioned Mr. Gillespie in a letter to her sister Catharine. Emily was speaking of going to Schenectady for the commencement of Union College, and she says, "A man there has fallen love with me—Mr. Gillespie, author of 'Rome as seen by a New Yorker.'"

he is still at Schenectady. And now farewell, dear Mrs. Nott. Do not *quite* forget me, away here from all my old friends.

Think of me kindly sometimes, pray for me that I may be useful to the poor Burmans, and ever believe me, my dear, *dear* friend,

Yours most affectionately,

Emily C. Judson

Source: Hanna family files.

Emily C. Judson to the *Columbian Magazine,* Fall 1846[129]—Boston to Maulmain

Outward Bound

And so, it is all over! The hurry, the bustle, the thousand cares attendant on departure are at an end, and the unusual excitement is about to give place to the dull monotony of a long sea voyage. It is all over, and here we stand, a lonely little company, looking into each other's face in something like bewilderment, as effectually severed from friends and country as though those kind beings had a moment since waited at our funerals. The last sob has had its answering sobbings; the last farewell has trembled upon lips that I had fain hoped would breathe it above my death-couch; the last touch of the loved hand, the last glance of the eye—ah me, it is well that life seldom darkens into days like this.

Still do I see those dear, dear faces thronging the wharf; still my eye peers eagerly among them for those best loved; those by whose side I have stood in joy and sorrow, whose slightest whisper long since forgotten now comes back flinging upon me the weight of a new heart-ache; those who bent fondly above me when my cheek paled and my eye grew dim, and, winning me back from the grave, rejoiced to see my foot once more firm. O but for one more *last* word with these! As my eye wanders in search of the friends of other days, it falls upon those of later date, but still beloved as truly if not as tenderly. Again and again the vision rises to my confused sense and passes and re-passes before my eye, face after face bearing familiar features standing out from the mass with the distinctness of reality. Again handkerchiefs are waved in thrice repeated adieu, and kisses are flung from fingers that have often, O so often twined with mine, but which I may never, never clasp again. Then come like a death signal the shrill cry of the boatswain, the quick rattling of ropes, and slowly we wheel away, striving for yet one more glance and yet one more, till wharf and carriage, new friends and old, are left behind together.

---

[129] This was published in the *Columbian Magazine* in August 1847. Emily's corresponded with Robert West, and his letters are dated March 3 and April 28, 1846; she promised to write exclusively for the *Columbian* with remuneration of fifty dollars an article.

And this close, narrow cabin, with its small window and low ceiling, is to be my home, not merely for days and weeks, but for long, weary months, without the possibility of change. Not one spot of green earth to set my foot upon, not a forest leaf to soothe my ear with the familiar sound of its rustlings, but a few planks for my promenade, and this incessant dashing, dashing, for daily and nightly music. I, who have never loved glittering spires and proud monuments, still strain my eyes for a last look at the tall shaft of granite rising from yonder battle hill and now but a shadowy line against the sky, turning them away only to look upon the burnished dome of the State House,[130] made visible by its glitter in the dim distance. Now both are lost, and I have looked my last upon the land of the robin and the violet, the land of kind hearts and free hands, the land of Sabbath bells and prayerful voices—my bright, my beautiful, my own beloved land. There, even the wild flower [sic] shooting from the split rock in the neglected forest, and the humble wild bird nestling in the green knoll by the wayside, are dearer to me than all the gold of the South or the treasures of Eastern India. I was cradled amid its rugged simplicity, lulled to my earliest slumber by the music of its rills, and fanned in my hours of play by the green boughs ever waving in its fair forests. Its mossy knolls have been my altars, its groves my temples, and its birds, and flowers, and pebbles, the beautiful books in which, side by side with the pages of inspiration, I have studied the character of Him who placed both them and me in this strange lovely world. It was the home of my infancy, the home or my childhood, the home of my youth, and thrice ten thousand times the home of my heart. "If there were no other world," O who would thus turn to voluntary exile? Father in heaven, fling Thy sunlight upon our trackless way, else are we indeed in darkness.

Hurra, hurra, how gayly we ride! How the ship caree[n]s! How she leaps! How gracefully she bends! How fair her white wings! How trim her hull! How slim her tall taper masts! What a beautiful dancing fairy. Up from my narrow shelf in the close cabin have I crept for the first time since we loosed cable and swung out upon the tide, and every drop of blood in my veins jostles its neighbor drop exultingly, for here is sublimity unrivaled. The wild, shifting, restless sea, with its playful waves chasing one another laughingly, ever and anon leaping up, shivering themselves by the force of their own mad impulse, and descending again in a shower of pearls; the soft azure curvature of the sky shutting down upon its outer rim as though we were fairly caged between blue and blue; and the ship, the gallant ship, plowing her own path in the midst, bearing human souls upon her tremulous breast, with her white

[130] Here Emily is describing two familiar sights to even modern day Bostonians, though probably these were more visible from the sea in pre-skyscraper eras. The first, "the tall shaft of granite rising from yonder battle hill," is the Bunker Hill Monument, an obelisk towering 221 feet above the historic Revolutionary War Battle of Bunker Hill which took place on June 17, 1775. Conceived in 1823, started in 1827, it was finished in 1843. In the editor's childhood it was a popular place to visit, and to make the long stairway trek to the top. The second would be the dome of the State House. Known as the "new" State House it was built in 1798 adjacent to Boston Common, at the height of Beacon Hill.

wings high in air and her feet in the grave. And then the tumult, the creaking of cordage, the dash of waters and the howling of Winds—"the wind and the sea roaring!" I have felt my heart swell and my blood tingle in my veins when I stood in the silent forests of Alderbrook, and I have looked up at the solemn old trees in awe mingled with strange delight; the awe and delight have both deepened at the blaze of the lightning and bellowing of the thunder amid the wild echoing rocks of Astonroga; and now, in this strange uproar, they come upon my heart and make it bound like the arrow from the bended bow. The trees were the temples built by the Almighty for His worship, and there is something awfully beautiful in their shadows; the lightnings "go and say unto Him, here we are!" and "He shut up the sea with doors and made the cloud the garment thereof, and thick darkness the swaddling band for it." And here as I stand poised upon the wild elements I feel myself near, very near to the only Protector who has a hand to save, and in the hollow of that all-powerful hand I rest in perfect security. God, my God, I go forth at Thy bidding, and, in the words of Thine own inspired poet, "Thou art my buckler, the horn of my salvation, and my high tower." The sea can not separate Thee from me, the darkness of midnight can not hide Thy face, nor can the raging of the storm drown Thy still small voice, My heart leaps joyfully as I trust in Thee.

On, brave little wrestler with the elements! On, right gallantly! I love the bounding, the dashing, and the roaring, and my heart shall know no faltering while "my Father is at the helm."

Hurra, hurra! Here we are upon a sea of fire! How the waves leap and sparkle, while, curling backward from their tops down their black sides, roll long wreaths of flame! The stars are quenched, and the heavy clouds go hurrying by in dismay as though they feared the fearful mandate had gone forth, the taper been lighted, and the hour was at hand when the "heavens should be rolled together as a scroll." The scene is wildly, startlingly beautiful. Those who look into such mysteries say that the fiery sea below us owes all its brilliancy to a small insect floating upon the surface of the wave. In these strange regions I can almost fancy them the torch-bearers of the mighty sea king. If we are to credit the gentlemen of the tarpaulin and pea-jacket, there is a coral palace just below us now, where his majesty of the trident holds his imperial court, but I have a suspicion that the deep might lay open to us greater wonders than ever glittered in ancient mythology or modern poetry. There is many a brave ship suspended fathoms deep, still floating, floating, floating, with the blue waves for sail and pennon, and rich treasures mouldering and rusting in her bosom. There secrets, which have made thrones tremble, and crowns bow, lie forever hid from the eyes of mankind. There knowledge slumbers with sealed eye; there wisdom folds her powerful pinion and forgets how she moved a world; there the star of beauty has set in utter darkness; there the tuneful finger of love thrills never more the palsied heart strings; and there goodness and purity, in their white vestments, wait the signal to mount to heaven. Greater wonders! Why, this same deep upon whose glittering breast we are now floating will at some future day fling back her locked portals, unfold her curtaining waves, while from her blue caverns will spring, strong in life and radiant in beauty, all whose hearts have said, "Thy will be done," when lying down to their strange rest. No monarch of mystic realms has reared his throne of "turkois and almondine" in those purple twilights, there treading pearl-strewed floors, listening to notes breathed from the crimson lips of silver shells, or winded on the pearly horns of water nymphs, and reclining within the bower formed by the branching jasper. No merry mermaid looses the golden fountain of her own enshrouding tresses, and bends her bright face to the mirroring wave; no fabulous naiad of the olden story laves her rosy limbs in the rainbow tide; and no pale Undine comes in shape of mortal maiden, to weep beneath the green bough in the starlight, or walk forth in gay vestments at noonday, with nodding plume and well-filled quiver, to lure the unwary to her cold, damp palaces. But greater than these lie beneath us, those who shall wear crowns beneath the stars—tread among the varying lights which, in the god-lighted atmosphere of the Eternal, flash from the sapphire, the emerald and jasper, the soft green chrysophrase, the blood-red hyacinth, and the purple amethyst, listen to the lays of angels, and recline on couches of transparent gold in the shadow of that tree whose "leaves are for the healing of the nations;" who shall plunge into all the wise mysteries of the universe, and dwell forever in the presence of Him whom no man can now see and live. Ah, there are richer treasures beneath us than ever found life in Grecian song or fable, or stirred the fingers of troubadours and minnesingers—the caskets which have held the precious purchase of the Son of God, and which shall be restored in glorified beauty when He takes them to the mansions which He is now preparing.

We are just "crossing the line"—that great brass rim which on Mr. B-'s globe used to "divide the earth into two parts called the Northern and Southern hemispheres." We mount the metallic ridge without any perceptible decrease of motion, and off we bound away, away! stretching southward into another world. Ha! How the wind blows! How the canvas swells! How the waves dash!

Hurra! Gallantly ride we in this skeleton ship, while the sunlight glints gaily on white bare mast and slender spar. Gallantly ride we over wave and hollow, over foam and rainbow; now perched upon the white ridge, poising doubtfully and trembling like a frighted steed; now plunging down, down into the measureless trough which seems yawning to engulph us forever. Wildly blows the gale, more and more wildly bound the mighty billows, with a roaring as though all the monsters of the deep were swarming around us. But not so. Neither the wide mouth of the shark, the brown back of the porpoise, nor the spouting nostril of the whale is visible; the brilliant dolphin in his opal jacket has retreated to his own haunts below the storm, and the little "Portuguese man-of-war" has drawn in the pink and purple fringes of his silver sail, and rolls like a cunning beetle from wave to wave, as light as the bubble from which he can not be distinguished. Even the albatross flapped his strong pinion and wheeled away when he saw the winds gathering dark in the heavens; the cape pigeon lingered a little as though caring lightly for the ruffling of his mottled plumage, and then spread his butterfly-embroidered wings and hurried after; but the stormy petrel, though small and delicate as the timid wren (I will take a lesson from thee, busy daring little spirit that thou art, bright velvet-winged petrel), scorns to seek safety but by breasting the gale. And here he remains, carousing amid the foam as though those liquid pearls, leaping high in air and scattering themselves upon the wind, had a magic in them to shield him from danger. He dips his wing in the angry tide as daintily as though it were stirred but in silver ripples; then he darts upward, and then plunges and is lost in the enshrouding foam. But no, he is again in air, whirling and balancing, wheeling and caree[n]ing, up and down as though stark mad with joyousness, and now he vaults upon the back of the nearest foam bank and disappears to rise again as before. And still the billows roar and bound and lash the sides of the trembling ship, and sweep with strange force her decks; and still we reel and plunge, down, down, surely. No, we are up again, leaping skyward; we pause a moment and—what a fearful pitch was that! Ah, my brain grows giddy, but still I can not hide myself in my dark cabin.

And now caree[n]ing and caracoling yonder, like an untamed steed that has freed himself from the trappings of civilization, comes a bark with sails close reefed like our own, and something that appears like the stripes of Holland flying at her stern. Ride we a race—the skeleton ship and bark—that we travel the waves so madly? Are these two immense ribbed things that seem to revel in the storm really of this upper earth, or are they dark spirit-creatures that come to us from a phantom world below? All the bark leaps from billow to billow I can almost fancy that I hear the voice of some poor Matthew Lee from her foam-shrouded deck—

> "You know the spirit horse I ride;
> He'll let me on the sea with none beside!"

I have heard of a "flying Dutchman " off this rude coast, and I should well nigh believe that the mystic churl had drawn near to spy out our belongings, but that our own sober Bostonian "cradle of liberty" is every whit as full of antics. But look, look! How our suspicious neighbor reels, dipping up whole decks full of surf; see her spring from the white yeast and leap to the clouds; and now, as I live, not the tip of a mast is to be seen, and she but a brace or two of rods distant! Still shines the sun and still the wind comes roaring from the clouds and howls among the rigging with a dismal tone, strangely contrasting with the glorious brilliance of the light. A thick white mist scattered from rich heavy foam-wreaths spreads itself over the face of the waters and becomes at once an iris curtain. Up curls the mist from every shivered billow—up, curl on curl, it winds in silvery beauty, and meeting the sun, falls back in gorgeous showers of million-colored rainbows. Beautiful, gloriously beautiful! The sea, even as "the earth, is full of thy riches."

Onward we trip buoyantly and blithely. Up from the chilling south come we to regions of perpetual warmth and sunshine. Up, hurrying on like the lithe roe-buck among his native hills, bounding and dancing, oh, so gayly! and here we are where sleep in purple mist the fair islands of Eastern India. Blithely, still blithely speed we onward, and still softer grow the breezes, while the light gushes warm and golden from the fleecy clouds, and far away by the verge of the horizon a slumbrous vail like silver gossamer is settling down on sky and wave. A piece of half-molten gold seems to have grazed the luxuriously sleepy blue from the south around to the west, leaving everywhere its traces rich and glowing, but with none of the harsh glare which is common to sterner skies. As it reaches the west it is entirely melted and circles around the setting sun, a girdle of glory but still subdued into a soothing softness. This is a rare East Indian scene, such as can not be copied where frosts have made the sun pale and set the clouds in a shiver. And now the sun nears the water, dips his lower disk in the tide, and drops down behind it with but little of the ceremony that marks his exit on land. And now for other beauties, since the storehouse of creation is exhaustless. But look upon the surface of the water! One half is of a pale flickering orange, while the other displays fold on fold of crimson, lost in the blackness of approaching night; and far behind us we are dragging in the wake of the ship long lines of green and amber and purple, each rarer than ever robed a Tyrian princess. A still dimmer haze, though all of a dark rich purple, creeps over the face of the sea as twilight deepens, and one by one the stars open their bright eyes on the misty scene below. Sweet, mild Maia Placidus, brilliant Canopus, and half of the southern cross are left behind; but we greet night-watchers better loved to-night, for lo, yonder, gleaming from its gray curtains, the polar star!

The polar star, ever the same in its unpretending, unobtrusive loneliness, has been made an emblem of faith and trust, a way-mark, a balancing point, and we feel lost when we look to the place it has occupied in the heavens and find it vacant. A welcome back, thou pale-eyed northern queen, lone pearl, of the earth-arching heavens; and a blithe welcome too to thee, old shaggy monarch of the icy regions, ever unmoved even by the sight of the huntsmen upon thy track with their hounds in the leash, ready to rend thy tough hide at the slightest signal. And there shines the noble Arcturus, he of whom the son of Amram sang from the plains of Midia after he had cast aside the princely purple of Egypt; asking in the name of his God, the great mechanist of the stars, "canst thou bind the sweet influences of the Pleiades or loose the bands of Orion? Canst thou bring forth Mazzaroth in his season? or canst thou guide Arcturus with his sons?" How long has that silver lamp been shining up in heaven? and who are the beings that bask in its light? Angels, creatures bearing the form of man, or those framed to exhibit the versatility of the Contriver's power, whose very mode of existence is utterly inconceivable? Has it ever fallen under the ban of sin? Can sorrow and death visit it? Probably before our little earth or even our fair solar system sprang from the moulding hand of the Architect it may be myriads on myriads of ages before "the stars sang together" at sight of the beautiful new creation—Arcturus moved in the midst of his sons, chaining them within their orbits by a subtle resistless power, and receiving from them the reflected light of his own smiles. The same large, mild eye, hundreds of centuries ago, looked down upon the sublime historian, the poet-chieftain of Israel, in his desert wanderings with his murmuring people; and the shepherds upon the star-lit plains of Chaldea gazed upon the beacon and braided with its rays strange mysteries. And yet that very orb, that proud, regal Arcturus, with his full unflickering blaze, may at this very moment be among the things which were and are not. The taper, whose rays may have been myriads of centuries traveling to us, could easily have been extinguished before the fires of our own system were lighted, and yet we stand wondering at the semblance. Ah, well, noble star! whether thou art or art not, I greet thy fair seeming right joyfully, for the light of other days is upon thee. The loved ones whose feet are now pointing to ours, with the diameter of the globe between, may look upon thy face even as we look.

And yonder is our own magnificent Jupiter, his large eye fully opened, and there is the northern crown, and there the heart of the royal Charles, and there bright Cassiopeia, and still beyond, the tiny sparklers forming the pale tresses of Berenice, and there—and there—and there—why they are old friends, everyone. I am home again.

Land ho, land! A succession of dark rich purple festoons are turning their convex side to the sky in the far distance, telling us that not more than twenty-five miles lie between us and the southernmost islands of the Nicobar chain. And that is really land! Happy as we have been in our little floating bird's-nest, my foot aches to press it.

Land ho, land! Another purple island, regal in the morning light. It sits like a pyramid upon the water, and tapers until its soft, shadowy outline is nearly lost in the clouds. Nearer and nearer we come, and several peaks are now visible, covered with something which seems like foliage, while bald gray cliffs, streaked with chalky lines, descend perpendicularly to the water. On we go, and the rocky sugar loaf of Narconidam fades in the dim distance.

Land at last—the strange land that for us bears the fond name of *home*. In a long chain, made up of irregular links, which it seems that a breath might dissever, stretches from the south far up to the head of the bay the shore of Burmah. The faint wind dallies about the deck, and creeps over brow and cheek with a soft, soothing deliciousness, but there is only a breath of it stirring, and that is "dead ahead." We have been beating landward with but little success during the past week, but patience! the goal is now in sight, and it matters little whether we reach it to-day or to-morrow, or the day after. Surely we will not murmur at a day more or less tacked to the end of a twenty weeks' voyage. Thank God, that He has spread the land before our eyes at last; that He has shielded us when wrath was stirring in the heavens and darkness was upon the Waters; that He has pinioned the wings of the wind, and said to the waves, "thus far shalt thou go, and no farther."

Last night a poor, tired little land-bird, with a head like blue violet in the spring-time, and a neck slender and most gracefully arched, entered at the window of the saloon, and nestled down on the cushions of the transom with the fond confidence of our own tuneful robin. It was a sweet harbinger, and most joyfully welcomed. Before the unsuspecting little sleeper opened its eyes this morning, it was seized and caged under a morah, where it still flutters, displaying through the bamboo bars its chameleon plumage in all the changeable shades which it has stolen from a tropical sun. It needs not the olive leaf to be a dove to us—the beautiful little stranger!

On—On—on—slowly—very slowly; but the land gradually becomes more distinct; the purple hue of the hills is changing to emerald; masses of trees appear like small clumps of shrubbery; the glass discovers to us the tiny sails of fishermen close in shore, and hark! The cry, "Amherst!" Ay, yonder point of land, with the badge of its degradation on its front, is Amherst, our first anchoring place. Nearer and nearer, tree by tree becomes visible as it appears in relief against the sky—the palm, the cocoa, and the tamarind; and, lo! on that green bank sloping to the water, the hopia shading the ashes of the sainted.[131] From the highest point rises the taper spire of a pagoda, and another is built on the rocky promontory that stretches into the bay. It must be a land of beauty—even at this distance we can but feel sure of that—but how dark! how dark! The Burman is not like

> "The poor Indian whose untutored mind
> Sees God in clouds and hears Him in the wind."

[131] The hopia tree stood over the grave of Ann Hasseltine Judson, the first wife of Adoniram Judson, who was buried in Amherst.

He has no God, not even the Great Spirit of the Indian's hunting ground, nor the frail deities of ancient mythology. The object of his worship is a man whose ashes are scattered to the four winds of heaven, and whose soul has been for thousands of years extinct. His system is one of cause and effect, and he believes that ages of suffering in the lowest hell will be the unavoidable effect of the sins he is daily committing, while his good deeds are only an offset to the evil. His future life is a long transmigratory round of toil and suffering; and the most glowing of his hopes, the acme of his promised bliss, is annihilation. And it is not merely one small nation that is hugging such misery—groveling in this terrible darkness; Buddhism in its various modifications is the religion of more than a third of the population of the world. To kindle the fire which shall illuminate such a people, though it be at first but the faint, fitful glimmer of a rush-light, how glorious! To plant the seed of one pure principle in natures so degraded, to place one bud of hope in the core of such misery, and watch its beautiful and beautifying expansion, to hold in hand the lever which after hundreds of years shall elevate a mighty nation, as the barbarians of the British Isles have been elevated by that same instrument, has a glory in it which no truly wise man would barter for the sceptre of an Alexander. Good can be done everywhere, and nothing is truer than that "missionaries are needed at home"; yet if I have but one morsel of bread, let me give it to the famishing; if I have a single flower, let me take it to the cell of the dying prisoner, on whose cheek the free air never plays, and who knows nothing of the pleasant sights and smells in which others are revelling.

We have approached as near the shore as safety will permit, and already the white sail of a pilot-boat is gliding across the water to meet us. It is preceded, however, by a boat-load of natives, with their broad muscular shoulders bared, and their gay patsoes spread over their heads, to protect them from the broiling sun. They bring fresh offerings of fruit, fish, and milk, for there is one of our number that is no stranger to them. What glad faces they bear! And how delicious the fruit tastes! Adieu to salt fish and sea biscuit. Ha! how every thing smells of land!

These men seem almost beautiful, coming from among the green trees, and certainly such an orange as this never grew before—never. For the land, for the land—away!

Ship *Faneuil Hall*, 1846

Source: A. C. Kendrick, *The Life and Letters of Mrs. Emily C. Judson*, 221–34.

Emily C. Judson to Miss Jane E. Kelly,[132] November 14, 1846—Lat. 5 N., Long. 93 E.

I find, dear Jane, that I have told you above that we should scarce be likely to welcome so fine a gale as that first one off the Cape. But I was mistaken. We have had another, which beat it all out and out. The wind blew a perfect hurricane, but it was astern, and so swept us on our way at a furious rate. A Dutch bark came within a few rods of us, and I assure you my heart went pit-a-pat when I saw it reeling and tumbling, though I was told that it went on quite as sedately as we did. At one minute it seemed leaping to the clouds, and at the next not even the top of a mast was visible, so low had it sunk behind the mountain billows. But the beauty of the scene was the showers of rainbows, for the sun was gloriously bright. This was off the Cape, where we may always expect gales; but a few days ago we had a succession of squalls, which were more dangerous than a continued gale. They come on without a moment's warning; and then to see the tarpaulins scramble, racing after each other up the rigging like so many rats, and shouting a chorus something in the tone of a bellowing bull, is, as Mark Tapley would say, "reg'lar fun." But we have now reached the simoom, and may expect to see Maulmain in a fortnight, or perhaps ten days. To-day we heard the chirp of a land-bird, probably from Sumatra, and the long, brown wreaths of sea-weed go drifting past us, as we have not seen them since we left the Bermudas. It is eighteen weeks to-day since we left Boston; so imagine, if you can, how the vicinity of land must affect us....

Last night we had a supper of dolphins, which, but for their being fried in rancid lard, would have been delicious. As it was, I only tasted them. In truth we have been reduced to pretty scanty fare, and I shall be quite willing to stick my teeth into an orange when we get ashore. The dolphin is very beautiful: rich brown on the back, and blue, and green, and gold, shaded into each other along the side to the belly, which becomes of a deep salmon hue, then pale rose, and then white. While dying, the color changes in rapid flashes, now deepening into almost blackness, and now the white extending to the streak of brown upon the back. One of those caught yesterday had several small fish in its stomach. The most curious of these was the toad-fish, about the size and shape of a full-grown dace, with a round bag on the under side [sic] three times as large as itself, which it can contract and expand at pleasure. A flying-fish was also taken out, and another creature a little larger than a silver dollar, and very nearly as flat and round. This would be a grand place for a naturalist like you. The captain has promised to try to get me a "Portuguese man of war," which, if I can preserve in spirits, I will send you. You will find a description in the books, but you can not [sic] imagine how beautiful it is.

---

[132] This is an addendum to a letter which was written September 25, 1846.

The sail is of ribbed silver, fringed with pink and purple; the body seems silver, and then the long strings of purple beads. I assure you he is a rare little fellow.

My letter will be scarcely readable, but they say I must use this good-for-nothing thin paper. Good bye, Jenny dear; God bless you, and may you be happy.

Affectionately,

Emily C. Judson.

Source: A. C. Kendrick, *The Life and Letters of Mrs. Emily C. Judson*, 218–21.

Abby Ann Judson to Emily C. Judson,[133] November 14, 1846—Bradford

My dear Father and Mother,

Last Wednesday it was just three months since I last wrote, and as you asked me to write to you once in three months, I will now do it. I would have wrote [*sic*] last Wednesday only it was a school day and I do not have as much time as I have on Saturday. School will close next Tuesday, and at present I stand in great awe of approaching examination for the trustees are going to examine me in both U. S. History and Arithmetic. I was marked four in History which is the highest mark, so I shall never have to study it again, not at this school at least. Aunt Mary[134] is very dangerously sick, indeed we do not know as she will ever get well. I believe she is not able to sit up. When you write to me I hope that you will tell me all about the voyage and if Henry[135] and Edward[136] are quite well. Tell them when they get old enough to talk how I used to love them and how I love them still. Kiss them each for me and you may be assured that I send a great many to you. I believe I said in my last that I was going to make you some clothes in the vacation, but as it is only two weeks, I thought that I would defer it until the one after which is four weeks.

---

[133] This letter had an addendum by Nancy Hasseltine, the daughter of one of Ann Hasseltine Judson's brothers. She addresses Adoniram as "Uncle" in her December 10, 1846 letter. Abby Ann was living in Bradford, Massachusetts, and studying at Bradford Academy, where Ann's family was involved in leadership.

[134] This is likely Mary Hasseltine, sister to Ann Hasseltine Judson.

[135] Henry Hall Judson, born July 8, 1842, was the son of Adoniram and Sarah Hall Boardman Judson. Henry was the sixth of their eight children, the fourth of five who survived. He remained in Burmah in 1845 when Adoniram and Sarah returned to the United States with the three older children. He returned with Emily in 1851 and went to live with her family in Hamilton, New York. Henry attended Brown University and Williams Collage; he enlisted in the army at the time of the Civil War in January 1864. Later that year, he experienced a debilitating accident attributed either to sunstroke or a horse kicking him in the head. He was married once—unhappily according to his own correspondence—and he eventually died in a veteran's home in 1918, the last of his siblings to die. Of this, the chaplain noted, "The end was a genuine example of Christian fortitude." See Rosalie Hall Hunt, *Bless God and Take Courage, The Judson Legacy* (Valley Forge PA: Judson Press, 2005) 291.

[136] See vol. 1, "Cast of Characters," s.v. "Judson, Edward."

Mr. Simons[137] has been to see me some time this week, and you may suppose that I was glad enough to see him. He showed me the likenesses of his children and I think they look very like them. He is going to spend the winter at the South and will take Tommy with him. Mr. Simons said something about you Father at Haverhill last Sunday in his sermon, but as I was not there I cannot tell you what. Juliet M. Bartlett asked me to tell you that she thanked you very much for the lock[138] which you gave her, and says that when you were here she did not have a single chance to thank you for it. Since I wrote last I have received a letter from Mrs. Wade,[139] and in it was a letter for you, but I did not send it to you because you would soon see her and she can tell you all that was in it that she wrote. In the part that was addressed to me she said that Mr. Osgood[140] and his wife and children were to embark the next month, and when Mr. Simons he said that Mr. Osgood would be in New York in a week or a fortnight. I shall be very glad to see them. Nancy says that she should like to write you a few lines[141] so I shall have to close pretty soon. I send you both a great deal of love. Please to tell all that I used to know in Burmah especially Emily and Mary Howard[142] that I want them to write to

---

[137] Thomas Simons was born in Wales. He was ordained on December 18, 1831, after graduation from the Newton Theological Institute and was appointed to missionary service on March 7, 1831. He sailed for Burmah on June 29, 1832, arriving in Maulmain on January 1, 1833. On June 23, 1833, he married Caroline Jenks Harrington in Maulmain, probably the widow of a missionary who had died, and between 1834 and March 1843, they had six children, two of whom died in June 1839. Caroline Simons died on May 1, 1843. Mr. Simons returned to America in May 1846. While in the United States, he visited with Abby Ann Judson at Bradford Academy; she would have known him from her years in Burmah. He returned to Burmah in November 1847, arriving in Maulmain April 19, 1848. His second wife was Lydia Lillybridge, who had sailed to Burmah with Adoniram and Emily Judson; they were married in Maulmain in 1851.

[138] This likely refers to a lock of Adoniram Judson's hair. Giving away locks of hair was popular at this time, and there are many references to this practice in letters within the correspondence.

[139] Deborah Wade was a missionary to Burmah; with her husband Jonathan, they were appointed in 1823. Adoniram Judson called them "his dearest and best of friends." Much of their work was in the jungle communities following the path of George Boardman. They left for the United States on December 22, 1847. From the Hamilton, New York area, they stayed not far from the home of Emily's parents and sister; they visited the Anable-Sheldon families in Philadelphia. With a large group, they had left Boston on July 25, 1850, and returned to Burmah in February 1851.

[140] Rev. Sewall Osgood was a missionary in Maulmain who worked with and lived by Adoniram Judson. Judson and Osgood occupied two of the four homes in the mission compound and lived so close that it "allowed me the pleasure and profit of almost hourly intercourse." He arrived in Burmah in 1834. His first wife Elhira Brown Osgood died on October 5, 1837, in Maulmain. On July 8, 1838, he married Sarah Thomas, the widow of the Reverend Jacob Thomas, with Adoniram Judson offi- ciating at the wedding. He spoke in the letters to Emily, of which there are five between July 1850 and April 1852, of Adoniram Judson as his "most intimate friend." He never personally met Emily, as he had returned from the field prior to 1846. At the time of his letters, he was working with the American Baptist Missionary Union as a district secretary. In 1845, just as they were leaving for the United States, Sarah and Adoniram Judson gave care of Charley, too young to make the trip, to Mr. and Mrs. Osgood. Charley died not long after their departure. Mr. Osgood visted Adoniram, Elnathan, and Abby Ann in the United States. His third wife was Caroline Wait; they were married December 30, 1850 at Saratoga, New York.

[141] See the letter written to Adoniram Judson from Nancy Hasseltine dated December 18, 1846. It completed page 3 of Abby Ann's letter.

[142] Hosea and Theresa Howard were in Maulmain as missionaries with Adoniram Judson. Mr. Howard's responsibility was to run one of the schools that the mission maintained. Mrs. Howard was involved in that work as well. In one letter, he claims that they worked there with Adoniram Judson longer than any other missionaries. Emily and Mary were their daughters; Abby Ann knew them from her time in Burmah.

---

me and that I shall write to them whenever I have an opportunity. But I must close for Nancy wants room to write. Farewell dear Father and Mother.

Your ever most affectionate daughter

Abbie Ann Judson

P.S. You will note the change which I have made in the manner of spelling my name. When you write to me please to direct it Abbie.

Source: American Baptist Historical Society, AJ 10, no. 302.

Emily C. Judson to Catharine Chubbuck November 28, 1846— Amherst

Well, Katie, here we are at last in queer, ridiculous, half-beautiful, half-frightful, exceedingly picturesque Burmah. We took in a pilot yesterday, and this morning came to anchor in full view of all the greenery of the odd little promontory named Amherst. The old weather-beaten wooden pagoda, stationed away out in the water, and fully visible only at low tide, is overlooked by a charming sister on the bluff above, clad in bridal whiteness, with gilded ornaments, and odd surroundings of various sorts, that I can hardly describe at this distance. How my heart bounded, and every nerve thrilled, as I yesterday watched the purple hills, gradually resolving themselves into the radiant flush of real life, until the green trees stood out in beautiful relief against the blue above them, and the brown roofs of cottages nestling among humbler greenery, became distinct enough to be guessed at. After a five months' surfeit of brackish ocean breezes, to drink in such an air as this!—actually freighted with the odor of fresh turf, and the delicate breath of fading grasses, and the perfume of delicious fruits and rich tropic blossoms.

We were visited last evening, before the pilot came off, by a boat load [sic] of nearly naked Madrasees—great athletic looking fellows, some of our party remarked; but as they mingled with our crew, their inferiority of stature could not but be noted, and their finely rounded limbs struck me as displaying more of the grace and beauty of a woman than the bold, muscular development of the athlete. They are erect, with their round bullets of heads finely, even royally balanced, a graceful carriage of body, a pliability of limb that would do no discredit to one of their own serpents, and, of course, great agility in their movements; but in a contest of mere strength, I should scarcely doubt that one of our sailors would be a match for a half dozen of them. The pilot is a Portuguese, fat, square, and heavy. Catch any stress of wind or weather disturbing *his* equilibrium. He states with a very magisterial sort of an air the impossibility of taking the ship up to Maulmain, as the river is not navigable by so large a vessel at this season; so I suppose we shall go up in boats.

We were scarcely anchored this morning when a boat of six or seven men came bounding toward us, who, by the fluttering of gay silks, and the display of snowy jackets and turbans, were judged to be something above mere boatmen. As they drew sufficiently near to be distinguishable by their features, one of our number who had been for some time silently watching them from the side of the vessel, leaned far over for a moment gazing at them intently, and then sent forth a glad wild hail. In a moment the glancing of oars ceased, a half dozen men sprang to their feet to the imminent peril of the odd nut-shell in which they floated, and a wilder, longer, and if possible more joyous cry, showed that the voice of the salutation was recognized. Christian beckoned me to his side. "They are our Amherst friends" he said; "the dear, faithful fellows!" And these were some of the Christians of Burmah! the pioneers of a nation! Men born in idolatry, Bought out by the Saviour, while yet buried in the black depths of heathenism, redeemed and marked for His crown in glory! What a sublime thing to be a missionary! In a few moments the men had brought the boat along side [*sic*], and were scrambling up the sides of the vessel. How the black eyes danced beneath their grave brows, and the rough lips curled with smiles behind the bristling beards! Then came a quick grasping of hands, and half-choked words of salutation, in a strange, deep guttural, which he only to whom they were addressed could understand; while I, like the full-grown baby that I am, retreated to the nearest shadow, actually sobbing; for what, I am sure I do not know, unless I might have fancied myself a sort of flood-gate for the relief of other people's eyes and voices. However, though it had been pretty strongly intimated that "mamma" must not be out of sight, just at present, I do not think her madamship was missed until she had made herself tolerably presentable, and then she was again beckoned forward. The Burmans gave my hand a cordial American grip, but their dusky palms were so velvety that I do not think even your fingers would have complained under the pressure. Then a venerable old man, who, as I afterward learned, is a deacon in the church, came forward, and bending his turbaned head respectfully, commenced an animated address, waving his hand occasionally to the troop behind him, who bowed as in assent. I have no doubt it was a rare specimen of eloquence, but, of course, I could not understand a word of it, and could only curtsey and simper very foolishly in acknowledgment. You will laugh when I tell you I have seldom been so embarrassed in my life. I soon learned that the men had reserved nicely matted seats for us in the boat, and that several of their wives and daughters were waiting at the jetty, with cart and oxen, to take me up to the village. Off ran I for my bonnet, but somebody very peremptorily interfered, declaring that a certain pair of thin cheeks were quite thin enough already for their owner's good; and, moreover, that it was very foolish to waste life by keeping the heart all of a flutter, asserting that mine made a dozen trills and quavers, while that of a sensible person took but one moderate step.

Our visitors had brought us bottles of milk, eggs, fish, shrimps, yams, sweet pota-toes, plantains, and oranges for our comfort, and while they were unloading their treasures, I borrowed the captain's glass, and took a long look at the jetty. I could see, now that I knew they were actually there, the women grouped along the beach, and another object, which I was told was the cart and a pair of cream colored oxen, standing farther back upon the greensward. My feet fairly ached to press that soft carpet of earth and vegetation, but even the strong men who came for me acknowl-edged that "mamma" was too small for the undertaking, and so went away alone.

Now, darling, you know I am not a Niobe; you know I always did try to steer clear of certain sentimental indulgences, because they were sure to bring on headache without leaving any mortal good in return. You know I say that I am not one of "earth's sorrowful weepers," but somehow I did get *overtaken* this time. Down into my cabin I went, every nerve in me quivering, and treated my pillow to a regular tear-bath. "Twice of a single morning you ask? Twice of a single morning, dear—Or what is nearer the truth, the quarter deck operation continued. I was deep in the melting luxury, when the door was softly opened, and I knew that some person stood beside me. I did not move; but kept my face covered with the toler-ably well wetted bit of linen, that had divided my favors with the pillow; fortifying meanwhile my voice in anticipation of a question.

Presently I heard words, but though spoken close to my ear, they were not addressed to me. How that low, mellow voice crept down into my heart, calming its foolish agitation, imparting the strength of faith, illuminating its tremulous, shadowy depths with hope, and elevating it to a still, serene reliance on Him who can be touched with the feeling of our infirmities, simply because His nature though sinless, has vibrated to every earthly emotion.

Then how strange to be so thoroughly comprehended! Anybody else now would have thought that I was in a pet from the disappointment of not going on shore, or something else of the kind.

He knew, I can not [sic] tell how, but he told it all in that prayer as I never could have done—he knew, just how a faint heart feels, suddenly pressed upon with a view of moral sublimity to which it is for the moment inadequate; he knows what it is to have the doors of time, all shut and barred, and the long vista of eter-nity stretching in solemn perspective before the shrinking soul, and he knows just what is needed at such a crisis.

I remember a soothing, balm-distilling influence, a feeling of perfect security and serenity, and then I went to sleep. When I awoke, the jolly boat with the officers and gentlemen passengers, Christian among them, had gone on shore, and with the exception of a half-hour devoted to the hopia tree, I have been writing to you ever since.

Source: A. C. Kendrick, *The Life and Letters of Mrs. Emily C. Judson*, 238–42.

Emily C. Judson to Friends in Boston, Early December, 1846

We had a long but most delightful voyage in the pleasant *Faneuil Hall*, with its fine accommodations, kind officers, and quiet, orderly crew; and between our internal resources, and the constantly varying character of the sea-scenery, we could find no time for ennui. Twenty weeks from the day on which we went abroad, we anchored off Amherst; and the next Monday morning, were lowered into a Burmese boat, to proceed up to Maulmain. I was most agreeably disappointed by my first view of the land of palms and mosquitoes. Our boat was very much like a long watering-trough, whittled to a point at each end, and we were all nestled like a parcel of caged fowls under a low bamboo cover, from which it was not easy to look out. But the shore, along side [*sic*] which we were pushed up stream by the might of muscle, was brilliant with its unpruned luxuriance of verdure, and birds, and flowers. Here some strange tree dropped its long trailers to the water, there the white rice-bird, or a gayer stranger, with chameleon neck and crimson wing, coquetted with its neighbor, and the wealth of green, bending below; and then followed rich blossoms of new shapes and hues, and bearing new names, some in clusters, and some in long amber wreaths, stained here and there with lemon and vermilion, and all bearing that air of slumbrous richness characteristic of the Indian climate. Our oarsmen were Amherst Christians, who seemed as wild with joy as the birds themselves (not that they were particularly bird-like in any other respect), and there was laughing and chattering enough to make any heart merry. The first, being a universal language, I had no difficulty in understanding, but the latter sounded to me even more outlandish than their gaudy patsoes, bare, brawny shoulders, and turbaned heads, appeared to the eye.

Source: A. C. Kendrick, *The Life and Letters of Mrs. Emily C. Judson*, 242.

Emily C. Judson to an Unknown Friend,[143] December 5, 1846

The Letter from Mrs. Judson—"*Fanny Forrester*" [*sic*]—announcing the arrival of the mission family in India, is dated "Maulmain, December 5, 1846." Mrs. Judson thus speaks of her new home:—

> I write you from my very pleasant but very odd-looking house, which I saw for the first time on Monday last. I am delighted with the appearance of things here. The fruits are mostly rich and healthful, the foliage exuberant and the weather perfectly charming. There is a delicious softness in the air. The people, although very degraded, are exceedingly interesting in appearance, and have faces full of intelligence. I should think the Burmans far superior to the Hindoos.
>
> Our city is a perfect Babel, so far as languages and dress are concerned. Besides English, Americans and Burmans, we have people from nearly all the nations of the East—Chinese, Hindoos, Malays, Karens, etc. Mussulmans, Armenians and Isrealites.
>
> There is now passing my window a singular procession; men running and performing various antics, wax images tricked out gorgeously, a large and magnificent carriage, adorned with some dozen gilded umbrellas, fringed with golden drops, crimson tents and other gay trappings, etc. etc.
>
> We had a long voyage—a hundred and forty days—but it seemed scarcely a tenth part of that to me, it passed so pleasantly. I enjoyed every moment of the time. I feel that I am on the right side of the world; God grant that greater good may come of it than my own happiness, though I am deeply grateful for that. Dr. Judson is quite well.

Source: *Newark Daily Advertiser* (Newark NJ), March 27, 1847.

Emily C. Judson to Miss Cynthia Sheldon, December 1846—Maulmain

Very dear Miss Cynthia,

Imagine me if you can sitting very demurely with my feet nearest you, or rather imagine yourself stretched out asleep with me for one of the legs to your bedstead. This being at a twenty weeks distance from any place [*sic*] you have ever seen

---

[143] This letter appeared in the *Newark Daily Advertiser* (Newark NJ), March 27, 1847. It is found on page 2, column 5.

before is a curious affair; and things could scarce be more unlike their namesakes the other side of the water if they had been manufactured in the moon. I like the country however, for altho' it is full of discomforts it is suited to my tastes. The most unpleasant thing to me, tho others seem not to mind it at all, is that the houses are constructed so that you are never sure of being alone, even when in bed, the natives all considering it a mark of respect to look in at your windows on passing. Then if you speak in one room you are heard all over the house—indeed, the house is one large room, the partitions being nothing more than screens extending a little ways above the head. The present officers of government with most of whom I have formed some acquaintance, thro' their love for my good husband, are delightful people, but they are soon to be "relieved" and we cannot tell what the next batch will be. The missionaries too are most of them superiour [sic] people, and by no means the awkward slatternly set that some persons (myself among the number) have considered them. From associating with English families of the highest breeding (which they do to a small extent and could do much more if they would) they have most of them acquired an case [sic] and polish of manner which they would scarce have gained in America. Tell A.M.,[144] she can form no idea of Mrs. Stevens[145] from her family friends in Boston. I have not seen but one or two ladies in America so perfectly lady-like. I tell you these comparatively trivial things because I think most people at home have a wrong impression. The ladies in the mission are mostly tasteful in their dress and furniture tho very plain and simple; and their children, from being constantly under elevating influences, appear better than any children that I have ever seen. There are of course different degrees of piety among them, but there seems to me on the whole far more *heart-religion* than I expected to find. I expected to *hear* a great deal about extrinsic matters as we do at home, and *see* but little of the spirit; but it is directly the reverse. It seems to me almost like a continual Sabbath among them thus far. But all these pleasant things amount to but little. We are contemplating a very serious business and the good doctor is more sad than I have seen him for six months. We are thinking of putting out a *feeler* toward Ava in the shape of a trip to Rangoon, and if possible a residence there. At your distance you will not be able to appreciate the nature of the step, but to us it is far more formidable than that of leaving America, for the difference between Maulmain and Rangoon is really much greater than the difference between Utica and Maulmain. Here we are perfectly safe under

[144] See vol. 1, "Cast of Characters," s.v. "Anable, Miss Anna Maria."

[145] Elizabeth Stevens arrived in Maulmain in February 1838; her husband was Edward Stevens. Elizabeth Stevens took six-month-old Edward Judson into her home when Sarah and Adoniram had to leave for the United States in 1845, and her care and nurture saved his life. She served forty-eight years in Burmah. She had extensive correspondence with Emily Judson, and her letters spoke of everyday life among the missionaries. When Emily returned to the United States, the letters from Mrs. Stevens brought news of friends and colleagues. Mrs. Stevens had a sister, Sarah Haven, in Massachusetts, who wrote a number of letters to Emily asking for information on the Stevens family.

the English government—there we are at the mercy of ignorant, capricious and tyrannical heathen men whose prejudices are all awake as soon as they see a white face. This difference extends to all the creature comforts—what you eat, drink and sleep on. As for *wearing* I think I shall adopt the Malay fashion which is rather pretty and requires but little care and a small quantity of material. I believe some of the ladies here think I am very cruel to urge the poor doctor after all his sufferings at Rangoon and Ava to attempt Burmah with all its dangers again, and I don't know but they are right; still he is very courageous about it and sad only on account of me and the children. It seems hardly right to either of us to settle down here at comfortable pleasant Maulmain and wait for poor Burmah to open *herself* to us (the great cry when we talk of going is "oh there is no opening at present") without a single attempt to try the door and see if it will not give way in our hands. It is our intention now to remain here a couple of months till I get a few words of the language and then commence our march toward the heart of Burmah. We are not fully decided, however, for some of the missionaries think the matter hopeless. I do not think myself over laden with missionary spirit—in fact, I am the same pewter six pence that "I used to was;" but I cannot sit idle or sit and prepare myself for writing Burman books even, while these gorgeous processions are passing everyday with offerings to idols and hundreds of gilded pagodas are rising from every hill. It don't [sic] require a very strong missionary spirit to run one's neck into danger in such circumstances. You will easily understand my willingness to go, when you recollect that I have been somewhat acquainted with poverty and hardship before, and that I can be very happy with a serious burden on my back. Beside I must acknowledge there is something rather pleasant to me in the tho't of suffering for Christ's sake even tho' these poor wretches that I pity with all my heart sh'd get no good by it.

You will receive with this letter forty dollars which Mr. Jones will pay to you, because we do not consider it quite safe to send an order on the board to you. We know you too well. Please receive the little sum from us, not as compensation for the trouble which I gave you in getting off—that I know money would scarce repay; and no amount, however great, would be sufficient to express my gratitude for your constant kindness. This little sum may however cover a small portion of the actual expense that you incurred on my account and so we still remain your debtors. I have just put up a box to send home by the ship that we came in. In it you will find, beside some things from Mrs. Bullard, a couple of packages for our people in Hamilton, a lacquered bonnet box for Mrs. Nott[146] and another for Miss

---

[146] See vol. 1, "Cast of Characters," s.v. "Nott, Urania Sheldon."

Kelly,[147] a small Chinese tea-pot for Mary Jones[148] and a dress for Anna Maria. If I don't have time to write A. M. more before the steamer leaves, which I fear I shall not, please tell her that white dresses are so very unfashionable here, never being worn except in the morning, that I could find no India muslin in town. The embroidered muslin that I send instead is worn by English ladies for evening dresses and will wash perfectly well. The flowers will look better for washing. I sent her what is here considered two dress patterns, for it seemed to me impossible to make a dress out of one. If, however, I sh'd be mistaken she may keep the remainder or give it to the one she would best like to see dressed like herself. I sh'd like to come out with her, but I have done with such dresses forever. The bonnet-boxes will not bear rough usage, but they keep out dust and moisture and for that reason are invaluable here. I think they will be found useful.

Please give my love to dear Mrs. Anable,[149] William and Mrs. William[150] and all the rest of the good people. Tell my son Courtland[151] that I have very nearly lost the hope of seeing him, and consider him a very undutiful boy therefore. Tell Henry[152] here is the place to make his fortune, and the sooner he comes the better.

Our cow gave a little milk to the last and arrived safely. She is a very popular madam—everybody flocks to see the American cow. Mr. Howard[153] had a couple of ponies all ready for us when we arrived, but the doctor did'nt [sic] like his and sold it. Mine is a darling and will serve for both of us as we can't very well both go out together. He has an engagement to ride tomorrow morning with Mr. Haswell[154] and Mrs. Stevens, for which I am glad as he has not been out since our arrival. We have had numerous invitations to dinner (among others from the governor's lady) but have declined all. Poor little Edward[155] is teething and makes me a deal of

[147] See vol. 1, "Cast of Characters," s.v. "Kelly, Miss Jane."

[148] Mary Jones was the wife of Morven Jones. They lived in the Utica area and were intimately familiar with Miss Cynthia Sheldon and the staff and student body of the Utica Female Academy. Mr. and Mrs. Jones, as well as Miss Sheldon, were members of the Bleecker Street Baptist Church where Mr. Corey was the pastor. In a December 1848 series of letters to Emily, Morven Jones described a terrible accident; a group from the church was standing on a bridge overlooking the Mohawk River, there to witness a baptism, and the bridge collapsed. At least one person died in that accident, and Mary Jones was severely injured.

[149] See vol. 1, "Cast of Characters," s.v. "Anable, Mrs. Alma Sheldon."

[150] See vol. 1, "Cast of Characters," s.v. "Anable, William Steward."

[151] See vol. 1, "Cast of Characters," s.v. "Anable, Courtland."

[152] See vol. 1, "Cast of Characters," s.v. "Anable, Henry Sheldon."

[153] See vol. 1, "Cast of Characters," s.v. "Howard, Hosea and Theresa."

[154] James Haswell had sailed for Burmah in 1835, arriving in February 1836 to work with the Talaings. His wife was Jane Haswell. James Haswell became a partner with Adoniram and Sarah Judson, and when Adoniram and Elnathan were born, Sarah turned over the translation of the Peguan Scripture to him. He served as a missionary for more than forty years.

[155] Edward Judson, born December 27, 1844, in Maulmain, Burmah, was the eighth child of Adoniram and Sarah Hall Boardman Judson and the fifth of their children to survive. Only a few months old when Sarah and Adoniram returned to America, Edward's life was saved by the nurture and care he received from Elizabeth Stevens. He loved Emily as the only "Mama" he had ever known and returned with her to the United States in October 1851. Edward, who was Eddy to his family, became a minister; he did mission work with the immigrants in New York City, and with the aid of the Rockefeller Family, he built the Judson Memorial Baptist Church in what is now Washington Park.

trouble, so you must not mind if my letter sounds very queer. I am interrupted every third line. You don't know how funny it seems to be Mama'd and missis'd by children and servants, and what a task I have making myself understood by the latter. My paper is out. Goodbye, dear Aunt Cynthia. God bless you and reward you for your kindness.

Emily C. Judson

Source: Hanna family files.

William D. Ticknor and Company to Catharine Chubbuck, December 9, 1846—Boston

We have two copies of "Alderbrook" put up to your address and will feel obliged if you will inform as how they may be forwarded to you.

Very respy,

W. D. Tichnor and Co.

Miss Catharine Chubbuck

Hamilton

N.Y.

Source: Hanna family files.

The Dedication of *Alderbrook*,[156] December 1847

To
Him who is henceforth to be
My guide through life, its sunlight and its gloom,
These few little flowers,
Gathered by the wayside before we had met,
Are half-tremblingly, but most affectionately
Dedicated.
May their perfume be grateful;
Their fragility be pardoned;
And
Heaven grant that no unsuspected poison may be
Found lurking among their leaves!
Fanny Forester

---

[156] In fall 1845, Emily published *Trippings in Author-land*, an anthology of her stories and sketches. *Alderbrook* included some material from *Trippings*, but it mostly included material written after *Trippings in Author-land* had been published.

Miss Nancy Hasseltine to Adoniram Judson,[157] December 10, 1846

My dear Uncle,

To relieve the anxiety and solicitude you must necessarily feel respecting Abby's[158] health, improvement, etc. permit me to say that she is doing well, particularly in her studies. Perfection is not to be expected in any child and time must be allowed to prune all the *excrescences* and prepare the vine to bear precious fruit. She has capital materials for making a first rate character—Has appeared perfectly contented with the exception of a short time when your sister visited us and she urged very much her going back to Plymouth[159] which for a time made her uneasy.

Aunt Mary[160] has been very sick for two months—most of the time her life has been despaired of but at present there is a little hope. Aunt A.,[161] Mother and the other members of our family desire much love to yourself and Mrs. Judson and sincerely regret that we had not the pleasure of an extended acquaintance. We long to hear of your safe arrival and happy settlement over your precious charge.

Believe me your aff. niece

Nancy J. Hasseltine

Written along the left margin of the first page of Abby Ann's letter: "We should be highly gratified to hear from yourself or Mrs. Judson at any time when your arduous labors will allow you time to favor us."

Source: American Baptist Historical Society, AJ 10, no. 302.

---

[157] This letter from Nancy Hasseltine was written on page 3 of a letter written by Abby Ann Judson to Adoniram and Emily. That letter was dated November 14, 1846.

[158] Abby Ann Judson, the first daughter and oldest child of Adoniram and Sarah Hall Boardman Judson, was born September 26, 1835. She saw her mother die on the Isle of St. Helena as they returned to the United States from Burmah. Just before leaving for Burmah with Emily, Adoniram Judson placed Abby Ann at Bradford Academy for her education. The family of Ann Hasseltine Judson was generous to Abby Ann and supportive of her interests and her future. On October 15, 1851, Abby Ann started a course of study at the Misses Anable's School in Philadelphia, and in fall 1853, she moved to New York City to take a teaching position in the home of Mrs. Maria Brown, a former missionary to Siam. She enjoyed a warm relationship with Emily, and her letters show that the two could speak freely with each other.

[159] For approximately four months after their return from Burmah, Adoniram placed Abby Ann with his sister Abigail Brown Judson in Plymouth. Abigail Judson was an eccentric individual, and while she loved her brother's children and intended to take some financial responsibility for them, there was obviously a significant generational gap. At this time at Bradford Academy, Abby Ann was in a wonderful environment, and the report on her in the first part of the letter demonstrates that she was responding. The thought of leaving all of that to go back to Plymouth with her aunt caused a great deal of nervousness.

[160] Mary Hasseltine, sister of Ann Hasseltine Judson.

[161] Abigail Hasseltine, sister of Ann Hasseltine Judson

Abby Ann Judson to Emily C. and Adoniram Judson, December 15, 1846—Lynn

My dear Father and Mother.

As you asked me to write to you once in three months you may think it strange that I write now but Mr. Backeller with whom I am staying said that I might write a quarter of a sheet full and he would send it so I will do so. They are very sick at Miss Hasseltine's. Aunt Mary[162] is very dangerously sick and they despair of her life. She was first attacked with the influenza, and had an attack of the palpitation of the heart. My cousin Rebecca is very sick with the typhus fever but I believe that now she is better. As they were so ill there Aunt Abby,[163] at first thought of sending me to Aunt Judson's[164] at Plymouth. But Aunt Emerson came over and said that she was going to Lynn the next morning if pleasant, but it was so stormy all of the next day that she defered [sic] going till the day after. The next morning we started at 9 o'clock, and, after riding all day we got there between 4 and 5 in the afternoon (we rode in a chaise). When we arrived at Lynn they told us that poor Mrs. Backeller was dead. She died on the first of Oct. after a long and painful illness. Perhaps you would like to hear some particulars of her sickness and death. She took her chamber the next week after you saw her. She did not leave her chamber after that except a few times when she went out to ride. She suffered exceedingly especially the last fortnight of her life. She vomited incessantly so that she was not able to converse but very little. She was perfectly sensible to the last and perfectly resigned. Her disease was a malignant disease of the liver. I am knitting a pair of stockings for myself. Last week on Monday My Uncle Eliphalet came for me to go to Salem and spend a few days. My Aunt Nancy and Uncle George were there. When I went to Salem I wrote a short letter to Skaneateles.[165] I returned to Lynn on Thursday. As they keep a shop here I have a nice time seeing the folks come in to buy and sometimes I try to wait on them myself. Perhaps you would like to hear me tell you how I spent Thanksgiving day. I had several little notes to be opened at dinner which were given to me at Bradford. In the morning I went out to Mrs. Cutler's, and spent the day there. In the evening we had some singers. A gentleman and his four sisters. The gentleman played on the melodian [sic] and the sisters sung several peices [sic]. Among other things they sung [sic] the Grave of Mrs. Judson for it has been set to music, and He doeth all things Well. The young ladies here send their kind regards to you. Father, I want to know

---

[162] Mary Hasseltine was a sister of Ann Hasseltine Judson. Abby Ann's letter of November 14, 1846 mentioned this.

[163] Abigail Hasseltine, sister of Ann Hasseltine Judson.

[164] See vol. 1, "Cast of Characters," s.v. "Judson, Abigail Brown."

[165] These are likely references to Abby Ann's maternal grandparents and to aunts and uncles related to her mother, Sarah Hall Boardman Judson.

whether you and Mother are not coming back to America when your dictionary is finished. Oh I wish that you would. Mrs. Cutler's little daughter Mary says that she loves you both right well. She sleeps with me in the night. I brought my United States History with me and study it now for we did not quite finish it last term and recite out of it to Mrs. Backeller's niece Sarah Smith. I love her dearly. She has been making me a hood to wear this winter. I go to Sunday School with Mary and Sunday before last I gave 10 cents to foreign missions. It was to support a little Assamese girl in Assam. I wish that it had been to help to support you then I should be giving to *you* some money which you gave to me. Last week I received a letter from Cousin Nancy[166] and she said that Aunt Abby was sick but not dangerously. I have been twice to Mary's school. Her teacher Miss Rogers is in and says that I am a naughty girl because I have not said anything about her. But I must close. I send you both much love. Kiss Henry[167] and Edward[168] for me. Good-by [*sic*].

Your ever affectionate daughter,
Abbie Ann Judson[169]

Source: American Baptist Historical Society, AJ 10, no. 301.

Emily C. Judson to Mrs. Hannah Gillette, December 20, 1846—Maulmain

My Dear Mrs. Gillette

A year ago I was sitting in your pleasant little parlor, never dreaming of such an overturn in life as this,[170] and very happy; but no happier than I am now. Now I have measured half the world by ship-lengths, and stand here (or rather sit) one of the four legs of your bedstead while you sleep. These turn-abouts in life really tip one's brains over curiously. I never quite got my ideas straight after crossing the equator until I came in sight of the north star again; and now things are worse than ever. Nothing here, not even a bird or tree, is like the vegetable or winged things across the water; and the few articles that bear a slight resemblance to those seen before must needs have new names. Little boys' trowsers are *bombees*, their frocks *engees*, and people don't lunch, they take *tiffin*....

---

[166] Nancy Hasseltine wrote a letter on December 10, 1846, and sent it with a letter that Abby Ann had written on November 14, 1846. She addressed Adoniram Judson as "Uncle."

[167] See vol. 1, "Cast of Characters," s.v. "Judson, Henry Hall."

[168] See vol. 1, "Cast of Characters," s.v. "Judson, Edward."

[169] In a post script to her November 14, 1846 letter, Abby Ann asked that the spelling of her name be changed to "Abbie."

[170] On December 25, 1845, Emily met Adoniram Judson in the parlor of the Gillette home in Philadelphia, where she had been staying for the winter.

I am delighted here with every thing [*sic*] so far as I have yet observed. To be sure there is little of what in America is considered comfort (what an outlandish oddity our house would be, set down in Delaware, 12th!) but there is a picturesque beauty—a mingling of awkward simplicity with magnificence quite as clumsy and awkward—a rich gorgeousness, a fantastic extravagance, a rudeness sometimes annoying, but oftener ludicrous—in short, the scenery, the works of art (there is no small degree of skill displayed in building a pagoda, and ornamenting the carriages that go up with offerings to Guadama), the manners of the people, the color of the sky, the atmosphere, are all in perfect keeping with each other, and all have an oriental air which is quite fascinating to me. The houses of the missionaries are the plainest possible, built of teak boards, and furnished with the same kind of wood, without varnish. The partitions between the rooms are mere screens, reaching a little above the head, so that a word spoken in one room is heard all over the house. To my eye, however, even these houses have an air of relative beauty about them which nicer ones would not have. If I were fond of new things, I should think it was because they were new and odd; but I think I was made for an uncivilized land....

Were we to settle down in this house with the comforts we should be able to secure, the pleasant English and missionary families about us, although in a very different condition from a pastor's family at home, my taste would be gratified, and I should, as far as the things of this world are concerned, be perfectly happy. But that is not to be. My conscience will not allow me to remain in delightful Maulmain while there is the slightest hope of my husband's being able, by going to a place of danger and privation, to do any thing for the miserable nation, at the door of which we are standing. I am not myself made for great things, but, when I see his heart turning that way, I can say "go," and when the trials come, I know I can cheer and comfort him. As soon as I can get a few words of the language—a couple of months, perhaps—we shall put off to Rangoon, and there wait an opportunity to creep into Ava....

I have discovered since I left America that I am incapable of the emotion of fear. I have been two or three times pretty severely tried in that respect. I may meet with things at Rangoon, however, that will make my hair bristle. God only knows, and quietly in my own closet I ask His direction and assistance; You and your dear good man will, I trust, help me ask, for none ever needed all the graces of godliness, combined with singular wisdom, more than I do just now. I love the cause of Christ with my whole heart, and I love, too, these poor wretches, who, in ignorance of, the ways of life, are going down to eternal misery. God make me useful to them. I do not believe in practicing self-denial for self-denials sake—I think that a relic of popery—but I should not shrink from suffering or even death in His cause. I pray that I may not be like Peter when I say *I never will*....

Your affectionate friend,
Emily C. Judson.

Source: A. C. Kendrick, *The Life and Letters of Mrs. Emily C. Judson*, 243–45.

The Reverend Doctor William Dean to Emily C. Judson,[171] December 1846[172]—Hong Kong

My dear Sister Judson

As I am sending packages to Calcutta I will put in a line for you; it may not be worth the postage—but never mind. I'll write. You may have heard that Bro. [ ] [ ] [ ] of [ ] have gone to [ ]—and two Bro. [ ] [ ] [ ] [ ] [ ] [ ] from U.S. Bro. S. Smith is soon to join Bro. Jones at Bankok where six Chinese have [ ] [ ] [ ] by Br. [ ]. Rev. and Mrs. Farmer [ ] [ ] [ ] on their way to [ ] [ ] [Note: Two lines are lost here.]

From [ ] [ ] [ ] of US Rev. and Mrs. Whelden [ ] (of three children) have joined the Canton Mission from the Southern Baptist [ ] [Note: A line is lost here.] and [ ] very well—I am spending my time with [ ] to Genius—it was [ ] but I fear it may [ ] [ ] the man who speared the pig! you know what—How do you succeed in book making in Burmese? Will you bind me a copy of your first and I'll see if I've forgotten all my Burmese—not much to loose [sic] you must know—but once I write [ ]—what do you call that? If there is no sense in that there is in this (Note: writer has a list down the page of Chinese characters) read it downwards and then see 2nd John [ ] Who [Note: Five lines are lost here.] Do you see or hear any thing [sic] of my old preceptor and friend Moung Shway Moung? How are those blue and black eyed [ ] sisters of yours? [Note: A line is lost here.] Did you see [ ] King of [ ] Did you [ ] [ ] [ ] at Morrisville [ ] [ ] has joined the Church. Oh [ ] [ ] me grace

With kindest regards to Dr. J.
I am Gratefully
Yours
W. Dean

Source: American Baptist Historical Society, this letter is unrecorded.

[171] The handwriting and poor copy quality of the microfilm leave rather large gaps in the transcription of this letter.
[172] This letter is undated. December 1846 is an approximation.

LETTERS

———✧———

JANUARY-APRIL 1847

Emily C. Judson to Mrs. Elizabeth Stevens, January 1847

My Dear Mrs. Stevens,

I have been all day divided between my desire to attend your meeting this afternoon (which I know will be interesting) and the awkwardness inseparable from my appearance in a Company of matrons, where I feel as though I had no right to be.

I do love the dear children that a saint in heaven has left me. I love them for their own sakes; for sweeter, more lovely little creatures never breathed; brighter, more beautiful blossoms never expanded in the cold atmosphere of this world. I love them for the sake of one still dearer, who had the power to break all the ties which were twined with tenfold strength about my heart; and I love them because they are immortal beings, because for them a Saviour died, even as for me. I love them; I pray to God to help me train them up in His fear and love.

I shall be very thankful, my dear Mrs. Stevens, for any advice you or the loved sisters who will meet with you to-day, can give me; for I know that I am utterly unfitted for this sweet burden which God has laid upon my heart and hands. Please ask them for their prayers, first in behalf of the orphans afar off;[1] next, in behalf of the little ones here,[2] that they may never know the want of a fond mother's care and love; and next, in behalf of the new, inexperienced mother, that God may give the wisdom, patience, gentleness, humility, and entire dependence on Him, necessary to their proper management; so that at last I may be able to lead them up to her who loved them even more than I, and say, "here are thine own jewels, polished for thy crown."

Believe me, my dear Mrs. Stevens, it is only the bashfulness attendant on a strange situation, and which it seems impossible for me to surmount, which keeps me from your meeting. May Jesus Christ be in your midst.

Affectionately,

E. C. J.

I send the children. Will you or Mrs. Haswell[3] be kind enough to take charge of them as formerly?

Source: A. C. Kendrick, *The Life and Letters of Mrs. Emily C. Judson*, 245–46.

---

[1] Of the Judson children, George Dana Boardman, Adoniram ("Pwen" or "Addy"), and Elnathan ("Elly") were with Dr. and Mrs. Calvin Newton in Worcester, Massachusetts. Abby Ann Judson was at Bradford Academy in Bradford, Massachusetts, with the family of Ann Hasseltine Judson.

[2] Henry Hall and Edward Judson were in Maulmain with Emily and Adoniram Judson.

[3] Jane Haswell sailed for Burmah in 1835, arriving in February 1836 to work with the Talaings. Her husband was James Haswell. She served as a missionary for more than forty years. Mrs. Haswell took in Henry Hall Judson when Adoniram and Sarah sailed for the United States in spring 1845. The correspondence between Emily and Jane Haswell reflects a warm relationship between the two.

Emily C. Judson to her Journal, January 1, 1847—Maulmain

Actually in Burmah! And is it really myself? Is the past year a reality, or am I still dreaming up there in Dominie Gillette's[4] chamber, where I lay down (seemingly) a year ago? If it be a dream, I pray God that I may never wake, for I believe that it would break my heart to be other than I am. Thank God, it is a reality—a blessed reality; and I am in the very spot I so longed to plant my foot upon, years and years gone by.[5]

Source: A. C. Kendrick, *Life and Letters of Mrs. Emily C. Judson*, 246; Hanna family files.

Mrs. Elizabeth L. Stevens to Emily C. Judson, January 1, 1847[6]

My dear Sister

I have been looking at the cot and, from the way the tape has been woven in to make a bottom, I am quite sure a comforter or very thick bed quilt folded would do better! Then the second mattress you spoke of sending—Edward[7] can tell you how the frame comes up round and if you have no spread or comforter I can lend you one if you let me know.

E. L. S.

Source: American Baptist Historical Society, AJ 19, no. 909.

---

[4] Following several successful pastorates, the Reverend A. D. Gillette was the founding pastor of the flourishing Eleventh Baptist Church in Philadelphia in 1839. With his wife Hannah and several children, he graciously opened their home to Emily Chubbuck when she came to Philadelphia at the end of March 1845 for her health. The connection had been made through Miss Cynthia Sheldon, a family friend of Mr. Gillette and his parents. A prominent Baptist, Mr. Gillette journeyed to Boston in December 1845 to accompany Adoniram Judson to Philadelphia for meetings, and on Christmas Day, he introduced Dr. Judson to Emily Chubbuck with the hope that Fanny Forester could be persuaded to write the memoir of Sarah Hall Boardman Judson. A. D. Gillette and his wife Hannah remained valued and trusted friends, not only with Emily, but with the Sheldon and Anable families. In 1852, Mr. Gillette moved to New York City where in the next decade he pastored two churches and then moved on to churches at Sing Sing, New York and Washington, DC.

[5] As a young woman, Emily had approached her pastor, Dr. Nathaniel Kendrick, about the possibility of becoming a missionary, to which he had counseled patience. Now, many years later, she indeed is on the mission field, fulfilling that early desire.

[6] This letter is undated. It seems natural, as it has to do with setting up house, to place it shortly after their arrival in Burmah.

[7] A native of Georgia, a graduate of Newton Theological Institute, and recently married to Elizabeth Haven, Edward Stevens arrived in Maulmain in February 1838. He was responsible for the native churches that were associated with the mission. A skilled linguist, Edward Stevens took on the work of finishing the dictionary after the death of Adoniram Judson. In April 1850, Mr. Stevens tenderly buried "Angel Charlie" in the chapel compound. Mr. Stevens served in Burmah for forty-eight years.

Mr. Charles B. Stout[8] to Emily C. Judson, January 1, 1847—New York

Dear Friend

The year in which you gave yourself to the Mission has passed away, and the foot-fall of to-day is upon another stepping stone of time. Since the July day which brought me your brief, but kind letter, I have intended to write: and now, I do from the festive scene of this happy Holyday—I pen these lines to you. A thousand thoughts throng upon my mind, as I realize that I am tracing characters to be read half way [*sic*] round the world; and it seems almost miraculous that this sheet should traverse earth's semi-circumference, and finally fall into your hands. It was my privilege a few evenings since (Dec. 30) to attend a "farewell meeting" in Oliver St, at which Brother and Sister Lord were dedicated to the China Mission. Dr. Dovoling [*sic*] read the "Missionaries' Farewell"—"Yes! My native land I leave thee!" in a most feeling manner. The Missionaries evinced a commendable calmness and self-possession during the exercises, which were of an interesting and affecting character. Our friends expect to sail on Monday the 4th Inst. Others will soon follow them to China—among them a sister of the late Mrs. Shuck, who has married a missionary under appointment. I have a dear and cherished friend, who preceeded [*sic*] you some four months to a heathen land. Mrs. Rebecca N. McMillan of the Madura Mission, Southern India. I commend her to your kindness, your sympathy, and prayer. It would give me pleasure to learn that you had commenced an acquaintance across the Bengal Bay. The spiritual pulse beats low at home, the lights of many seem to have gone out, and few enquire the way to Zion. As some items in the world of letters may be acceptable I subjoin a few— which may not have reached you. Your friend Mr. Willis,[9] has married again, and is

---

[8] Mr. Charles Stout first wrote to Emily on January 1, 1847. He received a letter from her in July the previous year as she was leaving Boston; apparently, it went to his wife, but it was inadvertently addressed to "Mr. Stout" instead of "Mrs." He identified himself as one who was interested in missions and as the secretary of the Young Men's' Mission Society of the Stanton Street Baptist Church. His letters in 1852, of which there were three, had to do with helping to secure materials that would be helpful to the writing of the memoir. From the *Baptist Encyclopaedia*: "Charles B. Stout was born at Flemington, N. J, in 1824. spent his youth in New Brunswick, became an active member of the Stanton Street Baptist church, New York; has been for years connected with the First or with the Remsen Avenue church in New Brunswick. He is the author of several books which have had an extensive sale; was one of the first to use the blackboard in Sunday-schools, and is widely known in the Sunday-school work as an able speaker and contributor to the magazines" (Cathcart, William. *The Baptist Encyclopedia* [Philadelphia: Louis H. Everts, 1881] 1114).

[9] Nathaniel Parker Willis was the editor, with General George Morris, of the *New Mirror*, a prominent literary magazine in New York. His "discovery" of Emily in the June 8, 1844 edition of the *New Mirror* catapulted her into literary fame and enabled her to command the highest prices for her articles and stories from the major magazines of that period. It began a new and glorious chapter in her life. Over the next two years, he became her friend, mentor, and confidant. His black-bordered letter of March 21, 1846, made it abundantly clear that her engagement to Adoniram Judson had come as a "death blow" and that he had expected to marry Emily upon his return that month from England. He returned several letters to Emily to demonstrate to her, lest she had forgotten, why he had felt right in that expectation. In volume 1, there is a timeline that presents in some detail the substance of their developing relationship, all from the letters Willis had written to Emily. When she received her letters back from Willis, she destroyed them, feeling that they would cast a negative shadow on her life and, because of that, the life and ministry of Adoniram Judson.

associated with Gen. Morris[10] in publishing a fine paper entitled "the Home Journal." Mrs. Willis is the (adopted) daughter of a Member of Congress, and is said to be *heir apparent* to a considerable fortune—hope she may get it, and Mr. W. return to his lamented Glenmary. A brighter star is playing in the literary world, and the query now is—"Who is Grace Greenwood?" But the lady keeps her secret well; better than some of her sisters according to Madame Rumor. Edgar A. Poe, whom you know by reputation at least is sick at his residence in this city, and suffering for bread! What a selfish world is this in which we live—how poorly paid the man of letters! Perhaps you were wise in withdrawing from the "primrose path" as you did. *Alderbrook*[11] we learned about two weeks since, (and) many have already taken it to their homes and to their (hearts). Right glad was I to meet in its pages things new and old [ ]. There was high-souled "Alfred Mason,"[12] and sweet "Nora Maylie," dear "Charley Hill" and "Rag Raffles," the rogue—the sportnelle [*sic*] "Ida Ravelin" and the "Dissatisfied Spirit," and then thy tender and touching "Farewell"! Would I could share in such devotion as yours, and as fully consecrate myself upon the Missionary Altar! And here I must correct a mistake, yours of July 7 was written not to "Mrs." but Mr. C. B. Stout; how the error prevailed, I know not, but as some of my intimates think mine is a womanly heart, you may have come to the same conclusion. However I hope this letter will not be less acceptable coming from the sterner sex. My better half (if indeed it be not wanting) is as yet undiscovered, no "bright peculiar star" has risen above the horizon of my afflictions, and I like the lonely islander "Must finish my journey alone."

A due respect perhaps requires that none should be said of the writer—the difficulty of writing of one's self, you have no doubt experienced, and therefore will more readily excuse brevity on this point. (If I had a rich cousin I might send you "a sketch.")[13] Charles B. Stout is a member of the Stanton St. Baptist Church in this city, and the Secretary of the Young Men's Mission Society. His business is to teach the young idea" [Note: The opening quotation marks are missing.]—a process with which you may not be unfamiliar. As Grace Greenwood has it, mine

[10] General George P. Morris was a partner with N. P. Willis at the *New Mirror* and a prominent literary figure in New York and Philadelphia. The original founder of the *New York Mirror* in 1823, beginning in 1843 with the *New Mirror*, he entered into a succession of publication enterprises with N. P. Willis. A writer, poet, and songwriter, Morris published a number of anthologies of both prose and poetry. When Willis went to Europe in 1845 after the death of his wife, he asked General Morris to guide Emily in her literary endeavors. Known universally as General Morris, his title came from his rank as a brigadier-general in the New York Militia.

[11] On December 9, 1846, Ticknor, Reed and Fields had sent Catharine Chubbuck two copies of *Alderbrook*, so we suspect it was published about this time.

[12] This is a listing of many of the stories and characters that appear in the pages of *Alderbrook*.

[13] Mr. Stout is referring to an original piece written by Emily in 1844 for the *New York Mirror* that was a prelude to the fame she acquired as Fanny Forester. Her initial letter to the editor spoke of a visit to New York by Emily and her "Cousin 'Bel'" and how they did not have the money to satisfy their desires as they were tempted by the shop windows of the city. The editor responded by inviting Emily to "write us therefore a sketch of 'Bel' and yourself," which Emily did, and it appeared a few weeks later. The piece was later published in *Trippings in Author-land* under the title "The Cousins—A Sketch."

is—"A name to but a few endeared / And all unknown to fame." But to return— my sympathies are warmly enlisted in the cause of Missions, and for five years I have aided the "home department." I feel for the far-off heathens, and for those peopling the wide-spread prairies of the West. Christians here are generally lamentably ignorant of Missionary facts—we know nothing of your trials and but little of your successes. Light! give us light, and men with money; would be given to the Heathen. The narrowing space warns me that I must draw to a close. I have written with all the freedom of an old acquaintance, and touched upon topics I thought likely would be interesting to you:—the letter I commend to Him who notes the sparrows fall. Permit me to hope you will answer this when convenient, and if desirable on your part, (as it certainly is on mine,) we will continue the correspondence. There may be hours when it would be a relief to turn to the land of your childhood, and write to those whose love and prayer are pledged to you. That you may be blessed below, and meet the good and the gifted above is the prayer of

Yours sincerely

C. B. Stout

185 Allen St. N.Y.

Source: American Baptist Historical Society, AJ 19, no. 888.

Adoniram Judson to Miss Abigail B. Judson,[14] January 1, 1847— Maulmain

My Dear Sister:

The accompanying Bible was packed in a large box that was never opened till my arrival here, or I should probably have left it with you, and saved it a double voyage, to which it is now consigned, in the hope that it will find a resting-place at last in the old mansion house, and frequently meet your eyes, and be received into your heart.

Edward,[15] my youngest, is just now sitting in a little chair to keep him still. He is just two years old.—A day or two ago I went out to the graveyard, and erected

---

[14] This letter is included in the Correspondence of Emily Chubbuck Judson as it reflects tenderly on the family life of Adoniram and Emily in Maulmain, and fills in some of the picture of the family relationships, the children, and the decisions having to be made. Adoniram and Emily had only been in Burmah about a month when this letter was written.

[15] Edward Judson, born December 27, 1844, in Maulmain, Burmah, was the eighth child of Adoniram and Sarah Hall Boardman Judson and the fifth of their children to survive. Only a few months old when Sarah and Adoniram returned to America, Edward's life was saved by the nurture and care he received from Elizabeth Stevens. He loved Emily as the only "Mama" he had ever known and returned with her to the United States in October 1851. Edward, who was Eddy to his family, became a minister; he did mission work with the immigrants in New York City, and with the aid of the Rockefeller Family, he built the Judson Memorial Baptist Church in what is now Washington Park.

the grave-stones that I procured in Boston, in memory of poor little Charlie[16]—the last act of duty and kindness that I can ever do for him.

Emily loves the children as if they were her own. We should be very happy here, but the interests of the mission seem to require that we should remove to Rangoon, and endeavor to gain some footing in Burmah proper. We are now making arrangements for such a removal, and expect to leave this before long. It seems to me harder to leave Maulmain for Rangoon than to leave Boston for Maulmain. But here there are several missionaries; not one there; and doubtless there are some inquiring souls who need a missionary to take them by the hand and guide them into the paths of truth and salvation. How long we shall be tolerated there under a despotic government, we know not; but we desire to commit our future destiny into the hands of our heavenly Father, with full confidence that he will order all things well.

We are always meeting with some article of clothing, or other use, to remind us of your kindness. The two large silver spoons you gave me are the only ones on our table; but I have found half a dozen of more common metal to supply the deficiency.

I did not think of writing you a letter just now; but as I was doing up the box containing the Bible, I thought I would just write a line that will cost you no postage. I shall send the box to Mr. Colby,[17] 22 Pemberton Square, Boston, and he will forward it to you. I have not yet heard a word from you, or the children, since I left you. Wrote you lately by overland mail.

Give my love to Mr. Harvey and family, and to other friends. My dear sister, I often think of you in your solitude. May God ever be with you, to protect and bless you. Do write me often, and tell me all about affairs in Plymouth, and the friends about you. Let us ever pray for one another. My late visit has endeared you to my heart far more than ever before.

---

[16] Charles Judson, the son of Adoniram and Sarah Hall Boardman Judson. He was born December 18, 1843. When Adoniram and Sarah were forced to sail for American due to her health, Charles was left with Sewall and Sarah Osgood, fellow missionaries in Maulmain. Charles died in August 1845, just before his mother Sarah Hall Boardman Judson was to die at the Isle of St Helena.

[17] A prominent businessman, Gardner Colby and his family lived in Pemberton Square in Boston before moving "to the country," Newton Centre, Massachusetts. Mr. Colby was a member of the Board of the American Baptist Missionary Union and an avid supporter of the missionary movement. In a letter after they sailed from Boston to Burmah, Emily mentions the extravagant hospitality extended to them in early July as they waited for the *Faneuil Hall* to embark. Adoniram and Emily stayed with the Colby family frequently.

Let me know whatever you hear about the children; and try, if possible, to visit Bradford[18] and Worcester.[19] You would be joyfully received at both places; and I have written to Miss Hasseltine[20] to allow Abby Ann[21] to visit you.

Ever your own brother,

A. Judson

Emily sends her love.

Emily C. Judson to her Journal, January 2, 1847

I have got a teacher, and made a beginning in the language, but the children absorb so much of my time that I can not [sic] study much. They are dear little fellows, but so full of mischief! Precious gems they are; may they not be spoiled by so inexperienced a polisher as I am.

Source: A. C. Kendrick, *Life and Letters of Mrs. Emily C. Judson*, 246.

Anna Maria Anable to Emily C. Judson, January 2, 1847

I hope you had a happy New Year dear Nemmy.[22] I assure you we all thought of you a good many times yesterday. Your picture looked down very complacently[23] upon the different groups collected in the parlour [sic] and my thoughts wandered over to Burmah a good many times. If I don't get a letter from you before long Miss I shall have my shadowy notions about you—already I begin to dread thinking of

[18] Ann Hasseltine Judson, Adoniram Judson's first wife, was from Bradford, Massachusetts. Bradford also was the home of Bradford Academy, where Abby Ann Judson was a student and where the sisters of Ann Hasseltine were situated.

[19] Worcester, Massachusetts, was the home of Dr. and Mrs. Calvin Newton. George Boardman went to live with them when he returned from Burmah as a child in 1835. Adoniram and Elnathan went to live with the Newtons in November 1845 upon their return from Burmah.

[20] This is a reference to Miss Abigail Hasseltine, a sister to Ann Hasseltine. Miss Hasseltine was the headmistress of Bradford Academy.

[21] Abby Ann Judson, the first daughter and oldest child of Adoniram and Sarah Hall Boardman Judson, was born September 26, 1835. She saw her mother die on the Isle of St. Helena as they returned to the United States from Burmah. Just before leaving for Burmah with Emily, Adoniram Judson placed Abby Ann at Bradford Academy for her education. The family of Ann Hasseltine Judson was generous to Abby Ann and supportive of her interests and her future. On October 15, 1851, Abby Ann started a course of study at the Misses Anable's School in Philadelphia, and in fall 1853, she moved to New York City to take a teaching position in the home of Mrs. Maria Brown, a former missionary to Siam. She enjoyed a warm relationship with Emily, and her letters show that the two could speak freely with each other.

[22] "Nem" or "Nemmy" was a name of endearment given to Emily by a small group of her intimate friends at the Utica Female Academy. Anna Maria Anable was "Ninny."

[23] In a letter of February 15, 1846, Emily said that she had been to see Mr. Rothermel and that he was painting a portrait of her for Anna Maria Anable. In latter correspondence, there were references to Freeman doing some paintings, one from the engraving of Emily done by John Sartain, possibly one of Anna Maria, and one of Adoniram Judson, who said he simply did not have time to sit for such a painting.

you as Mrs. Dr. Judson or Fanny Forester.[24] Don't you think you will always be my little Nemmy? No, I know you will not—you cannot, and that is what makes me cry almost every time I sit down to write to you. I have begun to write a good many times but give up after a page or two because I was writing so stupidly.

I rec'd a letter from Ticknor and Co.[25] last week asking to what address they should send my *Alderbrook*—so last eve'g came a large package to me from Boston (I had told them to forward Kate's[26] and Aunt U.'s[27] to me) I assure you it was the most precious New Year's gift I had rec'd. It is very handsomely got up and has already been through one edition. That is in three weeks. I have read it through I believe and it is remarkably well printed—I have not discovered any misprints.

The religious papers notice it very handsomely. Poor Dominie Gillette[28] is too ill to write a review so you may rest easy I think as regards your too troublesome friends. Friend G. is really seriously ill with some disorder of the lungs and will unable [*sic*] to preach the papers say till Spring. Can you imagine a family more to be pitied than theirs? Mrs. G. presented to her distressed and disappointed husband a fourth *boy* about a month ago. I am afraid the little fellow will have to be taken up by strangers he is so unwelcome to the friends.

By the way Nemmy whose marriage do you think I saw in the papers the other day? Joseph P. Neal's![29] and what's more he has married a mere little Baptist girl (I suspect) and her name is Emily! She was from Hudson. Well, how your old flames are marrying off! I don't believe any of them will be as [ ] as I, the infection seems to extend only among the rougher *sect*. I have heard that Willis[30] has caught a Tartar this time who means to make him walk straight. It is only rumour [*sic*] though—I know nothing of the truth of it. Mr. Wm Kirkland of New York is dead. He was drowned in the north river about six weeks ago. The circumstances were

---

[24] Emily Chubbuck Judson as Fanny Forester. See vol. 1, "Cast of Characters," s.v. "Chubbuck, Emily E." and "Forester, Fanny."

[25] Ticknor, or Ticknor, Reed and Fields, published *Alderbrook* and several of Emily's later works. There are a number of letters in the collection from Mr. Ticknor. On December 9, 1846, they sent two copies of *Alderbrook* to Catharine Chubbuck, Emily's sister in Hamilton.

[26] Sarah Catharine Chubbuck, "Kate," "Kit," or "Kitty" was Emily's older sister by ten months. Outside of the two terms at the Utica Female Academy, which Emily arranged for her, Catharine always lived at home with her parents in Hamilton, New York. The letters indicate opportunities for marriage, but she, for unknown reasons, remained single. She later helped to care for Henry and Edward Judson after their return from Burmah in fall 1851 when they moved into the Hamilton home with their "aunt" and "grandparents," and she was remembered by them as "dear old Aunt Kate—a dear friend."

[27] See vol. 1, "Cast of Characters," s.v. "Nott, Urania Sheldon."

[28] See vol. 1, "Cast of Characters," s.v. "Gillette, The Reverend Abram Dunn."

[29] Joseph Neal was a prominent member of the literary establishment in Philadelphia and became a part of Emily Chubbuck's circle of friends when she was there. Neal was well known and respected as a writer and editor; one of his best known works was the *Charcoal Sketches*. In 1842, he founded the *Saturday Gazette*, a successful publication that contained a great deal of humorous satire. Anna Maria Anable frequently referred to Neal as a beau for Emily. Mr. Neal married Alice Bradley in 1846; he died in 1847.

[30] See vol. 1, "Cast of Characters," s.v. "Willis, Nathaniel Parker."

very distressing to his family. Old Mrs. K.[31] his mother had a paralytic stroke soon after hearing of it from which she has but partially recovered. He had just avowed Unitarian principles and had published one number of a new religious paper. The family are [sic] in tolerably comfortable circumstances.

Miss Chaplin, Mrs. Eaton[32] and Miss Hotchkiss from Hamilton have visited us lately. Tell the Dr. his friend Mr. Wilder of Albany is going to spend next Summer in H. and if he likes it he will reside there. He has given a thousand dollars to their building a new church and the H. folks are delighted at having him there. Do you know Nemmy I do not like those H. people any too much as there seems to be a want of sincerity among them. I may be mistaken though and it is no matter if I am not.

There is not much going on here in Utica to interest you. Willie Dutton and Mary Dullibar [sic] were married this week—and Mary Pomaroy [sic] was married about a month ago. Mrs. Mayer gave a party this week which I attended. It was the first full dress party I had attended except a wedding one for a year and a half. Johnny [ ] came to [ ] me down there (you know it was out of town) and all the old beaux (my old admirers!) were there. I do not know whether it was because I was dressed remarkably well (I was I assure you) or whether because I had [ ] particularly amicable but when I returned I found myself highly flattered with the attentions bestowed upon me, and I began to doubt whether it was well for us who prefer *godliness* to be found often in such gay company. I do not dance any more [sic] and people have to have respect for the motive which led me to decline—and I know that I have a decided influence here for I can see it, but I must walk very cautiously. I feel it to be more difficult to pursue a consistent course here than if I had more religious society, for that reason I go out but little. There are enough professors of religion here, but there are few who make the interests of religion their first interest. O, I am sick of this half way religion. If I am a Christian at all I want to be one in earnest—I do not know as I have any evidence now that I am one—I have certainly no assurance of it.

I have been reading Edwards on the affections and it is certainly a very disheartening book. After searching it very carefully I came to the conclusion that I had never been converted. I could find in it no encouragement to think that I had ever been spiritually born, and even now while I am writing I feel that it is doubtful at least. Whatever religious feeling or principle I may have would naturally be the result of such an education as I have rec'd. I believe in the inspiration of the Bible

[31] Mrs. Kirkland lived in Utica and was active in church circles. In additon to William, there is also evidence of another son, Charles.

[32] The Reverend Doctor George W. Eaton was a distinguished professor and future president of Madison University and the Hamilton Theological Institution. He had a warm relationship with the Sheldon-Anable families, especially while they were at the Utica Female Academy. Mrs. Eaton was his wife.

and that God was manifest in the flesh and suffered death that all might live—but I cannot say he suffered for me. I have a kind of faith but I am afraid it is not Scriptural and some desire after holiness but they are very faint. I wish really that I had some good friend who could advise me, but I know that would be of no use— I must seek aid from above. I am going to spend the Feb'y vacation with Aunt U[33].—and shall have a good frank talk with the Dr.[34] He is a good man and will talk kindly and wisely to me and I can set him right on whatever wrong notions he may have of an old affair of mine. Aunt U. and Mary Pearson made us a short visit about a fortnight since and Aunt U. has not appeared so like herself since last Spring. Matilda Berthoud[35] has been making me a visit. Her home is a very [ ] [ ] since the death of her mother. She is anxious to come here next Spring and I think will come. She does not want to teach and I don't know what she will do. I feel as if she was on my hands and I must provide for her. If I knew of any one [sic] who was good enough for her I should try and do as most mothers would under similar circumstances—marry her off. You see—whatever notions I may have with regard to myself individually—I think most women had better marry and have some body [sic] to take care of them.

Then I have just been to see Mary Jones[36]—she sends a great deal of love to you. Did I tell you how poor Eugenia Damaux[37] had lost her sister Mary? Annette and her father have returned to France and now poor Eugenia is quite alone. The

---

[33] See vol. 1, "Cast of Characters," s.v. "Nott, Urania Sheldon."

[34] The Reverend Doctor Eliphalet Nott was the president of Union College in Schenectady, New York. An ordained Presbyterian minister, he was married to Urania Sheldon Nott, the sister of Miss Cynthia Sheldon and Mrs. Alma Anable and the aunt of Anna Maria Anable.

[35] Matilda was a friend of Anna Maria Anable and probably of Emily as well, for Anna Maria's and Miss Sheldon's letters refer to her. In one letter, Miss Sheldon tells how Anna Maria had gone to visit Matilda, and while there, Matilda's brother had taken Anna Maria for a buggy ride. Somehow the horse got frightened, and Anna Maria and her host were taken on a wild ride, which they survived by the heroic actions of the brother, the undaunted courage of Anna Maria, and the providence of God. In a letter shortly after their move to Philadelphia in 1848, Miss Sheldon says that Matilda is everything to them. She is perfectly happy being with them, and she adds that she is a "host in French." When Henry and Edward went to Hamilton to live with Emily's parents and sister, Matilda was one of the individuals considered to be employed to help with work around the house and with the care of the family.

[36] Mary Jones was the wife of Morven Jones. They lived in the Utica area and were intimately familiar with Miss Cynthia Sheldon and the staff and student body of the Utica Female Academy. Mr. and Mrs. Jones, as well as Miss Sheldon, were members of the Bleecker Street Baptist church where Mr. Corey was the pastor. In a December 1848 series of letters to Emily, Morven Jones described a terrible accident; a group from the church was standing on a bridge overlooking the Mohawk River, there to witness a baptism, and the bridge collapsed. At least one person died in that accident, and Mary Jones was severely injured.

[37] Eugenia Damaux was part of Emily's intimate circle of friends at the Utica Female Academy. Living in New York City, Eugenia suffered from some kind of eye problem that at times made life difficult for her; this was a matter of comment in many of the letters exchanged between the girls themselves and with Miss Cynthia Sheldon. In 1848, Eugenia was in New York living "at Mrs. Brown's—the same warm-hearted French girl as ever." In 1849, she married Johnny Edmonds, described as rich and pious, and they lived in Utica.

Browns are very kind to her. We very seldom hear from Mary Barber[38]—and I don't know what she is doing with herself.

Nell and Olivia[39] are having a rare time in Sheboygan.[40] Everything looks bright to them but Court[41] tells another sort of story. To tell the truth he would never do for a clerk and merchant. I wish (he) was good enough for a Minister—I should like very much to see him a good faithful clergyman. He has no fancy for this however, and will go on Lake Superior again probably.

We have had a visit from very good brother Giles, he is one of the most pious men I know of. I believe I have not written you before since the girls left[42] [ ] about six weeks since. We dreaded to have them go very much. We had all had such a charming Summer together, that I could not bear our little family circle should be broken—but I presume it is for the best. No doubt it will be a good thing for Molly,[43] if her health is spared and I hope Hatty's[44] health will continue to improve there. Molly writes in rare spirits. She enjoyed the journey on very much and every thing she sees interests or amuses her. Now Nemmy dear do write very often and tell me all about your house and your children and all the friends. Why, I [ ] a spe-

---

[38] Mary Barber was mentioned frequently in the Emily Chubbuck Judson letters; she was a student and then a teacher at the Utica Female Academy. There were ups and downs to that relationship; in fall 1845, apparently Mary had written to someone expressing what Anna Maria Anable called "ingratitude," and Mary had been banned from the Academy until she made proper apologies to Miss Sheldon. In a September 7, 1845 letter from Anna Maria, we learn that her remarks had been about Miss Cynthia Sheldon. In November 1847 Jane Kelly remarked that they had not heard from Mary in over a year. In 1848 Mary Barber was back at the Utica Female Seminary teaching with Jane Kelly. Though at this time Miss Sheldon had moved to Philadelphia, Mary Barber had been able to reconcile with her, and in later years we find Mary very close to the Sheldon—Anable families; later, there was considerable consternation on Miss Cynthia Sheldon's part in her correspondence with Emily about Mary's health, the seriousness of it, and Mary's impending death. These letters were written in April 1852. Miss Sheldon went to help transfer Mary to Albany in June 1852, where she would be better situated and perhaps have access to better doctors. On September 9, 1852, Anna Maria Anable wrote to Emily of Mary Barber's death.

[39] Olivia Williams Anable. See Anna Maria Anable's letter of September 27, 1846, for the news of Miss Williams's marriage to William Stewart Anable, Anna Maria's brother.

[40] After their marriage, William and Olivia Anable went to Sheboygan, Wisconsin, where Will was going to open a store.

[41] Courtland Anable was a younger brother of Anna Maria Anable. He held several positions over the years, and he studied at Hamilton College while he boarded for a time with Emily's parents. In 1853, he returned to Philadelphia where he preached his first sermon at the Eleventh Baptist Church. He was "Uncle Court" to Emily Frances Judson. In 1880, Courtland Anable was listed in the Massachusetts Census as an ordained minister serving in a church.

[42] Hatty and Molly had taken positions in New Orleans. Hatty returned to the home in which she had been previously situated. See the letter of Miss Cynthia Sheldon to Emily dated September 29, 1846.

[43] Molly was Mary Anable, a sister to Anna Maria and Hatty Anable.

[44] Harriet or "Hatty" or "Hattie" or "Hat" Anable was one of nine children born to Joseph and Alma Anable, and was a niece to Miss Cynthia Sheldon and Mrs. Urania Sheldon Nott. In 1841, she had added a note to a letter written by Miss Cynthia Sheldon to Emily. As early as November 1842 she was away, and a letter from Emily to Catharine Chubbuck said that "she (Miss Sheldon) expected that Hat would return as accomplished as Anna Maria." Her trips away were both educational and employment, as she worked as a private tutor in families that would bring her into their homes. In August 1843, she had just returned from Beonsen, in the vicinity of New Orleans, and was engaged to go again. A letter from Anna Maria on January 6, 1845 said that she would stay South for another year. About this time Miss Cynthia Sheldon mentioned her concern for Hatty's spiritual health. In May 1845 she was in New Orleans. She was home again in summer 1846, but a September 27 letter from Anna Maria said she had been asked by Mr. Roman with some urgency to return and she thought that she should. She was to return home from New Orleans in January 1849 after Anna Maria Anable had started the Misses Anable's School in Philadelphia in fall 1848. Harriet was fluent in French, having placed herself earlier in a French environment in New Orleans. Hatty died in 1858.

cial and peculiar interest in every body [*sic*] that has ever been to Maulmain. I see notices of one or two returning families and I really want to see them. Can it be that I should never see you and the Dr. again I cannot feel reconciled to it. Won't you turn right round to the Dr. and give him one good kiss for me and tell him to kiss you back and try and think it is a kiss from your own little Ninny.[45] O, how I wish that indeed I was standing by you both! I must write to Lydia.[46] Jul.[47] and Sarah[48] are [Note: Written along the right margin of page 6.] going to write themselves so I suppose they will tell you of their affairs. Casswell[49] is here and I like him right well.

    A. M.

Source: American Baptist Historical Society, AJ 13, no. 508.

Emily C. Judson to her Journal, January 5, 1847

It seems to me as though I do nothing but get up, turn round, and then go to bed again! I believe there never was such a novice in housekeeping; and then the children, and the language, and the thousand and one other botherations! I expected to make a rush at the language, take it by storm, then get a parcel of natives about me, and go to work in "true apostolic style." Not that I had the vanity to think

---

[45] "Ninny" was a name of endearment given to Anna Maria Anable by her most intimate friends at the Utica Female Academy. Emily was "Nemmy."

[46] Lydia Lillybridge was one of Emily's closest friends at the Utica Female Academy. When Emily made the decision to go to Burmah as the wife of Adoniram Judson and as a missionary, Lydia wanted to go with them. Emily spoke to Adoniram Judson of Lydia's extraordinary abilities, and Adoniram advocated her appointment before Dr. Solomon Peck and the Board of the American Baptist Missionary Union. Lydia was commissioned to go with them, in spite of the fact that she remained single. Always independent, outspoken, and unafraid to cause ripples in the missionary community, Lydia served on the mission field for twenty-eight years. She married missionary Thomas Simons in May 1851. See the timeline on the life and service of Lydia Lillybridge Simons in vol. 1.

[47] Julia Look was a student of Emily's at the Utica Female Academy and later a fellow teacher. A November 22, 1845 letter from Anna Maria encouraged Emily to stay in Philadelphia for the winter for her health and remarked that Julia had the hardest part because she was teaching Emily's composition class, and the students kept asking for Emily. In a September, 1847 letter, she was listed as one of the teachers at the Utica Female Academy. On September 23, 1849, Anna Maria wrote that Julia and Albert B. Casswell were married and came to visit with her. In one 1849 letter Julia spoke of another teacher who was teaching "our composition class." On October 27, 1850, Anna Maria Anable noted that she had had a son. She was one of a small number of people who addressed Emily as "Nemmy" in her letters.

[48] Sarah Bell Wheeler was a teacher at the Utica Female Academy, an intimate of Emily Chubbuck, and one of the few who addressed Emily as "Nemmy." In a September 1847 letter, she was listed as one of the teachers at the Utica Female Academy. There are a number of letters from Sarah Bell before and after her marriage to Charles Gould of Boston in October 1850. There are several letters clustered in the year or two after Emily left for Burmah and a number at the time of her return to America. Emily stayed with Charles and Sarah Bell Gould in October 1851 when she arrived in Boston after the long sea voyage from Burmah and then England. She stayed there a number of times following that. In 1851, Anna Maria Anable wrote of Sarah Bell: "Sarah is grown so lovely in person as well as character that she must assert a blessed influence on all with whom she comes in contact."

[49] In an 1849 letter to Emily, Sarah Hinckley tells her that Mr. Casswell and Julia Look have been married. In April and May 1853, there are two letters to Emily from Mr. Casswell. Apparently, he had invested some money for Emily, and the letters are a defense of the fact that he took a fee for the transaction; Emily had called the fee into question.

---

myself very apostle-like, but I know, O my Heavenly Father, that Thou canst bless the very meanest of Thy children if they but look up to Thee. And I will continue to look; for though my work is not what I expected, Thou canst bring great results from little causes. It is all of Thy ordering.

Source: A. C. Kendrick, *Life and Letters of Mrs. Emily C. Judson*, 246–47.

Emily C. Judson to her Journal, January 6, 1847

We are looking toward Rangoon, and I pray that we may succeed in going. God's "ways are not as our ways," and His time may be nearer than we suspect. But it is very, very pleasant here. Many think we are not wise in going to Rangoon, and perhaps we are not. But if God's time *should* be at hand, we might regret that we had held back. At any rate, it is good to stand in the way of His providences; and I do not wish to stay here until I become attached to the comforts of the place.

Source: A. C. Kendrick, *Life and Letters of Mrs. Emily C. Judson*, 247; Hanna family files.

Emily C. Judson to her Journal, January 10, 1847

This taking care of teething babies, and teaching darkies to darn stockings, and talking English back end foremost to teetotum John, in order to get an eatable dinner is really very odd sort of business for Fanny Forester.[50] I wonder what my respectable friends of the anti-F. F. school would say, if they could see my madamly airs. But I begin to get reconciled to my minute cares. I believe women were made for such things; though when I get settled, I hope to put in a mixture of higher and better things, too. But the person who would do great things well, must practice daily on little ones; and she who would have the assistance of the Almighty in important acts, must be daily and hourly accustomed to consult His will in the minor affairs of life.

Source: A. C. Kendrick, *Life and Letters of Mrs. Emily C. Judson*, 247; Hanna family files.

Emily C. Judson to her Journal, January 11, 1847

I did hope that when I got to the antipodes, I should find a spot where it was not a ladylike *duty* to spend half one's time on dressing and the other half in shewing

---

[50] Emily Chubbuck wrote under the *nom de plume* Fanny Forester. Asked about it once, she said, "Would anyone buy a book written by Emily E. Chubbuck?"

[sic] off the dress. But no; to "dress for calls" etc. etc. is quite as necessary here as at home. L.[51] is to meet the lady commissioner to night [sic], and she has been down to inquire what she shall wear. I am glad I decided not to go; and now I mean to resolve once for all on an independent course. I will never ape English fashions, in dress or in anything else; and I will never get entangled in English society. I mean to be an humble, quiet, useful missionary-wife; and I will hoard every moment of precious time as the miser hoards his gold.

Source: Hanna family files.

Emily C. Judson to her Journal, January 12, 1847

L.[52] had a pleasant evening and wishes I had been there. She says my notions about dress have changed; but it is not so. When I was in society it would have been wrong not to follow in some degree the prevailing fashion; but I am not in society here and never mean to be. My duty is to the heathen, and they cannot tell the difference between a stylish dress and a plain one. Something is due to my husband's taste, to my own sense of neatness and propriety and to my missionary associates. Beyond that I have fully resolved never to have anybody to please. As though I left everything in my own beautiful America to come out here and dawdle away my time among strangers and foreigners.

Source: Hanna family files.

Emily C. Judson to her Journal, January 13, 1847

It is late, and we have spent the greater part of the evening in talking over old times. O, how I rejoice that I am out of the whirlpool! Too gay, too trifling for a missionary's wife! That may be, but after all, gayety is my lightest sin. It is my coldness of heart, my listlessness, my want of faith, my spiritual inefficiency and inertness, my love of self, the inherent and every day pampered sinfulness of my nature, that makes me such a mere infant in the cause of Christ—not the attractions of the world. [Note: This has been added in someone else's handwriting: "mem. How to become spiritually minded."]

Source: A. C. Kendrick, *Life and Letters of Mrs. Emily C. Judson*, 247; Hanna family files.

---

[51] See vol. 1, "Cast of Characters," s.v. "Lillybridge, Miss," also the timeline "Lydia Lillybridge Simons."
[52] Ibid.

Emily C. Judson to her Journal, January 14, 1847

I did not think that I should feel so sad to be left alone only these few weeks; but the prospect actually makes my heart faint. We have been daily and hourly together ever since our marriage, and his presence is my very life. I hear his step now, as he goes from room to room, making all the arrangements in his power for my comfort. So thoughtful! so tender! so delicate! O, there are few on earth so blest as I! And how kind must be my heavenly Friend, to lead me in such a pleasant, path, and make a place for me in such a heart!

Source: A. C. Kendrick, *Life and Letters of Mrs. Emily C. Judson*, 247–48.

Emily C. Judson[53]

To An Infant
The glittering wing, that a leaf might crush,
A silvery voice, that a breath might hush,
A dew-drop, quivering on a flower,
The flickering blush of the sunset hour,
The chain of pearls round the brow of night,
That melts and is lost in the morning light,—
All things gentle, pure and free,
And fragile, are but types of thee.

Source: Emily Judson, *Alderbrook*, Volume I, Page 278.

---

[53] This poem and the one that follows it are two of six that appeared in the subsequent editions of *Alderbrook* after the first edition was published. We believe that these six were poems that Emily wrote (or rewrote as she did "The Weaver") on the journey from Boston to Burmah in the twenty weeks that they were at sea.

A Wish

'T is beautiful! 'tis beautiful.
    That soft, rich, half-veiled light,
Flung by the beams which warmed the day,
    Upon the brow of night.

So when life's golden day shall close,
    And on my mother's breast
I slumbering lie, may love still smile
    Upon my shadowy rest.

Source: Emily Judson, *Alderbrook*, Volume I, Page 278.

Emily C. Judson to her Journal, January 16, 1847

Not well to-day. I slept but an hour or two last night, and that very brokenly. I suppose it is foolish in me to allow this matter to weigh so heavily upon my spirits; but it is a little solace to my wounded vanity that I am not the only foolish one. If men who have been through prisons and all perils weep at such separations, surely such a weakling as I should not be put in a strait-jacket. The truth is, we poor humans are utterly baffled in attempting to estimate each other's sufferings. I will venture to assert that it required a far greater effort in Ann H. Judson to leave her husband (such a husband!) in Rangoon, and go to America alone,[54] than to play the heroic part in his presence, and for his sake, that she did at Ava.[55]

But dear J.'s going to Rangoon for two or three weeks is not my going to America, and I must try not to be quite a fool. What would people in America, who believe that missionaries are or ought to be destitute of natural affection, say to this struggle? But they can not [sic] know of it, and I shall be the last to tell. Let them think, if they like, that I came on a literary speculation, and so made merchandise of myself for ambition, as some have done for the sake of religion. How little they know the hearts of either of us. And what a blessing that God is omniscient!

Source: A. C. Kendrick, *Life and Letters of Mrs. Emily C. Judson*, 248; Hanna family files.

---

[54] Ann Hasseltine Judson embarked for the United States on August 21, 1822, in an effort to regain her fragile health. She returned to Burmah on December 5, 1823.

[55] When Adoniram suffered the terrible privations of prison during the Burmese-English war, it was the daily visits of Ann which brought hope and strength to see him through. Surely these visits were difficult for Ann, emotions and fears that no doubt she would try to control, if not hide.

Anna Maria Anable to Emily C. Judson, January 17, 1847[56]

Dear dear Nemmy[57]

How I wish I would know what you are about to night [sic]. I said I should not wish again till I heard, but Martha must make room for this little note. I have just laid down the Life of Lavarty [sic], and as I read I cannot help wondering whether you are much interested yet in the welfare of those "yaller [sic] boys and girls." There is something in the enthusiasm of those Germans that is quite inspiring—contagious. Should the German mind once become thoroughly awakened to spirituality in religion would there not be a nation of missionaries? The French and German both seem to me to have the elements of real apostolic zeal in them. I have been a good deal interested lately in reading accounts of the Moravian church. I suppose it is one of the purest establishments for so arbitrary a one that was ever formed. Now I don't mean to be any more [sic] prosy than I can help, tho' as it is Sunday night and after ten o'clock 'twould be some excusable. On second thought I won't write any more to night, so kiss good nighty.

Source: American Baptist Historical Society, AJ 13, no. 507.

Anna Maria Anable to Emily C. Judson, January 18, 1847[58]

What do you think I have been doing for a wonder? Nothing more nor less than reading some half dozen numbers of the "Home Journal."[59] You know Morris[60] and Willis[61] were editing together again didn't you? I have not had curiosity enough to look at the paper till this morning I read with the intention of subscribing if it was worth it, but Palms and Pico and Grace Kilawood [sic] have sickened me. I don't believe Willis has much to do with it. One thing shows the tender heartedness of his nature. Poe[62] has been ill, and he is poor and his wife is dying, but notwithstanding his former abuse of Willis, he has written him now a letter full of grateful hearty affection, which shows that tho' most of his friends had deserted him, Willis looking upon him as a man of genius had been kind to him. It is almost inconceiv-

[56] This letter has an addendum dated January 18, 1847.

[57] Emily Chubbuck. See vol. 1, "Cast of Characters," s.v. "Nemmy, Nem, or Nemmy Petty (Nemmie Pettie)." Also the chapter "Names of Endearment."

[58] This letter is an addendum to a letter dated January 17, 1847.

[59] This was a new magazine being published by N. P. Willis and General George Morris, who collaborated formerly with the Mirror and New Mirror.

[60] See vol. 1, "Cast of Characters," s.v. "Morris, General George."

[61] See vol. 1, "Cast of Characters," s.v. "Willis, Nathaniel Parker."

[62] Edgar Allen Poe. In an 1850 publication of poems by Edgar Allen Poe, there were significant contributions written as memorials by George Graham and N. P. Willis. Poe had a relationship with Fanny Osgood. For more information on this relationship, see vol. 1, "Cast of Characters," s.v. "Osgood, Fanny."

able how little interested I am in that sort of literature. I never look into *Graham*[63] now tho' it comes regularly to the house. By the way you have done the right thing on writing for the *Columbian*[64] and for any thing [*sic*] of that kind. I think that notwithstanding *Graham's* efforts that it stands higher than the other. I wish you *would* write for it once in a while. If for nothing else just to let folks know that you dared. Mrs. Conant[65] has written some for it. The *Christian Watchman*,[66] which I take is one of the best of religious papers—I think it is more interesting than the *New York Observer*. They always say just the right thing too about you and your books.

Ugh! how I wish we had a little tropical heat this cold blustery morning. I shrank into almost nothing and I feel as black and blue as the donor's book.

The term is drawing to a close and we are all busy. There is a concert to be attended to night [*sic*] and a picture to be seen to morrow [*sic*] and a sculptor's rooms to visit next day, and our music scholars must play in the school rooms, and next week Horace gets up a concert at which of course I must assist and then the trustees visit the school a whole week—now don't you pity me? I wish could [*sic*] wrap myself up in a blanket and lie under the stove like pussy.

I anticipate a nice time visiting Aunt U.[67] and if I don't have it I won't stay. I'll either go to W[ ] and see our sweet sister Sarah and her little boy, or I'll go to Troy

---

[63] George Graham was the editor of *Graham's Magazine*, one of the preeminent literary magazines of Emily's time. He took an interest in Emily Chubbuck as Fanny Forester; he mentored her and published every piece of writing that she could submit to him, and for it all, he remunerated her with the astounding sum of five dollars a page. In April 1845, when Emily was staying in Philadelphia with the Reverend and Mrs. A. D. Gillette, Mr. and Mrs. Graham were frequent visitors, often inviting Emily to tour parts of the city with them in their elegant carriage. That relationship picked up again when Emily returned to Philadelphia in fall 1845.

[64] The *Columbian* was one of the magazines that Emily had written for during the years of her literary career. After leaving for Burmah, she agreed to write exclusively for them; a long piece on her journey to Burmah was to be published in the August, 1847 issue. See the letters of Robert West dated March 3 and April 28, 1846.

[65] Anna Maria's negative comments about Mrs. Conant in her letter of July 31, 1848, are quite interesting, if not surprising. In a May 1846 letter, Emily said that she had found Mrs. Conant quite "agreeable." In spite of Anna Maria's feelings, Mrs. Conant was an accomplished scholar. She wrote a number of articles and books about the Bible and was considered competent in the biblical field. Earlier letters indicate that she called on Emily a number of times when she was in Hamilton, and the references are always cordial. When Emily returned to the United States, a warm letter from Mrs. Conant invited her to stay with her should she come to Rochester. After the publication of the Judson memoir, written by Francis Wayland in collaboration with Emily Judson, Emily planned to write an abridgement of those two volumes as a more popular offering. As Emily's health deteriorated in late 1853 and it became increasingly obvious that she would be unable to take on such a task, Mrs. Conant was asked to take the responsibility for that project, and eventually it was published as: *The Earnest Man: A Memoir of Adoniram Judson, DD, First Missionary to Burmah.*

[66] The *Christian Watchman* was a prominent religious paper that had been started in Boston in 1819. In these years (1838–1848), it was under the leadership of the Reverend William Crowell; Mr. Crowell wrote to Emily on July 10, 1846, asking her to contribute articles to the *Watchman* from Burmah.

[67] See vol. 1, "Cast of Characters," s.v. "Nott, Urania Sheldon."

and spend all the vacation frolicking with Master W. Judson Buckingham[68] who is the brightest, meanest little rogue that ever tore a mother's collars.

We receive letters from the girls every week. Hatty[69] likes her situation very much. Molly[70] is still with her tho' she talks quite largely about putting on a cap and spectacles and passing off for forty. It seems they think she is too young to teach. There are plenty of situations, but Mr. Roman won't let her go until he finds the right place. Poor Nora Westcott[71] is in Mississippi but dying of consumption. Lou Marble[72] had a letter from her sister last week. Mary Jerome also has the consumption. Sarah Hinckley[73] is in Virginia and wed I believe—but what a scattering there has been since last Spring. Lou is almost the only one of the old set left—and she seems to feel quite [Note: This is page 5 of the letter. It is written across and perpendicular to the text of page 4.] disconsolate. I pity Lou. She wants to write but she don't [sic] exactly know how—and she don't [sic] know what to do with herself any way [sic]. I wish she was [sic] a decidedly religious girl. She is very thoughtful but I don't think she is pious. She is resolved to stay with us—tho' she studies nothing but Music. I don't much wonder—for her talents are buried in that little village where her home is.

[68] Fanny Buckingham was the daughter of Fred and Martha Sheldon. She was a niece to Miss Cynthia Sheldon and a cousin to Anna Maria Anable. She was married to Mr. Buckingham, the second in command of the ill-fated steamship *Swallow*, which went down on the river with the loss of a significant number of passengers. (See the letter of Miss Cynthia Sheldon to Emily E. Chubbuck dated April 11, 1845.) Fanny Buckingham was mentioned in Anna Maria's letters of December 28 and 29, 1847. She had a young son Judson, and she was visiting Anna Maria.

[69] See vol. 1, "Cast of Characters," s.v. "Anable, Harriet."

[70] Mary Juliet Anable was born February 18, 1830 in Bethlehem, Albany County, New York, one of nine children born to Alma and Joseph Anable. She went to New Orleans with Hatty in 1847, but she returned home early in March 1848, and by 1849, she was working with Anna Maria in the Misses Anable's School in Philadelphia. Writing in March 1849, Hatty said of Mary, "She paints and draws, speaks French, plays the piano, sings, dances and is our mathematician. What should we ever do without her? She laughs from morning till night, and it is really refreshing to be with her." On December 26, 1860, she was married to Pierre Jacques Darey, the officiating minister being the Rev. Dr. Eliphalet Nott, her uncle. Mary died at the age of sixty-eight on April 20, 1898 in Ottawa, Ontario, Canada.

[71] Nora Westcott was one of the girls from the Utica Female Academy. On January 17, 1847, Anna Maria Anable noted that Nora was in Mississippi, though dying of consumption. In November 1849, Sarah Hinckley spoke of her death.

[72] In 1843, Miss Marble was a recent graduate of the Utica Female Seminary and wrote to Emily upon her return to Port Byron. In an 1848 letter to Emily, she was at the academy as a teacher and was fully involved there. According to a letter written by Sarah Hinckley in 1849, Miss Marble married and moved to New York City. In Emily's February 19, 1850 letter, she was referred to as "Lou Marble Wright." Then, in April 1851, Anna Maria mentioned that Louisa Marble Wright was now a widow, back living in Utica with her sister.

[73] Sarah Hinckley was one of the girls from the Utica Female Seminary; there are some letters from her in the collection. Sarah Hinckley was Emily's student at the Utica Female Academy. In an 1849 letter, Miss Hinckley reminisced about that time and brought Emily up to date on many of those who were there with her. She also spoke of the sad farewell when Emily left for Boston and then Burmah.

I suppose there are some letters on the way. I so hope you had a pleasant voyage. Letters have been received from Dr. Dean[74] from Java. It seems they had a delightful voyage. I have never told you what nice times Grand pa[75] and I have together since his sickness. We like the same kind of books and we agree on all subjects. If I like anything particularly nice I run to Grand pa with it and he is sure to like it too. O, he shares so much Christian patience under his afflictions that I love him better than ever for it. He is naturally impatient you know. Give my best love to the Dr. and don't allow one day pass without thinking kindly of this desolate child on this side of the world. Anna Maria

Source: American Baptist Historical Society, AJ 13, no. 507.

Adoniram Judson to Emily C. Judson, January 19, 1847—On Board the *Cecilia*

My Dearest Love,—

I awoke this pleasant morning thinking of you, and imagining how you were sleeping, and how you were getting up, and how you were employing yourself about the children and the house. It seems as if I had been associated with you for many years; and hardly knew how to deport myself in your absence. When I came out of my cabin this morning, we were losing sight of Maulmain, and are now in sight of Amherst. I write this line to send back by Captain Crisp, Sen., who is now on board. I received letters and accounts yesterday from my agents in Calcutta, and put them under the cover containing the other valuable papers; you had better look them over. I only noticed that the balance due me at the close of last year was two thousand six hundred rupees, which is much larger than I expected.

I feel in excellently good spirits in regard to making the attempt at Rangoon, though I see no particular reason to hope for success. I intend to do all that lies in my power, and am quite willing to leave the event in the hands of God. "Trust in

---

[74] The Reverend Doctor William Dean was a distinguished missionary to Hong Kong for more than fifty years. As the pastor of the local church in Morrisville, he baptized Emily Chubbuck when she was seventeen. There are nine letters in the correspondence from Mr. Dean, beginning after Emily's appointment to missionary service. After the death of Adoniram Judson, it was speculated, and not without reasonable support, that William Dean had an interest in taking Judson's place in Emily's life and affections. The later correspondence between Emily and Anna Maria Anable shows that Dr. Dean was often the butt of their ridicule, so something had happened to challenge that relationship. In 1854, when William Dean was courting Mrs. Maria Brown in New York City, Abby Ann Judson was working for Mrs. Brown as an in-house teacher for her children. For the complete story of William Dean's life and the many ways he touched the mission movement and the life of Emily Chubbuck Judson, see vol. 1, "Cast of Characters," s.v. "Dean, William."

[75] Deacon Asa Sheldon was the father of Miss Cynthia Sheldon, Urania Sheldon Nott, and Alma Sheldon Anable. Deacon and Mrs. Sheldon lived with their daughters and grandchildren as a part of the Utica Female Academy community. Mrs. Sheldon died January 29, 1847. Deacon Sheldon continued to have a room at the Utica Female Academy, where he died in March 1848. For many years, he led mealtime prayers for the academy family, and Deacon and Mrs. Sheldon were popular with the students, who often looked in on them.

God and keep your powder dry," was Cromwell's word to his soldiers. Trust in God and love one another is, I think, a better watchword. Let us do the duties of religion and of love, and all will be well. Conjugal love stands first. Happy those who find that duty and pleasure coincide. Then comes parental love and filial love; then love to associates, and then love all that come within our reach. I have been talking with Crisp this two hours, and you see I have become quite ethical.

Sweet love, I wish I could reason out the subject, and come to a satisfactory solution on your lips. Farewell for the present.

Ever thine, A. Judson.

Source: A. C. Kendrick, *The Life and Letters of Mrs. Emily C. Judson*, 251–52.

Adoniram Judson to Emily C. Judson, January 20, 1847—On Board the *Cecilia*

My Dearest Love,—

We are just passing between the two buoys off Amherst, the pilot's boat is coming off, and he will leave us in an hour. I write a line by him, but it may not reach you immediately. Another beautiful morning. The hopia tree[76] is just visible from the shore. I seem to have lived in several worlds; but you are the earthly sun that illuminates my present. My thoughts and affections revolve around you, and cling to your form, and face, and lips. Other luminaries have been extinguished in death. I think of them with mournful delight, and anticipate the time when we shall all shine together as the brightness of the firmament and as the stars for ever and ever.

I should be glad to get a line from you and the children before I lose sight of the coast; but it can not [sic] be. I trust I shall get something by the *Erwin*, in which Captain Antram is to take passage. Pray take care of yourself.—I left four books at the printing-office to be bound. Ask brother Ranney[77] about them, and when you get them, I should be glad to have you read the memoir of Hester Ann Rogers. Once more farewell, dearest and best. "Think of me sweet, when alone."

---

[76] This is the hopia tree that was lovingly placed at the head of the grave of Ann Hasseltine Judson. She died in Amherst in 1826. Little Maria Judson was buried there the next year.

[77] Thomas Ranney was appointed to missionary service in June 1843, arriving in Burmah in May 1844. He was an important part of the Judsons' lives while in Rangoon. He was superintendent of the printing press in Maulmain and business manager for the compound. Thomas Ranney went with Adoniram Judson on his last voyage, and thus was with him when he died. There is a letter in the collection from the *Aristide Marie* written five days before Adoniram Judson's death; one of the things he did at the time of death was to take some locks of his hair to bring to Emily. She later sent one of these locks to Adoniram's sister Abigail in Plymouth. Thomas Ranney provided the accounts of Adoniram's last voyage and his last hours of life. He also handled some of the financial matters for the mission and in the settlement of Adoniram Judson's estate. Thomas Ranney was married to Maria Gager, who died in 1857, and then to Mary E. Bennett, the daughter of missionaries Cephas and Stella Bennett.

Yours ever,
A. Judson

Source: A. C. Kendrick, *The Life and Letters of Mrs. Emily C. Judson*, 252.

Emily C. Judson to her Journal, January 20, 1847

All alone, and so lonely! My life is one continued heartache, for I continually feel as though he was dead. My family worship is broken by tears, for it is *his* business; and when I attempt to bless the food at meals, my voice sometimes utterly fails. Alone with the children about me, and trying to fill his place, I feel widowed indeed. I have but one refuge, and this helps me to live. I know too that he is praying for me.

Source: A. C. Kendrick, *Life and Letters of Mrs. Emily C. Judson*, 248–49; Hanna family files.

Emily C. Judson to Adoniram Judson January 20, 1847—Maulmain

My Own Blessed Darling,—

I have been exceedingly distressed about writing to you, for I thought you would be worried about us, and have no opportunity of hearing until your return. Captain Antram has, however, just sent word that he leaves early to-morrow morning, and so I sit down in my night-dress to tell you that all is going on like clock-work. There has been a robbery in the printing-office, and so I have got two of Mrs. Howard's[78] scholars to sleep with Moung Shway Kyo, and they do sleep! Captain A.'s servant made plenty of noise, and I walked fairly over them to the door, but they are snoring still. Little Edward[79] is quite well again, though I was obliged to go to Mrs. S.[80] about him again, being unwilling to call a physician, unless obliged to.

We have heard that the king is really assassinated. I am prepared for almost any thing [*sic*] strange, and I think that these various overturnings *must* turn up something favorable to our object. How good of you, darling, to write me those two sweet letters, when I didn't expect any! They made me cry, like the baby that I am, in gratitude. Oh, if we are ever safely together again, I will follow you wherever you

---

[78] A graduate of the Hamilton, New York seminary, Hosea Howard and his wife Theresa first sailed for Burmah in 1834, arriving in December that year. They were stationed in Maulmain as missionaries with Adoniram Judson, and Mr. Howard claimed in a letter to Emily that he had worked there with Adoniram longer than any other missionary. Mr. Howard ran schools that the mission maintained, a task in which he was ably assisted by his wife. Lydia Lillybridge was responsible to Mr. and Mrs. Howard when she arrived in November 1846. Mr. and Mrs. Howard left Maulmain for the United States in February 1850.

[79] See vol. 1, "Cast of Characters," s.v. "Judson, Edward."

[80] See vol. 1, "Cast of Characters," s.v. "Stevens, Elizabeth 'Bessie.'"

go, in spite of difficulties. Not that every thing [*sic*] is not pleasant now, but these separations are not good. I look in my room and through my dressing-room window up to the chapel for you every day in vain. And you;—I think of you, darling, although I write about myself. I think of you on the sea, perhaps in danger; on the land, alone and exposed to—what? Oh, if I could only know precisely what!

I have no choice at all between Maulmain and Rangoon. Decide as you shall think best. I know you will not let this world's comforts weigh with you, and yet you will be prudent.

Farewell, my "home," my life, my all but God and heaven. Farewell for a little while, but come as soon as possible. May the best blessing of Heaven be about thee, my precious, precious husband (my heart bounds with pride and pleasure as my pen first addresses thee by this title, darling); may the blessing of Heaven be upon thee, and all sad thoughts and remembrances be kept far away. So prays daily,

Thy loving wife,

Emily

I have not let the clock run down, nor neglected to feed the fowls!!

Source: A. C. Kendrick, *The Life and Letters of Mrs. Emily C. Judson*, 253–54.

Adoniram Judson to Emily C. Judson, January 23, 1847[81]—Off Rangoon

My Dearest Love,

We are just anchoring, and I write a line to be ready for any vessel that may be going out, as I go ashore. We have had a pleasant passage; but very light winds have kept us on our way till this Saturday morning, though, as you recollect, we went on board, at Maulmain, Monday forenoon. I know not what reception awaits me on shore, but shall endeavor to let you know before I close the letter.

Four o'clock, P.M. Dreadfully tired in getting my few things from the ship and through the custom house. I am now writing in Captain Crisp's brick house, who invites me to stay and make myself at home. Have yet seen no government people, nor any house that is to be let; so that I can write nothing definite about future prospects. I would not close this letter without something more satisfactory, but I hear that a vessel is just leaving for Maulmain; and I know you will be anxious to hear from me. You may be sure my heart remains in the right place; but I am too much exhausted to say how much I miss your presence, and long to see you once more.

---

[81] This letter has an addendum dated January 24, 1847.

Yours ever,

A. Judson

Evening. I have seen a large brick house, the one we heard of in Maulmain, for the upper part of which the owner demanded one hundred rupees a month, but I beat him down to fifty. It contains six or eight rooms, some quite large; but there are but few lights, and the place looks as gloomy as a prison. It is situated in a street of Mussulmans—not a foot of ground belonging to the upper story, except a path to a spacious cook house, and a shabby horse stable, but which might be improved. I shrink at taking you and the children into such a den, and fear you would pine and die in it. But the old town—the new I have not yet seen—looks much better than I expected, though very much inferior to Maulmain. No dust in the streets, which are paved most unevenly with brick, so that it is very difficult walking or riding. Tomorrow is Sunday, and I shall not go out much. Expect to have an interview with the governor, on Monday. The Portuguese magistrate, who tried to annoy the brethren last here, is absent at Amarapura. It is after ten o'clock; you have already retired, and I am going to creep under the curtains that were dear Abby's.[82] O my poor heart! It is torn into ten thousand pieces. How happy we shall be when we rest in the grave, and find ourselves together in paradise! Had a long discussion with—, and hope that he will give up his infidelity. Farewell, dear love. When I turn away from all the filth and wretchedness around me, and think of you, it seems like looking from hell to heaven. How can I take you from all the comforts of Maulmain, and shut you up in this den?

Source: Francis Wayland, *A Memoir of the Life and Labors of the Rev. Adoniram Judson, DD* (Boston: Phillips, Sampson, and Company, 1853) 2:272–74.

Adoniram Judson to Emily C. Judson, January 24, 1847[83]

Have taken a stroll through the place with Crisp. Great, crowded population. Immense field for quiet missionary operation. Several of the converts are coming to see me. Unless I meet with a decided repulse from the governor tomorrow, which nobody anticipates, my mind is about made up to prosecute the "Pass of Splugen." I am going to have a little worship with the converts, but must send off this letter without further delay. Expect to take return passage in the *Gyne*, which sails in three, or four, or five days.

Farewell again, dearest love.

---

[82] See vol. 1, "Cast of Characters," s.v. "Judson, Abby Ann."

[83] This letter is an addendum to a letter dated January 23, 1847.

A. Judson

Source: Francis Wayland, *A Memoir of the Life and Labors of the Rev. Adoniram Judson, DD*, 2:274.

Emily C. Judson to her Journal, January 27, 1847

As I lay alone upon my pillow to-day, my head racked with nervous pain, and the children frolicking about the rooms, many strange thoughts passed through my mind. What are God's designs toward me, that my life from the very cradle has been such an uninterrupted chain of discipline? Has He been preparing me for any unheard of sufferings? Does He intend to make me an instrument in accomplishing some mighty good? Or is all this designed merely to fit my own soul for the inheritance of the saints? If the latter, how ought I to labor and strive to improve by His strange dispensations! I have not yet seen thirty years, and such changes!—such varieties of fortune! I seem to have lived a century. I have been tried both by adversity and prosperity, by undeserved praise and by censure equally undeserved. I have toiled both by night and by day, have been pinched by want and overwhelmed by plenty, and all for what purpose? O, my Heavenly Father, bless unto me all Thy past dispensations, and prepare me for whatever Thou hast marked out for me in future. Make me a good wife, a good mother, and a good teacher of the heathen example which the native converts may safely follow.

Source: A. C. Kendrick, *Life and Letters of Mrs. Emily C. Judson*, 249; Hanna family files.

Adoniram Judson to Emily C. Judson, January 28, 1847—Rangoon

My Dearest Love,

The *Erwin* has just come in, and I have received your sweet letter. I expected to have left to-day in the *Gyne*;[84] but there is no depending on any thing [*sic*] you hear in this country of lies. Whether she will go tomorrow, or the next day, or the day after, I know not; and what is worse, here are—, and—, and—, who have just arrived. All want to crowd into the one only cabin of the *Gyne*, which I had engaged, and I cannot refuse them. I found another little vessel that is going to-morrow, by which I shall send this letter; but it has no cabin at all, nor any place where one could sustain life. But God orders all things well—the comforts and the discomforts, the bitter and the sweet, of this short, flitting life. Among the little vexations I meet with, your letter lies like a cordial in my inmost heart. I will not complain while you are alive, and well, and happy, my precious, darling wife. I am

[84] See the letter of Adoniram Judson to Emily Judson dated January 24, 1847.

glad, too, to hear such good accounts of the children.[85] Give my love to L.[86] I only wish that—was out here; but how it can be brought about, and how we could manage to have her with us in this country, I cannot tell.

Since I wrote last, I have seen the governor. He received me remarkably well—invited me to settle here—promised to give me a place for an English church, that the English might be induced to come to the place, and enjoy the "benefit of clergy"! He approve also of my prosecuting the dictionary, and spoke favorably of my going up to Amarapoora[87] and seeking royal patronage. I have engaged the brick house[88] I mentioned in my last; but I am afraid your spirits will sink to zero when you see it. We shall, however, be together; and we will try to keep one another's spirits up. Living here is more expensive than I thought. Two or three bottles of milk for a rupee, and eight loaves of very poor bread; but fowls and fish are cheaper. The police is well administered; and it is nearly as safe living here as in Maulmain. As to missionary efforts, nothing can be done openly. The system of intolerance is enforced more rigidly than ever. It is not as a missionary or "propagator of religion," but as a minister of a foreign religion, ministering to the foreigners in the place, that I am well received and patronized by the government. The young heir, and his younger brother, who is premier and heir-apparent, are rigid Boodhists, particularly the latter. Boodhism is in full feather throughout the empire. The prospects of a missionary were never darker. But let us aim to obtain the praise bestowed upon Mary—"She has done what she could." I have been to little Roger's[89] grave. There is room for the other children, and for either of us; and I fancy that he sleeps just as quietly here, as those who lie under the British flag.

Evening. I must put a stop to this scrawling letter, and send it to Brown's, in hope that it will reach you somehow. Farewell, my darling love. This separation has taught me more than ever how dear you are to me. May we live to be sources of happiness and promoters of holiness to each other. If we give up all to God, he will take care of us, and bring light out of darkness, and good out of evil, I do believe; and we shall praise him forever, that he led us through some dark ways in his blessed service.

How many expressions in your letter go to my heart, and take it captive! May the light of love and happiness shine around thee evermore is the prayer of

---

[85] The two children at home with Emily were Henry and Edward. Henry was four and a half years old, and Edward was two years old. 1578.

[86] See vol. 1, "Cast of Characters," s.v. "Lillybridge, Miss Lydia." Also the timeline "Lydia Lillybridge Simons."

[87] Amarapoora or Amarapura became the new seat of the Burmese government in 1841 after Ava had been heavily damaged by an earthquake.

[88] See the letter of Adoniram Judson to Emily Judson dated January 23, 1847. For Emily's description and impressions of this house and their experience with bats, see her letter to her sister Catharine Chubbuck dated March 15, 1847.

[89] Roger Williams Judson, the son of Adoniram and Ann Hasseltine Judson. He was born September 11, 1815, and died in May 1816.

Your ever affectionate husband,

A. Judson

Source: Francis Wayland, *A Memoir of the Life and Labors of the Rev. Adoniram Judson, DD*, 2:274–76.

Adoniram Judson to Emily C. Judson, January 29, 1847

My Dearest love,—

The vessel by which I wrote you last night is, I believe, still in the river. She has had the blue Peter (the sailing flag) hoisted ever since we have been here. Such is the endless delay of the place. The *Gyne*, in which I have engaged my passage, will not sail till next Monday; to-day is Friday. I think she will sail then, because Antram and the rest will be anxious to return. No further news. I have made all my inquiries, and done all my business here, and want to be off.

Your precious letter by Rozario came in this morning. I fold you in my inmost heart.

I forgot to mention that for several days I have suffered from an ophthalmic affection of the left eye. It is now better; but I don't like to write by lamp-light, as I am now doing.

So farewell, dear, dear wife, and kiss Henry[90] and Edward[91] for papa,[92] and Lydia[93] too, and keep one eye open in the night.[94]

Yours ever,

A. Judson

Source: A. C. Kendrick, *The Life and Letters of Mrs. Emily C. Judson*, 255.

[90] Henry Hall Judson, born July 8, 1842, was the son of Adoniram and Sarah Hall Boardman Judson. Henry was the sixth of their eight children, the fourth of five who survived. He remained in Burmah in 1845 when Adoniram and Sarah returned to the United States with the three older children. He returned with Emily in 1851 and went to live with her family in Hamilton, New York. Henry attended Brown University and Williams Collage; he enlisted in the army at the time of the Civil War in January 1864. Later that year, he experienced a debilitating accident attributed either to sunstroke or a horse kicking him in the head. He was married once—unhappily according to his own correspondence—and he eventually died in a veteran's home in 1918, the last of his siblings to die. Of this, the chaplain noted, "The end was a genuine example of Christian fortitude." See Rosalie Hall Hunt, *Bless God and Take Courage, The Judson Legacy* (Valley Forge PA: Judson Press, 2005) 291.

[91] See vol. 1, "Cast of Characters," s.v. "Judson, Edward."

[92] Adoniram Judson was "papa" to his children. At the time of his illness before his death, and Adoniram had gone to sea, Emily wrote a beautiful poem, "Prayer for Dear Papa."

[93] See vol. 1, "Cast of Characters," s.v. "Lillybridge, Miss," also the timeline on "Lydia Lillybridge Simons."

[94] In her letter of January 20, Emily wrote that there had been a robbery in the printing office.

Adoniram Judson to Emily C. Judson, January 29, 1847—Rangoon

To Fanny Forester[95] Judson

Tide ebbs and flows, day comes and goes,
The orbs inconstant shine;
One vestal lamp for ever glows,
The thought that thou art mine,

Though now, an exile far remote,
In foreign lands I pine
To catch a glance of thy bright eyes,
I know those eyes are mine.

Though seas and mountains interpose,
And elements combine
To bar the mutual, melting kiss,
I know thy lips are mine.

And though around thy graceful form
In vain I long to twine
My arms, and feel thy beating heart,
I know that heart is mine.

And joy it gives my inmost soul
That, as thy love is mine,
Thou know'st, beyond a shade of doubt,
My constant heart is thine.

Nor death shall loose the bonds of love,
Or cause me to resign
My claim upon thy lifeless form—
In the grave thou shalt be mine.

And when before the Throne we stand,
Arrayed in charms divine,
I shall be thine, and thou, my love,
Be ever, ever mine.

Source: A. C. Kendrick, *The Life and Letters of Mrs. Emily C. Judson*, 254–55.

---

[95] Emily Chubbuck wrote under the *nom de plume* Fanny Forester. Asked about it once, she said, "Would anyone buy a book written by Emily E. Chubbuck?"

Emily C. Judson to Her Journal, January 29 and 30, 1847

January 29, 1847. I am going on beautifully with the language; I do not believe it will be very hard for me.

January 30, 1847. Both children[96] are quite ill to-day, and I am full of cares. O, my poor little motherless boys! I do pray that our Heavenly Father may give me a soft and pitying heart toward you. It is so sad for such mere babies to be torn from their homes and put into a stranger's hands, especially a stranger so inexperienced as I am. How much I need to pray!

Source: A. C. Kendrick, *Life and Letters of Mrs. Emily C. Judson*, 249.

Emily C. Judson to the Rev. Mr. Corey,[97] January 31, 1847[98]— Maulmain

My Dear Mr. Corey,—

I am writing you, merely because I feel like doing so—because I think of you as you used to sit when I went bounding down to Aunt Cynthia's[99] room of a bright morning. I can not [*sic*] write a "missionary letter," and you will not disgrace me by letting anyone see a "common letter" such as I would have written on American soil. So then—to you just as I would chat with you if you were to step in now, and sit down by the square hole which we dignify by calling window. We should be alone, for the Doctor has been gone to Rangoon a couple of weeks, and I have sent the children out, now that the sun is nearly down, to have a frolic upon the grass. The first thing you did probably, would be to remark the difference between our barn-like looking house, and the comfortable ones in Utica; and I should tell you that a Utica house here would be tipped into the river. And so it would; for though they are mere board shanties in comparison, nobody could live in it; then, perhaps,

---

[96] Henry and Edward Judson.

[97] The Reverend Corey and Emily Chubbuck Judson had had a somewhat contentious relationship, with Emily often feeling the brunt of what seemed to be his harsh judgments. He had said something to her family at the time of her engagement to Adoniram Judson, and one letter from Emily suggests that in a conversation between the two of them over these issues, neither one of them would move off of their position. See the letter of Emily E. Chubbuck to Adoniram Judson dated April 13, 1846. This then must be seen as a letter fostering reconciliation.

[98] There is an addendum to this letter, dated February 2, 1847.

[99] Miss Cynthia Sheldon was in charge of the administrative and financial departments of the Utica Female Academy. Miss Sheldon and her sister Urania, who was literary principal, gave Emily Chubbuck a place at the academy in October 1840. They had deferred any cost to a future time when Emily could afford to reimburse them. Upon Miss Urania Sheldon's marriage in the late summer 1842 to the Reverend Doctor Eliphalet Nott, the president of Union College, and her subsequent move to Schenectady, Miss Cynthia Sheldon assumed a larger leadership role at the academy. Active and well-known in Baptist circles, Miss Cynthia was to become an important mentor, advisor, and friend to Emily until the time of Emily's death in 1854. She was the aunt of Emily's best friend, Anna Maria Anable, and was addressed by most as "Aunt Cynthia." In 1848, Miss Sheldon moved to Philadelphia to help Miss Anable with the startup of the Misses Anable's School.

I should tell you that Edward[100] cried in the night (last night), and as he is not well, I sprang up to go to him. As I stepped my foot upon the floor, it was like thrusting it into the fire. I immediately got a light, and found the floor black with ants—no uncommon thing. We are obliged to have our bedsteads stand constantly in water. I do not know whether or not I should tell you how the frogs hop from my sleeves when I put them on, and how the lizards drop from the ceiling to the table when we are eating. I do not think I should mention my feet; but you would see that I found it impossible to keep them still, and had them in immensely large shoes, and you would probably think of the ant-bites, especially as you would see several on the backs of my hands.

You would not need to be told that Maulmain is a beautiful place, for you would see it; still I think I should launch out somewhat in its praises. To my eye there is nothing in a land of frosts to compare with it. Our house, as it was built first, is much the poorest one in the mission, and the least pleasantly situated; but I would not exchange it for any thing [sic] belonging to a cold climate. Then the scenery around is perfectly charming. Just mount a little Burman pony, and come along with Mrs. Stevens,[101] Mrs. Haswell[102] and me, just as the mist is rising from the river in the morning. The hills are bristling with white and gilded pagodas; the tiny bells attached to them are giving out faint music; and at their base the mendicant priests wander about in their yellow dresses, looking the personification of the misery which they are dealing out to their fellows. You pity the poor wretches in spite of yourself. As you turn your back upon the hills, a scene unrivaled in picturesque beauty opens upon your view, and you involuntarily draw up in the middle of the street, and stand erect in your stirrups. The mist hangs like a silver vail [sic] above the river which is specked with very curious looking boats, and just before you lies, like a gem of emerald, the island of sacred water. On the right hand the land rises, in some parts precipitously, and here and there little houses like last year's hay-stacks, are stuck down in groves of various kinds of trees—the palm, cocoa, orange, lime, and jack, etc., etc. You are met all along the way by the turbaned heads of different nations; for Maulmain seems to be a place of general conference. A portly, king-like Mogul rolls by in his lumbering gazzee; a Jew in his own peculiar costume is wending his way to his merchandise, looking, poor fellow! little like a child of Abraham; the Chinaman toddles along in his high-toed shoes, and silken trowsers [sic]; the Indian from the other coast covers himself entirely with his white flowing drapery, making a very ghost-like appearance as he squats on the hillside, or glides along the street; the ugly Portuguese, aping the ungraceful

[100] See vol. 1, "Cast of Characters," s.v. "Judson, Edward."
[101] See vol. 1, "Cast of Characters," s.v. "Stevens, Elizabeth 'Bessie.'"
[102] See vol. 1, "Cast of Characters," s.v. "Haswell, Mrs. Jane."

English style of dress, jogs on his way in clerk-like fashion; and the Burman with his chequered *patso* thrown over his shoulders and descending to his knees, to protect him from the chill air of morning, steps from the road, and stares admiringly, exclaiming meanwhile at the courage of the English ladies. I believe both Burmans and Hindoos think English *women* braver and more daring than any of the *men* of the East. And though they are, most of them, fine, muscular-looking fellows, I think I should scarce fear a half-dozen. A robbery took place in our compound at the printing office,[103] since Dr. J.'s absence, and Miss Lillybridge[104] and I have but a timid Burman boy to garrison our weak fort, who I know would run at the least rustling of danger. If we can put on a bold front and stand erect, I suppose there is no danger here; but I am told we have a different kind of men—more savage—in Burmah proper. If we go to Rangoon God only knows what lies before us. Maulmain to my taste is pleasanter than any thing [*sic*] in America; though to a person of less romance (I find that I have romance, although I supposed it entirely worn out before I left America), there must be a great many blots upon the picture. Articles to eat and wear are sadly circumscribed, but the eye has a feast. And then, while I lay no claim to much missionary spirit, it *is* a comfort to pick the poor wretches out of the mire and filth, and give them the hope of a crown in heaven. There is a "romance" in that which makes me deem a residence in a Maulmain barn or a Rangoon prison, preferable to the most splendid American mansion or European palace.

I was just called to look at a *bong bong tantah*, as little Henry[105] calls it—a Burman funeral. It is a very splendid affair, and the music has been within hearing for a couple of hours. The dead is borne in a magnificent car of gold and scarlet, with offerings of fruit and flowers before, and a priest in his yellow robes at the side. It is a strange sight. I have written two long letters already, or I would describe it more particularly. My love to Mrs. Corey, and believe me, my dear sir,

Yours most sincerely,

Emily C. Judson

Source: A. C. Kendrick, *The Life and Letters of Mrs. Emily C. Judson*, 255–58.

---

[103] See the letter of Emily C. Judson to Adoniram Judson dated January 20, 1847.

[104] See vol. 1, "Cast of Characters," s.v. "Lillybridge, Miss Lydia."

[105] See vol. 1, "Cast of Characters," s.v. "Judson, Henry Hall."

Mrs. Elizabeth L. Stevens to Emily C. Judson, January 31, 1847[106]

My dear Sister,

Excuse my sending for your saddle this morning, one of our keys was missing. The pony jogged on nicely after his last evening's exercise. Do you not think you would ride better with your stirrup strap shorter?

I will try to get Mr. Vinton's[107] pony and ride with you[108]tomorrow.

Mr. and Mrs. Hough[109] have promised to come here to tea tonight and I *very much* wish you and Miss Lillybridge[110] would come. I shall send for Miss L. Don't say no. I'll try to lead things quiet so you need not be fatigued and you need not tire yourself beforehand enough even to give your hair an extra brush, certainly not change your dress. We need not mind them more than a mission family.

The spots were on the cover of the Magazine I believe when it came over on [ ]—beg pardon a thousand times—On the 162 p. of M. L. D. you will find the scene I referred to—"The bridal prayer." I read "Ally Fisher[111]" to Mrs. Brayton[112] last evening; she at first thought she could recognize the little girl.

You asked me the other day if I loved poetry. I shall do myself injustice not to say I have taste and heart enough to love dearly "Blow softly, gales! A tender sigh"[113]—Your having written that makes me happy in thinking of you as taking

---

[106] This letter is undated. It is placed on January 31, 1847, because Mr. and Mrs. Hough are invited to tea by Mrs. Stevens, but only Emily, which would suggest that Adoniram was not at the mission. We know also that the Houghs were to leave for America in February 1847.

[107] Calista Holman was born in Union, Connecticut, in April 1807. She married Justus Hatch Vinton on April 9, 1834, and together, they sailed for mission work in Burmah in July 1834. With her husband, she was stationed at Chummerah, Newville, and Maulmain, specializing in work with the Karens. She taught the Karen women and was the author of several hymnbooks in their language. Calista and Justus Vinton were the parents of three children. Mrs. Vinton died in Rangoon on December 18, 1864.

[108] In her letter to Mr. Corey dated January 31, 1847, Emily mentions that she often rode with Mrs. Stevens and Mrs. Haswell.

[109] George and Phoebe Hough were the first missionaries to be wholly called by the American Baptist Missionary Union. They worked in Burmah with Adoniram and Ann Judson. They arrived in Burmah in October 1816 and retired from missionary service in 1826; George Hough subsequently worked for the government as an interpreter and school superintendent, and Mrs. Hough worked as an educator. They remained friends with Adoniram Judson and many of the other missionaries. Their independence was problematical for many of the missionaries.

[110] See vol. 1, "Cast of Characters," s.v. "Lillybridge, Miss," also the timeline on "Lydia Lillybridge Simons."

[111] "Ally Fisher" was one of Emily's later stories; it appeared in vol.1 of the first edition of *Alderbrook*.

[112] Mary Fuller was born August 17, 1808 in Roxbury, Connecticut. She attended Brandon Academy in Vermont, and the Female Seminary in Warren, Rhode Island. She was married to the Reverend Durlin Brayton on October 2, 1837, and on October 28, 1837, they departed for Burmah. Durlin and Mary Brayton worked in Mergui until their departure for the United States on February 23, 1847. As this letter was being written by Elizabeth Stevens, Mary Brayton's departure home was imminent. Mary Brayton did not return to Burmah until March 1850. There are several letters from Mary Brayton to Emily; in one of them, she advocated strongly that missionary children should not be separated from their parents. Her only daughter Mary returned with her in 1850. Mary Brayton died on December 16, 1890 at Rangoon.

[113] "Lines Written Off St. Helena" was written on the *Faneuil Hall* as it passed St. Helena, where Sarah Boardman Judson had been buried; Emily wrote a tribute to her.

the place of her who wrote, "We part on this green islet love."[114] Those sweet sweet lines—you have no idea.

Written along the top margin of page 1: "The boy came over for milk this morning—I suppose you forgot to tell him."

Source: American Baptist Historical Society, AJ 19, no. 905.

Ms L. A. Kilham to Emily C. Judson, February, 1847

Will Fanny Forester[115] accept this little bag. [sic] It was woven when the bright and happy influence of *Alderbrook*[116] made the hours pass pleasantly and we thought of the sweet lady who had showed us with her genius far away in that strange land to which she had gone, and we felt that while we offered love and admiration to bright Fanny Forester we could give a fabric homage, and deeper reverence to the noble woman, who had laid the offering of her beautiful gifts on the altar of Missions.

Allow me, madam, to express the pleasure I have received from your works, and accept my warmest wishes for your happiness.

With much respect

L. A. Kilham

Source: American Baptist Historical Society, AJ 16, no. 786.

Emily C. Judson to the Reverend Mr. Corey, February 2, 1847[117]

I received a letter from Mr. Judson yesterday.[118] He had not seen the governor but had found a house which he says is "as gloomy as a prison." He writes, "I turn from all this filth and wretchedness to you; and how *can* I think of taking you from the

---

[14] This poem was written by Sarah Judson as in 1845, Sarah, Adoniram and the children approached Port Louis, the Isle of France, on their journey from Burmah back to America. Though Sarah had been sick, she was sufficiently improved, so Adoniram was comfortable to have her go ahead without him, and he would go back to Burmah to work on the dictionary. The parting was that of a husband and wife, to part for an interval until reunited. The poem contains many elements of their life together. Shortly after this was written, however, Sarah became sick again, and Adoniram changed his plans and pressed on to America with her. As they approached the Isle of St. Helena some seven weeks later, Sarah died, and she was buried there as Adoniram and the children returned to America.

[115] Emily Chubbuck Judson as Fanny Forester. See vol. 1, "Cast of Characters," s.v. "Chubbuck, Emily E.," and "Forester, Fanny."

[116] The first edition of *Alderbrook* was available as early as December,1846, for copies were sent to Catharine Chubbuck by the publisher on December 9.

[117] This is an addendum to a letter of January 31, 1847.

[118] See the letter of Adoniram Judson to Emily Judson dated January 23, 1847.

comforts of Maulmain into this den?" We shall go now unless the government absolutely forbids it, as soon as he returns. I am busy packing up again.

Source: A. C. Kendrick, *The Life and Letters of Mrs. Emily C. Judson*, 255–58.

Adoniram Judson to Emily C. Judson, February 2, 1847—Rangoon

My Darling,

We move from the *Gyne* to the *Thistle*, and from the *Thistle* back to the *Gyne*, according to the whims of Antram and Co. I dutifully follow in their wake. Yesterday we got all our things on board the *Thistle*; to-day we have changed our quarters to get more room. For a day or two I have had nothing about me but the clothes I have on. The *Thistle* drops down with this noon's tide, and I write this line to send by her. The *Gyne* says she will move with this evening's tide, but I guess not till to-morrow's. It is doubtful which will arrive first—both, probably, near the end of the week. I have received two precious letters from you, and have sent you several to which I am afraid that epithet can not [*sic*] be fairly applied. I have *some* desire to see your sweet face once more, and fold you in my arms. May we be blessed with a happy meeting! From all I hear, we shall be a fortnight, or three weeks or more, in Maulmain, before we get passage in the *City of London*. The longer I stay here the more tolerable a future residence appears. But it will be dull work, except so far as we find happiness in ourselves and in God. And there will be many external discomforts. I don't care so much for myself, but I hate to reward your kindness and love to me by dragging you into this forlorn, dreary place. They are pretending to put some polish on the upper story of "Green Turban's" den, against Madam's arrival. And they are taking some precautions against fire, according to my suggestions. Farewell, *Zwn mon*, my life, my love, and dear Henry[119] and Edward.[120]

Yours ever,

A. Judson

Source: A. C. Kendrick, *The Life and Letters of Mrs. Emily C. Judson*, 259.

---

[119] See vol. 1, "Cast of Characters," s.v. "Judson, Henry Hall."

[120] See vol. 1, "Cast of Characters," s.v. "Judson, Edward."

Adoniram Judson to Emily C. Judson, February 5, 1847—On Board the *Gyne*

My Darling Love,—

We sailed from Rangoon on the 3d, and must be near Amherst. In fact, the Martaban Hills are said to be in sight. I write a line to send up by some chance opportunity, in case we are detained a tide or so at Amherst. This little absence has taught me how much dearer you are now, my wife, than formerly, my—my lady-love—is that the word? Ah, you have been doing the thing ever since we were married, though I have repeatedly told you not to do it, and you faithfully promised, before Dr: K—,[121] to love, honor, and *obey*; you will not attend to the latter particular, but will keep going on making me love you in spite of myself. This is what you have done ever since we first met. However, I am determined to assert my right one of these days, and rise superior to all vain fascinations. Yes, when I get you into Burmah proper, we will see if you wont [sic] mind. Ah, darling love, what nonsense I am writing! Your last was the 24th of January. Twelve days have passed, and many things may have happened in that time affecting you seriously.

We have just anchored in full view of Amherst, and must wait six hours for the tide to turn. But it is impossible to write with all this chattering about me. What shall I say? It has been the plague of my life to be forced into the company of people whom I had no wish to see or hear. I hope the time will come when we shall be able to enjoy one another's society, and pursue our proper work, acquiring and using a heathen language for the dissemination of Gospel truth (the most glorious work that man can be engaged in), without the everlasting annoyance and din of company. But then, perhaps, you will get tired of me, and long for the society you formerly enjoyed. And I am sure I should not blame you, or think it at all strange. I only think it strange that you could make up your mind to follow "the fortunes of that lone missionary" so contentedly as you have. You say you love me because I am so good! Why don't you add—and so handsome? That would be equally appropriate. Ah, poor girl, you have been sadly taken in. Circumstances combined to make me a sort of lion at home, and I took advantage of my adventitious position to find my way to your heart. I almost condemn myself for a villain, and my only apology is that I could not help it. However, when I think of the affair in connection with religion and eternity, I feel that it has been my precious privilege to draw you from a situation of danger to one which, with the blessing of God, will conduce

---

[121] When Emily Chubbuck was in her teens, Dr. Nathaniel Kendrick was the pastor of the Baptist church in Eaton and also a professor in a local theological school; he eventually became the president of the Hamilton Literary and Theological Institution. At that time in her life, Emily spoke with him about becoming a missionary. Dr. Kendrick gave her the wise counsel of discernment, patience, and waiting. Adoniram and Emily turned to Dr. Kendrick to officiate at their marriage. He married Adoniram and Emily on June 2, 1846. A. C. Kendrick, in *the Life and Letters of Mrs. Emily C. Judson* (New York: Sheldon and Company, 1831), says that the marriage of Emily and Adoniram Judson was the last service for which Dr. Kendrick was able to leave his home. Other correspondents mention his continued frailty. He died on September 11, 1848.

to your highest, your everlasting benefit. And to attain such an end, I should not value another voyage to America, dearest and best.

Here we lie, with Amherst in sight from our cabin window. Amherst, whither I brought Ann,[122] and returned to find her grave; Amherst, whither I brought Sarah,[123] on returning from my matrimonial tour to Tavoy, and whence I took her away in the *Paragon*,[124] to return no more; Amherst, the terminus of my long voyage in the *Faneuil Hall* with Emily. The place seems like the centre of many radii of my past existence, though not a place where any of us have lived for any length of time. Ann never saw Maulmain; Sarah never saw Rangoon. If we should remove to the latter place, it would seem to me like beginning my life anew. May it be under more propitious auspices, and may the latter part of life make some atonement for the errors of the former. May you, my dearest, be happy, and useful, and blessed there! May we be luminaries to Burmah, and may our setting sun descend in a flood of light! Who shall paint the glories of the eternity before us? Eye hath not seen, nor ear heard, etc. I hope to get up to Maulmain some time to-morrow. So farewell once more, and, believe me to be, with ever growing affection and esteem,

Your devoted husband,

A. Judson

Source: A. C. Kendrick, *The Life and Letters of Mrs. Emily C. Judson*, 260–61.

Emily C. Judson to a Friend, February 12, 1847—Maulmain

Letter from Fanny Forester

We are favored with the use of a letter from Mrs. Judson to a friend in this country, written on the eve of Dr. Judson's departure from Maulmain to recommence operations at Rangoon, extracts from which will be interesting to our readers, both as showing the prospects of the undertaking, and as exhibiting a glance at missionary domestic life in that heathen city.

We beg to assure some of Fanny Forester's literary admirers, who were so shocked that she, so cultivated and so ethereal a being, should link herself to the destinies of a missionary, that Fanny is not only exceedingly happy, but writes—the letter is a private one to a lady to whom she writes as a daughter to a mother,—

---

[122] Ann Hasseltine Judson, Adoniram Judson's first wife. Ann was buried at Amherst. See the letter of Adoniram Judson to Emily C. Judson dated January 20, 1847. In that letter he mentioned being able to see from the ship the Hopia tree which was planted by her grave.

[123] Sarah Hall Boardman Judson, Adoniram Judson's second wife.

[124] The *Paragon* was the ship on which Adoniram and Sarah, and the three children, sailed to the United States in 1845. Sarah died at the Isle of St Helena.

with a most matronly and practical air, of "her two little boys, sweet, beautiful and affectionate," of her "house-keeping," etc. shewing [*sic*] that she is not in the clouds, but on the earth, acting well the art of a good missionary's wife.—*N. Y. Recorder*.[125]

Maulmain, Feb. 12th, 1847

My Dear Mrs.—

Boats were engaged this morning to take our few goods on board the ship which is to convey us to Rangoon, but we received a note from the captain which gives us a couple of days more. Mr. J. has been over—was gone nearly three weeks, and returned this day week. I cannot give you so correct an idea of things there in any other way as to quote from his letter, received during his absence.[126] He writes, "The governor received me remarkably well," etc., "approved my prosecuting the dictionary, and spoke favorably of my going up to Amerapore and seeking royal patronage. I have engaged the brick house mentioned in my last, but I am afraid your spirits will sink to zero when you see it. Living here is much more expensive than at Maulmain," etc. "The police is well administered, and I think it nearly as safe living here as in Maulmain. As to missionary effort nothing can be done openly. The system of intolerance is enforced more rigidly than ever. It is not as a missionary or 'propagator,' of religion, but as a minister of a foreign religion ministering to the foreigners in the place, that I am well received and patronized by the government. The new king and his younger brother, who is premier and heir apparent, are rigid Boodhists, particularly the latter. Boodhism is in full feather through the empire. The prospects of a missionary were never darker; but let us aim to obtain the praise bestowed upon Mary. 'She has done what she could.'" He adds, "I have been to little Roger's grave. There is room for the other two children and for either of us, and I fancy that he sleeps just as quietly here as beneath the British flag."

In another letter, speaking of the house, he says, "It contains six or eight rooms, and some quite large; but there are but few lights, and the place looks as gloomy as a prison. It is situated in a street of Mussulmans—not a foot of ground belonging to the upper story, (we have only the upper story,) except a path to a spacious cook-house and a shabby horse-stable. I shrink at taking you and the children into such a den, and fear you would pine and die in it."

So much for the letters, but things look much brighter since he has returned and told me about them. I think we shall manage to get plenty of sunlight into the

---

[125] This introduction was originally written for, and appeared in, *The New York Recorder*, a religious newspaper. From there, it was picked up by the *Newark* [NJ] *Daily Advisor*, June 4, 1847, page 1, column 6, and printed in its entirety. The Editor found it in the *Newark Daily Advisor*.

[126] These quotes are from the letter of Adoniram to Emily dated January 28, 1847.

"gloomy prison." Our religious prospects, however, I cannot brighten, except by remembering that God is able to bring light out of darkness.

Source: *Newark Daily Advertiser* (Newark NJ), June 4, 1847.

Anna Maria Anable to Emily C. Judson,[127] February 15, 1847—Utica

My dear Nemmy[128]

I am seated in Grandpa's[129] room to night to write to you of the first death that has occurred in our family not only since you sailed but for the last twelve years.

Our dear Grandma's chair by the hearth is vacant, and poor dear Grandpa is left to drag out his weary years-laden existence, and it is pitiful to witness his grief. He cannot by his heart devoted attention pour balm into his afflicted heart. He who wounded can alone heal, and to Him my dear Grandpa looks with most touching resignation. I have been very much in my Grandparents' room this Winter (for since Grandpa's illness last Summer it has seemed to me a holy place) and I know how many little tender attentions which he rec'd at her hands all constantly reoccurring to his memory. I need say nothing to you dear Nemmy of the virtues of my dear Grandma, of the delicate tenderness and child-like truthfulness and simplicity of character which endeared her so to a large circle of friends and connections. We miss her sweet smile of welcome as we open the door, and her gentle voice of invitation to sit down by her chair that she may hear what we say, and above all we shall miss her prayers—but we have still in our hearts and may we ever retain there the memory of her bright example and God grant that as they advance in life her children's children may imbibe more and more of that spirit of benevolent tenderness which characterized her. She died on Monday the 29th of Jan'y after a very short illness. She was 80 years old. Grand pa is 86 and they had lived together sixty three years. She complained of a cold on Saturday but we did not think her so ill as she had been many times previously and we apprehended no danger till the following Wednesday. Her illness was not very distressing but she had no strength left to resist even a slight attack. She was the first person Nemmy that I ever saw die and I happened to be left alone alone [*sic*] with her at that moment. Aunt U.[130] had come up in the night-train and as they apprehended no immediate danger they had gone for a few moments into Aunt C.'s[131] room. She

---

[127] There is an addendum to this letter that was written on March 30, 1847.

[128] Emily Chubbuck. See vol. 1, "Cast of Characters," s.v. "Nemmy, Nem, or Nemmy Petty (Nemmie Pettie)." Also the chapter "Names of Endearment."

[129] See vol. 1, "Cast of Characters," s.v. "Sheldon, Deacon Asa."

[130] See vol. 1, "Cast of Characters," s.v. "Nott, Urania Sheldon."

[131] See vol. 1, "Cast of Characters," s.v. "Sheldon, Miss Cynthia."

continued to breathe more and more quietly till she fell asleep not more than three minutes after they left the room. There was no struggle nor groan nor gasping, and tho I was watching intensely every breath all was so quiet when she breathed her last that I could not believe it was death.

<blockquote>
—"Life so sweetly ceased to be
It lapsed in immortality."
</blockquote>

I will not attempt to describe the scenes that followed—the bitter grief, the tears of mourning, and the prayers too. O, how affliction drives us to the throne of grace! We look up to see a Father's hand—and we ask tremblingly conscious of ingratitude at least—what have we done that thou has laid thine hand upon us? May we all as a family read this lesson nightly!

The funeral took place on Sabbath in the church. I am told the house and galleries were crowded and Mr. Corey[132] preached an excellent sermon on the text "Well done, good and faithful servant etc."

We sit in Grandpa's room now constantly. It's vacation and my work is here and my books are here. I read nothing now but what I can read aloud to him and to my dear mother[133] who is giving up some of her cares to a very good woman we have obtained as a kind of housekeeper. Grandpa's personal wants and comforts are as well attended to as ever, and he has children and grandchildren whose hearts are all devotion to him and who designs to be with him, but we can none of us supply to him Grandma's place. Yet, I fear we shall not have him long with us to

---

[132] Mr. Corey was the pastor of the Bleecker Street Baptist Church near the Utica Female Academy, and Miss Sheldon and many of the girls from the academy attended worship there. (Cynthis Sheldon, Alma Anable, Deacon Asa and Isabell Sheldon, Edward Bright, and Horace Hawley had been charter members of the church in 1838.) In April 1844, he wrote to Emily expressing dismay that at a school program one of the girls had read a composition justifying dancing as exercise; he spoke of this as a roadblock to the salvation of many. Then, on March 10, 1846, Emily indicated in a letter to Anna Maria that Mr. Corey had been critical of her relationship and impending marriage to Adoniram Judson. Miss Cynthia Sheldon wrote a number of times expressing Mr. Corey's regret and support, and in 1847, there were letters of reconciliation between Emily and Mr. Corey. In spring 1848, letters reveal that Mr. Corey's wife had died of consumption, her condition exacerbated by recent child-birth. She had left behind four children. In July 1849, Anna Maria Anable wrote of his impending marriage to Jane Backus, a good choice for this "rising man." Mr. Corey remained popular with the Sheldon-Anable families even after their move to Philadelphia in 1848. A March 2, 1852, letter from Charles B. Stout told of Mr. Corey's call to the Stanton Street Church in New York City, which Mr. Corey did not accept. Finally, in 1854, there was a pastoral letter from Mr. Corey to Emily on her illness and her possible death. He preached at the Bleecker Street Church as late as January 1867.

[133] Alma Sheldon Anable was the sister of Miss Cynthia Sheldon and Urania Sheldon Nott. Genealogy sources show that she married Joseph Hubbell Anable in Troy, New York on July 28, 1814, and that it was the second marriage for Mr. Anable. Born in 1773, he was forty-one at the time of the marriage, and Alma was likely considerably younger. He died in 1831, which explains why Alma Anable and her family lived and worked first at the Utica Female Seminary and then later at the Misses Anable's School in Philadelphia. Joseph and Alma Anable were the parents of nine children: Henry Sheldon Anable (b. June 21, 1815); William Stewart Anable (b. November 6, 1816); Anna Maria Stafford Anable (b. September 30, 1818), Cynthia Jane Anable (b. January 28, 1820); Samuel Low Anable (b. November 28, 1821); Harriet Isabella Anable, also known as Hatty or Hattie (b. December 18, 1823); Courtland Wilcox Anable (b. July 28, 1825); Frances Alma Anable, or Fanny (b. April 12, 1828); and Mary Juliet Anable (b. February 18, 1830).

sit in his corner and pray for blessings on his children. The longer I live the more I feel that the prayers of an aged saint are invaluable.

Source: American Baptist Historical Society, AJ 13, no. 504.

Abby Ann Judson to Adoniram Judson, February 16, 1847—Bradford

My dear Father,

Last Thursday was the day that you appointed for me to write on,[134] but I have not written till now. I have not received any letters from you but I hope to soon. Please to tell me how Henry[135] and Edward[136] are. I hope that they are both well. You have doubtedly arrived at Burmah by this time. What kind of a voyage did you have. I hope that you had a pleasant time without any storms. This term I study Geometry. All the rest of my studies are the same except United States History. I hope that Mother[137] is well. How are all the missionaries. I have lately seen Mr. Osgood[138] and since I last wrote Mr. Simons.[139] I was very glad to see them, as you may suppose. Mr. Osgood saw your portrait at Aunt Abby Haseltines[140] [sic], but he did not seem to think that it looked exactly like you. Last vacation Aunt Mary[141] and Cousins Thomas and Rebecca were sick with the typhus fever and Aunt Abby being apprehensive that I might be taken sent me to Lynn with Aunt

---

[134] On November 14, 1846, Abby Ann said in her letter that "last Wednesday it was just three months since I last wrote, and as you asked me to write to you once in three months, I will now do it. "

[135] See vol. 1, "Cast of Characters," s.v. "Judson, Henry Hall."

[136] See vol. 1, "Cast of Characters," s.v. "Judson, Edward."

[137] The reference is to Emily, whom Abby Ann called "Mother." All of the children called her "Mother" or "Mamma."

[138] Rev. Sewall Osgood was a missionary in Maulmain who worked with and lived by Adoniram Judson. Judson and Osgood occupied two of the four homes in the mission compound and lived so close that it "allowed me the pleasure and profit of almost hourly intercourse." He arrived in Burmah in 1834. His first wife Elhira Brown Osgood died on October 5, 1837, in Maulmain. On July 8, 1838, he married Sarah Thomas, the widow of the Reverend Jacob Thomas, with Adoniram Judson officiating at the wedding. He spoke in the letters to Emily, of which there are five between July 1850 and April 1852, of Adoniram Judson as his "most intimate friend." He never personally met Emily, as he had returned from the field prior to 1846. At the time of his letters, he was working with the American Baptist Missionary Union as a district secretary. In 1845, just as they were leaving for the United States, Sarah and Adoniram Judson gave care of Charley, too young to make the trip, to Mr. and Mrs. Osgood. Charley died not long after their departure. Mr. Osgood visted Adoniram, Elnathan, and Abby Ann in the United States. His third wife was Caroline Wait; they were married December 30, 1850 at Saratoga, New York. With all of his suggestions of "intimacy" and "his most intimate friend," Mr. Osgood stated that his life was so busy that he simply did not have the time to look through his papers for anything that would be helpful in writing the memoir.

[139] Thomas Simons was born in Wales. He was ordained on December 18, 1831, after graduation from the Newton Theological Institute and was appointed to missionary service on March 7, 1831. He sailed for Burmah on June 29, 1832, arriving in Maulmain on January 1, 1833. On June 23, 1833, he married Caroline Jenks Harrington in Maulmain, probably the widow of a missionary who had died, and between 1834 and March 1843, they had six children, two of whom died in June 1839. Caroline Simons died on May 1, 1843. Mr. Simons returned to America in May 1846. While in the United States, he visited with Abby Ann Judson at Bradford Academy; she would have known him from her years in Burmah. He returned to Burmah in November 1847, arriving in Maulmain April 19, 1848. His second wife was Lydia Lillybridge, who had sailed to Burmah with Adoniram and Emily Judson; they were married in Maulmain in 1851.

[140] This was Abigail Hasseltine, sister of Ann Hasseltine Judson.

[141] This was Mary Hasseltine, sister of Ann Hasseltine Judson.

Emerson.[142] I returned home to Bradford five or six weeks ago, and staid [sic] there about the same time. I spent Thanksgiving, Christmas, and New Years there. I believe that I gave an account of the manner in which I spent Thanksgiving in the letter I wrote while at Lynn so it is needless to repeat it here. I hung up my stocking Christmas Eve, and in the morning it was full of a variety of little articles. On the day before New Years I went to a fair which was got up by the Ladies of the Chapel Society to help build a chapel in Lynn. I bought several [ ] little things and gave them away for presents. I made three book-marks, and sold them for fifty cents. When I was at Lynn I went to Salem twice. The first time that I went was with Uncle Eliphalet, and the second with Brother George.[143] Uncle George and Aunt Nancy from Skaneateles were there.[144] I was very glad to see George for I had not seen him for some three or four years past. He is at college now and he said that Adoniram[145] and Elnathan[146] are quite well and very happy. I have not heard from then [sic] since. I saw a notice in the *American Messenger* (which I take) that 1000 persons had been converted in the churches belonging to Rangoon. It must give you a great deal of pleasure. We have a society here called the Chidlaw [sic] Society. I need not say that I am a member. This society is composed of those members of the Academy who wish to belong to it. It is for the benefit of the West. At present we are making up a lot of clothing. I have been making some tablets and other little things to sell, and give the money to the Society, and have already got 77 cents. The Society meets every Friday evening. When Mr. Osgood was here he told me that there was going to be some alteration in that lane, which runs by the side of the printing office but I don't recollect what. I had several little notes to

---

[142] See Abby Ann's letter to Adoniram and Emily dated December 15, 1846.

[143] George Dana Boardman, the son of George Dana Boardman and Sarah Hall Boardman, was born August 18, 1828, in Tavoy, Burmah. George returned to the United States in 1844 at the age of six and lived with Dr. and Mrs. Calvin Newton in Worcester, Massachusetts. He never saw his mother again. He attended Brown University in Providence, Rhode Island, graduating after taking a few years off for travel in the West. He went on to attend Newton Theological Institute, and in 1855, he married Miss Ella Covell. He served two churches before settling into the First Baptist Church of Philadelphia, where he served with distinction for thirty years. He formed a close relationship with Emily upon her return in 1851; when she gave him a copy of *An Olio of Domestic Verses*, she addressed it "Georgie—from Mamma."

[144] These are references to Abby Ann's maternal relatives; upon his return to America in 1845, Adoniram Judson went to Salem and Skaneateles to visit the parents and family of the recently deceased Sarah Hall Boardman Judson.

[145] Adoniram "Addy" Judson was born April 7, 1837, the second child and first son of Adoniram and Sarah Hall Boardman Judson. From November 1845 to October 1851, he lived with Dr. and Mrs. Calvin Newton in Worcester, Massachusetts. He then spent a year with Dr. and Mrs. Edward Bright in Roxbury, Massachusetts, and before entering Brown University, he was two years at Pierce Academy in Middleboro, Massachusetts. After his education and medical school, Adoniram served as a surgeon in the Civil War and became a prominent orthopedic surgeon with several books to his credit. He died in 1916. Over the years, he became vocal about the separation of missionary children from their parents.

[146] Elnathan "Elly" Judson was born July 15, 1838, the third child and second son of Adoniram and Sarah Hall Boardman Judson. From November 1845 to October 1851, he lived with Dr. and Mrs. Calvin Newton in Worcester, Massachusetts. He then spent a year with Dr. and Mrs. Edward Bright in Roxbury, Massachusetts, and before entering Brown University, he spent two years at Pierce Academy in Middleboro, Massachusetts. There are strong indications that Elnathan planed to become a missionary, and in fact, he did graduate from Union Seminary. In 1860, however, he suffered a serious sunstroke that subsequently caused serious mental impairment. For much of his life, Elnathan was confined to mental institutions. He died after a second paralyzing stroke in 1896; in the last years of his life, Elnathan was lovingly cared for by his sister Abby Ann Judson.

read at the dinner table on Thanksgiving day which some of the Academy girls gave to me to open at that time. I also wrote several to be opened on different times of that day. I send Mother and you a great abundance of love. I also send some to all that I used to know in Burmah. Tell Mah Byouk that I have not forgotten her or ever shall. Please to kiss dear Henry and Edward for me. Tell Emily and Mary[147] that I want them to write to me. Please to send the enclosed note to them. The part of the family [Note: The next to the last line of the letter is lost in the letter fold.] Rebecca send [sic] love to you and Mother.

Your ever most affectionate daughter
Abbie[148] A. Judson

Source: American Baptist Historical Society, AJ 10, no. 300.

Emily C. Judson to Miss Cynthia Sheldon, February 19, 1847[149]—On board the City of London

My dear Miss Cynthia,

We are now in the Rangoon river, a branch of the Irrawaddy, anchored to wait for the next tide. We shall not reach Rangoon before tomorrow morning. This morning when I went on deck, I could almost fancy myself caught in a trap from which it would be impossible to extricate myself. The river is narrow at the mouth, but widens with a sudden sweep, which makes it appear as though we were enclosed in a pair of nippers. However, the trap is not a very alarming one. We are in an elegant great English ship, as large and as good as the one we left America in, and have all the comforts we could ask for such a short trip. There is only one thing that troubles me. Yesterday the doctor was seized with a bowel complaint which in the night was followed by chills and fever. Indeed, this complaint has been hanging about him for two or three weeks. This morning he is a little better, but I am by no means at ease about him. I lay last night with my eyes shut so that he might not think he was keeping me awake and tho't over what I sh'd do if he were ill. We have no kind missionary friends to receive us at Rangoon, as at Maulmain, and I cannot speak enough of the language to make myself at all understood. We do not know whether the house is ready for us (the old Mussulman who owns it agreed to make some repairs) and getting through the customs house is a terrible operation. It will take three or four days in the regular course of things, but if there is no one to attend to it properly!—All these things looked like a mountain

[147] Childhood friends of Abby Ann's, the children of some of the other missionaries in Maulmain.

[148] On November 14, 1846, Abby Ann wrote in a footnote that she was changing the spelling of her name to "Abbie."

[149] We note that this letter was sent by ship to the Mission rooms in Boston, and then forwarded to Miss Sheldon on June 18, 1847.

in the night, but daylight always brightens my night-visions; now I am hoping for the best. One great trouble is, you cannot get a rag more than you have on your back, not even a mattress to sleep on, through the custom-house till *great my lords* please to let you. I think it would be perfectly right for the English to conquer all Burmah if only to teach them a little sense. It does seem to me as tho' they are a nation of fools. We chance to have a man aboard who understands the navigation of the river—otherwise there is no knowing when we sh'd get up—the government provides no pilots. Another thing which adds some to my anxiety is the *renewal* of little Master Edward's[150] troubles. We tho't the trip had quite cured him of his bowel complaint but yesterday it came on more furiously than ever. Don't you think I am in a great mess away off here among strange people of whose language and manners I am entirely ignorant. If the doctor only keeps well I have no dread of anything, but I am afraid the very efforts he makes to do so will make him worse. I write you this line now because the captain thinks there may be an opportunity to send on our arrival. I shall write again to some of you as soon as we are in our house. Meantime, continue to address letters to Maulmain, and they will forward them to us. There may be some way more direct, but we cannot tell yet. We left Lydia[151] very well, and doing nicely in her school. She is teaching English to a class of large girls. She works at the language as she always does at everything and I believe is beating me. This unpacking, assorting, and re-packing, the care of a family, tho' a small one, the additional cares occasioned by the doctor's absence, and the illness of the children, have been heavy draw-backs to me. I cannot get time for anything—scarce even to write a letter. I believe all the English ladies in Maulmain called upon me and I had the civility to return but one call. It is impossible to find time to be civil. There is one comfort in getting into our "Rangoon den," as the doctor calls it. These endless *calls* will be suspended, for there is nobody to call. English ladies in the east have no way of spending their time and they sit and bore you an hour or two, out of the most precious part of the day merely to dispel *ennui*. It is a very annoying practice. I sh'd like to have one person like sweet little Mrs. Stevens[152] (the missionary's wife) for a neighbour in Rangoon, and that is all the society I sh'd care for. But I'd rather be without any person near me who can understand a word of English (my husband of course excepted) than to be annoyed as I was in Maulmain. I hope grandfather and grandmother are yet alive,[153] and [Note: Written in the right margin of the address page.] grandfather is getting better. How I should like to see their dear faces once more—and all of you.

---

[150] See vol. 1, "Cast of Characters," s.v. "Judson, Edward."

[151] See vol. 1, "Cast of Characters," s.v. "Lillybridge, Miss," also the timeline on "Lydia Lillybridge Simons."

[152] See vol. 1, "Cast of Characters," s.v. "Stevens, Elizabeth 'Bessie.'"

[153] On February 15, 1847, Anna Maria Anable wrote a poignant letter to Emily telling of Grandmother Sheldon's death. That letter was not mailed until after March 30, 1846, and it would not have reached Emily until June or July.

Would'nt [*sic*] I jump up two feet at least if I could just be set down for one hour in your dining-room. I sh'd have a great many wonders to tell you—and a great many funny things too. Maybe I shall come to you some one of these years—there's no knowing. At any rate, don't forget me, for I think of you very very often. Remember me especially when you pray and believe me ever, Your sincerely affectionate friend,

Emily C. Judson

Written in the left margin of the address page: "Thinking that you must take some interest in all that interests me, I will tell you a small anecdote about my little Henry.[154] When he first came to us I had a great deal of trouble with him about saying his prayers at night and spent a great deal of breath in talking with him. I commenced by praying with him and finally succeeded in making him say a little prayer himself. The first day I came aboard ship I was horribly sea-sick, but I made out to creep from my cot after he was in bed and stand by his bed while he repeated his little prayer. I then said 'good night' but he reached his hand after me and exclaimed in surprise, 'You haven't prayed to God.' 'Mama is very ill and must go to bed' I said, half fainting and moving away. Suddenly he cried out in alarm, 'Mama, mama, God will send us to hell if we don't pray to him,' and there was the sound of tears in his voice. Don't you think I was thankful to see the little seed I had planted taking root so soon! He is only four and a half years old."

Source: Hanna family files.

Mrs. Elizabeth L. Stevens to Emily C. Judson, February 19, 1847— "*The Judson House*"

"Now my dear "little lady" don't open your bright eyes *too* wide while you ask, why are they over there?" The answer is soon given—our house is in ashes. Night before last some person who loved us none too well set fire to our roof and I hardly had time to arouse my children to escape with them barefooted in their night clothes. By the time I had got to the bottom of our front steps Edward[155] came to put into my hand a few little things which he had met with, in searching the drawer where I had months ago told him my mother's miniature would be found in case of fire, which I have always thought of as the first thing to be secured after the children. I had left the precious treasure in another place and before I could answer his question where to look the flames were raging so fearfully I could only say *let it go*.

[154] See vol. 1, "Cast of Characters," s.v. "Judson, Henry Hall."
[155] See vol. 1, "Cast of Characters," s.v. "Stevens, Edward."

Our mattresses, pillows and blankets from one bed were saved; these we have spread on the cots left in your room. For Eddy and Sarah[156] I have taken the temporary use of two of the quilts found in your bureau until I can make new mattresses for them. Not only our mission friends but many people of the place have showed us such kindness and also the Braytons,[157] who lost most of their outfit. But I have met with losses which neither friends nor money can make up to me; yet I feel it almost wrong to say even as much as that sorrowfully, it is so wonderful we were all preserved. Had I not been awakened (probably, Edward says, by the baby for other sounds do not usually much disturb me nights) so that I heard a man about and aroused Edward, we might not have been able to escape.

I had had two bottles of medicine prepared for you, but they are gone with the medical book. I hope to be able to borrow the work and again have the mixtures made. Do write me particularly about your health.

This evening I received my Nov. 29th overland from my mother and sister—the only letter I possess. Those hoarded treasures of sweet home words—the letters of many years—were in an instant devoured; but the memory of the happiness they gave me cannot so easily be taken from me by an earthly being. Sarah[158] wrote "Miss Vose told me Miss Nancy Hasseltine[159] had had a burning fever, and her recovery was considered very doubtful. Miss Abigail[160] had confined herself to her sister[161] and was almost worn out. Thomas was recovering from Typhus fever. Abby Ann[162] she said was very well. One little incident she told me of Abby. One day Nancy H. passed through the room where she was, and saw her intently pouring over a book. She looked over her shoulder and found she had a vol. of Dwight's Theology!"

The Steamboat *Atlantic* had been wrecked near N. London and among the 50 person lost was Mr. Armstrong one of the Secs of the Am. Board.

---

[156] Two of the children of Edward and Elizabeth Stevens. They were eight and six years old as this was written.

[157] The Reverend Durlin L. Brayton was born in Hubbardton, Vermont, on October 27, 1808. He graduated from Brown University and then the Newton Theological Seminary in 1837, at which time he was appointed to missionary service. On October 2, 1837, he married Mary Hawley Fuller, and they sailed for Burmah on October 28, 1837. They arrived in April 1838 and, passing through Amherst and Maulmain, arrived at Mergui in April 1840. In February 1847, they departed Maulmain for America due to Mrs. Brayton's ill health. Mr. Brayton returned to Burmah the following November, and Mrs. Brayton remained in America until arriving back in Burmah in March 1850. They had one daughter, Mary. Mary Brayton died December 16, 1890 in Rangoon; Durlin Brayton died April 23, 1900, also in Rangoon.

[158] Elizabeth Stevens had a sister who lived in Massachusetts; her name was Sarah Haven. There are nine letters from Sarah Haven to Emily in the correspondence. Sarah Haven was one of Emily's visitors in 1852–1853 when she was living in Providence, Rhode Island, and working on the Judson memoir with Dr. Francis Wayland.

[159] Nancy Hasseltine was a teacher, the niece of Ann Hasseltine Judson. In a letter, she referred to Adoniram as "Uncle."

[160] Abigail Hasseltine, Ann Hasseltine Judson's sister, was the headmistress of the Bradford Academy, where Abby Ann Judson was studying.

[161] On December 10, 1846, Nancy Hasseltine had mentioned the serious illness of Mary Hasseltine, another sister of Ann Hasseltine Judson.

[162] See vol. 1, "Cast of Characters," s.v. "Judson, Abby Ann."

Both mother and Sarah send you love and to "the good Dr. Judson" too as mother writes. Can you ever excuse such a looking scrawl? I took the paper from your bureau and this is the only quill we own and I could not [Note: Written in the right margin of the address page.] stop to get Edward to mend it. You may imagine I have had a little fatigue and excitement and do not feel like doing *anything* properly; certainly not like writing a nice, suitable looking and reading letter to Fanny Forester's[163] ladyship; and so with a kiss to my little Edward[164] and one for yourself I will subscribe myself

Yr. very aff.

Lizzie

Written in the left margin of the address page: "I have closed without telling you how very sorry I am about your loss.[165] Would you like Sarah to repurchase any of the things in Boston for you? She would be very happy to do anything for your comfort. Mrs. Ranney[166] had decided to buy your bonnet so that is saved."

Source: American Baptist Historical Society, AJ 19, no. 907.

Emily C. Judson to Anna Maria Anable, February 22, 1847[167]—Rangoon

Thank God, we are here at last, and able to see our way through to the end of present botherations, though we are by no means through. The poor Doctor escaped the fever which I dreaded, but is still quite ill with bowel complaint. He is, however, able to sit in the custom-house, unlocking his chests, etc., and waiting with exemplary patience the overhauling, and in some instances, *spoiling* of his goods. Amai! ama! You can have no idea of the impudence of these wretches. I have not seen our house yet; but they are beginning to get the goods which have passed the custom-house into it, and I shall go over to-morrow. We came ashore Saturday morning (it is Monday now), and on the invitation of an English captain of a schooner, took up our quarters at his house. He is married to a creole, one of the better specimens of the class, and at least far superior to any thing [sic] else in

---

[163] Emily Chubbuck Judson as Fanny Forester. See vol. 1, "Cast of Characters," s.v. "Chubbuck, Emily" and "Forester, Fanny."

[164] When Sarah Boardman left for the United States in 1845, Edward was but a few months old, and his health was precarious. Mrs. Stevens took him into their home and nursed him as her own, caring for him for almost two years until Adoniram returned with Emily. She literally saved his life. Elizabeth Stevens certainly would have felt an additional bond with Edward because of those shared years.

[165] We learn here that the fire that destroyed the Stevens home also destroyed some of the Judson's valuables. Adoniram was later to speak of two trunks lost at a value of 700 rupees; Emily estimated the value at closer to 1,000 rupees. See Adoniram Judson's letters to Edward Stevens and Thomas Ranney dated March 2, 1847.

[166] Maria Gager Ranney arrived in Maulmain in May 1844. Her husband Thomas was the superintendent of the printing press and business manager for the missionary compound. A letter from Lydia Lillybridge reveals that Mrs. Ranney had some responsibilities in the mission schools. She had no children; Maria Ranney died on April 26, 1857.

[167] This letter has an addendum to it dated February 23, 1846.

Rangoon. Captain Crisp's father knew the Doctor before the war, and the son is very kind. His house is built in English style, and is the best but one in town. But such a house! How you would stare to see it set down in Genesee street! It is very large, and built of brick with massive walls. The partitions are of brick, and the floors, even of the second story, of brick, thick and ugly enough. This is to prevent fire, for which the bamboo houses of the natives furnish most charming tinder. The walls and floors are pretended to be plastered inside, but the plastering is thin and unlike any thing you see in America, and, with the bricks, is broken away in thousands of places. Madam Crisp has kindly assigned us a couple of rooms in which that part of our luggage and that of our servants, which we were able to get ashore on Saturday, lies in most glorious confusion. There are mats (Burmese mats, remember,) spread upon the uneven floors, which have probably lain for years, for they are rotted and mildewed; and one of them in our sleeping-room has entirely disappeared, except the four tattered corners, leaving the red bricks and gray and white plaster very prominent. Then the broken and mildewed furniture! It is quite dangerous to attempt sitting down on chair or couch till you have examined into its capabilities; for ten to one the chair has a broken leg, and the couch a hole through the bottom, deftly covered with a cushion.

You have no idea of the troubles we passed through in reaching the happy state recorded on the last page. The captain of the *City of London*, a regular bear, insisted on our goods being taken from the ship on Sunday, and it was in vain that the Doctor pleaded both his principles and his illness; the ship must be emptied at any rate. We had discovered while aboard the reckless character of the captain, and the half mutinous state of the crew. You may imagine, therefore, our feelings when we laid down our weary heads on Saturday night. The articles could be taken from the ship without the Doctor's presence, but thence they would be conveyed to the custom-house, and he must be there if ever so ill. He was in great pain and very weak; but at last he said, "Why need we be troubled? To-morrow is peculiarly God's own day, and He will take care of it." He seemed to receive from this a little comfort, and before morning had a refreshing sleep. About day-light the captain came in to say that the goods might remain in the ship. "But why? You said yesterday that they could not remain." "The truth is, sir, my boys are bad fellows; they say they have worked three Sundays and wont [*sic*] work to-day, and I can't make them." We suppose that the wretches, wicked as they are, yet had kind feeling enough to take this stand for our sakes; for though we could have no communication with them, we dispensed some smiles, and smiles are rare things among them, poor fellows. And now how do you think I spent the half hour before commencing this page? Why, in the very important business of teaching Master[168]—to put on

[168] This was Edward Judson; in letter dated February 19, 1847, Emily referred to him as "Master Edward."

and tie his own shoes. Not that he is so brave as already to have learned the lesson, but he has made a very respectable beginning. The children in this country are ruined by domineering over servants, and I am determined to save mine from such a curse. I will teach them to help themselves, and to treat servants properly, if it requires my whole time. My nurse has a little girl who is so accustomed to be knocked about that she never thinks of defending herself from a white child. I put a stop to all such proceedings for my children's sakes.

Source: A. C. Kendrick, *The Life and Letters of Mrs. Emily C. Judson*, 267–70.

Emily C. Judson to Anna Maria Anable, February 23, 1847[169]

We had grand good luck yesterday. The Dr. dispensed presents right and left at the custom-house, and before dark his goods were all through. As soon as breakfast is over, I am going to help put things in proper trim. We shall sleep there to-night. I went to see the house last night, but reserve the description until we are settled in it.

Source: A. C. Kendrick, *The Life and Letters of Mrs. Emily C. Judson*, 267–70.

Adoniram Judson to Mr. Thomas S. Ranney, March 2, 1847

I thank you for your circumstantial account of the fire, which, with brother Stevens's gives me a pretty vivid idea of the affair. It was truly a dreadful affair. My loss is probably heavier than that of any other person, except brother Stevens himself. My best clothes and wife's, together with our most valuable utensils of various sorts, were packed in the two boxes that are burned. I estimate the value about seven hundred rupees; wife says nearer one thousand. But all these things are ordered well."

We have had a grand bat hunt[170] yesterday and to-day—bagged two hundred and fifty, and calculate to make up a round thousand before we have done. We find that in hiring the upper story of this den, we secured the lower moiety only, the upper moiety thereof being preoccupied by a thriving colony of vagabonds, who flare up through the night with a vengeance, and the sound of their winds is as the sound of many waters, yea, as the sound of your boasted Yankee Niagara; so that sleep departs from our eyes and slumber from our eyelids. But we are reading them some lessons which we hope will be profitable to all parties concerned, and remain,

[169] This letter was an addendum to Emily's letter to Anna Maria of February 22, 1847.

[170] See the letter of Emily Judson to Catharine Chubbuck dated March 15, 1847. It contains her impressions of what she called "Bat Castle."

Yours affectionately,

A. Judson

Source: A. C. Kendrick, *The Life and Letters of Mrs. Emily C. Judson*, 271–72.

Adoniram Judson to Rev. Edward Stevens, March 2, 1847[171]— Rangoon

Dear Bro. Stevens,

The Lord gave and the Lord has taken away—*Blessed be the name of the Lord*. My heart over flows [sic] with gratitude and my eyes with tears, as I pen those precious inspired words. There are some other lines, quant in garb, but rich in core, that are worth more than all your house and contents: "Blessed be God for all, for all things here below; For every loss and every cross to my advantage grow."[172] But I sympathize with you and dear sister—Bro. Bullard has also sustained a heavy loss. Bro. Brayton's[173] will not on the whole be any great loss. As to me—the leeks and onions[174] that were packed up in those two valuable boxes (with about 7 or 800 papers) were very bright to the eye and soft to the feel, and many of them we shall greatly need, if we live a year or two longer, but they have gone to dust and ashes, where I have seen many bright, dear eyes go to [ ] any pain of whh [which] I would have given those boxes ten times over. "Where are all the birds that sang, A hundred years ago, The flowers that all in beauty sprung, A Hundred years ago. The lips that smiled, The eyes that wild, In flashes shone, soft eyes upon. Where, O where are lips and eyes, The maiden's smiles, the lover's sighs, That lived so long ago?"

I am glad and thankful that N.T. and other Mn. [manuscripts]are not lost— though some are. And I am glad that so much interest has been excited in the Christian community of Maulmain. I am glad also that my house was empty and ready to afford you immediate shelter.

We arrived here the Saturday after leaving Maulmain. I got our things through the customs on the next Monday—a week ago yesterday. We now begin to feel a little settled, and are about commencing a routine of study and I only add, missionary labor, for though the Burmese converts are few and timid, the Karens flock

---

[171] Both Edward Stevens and Thomas Ranney wrote descriptive letters of the fire, and Adoniram Judson responded to both of them. These letters are in the vol. 2 of *A Memoir of the Life and Labors of the Rev. Adoniram Judson, DD* by Francis Wayland.

[172] These lines are from the writings of the "Late the Reverend D. G. John Leland."'

[173] See vol. 1, "Cast of Characters," s.v. "Brayton, The Reverend Durlin and Mary.

[174] This is an allusion to Numbers 11:5-6. The people of Israel, freed from their bondage in Egypt, were finding the harshness of the wilderness trying their patience, if not their souls. Looking back, they saw Egypt through the eyes of yearning, which made it more than reality had ever allowed. "We remember the fish, which we did eat in Egypt freely; the cucumbers, and the melons, and the leeks, and the onions, and the garlick: But now our soul *is* dried away: *there is* nothing at all, beside this manna, *before* our eyes." (King James).

in from different parts and occupy a good deal of my time—All the men under-stand Burman pretty well, and I have some interesting meetings among them.

Yours affect'y

A. Judson.

Source: Franklin Trask Library, Andover Newton Theological School, Newton Centre MA.

Emily C. Judson to the Editors of the Christian *Reflector*,[175] March 3, 1847[176]—Rangoon

To the Editors of the Christian Reflector:

Our first package of American papers has just been received, and I have taken a trip upon the inky columns, at more than railroad speed, back to the busy world I have left behind. I see fair, beautiful Boston, as when I strained my eyes to catch a last glimpse while it faded in the haze of distance on that memorable parting day. I go a little farther, and there are kind hands, and dear faces, and tearful eyes, and—. What if my own tears do fall and blot the paper? You will not think, I trust, that I love my new home any the less for remembering the old.

We had a long but most delightful voyage in the pleasant "Faneuil Hall," with its fine accommodations, kind officers, and quiet, orderly crew; and between our internal resources, and the constantly varying character of sea scenery, we could find no time for *ennui*. Twenty weeks from the day on which we went aboard, we anchored off Amherst; and the next Monday morning, were lowered into a Burmese boat, to proceed up to Maulmain. I was most agreeably disappointed by my first view of the land of palms and mosquitoes. Our boat was very much like a long water-trough, whittled to a point at each end, and we were all nestled like a parcel of caged fowls, under a low bamboo cover, from which it was not easy to look out. But the shore, alongside which we were pushed up stream by the might of muscle, was brilliant with its unpruned luxuriance of verdure, and birds and flowers.

Here some strange tree drooped its long trailers to the water, there the white rice-bird, or a gayer stranger, with chamelion [sic] neck and crimson wing, coquetted with its neighbor and the wealth of green bending below; and, then fol-lowed rich blossoms of new shapes and lines, and bearing new names, some in clusters, and some in long amber wreaths, stained here and there with lemon and vermillion, and all bearing that air of slumberous richness which I believe is a char-

---

[175] This letter was originally sent to the editor of the *Christian Reflector*, and a subsequent letter dated March 14, 1847, was sent to the editor of the *New York Commercial Advertiser* and printed in the *Newark Daily Advertiser* on August 11. These letters reveal the wonderful power of Fanny Forester's pen used in advocating the mission cause now so dear to her heart. She later wrote numerous articles for *The Macedonian*, one of the magazines of the American Baptist Missionary Union.

[176] This letter appeared in the *Newark Daily Advertiser* (Newark NJ), July 16, 1847. See p. 2, col. 5. The column heading read: Letter from Fanny Forrester [sic]—Mrs. Judson.

acteristic of the Indian climate. Our oarsmen were Amherst Christians, who seemed as wild with joy as the birds themselves, (not that they were particularly bird-like in any other respect,) and there was laughing and chattering enough to make any heart merry. The first, being a universal language, I had no difficulty in understanding, but the latter sounded to me even more outlandish than their gaudy patsoes, bare, brawny shoulders, and turbaned heads, appeared to the eye.

To my taste Maulmain is a beautiful place, with its curious, weather-stained houses, set down in spacious compounds, which are hedged round by the bamboo, and filled with tropic fruit-trees. To my taste, I say, because tastes differ widely, and mine, having been formed on the simple model of American country-life, would not be difficult to please. I have been told, however, by English ladies, that there were few towns in the East so entirely unexceptionable as a residence in every respect. For Rangoon, whither we came a little more than a week since, I cannot say so much. Indeed, the two places are so utterly unlike as to preclude any attempt at comparison. Maulmain has sprung up within the last fifteen years, and has all the sweet freshness of its youth about it;—but Rangoon is an old, dilapidated town, with no specimens of architectural splendor for romance to spread a single feather by, crumbling in its narrow streets, but still, more than half in ruins.

The government buildings are deserted, some of the fine tanks that it used to boast filled with rubbish, the moat dry, the gates taken away, and the stockade in most parts laid flat for street pavements. And *such* pavements! Corduroy roads are nothing to them. This desolation is occasioned by the last king's having made an attempt to remove the town from the river's edge, and leave the ground to money-making Jews, and a few English and Chinese. There are two Englishmen, ship captains, residing here now.

Our house ("Green Turban's Den," as we have named it, since it is nearer that than a lodge, or a hall, or a cottage) is on a Moorman street, an upper story, with a Jew's shop beneath it. It looks a little like civilization to see the children in their wide trowsers [sic], usually of crimson cotton, and their white, close fitting robes above, trudging off to school, with their satchels on their shoulders, even though we know that the extent of their learning is probably only to jabber the Koran; but it mars the picture some to watch from day to day and find no girls among them.

The Burmese women go into the streets as openly as the men, but the wife of the true Mussulman never feels the fresh air upon her cheek. Hereupon I should like to propound a question to physicians, but I forbear. Money is the Moorman's god, as the Jews'; and trade, trade, trade, I think must be the burden of his prayers to Allah. It is very certain that not a miser of them in this neighborhood neglects his prayers; for such a din as they make about our ears of an evening would get them a berth for the night in a Boston watch-house. The old Abrahamite below is far the quietest, but even his hurried voice, laden with Hebrew accents, sometimes makes its way up through the floor. As I write, I glance down into the street, and see a Burman priest, distinguishable by the shaven head and dirty yellow pasto, hugging the vessel in which he receives alms to his breast, and glancing first at one side of the street, and then the other, it appears to me a little anxiously. No one seems inclined to pay him any attention, and I am afraid the poor fellow will get no breakfast unless he turns some corner where he will find more Boodhism.

From my window I can see the tips of several pagodas, and through the openings of a bamboo roof opposite, I catch glimpses of a cross crowning a Romish church. The Catholics can do Protestant missionaries but little mischief here now, as the alarm of poor "father Brumo," at an invasion which he appears to consider a rising up of the Arch-fiend himself, clearly evinces. The new king is a rigid Boodhist, and all foreign religions are on a par in his eyes. Boodhism never was more popular throughout the empire than now. The king's brother, who is prime minister and heir apparent, pounds and cooks the rice for the priests with his own hands; and when he has occasion to impose a fine upon a Mussulman or any other foreigner, instead of receiving the money himself, he kindly advises the poor wretch to present it to the priests, and to buy merit for both, one profiting by the gift, the other by the suggestion. All *Mussulmandom* has been thrown into consternation of late, by the report that his most Boodhistical majesty, in an extreme fit of piety, had obliged three of their brethren to *eat pork*.

In the midst of all these things, the missionary of Christ would have cause for little encouragement, but that he knows he is enlisted on the side of an all powerful conqueror, who, in the end, and in his own good time, is certain of victory. Since our arrival about fifty Karens, some of whom desire baptism, have come to pay the teacher a visit; but only a few of the Burmese venture to show their faces. Ko Thalia, the good old pastor of whom you have often heard,—a mild patriarchal-looking man, who quite takes me back in my fancy to the early days of Christianity,— explains the difference. He says there are a great many Karen disciples, and when one of them finds himself in trouble with the government, they all band together, each contributes a few rupees, and so they help him out of his difficulty.

But the poor Burman is obliged to bear his own burden alone. The good old man is well qualified to judge, as he has himself both been in the stocks, and suffered in purse, for Christ's sake. Some of the Karens that came in never saw a missionary before, having been baptized by a native preacher. It was interesting, touchingly interesting, to hear how even these referred to the Bible—with what perfect confidence they presented it, in almost every remark they made, as their rule of faith and conduct; and I saw tears in eyes which one would suppose had looked on too many scenes to melt readily. A few years ago these men had no written language, and now they can nearly all read the Bible.

"The teacher" held Burmese worship last Sabbath in his study, though his audience was mostly composed of Karens. When I looked out upon the strange scenery made up of oriental beauty and oriental degradation and wretchedness, and saw the poor, half-frightened disciples, creeping along the narrow alley, back to the stairs leading to the upper chamber where they were to worship, I thought I had before me a vivid picture of the olden time and Scripture scenes. Thus met the first disciples, when those from whom we are descended were performing blasphemous and bloody rites in a rugged northern island, more barbarous and more degraded than the poor worshippers of an acknowledged nonentity that surround us here.

Yours, most sincerely,

Emily C. Judson

Source: *Newark Daily Advertiser* (Newark NJ), July 16, 1847.

Mrs. Stella K. Bennett to Emily C. Judson, March 8, 1847— Monmogon

My dear Mrs. Judson,

The suddenness with which Mr. Bennett[177] leaves for Maulmain prevents my writing you more than to acknowledge the receipt of your kind note by Mr. Wade[178] and to thank you for it. If my circumstances had permitted my writing at the time of your arrival in this country or for some time after, I should not have been so tardy in congratulating you on your marriage to one of my first and best friends in the Mission and in giving you a cordial welcome to all the joys consequent upon that marriage. Sorrows there are and enough too, connected with every situation in life—some are peculiar to Missionary life but missionaries have their peculiar joys too, and after many years participation of them, I can truly say I wish you no greater joy than to live and have health to labor long and hard for the

---

[177] Cephas Bennett arrived in Burmah in January 1830; his wife was Stella Bennett. Mr. Bennett remained the superintendent of the Baptist Press there for more than fifty years. He worked with Adoniram Judson on the printing of the Bible into Burmese and Karen. From the Utica area, the Bennetts sent their children back, and the girls were educated at the Utica Female Academy. The girls included Elsina (April 1828), Mary (November 1829) Ann (August 1833), Ellen (June 1835), and Sarah (June 1837).

[178] Jonathan and Deborah Wade were appointed missionaries to Burmah in 1823. Their relationship with Adoniram Judson was especially dear because of the early experiences they shared, including the death of Ann Judson. When she died and Adoniram returned to Amherst expecting to find her, he learned instead the news of her death. He never forgot the sight of Deborah Wade standing on the veranda holding little Maria in her arms. Much of their work was spent in the Karen jungle communities following the path of George Boardman. They returned home to America on December 22, 1847, and went back to Burmah in January 1851, just as Emily was returning to the United States. They were from the Hamilton, New York, area. They left for Burmah on July 25, 1850, and were in Maulmain by February 1851. Both died in Burmah; Deborah died at Maulmain in 1868, and Jonathan died in Rangoon in 1872.

good of those among whom you have chosen your home. I have very much wished to see you and Mr. Judson and Miss Lillybridge[179] but if you should go to Rangoon and remain there it is not probable we shall ever meet on earth. There are a thousand things about which I should like to inquire, but I dare say Mr. B. will trouble you enough in that line for us both.

Hope you have heard from Miss Sheldon[180] since we have, our last date from here was in Aug.

You have heard my health is poor but I am happy to say I have gained strength considerably here and trust I shall be able to attend to my usual duties in the school the coming rains. The loss of our beloved sister Mason[181] and now her husband is felt as one of the greatest afflictions that ever befell Tavoy. As things now are the prospect for both Karens and Burmans in this region looks dark, but no one knowing the state of Br. Masons health and of his mind can doubt the necessity for his withdrawal for the present from Missionary labor and while we who remain mourn that we can accomplish so little we must try to have faith that the Lord will carry forward his own work in *some* way, though we do not see it. We shall look with the deepest interest for the issue of Mr. Judson's removal to Rangoon should he go. Shall hope to hear from you occasionally, though you have reason to expect a very poor return for anything you will write. How do things appear as you anticipate? or otherwise. How do you succeed as mother? Do the dear boys[182] seem to know they are at *home* again and with Papa and Mama? How is Mr. Judson's health compared with what it was when he left M. to go home? How is your own health compared with what it was at home? Allow me to thank Mr. Judson here for a very kind note he wrote me last June, and with very kind regards to him,

> Believe me yours
> Very affectionally
> S. K. Bennett

Source: American Baptist Historical Society, AJ 12, no. 359.

---

[179] See vol. 1, "Cast of Characters," s.v. "Lillybridge, Miss," also the timeline on "Lydia Lillybridge Simons."

[180] See vol. 1, "Cast of Characters," s.v. "Sheldon, Miss Cynthia."

[181] Helen Maria Griggs was the second wife of Francis Mason; they married on May 23, 1830, the day before their ship left Boston for Burmah. Working at Tavoy with the Karen tribe, Helen Mason became close friends with Sarah Hall Boardman. Helen Mason had four children; she died on October 8, 1846 of "debility after child birth" four months after the birth of Francis.

[182] Henry Hall Judson, approximately four and a half years old, and Edward Judson, just two months beyond two years old.

Emily C. Judson to Catharine Chubbuck, March 14, 1847[183]

[Note: The first page of this letter is missing.]

study door. At first a cold chill crept to the very tips of my fingers, but in a moment more I saw that their stare was more one of curiosity than malice. There was a movement among the Burmans—a little fidgeting—but the doc. seemed not to observe the addition to his assembly, and went on as usual. At first all listened very attentively, but when he came to speak of Christ and his mission they broke into a low incredulous laugh and three of them arose and went away. The other two stayed until he had finished, and one of them, an old man with a devil's face, lingered a long-time afterward. But the doc. tho't it best to take no notice of him. During worship Edward[184] cried and I was obliged to cross the court with him. You may well believe that I was a little startled to see two respectable looking Burmans, with elegant great silk patsoes, sitting in the entrance room. Were these government spies and the cooly-looking wretches within jailors and executioners. It certainly looked like it. Well, spy away, tho't I, if you move an inch toward the door I whisper the alarm and there are disciples enough within to overpower you and get away. So I bro't my chair into the court and placed it in a position to command all the doors while I pretended to be watching Edward's sleep. They looked at me and whispered to each other and looked again, but I knew that they would'nt [sic] hurt *me*. And now what do you suppose they turned out to be? Why, two innocent chaps, nephews of the one of the disciples, who, tired of their own religion, came to find out more of ours than their uncle could teach them. Just as they went into the study my sava-byan-dan (interpreter) came in; and while the doc. held a sharp contest with them for two long hours, he listened most eagerly but said nothing. I trust his Boodhism rec'd a shock. I should'nt [sic] have mentioned the little alarms of today, as they turned out nothing, but it will give you something of an idea of our position.

Our house is on a Moorman street and for this reason particularly favourable [sic] to getting Burmans together for worship. There are some Burmese on the street, however, and a Jew's shop beneath. Over the way I see a kingly Mogul sit smoking his hookah nearly all the day, and a little to the right is one Armenian house. Last week a Burman was killed a few doors from us by robbers, but we are in comparatively little danger. They know that it is the custom of foreigners to keep fire-arms—beside our door fastens with a heavy iron chain and three Burmans sleep in the entrance room. The only possible danger is from the windows which they might enter by means of a ladder, as we are obliged to keep them open, but there is not much danger of it.—It is three weeks yesterday since we arrived in

---

[183] This letter is dated from the line that says it is being written three weeks and a day from they time they landed in Rangoon (February 20).

[184] See vol. 1, "Cast of Characters," s.v. "Judson, Edward."

Rangoon, and now, Kitty duck, let me tell you that I never spent three such happy weeks in all my life. We are in just the spot where we sh'd be and where we both are glad to be. [Note: A line here is written, and then marked out by Emily.]—we can go on with our work without interruption, and we do get on bravely. I study language and take care of the two babies and the doc. makes dictionary from morning till night. To be sure the natives come in (not half so much as we are hoping they will soon, though) but they have an object, and there is none of this fashionable dilly-dallying about it. Beside, I am at liberty to dress as I choose, and am getting strong under the thin loose clothing that the climate requires. The Maulmain fashionables are absolutely worse than the gayest New Yorkers, and you must screw yourself up in long waists and shapely whale-bones for *decency's* sake. Poor Lydia[185] is suffering terribly, for Mrs. Howard[186] will not even let her wear her pretty morning dresses. I protested against all such nonsense, pronounced the English leaders of the ton *provincialists* (a galling word) and told them that no *lady* in London or Paris ever dressed till after twelve. My positive and contemptuous air did a deal of good; but when you have a great object to accomplish and every moment seems precious you do not like to be subjected to such foolish annoyances. Here, we need never waste a moment without we choose, and I absolutely grudge the time I take up in writing my letters. There is an immense field before us, and after the rains (in about eight months) we mean to feel our way up to Ava. I do believe that God is with us, and I am all courage. If we go to Ava so soon I must study night and day to speak the language a little acceptably. Some missionaries I find have made a great mistake by thinking they could use the language before they were fit.

I have put off mentioning to you a serious loss which has saddened us a little, because I tho't it would probably trouble you a great deal more than it has us. In coming round here, we bro't but *very* few things with us. We gave [Note: Written in the right margin of the address page.] away a great deal, sold a little and packed the rest away to send for after the rains were over. In two chests we put everything valuable that we had on earth and these we stowed away in Mr. Steven's house. The very night after we left and before we were out of the river, his house was burnt to the ground and not a thing saved. Among the lost which it would be impossible to enumerate here were all the doc.'s bombazine clothes, fine flannels, every American shoe that he had, his spectacles both gold and silver, our silver forks (steel rusts so that we cannot use them in this country,) an [Note: Written in

---

[185] See vol. 1, "Cast of Characters," s.v. "Lillybridge, Miss," also the timeline on "Lydia Lillybridge Simons."

[186] Theresa Howard was born in New York; with her husband Hosea, she arrived in Burmah on December 26, 1834. They worked in Moulmein and Rangoon for sixteen years before sailing for the United States on February 28, 1850. Theresa Howard worked with her husband in the schools established by the mission. She died in Bloomington, Illinois, on July 14, 1868.

the left margin of the address page.] elegant great solar lamp that Mr. Newton[187] gave us, my Jane Kelly[188] tea spoons, my travelling-dress [sic] for which I paid fourteen dollars and which would be invaluable at Ava, a beautiful new mouselaine [sic] de laine, three dress patterns, one of which Miss Trevor gave me, all my *fine* flannels, linen pocket-handkerchiefs, linen chemise, silk-stockings (very useful here as the giver knew) thin night-dresses, napkins, towels etc. etc. etc. The things that we regret more as being the most needed are the doctor's shoes and glasses and the flannels for both of us. If I were coming out again, I would make up a half-dozen chemises of the thinnest gauze flannel for the hot season. I am already suffering from the thickness of common rule flannel and yet I cannot do without it. We lost by the fire about five hundred dollars.

Source: Hanna family files.

Emily C. Judson to the Editor of the *New York Comercial Advertiser*,[189] March 14, 1847[190]—Rangoon

We exchanged Maulmain for this city some three or four weeks since, and though we left English society and to a great degree English comforts behind, I find my new situation rather pleasant than otherwise, and have no fear of dying of hunger, heat or home sickness. As for the government, it is as oppressive as the depravity of human nature can make it. Grind—grind, crush—crush, is the policy, until industry is discouraged, energy deadened, everything like enterprise or independence exchanged for the most abject meanness of spirit, and men, without a single hope for this world or the next, crouch in the ashes of their miserable huts

[187] There are seven letters in this correspondence from Mr. and Mrs. Isaac Newton of New York City. In a June 1846 letter, Mrs. Newton indicated that they are "new friends," certainly of Emily. They obviously had considerable wealth, which they shared generously with Adoniram and Emily through packages and, upon Adoniram's death, an immediate check to Emily of $500. Mr. Newton called Adoniram his "friend." One of the letters invited Emily to stay with them in New York upon her return, and a later letter indicated that she had indeed done that. On May 15, 1846, Adoniram Judson inscribed a dedication to Mrs. H. H. Newton on the fly-leaf of a volume of Burmese hymns that had been compiled by Mrs. Sarah B. Judson: "Mrs. H. H. Newton From A. Judson/ The wings [ ] [ ] /[ ] are folded in St. Helena—New York—May 15th, 1846."

[188] Miss Jane Kelly was Emily Chubbuck's friend at the Utica Female Academy, and then she became a teacher with Emily at that institution. Miss Kelly became the literary principal in 1844 with the retirement of Mr. and Mrs. James Nichols from that position. During a period of Miss Kelly's illness in 1844, Emily filled in the position for her. Then, in 1848, when Miss Cynthia Sheldon moved to Philadelphia to help start the Misses Anable's School, Miss Kelly became the "headmistress" of the academy and successfully brought it into the future, though not without some initial disparagement from the Sheldon-Anable families.

[189] This letter was sent to the editor of the *New York Commercial Advertiser* and a subsequent letter dated March 3, 1847, was sent to the editor of the *Christian Reflector* and printed in the *Newark Daily Advertiser* on July 16. These letters show the wonderful power of Fanny Forester's pen used in advocating the mission cause now so dear to her heart. She later wrote numerous articles for *The Macedonian*, one of the magazines of the American Baptist Missionary Union.

[190] This letter appeared in the Newark Daily Advertiser, Newark, New Jersey, Wednesday Evening, August 11, 1847. Its heading was: Another Letter from Fanny Forester (a previous letter from March 3, 1847 had appeared July 16, 1847). Of this letter it said: "We extract from a long letter with which we have been favored from Mrs. Judson—Fanny Forrester [sic] of yore—the following interesting account of Dr. Judson's position and labors on the Burman mission:—*N. Y. Com. Adv.*

and pass their long days and nights like the dogs and bullocks which surround them. I like the Burmese character, as it would be but for this withering oppression. It has many fine traits, which the adoption of Christianity usually throws into bold and beautiful relief. But the Christians among them are obliged to worship by stealth, for religious intolerance, of the narrowest, sternest order, is the policy of all in power, from the lowest to the highest.

We worship in a private room of our own house, with the doors shut. Last Sabbath we had, to my eyes, a singularly interesting scene—the administration of the Lord's Supper. No Sabbath-bell called the little knot of worshippers together; no Sabbath stillness reigned in the air, speaking in wordless eloquence to the spirit; the hand of toil paused not for one single holy moment, but the voice of trade came up in boisterous tones from every open shed, mingled with a low, continuous murmuring from the distant market place [*sic*] Imagine me looking down into this street from the upper verandah of a large, oddly fashioned house, with solid, heavy masonry around and below, and open bamboo work waiting to be thatched above my head. I have taken this stand to watch the coming of our little band of disciples. The sun is low and the shadows all around are lengthening and slightly darkening. In the distance towers the point of many a gilded pagoda, tricked out in glittering trumpery; and nearer, a cross, beneath which an Italian priest repeats Latin formulas to a congregation of half-blood Portuguese, peeps from clustering green; and nearer still, a crescent hides itself in luxurious shadows. But to our own street.

Cautiously they come, some of the more timid with their patsoes gathered up in a knot, like coolies, and their small white jackets hidden in the folds, to give them a labor-like appearance. Entering a narrow alley at the left corner of the house, they creep around to the back, ascend a long flight of stairs, and when the last has entered, bolt the door behind them. And now behold me seated in a long, dark, narrow room, with massive walls and a low, heavy ceiling, from the beams of which lizards crawl to sun themselves at hot noon-day, and where nestle scores on scores of bats, to come thence with the darkness, and flit and flap their ugly wings above our heads all through the night. Now the day's sultriness is passed, and the last mellow rays of an Indian sun are streaming through the one unglazed window, making it appear, with all this dust floating in the atmosphere, as though we breathed flakes of gold. On either side of me is a pair of small, sweet blue eyes, bright with the mirth which the demure little lips have striven hard to banish looking into my face as they turn from the surroundings, to them so barren of interest, but not wonderingly nor discontentedly. Bright, beautiful blossoms! The sunshine of love is about them, and little do they think of the wilderness they are budding in, or how like the winged things of a better world the contrast makes them appear.

"The teacher" is in his usual seat by his study table: sitting, or reclining on mats in a half-circle around, are dark-faced men in oriental costume—eager, greedy, half-tearful listeners to a tale full of thrillingly intense interest, the passion of our Saviour. I do not understand much of what is said, but the voice now goes on evenly, as though balanced by many details, and now it swells gradually higher—fuller—and still fuller, and then dies away in a low sad cadence. For a moment there is a pause, unbroken by a breath. Then the subject is resumed, at first with rapid, earnest articulation—then the voice falters as though heavy with grief, the words following each other slowly and with hesitating tremulousness. The listener bends low in sorrowing silence, yet not so low but I can mark the quivering of the lips, and the pressing of white eye-lashes against tawny cheeks; and so the tale goes on, until the voice grows firm again and deepens into triumph. Then prayer ascends, while all these strange, bending figures press the door with their foreheads, and at the close utter the response with a solemn fervor.

And then—Oh! who could see the sacred cup which every Christian loves better than his life, the mystic symbol commemorative of our salvation, touch these newly tamed lips without feeling his blood tingle in its channels? Who? Thank God for the spirits, and there are many of them in fair, beautiful America, who are not narrowed down by the miserably short-sighted selfishness which cries "All for home"—spirits not wholly imprisoned in clay, nor cramped by the boundaries of time and space. Such will extend to our little band of disciples a kindly and sympathetic hand. They are but few—eleven in number present—but to me this small gathering is far more interesting than the most crowded assembly in America.

Eleven disciples! The number left after the traitor had withdrawn, more than eighteen centuries ago, when the sweet memorial was left us—even while the stroke of the hammer resounded from the cross and the band of armed men were gathering by the brook Kedron.

The sun disappears before the rite is concluded; and one by one the worshippers go out, slip the foot into the crimson sandal and creep cautiously down the stairs. The old man of patriarchal aspect, with the mild, meek face and almost timid air, left the worship of Gandama for that of Christ twenty years ago; and though there is no evidence of boldness in his face or manner, his feeble foot has never slipped nor his heart grown weary. He had suffered many a shameful indignity, been stripped of his goods, lain with his feet in the stocks and seen his friend prosecuted until death came to end his sufferings. And yet, when Europeans were obliged to flee, he continued, in his own quiet, prudent, unostentatious way, to go from house to house and keep alive the little spark which had been lighted just as the cloud of war settled upon the country.

"Through the grace of God I have been permitted to baptize one hundred and sixty-four," he said to me one day, in reply to a question I had asked; and the quiet happiness lighting up every feature as he spoke, I almost believe would have been even more persuasive than the eloquence of Paul when he made the proud Roman trouble. This old man is the pastor of the little native church, but it has been a long time since he dared to assemble its members. Our house affords some protection. The fine-eyed, intelligent seeming man near the door was formerly a writer in the employ of Government, and is one of the hundred and sixty-four most of whom, by the way, are scattered in the jungles, mentioned by the good pastor. The affection which he evinces for his spiritual father is quite touching. He is also a preacher, and assists the American missionaries in their literary pursuits. So you see the little blade that I mentioned is already putting out its branches.

The poor old woman that hobbled in with so much difficulty, and crouched upon the mat, is more than ninety years of age. She was once in respectable circumstances, her husband being engaged in the coinage of money, from which employment she takes her own title. But her husband is dead, her children too are dead, excepting one daughter, (a widow with seven dependent children and the Christian mother's persecutor) and the lone old woman is very, very poor. But twenty years ago she commenced laying up treasure in heaven, wealth which will hereafter prove an exhaustless mine; her heart is always from the desert in which her worn out body still lingers, away with her treasure.—Blessings on her drooping head and bending figure! She is ugly now, very ugly, but I look at the small, faded, watery eyes, the dark skin which seems to have been tanned and toughened for the wear of a long life, and the furrows ploughed no less by care than time, and think of a day when even she will be polished into a brilliant, precious jewel. She has a beautiful spirit even now.

Emily C. Judson to Catharine Chubbuck, March 15, 1847—Bat Castle (Rangoon)

Dear Kitty,—

I write you from walls as massive as any you read of in old stories and a great deal uglier—the very eye-ball and heart-core of an old white-bearded Mussulman. Think of me in an immense brick house with rooms as large as the entire "loggery,"[191] (our centre room is twice as large, and has no window), and only one small window apiece. When I speak of windows, do not think I make any allusion to glass—of course not. The windows (holes) are closed by means of heavy board

---

[191] The loggery was Emily's father's home. See Kendrick, *The Life and Letters of Mrs. Emily C. Judson*, 166. See also vol. 1, "Places, Events, Organizations, and Magazines," s.v. "Loggery, The."

or plank shutters, tinned over on the outside, as a preventive of fire. The bamboo houses of the natives here are like flax or tinder, and the foreigners, who have more than the one cloth which Burmans wrap about the body, and the mat they sleep on, dare live in nothing but brick. Imagine us, then, on the second floor of this immense den, with nine rooms at our command, the smallest of which (bathing-room and a kind of pantry) are, I think, quite as large as your dining-room, and the rest very much larger. Part of the floors are of brick, and part of boards; but old "Green Turban" white-washed them all, with the walls, before we came, because the Doctor told him, when he was over here, that he must "make the house shine for madam."[192] He did make it shine with a vengeance, between white-washing and greasing. They oil furniture in this country, as Americans do mahogany; but all his doors and other wood-work were fairly dripping, and we have not got rid of the smell yet; nor, with all our rubbing, is it quite safe to hold too long on the door. The partitions are all of brick, and very thick, and the door-sills are built up, so that I go over them at three or four steps, Henry[193] mounts and falls off, and Edward[194] gets on all-fours, and accomplishes the pass with more safety. The floor overhead is quite low, and the beams, which are frequent, afford shelter to thousands and thousands of bats, that disturb us in the day-time only by a little cricket-like music, but in the night—Oh, if you could only hear them carouse! The mosquito curtains are our only safe-guard; and getting up is horrible. The other night I awoke faint, with a feeling of suffocation; and without waiting to think, jumped out on the floor. You would have thought "old Nick" himself had come after you, for, of course, you believe these firm friends of the ladies of the broom-stick incipient imps. If there is nothing wickeder about them than about the little sparrows that come in immense swarms to the same beams, pray what do they do all through the hours of darkness, and why do they circle and whizz about a poor mortal's head, flap their villainous wings in one's face, and then whisk away, as if snickering at the annoyance? We have had men at work nearly a week trying to thin them out, and have killed a great many hundreds, but I suppose their little demoniac souls come back, each with an attendant, for I am sure there are twice as many as at first. Every thing [sic], walls, tables, chairs, etc., are stained by them. Besides the bats, we are blessed with our full share of cockroaches, beetles, spiders, lizards, rats, ants, mosquitoes, and bed-bugs. With the last the wood-work is all alive, and the ants troop over the house in great droves, though there are scattering ones beside. Perhaps twenty have crossed my paper since I have been writing. Only one cockroach has paid me

---

[192] See the letter of Adoniram Judson to Emily C. Judson dated February 2, 1847.

[193] See vol. 1, "Cast of Characters," s.v. "Judson, Henry Hall."

[194] See vol. 1, "Cast of Characters," s.v. "Judson, Edward."

a visit, but the neglect of these gentlemen has been fully made up by a company of black bugs about the size of the end of your little finger—nameless adventurers....

Emily

Source: A. C. Kendrick, *The Life and Letters of Mrs. Emily C. Judson*, 270–72.

Emily C. Judson to Miss Cynthia Sheldon, March 21, 1847—Rangoon

My very dear Miss Cynthia,

I am on missionary ground at last; and but for the certainty that the "Lord God omnipotent reigneth," very discouraging ground would it be. We are surrounded by false religions of every kind; and yet tied hand and foot.[195] Maulmain with its English comforts, charming society and well-ordered churches is an American town compared with this dreadful place. The city is all in a glitter with splendid kyoungs and gilded pagodas, and those who do not worship the Boodh have their other gods quite as false. The Parsee prostrates himself before the sun or some lesser fire of his own kindling, the Moorman calls loudly upon Allah, and the poor humbled Jew worships the Messiah of his imagination, yet to come. Scarce in advance of these are the professed believers in Jesus Christ—the Greeks, Arminians [*sic*] and Portuguese. We have attended the worship of the two latter. The Roman priest is but a year from Italy and the other not long from Arminia [*sic*], so they have their religion as pure as corrupt fountains could give, but such senseless mummery I never would have believed practised [*sic*] by men with heads on their shoulders.

The little church of Protestant disciples is very small, and exceedingly timid, for (poor fellows!) they have had occasion to know something of the tender mercies of an idolatrous government. A few of them creep round to our back door and up to the doctor's study of a Sunday to worship but the number is so very small that our courage is kept up only by knowing in whose hands are the hearts of all men. A week ago today a little Burman girl chanced to open the outer door after it had been barred; and when we rose from prayers I was startled to see several wild, savage looking men, nearly naked, sitting just outside the study. I was seated so between the doors that I could not see very well how many there were of them, but I counted five. I did not sit very easily, especially as I saw the doctor's Burmese assistants looking a little troubled and anxious, and while I was trying to invent an excuse to leave the room and see what was going on without, little Edward[196] began to cry. I immediately took him in my arms and went out. There were but five

[195] Burmese authorities allowed Emily and Adoniram Judson to go to Rangoon to work with the foreign Christian population there; they were restricted from preaching at all to the natives of Rangoon.

[196] See vol. 1, "Cast of Characters," s.v. "Judson, Edward."

of the wild men; but in crossing the court I saw two young intelligent looking Burmans in handsome silk patsoes, sitting in the entrance room, listening, watching, and whispering. The thought of government officers with their jailors or policemen flashing across my mind, and I paused to consider whether it would be best to give the alarm. Finally I placed my chair on one of the big sills which I wrote A. M.[197] about, where my eye commanded the whole house, pretending to watch Edward and listen to the preaching at the same time. After worship was over, we learned that the wild men were common coolies who had come to gratify curiosity; and the two young men were inquirers, nephews of one of the Christians. They came into the study; my teacher, a government interpreter, followed; and for an hour and a half the doctor talked with all his might—pulling down and building up. Today our whole assembly consisted of our own people, the Rangoon herd, two Maulmain disciples, and a Rangoon convert who desires baptism; and it is supposed that the occurrence of last Sabbath kept the others away. The two young inquirers were writers in the employ of the Ray Woon, and though we are confident that they were "good men and true" they might very well be taken for spies. I tell you all this that you may get some notion of our position and the weakness of the tiny church. Oh! Never were prayers needed more than we need them now—away here in this terrible place, with none to look to but each other and God. Do remember us every day, dear Aunt Cynthia,[198] and tell all who love the cause of missions which is the cause of Christ, to remember us for the sake of that, though they may have no love for us. You don't know how distressing it is to look about and feel that you can do nothing—nothing—or next to nothing. I believe he is very thankful (my precious husband) for the two or three inquirers that have been sent him, but only think what might be the result if he were allowed to go out and preach and distribute tracts. Such a proceeding, however, would send us back to Maulmain in double-quick-time; and we are very anxious to retain a footing here and perhaps proceed up to Ava.

The neighbourhood [sic] is just now in a great state of alarm on account of several robberies and murders. One man was shot down in our own immediate neighbourhood [sic]; and, beside that, there have been three killed and more wounded. They cannot reach us without a ladder and so we feel pretty safe; especially as we hope they may have had their spies out when we landed, and so know

---

[197] Anna Maria Anable was the niece of the Misses Urania and Cynthia Sheldon and the daughter of Joseph and Alma Sheldon Anable. Emily first met Anna Maria in fall 1840 when she went as a student to the Utica Female Academy; both Emily and Anna Maria became members of the faculty there. In these years, Anna Maria became Emily's dearest friend, and the extensive correspondence between the two reflects sensitive, flirtatious spirits and a deep intimacy. Emily was "Nemmy" to Anna Maria's "Ninny." In 1848, Anna Maria Anable, with the help of her extended family, moved to Philadelphia and started the Misses Anable's School there. At Emily's death in 1854, Anna Maria was given guardianship of Emily Frances Judson, daughter of Emily and Adoniram Judson.

[198] See vol. 1, "Cast of Characters," s.v. "Sheldon, Miss Cynthia."

we have nothing worth taking. Still, I must own that I should sleep a little sounder if the wretches were in irons. And how do you think our wise governour [*sic*] has [Note: Written the right margin of the address page.] set about establishing order? Why he has issued a permission to all the citizens to shoot down any man who may be seen in the street after ten in the evening.—We are in the midst of dangers, difficulties, and discouragements, and I am the same wicked one that you knew aforetime. Then there is none but me to hold up the hands and encourage the heart of the weary labourer [*sic*] (the noblest, purest, and truest of men) none but poor good-for-nothing me—do oh, do pray for us more earnestly.

Written along the left margin of the address page: "I am getting on in the language very well. Since our arrival we have all been in very good health. The hot season is coming on and everybody but me suffers. I enjoy it, especially since the burning up of my thin flannels. Our loss by the fire was severe, but we have managed to bear it very well. It was, of course, for the best.

"Please give my love to all that remember me kindly. I suppose I think of you all twenty-times where you think of me once. How I wish I could spend a little time with you independent of the bustle which spoiled my last few months."

With aff'ate sincerity—Emily C. Judson

Written along the left margin and top margin of page 1: "P.S. The last that I heard from Tavoy Mrs. Bennett[199] was quite ill—also Messrs. Wade[200] and Mason.[201] If Mrs. Brayton[202] sh'd visit Utica I hope you will see her. She is a simple-minded woman, but very lovely on account of her devoted piety."

Source: Hanna family files.

---

[199] Stella Bennett was the wife of Cephas Bennett; they arrived in Burmah in January 1830. Mr. Bennett remained the superintendent of the Baptist Press there for more than fifty years. From the Utica area, they sent their children back, and the girls were educated at the Utica Female Academy. The girls included Elsina (April 1828), Mary (November 1829), Ann (August 1833), Ellen (June 1835), and Sarah (June 1837).

[200] See vol. 1, "Cast of Characters," s.v. "Wade, Jonathan and Deborah."

[201] Francis Mason arrived in Maulmain in November 1830 and transferred to Tavoy in 1831. His first wife died, and he married Helen Maria Griggs just before leaving the United States. She died in Burmah in 1846; they were the parents of four children. A skilled linguist, Mr. Mason was fluent in twelve languages and translated the Scripture into two of the Karen dialects. In spring 1847, Mr. Mason was seriously ill, and the other missionaries were concerned about him. In September 1847, he remarried, and Adoniram Judson officiated the ceremony. His new wife was Ellen Huntley Bullard; originally from Vermont, she was the widow of Edwin Bullard, missionary to Burmah. Francis Mason died March 3, 1874 in Rangoon.

[202] Mary Fuller was born August 17, 1808, and served as a missionary to Burmah with her husband Durlin Brayton. She advocated strongly that missionary children should not be separated from their parents. Mary Brayton died on December 16, 1890, at Rangoon. See vol. 1, "Cast of Characters," s.v. "Brayton, the Reverend Durlin and Mary."

Newark Daily Advertiser,[203] March 24, 1847

Dr. Judson's Arrival in Burmah.—The *New York Recorder* has received a private letter from Mrs. Judson, which announces the arrival of the Mission family in Burmah after a passage of 136 days. Their voyage was a fine one—accommodations excellent. Mrs. Judson had found the cold air of the sea uncongenial, but it was believed that the tropical climate of Burmah would be favorable to her health.

In a postscript to his letter, dated December 15, Dr. J. says that he is once more in his own domicil [*sic*], preparing to recommence missionary operations.

Emily C. Judson to Lydia Lillybridge, March 27, 1847

I wrote you a little while ago that I was going on with the language swimmingly, and now you will be surprised to hear that I study only between seven and eight in the morning, and that by no means every day. My plan was to study during the day (what time I could spare from family cares), and write in the evening. Accordingly I began collecting my papers for the Memoir;[204] but before I had fairly entered upon my course my health failed from too close application. I must abandon either the study or the memoir, and so the former is waiting, as the latter, if delayed, would be too late. Writing always affected my nervous system, and writing and study together I shall never be able to practice.

Source: A. C. Kendrick, *The Life and Letters of Mrs. Emily C. Judson*, 273–74.

Miss Jane Kelly to Emily C. Judson, March 28, 1847

My dear Emily,

Could you have gazed through the long dim distance that stretches out between us, and looked on that eager breath-less little group that was gathered in Aunt Cynthia's[205] room yesterday morning, the sight of your eyes would have affected your heart. The blessings which each involuntarily called down upon your head, would have been to you an ample return for all the pain and trouble so many letters must have cost you. I must tell you, tho' you already know it, that I heartily rejoice to hear that you are so happy so cheerful, and so devoted to your great and good work. Go on, and prosper in your glorious mission as I know you will, you have the undaunted spirit full of hope and faith which must insure success.

Source: American Baptist Historical Society, AJ 17, no. 788.

---

[203] *Newark Daily Advertiser* (Newark NJ) March 24, 1847. See p. 2, col. 3.

[204] Emily was writing the memoir of Sarah Hall Boardman Judson, the second wife of Adoniram Judson.

[205] See vol. 1, "Cast of Characters," s.v. "Sheldon, Miss Cynthia."

Miss Cynthia Sheldon to Emily C. Judson March 29, 1847[206]—Utica

My dear dear Emily

Your letters have at length arrived, our hearts are full to overflowing on the occasion—well paid for months of restless anxiety—do you know our imagination had been wrought up to a fevered point—the countless gales and disasters at sea considered unprecedented in any former season had excited great fears for your safety—but here comes such glowing descriptions of storms—gales—tar tea etc.—that all hands here agree in thinking them the charm of a voyage—The Lord in great mercy preserved you all—and we are thankful. What would you have done without your good Doctor—I very much doubt having such cheerful letters under the same circumstances on any other account. Lydia[207] says we did not begin to know how good he is in Utica—can that be true—Now my dear E.—I have something against both of you that will be remembered as long as I live—but owing to my peculiar *composition* it is already forgiven—how do you think my conscience could be screwed to take the forty Dollars[208] for *what* I *know not*—any way it looks too much like a book concern I wot [sic] off—but here comes up the poor Burman boy in Mr. Bennett's[209] charge to whom I owe sixty Dollars this minute—this forty makes it easy to cancel that—do you not think this has helped much to put on the screws—The Burman boy shall bless you for this *mis*deed—and my peculiarity strengthens my faith in particular providence—your letter to dear father[210] is every thing [sic]—to him and to us—but oh you know not now the desolation reigning here—dear dear Mother—Anna M.[211] has told you has already been removed from us—and in what manner—poor dear father is trembling on the verge of the grave—His lone pillow and my long practice of seeing them both either sleeping or waking makes this midnight hour very, very sad to me—Yesterday dear father went twice to Church, and had his heart set on going in the evening too—but we prevailed on him to stay—his feelings are like Simeon of old, in view of that the Lord

---

[206] There is an addendum to this letter dated March 30, 1847.

[207] See vol. 1, "Cast of Characters," s.v. "Lillybridge, Miss," also the timeline on "Lydia Lillybridge Simons."

[208] See Emily's letter to Miss Cynthia Sheldon dated December, 1846, in which she speaks of a draft for payment for some things that Miss Sheldon had taken care of for her.

[209] See vol. 1, "Cast of Characters," s.v. "Bennett, The Reverent Cephas and Stella Kneeland."

[210] See vol. 1, "Cast of Characters," s.v. "Sheldon, Deacon Asa."

[211] See vol. 1, "Cast of Characters," s.v. "Anable, Miss Anna Maria."

---

has done for dear Fanny[212] and Henry[213] too—you well know our feelings "stand still and see the Salvation of God"[214]—is now more on my heart than any other passage—Mrs. Anable[215] is all heart and all feeling in these wonderful blessings— Cousin John Sheldon[216] is rejoicing in hope—Mr. Gratiot[217] cannot be far from the kingdom—Martha Lillybridge[218] found peace to her troubled soul two or three days before Fanny did—we have a daughter of Mr. Bingham the Missionary to our Indians, in school; she is a lovely girl—and now is seeking Jesus—others are affected—Miss Kelly[219] and all the teachers think our meetings are delightfully solemn. Mr. Westcott is very impressive—Still they manifest confidence in Mr. Corey[220]—and every thing [sic] is now promising for his increased [Note: Several words are lost at the bottom of the second page of the letter.] man I do not believe his judgment will ever again be so led astray as it was last spring[221]—he has suffered martyrdom almost on the account—your appeal for Missions my girl in father's letter will do great good—you live for purpose, and I could not hold from Mr.

---

[212] Fanny Anable was one of nine children born to Joseph and Alma Anable and was a niece of Miss Cynthia Sheldon and Mrs. Urania Sheldon Nott. The correspondence indicates that in April 1845 she was away from home studying and taking music lessons. These spring letters indicate that she was in Philadelphia, working in the home of and with the family of the Reverend A. D. Gillette. See Miss Sheldon's letter to Emily of November 30, 1845, in which she spoke of all that Fanny was doing to improve herself in the field of music, but also her concern for Fanny's interest in the party life and the "vanitie" which surround her." A March 30, 1847 letter from Anna Maria Anable told of Fanny's conversion following her grandmother's death. In September 1847, she was listed as one of the teachers at the Utica Female Academy. Fanny became a teacher with her sisters in the Misses Anable's School in Philadelphia.

[213] Henry Sheldon Anable was the oldest of the six children born to Joseph and Alma Sheldon Anable. He was born June 21, 1815. In August 1846, he was in the Milwaukee, Wisconsin, area and was thinking of settling there. In a September 27 letter, he said he might leave Utica to join William and Olivia in Sheboygan, Wisconsin. He was married to Rosanna Frick in Sheboygan, Wisconsin, on February 13, 1855, and died September 3, 1887, in Flushing, New York.

[214] The people referenced in this paragraph had been touched and changed by the winds of the revival Spirit that continued to be active in their local church. Miss Sheldon was generous in speaking of the effects and praising God for God's "Salvation."

[215] See vol. 1, "Cast of Characters," s.v. "Anable, Mrs. Alma Sheldon."

[216] On May 7, 1845, Anna Maria Anable referred to a "Cousin John Sheldon," who had seen Emily's brother, J. Walker Chubbuck in Wisconsin. This is likely the son of John Sheldon, brother of the Sheldon sisters (Cynthia, Alma, and Urania). Two letters from him are in the correspondence, one dated February 1, 1846 in which he speaks of coming from Washington, DC, to Philadelphia to see Emily and a second on February 7 in which he apologized for having to leave without properly saying "good-bye" to Emily.

[217] See vol. 1, "Cast of Characters," s.v. "Gratiot, Charles."

[218] Martha Lillybridge was the sister of Lydia Lillybridge, who went to Burmah with Emily and Adoniram Judson. Martha was at the Utica Female Academy. On May 28, 1848, Anna Maria wrote, "Martha is a very fine looking girl—but she lacks energy. I think we shall have her take Fanny's (Anna Maria's sister) place at Miss Martin's. It will suit her as she has no desire to shine as a teacher in a school."

[219] See vol. 1, "Cast of Characters," s.v. "Kelly, Miss Jane."

[220] See vol. 1, "Cast of Characters," s.v. "Corey, the Reverend D. G."

[221] Mr. Corey had made some disparaging remarks about the engagement of Emily and Adoniram, expressing his negative opinion as to Emily's suitability for becoming a missionary. There was great consternation on Emily and Adoniram's part, as well as their dearest friends.

Beebee[222] what would do the world good[223]—But this going to Rangoon is a serious business—we do feel it—Our prayer to God is you may both have *sustaining grace* we know not even now. What trials, deprivations, or persecutions abide you—we shall look for the steamers with deep solicitude hoping for letters—Mrs. Bennett[224] writes Nov. 12th—another son—better prospects for health etc.

Well as I know you prize every line from these parts—as we do from that far country—and I sometimes think distance strengthens the cords of affection—our hearts do yearn over the absent ones.

Source: American Baptist Historical Society, AJ 20, no. 1006.

Miss Cynthia Sheldon to Emily C. Judson, March 30, 1847[225]

A good letter just came from dear Olivia[226]—she is a darling endures heroically all the privations of the new country—Courtland[227] writes from the same post much in her praise—William[228] is very happy—full of hopes—we have felt deeply about Henry,[229] going—but we give him up now most cheerfully—the Lord will direct him.—Harriet[230] and Mary[231] write with so much feeling about dear Grandma's[232]

---

[222] Alexander Beebee was trained as a lawyer, but after experiencing strong religious convictions after the death of his first child, he became active in a Baptist church near Skaneateles, New York. In 1824, he observed that the Baptist denomination had only a few credible newspapers in the United States, none of them being in New York. In 1825, he became the editor of the *Baptist Register*, and over the next thirty years, it became a strong foundation for the rapidly growing Baptist churches of Central New York. During the course of Emily's engagement to Adoniram, Mr. Beebee must have said something reflecting the religious wisdom or judgment strongly expressed by many about the marriage of Adoniram Judson and Emily Chubbuck. Many of Emily's letters reflect the antagonism she felt for him. In July 1849, she wrote him a confrontational letter about something he had said. Morven Jones and Miss Sheldon, through continued efforts, did bring about a truce. Morven said that Emily had "no better supporter" than Mr. Beebee.

[223] In a letter written August 29, 1847, Miss Sheldon said, "Mr. Beebee called yesterday to see if we had letters from you by the last steamer—he is very greedy—and says the extracts he took from your letter to Mrs. Jones is lauded every where [sic] and he hopes you will rest assured that such communication is just what every body [sic] wants—the cause would be advanced ten fold if our Missionaries understood giving out such details."

[224] Stella Bennett, with her husband Cephas, arrived in Burmah in January 1830. Five of their seven children were born in Burmah, but they returned to the United States for education. The girls attended the Utica Female Academy, so Mrs. Bennett is frequently mentioned in the correspondence.

[225] This is an addendum to Miss Sheldon's letter of March 29, 1847.

[226] Olivia Williams Anable was married to William Stewart Anable, the second child and second son of Joseph and Alma Sheldon Anable. See the letter written by Anna Maria Anable on September 27, 1846. They lived in Sheboygan, Wisconsin, where Will Anable was in charge of a retail store.

[227] See vol. 1, "Cast of Characters," s.v. "Anable, Courtland."

[228] Born on November 6, 1816, in Albany, New York, William Stewart Anable was the second child and the second son of Joseph and Alma Sheldon Anable. In an August 31, 1844 letter, Miss Cynthia Sheldon reported to Emily that William had returned home, having "doff'd his sailor garb for age." He married Olivia Williams on September 24, 1846, according to a letter written on September 27 by Anna Maria Anable. They moved to Sheboygan, Wisconsin, where Will opened a store. William died February 9, 1863 in Virginia, California.

[229] See vol. 1, "Cast of Characters," s.v. "Anable, Henry Sheldon."

[230] See vol. 1, "Cast of Characters," s.v. "Anable, Harriet."

[231] See vol. 1, "Cast of Characters," s.v. "Anable, Miss Mary Juliet."

death—we have begged them to come home in June—Their last letters however make it doubtful—Mary wrote to Fanny a very impressive letter to improve the present time in preparation to meet dear Grandma in Heaven—and yours came on the day she found peace in believing—John Fuller has this morn'g surrendered to the Prince of peace I learn—do you know he is a decendant [sic] of Andrew Fuller and is thought to possess rare talents—Nine young men presented themselves with some twenty persons for prayer at the close of the sermon last evening—has Anna M.[233] told you we have actually bought our Meeting House four weeks ago—do you not think we feel it home now—and at this time some of our good members are working in mornings at the Baptistery—we have prayer meeting there in the aft'n and a crowded house in the evening—Mr. Beebee[234] subscribed fifty Dollars for our Church—no other from Broad St. have given a manifestation of even willingness to let us go forward—Mr. B. is a good man—means to do right—He is now heart and hand with you—Mrs. Nichols[235] spent last night with us—she is deeply afflicted by the death of her little Lucy—and our dear Sophie also died the 29th of Feb'y—Mr. Ward writes me a deeply affecting letter—he has three motherless children to rear the best he can—Mrs. H. has passed a week in the city, two visits to us—we feel to mingle sympathies—she loved dear Mother—and we all loved dear Sophy.

11 o'clock I was interrupted to day—am glad now my paper is not filled—a praying circle have just left my room—John Sheldon[236] and Henry led the devotions—Mr. Gratiot[237] is humbled in the dust before God, so child like, willing to be any thing [sic] or nothing for Christ—I can only feel to praise God—who doeth all things well—could you have heard Henry—humble fervent petition—you would with us say, Lord it is all we ask—his heart goes out for poor William in tears and groans—Dear Anna M. is a real missionary in the house—but I warn you to make no attempt to remove her the other side of the big waters[238]—she has much to do

---

[232] Grandmother Sheldon died on January 29, 1847. See the letter of Anna Maria Anable to Emily C. Judson dated February 15, 1847.

[233] See vol. 1, "Cast of Characters," s.v. "Anable, Miss Anna Maria."

[234] See vol. 1, "Cast of Characters," s.v. "Beebee, Alexander."

[235] Upon the marriage of Urania Sheldon to the Reverend Dr. Eliphalet Nott, the post of literary principal was occupied by Mr. and Mrs. James Nichols. Mrs. Nichols was a popular teacher at the school. Her health failed in February 1844, and Miss Jane Kelly replaced them. Shortly after that, Miss Kelly became quite ill, and Emily Chubbuck held the position until Miss Kelly's restoration.

[236] See vol. 1, "Cast of Characters," s.v. "Sheldon, Cousin John."

[237] See vol. 1, "Cast of Characters," s.v. "Gratiot, Charles."

[238] For about a year and a half after Emily's marriage to Adoniram Judson, Anna Maria spoke of the possibility of having a call to missions and joining Adoniram and Emily in Burmah. On March 31, 1847, Sarah Bell Wheeler said that Anna Maria was a devoted Christian, and she thought that one day Anna Maria would go to Burmah. She obviously put a lot of prayer and thought into the matter. The painful medical treatments she underwent in summer 1847 were intended to improve her general health. See her letter of June 19, 1847. In summer 1848, she decided that her call was to remain a teacher. Anna Maria moved to Philadelphia, and with her family, she opened the Misses Anable's School. She remained there until her death. She raised Emily Frances Judson here after the death of Emily Judson.

here—Urania[239] writes me last evening she had received a letter from you—she is interested in Fanny[240] and Henry thus far—they are going to N. York this week, will be absent most of their vacation—Mr. Jones[241] is quite sick—we greatly fear he will not recover—Heaven bless you—prayers go up for this—we need yours also.

C. S.

Source: American Baptist Historical Society, AJ 20, no. 1006.

Anna Maria Anable to Emily C. Judson, March 30, 1847[242]

Dear, dear Nemmy[243] how my heart rejoiced to receive your letters last week. I have not written since and sent this because when I wrote the above I was expecting daily a letter from you. O, how long it had been to wait. More than nine months! And I have been *so* anxious about you for the last three months. Emily I have felt severely reproved since you left us. I loved you too much. You were my Gods and my conscience. I was sufficed to love you as to show me the natural tendency of my heart to cherish ideas. I feel thankful daily that I have a heart to appreciate you, and that intimacy was so long uninterrupted—that I have for so long a time been allowed to observe the sprit of Christian liberality and forbearance which actuates you, and I *now* feel thankful that your good husband was sent just in the right time to kindle into [ ]ed person the high wrought Christian enthusiasm of your character. I feel grateful, for next to the sublime consciousness of genius in our own souls and of those higher qualities which qualify us for companionship with angels, must be the satisfaction of knowing that we have a full sympathy with such a character. Tell the Dr. I am deeply grateful for his regards expressed in your letters for me. He little knows how the deep devotion and firm resolution of his character has possessed me. Whenever I think of him which is not seldom I assure you I feel my faith strengthened and my courage renewed to fight manfully the "good fight" if at the

---

[239] See vol. 1, "Cast of Characters," s.v. "Nott, Urania Sheldon."

[240] See vol. 1, "Cast of Characters," s.v. "Anable, Fanny."

[241] Morven Jones was from Utica and attended Mr. Corey's Baptist church, as did many from the Utica Female Academy. In a letter, he spoke of being present at the Colby's in Boston early in July, 1846, just before Adoniram and Emily departed for Burmah. In one letter, she called upon them to get some information on the death of her sister Harriet for the book *My Two Sisters*. In another letter, he summarized articles about the early mission in Burmah in response to her circular looking for letters from Adoniram Judson in preparation for the memoir. A long newsy letter in 1848 tells of happenings in Utica and Hamilton and the Baptist Church of which Mr. Corey was the pastor. In October 1845, his letter has to do with collecting autographs, her autograph particularly. Later letters (December 9, 21, and 22, 1848) tell of a fall that seriously injured Mary Jones; she had been standing on a bridge watching a church baptism when the bridge collapsed; her injuries caused her family to fear for her life, and they were persistently disabling.

[242] This is an addendum to a letter started February 15, 1847. That letter spoke of the death of Anna Maria Anable's grandmother. There is a second addendum dated March 31, 1846.

[243] Emily Chubbuck. See vol. 1, "Cast of Characters," s.v. "Nemmy, Nem, or Nemmy Petty (Nemmie Pettie)." Also the chapter "Names of Endearment."

close of my course I may but find a crown of righteousness laid up for me with those who love our Lord's appearing. But oh, how much of divine assistance I need—I do hope that you and the Dr. will pray for me. Mine are temptations without and temptations within, but I am not going to be any more egotistical, only I do long sometimes for a good fruitful minister to give me a word of encouragement. You must not think that I am unhappy, for I am not. Mr. Corey[244] and the church and I have all got along very comfortably together by dint of minding our own business and we are having soon a precious season of revival. I cannot say that I am taken by surprise or that I am excited though we are having very exciting times in one sense. I know your heart will rejoice to hear of the conversion of dear Fanny[245] and Henry.[246] They have both been serious for some time—Fanny will write you herself, and Henry is ready to go any where [sic] if he can only do some good. The death of Grandma made a very deep impression on his mind. He is about as happy a young convert as ever I saw, and yet perfectly humble. May he be steadfast. John Sheldon[247] has been here for the last six weeks and he too is among the followers of the Lamb. Charles Gratiot[248] is deeply serious. He came home from church last night and begged his wife to kneel down and pray for him. This afternoon he and John and Henry have all been to prayer meeting. Now is not all this wonderful? It is the Spirit of God. Mr. Corey has had a Mr. Westcott[249] to assist him for a fortnight past and we have had preaching from him every eve'g. He is a man after my own heart, calm and convincing in his arguments, but warm and earnest in his feelings. I love him too for the manner in which he speaks of you and the Dr. The first sermon he preached was to the Church and he drew a contrast between the Dr. and Tom Payne as to influence. It was the most beautiful eulogy on your husband that you can imagine, and the beauty of it is that he is all unconscious of the peculiar state of feeling towards the "beloved missionaries." Horace, tho' he has been absent ever since on his Spring business heard all that, and Mr. Corey too is obliged to hear a good deal. The day your letters came they were both (Mr. W. and Mr. C.) in Grandpa's room and heard your letter to him. Mr. W. was so delighted that he begged to be allowed to take it to Mr. Beebee.[250] Mr. Corey thinks there never was

---

[244] See vol. 1, "Cast of Characters," s.v. "Corey, the Reverend D. G."

[245] See vol. 1, "Cast of Characters," s.v. "Anable, Fanny."

[246] See vol. 1, "Cast of Characters," s.v. "Anable, Henry Sheldon."

[247] See vol. 1, "Cast of Characters," s.v. "Sheldon, Cousin John."

[248] See vol. 1, "Cast of Characters," s.v. "Gratiot, Charles."

[249] Dr. Westcott was mentioned in a number of letters from Utica in early 1847. He was a preacher and preached in the Utica Baptist Church where Mr. Corey was the pastor and where a revival that had touched the lives of many of the Anable-Sheldon families took place.

such another man as Dr. Westcott, and yet Dr. Westcott, the first time he called was very desirous of seeing the portrait of Sister Judson,[251] and also of taking home "Alderbrook"[252] articles in the magazines! I don't know what possesses me to fill your head with these things, but we who are here yet cannot help rejoicing a little to see people that have run their heads into a noose get choked a little. I think Emily you must look with a little more favor on Br. Beebee for he has certainly behaved like a Christian in this affair if he has not been very wise. He has been *still* at least and all of his family have [sic] expressed the greatest interest. You know it *was* pretty hard for a man who meant to be friendly to have such a damper put upon his feelings. He came up to see Aunt C.[253] yesterday and she told him under what circumstances the thing was said and enlightened him a little as to the folly of Mr. Corey's course thro' it all.[254] He said he has had no personal feelings of resentment he knew—but he had felt that you might be governed by caprice. He has the most exalted opinion of your talents, and the utmost confidence in your sincerity etc. etc.—at any rate he thinks the Board has never sent out a missionary so *well qualified in every respect to do good*. I must hold it, I am afraid you will get vain over Mr. Beebee's salaciousness.

11' o'clock at night. I want to tell you dear Nemmy of what a little heaven on earth we are having in our house. Mr. Gratiot arose in the meeting to night and said but that he had wandered far from his prospects and now he wished the prayers of Christians that he might have grace to arise and go unto his Father's. We had prayers in Aunt C.'s room, John Sheldon and Henry Anable both leading in worship! Hank's great desire seems to be that he may be the humble instrument of doing some good. He looks upon Sheboygan now as a sort of missionary field.

Nemmy you were a blessed good child to write me such a good long letter but why didn't the dear Dr. give me one little message? I believe he *has* written and I am afraid it is lost. Or else may be you've quarreled and he does not like to tell of you. So you think I would like Burmah, and those dirty faced men are quite picturesque in their appearance after all! You don't say anything about the snakes, etc.

[250] In a letter written August 29, 1847, Miss Sheldon said, "Mr. Beebee called yesterday to see if we had letters from you by the last steamer—he is very greedy—and says the extracts he took from your letter to Mrs. Jones is lauded every where and he hopes you will rest assured that such communication is just what every body wants—the cause would be advanced ten fold if our Missionaries understood giving out such details." Mr. Beebee was the publisher of the *Baptist Register*.

[251] P. F. Rothermel was a well-known portrait painter in the Philadelphia area. In a letter of February 15, 1846, Emily said that she had been to see Mr. Rothermel and that he was painting a portrait of her for Anna Maria Anable.

[252] *Alderbrook* was a collection of Emily Judson's works, many of which she had written under the pseudonym "Fanny Forester." It was published in 1847; one of the last things that Adoniram Judson did before sailing for Burmah in July 1846, was to sign a contract with Mr. Ticknor of Ticknor and Company, publishers (or Ticknor, Reed and Fields).

[253] See vol. 1, "Cast of Characters," s.v. "Sheldon, Miss Cynthia."

[254] In the correspondence of early 1846, there is a good deal of consternation over the fact that Mr. Corey made some public comments expressing his misgivings as to the relationship between Adoniram Judson and Emily Chubbuck, and it took some time for Emily and her friends to work through their feelings regarding his attitude

Not a line from Lydia[255] to tell how you behave either nor whether your stories are true. I believe you have bribed Lydia and the Dr. so that you might have the story all your own way. I have *quarter* of a mind to accept of your invitation and come over and see for myself. I wish I was a man and could gad around the world as I pleased. So you didn't want Miss Blidgims a[256] bit on the passage 'cause the Dr. took such good care of you! Ah! you have learned to do without me and I must learn to do without you. It is a dreadful thought that I may no more see you on earth. Heaven grant that if it is so to be I may be prepared to meet you above. I shall wait anxiously for more letters from you telling of your designs with regard to Rangoon. Who knows but you are there now. I hope however that you will not be obliged to leave Maulmain yet a while.

Source: American Baptist Historical Society, AJ 13, no. 504 and 505.

Miss Sarah Bell Wheeler to Emily C. Judson, March 30, 1847[257]—Utica

My dear Nemmy.[258]

You don't know how glad our hearts were made by the good news we received from you last week.

We all rejoice that God spared your lives thus far, and hope that we shall hear of your health and happiness for many years. We often wish you here and when we get in Anna M's[259] room try to imagine what you are doing. Nemmy don't you love those dear little children?[260] I knew you'd make a good mother to them. Your dear Dr. is so kind to you that you would be [ ] to think for a moment that you are not one of the happiest beings in the world.

Nemmy I wish you could be with us now. For the last two weeks meetings have been held in our church every evening. A Mr. Westcott[261] from Stillwater (near Troy) has preached every evening, and God has greatly blessed this preaching of his word here.

Source: American Baptist Historical Society, AJ 22, no. 1113.

---

[255] See vol. 1, "Cast of Characters," s.v. "Lillybridge, Miss," also the timeline on "Lydia Lillybridge Simons."

[256] "Blidgims" and the variation "Blidgy" are used quite frequently and interchangeably as names of endearment for Anna Maria Anable. In April 1845, Anna Maria signed several of her letters "Ninny Blidgims." On May 8, 1846, Adoniram began a letter to Anna Maria "Dearest Blidgy," and on May 14, she addressed "Miss Ninny Blidgims." See vol. 1, "Cast of Characters," s.v. "Blidgims." Also "A Timeline for Bigims [sic] References."

[257] There is an addendum to this letter dated March 31, 1847.

[258] Emily Chubbuck. See vol. 1, "Cast of Characters," s.v. "Nemmy, Nem, or Nemmy Petty (Nemmie Pettie)." Also the chapter "Names of Endearment."

Miss Fanny Anable to Emily C. Judson, March 30, 1847—Utica

Dear Cousin Emily.

You do not know how much good your nice long note did me. I had no idea that you would ever have time to write to me, and it was such a good kind note, and just what I wanted, and it just in the right time, when I most needed a friend to give advice. I feel that God has been very kind to me, for every body [sic] seemed to take an interest in me.

I hope that Anna Maria[262] has told you how much our Heavenly Father has done for me, and that I now indulge hope that he has listened to my prayers. I pray that he will teach me to walk in His paths and spend the rest of my days in His service. I suppose A. M. has told of the evident change in Henry[263] and John Sheldon.[264] She has told all the news that will interest you, so that I don't know how to fill up the sheet.

I shall feel lonely enough when A. M. and Henry go away. I don't know what I shall do, I shall feel much like an only child and I am affraid [sic] I shall be spoiled; don't you think so? Matilda Berthoud[265] is here and is going to spend the Summer with us. She is to be my room mate [sic] when Anna Maria goes to Boston.[266] You cannot think how much she [Note: "Anna M." is written above the line.] thinks of Mrs. Colby.[267] She talks of her very often and says she is such a lovely woman.

I wish you had been here last Wednesday when your letters came; such flying about and such running up and down stairs you never saw. Oh! for a letter while it seemed as if you were here again. I wish you were here now, for I know you would love to have been in Aunt Cynthia's[268] room this evening and have seen John and Henry lead our prayer. It is after eleven oclock [sic] and our letters must go tomorrow, so I shall have to close my note soon. I had forgotten that you were once my Composition teacher, or I should have taken more time to write, but excuse it this time and another time I will do better.

[259] See vol. 1, "Cast of Characters," s.v. "Anable, Miss Anna Maria."

[260] In Burmah with Adoniram and Emily were Henry and Edward Judson. In the United States were George Boardman, Abby Ann, Adoniram, and Elnathan Judson.

[261] See vol. 1, "Cast of Characters," s.v. "Westcott, Dr."

[262] See vol. 1, "Cast of Characters," s.v. "Anable, Miss Anna Maria."

[263] See vol. 1, "Cast of Characters," s.v. "Anable, Henry Sheldon."

[264] See vol. 1, "Cast of Characters," s.v. "Sheldon, Cousin John."

[265] See vol. 1, "Cast of Characters," s.v. "Berthoud, Matilda."

[266] For more information on these medical treatments, see vol. 1, "Cast of Characters," s.v. "Anable, Anna Maria."

[267] Mary Colby was the wife of Gardner Colby, a prominent businessman and active Baptist layman. Mr. Colby was a member of the Board of the American Baptist Missionary Union and an avid supporter of the missionary movement. In a letter after they sailed from Boston to Burmah, Emily mentions the extravagant hospitality extended to them in early July as they waited for the *Faneuil Hall* to embark. Adoniram and then Emily stayed with the Colby family quite frequently over the years. Mrs. Colby was an active correspondent with Emily and supported her, her family, and the cause of missions.

[268] See vol. 1, "Cast of Characters," s.v. "Sheldon, Miss Cynthia."

Give my love to your dear good husband for me and remember me your old roommate[269] and affectionate

Fanny

Source: American Baptist Historical Society, AJ 12, no. 337.

Anna Maria Anable to Emily C. Judson, March 31, 1847[270]

I have a project in my head dear Nemmy[271] which I must tell you. You know my poor lame shoulders—Well, there is a physician in Boston who has had wonderful success in curing such cases, and I am going to put myself under his care this Summer. If this shoulder should be cured I should feel more pressure to be useful in the world. However I am not at all [ ] now on that scene while there are young persons coming to me almost hourly and asking what they shall do to be saved. I feel as tho' this was the place for me. What do you think Ninny Blidgims[272] does in such cases? Why she don't [sic] feel very much depressed by "responsibility" for she don't take much upon herself—she mostly directs them to read their Bibles and pray to God. He will convert them if they really *desire it*. Nemmy dear, you know I am tired of teaching Music. It is a good thing in itself and to be taught by some one [sic], but I think I have done enough at it. Now what sort of work do you think this child would make at the compositions? You know I cannot write—but after all, is that so necessary to the making a good teacher? We never expect to have a Fanny Forester[273] again, and I should not feel so humble about taking the class, as if you had just left. Jul.[274] does very well I believe, but you know she won't always be here, and thanks to my intimacy with you I feel some little confidence in my [Note: Three or four words are lost in a blank space that did not copy.] tell me frankly what you think [Note: Four or five words are lost in a blank space that did not copy.] I shall probably go to Boston in May and be absent all Summer.[275] I know

[269] Fanny Anable was working and studying in Philadelphia and staying with the Reverend and Mrs. A. D. Gillette during the winters that Emily was there, and the two had shared a room.

[270] This is a second addendum to a letter started February 15, 1847. It spoke of the death of Anna Maria Anable's grandmother. The first addendum is dated March 30, 1847.

[271] Emily Chubbuck. See vol. 1, "Cast of Characters," s.v. "Nemmy, Nem, or Nemmy Petty (Nemmie Pettie)." Also the chapter "Names of Endearment."

[272] See vol. 1, "Cast of Characters," s.v. "Blidgims." Also "A Timeline for Bligims [sic] References."

[273] Emily Chubbuck Judson as Fanny Forester. See vol. 1, "Cast of Characters," s.v. "Chubbuck, Emily" and "Forester, Fanny."

[274] See vol. 1, "Cast of Characters," s.v. "Look, Julia."

[275] For more information on these medical treatments, see vol. 1, "Cast of Characters," s.v. "Anable, Anna Maria."

Mrs. Colby[276] will be kind—and as Mrs. Bright[277] is in Roxbury and serious that I should come, I don't anticipate such a terribly tedious time as I otherwise should.

Give a great deal of love to Lydia[278] and ask her what she means by neglecting to write to her old chum? I sent letters to you which I thought would reach you by the middle of November. If I had time this morning I should write to L. notwithstanding.

I am going to get all those magazines and have a regular old fashioned time out. I have not read a line in *Graham*[279] or the *Columbian*[280] this Winter. There is no one that writes that I care anything about unless it is Mrs. Osgood.[281] Mrs. Childs I am tired [ ] indeed every one tires me but you. I do [ ] feel the need of education in my own mind. My mind if not a blank is certainly a great vagrant—wandering hither and thither in dreams and strange fancies. I wish if there is anything to it I could call it in and concentrate it on something just to prove to me that I am not a fool.

Nemmy who do you suppose has had the impertinence to write for the *Columbian* under the signature of 'Bel' Forester. I must say I felt provoked when I heard of it, for I doubt not it is some sentimental school-girl. It seems to me that name belongs to me[282] (didn't you give it to me?) *N'importe*. Kate[283] hasn't written

---

[276] See vol. 1, "Cast of Characters," s.v. "Colby, Mary."

[277] Mrs. Bright was the wife of Dr. Edward Bright, the corresponding secretary of the American Baptist Missionary Union. Dr. and Mrs. Bright took Adoniram and Elnathan Judson into their home in October 1851. They lived in Roxbury, Massachusetts.

[278] See vol. 1, "Cast of Characters," s.v. "Lillybridge, Miss," also the timeline on "Lydia Lillybridge Simons."

[279] See vol. 1, "Cast of Characters," s.v. "Graham, George."

[280] The *Columbian* magazine was published first by John Inman and then by Robert West. By early 1844, the *Columbian* was printing Emily's stories; this was before N. P. Willis and the *New Mirror* made her famous. With Graham, they readily agreed to pay her a top rate of five dollars a page for anything that she would write, and on several occasions, they tried to get Emily to write exclusively for them. They finally succeeded in this when she went to Burmah, for they obtained exclusive rights to all that she would send them at fifty dollars a story.

[281] Frances or "Fanny" Osgood presents an interesting counterpoint to Fanny Forester or Emily Chubbuck. Both writers achieved fame in the same period of time. Fanny Osgood was both a writer and poet, and in 1845, she wrote regularly for *Graham's Magazine*. Estranged from her husband, famed portrait painter Samuel S. Osgood, she began a relationship with Edgar Allen Poe, who became the editor and part owner of the *Broadway Journal* in March 1845. Poe had been helped to fame by N. P. Willis when the *New York Daily Mirror*, the paper that preceded the *New Mirror* and that made Fanny Forester famous, published "The Raven" in January. Fanny Osgood presented a poem to the *Broadway Journal* for publication, and Poe printed a poem in reply. This went back and forth for a number of months, and the two were soon involved in a relationship; it was commonly thought that Fanny Osgood's third child was fathered by Poe. All of this was being played out in the press in September 1845 when William Gillespie wrote his letter to Emily Chubbuck. The relationship with Fanny Osgood made Poe a pariah in the literary circles of New York within the year. In January 1845, Mrs. Osgood accused George Graham of not writing to her because of all of his correspondence with Fanny Forester. In June, just before sailing to Burmah, Emily mentioned in a letter that while in New York she stopped at Mr. Osgood's studio, hoping to make arrangements to see Fanny Osgood, but the meeting did not take place as she was out of town.

[282] "Cousin 'Bel'" was Anna Maria Anable and the "character" from Emily's letter to the *New Mirror*, which was published on June 8, 1844 and catapulted Emily to literary fame. The letter concerned Emily and Cousin 'Bel's visit to New York and their lack of money to enjoy the wares of the many shops they passed. She asked if the editor of the *New Mirror* would like to help them out.

[283] See vol. 1, "Cast of Characters," s.v. "Chubbuck, Miss Sarah Catharine."

me since New Years. I saw a beautiful piece of poetry of hers in a paper—she is getting quite a reputation as a poetess.

I must stop writing dear Nemmy. I doubt whether you will find this intelligible. Give my love—nay [Note: Written in the right margin of the address page.] adoration, veneration, reverence and—supply the next very if you please to the Dr. and ask him if he wants [ ] [ ] [ ] from poor little Miss Blidgims some [ ] or these little lines.

I have been afraid that I have written too often Nemmy. I know you have lots of correspondents, and some such interesting ones. What would n't [*sic*] I give if you could sit right down on this blessed settee by my side. I am afraid I should squeeze you to death.

Written in the left margin of the address page: "Hatty[284] and Mary[285] have both of them excellent situations but think once how the family is scattered. We want them home again.

"Don't forget me. I think of you—with those dear little children and your own house—write me all about it please. There's the bell. Kiss good bye."

Anna M.

Source: American Baptist Historical Society, AJ 13, no. 504 and 505.

Miss Sarah Bell Wheeler to Emily C. Judson, March 31, 1847[286]

Wednesday morning. My (dear) Nemmy[287]. I wish you could have been with us last night in Aunt Cynthia's[288] room. I have not told you that John Sheldon[289] is here, and that the future looks brighter to me now than ever before! John has been brought to feel his need of Christ's pardoning love, and is rejoicing in the forgiveness of his sins.

Henry[290] too. Nemmy you would hardly think him the same man. *Now* he loves to talk about religion, and God. Mr. Gratiot[291] went forward for prayer last night—and he is determined to live a Christian the rest of his life. A. M. has perhaps told you all this, but you would think and talk about them all the time if you were here.

---

[284] See vol. 1, "Cast of Characters," s.v. "Anable, Harriet."

[285] See vol. 1, "Cast of Characters," s.v. "Anable, Mary Juliet."

[286] This is an addendum to a letter dated March 30, 1847.

[287] Emily Chubbuck. See vol. 1, "Cast of Characters," s.v. "Nemmy, Nem, or Nemmy Petty (Nemmie Pettie)." Also the chapter "Names of Endearment."

[288] See vol. 1, "Cast of Characters," s.v. "Sheldon, Miss Cynthia."

[289] See vol. 1, "Cast of Characters," s.v. "Sheldon, Cousin John."

[290] See vol. 1, "Cast of Characters," s.v. "Anable, Henry Sheldon."

[291] See vol. 1, "Cast of Characters," s.v. "Gratiot, Charles."

Julia[292] intended to write in this package but there is not room. She will write the next time two weeks from this.

A. M. you would love more than ever if you could be with us now. She is a very devoted Christian, and I sometimes think she will one of these days go to Burmah. *She* would not object.

Nemmy my sister Lania had a little daughter named for me. Don't you suppose I feel honored?

Nemmy I am not making my "trousseau" now, and do not know how soon I shall. You know how anxious I was last spring that John would be a Christian, and that desire has been granted. He will return to Galura [*sic*] in a few weeks, and Nemmy will you pray for him, and for us all that we may be more devoted to the blessed Redeemer's cause![293]

I imagine that you may have been interrupted [ ] so many times while reading this little note by those children of yours.[294] Kiss them for me. We can't realize that you are so far away, and I believe one reason is this, that we are all creatures dependent upon one God for all things. Our prayers and desires are known and heard by our Heavenly Father.

Nemmy, we pray for you and your dear Dr. that God will keep, and bless you in whatever you do. My own love to Lydia[295] for I cannot write her this time. All friends are well and send very much love to you. They speak of you with affection, and [ ] delighted to know of your safe arrival in Maulmain.

God bless and keep you and your family. Do write us when you can Nemmy.

You have the love and best wishes of your friend

Sarah Bell Wheeler

Source: American Baptist Historical Society, AJ 22, no. 1113.

---

[292] See vol. 1, "Cast of Characters," s.v. "Look, Julia."

[293] There seems to be an indication in this letter and in the letter of November 26, 1847, that Sarah Bell Wheeler and John Sheldon were committed to or moving toward a commitment to marriage. However, by 1851, Sarah Bell Wheeler is married to Charles Gould, and Mr. Gould was a partner in a publishing firm (Gould, Kendall, and Lincoln) in Boston. Emily stayed with them for a few days upon her immediate return to America in October 1851.

[294] Henry and Edward Judson were living with Adoniram and Emily Judson. Henry was less than five years old, and Edward was a little more than two years old.

[295] See vol. 1, "Cast of Characters," s.v. "Lillybridge, Miss," also the timeline on "Lydia Lillybridge Simons."

Article from the *Baptist Memorial*,[296] April, 1847

Our acquaintance with and high estimate of the fair author, the present Mrs. Judson, prepared us more readily to appreciate the value of these charming volumes.[297] They contain much truth of the soberest and most useful character, set off in the coloring of fancy and genius. How any one [sic] could regard such writings—especially under the commendable circumstances which called them forth, a disqualification for her present missionary work, is strange. The volumes are indeed light reading; neither the bread nor meat of a healthy intellect; but may be sparingly used with great advantage as a condiment.[298]

Source: *Baptist Memorial*, April 1847, 6:118.

Miss Cynthia Sheldon to Emily C. Judson, April, 1847[299]

My dear dear One,

The days count slowly when we think of your letters—the first of next month is the time set to watch every mail. Heaven only knows with what intense anxiety that time is looked for. Anna M.[300] has no doubt told you every thing [sic]—but feelings of others. The delight with which we hailed your "Alderbrook" is abiding, every body [sic] speaks in high terms of it. Your closing piece my girl has touched the spring to every heart.[301] How dearly I love to retrospect the manuscripts in my room or your bedroom—of many of the stories as I read them in their present beautiful dress—could you and your dear Dr. see them. The sacrifice of money would be forgotten in the sure prospect of its being returned. The 2nd Edition has appeared already.

I cannot put in more than this scrap of paper in the package—Heaven preserve you both to greatly enjoy the work of the Lord. He has put in your hearts and hand to do—

ever yours

C. S.

Source: American Baptist Historical Society, AJ 21, unnumbered.

---

[296] *The Baptist Memorial, and Monthly Record, Devoted to the History, Biography, Literature and Statistics of the Denomination* was a monthly magazine published by Z. P. Hatch Publishers, New York. In 1850 the editor was the Rev. Enoch Hutchinson.

[297] *Alderbrook* was published toward the end of December 1846, and a second edition was soon necessary.

[298] This provides information about the problems that Emily, writing as Fanny Forester, had with the moralism of the church and the judgments they made upon the quality of her writing.

[299] This letter is undated. It is placed in April because of the reference to the appearance of the second edition of *Alderbrook*.

[300] See vol. 1, "Cast of Characters," s.v. "Anable, Miss Anna Maria."

[301] "Farewell to Alderbrook."

Miss Lydia Lillybridge to Emily C. Judson, April 1, 1847—Maulmain

How unlike the first of April at home! If I should tell you, dear Emily, that I have not for three weeks, had time to write you a letter, would you understand me? I sometimes wish that the days and weeks were twice as long—That note of yours was very acceptable, I assure you. You really had quite a budget of news from home. But you had not a word by the last steamer, and I'm not very sorry either; for "Misery loves company."—Poor Matilda![302]—Tell me something about Willis's[303] marriage if you can; and a great deal about "Mr. Corey's[304] pet."—How delightful it would be to engage in battle with those little airy creatures above your head![305]— Your loss by the fire[306] is much greater than I, at first, supposed. It is well that you early learned to live upon a little. All your nice dresses are gone, and I flatter myself that I shall now be able to make you *one* acceptable offering—that barege [*sic*] you let me have. Shall I send it by the next opportunity or keep it and send it with the pictures? At all events, you must have it before you go up to the Golden City.[307]

One of the points of my gold pen is broken off—the least bit in the world. I did it myself, with my own fingers. I have some idea of sending to Boston in a letter to be mended. Would you ask Mr. Peck,[308] or Mr. Colby,[309] or Mrs. C.[310] to attend to it?—Do you wish to know something of the state of affairs in this vicinity? Well, then I will tell you.

After the volcano of selfishness and vengeance had been in a state of eruption for nearly three months, almost constantly, its violent perturbations were quelled to a very considerable degree—(that is, about the time the Bishop left the city,) so much so, that hopes have been entertained at times, that its tremendous fires were

---

[302] See vol. 1, "Cast of Characters," s.v. "Berthoud, Matilda Berthoud."

[303] Nathaniel Parker Willis was the editor, with General George Morris, of the *New Mirror*, a prominent literary magazine in New York. He discovered Emily, published her writing in the magazine, and pursued a romantic relationship with her that eventually failed.

[304] See vol. 1, "Cast of Characters," s.v. "Corey, the Reverend D. G."

[305] In March, Emily wrote about her living conditions in Rangoon, including the "denizens of the Night" who swarmed around them in "Bat Castle." See her letters of March 15, 1847.

[306] Shortly after their departure to Rangoon, there was a fire at the mission compound in Maulmain, and Adoniram and Emily lost two large trunks of their most treasured possessions, which had been stored in the home of Edward and Elizabeth Stevens. In several letters they estimated the loss at between seven hundred and a thousand rupees.

[307] Adoniram and Emily hoped fervently that their time in Rangoon would open the door for them to go to Ava, which had long been the goal of Adoniram Judson.

[308] The Reverend Doctor Solomon Peck was for twenty years the executive secretary of the American Baptist Missionary Union. Many believed him to be hard, stern, and judgmental, and from some of his comments, it is easy to understand that perception. Dr. Peck and Emily did not always have the easiest of relationships. She felt in him the judgment that came from many in the church at the announcement of her impending marriage to Adoniram; that judgment concerned her "secular" past and concern that she was not an appropriate companion for the veteran missionary. On July 18, 1849 Emily wrote a blistering letter of defense to Dr. Peck in response to a letter from him of February 20, 1849; her letter framed how she viewed his perception of her, and her response was meant to set the record straight. There are eleven letters in the collection from Solomon Peck to Emily.

[309] See vol. 1, "Cast of Characters," s.v. "Colby, Gardner."

[310] See vol. 1, "Cast of Characters," s.v. "Colby, Mary."

entirely subdued; but subsequent outbreaks have shown that they are all the time fomenting inwardly, and gathering so much force as to render a safety valve quite necessary, though the explosions are much less frequent and violent, than formerly. *Comprenez vous?*

Dear Emily, when I think what a desirable home I have lost (should you not think it *strange* if I did not reflect on the subject *sometimes?*)—a house where piety reigns, and the atmosphere is love—and that this loss was occasioned by *one seemingly harmless step*,—by *one unintentional offence*. I feel like an *ignorant, unfortunate* child, disinherited—like an orphan without relations; for I did heartily feel, all the confidence in you, and yours, that a child feels in a parent. I sometimes think, that I am undergoing a sort of discipline, that I may be more effectually taught to place all my confidence, and hopes of happiness in our Heavenly Father.—The Beechers[311] were here to dinner yesterday for the first time. No very important news from Obo. Mr. Harris's[312] little boy has been sick for sometime, but is better.—

5 o'clock P.M. Yours of the 27th has just arrived. Need I tell you that I am thankful for it?—I would give a great deal, if I could study with you from "7 to 8 o'clock" that is, if you translate that hour; for I get along *very* slowly.—I'm *very* glad that you have commenced that memoir.[313] Do try to induce the Dr. to write his own. *Try* hard.—It would be very pleasant to teach those Jewesses. I told Mr. and Mrs. [ ] Howard[314] what you said, but thought I would wait till I found that you were in earnest, before I "asked consent." With regard to my own willingness—I'm willing to do whatever seems to be for the best. I should never wish to go, unless the Dr. were convinced [Note: "That it was best," is written and then crossed out.] without any of your influence, that it was for the best.—I've been a little in doubt of late, as to what portion of my time I ought to spend in the study of the language, etc. what, in teaching English. According to present arrangements, three hours a day for Burmese, seems to be the greatest amount of time that I can command reg-

---

[311] Mr. and Mrs. John Sydney Beecher sailed to Burmah with Adoniram and Emily Judson; they served there from 1846 to 1866.

[312] Norman Harris was born February 19, 1813 in Becket, Massachusetts. He attended Columbia College and Hamilton Literary and Theological School, graduating in 1844. Olive Celina Wadsworth was also born in Becket, Mass July 6, 1814. They were married on August 9, 1844, and were appointed to missionary service on October 28, 1844. In July 1846, they sailed to Burmah with the newly married Adoniram and Emily Judson. Olive Harris died in childbirth on November 23, 1853, in Shwegyin, Burma. In 1856, Norman Harris married for the second time; Miranda Harris died of fever in September that very same year. Norman Harris left the mission field shortly after the death of his wife Miranda and returned to the United States. There, in June 1858, he married for the third time; his third wife was Julia Wadsworth Chapman, the sister of his first wife, Olive Celina Wadsworth. Norman and Julia Harris returned to Burmah in 1858, though not under the auspices American Baptist Missionary Union; they were reappointed as missionaries in 1861. Norman Harris died March 1, 1884 in Hamilton, New York. Julia Harris died in September 1905.

[313] Emily was writing the memoir of Sarah Hall Boardman Judson.

[314] Hosea and Theresa Howard were in Maulmain as missionaries with Adoniram Judson. Mr. Howard's responsibility was to run one of the schools that the mission maintained. Mrs. Howard was involved in that work as well. In one letter, he claims that they worked there with Adoniram Judson longer than any other missionaries. Mr. Howard's responsibility was to run schools that the mission maintained, a task in which he was ably assisted by his wife. Lydia Lillybridge was responsible to Mr. and Mrs. Howard when she arrived in November 1846. Mr. and Mrs. Howard left Maulmain for the United States in February 1850.

ularly; and even this, I do not always spend, for one study hour comes after tea, and not [Note: Written in the right margin of the address page.] notwithstanding [sic] my greatest exertions to the contrary, I must often spend the evening with company, either at home or abroad, or else render myself very conspicuously odd by doing otherwise. I rise, or intend to rise at five, or half-past, or as soon as it is light be it ever so early. Then dressing, walking, dressing again, reading, etc. etc. occupy the time until twenty minutes before eight, when the family attend worship. At nine I go to the school room to spend two hours; there I listen for half an hour to the Burmese recitations—then another half hour is spent in translating. Afterwards two hours more in the school room—then one hour for rest etc. etc. from three, to four, with my Burmese teacher. Then comes dinner [Note: Written in the left margin of the address page.] with all its train of lazziness [sic]. The rest you know. (Don't you feel very much obliged for this interesting sketch?) You see that I spend more time with English, than with Burmese (and it was just so when you were here) and if you had disapproved of my course, you *would* have told me, I suppose; still, I should like your opinion distinctly, for there are some who think like this—Your great object in coming to this country was to give the *Burmese* religious instruction in their own language—therefore, you ought not to let *any thing* [sic] hinder you in acquiring that language—You might as well have taught the English at home—or some what [sic] in this style—After all, I do not think precisely so; for it is important that these English girls should be rightly educated—and they are mostly orphans, and [Note: Written along bottom margin of the address page.] as there is no provision made by government, for the education of girls, they would probably be not any better than the heathen around them if they were not *here*. There is no doubt but that some of them have been saved from becoming prostitutes by being placed here. I think it very much like missionary work to teach them, still I do not feel satisfied to spend so little time on the language. Let me hear the pro's and con's.

Written along the left margin of page 1: "I don't know precisely what Mr. and Mrs. H. think, though I am satisfied that they do not really think it best for me to teach one hour less, even for five or six weeks. One thing I know—that is—that I shall never make much progress in Burmese, until I spend more time in translating."

Written along the left margin of page 3: "With much love to your self, your Dr., and little Henry[315] and Edward.[316] Kiss them all for me, and write soon, if not more than ten words. I am your affectionate Lydia."

Source: American Baptist Historical Society, AJ 17, no. 775.

---

[315]See vol. 1, "Cast of Characters," s.v. "Judson, Henry Hall."
[316] See vol. 1, "Cast of Characters," s.v. "Judson, Edward."

Mrs. Deborah Wade to Emily C. Judson,[317] April 2, 1847—Tavoy[318]

My dear Sister Judson

Be assured your kind sisterly note gave me very much pleasure though from circumstances of trial and sorrow the answer has been delayed even longer than I had intended. The care and fatigue of setting off the little Masons[319] for America, and Mr. Wade[320] for Maulmain in a boat, was quite too much for my feeble strength, after which my anxious care for poor Mr. Mason, who seemed in a sinking state, and his mind bordering on derangement, has nearly unfitted me for the common duties of life. And then the care of his outfit to England devolved upon me, the other Sisters being then at the sea-side. I am now however beginning to feel rested, and hope not again to neglect my correspondents as I have of late. I have felt very keenly the deep disappointment of not seeing my old and dearly beloved friend and Brother Judson, either in Tavoy or Maulmain, but it must be in some way for the best, so I am silent. Both the former Mrs. Judsons[321] being to me such very dear Sisters, I naturally felt desirous of a personal interview with yourself, having reserved for you the same place in my best affections. Mr. Wade's acquaintance with your husband, (together with the letters from Utica) are, the next thing to a personal interview, so that I hope we may both throw aside the reserve of strangers, and correspond frequently and freely. The Home of your honored parents being the same as the loved Home of my childhood, you will naturally feel a warm interest in a spot so dear to me.—This is very sweet to my feelings. Let me always hear something of that dear family circle when you get letters—How many Brothers and Sisters have you? How many of them live at Hamilton? I felt it very kind of you and Br. Judson to call on the little remnant of my father's family. It gave them all very great pleasure. I want to ask many questions about them, when

---

[317] This beautiful letter was written to welcome Emily to the mission field. Mr. and Mrs. Wade had worked with Adoniram Judson for many years, as far back as Ann Judson's life and ministry and including Sarah Boardman Judson's life. Mrs. Wade also came from the Hamilton, New York, area, so there was a connection there as well.

[318] Tavoy was a small city in Tenasserim Province; located on a plain on the Tavoy River and surrounded on three sides by mountains, it had a population of 9,000 inhabitants. It was approximately forty miles from the ocean. It was a prominent Buddhist center with more than 100 monasteries. George and Sarah Boardman started a ministry here in March 1828. After the second English-Burmese war in 1852, a great deal of Tavoy came under the jurisdiction of the British, and significant new work was started. As a part of this, Francis Mason translated the Scripture into Sgau Karen, and Durlin Brayton had translated the Bible into Pwo Karen.

[319] Helen Mason died in October 1846. Previous letters suggested that Mr. Mason was so distraught that friends feared for his health, both physical and mental, and this letter seems to confirm that. With all of this, it appears that the Mason children were returning to the United States, as most of the missionary children did.

[320] Jonathan Wade was appointed as a missionary to Burmah in 1823. Wade's relationship with Adoniram Judson was especially dear because of the early experiences they shared, including the death of Ann Judson. Much of their work was spent in the Karen jungle communities following the path of George Boardman. They had returned home to America on December 22, 1847, and returned to Burmah in January 1851, just as Emily was returning to the United States. They were from the Hamilton, New York, area. They left to return to Burmah on July 25, 1850, and were in Maulmain by February 1851. Both died in Burmah. Deborah died at Maulmain in 1868, and Jonathan died in Rangoon in 1872.

[321] Ann Hasseltine Judson and Sarah Hall Boardman Judson.

we meet. Do you and Dr. Judson think of living *always* in Rangoon? *That* too, you know is one of my old Homes. Many fond recollections still cluster around that *first* Indian home, and those *first* scenes of my Missionary life. Please to ask Dr. Judson to describe to me the place, and House where you live, that I may know where to visit you in spirit. How are the dear children?[322] Do you find the task of educating them more difficult than you anticipated? I have thought much of you in the deportment of your duties, as I who like yourself have been unaccustomed to the care of children, have had little Motherless Ones, come to me for a home. Have you been able to secure ready and cheerful *obedience* from your little charge? It seems to me this is the only *good* foundation for what we hope may become an amiable, and Christian character. Do you not think with me that a constant study to make the little beings committed to us *happy*, and to indulge all their wishes as far as we *safely* may, quite compatible with the requisition of *prompt* obedience? I learn you suffer less by the fire which consumed Br. Stevens'[323] House. May I enquire if the loss was of much value?[324] With regard to letters [ ] of my beloved Sister Judson, I am sorry I have nothing of my own to assist you in the Memoir.[325] I have preserved very few of the letters of any of my friends and how being hasty productions, and sometimes confidential, I always destroyed them. I now deeply regret having done so, as her frequent warm expression of religious sentiment, and feeling, would have afforded many precious *gems* for the Memoir—and with regard to traits of character [ ] what Br. Judson published in the Magazine is exactly what I would have said—I have however procured from Mr. Mason a bundle of original letters, which I hope you may find useful—I shall forward them to Maulmain with this letter. And now I must stop, lest I fear you have never been accustomed to reading such a scrawl. I hope however you will make it out, and believe me—

Your very affectionate sister

D. B. L. Wade

Mr. Wade desires to write his best love to yourself as well as Br. Judson and the dear children.—I have tried in vain to recall to memory the interview you mention

---

[322] Henry and Edward Judson were living in Rangoon with Adoniram and Emily.

[323] Edward and Elizabeth Stevens were missionaries to Burmah. They arrived in Maulmain, Burmah, in February 1838. There are twenty-four letters in the correspondence from them. Mrs. Stevens took Edward Judson into her home when Sarah and Adoniram had to leave for the United States in 1845, and her care and nurture saved his life. The home of Elizabeth and Edward Stevens burned to the ground in 1847, and two trunks being stored for Adoniram and Emily were destroyed; these trunks held all of their excess clothes and precious mementos, which they had not wanted to bring to Rangoon with them. Mr. Stevens buried Charles Chubbuck (Emily's "Angel Charlie") in April 1850. Edward Stevens also accepted the responsibility of finishing the dictionary after the death of Adoniram Judson.

[324] On February 17, 1847, shortly after they left Maulmain for Rangoon, a fire in the mission compound at Maulmain destroyed two trunks of Adoniram and Emily's clothing and personal articles; much of the loss had been personal gifts of great sentimental value. In different letters the loss was estimated between seven hundred and a thousand rupees.

[325] At this time, Emily Judson was beginning to write the memoir of Sarah Boardman Judson and collecting the materials she would need for the project.

when I was in America. I well recollect going to the house of Mrs. Gilman[326] as I had been acquainted with the family in my girlhood—but I have been sadly forgetful of strangers, though interested in them at the time. Have you any society at all in Rangoon? I fear your health will suffer from the dreadful heat of that town at this season of the year. Tell dear Br. Judson that Mr. Wade has engaged a delightful season with each branch of his Karen flock this season. He was not able to cross the mountains to Mata after returning from Maulmain so that from 150 to 200 of the Karens came over to the foot of the mountain on this side and built a temporary Zagat on the banks of that pretty stream where our dear Brother Boardman[327] finished his labors. He enjoyed the meetings *very much*. Br. Judson will recollect the two Karens who went to Maulmain from Tavoy to learn to read Karen, while we were in America—well, one of them was *ordained* by Mr. Wade and Cross at that meeting, and 19 more were baptized. The other Karen is expected from the Lusetts [*sic*] soon, to receive ordination likewise.—They are both "revival preachers." Nearly a whole family will sometimes be melted into tears under their preaching, and especially under their *prayers*. Paun Kon Nuosan was ill at the time he was among his Karens and could not of course baptize. Mr. Wade has baptized 35 this season, and the only one suspended has been restored. We have about 750 in the communion at the Church at this station, and a Burman church of 15 to 20. I still feel a [ ] interest in the old Pastor of the Rangoon church, and the few scattered members who remain in that Country. How are your lungs affected by the elements of India thus far?—

D. B. L. Wade

Source: American Baptist Historical Society, AJ 22, no. 1121.

The Reverend Doctor William Dean to Emily C. Judson, April 23, 1847 —Hong Kong

My dear friend Emily

I shall not indulge you with an avowal of all the pleasure I enjoyed in the perusal of your letter of Feb. 4th. It is enough for you to know that I am giving you

---

[326] On August 26, 1844, Miss Cynthia Sheldon wrote to Emily Chubbuck to ask if she knew of someone who could come to Utica and work with a young student who needed a caregiver. The young student was seven years old, the daughter of Cephas and Stella Bennett, missionaries to Burmah. Emily wrote back on August 28 to speak of a Miss Gilman, a teacher she had known, as a candidate. On August 29, Emily wrote that Miss Gilman felt that she could not take the position for family reasons; at the end of the letter, Emily added a postscript, saying that Miss Gilman had changed her mind and would, in fact, accept the position if it were offered to her. Emily wrote more on September 2, 1845, and on September 3, 1845, Miss Sheldon wrote to Emily to say that she had decided in favor of Miss Gilman. Emily wrote a note to Miss Gilman on the letter she had received from Miss Sheldon and passed it on. In a letter written April 15, 1845, Anna Maria is talking of the girls dispersing as the term ended, and she noted that "the stage has come for Miss Gilman," and Miss Gilman was delivering a note to Emily's sister Catharine Chubbuck.

this "apology" for another of the like from the same pen. You kindly invite me to come to your "hearthless" home and inspect your housekeeping, but howsoever many attractions it may offer, I shd be half afraid to visit that "strangely beautiful land" and mingle with your "winged" company[328] with "blue eyes." I have so long been accustomed to look upon the half denuded, featherless beings that inhabit this lower world, that I shd not feel at home I fear in your fairy land. Still I must say I feel some little curiosity to see how that little timid girl, I once saw in Morrisville,[329] manage so many pairs of "blue eyes" and make things go in missionary life. You may well say that *you* can do without rose-bushes and music-boxes, and that your days of romance are just beginning—and all that sort of thing—but how you suppose that *I*, who have no "blue eyes" to look upon, can get along comfortably without such artificial means, is, more than I can comprehend. Then you come out upon me with a tirade of abuse because I did not *steal* a certain lady's heart and become a miss'y to Burmah. Pray how shd I have know, twelve years ago, that you were going to *Burmah* and instead of *stealing*, I seem to have been more successful in *stealing* all the lady's [*sic*] hearts.

It *was* certainly very "inconsiderate" in [*sic*] me to leave home as I did, but really our Amn flower garden has been so culled of its blossoms that I could'nt [*sic*] "pick" a rose which possessed any fragrance, and at the same time was not in danger of wilting under this tropical sun.

I feel much interest in your proposed attack upon Rangoon but fear you may suffer not so much from the "filth," tho I doubt not you will find enough for health, but for the want of exercise and fresh air. But why do I intrude my advice while you have better counsel nearer home. Do you heed it? But how am I situated for happiness and usefulness? If I fail in either it surely is not the fault of my *situation*—but still the failure is too true in relation to both, and particularly the latter. As to *usefulness* I must confess without affected humility, that mine dwindles into a very little, and you may justly suppose that this connection adds not greatly to my *happiness*. To be candid, the work of discipline in the little Church, the clearing away of the rubbish, and gathering up the fragments, since my return does not tend greatly to render me sanguine in relation to the results of my labors. I am still endeavoring to go on. One of our Chinese Ch. Members has been excluded, one became stronger, and one got *married*! I have baptized two since my return and a few more seem to be lingering about the fold and wld require less coaxing for them

[327] George Dana Boardman was the first husband of Sarah Hall Boardman Judson. Mr. Boardman died in 1831 after several days in the jungle, where he had gone to see some of his beloved Karens baptized. This strained his frail health beyond endurance.

[328] In her March 14 and 15, 1846 letters, Emily gave her sister Catharine a picture of the "other inhabitants" of their home—the bats, lizards, scorpions, beetles, nameless bugs, and the like. She probably had written similar descriptions to William Dean, and hence his reference to the "winged company."

[329] In spring 1834, just before he left for missionary service, Dr. Dean had baptized the seventeen-year-old Emily Chubbuck. At that time, he was serving as an interim pastor at the Baptist church in Morrisville.

to enter in, than a lamb I once knew in my native country—Indeed it is my great trouble to keep Chinamen *out of the Church* after they receive the first lessons in Christianity—as they then think that they request nothing but baptism to finish [ ] [ ]. By this don't understand me that I preach *baptism* among my first lessons, and in fact I have scarcely ever alluded to the subject by way of explanation or exhortation during my ministry among the Chinese. The reason is that they are so much accustomed to a religion of external forms that they readily seize upon the outward garb of our religion vainly thinking if they can get it on, they are *Christians*—And then again there is in the character of the Chinese such an almost indomitable love of gain that they vainly think that by getting into the Church they ensure their support. Against this I have had to fight and since my return have printed, (as the only thing in this publishing line) a tract of ten or a dozen pages on that subject. I suppose you have the same thing to contend with among the Burmese, but I hope in a modified form.

We have not yet baptised [*sic*] the first Chinese *woman*, and I know of no one who affords proof of being worthy—tho' a few are under Christian influence. I have the supervision of two stations out of Hong Kong and two Chapels here, and have been trying to prepare the *Acts* with Marginal Reference, for the press—now in the 10th Chap. Work slowly and often interrupted—quite alone and pressed down with an intolerable load of laziness—I have a letter from Revd Marsena Stone pastor of Eaton Church, date Jany 1st 47—says my "friends here are all well"—Saw Deacon Com[ ]—Morrisville Ch. no pastor—Eaton Ch. prosperous. Dr. Kendrick[330] still alive and *very happy*—tho a great sufferer. Hamilton Institution never more prosperous—Abolitionism still rampant. Our Board again in want of funds!!! Which is the more pitiable, the miserly Churches or the miserable heathen?

Written in the left margin of the address page: "Mr. Shuck and party are to go to Shanghai—and we hear of Methodists, Sabbatarians and Abolitionists all coming to China but know of no one but Bro Lord from our Board to join us, and I am likely to be left *quite alone*. Still not lonely as I have just heard of the death of Mrs. Barker the mother of the late Mrs. [ ]."

Written in the right margin of the address page: "Kindest remembrances to Dr. Judson and much love for the blue eyed boys[331]—How old are they? And what do you do with them beside *watching them* to sleep?—Who have you with you from the Messr party? The Beechers?[332] Please mention me kindly to any who may enquire after"

Your old friend and bro
William Dean

---

[330] See vol. 1, "Cast of Characters," s.v. "Kendrick, Dr. Nathaniel."

[331] Henry and Edward Judson were living with Adoniram and Emily in Rangoon.

[332] Mr. and Mrs. John Sydney Beecher sailed to Burmah with Adoniram and Emily Judson; they served there from 1846 to 1866.

Written along the left margin of page 1: "Many thanks for your definition of trippings[333]—quite intelligible now even to *me*. Stupid! That I shd not have understood before—pray dear one some of your trippings—Rangoon."

Source: American Baptist Historical Society, AJ 15, no. 594.

Miss Lydia Lillybridge to Emily C. Judson, April 23, 1847[334]—Maulmain

O Emily!

If I could see you, I could give you an interesting account of my affairs. As it is, I can give you only a few dull hints. Mr. Ingalls[335] has been here and spent a couple of hours, and—would you believe it, if I should tell you that I was almost overpowered by his address? He gave such a thrilling account of his interesting field of labor—of the need of assistants—and of its claims upon *my* attention, as to make me willing to leave this place and go over to Arracan immediately. (with a few provisions.) Would you and the Dr. give your consent if it were asked? But I must not put any more such thoughts on paper, or you will think that my head is really turned.

Source: American Baptist Historical Society, AJ 17, no. 774.

Miss Jane Kelly to Emily C. Judson April 23, 1847[336]—Utica[337]

April 23rd Fri. eve.

It is several weeks since I began this letter, I was prevented finishing it at the time, by the meetings and Miss C.[338] advised me to defer writing as she and A. M.[339] were writing you all about the revival, Grand-Ma's[340] death and other matters. This evening A. M. came up to my end of the table after tea with your letter in her hand (Can you see just how we looked) and read it to us. I felt that you were

---

[333] Emily's book of stories and sketches was published in fall 1845 under the title *Trippings in Author-land*. In his July 3, 1846 letter to Emily, Dr. Dean asked her to explain to him the significance of "Trippings."

[334] This letter has an addendum, dated May 21, 1847.

[335] Lovel Ingalls was born August 21, 1808, in Worcester, New York. He was ordained October 2, 1834 in Boston, New York, and graduated from the Hamilton Literary and Theological Institute in 1837. In September 1834, he married Marcia Dawes of Cummington, Massachusetts; Miss Dawes had been educated at Cummington Academy. They first sailed for Burmah in 1835, arriving at Amherst February 20, 1836. They were stationed at Mergui and then Maulmain in May 1845; Marcia Dawes Ingalls died on November 9, 1845, at Maulmain. Lovel and Marcia Ingalls were the parents of three children. Mr. Ingalls went to Akyab in 1846 and returned to the United States beginning May 1850. He went back to Burmah in December 1851. His second wife was Marilla Amelia Baker, and they married December 23, 1850 at Troy, New York. Mr. Ingalls died at sea on March 14, 1856.

[336] This letter is an addendum to the letter of March 28, 1847.

[337] This letter has an addendum dated April 23, 1847.

[338] See vol. 1, "Cast of Characters," s.v. "Sheldon, Miss Cynthia."

[339] See vol. 1, "Cast of Characters," s.v. "Anable, Miss Anna Maria."

---

really with us again in [ ] persona, the letter was so like you. Your philosophical coolness, or rather your Christian cheerfulness is quite my admiration. To a "Soul of Whim" you somehow manage to attract an amazing quantity of the commodity called common sense. And so you have really transformed yourself to the other end of the earth, and have formed yourself into a devoted exemplary little wife, and mother, while we, poor mortals, have been living here much after the old fashion, having a very hum-drum sort of life looking and feeling for all the world just as we did when you left. You can see us just as we *are* any moment, I wish we could form as perfect a picture of your where-abouts, and what-abouts. There would be real satisfaction in taking aerial trips across the world, if one could really light upon any thing [sic] which looked or seemed like reality. When you get settled in your new home do give me a few elements that I can compare with a picture that will seem life-like. It is too often my ill fortune to write to my friends detailed accounts of matters about which they are perfectly familiar so to save you the trouble of reading a tedious and twice told tale I got A. M. to tell me what she had been writing you. She has told you all about the revival in the Church and in the city and how much cause we all have to rejoice that so many of our dear friends have been brought into the Kingdom. She has told of Hat[341] and Molly,[342] and all about Henry's going west, and also her own trip to Boston.[343] I'm so selfish that I don't feel quite satisfied with her plan. We all feel very unwilling to part with her. I cannot learn that you have been informed of Sophia Ward's death. She died a few weeks after the birth of a son, she was struck with paralysis and not aware of her condition. She has left three little boys and a devoted husband to mourn her loss. Mrs. Nichols has lost her Lucy and is much afflicted. I have not heard from

---

[340] Deacon Asa and Mrs. Sheldon were parents to Cynthia Sheldon, Urania Sheldon Nott, and Alma Sheldon Anable. They had rooms at the Utica Female Academy where two of their three daughters were employed, and they were very popular with the students. After she married and moved to Schenectady, Mrs. Nott would often write and encourage Emily and the other girls to drop in on her parents whenever possible. Mrs. Sheldon died on January 29, 1847, and Deacon Sheldon died in March 1848. On February 15, Anna Maria had written of Mrs. Sheldon's death on January 29, though she did not mail the letter until after March 30, 1847.

[341] See vol. 1, "Cast of Characters," s.v. "Anable, Harriet."

[342] See vol. 1, "Cast of Characters," s.v. "Anable, Miss Mary Juliet."

[343] Anna Maria Anable spent summer 1847 in Boston, Massachusetts, taking some painful medical treatments to correct a skeletal condition with her shoulder. "Did I tell you I was coming here and for why? I am now sitting in a pair of excruciating steel corsets and every morning I go to a cross old bone setter here and take a medicated bath and get my shoulder shampooed. Tho' not a very pleasant operation—particularly the wearing the corsets (they cause me constant pain)—yet I am [ ] confident about being benefited and ultimately cured. I have already grown three quarters of an inch in a fortnight, from the straightening of my spine. I have been here now about three weeks." On April 26, 1848 she wrote: "My shoulder is quite strong and my shape is very much improved."

Mary Barber[344] since you left. Mr. Gratiot[345] saw her for a few moments on his way to Canada. She was well. Her old friend Mr. Milliancy [sic] is mayor, and what is better, is the most devoted lover of a husband the world has seen. Miss Breize [sic] is in the last stages of the consumption. The particulars of Nora's happy death you have already had. Eugenia's[346] health is better this spring than it has been in several years but we are not to see her this summer. My brother is in the Bellevue Hospital—he went to New York soon after you left the country and entered on his studies and is really going to be a physician. Speaking of physicians remind me that I am to tell you about Dr. Bagg's engagement to Maria Fa[ ]. You know all about Sarah Gold's matrimonial affairs, she is to be married very soon I believe. As I'm not sure you know any thing [sic] about this thing I'll add she is to marry the rich Mr. Dexter of Whiteston who has recently returned from his travels. Cornelia Kirkland has been quite out of health this winter, her friends are fearful that she is going to have settled upon her the disease her mother died of. Louisa Marble[347] still boards with us, and is reading some, and writing considerable. She is engaged now writing a Sabbath School book which I have not seen. She will not remain with us but a few weeks longer. Fanny is to be married in the course of a few months. The number of our boarders is increasing, but nearly all our girls are strange to you, not so our teachers, they are all as you left them, and the prospect is we shall not have any changes for some time. The school continues to be pleasant and is gradually growing larger. This is a bright sunny morning (Saturday) but it is cold while I am sitting by the side of my stove, you are suffering from heat.

Now taken it for granted my dear Emily, that you would be glad to hear of all the changes that have taken place since you left and of some that are to take place in the future and so will offer no apology for filling my sheet with such matter. Since commencing this letter I have been thinking of the changes we have experienced for the last few years, and am astonished at their number and importance. I am sometimes filled with strange apprehensions about the future, both as it regards my friends, and myself and yet I cannot believe that there are to be as many changes in the future, as there have been in the past. If we are Christians, we shall be prepared for what God has in reserve for us. To his protection let us commend ourselves for he alone can direct our steps. I was prepared to hear a favorable account of your voyage, and your new home and duties from you but did not feel

[344] See vol. 1, "Cast of Characters," s.v. "Barber, Mary."

[345] Charles Gratiot grew up in St Louis, where his father was an army engineer responsible for developing the Port of St. Louis. He married Ann Sheldon, who was a cousin of Miss Cynthia Sheldon, Mrs. Urania Sheldon Nott, and Alma Sheldon Anable. Together, Charles and Ann Gratiot had six children. Because they often lived with the Sheldon family, their letters contain a great deal of him. Letters in 1847 speak of his religious awakening; those of 1849 speak of his leaving for the California gold fields. In 1853, Charles Gratiot applied for a grant of 400 acres in Illinois, and he already owned 148 acres.

[346] See vol. 1, "Cast of Characters," s.v. "Damaux, Eugenia."

[347] See vol. 1, "Cast of Characters," s.v. "Marble, Miss."

sure that Lydia[348] would find all things in her new world just to please her. Her letters which have assured us of her continued devotion to her work and her finding things better than she expected have given us much pleasure. I really believe she has now got into the niche that was meant for her. When you leave Maulmain I trust you [ ] your mantle fall upon her, that is, impart to her your letter writing gift, or at least inclination. She has enough of the gift, but is burying it, so in all things just present the case to her in the light of a duty if you can and in so doing you will confer a favor on a score of her friends, here at home who want to hear from her. Remember me affectionately to your dear husband, I bless him in my heart every time I think of him, for his devotion to you, and his willingness to enter again upon a life of such toil and suffering as he has marked out for himself. My daily prayer for you is, that you may be blessed as you desire and deserve to be. Write to me if you can spare the time [Note: Written along the left margin of page 4.] from other and more important duties and believe me to be your devoted friend

Jane Kelly.

Written along the left margin of page 2: "Kiss your little children. I love them because you do."

Source: American Baptist Historical Society, AJ 17, no. 788.

Miss Julia A. Look to Emily C. Judson, April 25, 1847[349]

My dear Mrs. Judson,

Your very kind and delightful note was received a long time ago and should have been answered as long since but for some bad reason or other, I have been just a day too late for every package that Anna M.[350] has mailed for you. I shall not try to tell you how relieved and delighted we were to hear of your safe arrival, and that you were pleased with Burmah. I *wish* I could sit on some little stool beside you and your dear Dr. this evening. I'd ask a string of questions longer than from this our room over your and Anna M's to beyond where J. Williams lives. Since I cannot I'll tell you all about ourselves and myself, and wait for you to tell me all I would ask. Sarah Bell[351]—the mean [ ] thing comes and casts the light of her eyes over my shoulder and says "This looks school ma'arm-ified." Of course it does— how could it be any thing [sic] else. When you left I was preparing to go to my Virginia home for the first time. I went—and had the most delightful time that can

---

[348] See vol. 1, "Cast of Characters," s.v. "Lillybridge, Miss," also the timeline "Lydia Lillybridge Simons."

[349] This letter is undated. It is placed in April because she mentions the late spring in Utica.

[350] See vol. 1, "Cast of Characters," s.v. "Anable, Miss Anna Maria."

[351] See vol. 1, "Cast of Characters," s.v. "Wheeler, Miss Sarah Bell."

well be imagined. Everything was just as pleasant as could possibly be. I rode on horse-back, walked, ate peaches and cream, and did every thing [*sic*] else that was cunning. But those days like other vacation days are over—and we are already beginning to look forward ten weeks to our next long vacation. I spent two weeks with Susan last winter. I sent your note for her to read and in her last letter she sent love and her best wishes to you. Our school has changed a good deal during the last year. The Bacons and Wilmores are away for the summer—But strangers have come to fill their places. I have a *very* nice composition class but—poor things! I only wish they could be better [ ]. I try and try to remember something you used to tell us which [ ] I have not already repeated a dozen times and fortunately I now and then light on some thought or expression which had hidden in an unrummaged [*sic*] corner and so escaped my big[ ] research. But not safe even there my friend—thee must be dragged out and publicly executed on the school room platform on Friday morning. You already know that Anna Maria is to spend the summer in Boston[352] but—and you can guess how much we shall miss her. If we could only look in upon you, and see your little children, and what a nice mother Nemmy[353] makes—why—why—I can only *say*, we should be *very* glad, but feel a great deal more than is there so family expressed. Mr. Walraell has gone to Mexico to fight for his country, and receive the volunteer $12 bounty and sixty acres of wild land. I hope no Northern will take advantage and invade while Walraell is away—Think how unprotected we are! Sarah Bell, Helen Blasdell and myself have been out on tan bark walking since tea. The trees are just beginning to grow green and though this spring is a whole month later than the last—we are now having warm pleasant weather.

My dear Nemmy I know you have *every* body [*sic*] to write to, while there are so many of us to write to you—but do send me at least a note with the packages. If I were near you to night I'd certainly ask for a good night kiss both from you and your dear Dr. even it should make Lydia[354] stare as much as it did once.

Good bye—My dear friend—He can bless you and yours—
Julia L.

Source: American Baptist Historical Society, AJ 17, no. 763.

---

[352] For more information on these medical treatments, see vol. 1, "Cast of Characters," s.v. "Anable, Anna Maria."

[353] Emily Chubbuck. See vol. 1, "Cast of Characters," s.v. "Nemmy, Nem, or Nemmy Petty (Nemmie Pettie)." Also the chapter "Names of Endearment."

[354] See vol. 1, "Cast of Characters," s.v. "Lillybridge, Miss." Also the timeline "Lydia Lillybridge Simons."

LETTERS

———⚬———

MAY–AUGUST 1847

Miss Lydia Lillybridge to Dr. Solomon Peck, May 20, 1847[1]—
Maulmain Burmah

My dear Mr. Peck,

Your kind letter of October 21st, was received in January and afforded me much, very much pleasure, for which you have my warmest thanks—You have already heard, no doubt, of the safe arrival and pleasant voyage of the company that left you in July last,[2] and would like to know how I like my new situation. In most respects, I was very agreeably disappointed. The pleasant, retired situation of the school—the tasteful arrangement of things about the mission compound, and the air of elegance about the house which was to be my home, delighted me, and I was no less surprised, and delighted, with the neat, orderly appearance of the school, together with the advancement of the pupils in their studies—We arrived just in time to attend the examination at the close of the term. During the vacation, which continued a month, I applied myself to the study of the Burmese language.

Since the first of January, I have spent four hours a day in teaching, and three (generally) in acquiring the language. In this, my progress is slow, and would be if I studied all the time, for I am naturally slow about every thing [sic] of the kind. I am happy to be able to teach in English while I am learning, otherwise, I would feel that I was doing no good for a long time. I feel very much interested in the school, and quite at home in it. There are now about thirty in the girl's department, seventeen of whom, attend to English four hours in the day, and to Burmese one. The remainder devote two hours to English, and three, to Burmese.—Though I feel that by the blessing of God, I may do much good here, yet I should feel that I was doing much more if I were teaching those who would not receive any religious instruction at all, without my efforts—

Mrs. Howard[3] is untiring in her exertions, and has accomplished wonderful improvements in those under her charge. There are very few individuals who could carry on all departments with so much efficiency.

The constant care of so many children, is quite too much for her, and I'm sure that she cannot endure it much longer. I should be quite willing to take upon myself the care of the domestic department of the school if I were sure that it would be best for me to do so; but then I should have scarcely any time for

---

[1] This is one of four letters included in the correspondence from Lydia Lillybridge to Dr. Solomon Peck, the executive secretary of the American Baptist Missionary Union. These letters are included because the life and experience of Lydia Lillybridge and Emily Chubbuck Judson are so closely tied, and they inform us as to life in Burmah within the missionary family.

[2] Sailing on the *Faneuil Hall* were Miss Lydia Lillybridge, Reverend and Mrs. Norman Harris, Reverend and Mrs. John Sydney Beecher, and Dr. Adoniram and Mrs. Emily Judson.

[3] Theresa Howard was born in New York; with her husband Hosea, she arrived in Burmah on December 26, 1834. They worked in Maulmain and Rangoon for sixteen years before sailing for the United States on February 28, 1850. Theresa Howard worked with her husband in the schools established by the mission. She died in Bloomington, Illinois, on July 14, 1868.

studying the language, and Mrs. H. herself, does not think it would be wise for me to do it now.

But the care of her own numerous family is as much as she ought to have.

You see that I was very soon separated from the dear family of Dr. Judson.[4] It did not once occur to me, before leaving home, that such a wide separation would ever come to pass, and for a little time, I felt like a fatherless—motherless, child, for I did look to them for counsel and admonition, with all the warm confidence that a child feels towards a parent. I felt that God by his providence was teaching me; not to lean upon any earthly arm—but to place all my hopes of happiness in him alone.

As I could do nothing at present, in the way of teaching at Rangoon, this separation seemed to be for the interest of the Mission which I desire to promote, and I could say nothing against it.

However I feel myself highly favoured in having a home in such a kind-hearted, candid, and intelligent family as that of Mr. Howard's.[5] I have seldom met with an individual so habitually and heartily prayerful as he.

As it regards the good things of this life they altogether exceed my expectations, and I often feel that I have to many of them [sic].

If I had known all the circumstances connected with some of my predecessors being here, I think I should never have decided to come. But I do not regret my decision, for, though I often have doubts about having "run before I was sent," I again often feel that Providence directed my way, and that he will accomplish that for which he brought me here. Still, I fear that I shall not fulfil the expectations of the Board, of yourself, and of other Christian friends. Do not cease to pray, dear Sir, that God will lead me, and guide me, and cause me to do, and suffer all his will.

Accept my thanks for the volume of devotional exercises, which you presented me. While reading them, I have been encouraged, strengthened, quickened.

The kindness shown me by yourself and family, and the regard you have manifested for my welfare, have led me to write very freely and familiarly—perhaps, too much so. If so, do excuse me, and write as often as you can, if only a few lines.

Please present my kindest regards to Mrs. Peck, and her parents. I shall long remember the delightful visit I had with them at Andover. Kiss the little girls for me, and tell them not to forget that they were to write to me. I should be very grateful for a letter from Mrs. P.

With much respect, I am yours,

Very affectionately,

Lydia Lillybridge

---

[4] In mid-February, Adoniram and Emily Judson left for Rangoon, hoping to be able to use that as a launching pad to get into Ava.

[5] See vol. 1, "Cast of Characters," s.v. "Howard, the Reverend Hosea and Theresa."

Rev. Mr. Peck

Secretary of the Baptist Board of Foreign Missions.

Please send the Daguerreotype likeness to Miss Martha Lillybridge, Female Academy, Utica, N.Y. and charge the same to my account. L. Lillybridge.

Miss Lydia Lillybridge to Emily C. Judson, May 21, 1847[6]

Well, your letter did come at last, but I began to think it never would come. I've not been so much out of patience waiting for a letter, since I have been here. If I thought it be any punishment to you, I wouldn't write you a word for two months; but I've concluded that *writing* to you will be the most effectual punishment I could inflict.

What bundles of news you had from home! I've not received a word from home by this month's steamer, and if you have any thing [*sic*] for me in yours, I hope you'll send it on quickly—You wrote as if you thought I really had some intention to leave this school for the other.[7] There is no such intention, and I did not think of giving you such an idea; but since I wrote you, one of our ship's company has seriously proposed the subject for my consideration. Don't mention it though—for there are broils enough already before the brethren, without this particular. I have not [Note: "mentioned" is written and crossed out.] stated this thing fully to any one [*sic*], before. I stand more firmly at my post than at any time [*sic*] before; not that I am unwilling to go there at any time [*sic*] the Board wish me. But I cannot see why this school is not as important as that. I have not time to write you all about the quarreling. Mr. Howard,[8] (meek man!) has to take the buffeting on every side. What would people at home say, if they knew all? Wouldn't they withhold some of their ill-timed, soul-destroying praise? This striving to be the greatest, will not be effectually put down, until a Heavenly Power puts the spirit of a little child into their hearts.

[6] This letter is an addendum to a letter started April 23, 1847.

[7] On April 23, 1847, Lydia spoke of Mr. Ingalls and of his looking for teachers to come to the mission at Akyab. Though Emily would not yet have that letter, it was sent with this one, and word no doubt circulated in the small missionary family and spread quickly beyond Maulmain.

[8] See vol. 1, "Cast of Characters," s.v. "Anable, William Steward."

Mrs. Stevens[9] and I, have some nice times. She is a darling little creature. Mrs. Haswell[10] too, is a sensible sort of a woman, that I like much—What shall I say more?—My brain is cooled a little, since I first commenced the letter. Mr. I.[11] intended to go in the steamer which leaves tomorrow, but it will not stop at his port; so he is obliged to stay another month. I had concluded, however, not to accompany him, so that it is no great disappointment to me. Mrs. Haswell's brother wrote her that Mr. J. was about to be married. Do you know to whom?

Martha[12] told me in her last letter that her Christmas present, was a copy of *Alderbrook*.[13] You have been very expeditious about that memoir;[14] but I don't believe a word you say about your knowledge of Burmese.[15]

Mr. Howard baptized three of our girls, last Sunday, and one young man, a Tamul. Two of the girls, we hope have been converted lately, the others asked for baptism a year ago.

Sometimes, I think my scholars are doing well, and sometimes, I think they are not. It is drill, drill, drill; day after day I have to pound Arithmetic and Grammar into their brains with my tongue and teeth.

[9] Elizabeth Stevens arrived in Maulmain in February 1838; her husband was Edward Stevens. Elizabeth Stevens took six-month-old Edward Judson into her home when Sarah and Adoniram had to leave for the United States in 1845, and her care and nurture saved his life. She served forty-eight years in Burmah. She had extensive correspondence with Emily Judson, and her letters spoke of everyday life among the missionaries. When Emily returned to the United States, the letters from Mrs. Stevens brought news of friends and colleagues. Mrs. Stevens had a sister, Sarah Haven, in Massachusetts, who wrote a number of letters to Emily asking for information on the Stevens family.

[10] Jane Haswell sailed for Burmah in 1835, arriving in February 1836 to work with the Talaings. Her husband was James Haswell. She served as a missionary for more than forty years. Mrs. Haswell took in Henry Hall Judson when Adoniram and Sarah sailed for the United States in spring 1845. The correspondence between Emily and Jane Haswell reflects a warm relationship between the two.

[11] Lovel Ingalls was born August 21, 1808, in Worcester, New York. He was ordained October 2, 1834 in Boston, New York, and graduated from the Hamilton Literary and Theological Institute in 1837. In September 1834, he married Marcia Dawes of Cummington, Massachusetts; Miss Dawes had been educated at Cummington Academy. They first sailed for Burmah in 1835, arriving at Amherst February 20, 1836. They were stationed at Mergui and then Maulmain in May 1845; Marcia Dawes Ingalls died on November 9, 1845, at Maulmain. Lovel and Marcia Ingalls were the parents of three children. Mr. Ingalls went to Akyab in 1846 and returned to the United States beginning May 1850. He went back to Burmah in December 1851. His second wife was Marilla Amelia Baker, and they married December 23, 1850 at Troy, New York. Mr. Ingalls died at sea on March 14, 1856.

[12] Martha Lillybridge was the sister of Lydia Lillybridge, who went to Burmah with Emily and Adoniram Judson. Martha was at the Utica Female Academy. On May 28, 1848, Anna Maria wrote, "Martha is a very fine looking girl—but she lacks energy. I think we shall have her take Fanny's (Anna Maria's sister) place at Miss Martin's. It will suit her as she has no desire to shine as a teacher in a school."

[13] *Alderbrook* was a two volume collection of Emily's poems, sketches and stories that was first published in December 1846.

[14] Emily was engaged in writing the memoir of Sarah Hall Boardman Judson.

[15] In her letter of April 1, 1847, Lydia spoke forcefully of the need to understand the Burmese language; she was not able to spend the time she felt she needed on learning it, and she was sure that with Emily's schedule, she was not making a priority of it as well. She was adamant that if they had come to proclaim the gospel to the natives, they had to learn the language in order to do it.

Mr. Mason[16] returned by the last Steamer[17] with health much improved, and is to spend the rainy season at Newton in Mr. Vinton's[18] family.

I shall not punish you again, in a long time. If you ever write again, tell me something of the children. If I could kiss *sweetly*, I'd say—Kiss the Dr. for me.

From your affectionate

Mrs. Judson Lydia

Has Miss Cynthia[19] written you a long letter yet?

Source: American Baptist Historical Society, AJ 17, no. 774.

Emily C. Judson to Adoniram Judson,[20] May 1847

To My Husband

'Tis May, but no sweet violet springs,
    In these strange woods and dells;
The dear home-lily never swings.
    Her little pearly bells;
But search my heart, and thou wilt see
What wealth of flowers it owes to thee.

[16] Francis Mason arrived in Maulmain in November 1830 and transferred to Tavoy in 1831. His first wife died, and he married Helen Maria Griggs just before leaving the United States. She died in Burmah in 1846; they were the parents of four children. A skilled linguist, Mr. Mason was fluent in twelve languages and translated the Scripture into two of the Karen dialects. In spring 1847, Mr. Mason was seriously ill, and the other missionaries were concerned about him. In September 1847, he remarried, and Adoniram Judson officiated at the ceremony. His new wife was Ellen Huntley Bullard; originally from Vermont, she was the widow of Edwin Bullard, missionary to Burmah. Francis Mason died March 3, 1874 in Rangoon.

[17] See the April 2 letter from Deborah Wade to Emily, in which she speaks of Mrs. Mason's death, the illness of Mr. Mason, and her efforts to get him ready to board the steamer for his voyage.

[18] Justus Hatch Vinton was born in Willington, Connecticut, in 1806. He attended the theological school at Hamilton, New York, and was ordained in June 1834. In July that same year, he sailed as a missionary to Burmah. His wife was Calista Holman Vinton; they were married April 9, 1834. They worked with the Karens at Chummerah, Newville, and Maulmain, where he had charge of the Karen theological seminary. At the end of 1847, they left for the United States, returning to Burmah and work at Rangoon in July 1850. Justus Vinton died in Kemendine, Burmah, on March 31, 1858. His wife, Calista Holman Vinton, died in Rangoon, Burmah December 20, 1864. Mrs. Vinton taught the Karen women and was the author of several hymnbooks in their language.

[19] Miss Cynthia Sheldon was in charge of the administrative and financial departments of the Utica Female Academy. Miss Sheldon and her sister Urania, who was literary principal, gave Emily Chubbuck a place at the academy in October 1840. They had deferred any cost to a future time when Emily could afford to reimburse them. Upon Miss Urania Sheldon's marriage in the late summer 1842 to the Reverend Doctor Eliphalet Nott, the president of Union College, and her subsequent move to Schenectady, Miss Cynthia Sheldon assumed a larger leadership role at the academy. Active and well-known in Baptist circles, Miss Cynthia was to become an important mentor, advisor, and friend to Emily until the time of Emily's death in 1854. She was the aunt of Emily's best friend, Anna Maria Anable, and was addressed by most as "Aunt Cynthia." In 1848, Miss Sheldon moved to Philadelphia to help Miss Anable with the startup of the Misses Anable's School.

[20] Arabella Wilson, in her book *Lives of the Three Mrs. Judsons*, has a portion of this poem. She identifies it as having been "written in Rangoon during a time of great physical suffering." (New York and Auburn: Miller, Orton, and Mulligan, 1856).

The robin's voice is never heard,
From palm and banyan trees,
And strange to me each gorgeous bird,
Whose pinion fans the breeze;
But love's white wing bends softly here,
Love's thrilling music fills my ear.

The heavy rain unceasing falls;
Winds hurry to and fro;
The damp mould gathers on our walls,
So dreary, dark, and low;
Dull shadows throng my aching brow,—
My heart is never shadowed now.

Sometimes we tread the busy street;
Dark, bold eyes on us gleam,
As patter onward sandaled feet,
In one continuous stream,—
The conquered sons of old Pegu,
The rich Mogul, the cringing Jew,

The subtle, soft Armenian,
The Parsee in his pride,
The quaint "celestial" artisan,
The slave from Cassay's side,
The Burman in his pomp and power,
Whose jealous brows upon us lower;—

None, none to greet us kindly here!
Their ban is on our door;
Of Jesus Christ, with frown and sneer,
They speak like men of yore;—
Not mine to brave the glance of hate,
But bravely will I share thy fate.

The pure, the beautiful, the good,
Ne'er gather in this place,
None but the vicious and the rude,
The dark of mind and face;
But all the wealth of thy vast soul,
Is pressed into my brimming bowl.

Where fragrant cocoa blossoms hang,
Or in the citron's shade,
My brothers' voices never rang,
My sisters never played;—
I love them none the less, that thou
Canst make me scarcely miss them now.

Yet think oft of one sweet home,
My father—mother—Kate;[21]
And tender, tearful memories come,
And clinging round me wait;
But at one Bound they vanish all—
Thy footfall in the dim, old hall.

Here closely nestled by thy side,
Thy arm around me thrown,
I ask no more. In mirth and pride,
I've stood—oh, *so* alone!
Now, what is all this world to me,
Since I have found my world in thee!

Oh, if we are so happy here,
Amid our toils and pains,
With thronging cares and dangers near,
And marred by earthly stains,
How great must be the compass given
Our souls, to *bear* the bliss of heaven.

Source: Arabella M. Wilson, *Lives of the Three Mrs. Judsons*, (New York and Auburn: Miller, Orton, and Company: 1856) 369–70, has portions of this poem; Emily Judson, *An Olio of Domestic Verse*, (New York: Lewis Colby, 1852) 153–56.

The Reverend Doctor William Dean to Emily C. Judson, May 21, 1847—Hong Kong

My dear Sister Emily,

I was more than half disappointed in finding nothing fr. last mail with your signature, still those disappointed hopes like too many others mainly indulged might have been unauthorized—and my disappointment might have been a just punishment for my presumptions. You may have heard that Dr. Duncan, with broken

[21] See vol. 1, "Cast of Characters," s.v. "Chubbuck, Catharine."

health, has just embarked for New York and Mr. and Mrs. Lord have proceeded on their way to join Dr. Magowen at [ ]—"and I only am escaped *alone* to tell thee"— Not a missionary of our Board within a thousand miles of me. Still in a philosophic way I manage to surround myself with the best of friends and engross myself in the best of works. During my snatching glances at English books I have read "The Old Purchase"—(Written with a *stiff-quill*—) and have looked over the Reviews—The last No (Jan/47) of the "Edinburgh" has a good article on "David Hume" but I was most interested in reading the "Pensees de Pascal" and also pleased to see so honorable tribute to Religion and its advocates in the "Edinburgh."—My "Acts" with, "marginal notes and references"—advances but too slowly. Some days a page— more or less—and some days not at all! It is painfully analogous to my daily employments wh. so largely partake of "Notes and references," that little is done with the *Text* of human life. If you doubt this now you may be more believing when I assure you that I am daily astray in the *multifarious* capacity of Chairman, Secretary, Treasure, and Librarian of the Mission; Gen. Superintendent of Chinese preaching, Schools, printing, revising and preparing tracts and the Scriptures; housewife, gardener, and cow-keeper for the Mission; Commission-agent and Postmaster General for the missionaries at the surrounding Stations—Home- Secretary and Gen. Correspondent to Foreign Parts—etc. etc. etc.—Whew! what a string of titles! what a man of business!—hem!—How pleasing to human nature to have "full swing!"—No discords—no dissenting votes—propose measures and pass resolutions *unanimously*—(Unus Animus) You may rest assured that there is not a more *harmonious* missn [sic] station in all the East! A perfect *model* of *una- nimity* in feeling and *oneness* of effort. Really it whd be delightful for you to look in upon a compound of so much missy [sic] harmony and domestic concord. It would afford me *very great* pleasure to give you ocular proof of all I have stated and I leave it for you to decide whether it is not a sight worth a voyage to China?—

—Here I have been called off by some of my "Marginal References"—a chi- naman just called with half a dozen attendants for some medicine for a sore leg—and I just directed the boy to bind him up with a plaster and sent him off with a book and an exhortation to throw away his idols and worship God—So you per- ceive I might add to my list of duties that of *Surgeon* and *Apothecary*—But I hear you say, "Enough of this"—

I hear that Mr. Shuck and party were to sail from Boston on the 8th March in the "Ashburton"—and are destined to *Shanghai* (not Canton) where the $10,000 Church is to be erected for wh. Mr. S. has been collecting funds, from "Dan to Beersheba." Have you a $10,000 Chapel in Rangoon? I have a nice one at Hong Kong wh. cost *one* thousand dollars, and I had the pleasure of having it *full* of Chinese last Sabbath—and I think it is quite large enough for me—indeed till last

Sunday it had not been more *than half* filled at any time since my return from America. We have also a small chapel in the Bazar [*sic*] where we have one service on the Sabbath. So you see I have *two chapels* and *two houses* and missionary associates—

What a mistake that I did not foresee and provide against such a dilemma while in the U.S. But pray don't blame a poor man who did all he could—

With kindest assurances to Dr. Judson

Believe me

Very Sincerely

Yr br

W. Dean

Source: American Baptist Historical Society, AJ 15, no. 593.

Mrs. H. H. Newton to Emily C. Judson, May 28, 1847—New York

My dear Mrs. Judson—I can assure you, your kind letter was received with heartfelt pleasure. I *could* not, when we parted ask such a favour [*sic*]—for I knew your large circle of friends had a prior claim to your affection and that your correspondence with them must, necessarily be a great tax on your time—I shall ever feel grateful to your kind husband for allowing me the pleasure, of becoming acquainted with one, whose friendship I *prize* and in whose welfare I shall ever take a deep interest. If, amongst your numerous cares, you can again spare me a small portion of your time—I shall be very glad and if Mr. Newton[22] or myself can in any way assist you we shall feel happy in so doing. Your letters to us we shall consider *to us alone*—

I felt a sort of sadness steal over me when I ascertained you were to leave Maulmain for really I heard so much of that spot from the lips of your husband I almost fancied I could find your house, with the beautiful tree on the corner—then too it seemed a bright spot in dark Burmah—May the God of all grace ever direct your steps—

I am thankful your first impressions are pleasant—you can really find something to *admire* in that far off benighted land—some *green* spots—may it ever be so. I certainly think a *cheerful* contented mind is one of the greatest earthly blessings—

[22] There are seven letters in this correspondence from Mr. and Mrs. Isaac Newton of New York City. In a June 1846 letter, Mrs. Newton indicated that they are "new friends," certainly of Emily. They obviously had considerable wealth, which they shared generously with Adoniram and Emily through packages and, upon Adoniram's death, an immediate check to Emily of $500. Mr. Newton called Adoniram his "friend." One of the letters invited Emily to stay with them in New York upon her return, and a later letter indicated that she had indeed done that. On May 15, 1846, Adoniram Judson inscribed a dedication to Mrs. H. H. Newton on the fly-leaf of a volume of Burmese hymns that had been compiled by Mrs. Sarah B. Judson: "Mrs. H. H. Newton From A. Judson/ The wings [ ] [ ] /[ ] are folded in St. Helena—New York—May 15th, 1846."

I am well aware I have but little idea of the misery of the heathen but I can feel for those whom God puts the desire in to their hearts to leave comforts and friends to labour [sic] in his service—I hope you will take care of *yourself*.

I never did think it right for the wife of a missionary to tax every energy she possesses to the full extent—why should she work and *slave* so much more than a wife and Mother here?—as a general thing too much is expected of her—If she is a comfort and helper to her husband and a faithful mother to his children—her cares and responsibilities are great—then the enervating influence of the climate—I had a very pleasant interview with Mr. and Mrs. Osgood[23]—we spoke of *you* often—How very much they are attached to Dr. Judson! I showed Mrs. O. your likeness—how much I think of that—how often I think of you sitting in the Artist's room[24]—and I can see you *hiding* away one of your hands. How often I have wished I had Dr. Judson behind your chair arranging your att[ ]!—

Since you left we have had quite a change in our family. George was married on the 10th December the day you arrived at Maulmain—his health seemed so feeble our Physician advised a sea voyage—he with his wife and Frances sailed on the 9th Feb. the journey this far has been of great benefit to him and we hope he will return to his home and friends quite well—I was desirous for Frances to accompany them—of course such a journey would be of great benefit to the minds of any young person—I was quite remiss in not saying where they sailed to—It was Liverpool—they will I suppose spend most of their time in Italy and Switzerland. Remember them in your prayers—if they only possess the pearl of great price, th*ey are* safe—I thank you sincerely for your kind remembrance of us—the vases I shall ever prize as your gift—they have not yet arrived—when they do, and if my life is spared—the next time I attempt a letter to you I will tell you where I have placed them—and then you'll see if it corresponds with your imagination.

I have always felt a very great reluctance to letter writing especially for the last several years because in the first place, I have no talent for it and in the next place

[23] Rev. Sewall Osgood was a missionary in Maulmain who worked with and lived by Adoniram Judson. Judson and Osgood occupied two of the four homes in the mission compound and lived so close that it "allowed me the pleasure and profit of almost hourly intercourse." He arrived in Burmah in 1834. His first wife Elhira Brown Osgood died on October 5, 1837, in Maulmain. On July 8, 1838, he married Sarah Thomas, the widow of the Reverend Jacob Thomas, with Adoniram Judson officiating at the wedding. He spoke in the letters to Emily, of which there are five between July 1850 and April 1852, of Adoniram Judson as his "most intimate friend." He never personally met Emily, as he had returned from the field prior to 1846. At the time of his letters, he was working with the American Baptist Missionary Union as a district secretary. In 1845, just as they were leaving for the United States, Sarah and Adoniram Judson gave care of Charley, too young to make the trip, to Mr. and Mrs. Osgood. Charley died not long after their departure. Mr. Osgood visted Adoniram, Elnathan, and Abby Ann in the United States. His third wife was Caroline Wait; they were married December 30, 1850 at Saratoga, New York. With all of his suggestions of "intimacy" and "his most intimate friend," Mr. Osgood stated that his life was so busy that he simply did not have the time to look through his papers for anything that would be helpful in writing the memoir.

[24] Emily had a portrait painted for Anna Maria by famous artist P. F. Rothermel. With that, she commissioned John Sartain, the famous engraving, to do an engraving. This ended up as the portrait in *Alderbrook*. Then, in the few months before they sailed, Emily spoke of having the artist Freeman paint some portraits of Anna Maria and Adoniram (who said he did not have time to sit for a portrait).

my time is so much occupied with my family I almost *dread* taking up my pen. My friendship and love for you have alone directed me to make the attempt—so my dear friend must "take the will of the deed."

I hope your own health and happiness may be preserved and may the blessing of Him who dwelt in the bush—dwell with you and those you love. My dear husband unites with me in aff to yourself and Dr. Judson.

Yours with sincere love

H. H. Newton

The ballard [sic] you speak of shall be coppied [sic] and sent to the Mission rooms to be sent by the first opportunity.

Source: American Baptist Historical Society, AJ 18, no. 860.

Emily C. Judson to Catharine Chubbuck, May 30, 1847[25]—Rangoon

My Dear Katy,—

We are in a charming coil just now, and though it is Sabbath day, have had no worship in Burmese. Night before last we had secret information that the Ray-Woon had ordered our house to be watched; and but for that information, before this time (for it is evening) our assembly of Christians would have been shut up in prison, suffering the lash, the stocks, or even worse torture. The Ray-Woon is a very cruel man, and it is said that the screams of poor tortured wretches are heard almost incessantly, night and day, to issue from his house. He is the second in power, but the governor is a weak man, over seventy years of age—a regular old woman in "hose and doublet"—patso and goung-boung, I mean. The man whom the Doctor baptized came in with his father-in-law. One of our people met them on the way and told them of the danger, but they were anxious to come, and managed to provide against it. The old man asked baptism for his son, a fine fellow about twenty, and the young man made known his wish to go over to Maulmain and prepare to preach. The Doctor came to my room, after they were gone, all animation; but he is sad again now....

Source: A. C. Kendrick, *The Life and Letters of Mrs. Emily C. Judson*, 274–78.

---

[25] This letter has an addendum dated May 31, 1847 and a second dated June 2.

Emily C. Judson to Catharine Chubbuck, May 31, 1847[26]

Last night, after trying in vain to comfort my poor husband, as he walked with clouded face up and down my room, by saying that God would take care of His own cause, etc., all of which he of course understands and feels more than I do, I was obliged to give up and sit down in silence. At last I turned suddenly to him, and inquired, "Would you like to know the first couplet that I ever learned to repeat?" I suppose he thought I was trifling, for he only turned his head, and said nothing. "I learned it," continued I "before I could read, and I afterwards used to write it every where [sic]—sometimes, even, at the top of the page, when I was preparing the story on whose success more depended than its readers ever dreamed." I had gained his attention. "What was it?" he inquired.

> "Beware of desperate steps; the darkest day,
> (Live till to-morrow,) will have passed away."

"I declare," said he with energy, and his whole face brightening, "if I could only believe in transmigration, I should have no doubt that we had spent ages together in some other sphere, we are so alike in every thing [sic]. Why, those two lines have been my motto; I used to repeat them over and over in prison, and I have them now, written on a slip of paper, for a book-mark." He stood a few moments, thinking and smiling, and then said, "Well, one thing you didn't do: you never wrote 'Pray without ceasing' on the cover of your wafer box." "No; but I wrote it on my looking-glass." This furnished one of our never-ending subjects, and we chatted away almost as cheerfully as if there had been no Vesuvius under our feet.

Source: A. C. Kendrick, *The Life and Letters of Mrs. Emily C. Judson*, 274–78.

Emily C. Judson to Catharine Chubbuck, June 2, 1847[27]

Just one year to-day since I stood before good old Doctor Kendrick, and said the irrevocable, "love, honor, and obey."[28] It was on many accounts a day of darkness, but it has dragged three hundred and sixty-five *very* light ones at its heels. It has been far the happiest year of my life; and, what is in my eyes still more impor-

---

[26] This letter is an addendum to a letter started May 30, 1847; a second addendum is dated June 2, 1847.

[27] This letter is an addendum to a letter started May 30, 1847; a second addendum is dated June 2, 1847.

[28] When Emily Chubbuck was in her teens, Dr. Nathaniel Kendrick was the pastor of the Baptist church in Eaton and also a professor in a local theological school; he eventually became the president of the Hamilton Literary and Theological Institution. At that time in her life, Emily spoke with him about becoming a missionary. Dr. Kendrick gave her the wise counsel of discernment, patience, and waiting. Adoniram and Emily turned to Dr. Kendrick to officiate at their marriage. He married Adoniram and Emily on June 2, 1846. A. C. Kendrick, in *the Life and Letters of Mrs. Emily C. Judson* (New York: Sheldon and Company, 1831), says that the marriage of Emily and Adoniram Judson was the last service for which Dr. Kendrick was able to leave his home. Other correspondents mention his continued frailty. He died on September 11, 1848.

tant, my husband says it has been among the happiest of his. We have been in circumstances to be almost constantly together; and I never met with any man who could talk so well, day after day, on every subject, religious, literary, scientific, political, and—and nice baby-talk. He has a mind which seems exhaustless, and so, even here in Rangoon, where all the English I hear, from week's end to week's end, is from him, I never think of wanting more society. I have been ill a great deal, but not in a way to hinder him; and he treats me as gently and tenderly as though I were an infant....

As for living, I must own that I am within an inch of starvation, and poor little Henry[29] says, when he sits down to the table, "I don't want any dinner—I wish we could go back to Maulmain." His papa does better, for he never has a poor appetite. For a long time after we first came here, we could get no bread at all; now we get a heavy, black, sour kind, for which we pay just three times as much as we did at Maulmain. You will say "Make it." What shall I make it of? or a biscuit, or pie, or any thing [sic] good? And when it is made of nothing, what shall I bake it in? Our milk is a mixture of buffaloes' milk, water, and something else which we cannot make out. We have changed our milk-woman several times, but it does no good. The butter we make from it is like lard with flakes of tallow. But it is useless to write about these things—you can get no idea. I must tell you, however, of the grand dinner we had one day. "You must contrive and get something that mamma can eat," the doctor said to our Burmese purveyor; "she will starve to death." "What shall I get?" "Anything." "Anything ?" " Anything." Well, we did have a capital dinner, though we tried in vain to find out by the bones what it was. Henry said it was *touk-tahs*, a species of lizard, and I should have thought so too, if the little animal had been of a fleshy consistence. Cook said he *didn't know*, but he grinned a horrible grin which made my stomach heave a little, notwithstanding the deliciousness of the meal. In the evening we called Mr. Bazaar-man. "What did we have for dinner to-day?" "Were they good?" "Excellent." A tremendous explosion of laughter, in which the cook from his dish room joined as loud as he dared. "What were they?" "Rats!" A common servant would not have played such a trick, but it was one of the doctor's assistants who goes to bazaar for us. You know the Chinese consider rats a great delicacy, and he bought them at one of their shops.

As for the house, it was very comfortable during the hot weather, for there is a brick floor overhead, but we suffer very much since the coming on of the rains. We are obliged to get directly before the window in order to see, and we suffer unac-

---

[29] Edward Judson, born December 27, 1844, in Maulmain, Burmah, was the eighth child of Adoniram and Sarah Hall Boardman Judson and the fifth of their children to survive. Only a few months old when Sarah and Adoniram returned to America, Edward's life was saved by the nurture and care he received from Elizabeth Stevens. He loved Emily as the only "Mama" he had ever known and returned with her to the United States in October 1851. Edward, who was Eddy to his family, became a minister; he did mission work with the immigrants in New York City, and with the aid of the Rockefeller Family, he built the Judson Memorial Baptist Church in what is now Washington Park.

countably from the damp air. We frequently shut all up, and light candles at noon. The doctor has severe rheumatism in his writing shoulder and constant headache, but his lungs do not trouble him so much as during the first storms. For myself, I am utterly prostrated; and, although I have taken care of everything and written a little, I have not sat up an hour at a time for six weeks. I have my table by my couch and write a few lines, and then lie down. The wooden ceiling overhead is covered with a kind of green mould, and the doors get the same way in two days if they are not carefully rubbed. Now, do you think I am in any way discontented, and would go back to America to live in a palace? Not I. I am ten times happier than I could be there. And then we are so, so happy in each other—We are frequently startled by echoing each others unspoken thoughts, and we believe alike in everything. You know I have always scolded, because nobody—minister nor people—was really orthodox in religious opinion. Well, he is strictly and thoroughly orthodox. At first I was a little annoyed by what seemed to me a taint of Guionism, Oberlinism, or something of that sort. I said nothing, however, but took to reading all those books with him, "for information." We went through all the numbers of the Methodist "Perfectionist"; took story after story and weighed it with the Bible and common sense; then we sifted Upham thoroughly, through all his growing and tiresome heaviness; and last of all, took up Madame Guion.[30] This last is really disgusting, and I consider her quite as much a patient for Dr. Brigham as Joan of Arc or any other monomaniac, though I believe, notwithstanding her very apparent unamiability, she had grace. Well, the amount of all is, we agree perfectly on all these topics.

Source: A. C. Kendrick, *The Life and Letters of Mrs. Emily C. Judson*, 274–78.

Emily C. Judson to Miss Cynthia Sheldon, June 16, 1847—Rangoon

Trouble on trouble—trouble on trouble! You could scarce imagine, dear aunt Cynthia,[31] people in a worse condition than we are now. Last Saturday evening Dr. J. came into my room with rod eyes and a voice all tremulous with weeping. "We must be at the worst now," he said; "and in all my troubles in this dreadful country, I never before looked on so discouraging a prospect. We are hunted down here like wild beasts; watched by government and plotted against by Catholic priests. The churches at home have made no provision for our going to Ava, the governor is importuned to send us out of the country, the monsoon is raging, and we could not go to Maulmain if we wished, and you are failing every day—it seems to me dying

---

[30] Jeane Marie Guion was a Christian mystic. She was born in the mid part of the seventeenth century. Adoniram quoted her in a letter to Emily dated April 3, 1846.

[31] See vol. 1, "Cast of Characters," s.v. "Sheldon, Miss Cynthia."

before my eyes—without the possibility of obtaining either medicines or a physician." It was all true except the last. I have suffered severely from the rain, but people like me "die" too many times to be much alarmed by anything that comes upon themselves. But it is a very sickly time, almost everybody is ill and funeral processions pass our house every day. There has been of late a funeral feast in nearly every house in our neighborhood, and the constant tap-tap of nailing up coffins in the night is dreadful.

I was speaking of Saturday evening. That same night Dr. J. was seized with terrible pains in the bowels, etc., which he thought was diarrhea. On Sunday he took laudanum injections, and was easier; but in the night the disease showed itself a dysentery of the worst form which we could find in our books. He had never had it before, either himself or in his family, and was utterly at a loss to know how to treat it. No two books agreed, and you know there is no medical adviser in the place. I begged him to take calomel, and he would have administered it to any other person, but in his own case he procrastinated. [sic] He has taken various medicines, and thus checked the disease; but last night (to-day is Friday) he became alarmed, and for the first time took a dose of rhubarb and calomel. I am afraid, however, it is too late, for he is in a terrible condition this morning. The last resort is a sea voyage, which at this season of the year is a desperate thing. Nothing goes from this port but little native vessels, with no accommodations for a well man, much less a sick one; and they are frequently wrecked. It would be utterly impossible to find one large enough to take in me and the children (the latter must, of course, go where I do), and if he goes alone, I think of the terrible suspense which awaits me for four, five, or six weeks, and the sufferings to which he must be exposed. He says only a matter of life and death could induce him to leave me with the children, and the people who are only children of larger growth, in my present condition. (I do not sit up an hour at a time.) If he goes, he must take our most intelligent man, but he, alas! is a most indifferent nurse.

Yours, etc.,

By "too late," I meant too late for any thing but a sea voyage; of that we have strong hopes.

Source: A. C. Kendrick, *The Life and Letters of Mrs. Emily C. Judson*, 278–79.

Emily C. Judson to Anna Maria Anable, June 16, 1847[32]

Dear Anna Maria,—

The Doctor is awake, but we can not [sic] tell yet whether he is better or worse.[33] He is evidently passing a crisis of some sort. The music and mourners have set up their screeching and howling at a house nearly opposite, and men are busy decorating the funeral car in the streets. We seem to be hemmed in by death. Suppose it should come here; there would be only servants to bury the dead! Something is the matter with Edward.[34] He was wakeful all night, and this morning he screams out suddenly when at his play as in pain, and runs to me as fast as he can. Poor little fellow! he can not [sic] tell his trouble. I have just quieted him, and take the moment to write while his head lies in my lap.

Source: A. C. Kendrick, *The Life and Letters of Mrs. Emily C. Judson*, 279–82.

Emily C. Judson to Anna Maria Anable, June 19, 1847[35]

Saturday. The Doctor says "the back-bone of his disease is broken." If it is, I am afraid there are two back-bones, for I think I never knew a person suffer so severely.[36] I have made Henry[37] a little bed on the floor, and he is groaning in a burning fever. If he is ill he will be very troublesome. I have given him a powerful medicine, and may get the start of the disease; it is Rangoon fever; he was seized suddenly and violently. Edward,[38] also, was troubled some in the night, and acts as strangely as yesterday. He scarcely ever cries, yet screams seem forced from him as by a sudden blow. He runs to me, but recovers in a moment, and goes back to play. There is something very alarming in this, knowing the brave little fellow's disposition as I do.

Source: A. C. Kendrick, *The Life and Letters of Mrs. Emily C. Judson*, 279–82.

---

[32] This letter was written over a two-week period. It has addenda dated June 19, June 20, and July 1, 1847.

[33] See the letter from Emily C. Judson to Miss Cynthia Sheldon dated June 16, 1847.

[34] See vol. 1, "Cast of Characters," s.v. "Judson, Edward."

[35] This is the second of four segments of a letter written over a two-week period—June 16, 19, 20, and July 1, 1847.

[36] See the letter of Emily C. Judson to Miss Cynthia Sheldon dated June 16, 1847, and her letter to Anna Maria Anable dated June 16, 1847.

[37] Henry Hall Judson, born July 8, 1842, was the son of Adoniram and Sarah Hall Boardman Judson. Henry was the sixth of their eight children, the fourth of five who survived. He remained in Burmah in 1845 when Adoniram and Sarah returned to the United States with the three older children. He returned with Emily in 1851 and went to live with her family in Hamilton, New York. Henry attended Brown University and Williams Collage; he enlisted in the army at the time of the Civil War in January 1864. Later that year, he experienced a debilitating accident attributed either to sunstroke or a horse kicking him in the head. He was married once—unhappily according to his own correspondence—and he eventually died in a veteran's home in 1918, the last of his siblings to die. Of this, the chaplain noted, "The end was a genuine example of Christian fortitude." See Rosalie Hall Hunt, *Bless God and Take Courage, The Judson Legacy* (Valley Forge PA: Judson Press, 2005) 291.

[38] See vol. 1, "Cast of Characters," s.v. "Judson, Edward."

Anna Maria Anable to Emily C. Judson, June 19, 1847—Boston

Dear Nemmy[39]

Your good long letter from Rangoon dated Feb'y came day before yesterday and did n't [sic] I have a feast tho' here all alone? It was very kind of you to take the time to describe your house so minutely[40]—I can imagine how every room looks, and as you say it does not look so bad neither. You have continued to give an air of comfort to those gloomy walls I know, and if you'll promise that the den won't admit snakes I think I'll accept of your polite invitation to occupy some of your spare room—only don't tuck me over among the dishes (the only room I see which you or the Dr. have not appropriated). I am afraid some Burman thief would break in some night and seize me for an offering on some of their heathenish altars.

I am very glad you concluded not to get up that bit of "misery" about the loss at Maulmain[41]—and I must say you bear it with astonishing fortitude. I hope you will not yet a while be seriously inconvenienced by it—When you want the things very badly they'll come I think. O' Twas too bad though to lose all your pretty things! I cannot imagine how the Dr. came to leave so many necessary things behind—his shoes, spectacles etc. Well, as you say it is all right—for some wise purpose doubtless, or it would not be.

The ladies here are sewing for Mrs. Stevens[42] and some church or other has already made a box for Mrs. Bullard[43] and sent it. I wish I was not making such a big hunt on Aunt Cynthia's[44] parlor myself this Summer. I should like to make a box of things for you all by my self [sic] while I am here. Did I tell you I was coming here and for why? I am now sitting in a pair of excruciating steel corsets and every morning I go to a cross old bone setter here and take a medicated bath and get my shoulder shampooed.[45] Tho' not a very pleasant operation—particularly the wearing the corsets (they cause me constant pain)—yet I am quite confident about being benefited and ultimately cured. I have already grown three quarters of an inch in a fortnight, from the straightening of my spine. I have been here now about

[39] "Nem" or "Nemmy" was a name of endearment given to Emily by a small group of her intimate friends at the Utica Female Academy. Anna Maria Anable was "Ninny."

[40] We would note that in a previous letter, Anna Maria asked Emily to do exactly what she did—describe the house in which they were living.

[41] Shortly after their departure to Rangoon, there was a fire at the mission compound in Maulmain, and Adoniram and Emily lost two large trunks of their most treasured possessions which had been stored in the home of Edward and Elizabeth Stevens. In several letters the estimated the loss at between five hundred and a thousand rupees.

[42] See vol. 1, "Cast of Characters," s.v. "Stevens, Elizabeth 'Bessie.'"

[43] A missionary widow, Mrs. Bullard married the Reverend Francis Mason in September 1847. He had lost his wife in 1846.

[44] See vol. 1, "Cast of Characters," s.v. "Sheldon, Miss Cynthia."

[45] Anna Maria Anable spent summer 1847 in Boston, Massachusetts, taking some painful medical treatments to correct a skeletal condition with her shoulder. On April 26, 1848 she wrote, "My shoulder is quite strong and my shape is very much improved."

three weeks—At first I went to Mr. Colby's,[46] and they received me most kindly and cordially. Mrs. C. has been in Brooklyn most of the Spring on account of her health—she has been miserable (by the way I think she feels a little slighted that you have not written to her) but is now much better. They have just moved into the country at Newton. Mr. C. has purchased a farm there and is going to build this year, so they have taken a final leave of dear Pemberton Square. I am boarding at Mrs. Joshua Lincoln's of the firm Gould, Randall and Lincoln, and I find them a very pleasant family. They are good, consistent Christians, and I consider myself very fortunate that they would take me in. My coming here was Mr. Colby's doings I shall probably have to remain here some four months—perhaps six before I can be permanently cured. As I am paying four dollars a week for board independently of washing and my *daily* visits to the Dr. are a dollar or more independent of medicines you see it will be an expensive Summer to me. Is it not fortunate for me that I have such a good, kind, sympathizing Aunt Cynthia? Ah, I am afraid her heart would fail her if she knew what ulterior object I had in view in coming here[47]— that you may not have the [ ] about me that she and mother had, I will tell you that the course I am pursuing is calculated to improve my general health as well as to correct the defect in my frame. I must go back to Utica and tell you about matters there, as, owing the hurry of coming away I could not write you by the last steamer. Aunt C. will tell you most of the news, but I am afraid she will forget to tell you of an accident that occurred at our last baptism! It was a lovely Summer's day and there were fifteen to be baptized in the Mohawk, so that an immense

[46] A prominent businessman, Gardner Colby and his family lived in Pemberton Square in Boston before moving "to the country," Newton Centre, Massachusetts. Mr. Colby was a member of the Board of the American Baptist Missionary Union and an avid supporter of the missionary movement. In a letter after they sailed from Boston to Burmah, Emily mentions the extravagant hospitality extended to them in early July as they waited for the *Faneuil Hall* to embark. Adoniram and Emily stayed with the Colby family frequently.

[47] For about a year and a half after Emily's marriage to Adoniram Judson, Anna Maria spoke of the possibility of having a call to missions, and joining Adoniram and Emily in Burmah. On March 31, 1847, Sarah Bell Wheeler said that Anna Maria was a devoted Christian, and she thought that one day Anna Maria would go to Burmah. She obviously put a lot of prayer and thought into the matter. We would suspect that the painful medical treatments she underwent in summer 1847 were intended to improve her general health (see her letter of June 19, 1847). In the end, in summer 1848, she decided that her call was to remain a teacher, and Anna Maria moved to Philadelphia, and with her family opened the Misses Anable's School. She was to remain there until her death. It was here that she raised Emily Frances Judson after the death of Emily Judson.

crowd had congregated. Mr. Corey[48] had baptized eleven when a part of the bridge gave way, and it is supposed some fifty persons were precipitated on the stones and in the water below. One man only was killed but several were injured. Poor Mary Jones[49] was hurt rather more than any one [sic] else—her shoulder blade is broken it was supposed in two places. She will probably recover the use of her arm but it will be a tedious case. Fanny[50] who fell by her side was not injured one particle. Some one [sic] who watched her said she clung fast to her parasol which was open and lighted on the rocks below like a feather. We had no idea that she fell (as she had strayed away from the rest of the girls) until it was all over. Of course there were rumours [sic] going around the city for a week or two; it was said that James Williams (who is mayor) said he should put a stop to Mr. Corey's gathering such crowds together on Sunday!! They were afraid of such an accident the day I was baptized. Would n't [sic] it have been considered a righteous judgement [sic] if it had occurred then? By the way, Charley [ ] has just married a Baptist wife. I hope she won't do as so many persons do now-a-days—leave her own church to go with her husband. I don't know what Johnny Edmonds will do now—I think Eugenia[51] and he had better [ ] together. They are both such staunch Episcopalians. Johnny

[48] Mr. Corey was the pastor of the Bleecker Street Baptist Church near the Utica Female Academy, and Miss Sheldon and many of the girls from the academy attended worship there. (Cynthis Sheldon, Alma Anable, Deacon Asa and Isabell Sheldon, Edward Bright, and Horace Hawley had been charter members of the church in 1838.) In April 1844, he wrote to Emily expressing dismay that at a school program one of the girls had read a composition justifying dancing as exercise; he spoke of this as a roadblock to the salvation of many. Then, on March 10, 1846, Emily indicated in a letter to Anna Maria that Mr. Corey had been critical of her relationship and impending marriage to Adoniram Judson. Miss Cynthia Sheldon wrote a number of times expressing Mr. Corey's regret and support, and in 1847, there were letters of reconciliation between Emily and Mr. Corey. In spring 1848, letters reveal that Mr. Corey's wife had died of consumption, her condition exacerbated by recent child-birth. She had left behind four children. In July 1849, Anna Maria Anable wrote of his impending marriage to Jane Backus, a good choice for this "rising man." Mr. Corey remained popular with the Sheldon-Anable families even after their move to Philadelphia in 1848. A March 2, 1852, letter from Charles B. Stout told of Mr. Corey's call to the Stanton Street Church in New York City, which Mr. Corey did not accept. Finally, in 1854, there was a pastoral letter from Mr. Corey to Emily on her illness and her possible death. He preached at the Bleecker Street Church as late as January 1867.

[49] Mary Jones was the wife of Morven Jones. They lived in the Utica area and were intimately familiar with Miss Cynthia Sheldon and the staff and student body of the Utica Female Academy. Mr. and Mrs. Jones, as well as Miss Sheldon, were members of the Bleecker Street Baptist Church where Mr. Corey was the pastor. In a December 1848 series of letters to Emily, Morven Jones described a terrible accident; a group from the church was standing on a bridge overlooking the Mohawk River, there to witness a baptism, and the bridge collapsed. At least one person died in that accident, and Mary Jones was severely injured.

[50] Fanny Anable was one of nine children born to Joseph and Alma Anable and was a niece of Miss Cynthia Sheldon and Mrs. Urania Sheldon Nott. The correspondence indicates that in April 1845 she was away from home studying and taking music lessons. These spring letters indicate that she was in Philadelphia, working in the home of and with the family of the Reverend A. D. Gillette. See Miss Sheldon's letter to Emily of November 30, 1845, in which she spoke of all that Fanny was doing to improve herself in the field of music, but also her concern for Fanny's interest in the party life and the "vanitie" which surround her." A March 30, 1847 letter from Anna Maria Anable told of Fanny's conversion following her grandmother's death. In September 1847, she was listed as one of the teachers at the Utica Female Academy. Fanny became a teacher with her sisters in the Misses Anable's School in Philadelphia.

[51] Eugenia Damaux was part of Emily's intimate circle of friends at the Utica Female Academy. Living in New York City, Eugenia suffered from some kind of eye problem that at times made life difficult for her; this was a matter of comment in many of the letters exchanged between the girls themselves and with Miss Cynthia Sheldon. In 1848, Eugenia was in New York living "at Mrs. Brown's—the same warm-hearted French girl as ever." In 1849, she married Johnny Edmonds, described as rich and pious, and they lived in Utica.

has joined the church. He is a clever little soul and has money enough to take care of her, so I should like to see them united, but—There is no use in arranging these matters for our friends. Johnny has a will of his own and Eugenia—I should not very much wonder if she and William Kelly should make a match by and by. William is practicing medicine in New York under very favorable auspices and is very kind to Eugenia. It is a notion of Aunt Urania's.[52]

By the way Aunt U. and I are getting on quite good terms again.[53] I believe if ever any body [sic] tried to put another right on—of one's heart by force, Aunt U. has tried within the last year to great mischief, but she can't come it [sic]. I will creep back again once in a while. About a week before I came on here; she was in Utica and I happened down in Aunt C's room just when she had been making a speech which almost killed Aunt C. As usual her own feelings had been dreadfully injured by some trifling thing and in the midst of her tears and complaints I felt called upon to take up the cudgel in Aunt C's behalf—I berated her most soundly and from Aunt O. [sic] she flew to me. We had last year's proceedings all over again and I ended by telling her that had I the thing to do over I should not confer with flesh and blood *at all*, but immediately by our conviction of duty do what was required of me.

We have been on much better terms since then. I stopped a couple of days in Schenectady and it seemed as if she could not do too much for me. She has all sorts of plans for her [ ] future, but—ah, me! I am an ungrateful child.

Written along the left and top margin of page 1: "Mrs. Stevens[54] writes that she is so sorry on your account about the fire. The loss she says can be made up, but you lost all your valuables. In case I should be in earnest about coming you must tell me what to bring.

"While I think of it—I have learned all about the Willis' here. They are a queer family always having some domestic quarrel. Nat they say is the best tempered of all—keeping clear of all their difficulties. Dea. Willis is a queer old man. The whole family came near being excluded from the church once owing to the old man's obstinacy. No wonder Nat is queer in religious matters. I cannot learn any-

[52] Urania Sheldon had been the literary principal of the Utica Female Academy in fall 1840 when Emily Chubbuck came to study there. Emily was able to afford this wonderful education through the generous offer of Miss Sheldon and her sister Cynthia, the executive and financial head of the academy, to defer tuition. Urania Sheldon left in late summer 1842 upon her marriage to the Reverend Doctor Eliphalet Nott, the president of Union College in Schenectady, New York. Because of the distance separating them, Emily's relationship with Urania Sheldon Nott did not develop the intimacy that grew between Emily and Miss Cynthia Sheldon. Urania Sheldon Nott remained a mentor, advisor, and friend to Emily in the years of her writing, her missionary endeavors, and upon her return to America in 1851. She was also the aunt of Anna Maria Anable.

[53] Anna Maria asked Adoniram Judson to baptize her by immersion before he and Emily left for Burmah, and that baptism took place on June 7, 1846. Urania Sheldon Nott was critical of this; Emily's note to her of July 7, 1846, related to some of the issues. The relationship seemed fractured for a number of months. Later in this paragraph, there is evidence of another confrontation that seemed to clear the air almost a year later.

[54] See vol. 1, "Cast of Characters," s.v. "Stevens, Elizabeth 'Bessie.'"

thing particular about his wife—they say however that he is determined to be a much better man than formerly."

Source: American Baptist Historical Society, AJ 13, no. 503.

Emily C. Judson to Anna Maria Anable, June 20, 1847[55]

Sunday Eve. It is out at last. Edward[56] awoke this morning, his face so swollen that his eyes are nearly closed, shining, and spotted purplish. We could not imagine what was the matter, but he was very feverish, and I knew he must have something immediately. I consulted the Doctor and my Burman woman, but neither of them could give me the slightest inkling of the disease.

Source: A. C. Kendrick, *The Life and Letters of Mrs. Emily C. Judson*, 279–82.

Miss Lydia Lillybridge to Emily C. Judson, June 23, 1847—Maulmain

My dear Emily,

You think you have been neglected by your friends here. But how should they know the reason of your not answering their letters—whether it was illness or sheer indifference, so long as no one had told them? Mrs. Stevens[57] really felt a delicacy about writing to you again before receiving any thing [*sic*] from you. She sometimes says—"What do you suppose the reason is, that she does not write to us?" I know that she feared that it was a want of interest in [Note: "Her" is written and crossed out.] us. We think, however, that you have an excellent reason, and are very sorry to hear of that trouble in your head. What is the reason? I suppose it is the rainy weather, the constantly damp atmosphere.

From all accounts, I concluded that you are enjoying some of the "romance" of the missionary life. Can you lie down at night and sleep in peace? I do not yet believe, that you will come back to Maulmain. As I understand it, the Doctor has a standing permission from the Board to go to Ava whenever there is an opening, and every body [*sic*] knows that they consider this an important movement, and that, rather than retard it, they would probably withdraw the necessary funds from almost any department of their Missions. So, Mr. H.[58] thinks, if I am not mistaken.

I did not have a word from home by either of the last two steamers. I think my letters have been miscarried else have stopped to rest somewhere. You have a letter lodged in London as well as myself. But mine will come next month, I suppose. You

---

[55] This is the third of four segments of a letter written over a two-week period—June 16, 19, 20, and July 1, 1847.

[56] See vol. 1, "Cast of Characters," s.v. "Judson, Edward."

[57] See vol. 1, "Cast of Characters," s.v. "Stevens, Elizabeth 'Bessie.'"

say that you do not know how much in earnest I was, about that important affair. I was in earnest when I said that I was willing to go to Arracan,[59] provided the Board wished to have me go, and there was a suitable home or boarding place for me, for I think I could be more useful there. I was in earnest too when I told you that I had concluded not to go with Mr. I.[60]

What *strong* expressions you make! "Not a woman upon earth, etc." There are exceptions to all rules. I have heard so, at least. Again, "God never blesses celibacy." Didn't he bless Paul, the Apostle? I imagine that there are some sad realities which you have not experienced. As for "hard, iron paths," they may be expected in all states; and one of my mottos is "of two troubles, choose the least." Though I do not think so highly of Mr. I. as the Doc. and some others do, I really pitied him when I thought of his going back alone—not *one* missionary there. But he will not stay long alone, I suppose; for I understand that he has determined to go to America at the close of the rains. (I wish you would not mention it though; at least, as coming from me.)

The people here are a little disappointed, I suppose, to think that I did not conclude to go. There must have been a most tremendously overwhelming influence to induce me to take such a step within six months after my arrival in the country. It seems to me, that I would not have gone with any man upon earth, even if I had been swimming in love. You will say that I am a foolish child. Well, be it so. I will say with the old woman, "I'm a happy fool then."—Things in school go on about as usual,—in the house, a little better than usual, and I will tell you why, when I see you. My Burmese as slowly as ever.—I suppose that you've heard that three of the girls have been hopefully converted recently, and that four have been baptized. Excuse this scribbling. I did not [Note: Written in the left margin of page 2.] intend to have such a long scrawl.

Written along the left margin of page 1: "Kiss little Henry[61] and Edward,[62] and tell them that '*Mrs.*' Lillybridge would like dearly to kiss them herself. I hope the Doctor will be better when we hear again. From your affectionate"

Lydia.

Source: American Baptist Historical Society, AJ 17, no. 773.

---

[58] Hosea Howard first sailed for Burmah in 1834, arriving in December that year. His wife was Theresa, and they had been married just before departure. Hosea Howard was a recent graduate of the Theological Seminary in Hamilton, New York. They were stationed in Maulmain as missionaries with Adoniram Judson, and he was to claim in a letter to Emily that he had worked there with Adoniram longer than any other missionary. Mr. Howard's responsibility was to run schools that the mission maintained, a task in which he was ably assisted by his wife. It was to Mr. and Mrs. Howard that Lydia Lillybridge was responsible when she arrived in November 1846. Mr. and Mrs. Howard left Maulmain for the United States in February 1850.

[59] See the letter of Lydia Lillybridge dated April 23, 1847. Also the chapter "Lydia Lillybridge Simons."

[60] See vol. 1, "Cast of Characters," s.v. "Ingalls, The Reverend Lovel."

[61] See vol. 1, "Cast of Characters," s.v. "Judson, Henry Hall."

[62] See vol. 1, "Cast of Characters," s.v. "Judson, Edward."

The Reverend Abram Dunn Gillette to Emily C. Judson, June 24, 1847[63]—Philadelphia

June 24, 1847
No 69 North Twelfth St Philadelphia

Dear, very dear Friend

We have received your letters written soon after your arrival in Burmah—likewise those of a later date telling us the sad story of your losses by fire[64]—W[e] sympathize with you, we do indeed—but we do not intend to let sympathy waste itself in sighs—Already our Mrs. Robarts[65] and Mrs. G.[66] beginning—and we hope to have a box ready to go soon. Mr. Abbott[67] expects to depart in the fall early—and if it is possible we shall send by him—

I regret that you did not say in your last what you most need. You must make free with us ever while you live and do so, as what we do shall be done if possible, most to your advantage. Dear Mr. J. can write to our little wife all particulars etc.—and as she is quiet and ever ready to be busy as usual—she will be happy and ready to do as need may be—

I presume she has already been heard from in Burmah, as having taken charge of another *Boy*, which entirely owing to circumstances, during the ever memorable winter of 1846, I call the missionary boy—what he is to be, we of course know not, but what he *is*—his fine Mother will speak in his behalf. James, Walter and Dany—

---

[63] This letter has an addendum dated June 28, 1847.

[64] On February 17, 1847, shortly after they had left Maulmain for Rangoon, a fire in the mission compound at Maulmain destroyed two trunks of Adoniram and Emily's clothing and personal articles.

[65] Mr. and Mrs. W. S. Robarts were active in Philadelphia Baptist circles. They were frequent visitors to the home of the Reverend and Mrs. A. D. Gillette, and later to the Misses Anable's School which Anna Maria Anable and her extended family had started in Philadelphia in 1848. In his biography of his father, Edward Judson mentioned that Adoniram Judson had stayed at the Robarts' home when he came to Philadelphia in December 1845, where he was to meet Emily Chubbuck. A. C. Kendrick said, "(Mr. Gillette and Dr. Judson) arrived in (or out of) due time in Philadelphia, and Dr. Judson was welcomed to the house of Mr. and Mrs. W. S. Robarts, who became warm personal friends, as they were already active friends of the mission cause." In 1846, with the engagement of Adoniram Judson and Emily Chubbuck, the Correspondence indicates some hard feelings towards Mrs. Robarts for comments that were made disparaging the coming marriage and missionary service. This is to be found in Emily's letter to Adoniram dated February 6, 1846; Mrs. Robarts seemed to be accusing Emily of worldliness—when all the time, Emily was quick to say, Mrs. Robarts was engaging in the same activity of which Emily was accused. The Correspondence also indicates a satisfactory healing of the relationship. In January 1849 Miss Sheldon told Emily that Mrs. Robarts had placed their daughter Mary in the Misses Anable's School.

[66] Hannah Gillette was the wife of the Reverend A. D. Gillette, pastor of the Eleventh Baptist Church in Philadelphia. Emily stayed with them when she came to Philadelphia in spring 1845 for her health, and she returned in November. In the parlor of their home, she met Adoniram Judson on Christmas Day 1845. Mr. and Mrs. Gillette became strong friends and supporters; Mrs. Gillette played an important part in getting Emily's outfit together for her life in Burmah.

[67] Elisha Abbott was born October 23, 1809 in Cazenovia, New York. He graduated from the Hamilton Theological Institute and was ordained August 25, 1835. He wife was Ann P. Gardner, and they were married April 2, 1837. Though they were appointed for work in Telagus, India, that changed upon their arrival, and they went to Maulmain in April 1837. They continued on to Rangoon shortly after that. In March 1840, they established the station at Sandoway. Mrs. Abbott died in Sandoway on January 27, 1845. Mr. Abbott left for the United States in November 1845, returning in August 1847. At one point in the correspondence, Mr. Abbott was mentioned as a possible husband for Lydia Lillybridge.

[68] These are the children of Hannah and A. D. Gillette. They had six children.

and now *William*[68] are all good children. The three eldest have much to say of you both, and Walter resolves on going a Missionary to *China*. I think he is not a little influenced in his decisions in favor of the Celestials, on account of certain defects, and rivalship [*sic*] of which a residence in Burmah would vividly remind him—poor chap—he is evidently *cut* in that quarter. Yet he is young and can out grow [*sic*] the wound, and even if a scar remains, it will only be a remembrance of pleasant scenes past—pleasantly.

The Literary gossip has given place to the sober conclusion, that after all you both had a right to love and marry each other and go where you pleased—and some writers begin to think there may come as much good to Mankind from the flight of the *Fairy* to tropical regions and the consecration of herself to the welfare direct of a needy and perishing race, as from having worn out early, as she must have done, in scribbling for the gratification of Americans.

We left Boston after your departure the following Monday—went up thro N. Hampshire to Bellowsfall, Vt—staid [*sic*] all night—next day crossed the green mountains for the first time, (I having been on the top of them before,) and on Wednesday morning arrived at my good old mother's home in Cambridge Washington County, which you Cozen [*sic*] Emily say in your letter, is "all carved up" by scenes in Burmah. Well be it so, only say or admit, that it exists, for it is my *childhood home.*—and while you remember childhood I will remember my native brook, all lined with Alder bushes—and water cresses, and full of little sparkling pebbles and shiney [*sic*] fish.—By the way *Alderbrook*[69] is gaining fast into the parlors, and par boiled [ ]iens of our slow, but sure Citizenhood [*sic*], I find it often where I did not expect to.

Our last Boy was born Nov 12, 1846 and on the same day, I was attacked with pneumonia and did not preach until March and then only occasionally—I hope I have recovered—yet my breast and lungs are not as sound as they once were. Br. Thomas Malcom, son of Dr. M. supplied my people greatly to their satisfaction, and profit. Our house keeps full of attentive worshippers—a good company have been added to us by Baptism, and I expect to bury two with Christ in that ordinance next Lord's Day—

I left home the Twelfth of May for Cincinnati and attended the Missionary Union—We had a goodly representation from New England, N. York and the Middle States, and many from the west. The scene was delightful—not a jar, or a subject foreign to the mission cause was introduced. I have attended all the anniversaries for twelve years last past, and never before had the privilege of feeling that we were indeed, what we professed—Delegates only to a mission body—Our

---

[69] The first edition of Emily's second collection of stories and sketches, *Alderbrook*, was released by Ticknor, Reed and Fields in early December, 1846. A second edition with added material was released in April 1847.

funds have increased, and we are doing more worth by ourselves than we ever did when all the States were with us "Deus Deo."[70] Our Southern brethren are also rousing up, and doing well. A missionary spirit is extending—I am confident that it is an improved spirit, our intelligent action from pure love to Souls and the glory of the Master. A giving and acting not from mere moral impulses, but from *holy purpose*. Yet also the tithe is not done that might be, or that should be—and I hope will be.—

I returned from the west by way of Lake Erie on whose treacherous waves—I was tossed by a Tempest forty eight hours—with little hope of getting on shore except as Paul's company did on broken piece [*sic*] of the ship and cargo.—Yet the Lord preserved us. I spent a day at Niagara—that eternal tide of rushing waters, whose roar is ceaseless and whose grandeur and sublimity are surpassing.—

On my way I did not fail to stop at Utica Seminary—I went round into the west back door about eleven o'clock at night, and as I passed thro the yard, four *chaps* of blushing *twenty hood*, met me departing from a serenade which they had been giving the girls—and as the latter were night cap on—looking thro the green blinds and some of the freer ones, looking with cap and [ ] out, hung literally, and far out of the windows. I of course, met with quite a *gallant* reception, not at all unpleasant to me. If I am not young in years I have a young heart—at least I am very certain it feels just as it used to when it beat in unison to other young hearts.

I of course found Miss Cynthia[71] in her room *stall* on *finger* and pen in hand, holding converse with her many absent correspondents. Mrs. Anable[72] was also yet up. I had a cordial welcome—a warm supper and not less than many questions to answer. You must remember—we had not met since—the introduction I gave to *Fanny Forrester*,[73] and the Apostle of Burmah[74]—need I add you were both spoken of.

---

[70] Here Mr. Gillette is speaking of the historic breakaway of the Southern churches to form the Southern Baptist Convention in 1845. The issues of contention were reflections of those that eventually would erupt in the Civil War.

[71] See vol. 1, "Cast of Characters," s.v. "Sheldon, Miss Cynthia."

[72] Alma Sheldon Anable was the sister of Miss Cynthia Sheldon and Urania Sheldon Nott. Genealogy sources show that she married Joseph Hubbell Anable in Troy, New York on July 28, 1814, and that it was the second marriage for Mr. Anable. Born in 1773, he was forty-one at the time of the marriage, and Alma was likely considerably younger. He died in 1831, which explains why Alma Anable and her family lived and worked first at the Utica Female Seminary and then later at the Misses Anable's School in Philadelphia. Joseph and Alma Anable were the parents of nine children: Henry Sheldon Anable (b. June 21, 1815); William Stewart Anable (b. November 6, 1816); Anna Maria Stafford Anable (b. September 30, 1818), Cynthia Jane Anable (b. January 28, 1820); Samuel Low Anable (b. November 28, 1821); Harriet Isabella Anable, also known as Hatty or Hattie (b. December 18, 1823); Courtland Wilcox Anable (b. July 28, 1825); Frances Alma Anable, or Fanny (b. April 12, 1828); and Mary Juliet Anable (b. February 18, 1830).

[73] Emily Chubbuck wrote under the *nom de plume* Fanny Forester. Asked about it once, she said, "Would anyone buy a book written by Emily E. Chubbuck?"

[74] While in Philadelphia for her health, Emily stayed with Mr. and Mrs. Gillette. A prominent Baptist pastor, Mr. Gillette introduced Adoniram Judson to Emily Chubbuck in the parlor of the Gillette home on Christmas Day 1845.

Our interview was mingled with pleasurable sadness—we went into Mrs. S's now only grandfather's[75] room—poor old pilgrim, he lay in his bed—lonely bed—one was not there—she who lain [sic] in his arms, pillowed on his bosom, and been his solace and comfort days and nights for sixty three [sic] years, had left her place of repose on earth and was pillowed with the beloved Disciple on Jesus' breast.

We talked and wept, and prayed—and at three o'clock A.M. parted without one wink of sleep, or a feeling that inclined to it, and at eight I was with Prof. Pierson and spent the day with him—his and Dr. Nott and Mrs. Nott[76] and old familiar friends—

I have as yet written but little of what the world calls News—I do not know of anything which I think would interest you to hear, which does not reach you thro other channels.

Mr. and Mrs. Robarts[77] are as usual—and be assured, Mrs. Judson is almost all in all in that quarter—no fear—no dissenting—no mistake, true as the needle to the pole, you may rely upon that—indeed, henceforth, and forever.

My little Boy Willy has just called me from my table, to take him out of his cradle, and he now sits on his blanket, on the floor of my study, second story back room—and is playing with my shirts, brush, and [ ] box and looks as if he knew something, tho he says not a word, unless it be that he speaks in Burman—for I do not understand his language tho his doting Mother doubtless knows every word—upon the principul [sic] I suppose—"Street sounds are signs of ideas," a saying I wish was true, for I never had any lack of sounds, but of *ideas* I am not so certain.—We have delightful weather, prospect of generous crops, and a supply for starving Ireland—Really we are now in a peculiar position as a nation—feeding the children of the Monster Mother Church in Europe—with potatoes—and these of Mexico with grape shot and canister comb shells and bullets[78]—so we go—Br. Jonathan is a queer genius—and can do two things widely different at the same time. Instance, he can *whistle, whittle* and *guess*—all in the same moment, and I am not sure but that he can *calculate* at the same time.

Do write us often—if it be but short, and yet we hope to get long letters and fail not Dear Emily to indulge that sweet muse—[ ] sings of the Sainted one whose

---

[75] Deacon Asa Sheldon was the father of Miss Cynthia Sheldon, Urania Sheldon Nott, and Alma Sheldon Anable. Deacon and Mrs. Sheldon lived with their daughters and grandchildren as a part of the Utica Female Academy community. Mrs. Sheldon died January 29, 1847. Deacon Sheldon continued to have a room at the Utica Female Academy, where he died in March 1848. For many years, he led mealtime prayers for the academy family, and Deacon and Mrs. Sheldon were popular with the students, who often looked in on him.

[76] See vol. 1, "Cast of Characters," s.v. "Nott, Urania Sheldon."

[77] See vol. 1, "Cast of Characters," s.v. "Robarts, Mr. and Mrs. W. S."

[78] This was the time of the Mexican War; previous letters spoke of President Polk and of men signing up for a twelve dollar bonus and a promise of sixty acres of land.

frail form found rest on Helena's rock bound coast[79]—I am Mrs. Brown of Assam—Mr. Day and Mr. Osgood[80]—Mrs. B is a gem of purest ray serene—a charming woman—a choice spirit—

May all goodness rest upon you. My heart shall be as your heart—the Lord being [ ].

A. D. Gillette

Source: American Baptist Historical Society, AJ 16, nos. 718, 719.

Mrs. Hannah Gillette to Emily C. Judson, June 24, 1847

My dear Cousin Emily

How can I reala[ ] that I now address you as the veritable little cousin Emily of 1846. What magic has transported the immortal Fanny[81] on the other side of the globe and called her Mrs. Judson? Surround her with new scenes, a new tongue a new house new hopes and new fears (shall I add): sure it is all right and we must be content, but if I could only drop in and take tea some day we could settle the difficulty of your leaving us so much better.

Oh sad—sad—was it not? When the parsonage was visited with an other [sic] boy—well so it was some people think it almost sinful for me to have inflicted upon the community the support of another *boy*,[82] and really I have been told I ought make an apology, but I insist upon it I have a perfect right to do so I presume in the matter as to the merits of the boy. Why the fact is he is worth any half dozen of girls you ever saw—but for [ ] you take up the cry of "Sour Grapes," I for bear— Fanny Forester may arrive some day when we shall prepared [sic] to appreciate the female sex—how [ ] on the little boys you so much love—Oh how I would like to see them; kiss them again and again for us[83] and perhaps some day we can do it for ourselves.

Oh that cruel fire at Maulmain[84] how sad that you should have lost all your valuable stock of supplies—do cousin Emily write us the particular articles you most need and we will try and replace them as far as [ ] in our power—but I fear

---

[79] The reference is to Sarah Hall Boardman Judson, who died September 1, 1845, as the Judson family returned to the United States because of her health. She was buried on the Isle of St. Helena. Emily was writing the memoir of Sarah Boardman Judson.

[80] See vol. 1, "Cast of Characters," s.v. "Osgood, The Reverend Sewall."

[81] Emily Chubbuck Judson as Fanny Forester. See vol. 1, "Cast of Characters" and "Forester, Fanny."

[82] In the letter from the Reverend A. D. Gillette dated June 24, 1847, he mentioned the birth of William Gillette the prior November.

[83] This is a reference to Henry and Edward Judson, sons of Adoniram and Sarah Hall Boardman Judson who had been left in Burmah when the family returned to the United States in 1845. Emily became their "new Mamma."

[84] On February 17, 1847, shortly after they left Maulmain for Rangoon, a fire in the mission compound at Maulmain destroyed two trunks of Adoniram and Emily's clothing and personal articles; much of the loss had been personal gifts of great sentimental value. In different letters the loss was estimated between seven hundred and a thousand rupees.

they never can be replaced in full—I presume the friends in Utica will do all they can to supply your deficiencies.

We have no especial news to communicate. We are not passing through the same changes that you do or in any degree to be compared—there is not much to disturb the monotony of City life—last week we passed through a season new and sad to us.

A stranger found his way to our door in a sick and exausted [sic] condition, having traveled from the West—sent on by Physicians to go to sea as the only hope for life—he arrived poor fellow without money without a friend in the world, could not be received in the hotel on account of his sick condition—and having heard of Mr. G. in the far city of St. Louis enquired for us—we took him in and after bathing the poor fellow [ ] and giving him nourishment he quietly lay down *and died*—it was all he wanted he was prepared for death a good faithful servant studying for the ministry, but his work was done in his youth. We had three Physicians to see him all agreed he died of exaustion [sic] and probably from not having allowed him sufficient nourishment, and together with the fatigue of traveling, one week to night he breathed his last. We buried him and called in strangers to prepare the last service on earth he [ ] require—Indeed dear Emily it was quite a scene of novelty and sadness to us the first time the boys have now looked on death and the impression I hope will be of lasting benefit to their minds.

Mrs. Robarts[85] and family are well. I presume she will write or Mr. R. in her stead—she speaks of you as all in all—and regrets from her soul the past—I know but don't think it—Dear Em. She does love you now and I think [ ] always, but was not quite certain of the propriety of *her dear* Dr. taking Fanny F.

I must close then I suppose Mr. G. has written all the important news—don't neglect us dear—I know you have *many friends* but none love you more than do your friends in 69[86]—Love to the Dr. Oceans for your own dear self from your affectionate

Mrs. H. J. Gillette

Phil. Mrs. Emily Judson

Source: American Baptist Historical Society, AJ 16, no. 718.

---

[85] See vol. 1, "Cast of Characters," s.v. "Robarts, Mr. and Mrs. W. S."
[86] The street address of the Gillette home is 69.

The Reverend Abram Dunn Gillette to Emily C. Judson, June 28, 1847[87]

It is Monday June 28, 1847, and as my little wife, the Witch, would not fill up this sheet, because she did not believe you would take time to read it, I will, for read, or not, there is a satisfaction in writing, which cannot be denied of—I suppose I often *talk* when my auditors hear little I say—yet I have the satisfaction of talking, or as poor [ ] says—"it gratifies the sentiment."

Yesterday was Lord's Day—and I baptised [*sic*] two lovely young Disciples, a female and a male—a full house witnessed with great apparent solemnity the solemn service—I trust Heaven owned the Deed.

We are now in the midst of hot weather. Thermometer is ninety four and six in the shade and one hundred twenty in the Sun—*whew*—I do not suppose your house is much warmer in Rangoon—It is a growing season, and all our crops in the country look well.

I hope as the Lord devises liberal things for his people, they may freely return liberally into his treasury.

The Lord bless—keep you ever—

A. D. Gillette

Source: American Baptist Historical Society, AJ 16, nos. 718, 719.

Anna Maria Anable to Emily C. Judson, June 29, 1847—Boston

Dear dear Nemmy[88]

I would give far more than "plent[ ] prayers" if I could lay my head down in your lap this afternoon and cry my cry out there, for it seems as if the very effort to weep as I have to the Dr.[89] has called forth more tears than I have shed before since you left. I hardly dare send that letter[90]—it seems so real and decisive a step, and

---

[87] This is an addendum to a letter started June 24, 1847.

[88] Emily Chubbuck. See vol. 1, "Cast of Characters," s.v. "Nemmy, Nem, or Nemmy Petty (Nemmie Pettie)." Also the chapter "Names of Endearment."

[89] The reference is to Adoniram Judson and to the letter she has written him on this same date of June 29, 1847.

[90] For more on Anna Maria Anable and a possible call to missionary service, see vol. 1, "Cast of Characters," s.v. "Anable, Anna Maria."

yet some power impels me to. O, what visions of home—of mother,[91] Hatty,[92] Molly,[93] Fanny,[94] all, circumstances come crowding to my mind. It seems to me that I *cannot* leave them. Then I look forward into the future and the most gloomy forebodings throng around it. I cannot begin to describe to you what they are—but tell me Nemmy for you have been there now long enough to know—is it worth while making the sacrifice? This that I propose now is a very different thing from going out far from responsibility—with liberty to come back any time I pleased. You know me Nemmy pretty thoroughly and you know under what circumstances my courage would fail. Were I in Lydia's[95] place now [ ] as I should perhaps that all this sacrifice had been in vain—that I could have done as much good at home had I the same disposition I am afraid I should sink under it. *I cannot bear to live under a mistake.*

I shall cast all these thoughts behind me and live till I get your and the Dr.'s answer simply—as though I am going to stay home always. Answer me candidly though. Don't let anybody influence you. Aunt C.'s[96] suspicions are awakened and she said she should write you about it.[97] Don't mind her. Advise me just as you would were I sitting in your little study with no eye but that of God upon us. Perhaps you and the Dr. will wonder why so suddenly I have taken a notion to come

---

[91] See vol. 1, "Cast of Characters," s.v. "Anable, Mrs. Alma Sheldon."

[92] Harriet or "Hatty" or "Hattie" or "Hat" Anable was one of nine children born to Joseph and Alma Anable, and was a niece to Miss Cynthia Sheldon and Mrs. Urania Sheldon Nott. In 1841, she had added a note to a letter written by Miss Cynthia Sheldon to Emily. As early as November 1842 she was away, and a letter from Emily to Catharine Chubbuck said that "she (Miss Sheldon) expected that Hat would return as accomplished as Anna Maria." Her trips away were both educational and employment, as she worked as a private tutor in families that would bring her into their homes. In August 1843, she had just returned from Beonsen, in the vicinity of New Orleans, and was engaged to go again. A letter from Anna Maria on January 6, 1845 said that she would stay South for another year. About this time Miss Cynthia Sheldon mentioned her concern for Hatty's spiritual health. In May 1845 she was in New Orleans. She was home again in summer 1846, but a September 27 letter from Anna Maria said she had been asked by Mr. Roman with some urgency to return and she thought that she should. She was to return home from New Orleans in January 1849 after Anna Maria Anable had started the Misses Anable's School in Philadelphia in fall 1848. Harriet was fluent in French, having placed herself earlier in a French environment in New Orleans. Hatty died in 1858.

[93] Mary Juliet Anable was born February 18, 1830 in Bethlehem, Albany County, New York, one of nine children born to Alma and Joseph Anable. She went to New Orleans with Hatty in 1847, but she returned home early in March 1848, and by 1849, she was working with Anna Maria in the Misses Anable's School in Philadelphia. Writing in March 1849, Hatty said of Mary, "She paints and draws, speaks French, plays the piano, sings, dances and is our mathematician. What should we ever do without her? She laughs from morning till night, and it is really refreshing to be with her." On December 26, 1860, she was married to Pierre Jacques Darey, the officiating minister being the Rev. Dr. Eliphalet Nott, her uncle. Mary died at the age of sixty-eight on April 20, 1898 in Ottawa, Ontario, Canada.

[94] See vol. 1, "Cast of Characters," s.v. "Anable, Fanny."

[95] Lydia Lillybridge was one of Emily's closest friends at the Utica Female Academy. When Emily made the decision to go to Burmah as the wife of Adoniram Judson and as a missionary, Lydia wanted to go with them. Emily spoke to Adoniram Judson of Lydia's extraordinary abilities, and Adoniram advocated her appointment before Dr. Solomon Peck and the Board of the American Baptist Missionary Union. Lydia was commissioned to go with them, in spite of the fact that she remained single. Always independent, outspoken, and unafraid to cause ripples in the missionary community, Lydia served on the mission field for twenty-eight years. She married missionary Thomas Simons in May 1851. See the timeline on the life and service of Lydia Lillybridge Simons in vol. 1.

[96] See vol. 1, "Cast of Characters," s.v. "Sheldon, Miss Cynthia."

[97] See the letter from Miss Cynthia Sheldon to Emily dated March 30, 1847; see also her letter August 22, 1847. She strongly stated her opposition to any thought of Anna Maria leaving them, even for a missionary cause.

---

as a missionary. I cannot exactly tell why, but since I have been in Boston[98] it has seemed to me vain to think of courses any other way. I should meet with opposition from every member of my family every step of the way—and I'll tell you just where the ground of opposition would be—That affection for you would had me to make a sacrifice which love to God could never accomplish. Now this I think would be acting an untruth, for it seems to me now that I might have talked for years about going as I have talked some months since without taking one step of the way.

I shall say nothing at home about this till I return which will probably be in August or Sept.—my present pace is to make my self physically qualified for such a work. Thank God mother will not oppose me. She has been a dear praying mother all her days, and she hopes God has heard her prayers for six of her children. Now if He asks for one of them for his special service and she is convinced it is God that asks—she will not refuse.

Every body [sic] here in Boston seems to think I shall go to Burmah one of these days. Mr. Colby[99] said they would send me. Mrs. Lincoln[100] asked me quite seriously the other day if I was not thinking of it and even old lady Baldwin asked me very bluntly one day why I did not go? It is *enough* to set any body [sic] to thinking when every body [sic] thinks the same thing for one.[101]

You don't know what a dear good little Mrs. Lincoln I am staying with. Mr. L.[102] is I rather think that wonder of book publishers—a noble hearted man.

He wants very much to publish[103] something of yours. He says he will give you 20 per cent for any thing [sic] you will send him. By-the-way did you ever give Graham[104] an article entitled a Dream? Somehow he has got hold of the "Winged

---

[98] For more information on these medical treatments, see vol. 1, "Cast of Characters," s.v. "Anable, Anna Maria."

[99] See vol. 1, "Cast of Characters," s.v. "Colby, Gardner."

[100] Mrs. Lincoln was the wife of Joshua Lincoln, a prominent Baptist layman and a partner in Gould, Kendall, and Lincoln. Anna Maria Anable boarded with Mr. and Mrs. Lincoln when she stayed in Boston in summer 1847 for medical treatments. Mrs. Lincoln was a strong supporter of missions. She was a sister of Charles Gould, who married Sarah Bell Wheeler of the Utica Female Academy.

[101] These references to Anna Maria thinking about missionary service go on for about a year. Then, she wrote a letter on April 26, 1848, in which she speaks of their move from Utica to Philadelphia, of her mother and Miss Sheldon taking on fewer responsibilities, and of Anna Maria starting a new school there. She states clearly that after considerable thought she understands that this is where she feels she belongs, though she will remain open to the possibility that God may use her.

[102] A prominent Baptist, Mr. Joshua Lincoln was a member of the firm Gould, Randall, and Lincoln, publishers.

[103] The company of Gould, Kendall and Lincoln had previously published the *Memoir of Ann Hasseltine Judson*, the *Memoir of George Dana Boardman*, a book on *Baptism* in 1846 by Adoniram Judson.

[104] George Graham was the editor of *Graham's Magazine*, one of the preeminent literary magazines of Emily's time. He took an interest in Emily Chubbuck as Fanny Forester; he mentored her and published every piece of writing that she could submit to him, and for it all, he remunerated her with the astounding sum of five dollars a page. In April 1845, when Emily was staying in Philadelphia with the Reverend and Mrs. A. D. Gillette, Mr. and Mrs. Graham were frequent visitors, often inviting Emily to tour parts of the city with them in their elegant carriage. That relationship picked up again when Emily returned to Philadelphia in fall 1845.

Watcher"[105] I think it must be copied from one of the daily papers on which Ticknor[106] said he should publish it [Note: Written above this is: "Graham gives no credit."] With the two articles he has continued to keep a little in advance of the *Columbian*[107] in the signature of F. F.[108] for the latter has issued but one piece of yours called Peter. It came out in the June Number. By the way Mr. Bright[109] and any body [*sic*] else I find thinks that you will receive the money for your writings. He was talking about it at dinner the other day and when I told him how matters stood both Mr. Lincoln and Mrs. B. exclaimed against the injustice of the thing. Whereupon Mr. B. took occasion to say "That he did not think there was a lady in the missionary field who had made greater sacrifices in giving than Mrs. J." Mr. L. was very desirous to have a certain book written which no one in the denomination could write like Mrs. J. Mr. B. told him to get you to do it and he would see that the board did not get the profits.[110] I'll tell you all about it when I come?

"*Alderbrook* sells well—The fourth edition is just out but they are small editions Mr. Ticknor says. Fields[111] is in Europe just now.

Mr. and Mrs. Eddy[112] treasurer of the Union took tea here the other evening with Mr. and Mrs. Bright. The Eddy's are real lively people. Mrs. E. is considered .

---

[105] "The Winged Watcher" is a poem written by Fanny Forester as she sailed to Burmah. A copy of this poem is available in the Houghton Library at Harvard University, in the James Fields collection; Mr. Fields was a partner in the publishing firm of Ticknor, Reed and Fields. There is a note with the poem in the handwriting of Adoniram Judson; it says that the poem was written "Off the Cape of Good Hope, September, 1846." Mr. Judson went on to say, "My dear Mr. Fields, Mrs. Judson sends you the accompanying lines, thinking, that you may be glad to make use of them to remind the public of the existence of *Alderbrook*, and facilitate the progress of that publication."

[106] William Ticknor was the principle of William Ticknor Publishing Company, which later became Ticknor, Reed and Fields. Mr. Ticknor published *Alderbrook* in December 1846, a second edition early in 1847, and several of Emily's other books in 1852 and 1853. There is considerable correspondence, which stopped abruptly when the publishing contract for the Judson memoir was awarded to another publisher.

[107] The *Columbian* magazine was published first by John Inman and then by Robert West. By early 1844, the *Columbian* was printing Emily's stories; this was before N. P. Willis and the *New Mirror* made her famous. With Graham, they readily agreed to pay her a top rate of five dollars a page for anything that she would write, and on several occasions, they tried to get Emily to write exclusively for them. They finally succeeded in this when she went to Burmah, for they obtained exclusive rights to all that she would send them at fifty dollars a story.

[108] Emily Chubbuck Judson as Fanny Forester. See vol. 1 "Cast of Characters," s.v. "Chubbuck, Emily" and "Forester, Fanny."

[109] Upon her return to America in 1851, Emily Judson had a close relationship with Dr. Edward Bright, the corresponding secretary of the American Baptist Missionary Union. They knew one another previously in New York, as he worked with the *Baptist Register*, a prominent regional newsletter, at the time of Adoniram and Emily's marriage. He was appointed corresponding secretary the end of May 1846, just prior to Adoniram and Emily's departure for Burmah. Dr. Bright helped Emily with many of her business affairs, he carried on the publishing details of the Judson memoir because of a serious illness in Dr. Wayland's family, and he and his wife took in Adoniram and Elnathan Judson for a year beginning in October 1851. He, with Dr. Edward Granger, was the executor of the estate of Emily Chubbuck Judson.

[110] The American Baptist Missionary Union had a policy that no missionary could accept remuneration for anything they wrote, that the income would go instead to the Mission Board. This standard had been proposed years earlier by Adoniram Judson and accepted as protocol. There had been conversations about changing this rule for Emily as she wrote the memoir of Sarah Hall Boardman Judson. Now it appears in this discussion that yet another exception to the policy is being discussed.

[111] James T. Fields became a partner with Mr. Ticknor in Ticknor, Reed and Fields.

[112] A native of Providence, Rhode Island, and a graduate of Brown University in 1822, Richard Eddy was a businessman, and for four years, he was the deputy collector for the Port of Providence before assuming responsibilities as treasurer of the American Baptist Missionary Union in 1845. He held the treasurer's responsibility for nine years before resigning for health reasons.

one of the most pious women in the city, but there is no ostentation about her. I should think she was one of Upham's Christians—she seems to love every body that loves God, and to make no fuss about it. By the way, I am not going to read any [Note: Written along the right margin of page 3] more religious books It's enough to set one crazy. The Book is the best book after all.

[Note: The letter continues on page 3.] 10 1/2 o'clock ev'g. Mr. Jones has just gone away and he certainly is the most *pokey* man for a Missionary that ever I saw. Why I do not believe he knows what enthusiasm means. When I found he had been at Rangoon I tried to get him to give me some description of it, but all he could say was that "they could n't [sic] say much for it"—and as a field of Missionary labor he did not see what you could expect to accomplish etc. If I was influenced at all by what he says I should burn up these letters and think no more of being a Missionary. He thinks a man or woman who goes out single is only half a pair of scizzors [sic] etc. and so on. He and I always dispute this last point and the funny of it is that he is going to take a single lady out with his wife. He can't get a whole pair of scizzors [sic] to go so he is obliged to take up with this half one. By the way the board invited this lady to go—*she has rec'd a call.* According to a resolution passed at Cincinnati the board can give any one a call to go on a Mission whom they think, suitable. Don't you think I could make Mr. Bright and some of the other good ones think I was suitable enough for them to give me call? I am going to spend a day or two with Mrs. B. this week and I mean to try. I think I shall let-it-rest-there. If it is to be that I go, I shall receive a call, [ ]! to me I hear the Dr. laugh at the idea of 'Bel'—Forester's[113] receiving a call from the board of missions. Would n't [sic] it be funny? Strange things do happen tho' in this world of ours.

Good night Nemmy darling. I would get a great many sweet good night kisses if I was in Green Turban's[114] den would n't [sic] I? How long it will be before I get an answer to this! I wish there was a magnetic telegraph between this and Burmah.
    Anna M.

Written at the bottom of page 4 perpendicular to the rest of the text: "Nemmy darling, on reading over my letter I find I have asked perhaps too abruptly for advice in this matter—particularly as I propose to act contrary to your previously expressed opinion. But I trust to our friendship. You know I *am alone*—mother, brothers, sisters and friends must be left if I embark in this cause. You know too how jealous friends are of such a friendship as ours and how much reason they would have for jealousy could I leave them as I propose some months since. You know I love you Nemmy with all my heart,—but—I cannot help thinking that you

---

[113] "Cousin 'Bel'" was Anna Maria Anable and the "character" from Emily's letter to the *New Mirror*, which was published on June 8, 1844 and catapulted Emily to literary fame. The letter concerned Emily and Cousin 'Bel's visit to New York and their lack of money to enjoy the wares of the many shops they passed. She asked if the editor of the *New Mirror* would like to help them out.

and I both love Christ—more than when our friendship began, so you are now doubly endeared to me.

"They don't think I am falling into a *canting* way. I am afraid you will, I write so much about myself."

Source: American Baptist Historical Society, AJ 13, no. 502.

Anna Maria Anable to Adoniram Judson, June 29, 1847[115]—Boston

My kind friend

I have been mortified every time I have thought of the foolish little note I wrote you two months since, and I should not venture to obtrude again were I not in a great dilemma out of which no one can help me so well as yourself. So upon your benevolence I again throw myself.

You know of course that I have ever since you left us written more or less seriously to Emily about going over to you, and your kind indulgence of what must have seemed a whim encourages me to think you will give me a patient hearing, and candid advice when I propose a serious reality. From a note which I rec'd from Lydia[116] in May, I think you must all have somewhat mistaken my motives, or rather I must have expressed myself too blindly and thoughtlessly to be understood.

It has not been without a design of devoting myself more entirely to the extension of truth that I have thought of leaving home, but it is true that I have heretofore had no thought of connecting myself ostensibly with the Mission. There has seemed to me something unfeminine and revolting to my notions of propriety in the thought of a young lady's presenting herself before a body of men to have them discuss her merits or demerits as a candidate for appointment to a missionary work. I would much have preferred to go out independent of the board and to be able to support myself when there, but that plan would have crippled my means of usefulness as well as perhaps fostered too much my pride and independence of spirit. Whether I can so far overcome those dispositions, as to make application to the board will depend very much if not entirely on your opinion of my qualifications for such a work. This is when I need direction. You will know something of the experience of my heart in religious matters, if Emily has read you those portions of my letters for I have written to her with great frankness.

My evidence of my own personal acceptance with God which I have long been seeking is no clearer than formerly, but in Christ as the Redeemer of mankind and in all the truths of revelation I see such loveliness that my heart is involuntarily

---

[114] One of the names used by Emily for the landlord of "Bat Castle" in Rangoon where they lived.

[115] This letter is the second lengthy letter dated June 29, 1847.

drawn out in the warmest affection. This gives me courage to hope that my nature is renewed, for I suppose one cannot at the same time love and hate God. However it may be with regard to my past experience, if I can at all understand my heart now, my desire is, to be in all things conformed to the will of God, and entirely consecrated to his service.

Now, if I overleap a few years, and review this life in the light of eternity, where, as I heard a clergyman say not long since there will be but two great objects of interest—God—and a redeemed spirit, the Cross is such a marvel to me, such a miracle of love, that I want to raise it up to the eye of every human being—but particularly to those who for so many centuries have been suffered by the indifference of the church to be in ignorance of it. I find within me some sympathy with the feelings which actuated Swartz, which burned in the breast of Pearce, and (I need not go so far back) which has actuated and still inflames you in your life-time consecration to this great object.

Many of course will say, why go abroad to accomplish your object? There is plenty of opportunity for doing good at home etc. etc. I can only say in answer— that there are plenty at home to work if they will and but *very* few to go abroad.

There is a Providence in all these things. I never should think of going to Burmah had I not such kind kind friends there as you and Emily. I did not know as I should desire to go were you still in Maulmain, but ever since you have talked of going into Burmah Proper, I have felt a great desire to contribute my little mite of strength in helping on the great work which I feel sure is to be done there.

Shall I tell you how I expect to be of any assistance? You will of course know best what I can do (and I may be under your especial direction may n't [sic] I?) but lest you should fear I am getting romantic, let me tell you that I do *not* exactly expect "to take a department in Mrs. _____'s Female Seminary." I have a notion however, which may see to you quite as romantic, of learning the language, visiting the natives' huts, talking with them, reading to them etc. etc.

Imagination pictures to me a thousand scenes revolting to a cultivated taste which engaged in such pursuits, but—the world was in as bad a state when our Divine Master descended from a Heaven of purity and love to dwell among us, and He has said "It is enough if the servant be as his master etc."—

The only question in my mind is this—Is it right for a person perplexed as I so often am about the state of my own heart, to engage in such a work. You will tell me to ask counsel of God—I do—and I sometimes think my Saviour [sic] means to teach me in this way what is the true life of faith. I have written you a long, egotistical letter and you know all my difficulties, but to that same attitude to which I appealed for a hearing in the commencement of it do I trust now for an answer to my queries, and should you advise me to come, I must trust still to your kindness for a welcome and a home. I do not fear much for the latter, for the benevolence [Note: Written along the left margin of page 3.] which opened its arms to me so readily as a friend, will not reject me, if it is right I should come, when I present myself as a friend and little "helper" too. Very respectfully and affectionately

Anna M. Anable

Source: American Baptist Historical Society, AJ 6, no. 78.

Adoniram Judson to Mrs. Elizabeth Stevens, June 30, 1847[117]— Rangoon

Dear Sister,

I have heard Mrs. Judson say, two or three times, that she ought to write you; so I thought I would supply her deficiency. She has been very ill, with a combination of nervous complaints, and become "as thin as the shad that went up the Niagara." I was taken with dysentery two or three weeks ago, and had the hardest time that I ever knew since I have been in the mission. Henry[118] lost his appetite, and grew thin with fever—And in the midst of it, poor little Edward[119] was seized with the erysipelas, and his eyes and face swelled so that he was not recognizable. At length several frightful sores opened, and are still discharging. Government troubles came thick upon us and the converts. The season of Lent arrived, and for four months no flesh or fowl—nothing but fish—is procurable, except by stealth, and at a great price. We had depended chiefly on fowl soup, and now it seemed as if we must die. However, we kept on breathing—

Only think that next July 11, will be the anniversary of our sailing from Boston, and I shall not then have received—except two short letters from Abby

---

[116] See vol. 1, "Cast of Characters," s.v. "Lillybridge, Miss," also the timeline on "Lydia Lillybridge Simons."

[117] This letter from Adoniram Judson to Elizabeth Stevens is included in this correspondence because of its portrayal of the Judson family at this time in Rangoon.

[118] See vol. 1, "Cast of Characters," s.v. "Judson, Henry Hall."

[119] See vol. 1, "Cast of Characters," s.v. "Judson, Edward."

Ann,[120] and ditto from Mr. Peck[121]—a single communication from the thousands of warm friends I left at home!

Better sing "Vive," etc., over the graves of friendship, and all things here below, except—except what? *love*; and that we will cherish in the young corner of our hearts, an oasis in the desert.

Yours affectionately,

A. Judson

Source: Francis Wayland, *A Memoir of the Life and Labors of the Rev. Adoniram Judson, DD*, 2:293.

Emily C. Judson to Anna Maria Anable, July 1, 1847[122]

I was interrupted suddenly by my invalids while writing the above sentence; since then I have had as much trouble as my worst enemy could wish. I was about telling you that I gave Edward[123] a dose of calomel at a venture in the morning, and that in the afternoon I thought of poor F—, and decided that the disease was erysipelas. The fever had by this time abated, and the spots on his face become red, instead of purple. I think my dose of calomel saved his life. I searched all my books and gave gentle remedies afterward; but the sweet little fellow is still a great sufferer. Both the Doctor and Henry[124] were better that day. I went to bed late at night with one of my very worst nervous headaches. I was awakened from troubled sleep by Edward's screams; but as soon as I raised my head I seemed to be caught by a whirlwind, and fell back helpless. As soon as possible I made another attempt, and this time reached the middle of the room, where I fell headlong. I did not venture on my feet again, but crept to the bed on my hands and feet, and finally succeeded in soothing him. All this time the Doctor was groaning terribly, and he managed between his groans to tell me that he was in even greater agony than when he was

[120] Abby Ann Judson, the first daughter and oldest child of Adoniram and Sarah Hall Boardman Judson, was born September 26, 1835. She saw her mother die on the Isle of St. Helena as they returned to the United States from Burmah. Just before leaving for Burmah with Emily, Adoniram Judson placed Abby Ann at Bradford Academy for her education. The family of Ann Hasseltine Judson was generous to Abby Ann and supportive of her interests and her future. On October 15, 1851, Abby Ann started a course of study at the Misses Anable's School in Philadelphia, and in fall 1853, she moved to New York City to take a teaching position in the home of Mrs. Maria Brown, a former missionary to Siam. She enjoyed a warm relationship with Emily, and her letters show that the two could speak freely with each other.

[121] The Reverend Doctor Solomon Peck was for twenty years the executive secretary of the American Baptist Missionary Union. Many believed him to be hard, stern, and judgmental, and from some of his comments, it is easy to understand that perception. Dr. Peck and Emily did not always have the easiest of relationships. She felt in him the judgment that came from many in the church at the announcement of her impending marriage to Adoniram; that judgment concerned her "secular" past and concern that she was not an appropriate companion for the veteran missionary. On July 18, 1849 Emily wrote a blistering letter of defense to Dr. Peck in response to a letter from him of February 20, 1849; her letter framed how she viewed his perception of her, and her response was meant to set the record straight. There are eleven letters in the collection from Solomon Peck to Emily.

[122] This is the fourth of four segments of a letter written over a two-week period—June 16, 19, 20, and July 1, 1847.

[123] See vol. 1, "Cast of Characters," s.v. "Judson, Edward."

[124] See vol. 1, "Cast of Characters," s.v. "Judson, Henry Hall."

first seized. I was unable to do any thing [*sic*] for him, however, and so crawled over to Henry's cot. Oh, the predicament that he was in!

I expected that both Edward and the Doctor would die, and you may imagine that I had one long cry before I began to contrive what I should do in case the worst should come. The vessel had gone off to Maulmain that very day, and it would be at least a week before another would sail. The amount of the whole is, that the Doctor had a most dangerous relapse, from which he has not yet recovered, though probably out of danger. Henry is left a pale, puny child, without appetite; and poor Edward, really the greatest sufferer, is still in an alarming situation. There is an abscess in his forehead and the acrid matter has eaten back into the bone, we can not tell how far; there is another immense one on the back of the head in a shocking state, and two lesser ones on his neck. We read our books and do the best we can; and are very grateful that we can keep the fever off, and that with this open house and damp air he does not take cold. He is the loveliest child that I ever saw; there is something which seems to me angelic in his patience and calmness. He could not help crying when his papa lanced his head; but the moment the sharpest pain was over, he nestled down in my bosom, and though quivering all over, he kept lifting his eyes to my face, and trying to smile, oh, so sweetly! He watched his papa while he sharpened the lancet to open another, and when it was ready, turned and laid his little head on his knee of his own accord. Just when we were at the worst my nurse was taken ill with fever. She had it lightly, however, so that her husband (my cook) took care of her, instead of burdening me with another patient. You will say that I write of nothing but my husband and children. Of course not; I think of nothing else.

Nemmy[125]

Source: A. C. Kendrick, *The Life and Letters of Mrs. Emily C. Judson*, 279–82.

Mrs. Elizabeth L. Stevens to Emily C. Judson, July 17, 1847—Maulmain

My Very Dear Mrs. Judson

Your good husband writes me that you are "as thin as the shad that went up the Niagara.[126] I am sure you were as thin as you could be when you left this, so I cannot fancy what your present appearance can be. Before you quite lose all materiality do come round here and live with us beef steak and bread and milk sort of people awhile. The association perhaps would be mutually beneficial. If I could

[125] Emily Chubbuck. See vol. 1, "Cast of Characters," s.v. "Nemmy, Nem, or Nemmy Petty (Nemmie Pettie)." Also the chapter "Names of Endearment."

[126] See the letter of Adoniram Judson to Mrs. Elizabeth Stevens dated June 30, 1847.

become a little speck intellectualized and you a good deal matur[ ] it certainly would be an improvement to us both.

I wish I knew more about the prospect of a good vessel from Rangoon here so that I might know when to anticipate the pleasure of seeing you.[127] Will you not again make your home with us while getting settled? [ ] has any one written you [ ] Mrs. Haswell's[128] [ ] [ ] [ ] three weeks old. The other prominent [ ] of mission news just now is Mrs. Vinton's[129] decision to go to America with Mr. Mason[130] who goes soon to Tavoy to try to persuade Mrs. Bennett[131] to accompany them. Should Mrs. B. go Mrs. Bullard[132] is to take permanent charge and remain for 8 or 10 years if Mr. Mason's little Francis—he does not think it best to take a young child home.

Mission matters are now flowing smoothly as need be. Mr. Vinton[133] is as friendly and good as we could wish—he is a most superexcellent man, except now and then he gets ultra about some things.

With kindest love and much real sympathy notwithstanding I have written no more sadly about your health and deprivations and the illnesses. The dear children added.

Written along the left and top margin of page 1: "Believe me very aff'ly Yrs. E. L. S.

"Kindly tell Mah Laat, I received her letter and that her daughter appears to be doing extremely well. Emma also gives good accounts of the little boy William."

Source: American Baptist Historical Society, AJ 19, no. 906.

---

[127] Life in Rangoon was most difficult for Emily and Adoniram, Henry and Edward. The house is labeled "Bat Castle" because of the bats, lizards, and other "creatures of the night" that inhabit it; Emily has been sick, unable to be off of her bed very much, then Adoniram took severely ill, and then the two boys became ill as well. Now, it appears that the decision has been made for them to return to Maulmain. In fact, they left Rangoon the end of August, arriving in Maulmain on September 5, 1847.

[128] See vol. 1, "Cast of Characters," s.v. "Haswell, Mrs. Jane Haswell."

[129] Calesta Holman Vinton was the wife of Justus Hatch Vinton. From Connecticut, they first came to Burmah in December 1834. Their main ministry was with the Karens. Mrs. Vinton taught the women and was the author of several hymnbooks in their language. They returned to the United States in 1848, returning to Burmah in July 1850. In 1851, they moved to Rangoon. Mrs. Vinton died in December 1864. Mr. Vinton died in March 1858.

[130] See vol. 1, "Cast of Characters," s.v. "Mason, The Reverend Francis, Helen, and Ellen."

[131] Stella Bennett was the wife of Cephas Bennett; they arrived in Burmah in January 1830. Mr. Bennett remained the superintendent of the Baptist Press there for more than fifty years. From the Utica area, they sent their children back, and the girls were educated at the Utica Female Academy. The girls included Elsina (April 1828), Mary (November 1829), Ann (August 1833), Ellen (June 1835), and Sarah (June 1837).

[132] Mrs. Bullard was the widow of missionary Edwin Bullard. In September 1847, she married Francis Mason, who had lost his wife the previous year. Adoniram Judson married them in Maulmain. When this letter was written in July 1847, there was no hint of a relationship, much less marriage, between Mr. Mason and Mrs. Bullard.

[133] Justus Hatch Vinton was born in Willington, Ct., in 1806. He attended the theological school at Hamilton, New York, was ordained in June 1834 and in July that same year he sailed as a missionary to Burmah. His wife was Calista Holman Vinton; they were married April 9, 1834. They worked with the Karens at Chummerah, Newville, and Maulmain, where he had charge of the Karen theological seminary. At the end of 1847 they left for the United States, returning to Burmah and work at Rangoon in July 1850. Justus Vinton died in Kemendine, Burmah March 31, 1858. His wife, Calista Holman Vinton, died in Rangoon, Burmah December 20, 1864. Mrs. Vinton taught the Karen women, and was the author of several hymnbooks in their language.

Anna Maria Anable to Emily C. Judson July 30, 1847[134]—Boston

Dear Nemmy,[135]

I am almost ashamed to write you so often but I cannot help it. I have been spending a couple of days with the Colby's[136] at Newton. Mrs. Colby sends a great deal of love to you. She has rec'd no letter yet? The more I see of the Colby's the better I like them. I always liked them, but they bear acquaintance well. Besides going out into the country occasionally to see a friend, I am passing the Summer in the most quiet manner possible I can, nothing for society and just go from my boarding place to the Dr.'s,[137] and saunter down Washington, St. and home again. Once in a while, however I get up something of absorbing interest—for this last fortnight I have been all engrossed in making some things for you my darling. If wishing would do any good, you should have not only a box but a cargo of things sent over to you. I supposed we should have an opportunity of sending by Mr. Abbott[138] who leaves in about a fortnight but he is going overland (it is not quite decided but Mr. Bright[139] thinks so) and we shall now have no chance to send till October. There is one thing gained by it—we shall have all the more time to make things. I wish I knew just what would be nice for you. I suppose clothes for the boys will always be acceptable. I shall try to use some judgment in the selection of the few articles I shall make myself. I rather think they will make up a box for you in Roxbury.[140] Every body [sic] feels great sympathy for you in your loss.[141] You can't conceive how your letter dated March 29th struck me. It came just after I had written to the Dr. and it seemed to be almost an answer, and yet so strange is the human heart no sooner did I know that there surely was some way in which I might be instrumental of doing some good there, then I began to feel very indifferent about it. Notwithstanding these changes of feeling, I have some principle in me, and an abiding conviction that sooner or later I shall be with you.[142] You and the Dr. will teach me how to behave myself properly won't you? I read your letter to

---

[134] This letter is an addendum to Anna Maria's letter of July 30, 1847.

[135] Emily Chubbuck. See vol. 1, "Cast of Characters," s.v. "Nemmy, Nem, or Nemmy Petty (Nemmie Pettie)." Also the chapter "Names of Endearment."

[136] See vol. 1, "Cast of Characters," s.v. "Colby, Gardner."

[137] For more information on these medical treatments, see vol. 1, "Cast of Characters," s.v. "Anable, Anna Maria."

[138] See vol. 1, "Cast of Characters," s.v. "Abbott, The Reverend Elisha."

[139] On the relationship of Emily Judson and Edward Bright, see vol. 1, "Cast of Characters," s.v. "Bright, the Reverend Doctor Edward, Jr."

[140] Roxbury, Massachusetts was the home of Dr. and Mrs. Edward Bright. Dr. Bright was the Corresponding Secretary of the American Baptist Missionary Union.

[141] On February 17, 1847, shortly after they left Maulmain for Rangoon, a fire in the mission compound at Maulmain destroyed two trunks of Adoniram and Emily's clothing and personal articles; much of the loss had been personal gifts of great sentimental value. In different letters the loss was estimated between seven hundred and a thousand rupees.

[142] For more on Anna Maria Anable and a possible call to missionary service, see vol. 1, "Cast of Characters," s.v. "Anable, Anna Maria."

Mr. and Mrs. Eddy[143] and she read me hers—she said she had thought of me as soon as she read yours. I did not tell her how *much* I had thought of going and yet she knows enough about it, if the board ever should think it best to send a teacher to Rangoon. It seems Mrs. Binney[144] has written some most eloquent appeals to the board for an assistant in a *normal school* at Maulmain, and they will feel bound to send her one I suppose. Mrs. E. asked me if I didn't want to go. I told her *no*. Mrs. Eddy is a darling woman. She was very much gratified at getting your letter and in reading "Outward Bound" in the *Columbian*.[145] Have you sent any article for the C. since you have been on land? You must let me know what you do in that time for I should not like to lose anything of yours. Tell the Dr. his little Abby[146] is considered quite a genius here. She has written a sermon with the three heads and application all in apple-pie order and you would think it was a minister *for* [ ]. The only childish thing I have heard of her saying was when Mrs. Colby told her she was going to live in the country. "Dear, dear," says Abby, "what shall I do for a stopping place now when I come to Boston?" It pleased Mrs. C. vastly.

Anna Maria Anable to Emily C. Judson, July 31, 1847[147]

Now Nemmy[148] darling my package has come from the *Faneuil Hall*[149]—and where did you pick up in such an out of the way place as Maulmain such a beautiful muslin as that? Why I don't believe any body [sic] else has got such a handsome dress in all Boston? Embroidered muslins are all the fashion, but I don't see anything in the stores that compares with it. It is almost too nice for me to flonish [sic] here, but I mean to have it made up elegantly and when I am presented to His Royal Highness at Ava may be [sic] I shall "grace it" as old Mary used to say. If I go to Providence to commencement however I shall be tempted to have it made up

---

[143] Mr. Richard Eddy was the treasurer of the American Baptist Missionary Union.

[144] Juliette Binney arrived in Burmah in April 1844. Her husband was Joseph Binney, who opened the Karen Theological School in Maulmain for training indigenous pastors for the Burmese Church. They both worked in establishing general education possibilities for the Burmese people. She returned to the United States in 1850 because of her health. He returned in 1859, moving the seminary to Rangoon.

[145] The *Columbian* magazine was published first by John Inman and then by Robert West. By early 1844, the *Columbian* was printing Emily's stories; this was before N. P. Willis and the *New Mirror* made her famous. With Graham, they readily agreed to pay her a top rate of five dollars a page for anything that she would write, and on several occasions, they tried to get Emily to write exclusively for them. They finally succeeded in this when she went to Burmah, for they obtained exclusive rights to all that she would send them at fifty dollars a story. The story mentioned here is in the correspondence dated fall 1846.

[146] See vol. 1, "Cast of Characters," s.v. "Judson, Abby Ann."

[147] This letter is an addendum to Anna Maria's letter of July 30, 1847.

[148] Emily Chubbuck. See vol. 1, "Cast of Characters," s.v. "Nemmy, Nem, or Nemmy Petty (Nemmie Pettie)." Also the chapter "Names of Endearment."

[149] The *Faneuil Hall* was the ship on which Adoniram and Emily sailed to Burmah. In her letter to Miss Cynthia Sheldon dated December 1846, Emily mentions that she is sending some things back to various people, and the gift for Anna Maria Anable is on that list.

immediately. You fulfilled my orders most beautifully Nemmy and I believe I have not had the grace to thank you before. The truth is I was afraid [ ] to gratify a whim of mine you had put yourself to some inconvenience and I was mortified. I do thank you, for it is so long since I have bought me a pretty frock that I had almost forgotten what was pretty. It makes me almost want to go to a great party again and *create a sensation*. I guess I could do it in that dress. I must tell you how "bewildered" good Mr. Shaw[150] at the Miss. Rooms got at the Dr.'s memorandum of an embroidered dress for dear cousin 'Bel.'[151] It seems they overhaul all the packages at the custom house and Mr. Lincoln[152] told him if there was anything *for Miss Anable* to retain it. So, he went poking down to terribly mystified Mr. Stowe memorandum in hand to see if the two had any connection with each other to the infinite amusement of the firm of G. R. and L.[153]

Written along the right margin of the address page: "I expect Aunt Urania and Dr. Nott[154] here next week, and shall then be able to decide whether I stay here more than a month longer or not. I don't much think I shall. I don't know as I shall ever be perfectly straight but I am much better off than I was before I came here and—if I take care of myself I have the prospect of a cure. If my physician thinks it best I shall stay till Dec. or Jan'y. I had almost forgotten to say that the other package I have [Note: Written along the left margin of the address page.] sent on to Kate[155] with the exception of the night gown which I shall send right straight back to you my darling, for I know you will find it useful some time or other. Since the fire at M. you will find there is a great dearth of such like pretty things in your wardrobe.[156] The other things I should have accepted with pleasure but I have just had a whole piece of linen made up and shall not need any more next six years."

---

[150] Thomas Shaw worked in the Mission Rooms of the American Baptist Missionary Union in Boston. He wrote Emily two letters in December 1851 about some shipping containers that had arrived for her. It is likely that they were items shipped from her breaking up household in Burmah. In November 1851, Charles Gould spoke of him as "Captain Shaw."

[151] "Cousin 'Bel'" was Anna Maria Anable.

[152] A prominent Baptist, Mr. Joshua Lincoln was a member of the firm Gould, Randall, and Lincoln. In 1847, while in Boston for her medical treatments, Anna Maria Anable stayed with the Lincoln family. Mr. Lincoln was active in Massachusetts and national Baptist circles.

[153] Mr. Joshua Lincoln's publishing firm was Gould, Randall and Lincoln.

[154] See vol. 1, "Cast of Characters," s.v. "Nott, Urania Sheldon."

[155] Sarah Catharine Chubbuck, "Kate," "Kit," or "Kitty" was Emily's older sister by ten months. Outside of the two terms at the Utica Female Academy, which Emily arranged for her, Catharine always lived at home with her parents in Hamilton, New York. The letters indicate opportunities for marriage, but she, for unknown reasons, remained single. She later helped to care for Henry and Edward Judson after their return from Burmah in fall 1851 when they moved into the Hamilton home with their "aunt" and "grandparents," and she was remembered by them as "dear old Aunt Kate—a dear friend."

[156] On February 17, 1847, shortly after they left Maulmain for Rangoon, a fire in the mission compound at Maulmain destroyed two trunks of Adoniram and Emily's clothing and personal articles; much of the loss had been personal gifts of great sentimental value. In different letters the loss was estimated between seven hundred and a thousand rupees.

Written along the bottom margin of the address page: "Jane Kelly[157] has gone to Binghamton with Mary Spencer.[158] The [ ] are all staying at the Rockland House down on the beach. I spent one day with them."

Written along the left margin of page 1: "Nemmy you are a blessed good child to write me so often—but I wonder if the Dr. has forgotten me altogether. He has never sent me a single message except of consent to my coming since he left. Domestic felicity certainly must have a tendency to make a body selfish."

Written across the top margin of page 1: "I wonder if Aunt C.[159] will tell you the news—*Jimmy Watson's got a son.*

"I don't know why I should feel disposed to laugh about it but I stopped to have a good shaking. I wonder if the little fellow looks like his father. If he takes after either father or mother he'll have a nose that's destined to rise in the world. Advise Nemmy sweet—let me know when you intend to take up yourself any such responsibilities and I will make preparations accordingly."

Anna M.

Source: American Baptist Historical Society, AJ 13, no. 501.

Mrs. Elizabeth L. Stevens to Emily C. Judson, August, 1847[160]

My dear Sister,

It seems that it is at last arranged that Mrs. Ranney[161] goes down with her husband—I hope the trip will do her good and you also and that you will all soon be safe home again. Do you know I never was much of a believer in sending off sick folks; I think they need their friends around them.

Now what do you think Dr. Morton[162] has prescribed this morning? That you come up and stop here till you can get started off on a voyage. I suppose he thinks

---

[157] Miss Jane Kelly was Emily Chubbuck's friend at the Utica Female Academy, and then she became a teacher with Emily at that institution. Miss Kelly became the literary principal in 1844 with the retirement of Mr. and Mrs. James Nichols from that position. During a period of Miss Kelly's illness in 1844, Emily filled in the position for her. Then, in 1848, when Miss Cynthia Sheldon moved to Philadelphia to help start the Misses Anable's School, Miss Kelly became the "headmistress" of the academy and successfully brought it into the future, though not without some initial disparagement from the Sheldon-Anable families.

[158] On February 28, 1848, Anna Maria Anable wrote to Emily, saying, "Mary Spencer has just returned from Albany. It is said she is engaged to John James, a handsome young widower with three children, and two or three hundred thousand $'s."

[159] See vol. 1, "Cast of Characters," s.v. "Sheldon, Miss Cynthia."

[160] This letter is undated; it fits best in August 1847, as Emily and Adoniram were planning to move from Rangoon back to Maulmain.

[161] Maria Gager Ranney arrived in Maulmain in May 1844. Her husband Thomas was the superintendent of the printing press and business manager for the missionary compound. A letter from Lydia Lillybridge reveals that Mrs. Ranney had some responsibilities in the mission schools. She had no children; Maria Ranney died on April 26, 1857.

[162] Doctor Morton was a physician who worked with the missionaries in Maulmain, Burmah. He delivered Emily Frances Judson in December 1847 and was present when Charles Judson ("Angel Charlie") was stillborn in April 1850. He was a valued and trusted advisor to the mission families.

our big dining room or something or other will help in the case. Now don't you believe you can persuade Mr. Judson to come? As a second attraction after the big dining room I must mention one renowned "John Simons," the cook, who will do his very *super*—better most in the line of niceties.

You need not be concerned about lodging places. I will arrange that to my own satisfaction and I hope to yours with the least bit of trouble that ever was. You can have my bedroom and Henry[163] and Edward[164] can sleep in Eddy's[165] room. E. and I can occupy the front spare room—you cannot tell how easily and nicely I can arrange it all. I know you will say "so many children will make so much noise it will never do." Leave that to me—there is nothing like trying, and noisy as my chaps are I believe they *can* be still, if not they can go over to the chapel and play all day.

I am disappointed not to go to help you up but very likely my room will be better than my company [ ] [Note: Written along the left margin of page 1.] if you had not the better substitute of Mrs. B's.

Yrs. Very aff'ly

E. L.Stevens

Source: American Baptist Historical Society, AJ 19, no. 895.

Catharine Chubbuck to J. Walker Chubbuck, August 7th, 1847[166]— Hamilton

My dear Walky

It seems you are determined not to let us know any thing about your own dear self or any body [sic] in your section of country—here it is almost four months since you left home, and not a single word from you yet. Now don't be frightened and think I'm going to give you a tremendous scolding, it's no such thing, though truth to say I think you are quite deserving of it, but then I've given up scolding this summer entirely, for I don't think it's very lady like to do so, and besides I've nothing under the sun to make me scold. But really I did think you would be more true to your promises to mother.[167] She has been in a perfect fever for two months, for fear something terrible had befallen you sometimes thinking you were *certainly*

---

[163] See vol. 1, "Cast of Characters," s.v. "Judson, Henry Hall."

[164] See vol. 1, "Cast of Characters," s.v. "Judson, Edward."

[165] Edward Stevens was the oldest son and child of Elizabeth and Edward Stevens; he was born December 17, 1838.

[166] This letter from Emily's sister Catharine to their brother Walker is included because it describes Emily's family in Hamilton, New York, as life went on in her absence. Catharine describes the fire that destroyed many of Emily and Adoniram's possessions left behind as they moved to Rangoon for ministry there.

[167] Emily's mother, Lavinia Richards Chubbuck, was born June 1, 1785, at Goffstown, New Hampshire, the eldest of thirteen children. She married Charles Chubbuck on November 17, 1805, at Goffstown, New Hampshire. Four of her children were born at Goffstown, and moved with Charles and Lavinia Chubbuck to Eaton, New York in September 1816; they were Lavinia, Benjamin, Harriet, and John Walker. Sarah Catharine, Emily, and Wallace were all born in Eaton.

sick or you would write, but then I have all the time tried to make her believe that it was more likely that you had run away. I hav'nt [*sic*] succeeded very well however, in making her believe this. I suppose it was necessary for me to give her the cause for running away, but I could'nt [*sic*] think of but two things one was to find a wife, and the other to get rid of buying me that wedding dress. If you have run away Sir, you better run back and tell us what for. I think it's very strange, we hav'nt [*sic*] heard a word from Uncle Holland's since you left. I don't know but you made a bargain with them to cheat us out of all the letters. I said once I would'nt [*sic*] write to you first, but I began to think I would being it was Walk Chub but I'm only going to write a little short one now because I'm in a great hurry, commencement is just at hand, and of course you know we must prepare for a great deal of company, for I suppose we shall have a greater crowd than usual this time. We are to have Dr. Fuller a slaveholder here to preach to us, and of course we suppose that will draw a crowd. Do you know boy that you ought to be here to attend the exercises? I think of selecting one from among the graduates to stand up with my new wedding gown that you are going to give me and I am sure you ought to be here to help me. Things go on pretty much after the old sort here. Mother has been pretty sick twice this summer but is able to go about the house, her cough is bad though. She has taken three or four bottles of that medicine and thinks it helps her. Our boarders[168] have all left now I don't know whether they will come back or not. I hope Miss Beebee will though for she is first rate company. Wallace[169] is in school yet in Peterboro and for aught I know doing very well—his health is not very good. We heard from Emily every month while she was in Maulmain, but now our letters are irregular it is now seven weeks since the last letter came, and we are dreading to hear again for they are in such a dangerous place that we are afraid for them. The king at Rangoon is a bigoted Boodhist and of course you know they will have to be very cautious what they say and do. It seems a hazardous undertaking for them to live there, but may be [*sic*] it is for the better. The doctor had baptized one convert there, and there are several inquirers. Poor Nemmy[170] met with a sad loss the night after they left Maulmain, or rather I might say the Dr. and she. They took only a few things to Rangoon, gave away some things, and packed the rest away to

---

[168] The Chubbucks took in boarders on a regular basis to supplement their income. Courtland Anable, brother of Anna Maria Anable, was one of those boarders. Most, if not all, were from the college/seminary at Hamilton.

[169] Born January 1, 1824, William Wallace Chubbuck was six years younger than Emily. During these years of Emily's correspondence, Wallace lived at or near home and worked at different occupations including printing, office work, and teaching. Emily wrote of him as capable in many areas, but seeming to lack ambition at times. He proved to be a strong support for the Chubbuck family over these years, and at the time of her death in 1854, Wallace had become one of Emily's primary caregivers. After February 1854, she dictated all her letters to him because of her failing strength. Wallace was active in newspaper and political activities; he also worked with at least one of the legislative committees in Albany. He was married in July of 1854; he died in August of 1861.

[170] Emily Chubbuck. See vol. 1, "Cast of Characters," s.v. "Nemmy, Nem, or Nemmy Petty (Nemmie Pettie)." Also the chapter "Names of Endearment."

send for after the rains were over. The night after they left and before they were out of the river Mr. Steven's[171] house where their goods were stored was burnt to the ground and not a thing saved. They merely escaped with their lives in their night clothes. It has left our folks pretty destitute but still they don't complain. All the doctor's bombazine clothes, shoes, dresses, flannels, and every thing [sic] you could mention almost they lost, it is very hard, but right I suppose. I am going to try to send a box this fall. To be sure we can't send a great deal but then every little helps, and in that country particularly. I would write more but have neither time nor room. Our folks send a great of love. Write do to Your affectionate

    Kitty

Source: Jerome Walker Chubbuck Collection, Wisconsin Historical Society Archives, Madison WI.

Adoniram Judson to Miss Lydia Lillybridge, August 12, 1847[172]— Rangoon

My Dear Lydia,

    I have never written you, because I know that Emily is frequently writing you, and that you will, or ought to, take all she writes as coming from us both. For the same reason I have never written to—till just now, in answer to a note from her. So having perpetrated that anomaly, I am not venturing on another, like the monkey who, having in an unlucky hour said A, was whipped to make him say B. However, the comparison is imperfect, in that there is no whipping needed to make me write to those I love. We have frequently wanted you with us here, and once seriously thought of it, in connection with a projected school; but the folly of the thought soon became apparent in the more evident precariousness of our own situation. I hope you pass your time not sadly or unhappily, though the study of a foreign language and getting used to a new school in a foreign land are not very epicurean occupations. But we must sow before we reap; and though our whole life should prove to be but sowing time, the harvest of eternity will produce ample returns.

    You are enough acquainted with Emily to know how happy I must be in her society. My sojourn in Rangoon, though tedious and trying in some respects, I regard as one of the brightest spots, one of the greenest oases in the diversified

---

[171] Edward and Elizabeth Stevens were missionaries to Burmah. They arrived in Maulmain, Burmah, in February 1838. There are twenty-four letters in the correspondence from them. Mrs. Stevens took Edward Judson into her home when Sarah and Adoniram had to leave for the United States in 1845, and her care and nurture saved his life. The home of Elizabeth and Edward Stevens burned to the ground in 1847, and two trunks being stored for Adoniram and Emily were destroyed; these trunks held all of their excess clothes and precious mementos, which they had not wanted to bring to Rangoon with them. Mr. Stevens buried Charles Chubbuck (Emily's "Angel Charlie") in April 1850. Edward Stevens also accepted the responsibility of finishing the dictionary after the death of Adoniram Judson.

[172] This letter of Adoniram Judson to Miss Lydia Lillybridge is included because of its descriptiveness of his relationship with Emily and their mutual relationship with Lydia.

wilderness of my life. May God make me thankful for all the blessings which have hitherto fallen to my lot, and for the hope of those richer blessings which are concealed by the cloud of sense from our spiritual vision. If this world is so happy, what must heaven be? And as to trials, let us bear up under them, remembering that if we suffer for Christ's sake, with him we shall reign.

Yours affectionately,

A. Judson

Source: Francis Wayland, *A Memoir of the Life and Labors of the Rev. Adoniram Judson, DD*; (Boston: Phillips, Sampson, and Company, 1853) 2:295.

Adoniram Judson to Anna Maria Anable,[173] August 17, 1847—Rangoon

My dearest Anna Maria,

Forgot you![174] No indeed,—you know better, though you run on at such a rate. We think of you and talk of you every day. I suppose I can truly say, that there is not a person in the country, that we unitedly love so much as you. And yet I have never written you. Why? Because *she* writes you constantly, and I somehow felt, that you would take all she wrote, as coming from us both. And you must do so— for we think and feel alike on every point. We sometimes wonder, that brought up in such different ways—in different countries—and in almost different eras of the world, we should be so perfectly one. There is but a single thing we quarrel about—that whereas she once promised to "love honor and obey," and I tell her to stop making me love her at such a rate, she will not obey, but keeps willfully going on in her own way. To you I can write freely, for you know her well. I suppose that we are the only two persons who are thoroughly acquainted with her and are able to appreciate her varied excellencies.

We have had a tedious time of it in Rangoon—(though so happy in some respects), but we have done our duty and ascertained some important points. We intended to go on to Ava,—but the state of the mission funds is such as to forbid that mission for the present—and indeed compel us to return to Maulmain. But to that measure,—I am impelled (contrary to Nemmy's[175] wishes) by another consideration. There is an event in prospect, which fills me with the liveliest

[173] Adoniram Judson asked all of his correspondents to destroy any letters they had from him, and many of them complied with his request. Because of this, few of his personal letters exist; several remain to Anna Maria Anable, including this one. There is also a November 26, 1848 letter to Abby Ann Judson about the state of her religious faith.

[174] In most of her letters, Anna Maria asks Emily if the doctor has forgotten her.

[175] Emily Chubbuck. See vol. 1, "Cast of Characters," s.v. "Nemmy, Nem, or Nemmy Petty (Nemmie Pettie)." Also the chapter "Names of Endearment."

apprehensions and makes it exceedingly desirable, in my view, that we should be in Maulmain about the close of the year.—[176]

I never think of the privilege of baptizing you,[177] but with the most heart-felt satisfaction and the deepest gratitude to God, and the more so, because I am sure you will never regret the measure—I am sure, whether aware of it your self or not, that it will tend through life, greatly to form and elevate your character. God will bless you for that act of obedience through life and through eternity. Shall we ever welcome you to our arms and our hearts in this country? We often speak of it,—but how can it be? Next to that we should delight to hear of your being settled in Boston—you would seem to be nearer to us, and would be with the dear Colby's[178] and Harris' and other dear and precious friends in that vicinity. But our earthly changes will be soon passed,—we shall live in the glory of Heaven. When I regret the loss of some blessed spots in America, I say "If God through every change can keep this earth so good and fair, We raise our eyes to heaven and say, What beauty must be there." Oh, dear friend, what is love, what is happiness here, compared to that which is just before us ?—purchased for us by the blood of the ever-blessed, adorable Lamb—Ever yours

Most affectionately

A. Judson

Source: Hanna family files.

Miss Cynthia Sheldon to Emily C. Judson, August 22, 1847[179]

My dear dear Emily,

Your letter came bearing date March 26th—O could you know how eagerly every word from your pen is read here, it would afford you comfort. The Lord has been good to us since my pen has lain dormant—The only reason I have deferred is knowing dear Anna M.[180] writes you about every month—and our family being

---

[176] This is as close as Adoniram Judson gets to announcing the impending birth of Emily Frances Judson, who was born December 24, 1847.

[177] Adoniram Judson baptized Anna Maria Anable on June 7, 1846, their last Sunday in Utica before leaving for visits with the Judson children and going to Boston for final preparations for their journey to Burmah. Anna Maria's change to Baptist was unpopular with Aunt Urania Sheldon Nott, a Presbyterian.

[178] See vol. 1, "Cast of Characters," s.v. "Colby, Gardner."

[179] This letter has an addendum dated August 29, 1847.

[180] Anna Maria Anable was the niece of the Misses Urania and Cynthia Sheldon and the daughter of Joseph and Alma Sheldon Anable. Emily first met Anna Maria in fall 1840 when she went as a student to the Utica Female Academy; both Emily and Anna Maria became members of the faculty there. In these years, Anna Maria became Emily's dearest friend, and the extensive correspondence between the two reflects sensitive, flirtatious spirits and a deep intimacy. Emily was "Nemmy" to Anna Maria's "Ninny." In 1848, Anna Maria Anable, with the help of her extended family, moved to Philadelphia and started the Misses Anable's School in Philadelphia. At Emily's death in 1854, Anna Maria was given guardianship of Emily Frances Judson, daughter of Emily and Adoniram Judson.

all scattered makes great drafts on my pen—We have at this time arranged to get seven weeks vacation. Where has it fled—now two weeks remaining—it has been work work [sic] indoors—to get settled for the coming year—and would you believe it our Trustees are really giving the entire inside of the house a nice white dress of paint. They could not have it begun of course till the last minute—and we now are in the middle of it—yet with *fine* prospects for getting through and settled next week—on the very day the school commences—Their ambition has incited mine a little—the halls are papered—rooms painted round the carpets and floor of the 2d hall—They now look clean as other people's rooms—The 2d hall is under going the same—the stairs too—school room walls and tables are drab—the white paint will show these to advantage—I am really becomeing [sic] strangely attached to the walls of this house as witness or memento of by gone days—calling up at every bidding our scattered family—with those who have found their final resting place—dear dear Mother[181] with her attachment to neatness is ever before me, if father's lone room seems neglected, or is undergoing any improvement—her table with the little boxes—and chair, has the same place. I have been so fearful of the affect of this month on dear father[182] that I am really thankful to count the days as gone—he is very weak when the weather is sultry—the last few days he has been very comfortable—this day he has been to Church three times—Mr. Kingsford preached this evening for us to a very full house—Mrs. K. is with him—she is truly an evergreen—no change—they are making a hasty excursion—go to Hamilton tomorrow—will *stop with* us Tuesday as they return—she has now a flourishing *school at* Richmond—

Mr. Loring died suddenly a week ago last night—Mr. Corey[183] had gone to Hamilton, they sent for him to preach the funeral sermon last Monday—this dispensation of providence has produced much feeling—a loud call to be ready—the poor family are greatly afflicted—Mr. Humphrey from Albany was in Church this evening—Dr. Fuller was our guest one night last week—he went to Hamilton to deliver the address before the Society of Enquiry—on Sabbath evening—It was an all powerful appeal from the text "The poor have the Gospel preached to them"—Mr. Knapp gave us a loud Amen to it—and it is said all the opposers to Dr. Fuller[184] coming felt the same—he however knowing there had been hostility determined to withdraw, and the next morning came to Utica—he is one of the most delightful men I have ever seen—and deplores the existence of slavery as

---

[181] Isabell Sheldon, the mother of Cynthia Sheldon, Urania Sheldon Nott, and Alma Sheldon Anable, died January 29, 1847. See the letter of Anna Maria Anable of February 15, 1847.

[182] See vol. 1, "Cast of Characters," s.v. "Sheldon, Deacon Asa."

[183] See vol. 1, "Cast of Characters," s.v. "Corey, the Reverend D. G."

[184] In a letter to her brother, Walker, dated August 7, 1847, Catharine Chubbuck had mentioned Dr. Fuller as a slaveholder, and his coming to speak had elicited some controversy.

much as we northerners do—your boxes[185] to Urania[186] and Jane[187]—with all other things came safely two weeks since—They are much admired—Jane made a two weeks visit in Binghamton then west on to Schenectady—she is the most popular lady in the country—Mr. Spencer says so—They are very much afraid she will marry Mr. Walcott, although he has not taken the first step towards it—but I think very likely she will get married some time—If that should come round—what do you think I would do without Anna M.—she has sent me your last letter—with a hint from her own pen that she would like to take the school you proffer to her—I have written to her about it—If the Lord will—you are in Ava by the time she could get there—The good providence of God has taken Lydia[188] to those shores—and now it appears to me providence indicates that Mrs. Bullard[189] should take Lydia's place—and she join you[190]—the dear girl would be much happier than where she is for she has found out for herself that you and the Dr. are every thing to her—she takes unwearied pains to make us all feel that gratuitous advice on a certain occasion was thrown away—you are her only friend—I do wish she was with you—The good of the cause requires Anna M. to stay here—nothing could appear more preposterous than for her to go out unmarried, every body would say it was the height of romance—very few forgive such folly—and if she could get appointed by the Board for Rangoon—justice to that body would not permit her to leave it without her life was endangered if it was important to sustain the school—you would not be there if providence directs another field—

My heart is indeed full—I know she seeks consecration to the work of God in the earth—heaven grant her own feelings may accord with direct providence—she will find this work to do in whatever allotment.

Source: American Baptist Historical Society, AJ 20, no. 1004.

---

[185] In her December, 1846 letter, Emily wrote that she was sending some gifts back to her many friends and supporters.

[186] See vol. 1, "Cast of Characters," s.v. "Nott, Urania Sheldon."

[187] See vol. 1, "Cast of Characters," s.v. "Kelly, Miss Jane."

[188] See vol. 1, "Cast of Characters," s.v. "Lillybridge, Miss," also the timeline on "Lydia Lillybridge Simons."

[189] Mrs. Bullard was the widow of missionary Edwin Bullard. In September 1847, she married Francis Mason, who lost his wife the previous year. Adoniram Judson performed their wedding ceremony in Maulmain.

[190] In February, Emily and Adoniram moved from Maulmain to Rangoon; in letters to follow, Lydia Lillybridge spoke of teaching there. In her April 1, 1847 letter, she wrote that she realized how much Emily and Adoniram mean to her; nevertheless, she said she would not come to Rangoon without the Adoniram's blessings. At this time, Adoniram and Emily made the decision to return to Maulmain.

Anna Maria Anable to Emily C. Judson, August 25, 1847—Boston

Dear Nemmy[191]

I am just on the move for home and have but a few minutes to write. Your last *interesting* communication *was received* while I was at Newton anniversary. I held the news to myself[192] with exemplary self-denial until day before yesterday. I then thought Mrs. Colby[193] might as well know it as not and she would be the best counselor for me. She will send you a inst. [*sic*]. I have attended to all your commissions and had the things sent to the rooms.[194] I shall see Mr. Shaw[195] this morning and give him a special charge about the box. I am in hopes that a vessel will leave before Nov. but they say it is doubtful. Too bad isn't it? I was just interrupted by a letter from Kate[196] complaining of you not writing. I am going to try and get out to see your mother[197] and Kate when I go home. I may as well send you now the list of articles which I have purchased.

Hoods own $2.75
looking book 1.00
Prayer book 1.75
slippers 1.00
knit bands 1.00
hardware 1.88
Scotch dish 1.62
flannel and linen 3.50
20.00

---

[191] Emily Chubbuck. See vol. 1, "Cast of Characters," s.v. "Nemmy, Nem, or Nemmy Petty (Nemmie Pettie)." Also the chapter "Names of Endearment."

[192] Anna Maria Anable had been thinking and talking with Emily and Adoniram Judson about joining them in Maulmain as a missionary. In summer 1847, Anna Maria Anable was in Boston undergoing painful medical procedures to repair her shoulder and spine and to improve the general state of her health for such service.

[193] Mary Colby was the wife of Gardner Colby, a prominent businessman and active Baptist layman. Mr. Colby was a member of the Board of the American Baptist Missionary Union and an avid supporter of the missionary movement. In a letter after they sailed from Boston to Burmah, Emily mentions the extravagant hospitality extended to them in early July as they waited for the *Faneuil Hall* to embark. Adoniram and then Emily stayed with the Colby family quite frequently over the years. Mrs. Colby was an active correspondent with Emily and supported her, her family, and the cause of missions.

[194] The offices of the American Baptist Missionary Union in Boston were referred to as the "Mission Rooms" or simply "the rooms."

[195] Thomas Shaw worked in the Mission Rooms of the American Baptist Missionary Union in Boston. He wrote Emily two letters in December 1851 about some shipping containers that had arrived at the rooms for her. These are likely items that were shipped after the breaking up of her household in Burmah. In November 1851, Charles Gould spoke of him as "Captain Shaw."

[196] See vol. 1, "Cast of Characters," s.v. "Chubbuck, Miss Sarah Catharine."

[197] Emily's mother. See vol. 1, "Cast of Characters," s.v. "Chubbuck, Lavinia Richards."

The other things that will be wanted for the little stranger[198] I shall get in Utica and try to have them by the next vessel which Mr. Shaw says (I have just seen him) may sail in a month. I shall also take the flannels home with me to make. I go day after tomorrow. I shall send in the box Punch and Yankee Doodle for the old children to laugh at and some similar things for the little ones. I could not find a copy of "Obadiah" but I think Punch will do as well. I wish I could get the back numbers with Mrs. Cander illustrated [sic]. By the way I have met here the drollest genius of a professor from way down east who entertained us one evening at Mr. Colby's with an original criticism on Fanny Forester's[199] style of writing. He has a great fancy for June Saxon and he says F. F. and Lamar Blanchard know how to write it. He is professor of belle letters and says he gives your stories to his boys to study, and furthermore if grave theologians would study them and talk in that style to their congregations they would have far more attentive audiences than they now have. He went with me to get Hoods [ ] Punch etc. and has some other books which I told him to get for you. He perfectly understands what you want and if I dared I would send you some of the books he mentioned. They cost a sight too.

I rather think he will write to you. If I see him again I mean to tell him to. He preached last Sunday and I have almost lost my heart.

Nemmy I wish I could say something to keep up your spirits. Make a desperate effort and get through with it as you have with other things. Though I am grateful for the confidence which inclines you to make me such a present yet I will not suffer myself to think anything evil can happen. You may depend upon tho' should the shield come to me *I should live for it*. Good bye. Anna M.

Source: American Baptist Historical Society, AJ 13, no. 500.

Mrs. Sarah L. Haven to Emily C. Judson, August 26, 1847—Boston

My dear Mrs. J.

Your tiny note dated Feb. 6th was long in reaching me, but it was most welcome and warmly prized. I thank you for your thoughtfulness, and shall much value the corsets that have taken two voyages on my account, and the note of the defacted [sic] one, which came with them. Did you think I could write ere this? Indeed I did not venture to until I had received a sort of permission, such as your

---

[198] This reference is to the impending birth of Emily Frances Judson, which took place on December 24, 1847. On August 17, 1847, Adoniram Judson wrote to Anna Maria about their return from Rangoon to Maulmain. He said: "There is an event in prospect, which fills me with the liveliest apprehensions and makes it exceedingly desirable, in my view, that we should be in Maulmain about the close of the year." Anna Maria did not receive this letter until November; Emily would have had to have written the news in May.

[199] Emily Chubbuck Judson as Fanny Forester. See vol. 1, "Cast of Characters" s.v. "Chubbuck, Emily" and "Forester, Fanny."

note afforded me. I know well the thousand claims superior to mine upon every moment of leisure you may have, and should most reluctantly intrude. The "long letter" you were kind enough to say you were anxious to write, I need hardly tell you, I should be exceedingly delighted to receive.

I am so happy, dear Mrs. J., that you and my Lizzie[200] love each other so well. Your affectionate expressions with regard to her have still more deeply endeared you to us. Lizzie expected to love you before she saw you, and since your arrival she has constantly written of enjoying you very much, and loving you dearly—she writes, that you meet your [ ] duties beautifully—May heaven ever smile upon your head and home!—

I wish you could be together quite consistently with duty. I know your society would be so much to my sister, and I feel that you too must enjoy hers.—It seems desolate for you to be at Rangoon[201]—so isolated—But you have a brave loving heart, and I doubt not enjoy a great deal with your husband and sweet children, besides having those peculiar consolations, which only those know who are called to make sacrifices for Christ's sake.

We grieved for you and Dr. J., that you should sustain so severe a loss so soon after your arrival.[202] I felt at first quite [ ] to the thought that your nice, pretty things were gone—I think if any people in this world desire comforts, missionaries do, and my will must be to shower them upon them. But God knows best and He orders each event.

Miss Anable[203] returns to Utica this week. She has been in Boston[204] this week in favorable season for forming acquaintances which might have been agreeable to her; our meetings have been thin, and we have had no social gatherings. We wish as much she was to be in Boston with us this autumn and winter. But perhaps the few, who now know her, would love her too well if she remained longer, and future parting would be all the harder. Every one [sic], who has seen her, thinks her a most interesting, sweet girl. I am glad you have so kind and lovely a friend.

The Colbys[205] are at Newton Centre. We regretted their leaving Boston, and I am sure I did their leaving that house so particularly associated with June 46.[206]—

---

[200] "Lizzie" was Mrs. Elizabeth Stevens, missionary to Maulmain, Burmah. Sarah Haven was a sister of Elizabeth Stevens Stevens.

[201] Emily and Adoniram, with Henry and Edward, moved to Rangoon in mid-February in hope that it would be a stepping-stone to move on to Ava. The Board of the American Baptist Missionary Union sent word that such a move would not be financially possible at that time; with that communication and for several other reasons, Emily, Adoniram, Edward, and Henry were in the process of moving back to Maulmain.

[202] On February 17, 1847, shortly after they left Maulmain for Rangoon, a fire in the mission compound at Maulmain destroyed two trunks of Adoniram and Emily's clothing and personal articles; much of the loss had been personal gifts of great sentimental value. In different letters the loss was estimated between seven hundred and a thousand rupees.

[203] See vol. 1, "Cast of Characters," s.v. "Anable, Miss Anna Maria."

[204] For more information on these medical treatments, see vol. 1, "Cast of Characters," s.v. "Anable, Anna Maria."

[205] See vol. 1, "Cast of Characters," s.v. "Colby, Gardner."

[206] Emily and Adoniram Judson stayed with the Colbys prior to their departure in July 1846 for Burmah.

Perhaps the country will be more favorable for Mrs. Colby's health, and for the training of the boys; but we miss them in our church, and I with many others, miss their pleasant society.

Mrs. Kilham was very much gratified with your message of love to her. She did not expect you would remember her so kindly—She was very ill last Spring, but is now quite well and interesting and lovable as ever.

My cousin Mary is making a very good minister's wife; almost too good we think, for she will not leave her husband and people to visit us half as often as we wish to see her. Her mother's home is with her.

My mother sends special love to you, and so does my sister Emma, whom I think you could love very much, if you knew her well indeed as very few do.

I am, my dear Mrs. J, yours very affectionately

Sarah L. Haven

Source: American Baptist Historical Society, AJ 16, no. 675.

Miss Cynthia Sheldon to Emily C. Judson, August 29, 1847[207]

Dear E. I am determined to send this off by morning mail. Anna M.[208] I suppose arrived in Troy[209] yesterday will come to Sch.[210] tomorrow and home Thursday with Jane[211] and Eugenia[212]—she was expected at home again—Brother Dan came on 11 o'clock last night stopt [sic] [ ] one train only. They all well in Troy.

Mr. Beebee[213] called yesterday to see if we had letters from you by the last steamer—he is very greedy—and says the extracts he took from your letter to Mrs. Jones[214] is lauded every where [sic] and he hopes you will rest assured that such communication is just what every body [sic] wants—the cause would be advanced

---

[207] This letter is an addendum to a letter dated August 22, 1847.

[208] See vol. 1, "Cast of Characters," s.v. "Anable, Miss Anna Maria."

[209] Miss Cynthia Sheldon had a brother, Fred Sheldon, who lived in Troy, New York, with his wife and family.

[210] Schenectady was the home of Miss Sheldon's sister, Urania Sheldon Nott, whose husband, the Reverend Doctor Eliphalet Nott, was the president of Union College in that city.

[211] See vol. 1, "Cast of Characters," s.v. "Kelly, Miss Jane."

[212] See vol. 1, "Cast of Characters," s.v. "Damaux, Eugenia."

[213] Alexander Beebee was trained as a lawyer, but after experiencing strong religious convictions after the death of his first child, he became active in a Baptist church near Skaneateles, New York. In 1824, he observed that the Baptist denomination had only a few credible newspapers in the United States, none of them being in New York. In 1825, he became the editor of the *Baptist Register*, and over the next thirty years, it became a strong foundation for the rapidly growing Baptist churches of Central New York. During the course of Emily's engagement to Adoniram, Mr. Beebee must have said something reflecting the religious wisdom or judgment strongly expressed by many about the marriage of Adoniram Judson and Emily Chubbuck. Many of Emily's letters reflect the antagonism she felt for him. In July 1849, she wrote him a confrontational letter about something he had said. Morven Jones and Miss Sheldon, through continued efforts, did bring about a truce. Morven said that Emily had "no better supporter" than Mr. Beebee.

[214] See vol. 1, "Cast of Characters," s.v. "Jones, Morven and Mary."

ten fold if our Missionaries understood giving out such details—Eld. Bennett thinks you the strongest woman out—All eyes and hearts he says are turned towards your movement in Rangoon—he has strong confidence the Dr. will get to Ava—and that the Lord will bless him there—All deplore your loss by fire[215]—I fear you will almost suffer before things get there—Anna M. advised waiting for the missionaries—Mr. Abbott[216] going the overland route disappointed us—and we now wait for the sailing of Mr. Danforth and Stoddard in October—I wait for Anna M.'s return to apply rightly the $60 which I have considered yours since the fire—I *had not* sent it to Mr. Bennett for the scholars—Courtland[217] is to return very soon and study law here—we need him and his heart is quite set on that proffesion [sic]—Henry[218] is to come for good next week—he found a church constitution and they have now secured an excellent minister, his whole heart is in the work—William and Olivia[219] keep house very snugly. The boys board with them— Isabella Williams has been sick since May. She is evidently sinking to her grave—

The Bennett's have made their visit to Schenectady—Homer very glad to get back—I do wish you could see our bright house—even the basement looks new— shall I send you some mixed paint for you to cover the [ ] oil[220] in your Walled Mansion—Mrs. Brown from Assam called here recently—she told of Mr. Brown making the first [ ]—and that it now is much sought for among the natives—she is a darling woman—we concocted a fine plan to have a first rate school established

[215] On February 17, 1847, shortly after they left Maulmain for Rangoon, a fire in the mission compound at Maulmain destroyed two trunks of Adoniram and Emily's clothing and personal articles; much of the loss had been personal gifts of great sentimental value. In different letters the loss was estimated between seven hundred and a thousand rupees.

[216] See vol. 1, "Cast of Characters," s.v. "Abbott, The Reverend Elisha."

[217] Courtland Anable was a younger brother of Anna Maria Anable. He held several positions over the years, and he studied at Hamilton College while he boarded for a time with Emily's parents. In 1853, he returned to Philadelphia where he preached his first sermon at the Eleventh Baptist Church. He was "Uncle Court" to Emily Frances Judson. In 1880, Courtland Anable was listed in the Massachusetts Census as an ordained minister serving in a church.

[218] Henry Sheldon Anable was the oldest of the six children born to Joseph and Alma Sheldon Anable. He was born June 21, 1815. In August 1846, he was in the Milwaukee, Wisconsin, area and was thinking of settling there. In a September 27 letter, he said he might leave Utica to join William and Olivia in Sheboygan, Wisconsin. He was married to Rosanna Frick in Sheboygan, Wisconsin, on February 13, 1855, and died September 3, 1887, in Flushing, New York.

[219] Born on November 6, 1816, in Albany, New York, William Stewart Anable was the second child and the second son of Joseph and Alma Sheldon Anable. In an August 31, 1844 letter, Miss Cynthia Sheldon reported to Emily that William had returned home, having "doff'd his sailor garb for age." He married Olivia Williams on September 24, 1846, according to a letter written on September 27 by Anna Maria Anable. They moved to Sheboygan, Wisconsin, where Will opened a store. William died February 9, 1863 in Virginia, California.

[220] See Emily's letters of February 1847, in which she vividly described their new home in Rangoon, and how everything—walls, floors, and furniture—had been heavily oiled.

here for Missionaries' children—Mr. Bennett[221] writes in his last that if Mrs. B.[222] is not materially benefited by the change she was seeking in March—that there was no alternative to her coming home. Now don't you think with me that she would be just the one to look after Missionaries' children and their lot of ground here is large—and I do believe the Baptists in Utica would raise a fine building—The Board would apply and concentrate funds to make them very comfortable—her daughter would be fine material for operations—If nothing happened to take us away all the higher studies or any benefit from our school should be secured to the pupils gratis—could we not have some strong women growing up in this way—boys too cared for and provided some way with the same advantages—Utica being the site of operations—I do believe Mr. and Mrs. Bennett ought to come home next year and still be in the employ of the board—what would the Dr. think of this plan—If well—the Board would *take* a hint from him better than any other—and recall Mr. B. saving them all the anxiety about deciding for themselves—I do not believe in the obligation of Missionaries to remain there to the sacrifice of life— and when they went last it was thought probable Mr. B. would have a return of the liver complaint in a few years—but poor Mrs. B. has been the sufferer—they would rather die than have it appear they were recreant to the cause—Mr. B. wrote me from Maulmain in March—he regretted very much not seeing you and the Dr. there—They need advice—encouraging—a door of hope opened to them in some way—a word from the Dr. and you to them would do great good—Anna M. and Ellen are doing finely—Mary[223] is coming next term to school—Elsina[224] is married in Homer—that is very well—Sarah is doing finely—Jane Hawley[225] has passed the summer in Wisconsin—Horace has now gone for her—we have Cousin Ann[226]

---

[221] Cephas Bennett arrived in Burmah in January 1830; his wife was Stella Bennett. Mr. Bennett remained the superintendent of the Baptist Press there for more than fifty years. He worked with Adoniram Judson on the printing of the Bible into Burmese and Karen. From the Utica area, the Bennetts sent their children back, and the girls were educated at the Utica Female Academy. The girls included Elsina (April 1828), Mary (November 1829) Ann (August 1833), Ellen (June 1835), and Sarah (June1837).

[222] Stella Bennett was the wife of Cephas Bennett; they arrived in Burmah in January 1830. Mr. Bennett remained the superintendent of the Baptist Press there for more than fifty years. From the Utica area, they sent their children back, and the girls were educated at the Utica Female Academy. The girls included Elsina (April 1828), Mary (November 1829) Ann (August 1833), Ellen (June 1835) and Sarah (June 1837).

[223] These are all daughters of Cephas and Stella Bennett, missionaries to Burmah.

[224] Elsina Bennett, born in April 1828, was the daughter of Cephas and Stella Bennett, missionaries to Burmah. Elsina was a student at the Utica Female Academy.

[225] Jane Sheldon Hawley was the daughter of John Sheldon and was a niece of Miss Cynthia Sheldon, Mrs. Urania Sheldon Nott, and Mrs. Alma Shelton Anable. She married Horace H. Hawley in 1841. Miss Sheldon was leaving for Wisconsin where the wedding took place, and Emily wrote of this on May 7, 1841. Horace H. Hawley worked in the publishing business and was instrumental in helping Emily with the publication of her earlier books as well as giving her guidance as she struggled with publishers, copyright issues, and other matters relating to publication.

[226] Ann Sheldon was a younger cousin of Miss Cynthia Sheldon, Mrs. Alma Sheldon Anable, and Mrs. Urania Sheldon Nott. She married Charles Gratiot, the son of a prominent army officer and engineer who opened the port of St. Louis. Because Charles and Ann Gratiot often lived with the Sheldon-Anable families, both at Utica and in Philadelphia after 1848, they were often mentioned in the correspondence. They had six children, one of whom was born very close to the birth of Emily Frances Judson. The letters reveal how Ann coped in her husband's absence when he went west during the gold rush to seek his fortune.

and the children here—Mr. Gratiot[227] occasionally—they have delightful rooms by connecting Henry's room with Anna M. Music room—nicely furnished—nursery up stairs—The piano is in the library—Mr. Gratiot really lives religion—only he has not yet put on Christ.[228]—Mr. Corey[229] has gone to New York for a short trip—not very well—Louisa Marble[230] was with us till June—went home at that time to see Fanny married to a young Episcopal Clergyman settled at Waterville—Louisa called here yesterday on her way there—she wrote a pretty historical story of the Wallensen [sic] which I gave to Mr. Gillette[231] for the Publication Society[232] in June—have not yet heard from it—hope it will come out—Louisa is greatly attracted to you.—

Mary Colgate[233] spent Thursday Morn'g here on her way to Niagara—she is greatly improved—Joan Louisa Campbell died on the 19th inst. at the residence of her husband's father in Buffalo—she had been sick a year.

It has not been in my power to go to Hamilton to see your dear Mother[234]—for I cannot leave father[235]—I hope your Mother and Catharine[236] will come here this fall—They were well at Commencement. Harriet[237] and Mary[238] have been well thus far or were the 15th—Mary was going the next day to spend some time with

---

[227] See vol. 1, "Cast of Characters," s.v. "Gratiot, Charles."

[228] In letters of the end of March 1847, Miss Sheldon and Anna Maria Anable both speak of a local revival in their Baptist church under the leadership of Mr. Corey and how many of their family lives were touched. The list included Fanny Anable and Cousin John Sheldon, and the comment was made that Mr. Gratiot "Cannot be far from the kingdom."

[229] See vol. 1, "Cast of Characters," s.v. "Corey, the Reverend D. G."

[230] In 1843, Miss Marble was a recent graduate of the Utica Female Seminary and wrote to Emily upon her return to Port Byron. In an 1848 letter to Emily, she was at the academy as a teacher and was fully involved there. According to a letter written by Sarah Hinckley in 1849, Miss Marble married and moved to New York City. In Emily's February 19, 1850 letter, she was referred to as "Lou Marble Wright." Then, in April 1851, Anna Maria mentioned that Louisa Marble Wright was now a widow, back living in Utica with her sister.

[231] Following several successful pastorates, the Reverend A. D. Gillette was the founding pastor of the flourishing Eleventh Baptist Church in Philadelphia in 1839. With his wife Hannah and several children (they would eventually have six), he graciously opened their home to Emily Chubbuck when she came to Philadelphia at the end of March 1845 for her health. The connection had been made through Miss Cynthia Sheldon, a family friend of Mr. Gillette and his parents. A prominent Baptist, Mr. Gillette journeyed to Boston in December 1845 to accompany Adoniram Judson to Philadelphia for meetings, and on Christmas Day, he introduced Dr. Judson to Emily Chubbuck with the hope that Fanny Forester could be persuaded to write the memoir of Sarah Hall Boardman Judson. A. D. Gillette and his wife Hannah remained valued and trusted friends, not only with Emily, but with the Sheldon and Anable families. He moved from Philadelphia to New York in 1852.

[232] This is the American Baptist Publication Society, the board of which Mr. Gillette was a member.

[233] Mary Colgate was the name of both the wife and the daughter of William Colgate, the prominent industrialist and manufacturer. This Mary Colgate mentioned is likely the daughter. On her trips back and forth from Utica to Philadelphia, Emily visited and stayed overnight with the William Colgate family in New York. There are letters in the correspondence from William Colgate, his wife Mary Gilbert Colgate, his son James Colgate, and his daughter-in-law, Mrs. Ellen Hoyt Colgate.

[234] Emily's mother. See vol. 1, "Cast of Characters," s.v. "Chubbuck, Lavinia Richards."

[235] See vol. 1, "Cast of Characters," s.v. "Sheldon, Deacon Asa."

[236] See vol. 1, "Cast of Characters," s.v. "Chubbuck, Miss Sarah Catharine."

[237] See vol. 1, "Cast of Characters," s.v. "Anable, Harriet."

[238] See vol. 1, "Cast of Characters," s.v. "Anable, Miss Mary Juliet."

Harriet—Mary Adams[239] was expected in the country too—they are probably all together now—they are looking forward to June—all design concerning them.

Heaven bless you my girl—bless your husband—and bless your united labors. Dear father and Mrs. Anable[240] send heartfelt greetings—the big tears roll down their cheeks when a letter comes from you—will you write often and every thing [*sic*]—I should have sent this before—only I waited to know when we could forward a box. Kiss the children[241] for me—tell them Aunt C. expects to see them when the Mission School is started.

Ever your attached friend

C. Sheldon

Source: American Baptist Historical Society, AJ 20, no. 1004.

---

[239] Mary Adams was related to the Utica Female Academy. Her letter to Emily in October 1845 was almost a whimsical piece of fantasy with literary pretensions. It reflected a fairly close relationship. A second letter in December 1845 was similar. The letters were written from New Orleans, and she spoke of Hatty Anable as being near to her. On January 29, 1849, Anna Maria Anable wrote, "Hatty says Mary Adams is going to marry Gardner Green of Norwich,—a very fine young man, of invention, fortune, piety and all that Mary's heart was sighed for." On July 8, 1850, Mrs. Urania Sheldon Nott spoke of attending this wedding in New York.

[240] See vol. 1, "Cast of Characters," s.v. "Anable, Mrs. Alma Sheldon."

[241] Henry and Edward Judson were the sons of Adoniram Judson and Sarah Hall Boardman Judson. They lived in Maulmain with Emily and Adoniram Judson.

LETTERS

—◆—

SEPTEMBER–DECEMBER 1847

Doctor Edward Bright Jr.[1] to Emily C. Judson, September 1, 1847—Boston

My dear Mrs. Judson:—

I cannot allow the Steamer of the day to depart without acknowledging the receipt of your most welcome favor of the 19th April. I intended to give you a long letter in return, but it has been utterly impracticable for me to do so—owing to the unusual pressures of official duties. Such a letter shall be forthcoming, however. In the mean time [*sic*] I wish to bespeak for our little *Macedonian* as many short articles descriptive of the scenes around you as you can consistently write. The *Macedonian* has a circulation of about 20,000, and we intend to double the number and to make it if possible a *highly effective* agent in opening the eyes, hearts and purses of the *masses* of our people to the claims of the missionary enterprise. It is in no sense the rival of the Magazine, nor do I ask for it any of the *official* communications which belong to my associate the foreign Secretary. But thro' the *Macedonian* you can reach the hearts of thousands by opening scenes which you would not think, perhaps, of describing in the Magazine. Our missionary periodicals must be sustained, and our missionaries can do more for them than *all* others. Your letters have been eagerly sought for publication, and, perhaps, you will think some of your friends have too readily yielded to the importunity of our news-paper editors. They intended well, however, and the letters will do good.

Give me the pleasure of receiving a letter or article for the *Macedonian*[2]—*very soon*, and *very often*. Dr. Wayland[3] is writing a series of short Missionary Sermons for it, and with the help of the Missionaries—it will do a good and great work.

We are now living in Roxbury—a very pleasant place—as you will remember. Mrs. B. and our four children are well. I am doing what I can to *systematize* and invigorate the *home works* of missions. We hope it is becoming the *fixed* purpose of our people to do more for the cause.

---

[1] Upon her return to America in 1851, Emily Judson was to have a very close relationship with Dr. Edward Bright, the corresponding secretary of the American Baptist Missionary Union. They had known one another previously in New York, as he worked at the time of Adoniram and Emily's marriage with the *Baptist Register*, a prominent regional newsletter. Prior to working as a publisher, he had been, in 1838, the founding pastor of the Bleecker Street Baptist Church in Utica. He was appointed corresponding secretary the end of May 1846 just prior to Adoniram and Emily leaving Boston for Burmah. Upon Emily's return from Burmah in October of 1851, Adoniram and Elnathan went to live with Dr. and Mrs. Bright for a year. Dr. Bright was to help Emily with many of her business affairs; he carried on the publishing details of the Judson Memoir because of a serious illness in Dr. Wayland's family. He, with Dr. Edward Granger, was to be the executor of the estate of Emily Chubbuck Judson.

[2] This will be the first of a constant stream of requests from Dr. Bright for material for the *Macedonian*. At times the needs of the magazine seemed to Emily to be insatiable.

[3] Dr. Francis Wayland was the president of Brown University in Providence, Rhode Island. A prominent Baptist leader and active in denominational activities, he was a proponent of missions. In 1851, upon Emily's return from Burmah, Dr. Wayland was asked to write the definitive memoir of Adoniram Judson. Beginning in December that year, Emily moved to Providence to work with him on the project; she was there until June and then returned frequently over the next year before it was finally published in September 1853. A warm friendship developed between Dr. Wayland and Emily.

We have all watched with intense interest for tidings from Rangoon since the Doctor's removal there. Multitudes have called and are calling daily in prayer to God—in his and your behalf. May the blessing of Christ our Savior be with you for ever [sic]. But I must stop—or this letter will fail to go. Remember me and Mrs. B. to Dr. J.—and be assured of our undiminished interest in all that concerns your persons and labors.

In great haste.

Yours most cordially

Edw. Bright Jr.

Source: American Baptist Historical Society, AJ 14, no. 553.

Mrs. Sarah Colby[4] to Emily C. Judson, September 1, 1847—Danvers

My Dear Mrs. Judson

If in consequence of my suffering your very welcome letters to remain so long unanswered, I fail to convince you of the high value I attach to it. I hope I shall not fail in assuring you of the increased love, and interest I feel for you by every communication from you to whomsoever addressed which come under my eye—The great amount of labors you accomplish fills me with admiration at the wonderful application and perseverance of your [ ]—While passing through scenes which almost every other person would feel were preparatory to usefulness, and quite sufficient to occupy thought, *you* have given to the world, under the title of *Alderbrook*,[5] your republished works, and have by this means enabled all who had not before known what was the character of your writings, to perceive that the brevity of thought and expression, the graphic delineation of truth and moral principle of Fanny Forester,[6] and by no means unworthy the bosom friend, and companion of our venerated Judson—and the letters you have written so full of interest, and so well calculated to keep alive the interest in yourself, and the cause in which you are engaged—the life of Mrs. Judson, which you tell us you have completed,[7] and which we are looking for with pleasing anticipations—all performed in the midst of trial by sea, and trial by wind, a foreign language, and foreign and barbarous [ ] to contend with—Husband and children to care for.

---

[4] Sarah Colby was the mother of Gardner Colby.

[5] *Alderbrook* was a collection of Fanny Forester's stories, poems, and sketches and was a sequel to *Trippings in Author-land*. The first edition came out in December 1846, and in April, a second edition was published.

[6] Emily Chubbuck wrote under the *nom de plume* Fanny Forester. Asked about it once, she said, "Would anyone buy a book written by Emily E. Chubbuck?"

[7] Emily was commissioned to write the memoir of Sarah Hall Boardman Judson.

Unpacking and [ ] packing—Moving,[8] unpacking and [ ]—all frame the uncommon ability you possess—And when I consider the view your present elevation enables you to take of the wants, and more, of the world, the requirement of God, and the glories of the better land, I feel assured that the talent which has shone with so much lustre [sic] under different circumstances—will hereafter achieve more splendid results—I have sometimes thought, when I have seen with what avidity every thing [sic] you have written [ ] seized upon by Editors and that had your motive for going to Burmah been none other than ambition for literary fame, you could not have chosen a more direct way to secure that object—My prayer is that your heart and soul may be entirely consecrated to God and your precious gifts so richly cultivated, may be employed with all its powers in promoting the glory of God, and the good of souls—If you recollect my saying to you that I felt an uncommon congeniality of soul with you, and regretted my want of education, or cultivation if you please—you will understand me when I tell you that when I read in one of your letters to Miss Anable[9] this clause—"O I can never be a [ ] Missionary, but I hope to do some good," my heart leaped in sympathy with the sentiment—and I have thought of it many times since—I do hope our heavenly Father is not displeased with a cheerful performance of duty, though it sometimes assumes the appearance of levity, in the minds of more sober labourers [sic] in the same field.—I should have written to you long before but residing most of the time in Danvers with my daughter prevents my knowing when a ship is to sail—and my letters not being worth the postage overland, I have deferred it—I wish I had something to tell you of what I have accomplished, but *I* live in the same dull routine of *nothings*—enjoying the blessings of providence and the rich provisions of gospel privileges, without realizing any improvement, or feeling satisfied with the performance a single duty—My health is generally excellent and I often tremble when I think, that where much is given much is required—Son Gardner[10] has purchased a small farm in Newton, near the Institution,[11] where he is now building a

---

[8] Emily and Adoniram Judson landed in Maulmain on November 30, 1846; in mid-February 1847, they moved to Rangoon in the hope that it would be a stepping-stone to Ava.

[9] Anna Maria Anable was the niece of the Misses Urania and Cynthia Sheldon and the daughter of Joseph and Alma Sheldon Anable. Emily first met Anna Maria in fall 1840 when she went as a student to the Utica Female Academy; both Emily and Anna Maria became members of the faculty there. In these years, Anna Maria became Emily's dearest friend, and the extensive correspondence between the two reflects sensitive, flirtatious spirits and a deep intimacy. Emily was "Nemmy" to Anna Maria's "Ninny." In 1848, Anna Maria Anable, with the help of her extended family, moved to Philadelphia and started the Misses Anable's School in Philadelphia. At Emily's death in 1854, Anna Maria was given guardianship of Emily Frances Judson, daughter of Emily and Adoniram Judson.

[10] A prominent businessman, Gardner Colby and his family lived in Pemberton Square in Boston before moving "to the country," Newton Centre, Massachusetts. Mr. Colby was a member of the Board of the American Baptist Missionary Union and an avid supporter of the missionary movement. In a letter after they sailed from Boston to Burmah, Emily mentions the extravagant hospitality extended to them in early July as they waited for the *Faneuil Hall* to embark. Adoniram and Emily stayed with the Colby family frequently.

[11] Newton Theological School was founded in 1825 for the education of Baptist clergy. Mr. Colby was on the board of the school.

home—Miss Anable has probably told you of her visit to Boston and the cause of it[12] and its results—My Son's removal from Boston has broken up my home there, where I prefer to be, and I am more decidedly making it home with my daughter, who with her excellent husband, do all in their power to promote my happiness— the people are kind and have as much intelligence as is usually found in country churches—Piety has been at a low ebb among them, notwithstanding the faithful preaching of Wm Eaton, who had for months past been feeling much for Xian [*sic*] here—God has appeared and by the hand of an incendiary has burned up their Holy and beautiful house where their fathers worshiped not sparing any vestige to show that it had been—it was a neat pretty house, and *all paid for*—but there was *no insurance*—It will cost much money, labour [*sic*] and pain, to erect another house equally adapted to the place—the people were almost *at their wits* end, but are now *rallying*, and have become much interested in collecting together means, to erect a new house—But what is this fire and loss of property, compared with the fire at Maulmain[13]—It grieves me to think you lost so many of friendship's momen- toes [*sic*]—your kindness in writing however is assurance that you have not needed such things to keep in remembrance those who love you in your native land.

Source: American Baptist Historical Society, AJ 15, no. 598.

Anna Maria Anable to Emily C. Judson, September 26, 1847—Utica

Dear Emily

I was very much disappointed in not receiving a letter from you this last month. In your present situation I shall of course be doubly anxious about you, but I trust darling that all will go well with you. I am very much troubled that the exe- cution of the commission you gave me is necessarily so long delayed. Your letter did not arrive till last month and there is no vessel sailing for Calcutta till next month. I hope however that in a fortnight the things will be on their way. According to your expectations the little stranger[14] will have come to light before you can receive this letter even—I pity the little thing if it is depending on supplies from

---

[12] Anna Maria Anable spent summer 1847 in Boston, Massachusetts, taking some very painful medical treatments to correct a skeletal condition with her shoulder. "Did I tell you I was coming here and for why? I am now sitting in a pair of excruciating steel corsets and every morning I go to a cross old bone setter here and take a medicated bath and get my shoulder shampooed. Tho' not a very pleasant operation—particularly the wearing the corsets (they cause me constant pain)—yet I am [ ] confident about being benefited and ultimately cured. I have already grown three quarters of an inch in a fortnight, from the straightening of my spine. I have been here now about three weeks." On April 26, 1848 she wrote: "My shoulder is quite strong and my shape is very much improved."

[13] On February 17, 1847, shortly after they left Maulmain for Rangoon, a fire in the mission compound at Maulmain destroyed two trunks of Adoniram and Emily's clothing and personal articles; much of the loss had been personal gifts of great sentimental value. In different letters the loss was estimated between seven hundred and a thousand rupees.

[14] The reference is to the impending birth of Emily Frances Judson, who was born on December 24, 1847.

America for its wardrobe. Fortunately infancy is delightfully indifferent as to its apparel. A baby makes a fuss only when its stomach is empty. The what withal it shall eat is more important to it than the where withal it shall be clothed. That makes me think Nemmy[15]—what a ruinous child that will be to you in the way of pies and cakes, by and bye. It is well I have put up the pie-pans and the cookery book. Poor little thing! I am afraid it will suffer if you continue to think that "Whisky saltish [sic]" was the ingredient wanting in your cake. Ah! Nemmy I wish I was there [sic] to cook up some nice little little [sic] dishes for you. I always think of you when we have anything extra, and if wishing were of any use you would have had many a batch of pies and cakes this Summer.

The last I wrote you I was in the hurry of leaving Boston. I spent two or three days in Troy.[16] Fanny's[17] little Henry Judson is certainly the most astonishing child I ever saw. He is only twenty months old and already his powers are so versatile that he entertains the whole family and all the visitors with his incessant pranks. Buckingham grows a better and better man every year. Did I tell you that he had become pious. Fred and Anna are keeping home in very pretty style. I spent a couple of days also with Sam'l and Sarah at Westerlo.[18] They have a sweet little boy nine months old,[19] and Sam is doing finely on his farm. I stopped over one night in Schenectady. The Dr.[20] is in miserable health just at present tho we hope he will be better. He suffers very much from rheumatism, and Aunt U.[21] is constantly occupied with him. On coming home I found the house all in such beautiful trim that I hardly knew it. It was all newly painted and papered and carpeted, and it has made such a difference that I assure you I am proud to welcome my friends to my nice

---

[15] "Nem" or "Nemmy" was a name of endearment given to Emily by a small group of her intimate friends at the Utica Female Academy. Anna Maria Anable was "Ninny."

[16] Fred and Martha Sheldon, a brother of Miss Cynthia Sheldon, Mrs. Urania Sheldon Nott, and Alma Sheldon Anable, lived in Troy, New York.

[17] Fanny Buckingham was the daughter of Fred and Martha Sheldon. She was a niece to Miss Cynthia Sheldon and a cousin to Anna Maria Anable. She was married to Mr. Buckingham, the second in command of the ill-fated steamship *Swallow*, which went down on the river with the loss of a significant number of passengers. (See the letter of Miss Cynthia Sheldon to Emily E. Chubbuck dated April 11, 1845.) Fanny Buckingham was mentioned in Anna Maria's letters of December 28 and 29, 1847. She had a young son Judson, and she was visiting Anna Maria.

[18] Samuel Low Anable was born November 28, 1828. he was the fifth child, third son of Joseph Hubbell Anable and Alma Sheldon Anable. He was to marry Sarah Babcock on September 24, 1844. In a September 26, 1847 Anna Maria Anable said that she had stopped to see Samuel and Sarah at their farm in Westerlo, New York.

[19] William J. Anable was born October 27, 1846.

[20] The Reverend Doctor Eliphalet Nott was the president of Union College in Schenectady, New York. An ordained Presbyterian minister, he was married to Urania Sheldon Nott, the sister of Miss Cynthia Sheldon and Mrs. Alma Anable and the aunt of Anna Maria Anable.

[21] Urania Sheldon had been the literary principal of the Utica Female Academy in fall 1840 when Emily Chubbuck came to study there. Emily was able to afford this wonderful education through the generous offer of Miss Sheldon and her sister Cynthia, the executive and financial head of the academy, to defer tuition. Urania Sheldon left in late summer 1842 upon her marriage to the Reverend Doctor Eliphalet Nott, the president of Union College in Schenectady, New York. Because of the distance separating them, Emily's relationship with Urania Sheldon Nott did not develop the intimacy that grew between Emily and Miss Cynthia Sheldon. Urania Sheldon Nott remained a mentor, advisor, and friend to Emily in the years of her writing, her missionary endeavors, and upon her return to America in 1851. She was also the aunt of Anna Maria Anable.

home.[22] Courtland [23]came in a few days after my return and has entered Mr. Spencer's law office. While he continues his studies he will take one or two classes in the school. Henry[24] and Mr. Gratiot[25] are both here to day (Sunday) and it seems quite like old times.

Eugenia Damaux[26] has been spending the last fortnight here. She has suffered almost death during the past year from an internal scrofulous humour [sic] which is connected with her disease of the eyes also. Now that she knows what is the matter she is in a way to be cured and her health at present is better than it has been for five years. Every new trial for poor Eugenia has the effect of softening her character and making her more and more lovely.

Matilda Berthoud[27] has made me a visit also since my return, and last week the Lincoln's[28] came on to see "our folks." Mr. Hague of Boston happened to be in town at the same time and last Saturday week we made up a delightful party for Trenton. The Bostonians began to think "I guess" that there is another city besides Boston and that is—Utica. Next Tuesday eve'g we are going to have a grand wedding here and who do you think are to be married? Brayton and Sarah Mills. Every body [sic] is delighted with it—on both sides of the house and all the city particularly.

Sarah is twenty-two and Brayton is twenty nine, but you know he looks all of thirty five and she is so lovely that I think he has made a great bargain as we say

[22] See Miss Cynthia Sheldon's letter of August 22, 1847, for all of the work being done at the Utica Female Academy in preparation for the opening of the term.

[23] Courtland Anable was a younger brother of Anna Maria Anable. He held several positions over the years, and he studied at Hamilton College while he boarded for a time with Emily's parents. In 1853, he returned to Philadelphia where he preached his first sermon at the Eleventh Baptist Church. He was "Uncle Court" to Emily Frances Judson. In 1880, Courtland Anable was listed in the Massachusetts Census as an ordained minister serving in a church.

[24] Henry Sheldon Anable was the oldest of the six children born to Joseph and Alma Sheldon Anable. He was born June 21, 1815. In August 1846, he was in the Milwaukee, Wisconsin, area and was thinking of settling there. In a September 27 letter, he said he might leave Utica to join William and Olivia in Sheboygan, Wisconsin. He was married to Rosanna Frick in Sheboygan, Wisconsin, on February 13, 1855, and died September 3, 1887, in Flushing, New York.

[25] Charles Gratiot grew up in St Louis, where his father was an army engineer responsible for developing the Port of St. Louis. He married Ann Sheldon, who was a cousin of Miss Cynthia Sheldon, Mrs. Urania Sheldon Nott, and Alma Sheldon Anable. Together, Charles and Ann Gratiot had six children. Because they often lived with the Sheldon family, their letters contain a great deal of him. Letters in 1847 speak of his religious awakening; those of 1849 speak of his leaving for the California gold fields. In 1853, Charles Gratiot applied for a grant of 400 acres in Illinois, and he already owned 148 acres.

[26] Eugenia Damaux was part of Emily's intimate circle of friends at the Utica Female Academy. Living in New York City, Eugenia suffered from some kind of eye problem that at times made life difficult for her; this was a matter of comment in many of the letters exchanged between the girls themselves and with Miss Cynthia Sheldon. In 1848, Eugenia was in New York living "at Mrs. Brown's—the same warm-hearted French girl as ever." In 1849, she married Johnny Edmonds, described as rich and pious, and they lived in Utica.

[27] Matilda was a friend of Anna Maria Anable and probably of Emily as well, for Anna Maria's and Miss Sheldon's letters refer to her. In one letter, Miss Sheldon tells how Anna Maria had gone to visit Matilda, and while there, Matilda's brother had taken Anna Maria for a buggy ride. Somehow the horse got frightened, and Anna Maria and her host were taken on a wild ride, which they survived by the heroic actions of the brother, the undaunted courage of Anna Maria, and the providence of God. In a letter shortly after their move to Philadelphia in 1848, Miss Sheldon says that Matilda is everything to them. She is perfectly happy being with them, and she adds that she is a "host in French." When Henry and Edward went to Hamilton to live with Emily's parents and sister, Matilda was one of the individuals considered to be employed to help with work around the house and with the care of the family.

here. The young married Society here is going to be charming. Brayton will live here—Dr.'s Bagg and Potter will soon be married and I presume that Mary Spencer[29] and Seward will make a match. I have not yet called on Chas [ ] wife but they say she is a lovely woman. They all seem so delighted to have me back that I am become quite charmed with the idea of being the pet old maid among them. Before I can do that however I shall have to get Augusta[30] married to Mr. Wolcott.

My figure, health and spirits have been very much improved this Summer.[31] Aunt U. thinks the benefit to the former is almost miraculous. If I go on improving till Spring I shall be quite smart enough to start for Burmah.[32] Ah! me. I am afraid I have done wrong to write so much about it. No I have n't [*sic*] tho' I could not help it at the time and should I see it now to be clearly my duty I trust I should not hesi-tate. I do not believe however that I shall ever get up such a sense of duty again—every letter I receive from you or Lydia[33] checks it a little. Aunt C.[34] had a note from Lydia this month and I had one last. She will turn out nice at last you

[28] A prominent Baptist, Mr. Joshua Lincoln was a member of the firm Gould, Randall and Lincoln, publishers. In 1847, while in Boston for her medical treatments, Anna Maria Anable stayed with the Lincoln family. Mr. Lincoln was active in Massachusetts and national Baptist circles.

[29] On February 28, 1848, Anna Maria Anable wrote to Emily, saying: "Mary Spencer has just returned from Albany. It is said she is engaged to John James, a handsome young widower with three children, and two or three hundred thousand $'s."

[30] Augusta Crafts is mentioned frequently in the letters written from the Utica Female Academy. A number of references chron-icle her very strong opinions; many of these were spoken against N. P. Willis and Emily's relationship to him (Mrs. Crafts did not approve of either). In an April 30, 1845 letter Anna Maria Anable said, "The Dr. is not engaged nor isn't going to be to Mary Spencer I imagine, and tho' Mrs. Crafts intimated very strongly that there was *some one* he had his eye upon, he denied it to me strongly and scolded about Mrs. Crafts gossiping tongue."

[31] For more information on these medical treatments, see vol. 1, "Cast of Characters," s.v. "Anable, Anna Maria."

[32] For about a year and a half after Emily's marriage to Adoniram Judson, Anna Maria spoke of the possibility of having a call to missions and joining Adoniram and Emily in Burmah. On March 31, 1847, Sarah Bell Wheeler said that Anna Maria was a devoted Christian, and she thought that one day she would go to Burmah. She obviously put a lot of prayer and thought into the matter. Her painful medical treatments in summer 1847 were likely intended to improve her general health. See her letter of June 19, 1847. In the end, in summer 1848, she decided that her call was to remain a teacher, and Anna Maria moved to Philadelphia. With her family, she opened the Misses Anable's School. She remained there until her death. She raised Emily Frances Judson here after the death of Emily Judson.

[33] Lydia Lillybridge was one of Emily's closest friends at the Utica Female Academy. When Emily made the decision to go to Burmah as the wife of Adoniram Judson and as a missionary, Lydia wanted to go with them. Emily spoke to Adoniram Judson of Lydia's extraordinary abilities, and Adoniram advocated her appointment before Dr. Solomon Peck and the Board of the American Baptist Missionary Union. Lydia was commissioned to go with them, in spite of the fact that she remained single. Always independent, outspoken, and unafraid to cause ripples in the missionary community, Lydia served on the mission field for twenty-eight years. She married missionary Thomas Simons in May 1851. See the timeline on the life and service of Lydia Lillybridge Simons in vol. 1.

[34] Miss Cynthia Sheldon was in charge of the administrative and financial departments of the Utica Female Academy. Miss Sheldon and her sister Urania, who was literary principal, gave Emily Chubbuck a place at the academy in October 1840. They had deferred any cost to a future time when Emily could afford to reimburse them. Upon Miss Urania Sheldon's marriage in the late summer 1842 to the Reverend Doctor Eliphalet Nott, the president of Union College, and her subsequent move to Schenectady, Miss Cynthia Sheldon assumed a larger leadership role at the academy. Active and well-known in Baptist circles, Miss Cynthia was to become an important mentor, advisor, and friend to Emily until the time of Emily's death in 1854. She was the aunt of Emily's best friend, Anna Maria Anable, and was addressed by most as "Aunt Cynthia." In 1848, Miss Sheldon moved to Philadelphia to help Miss Anable with the startup of the Misses Anable's School.

may depend upon it. It seems Mr. Ingalls[35] has made an unsuccessful visit to Maulmain.[36] Lydia is made of stern stuff I tell you and her pride is up about being married.[37] She means to have it understood that she is a missionary in good earnest.

Did you know that Jones made any overtures to her while in Boston? I suspect he did. He and his wife with a Miss Morse—an excellent woman, whom you would love sailed the 6th of this month. Since I have been absent brother Beebee[38] has worked on the feelings of Aunt C.[39] and Mary Jones[40] till they let him publish your letters to them.[41] They were excellent letters but still I thought it was proper to put a stop to that sort of fun. Kiss good night darling and

Written along the right margin of page 4: "let me hear from you every month. Anna M."

[35] Lovel Ingalls was born August 21, 1808, in Worcester, New York. He was ordained October 2, 1834 in Boston, New York, and graduated from the Hamilton Literary and Theological Institute in 1837. In September 1834, he married Marcia Dawes of Cummington, Massachusetts; Miss Dawes had been educated at Cummington Academy. They first sailed for Burmah in 1835, arriving at Amherst February 20, 1836. They were stationed at Mergui and then Maulmain in May 1845; Marcia Dawes Ingalls died on November 9, 1845, at Maulmain. Lovel and Marcia Ingalls were the parents of three children. Mr. Ingalls went to Akyab in 1846 and returned to the United States beginning May 1850. He went back to Burmah in December 1851. His second wife was Marilla Amelia Baker, and they married December 23, 1850 at Troy, New York. Mr. Ingalls died at sea on March 14, 1856.

[36] Lovel Ingalls sought to persuade Lydia to teach at Arracan, where he was a missionary. There was also a suggestion of marriage to him. See Lydia's letters dated April 23 and May 21, 1847.

[37] Suggestions had been made about Lydia marrying Elisha Abbott and then Lovel Ingalls. Lydia Lillybridge finally married Thomas Simons, also a missionary to Burmah, in May 1851, after Emily returned home.

[38] Alexander Beebee was trained as a lawyer, but after experiencing strong religious convictions after the death of his first child, he became active in a Baptist church near Skaneateles, New York. In 1824, he observed that the Baptist denomination had only a few credible newspapers in the United States, none of them being in New York. In 1825, he became the editor of the *Baptist Register*, and over the next thirty years, it became a strong foundation for the rapidly growing Baptist churches of Central New York. During the course of Emily's engagement to Adoniram, Mr. Beebee must have said something reflecting the religious wisdom or judgment strongly expressed by many about the marriage of Adoniram Judson and Emily Chubbuck. Many of Emily's letters reflect the antagonism she felt for him. In July 1849, she wrote him a confrontational letter about something he had said. Morven Jones and Miss Sheldon, through continued efforts, did bring about a truce. Morven said that Emily had "no better supporter" than Mr. Beebee.

[39] See vol. 1, "Cast of Characters," s.v. "Sheldon, Miss Cynthia."

[40] Mary Jones was the wife of Morven Jones. They lived in the Utica area and were intimately familiar with Miss Cynthia Sheldon and the staff and student body of the Utica Female Academy. Mr. and Mrs. Jones, as well as Miss Sheldon, were members of the Bleecker Street Baptist Church where Mr. Corey was the pastor. In a December 1848 series of letters to Emily, Morven Jones described a terrible accident; a group from the church was standing on a bridge overlooking the Mohawk River, there to witness a baptism, and the bridge collapsed. At least one person died in that accident, and Mary Jones was severely injured.

[41] In a letter written August 29, 1847, Miss Sheldon said, "Mr. Beebee called yesterday to see if we had letters from you by the last steamer—he is very greedy—and says the extracts he took from your letter to Mrs. Jones is lauded every where and he hopes you will rest assured that such communication is just what every body [sic] wants—the cause would be advanced ten fold if our Missionaries understood giving out such details."

Written upside down along the top margin of page 1: "Have you heard of poor Neal's[42] death. Some two months since he died of inflammation of the brain. The Oct. Col.[43] Has just come out with your Angel's [ ] in it. 'Tis a beautiful story."

Source: American Baptist Historical Society, AJ 13, no. 499.

Anna Maria Anable to Emily C. Judson, September 27, 1847

I forgot to mention Nemmy[44] in my last note that among the things I left in Boston to be sent on to you—a doz. napkins and towels were hemmed by Martha Mrs. Lincoln's[45] servant girl. She is a good girl and devoted to the Missionarys. [*sic*] She would go in a moment as a servant in a Missionary's family if the climate would agree with her, and she would be invaluable to you. She does all of Mrs. Lincoln's work, washing, cooking and all, and is very fond of children. If you should really want such a girl I do not doubt but that you get one. Martha and I had many a talk about going to Burmah together.[46] Prof. Anderson[47] left a copy of the Civilization of the Inca's or History of Peru for you by Prescott. It is a delightful looking book and I am going to read it as we have it in the house. The little wardrobe comes on pretty well.[48] I could not keep it entirely a secret and get anything done—but only those know it who are at work on something and they all

[42] Joseph Neal was a prominent member of the literary establishment in Philadelphia and became a part of Emily Chubbuck's circle of friends when she was there. Neal was well known and respected as a writer and editor; one of his best known works was the *Charcoal Sketches*. In 1842, he founded the *Saturday Gazette*, a successful publication that contained a great deal of humorous satire. Anna Maria Anable frequently referred to Neal as a beau for Emily. Mr. Neal married Alice Bradley in 1846; he died in 1847.

[43] The *Columbian* magazine was published first by John Inman and then by Robert West. By early 1844, the *Columbian* was printing Emily's stories; this was before N. P. Willis and the *New Mirror* made her famous. With Graham, they readily agreed to pay her a top rate of five dollars a page for anything that she would write, and on several occasions, they tried to get Emily to write exclusively for them. They finally succeeded in this when she went to Burmah, for they obtained exclusive rights to all that she would send them at fifty dollars a story.

[44] Emily Chubbuck. See vol. 1, "Cast of Characters," s.v. "Nemmy, Nem, or Nemmy Petty (Nemmie Pettie)." Also the chapter "Names of Endearment."

[45] Mrs. Lincoln was the wife of Joshua Lincoln, a prominent Baptist layman and a partner in Gould, Kendall, and Lincoln. Anna Maria Anable boarded with Mr. and Mrs. Lincoln when she stayed in Boston in summer 1847 for medical treatments. Mrs. Lincoln was a strong supporter of missions. She was a sister of Charles Gould, who married Sarah Bell Wheeler of the Utica Female Academy.

[46] For more on Anna Maria Anable and a possible call to missionary service, see vol. 1, "Cast of Charcters," s.v. "Anable, Anna Maria."

[47] See Anna Maria Anable's letter of August 12, 1847, where she mentions the professor for the first time. Any hopes that this relationship might become serious were dashed when some months hence she was to receive a letter saying that the professor had spent some time in Providence, Rhode Island where he met someone, and they were to be married.

[48] This is a reference to the expected arrival of Adoniram and Emily's baby in December 1847. Emily Frances Judson was born on December 24. Anna Maria had been asked to put together a wardrobe for the baby.

keep quiet. As Cousin Ann is expecting to be confined in Dec.[49]—it is very natural for the other teachers to suppose we are making something for her. Olivia[50] also is expecting to make a pass in Dec.—what a momentous month it will be. Jul[51] and Sarah Bell[52]—Jane[53] and Fanny[54] are all that know it among the teachers. Aunt C.[55] is going to write so I'll good bye again—I have given up sending any messages to the Doctor. I see he has forgotten all about me. Do not you dear Nemmy forget me, but love me always as I love you.

Anna M.

Source: American Baptist Historical Society, AJ 13, no. 498.

[49] Ann Sheldon was a younger cousin of Miss Cynthia Sheldon, Mrs. Alma Sheldon Anable, and Mrs. Urania Sheldon Nott. She married Charles Gratiot, the son of a prominent army officer and engineer who opened the port of St. Louis. Because Charles and Ann Gratiot often lived with the Sheldon-Anable families, both at Utica and in Philadelphia after 1848, they were often mentioned in the correspondence. They had six children, one of whom was born very close to the birth of Emily Frances Judson. The letters reveal how Ann coped in her husband's absence when he went west during the gold rush to seek his fortune.

[50] Olivia was married to William Stewart Anable, the second child and second son of Joseph and Alma Sheldon Anable. See the letter written by Anna Maria Anable on September 27, 1846. They lived in Sheboygan, Wisconsin, where Will Anable was in charge of a retail store.

[51] Julia Look was a student of Emily's at the Utica Female Academy and later a fellow teacher. A November 22, 1845 letter from Anna Maria encouraged Emily to stay in Philadelphia for the winter for her health and remarked that Julia had the hardest part because she was teaching Emily's composition class, and the students kept asking for Emily. In a September, 1847 letter, she was listed as one of the teachers at the Utica Female Academy. On September 23, 1849, Anna Maria wrote that Julia and Albert B. Casswell were married and came to visit with her. In one 1849 letter Julia spoke of another teacher who was teaching "our composition class." On October 27, 1850, Anna Maria Anable noted that she had had a son. She was one of a small number of people who addressed Emily as "Emily" and as "Nemmy" in her letters.

[52] Sarah Bell Wheeler was a teacher at the Utica Female Academy, an intimate of Emily Chubbuck, and one of the few who addressed Emily as Nemmy. In a September 1847 letter, she was listed as one of the teachers at the Utica Female Academy. There are a number of letters from Sarah Bell before and after her marriage to Charles Gould of Boston in October 1850. There are several letters clustered in the year or two after Emily left for Burmah and a number at the time of her return to America. Emily stayed with Charles and Sarah Bell Gould in October 1851 when she arrived in Boston after the long sea voyage from Burmah and then England. She stayed there a number of times following that. In 1851, Anna Maria Anable wrote of Sarah Bell: "Sarah is grown so lovely in person as well as character that she must assert a blessed influence on all with whom she comes in contact."

[53] Miss Jane Kelly was Emily Chubbuck's friend at the Utica Female Academy, and then she became a teacher with Emily at that institution. Miss Kelly became the literary principal in 1844 with the retirement of Mr. and Mrs. James Nichols from that position. During a period of Miss Kelly's illness in 1844, Emily filled in the position for her. Then, in 1848, when Miss Cynthia Sheldon moved to Philadelphia to help start the Misses Anable's School, Miss Kelly became the "headmistress" of the academy and successfully brought it into the future, though not without some initial disparagement from the Sheldon-Anable families.

[54] Fanny Anable was one of nine children born to Joseph and Alma Anable and was a niece of Miss Cynthia Sheldon and Mrs. Urania Sheldon Nott. The correspondence indicates that in April 1845 she was away from home studying and taking music lessons. These spring letters indicate that she was in Philadelphia, working in the home of and with the family of the Reverend A. D. Gillette. See Miss Sheldon's letter to Emily of November 30, 1845, in which she spoke of all that Fanny was doing to improve herself in the field of music, but also her concern for Fanny's interest in the party life and the "vanitie" which surround her." A March 30, 1847 letter from Anna Maria Anable told of Fanny's conversion following her grandmother's death. In September 1847, she was listed as one of the teachers at the Utica Female Academy. Fanny became a teacher with her sisters in the Misses Anable's School in Philadelphia.

[55] See vol. 1, "Cast of Characters," s.v. "Sheldon, Miss Cynthia."

Emily C. Judson to Doctor Edward Bright,[56] October 1, 1847—Maulmain[57]

Sketches of Scenes in Rangoon

My Dear Mr. Bright,—

I do not know whether others find the sight of eastern scenery and eastern men awakens fresh interest in the narrative part of the word of God; but really I would come all the way from America for the sake of reading the Bible with my new eyes.

"I have seen all this before!" was a feeling that flashed upon me more frequently at Rangoon than here, producing a momentary confusion of intellect, that almost made me doubt if "I was I;" and then came the reflections, when!—how!—where! and finally it would creep into my mind; why I learned about it in Sabbath school when I was a little child. The effect was to annihilate time and bring the days of the Saviour very near; and the strength of the ideal presence has been by no means unprofitable to me.

But there were peculiarities in my situation which I think I have never yet mentioned. There I was in the identical town of which I had read with such eager curiosity when I was a little child away in the central part of New York; and which then seemed to me about as real as a city belonging to the moon. And stranger still, I was actually associated with one of the movers in scenes, the bare recital of which had, in years gone by, thrilled on my nerves with greater power than the wildest fiction. Oh, how memory, and imagination, and various strangely mingled emotions wrought together in my mind, when I looked upon all that remained of that in which the first words of life that Burmah ever heard were spoken more than a quarter of a century ago. And you will readily believe that the baptismal waters which were parted by the first convert from this nation were to my eye unlike any other waters in the world. I could not, if I were to attempt it, give you any thing like an insight into my feelings as I stood under the shadow of the cocoa and lime trees on the banks of that beautiful pool, and gazed down into the clear waters. How angels must have rejoiced over that penitent! the first link in a precious chain which is to reach down to the remotest times!

[56] Upon her return to America in 1851, Emily Judson had a close relationship with Dr. Edward Bright, the corresponding secretary of the American Baptist Missionary Union. They knew one another previously in New York, as he worked with the *Baptist Register*, a prominent regional newsletter, at the time of Adoniram and Emily's marriage. He was appointed corresponding secretary the end of May 1846, just prior to Adoniram and Emily's departure for Burmah. Dr. Bright helped Emily with many of her business affairs, he carried on the publishing details of the Judson memoir because of a serious illness in Dr. Wayland's family, and he and his wife took in Henry and Edward Judson for a year beginning in October 1851. He, with Dr. Edward Granger, was the executor of the estate of Emily Chubbuck Judson.

[57] Adoniram and Emily left Rangoon the end of August 1847 and were back in Maulmain on September 5. Since this was written in Maulmain, it is placed on October 1. This was probably an article for *The Macedonian*, the American Baptist mission magazine.

With a similar, dreaming, wondering feeling, as though walking among shadows and skeletons, I wandered about the grounds occupied by the old mission house. The building was torn down after the war, and the place is now covered by a garden of betel, so thickly planted that it was with great difficulty we could make our way among the long creepers which had climbed far above our heads. This self-same soil had once been trodden by feet elastic with youth and vigor, and bounding with such hopes as God grants to those who trust their all to Him.

"The house must have been somewhere here," remarked one of those beings of the past (not a shadow), close at my elbow; "that mound was the site of an old pagoda, and I leveled it as you see. But there is a nice well somewhere—that will be a sure mark."

A plainly dressed, sober faced, middle aged Burman had been regarding our movements for some time with curiosity, and he now ventured on a remark.

"I am looking for a good well from which I drank water many years ago," was the reply. "It was close by my house, and was bricked up."

"Your house!" repeated the man with astonishment.

"Yes, I lived here formerly."

The Burman turned his eye on the tall betel vines with a kind of wondering incredulity; and then back upon our faces.

"It was in the reign of *Bo-dan-parah* (the fourth king from the present reigning monarch)."

If, my dear Mr. Bright, some modern looking personage should walk into your parlor and announce himself as the "Wandering Jew," I doubt whether your smile and shrug would be quite so significant as were those of our new friend. There was the well, however, a proof against imposture; and the next moment it was evidently so regarded by the Burman, for he led the way to it without speaking. It was a large square well—the bricks all green with moss, or silvered by lichens—almost as good as new, and quite superior to anything in the neighborhood. It could not be looked upon without some emotion; and the man stood by us listening to all our remarks as though he hoped to hear something he might understand; and when we went away he followed a little, and then stood and gazed after us in wondering silence.

Another of our visiting places was the but half enclosed neglected English grave-yard. The first child of European parents born in Burmah had been buried there; and there was a strong tie between that mouldering little one and ourselves. Over the grave of *little Roger*[58] stood, but slightly broken, the rude brick monument which was built thirty-three years ago; and a tall azalea, very much like those which perfume the forests of our New York, had grown out from the base almost overshadowing it. It was strange to stand and muse beside that little grave, with

[58] Roger Williams Judson, born September 11, 1815 and died May 1816, was the son of Adoniram and Ann Hasseltine Judson..

one parent by my side, and the other so irrecoverably a being of the past. Oh, how she had wept there!—and how human she grew—she whom I had formerly only wondered at—while my own tears started in sympathy....

Most truly and sincerely yours,
Emily C. Judson

Source: A. C. Kendrick, *The Life and Letters of Mrs. Emily C. Judson*, 282–84.

Mrs. Elizabeth L. Stevens to Emily C. Judson, October 1, 1847[59]

My much loved Mrs. J.

Your dear little Edward's[60] high chair is here still; shall we send it over today or run the risk of its being thought of tomorrow morning?

I am anxious to know how you rested and whether you are relieved of that nervous distress yet.[61]

It is one year today since my angel boy's last Sabbath with us.[62] I carried him to Burmah worship as usual and on his coming home he lay down in the swing cot (your little Edward's) and when we took him up the sweet lamb's little head fell. When I mentioned it to Mrs. Osgood[63] she said "little Charley[64] lived but three days after his neck gave way and soon after his neck failed his back also gave way"—but my little Calvin sat up till Wednesday evening. On Thursday his very beautiful eyes, Mr. Judson will tell you they were so—closed forever on us here, as he quietly lay in that same dear cot. His illness and dear Charley's were almost precisely alike in progress, and their appearance in their paleness and emaciation so much the same. They will always be closely associated in my memory; and now

[59] This letter is undated. It is placed in October after Emily and Adoniram Judson had returned from Rangoon. They had intended to stay with Mr. and Mrs. Stevens until they could settle into their own place, so it would be natural that Edward's high chair was still with Mrs. Stevens.

[60] Edward Judson, born December 27, 1844, in Maulmain, Burmah, was the eighth child of Adoniram and Sarah Hall Boardman Judson and the fifth of their children to survive. Only a few months old when Sarah and Adoniram returned to America, Edward's life was saved by the nurture and care he received from Elizabeth Stevens. He loved Emily as the only "Mama" he had ever known and returned with her to the United States in October 1851. Edward, who was Eddy to his family, became a minister; he did mission work with the immigrants in New York City, and with the aid of the Rockefeller Family, he built the Judson Memorial Baptist Church in what is now Washington Park.

[61] A letter from Emily to her sister Catharine dated October 4, 1847, describes in some detail the events and the family illnesses that preceded their leaving Rangoon and then the illness that struck Emily on the voyage from Rangoon back to Maulmain.

[62] The missionary records of the American Baptist Missionary Union simply note in the file for Edward and Elizabeth Stevens that "two boys died Maulmain."

[63] This was the second wife of the Reverend Sewall Mason Osgood. His first wife, Elhira Brown Osgood, died in October 1837. He married Sarah Maria Willsey Thomas, the widow of the Reverend Jacob Thomas, on July 19, 1838. Sarah Osgood died July 13, 1849, after their return to the United States.

[64] "Charley" was Charles Judson, the son of Adoniram and Sarah Hall Boardman Judson. He was born December 18, 1843, and died in August 1845. Because he was so young, Charley had been left behind with Mr. and Mrs. Osgood, as Sarah and Adoniram hurried their voyage to the United States, hoping that the sea and the journey would be restorative to Sarah. She died on the way home, on September 1, 1845, on the Isle of St. Helena.

these lowly lads are close together and their bright spirits together also. Do you not think it right to feel that Charley's Dear Mother[65] will watch and love my sweet boy with peculiar interest? For she did love him here.

With much affection

Yours E.

Source: American Baptist Historical Society, AJ 19, no. 894.

Emily C. Judson to Catharine Chubbuck, October 4, 1847[66]— Maulmain

Dear Kitty

I have just rec'd (today) your letter groaning over the Rangoon expedition, when we have been comfortably and happily housed in this place for four weeks. However, there was no harm done by the groaning for I can assure you we have had our full share of hardships to endure. I believe I hav'nt [sic] written you since our terrible illness. I think it was about the last of June,[67] just when our government difficulties were heaviest, that the Doct. was seized suddenly with dysentery. He has never been so ill since he first came to India—indeed, never in his life. No physician could be had, of course, but we had a chest of medicines and several good medical books. He grew rapidly worse, until we were obliged to conclude that nothing but a sea voyage would save him. It was in the midst of the monsoon, and there were only little native vessels in port, in which it was extremely dangerous to embark on account of the storms, and in which a well man would suffer, even though he were safe. He engaged a passage in one of these, however, and I was to stay behind with the children. But the vessel did not sail as soon as we expected, and the fifth day from the attack, his disease seemed to take a favourable [sic] turn; but on that very day our eldest boy, Henry,[68] was seized with fever! For several days I had observed that little Edward[69] frequently cried out, as tho' in pain when playing about the floor and sometimes too in the night, but I had been in too much

---

[65] Sarah Hall Boardman Judson.

[66] This letter has an addendum dated October 22, 1847.

[67] A letter Emily Judson wrote to Anna Maria Anable dated July 1, 1847, gives a very similar description of the illness that seized Adoniram Judson and the children.

[68] Henry Hall Judson, born July 8, 1842, was the son of Adoniram and Sarah Hall Boardman Judson. Henry was the sixth of their eight children, the fourth of five who survived. He remained in Burmah in 1845 when Adoniram and Sarah returned to the United States with the three older children. He returned with Emily in 1851 and went to live with her family in Hamilton, New York. Henry attended Brown University and Williams Collage; he enlisted in the army at the time of the Civil War in January 1864. Later that year, he experienced a debilitating accident attributed either to sunstroke or a horse kicking him in the head. He was married once—unhappily according to his own correspondence—and he eventually died in a veteran's home in 1918, the last of his siblings to die. Of this, the chaplain noted, "The end was a genuine example of Christian fortitude." See Rosalie Hall Hunt, *Bless God and Take Courage, The Judson Legacy* (Valley Forge PA: Judson Press, 2005) 291.

[69] See vol. 1, "Cast of Characters," s.v. "Judson, Edward."

trouble to give it much attention. But he awoke the next morning after his brother's attack, a shocking sight—his beautiful little face a shining purple, and so swollen that he could'nt [sic] open his eyes. My first impression was that he had been bitten by some poisonous serpent, but that seemed so incredible in the upper story of a tight brick house. [Note: A line at the top of the page is lost.] that I soon abandoned the idea, tho' neither the Doct. nor the natives could [ ] what was the matter. He was in a burning fever, and in my first alarm, knowing that something must be done at once, I administered a powerful dose of calomel, which I now suppose saved his life. The fever gradually subsided, the purple faded to a red, but the swelling seemed to increase rather than diminish. It was in a kind of desperation that I turned over the medical books that day, for I had no hint to direct me. At last, by pure accident, my eye lighted on the word *erysipelas* at the top of a page and the truth flashed on me at once. The bleak winds from the river came sweeping through our open windows, and it rained incessantly, so, that parts of the floor were never dry—in my anxiety for his father, I had neglected to keep my usual watch over the poor little fellow, and he had to [ ] a cold, which exhibited itself in this alarming manner. I had but one native woman about me, not worth so much when well as an American girl ten years old, and she began to exhibit feverish symptoms, which made me afraid I should not only lose her assistance but have another invalid on my hands. That day the vessel sailed, without the doctor, for he thought himself improving; and if he had'nt [sic], could not of course have left me in that predicament. I had been for a long time unable to retain anything on my stomach but burned bread and brandy [Note: A line is marked through.] first of January you will understand the reason why and was so excessively weak that I could'nt [sic] walk across the room without trembling. People can't afford night watchers under such circumstances, and we all went to bed as usual. The first that I knew I was awakened by one of Edward's frightful screams; and, as I sprang from the bed, I became aware that the doctor was rolling and groaning as though in great agony. The room was large and I had not got more than half across it when I fell headlong from faintness and giddiness. For a minute I was lost to everything— then I rallied, and not daring to trust myself to my feet again crawled to Edward's cot and soon discovered the cause of the scream. The fever had returned, and his little brain seemed literally on fire. I knew he suffered dreadfully, but, few grownup men would have endured it so nobly. From his cot I went to Henry's. He had been taking medicine, and miserable as I was, I had his bed to change and himself to bathe, he crying all the time at the top of his lungs. Oh, you cannot imagine the horrours [sic] of that night! The rain was pouring down, the wind sighing and wheezing most dismally, dogs howling along the streets in immense packs, and there was a constant regular tap, tapping—the sound of a hammer driving nails into the coffin of a dead man opposite. "There will be two corpses in this house soon," I thought, "and who will bury my dead?" The Doctor, I suppose by some exertion during the day, had brought on a relapse, and was worse than ever. I made up my mind that both he and Edward *must* die. But it was not so ordered. Several abscesses formed on little E's head and neck, which his father was after awhile well enough to lance and all gradually recovered. But our troubles were not quite ended. You know we went to Rangoon with the intention of seizing the first favourable [*sic*] opportunity to proceed to Ava. Just before our illness we rec'd the astounding intelligence that there was no money—ten thousand rupees less than they asked and absolutely need had been sent to Maulmain and in disposing of their receipts as economically, they had entirely neglected to provide for us. Of course there remained nothing for us, but to come back. It was a bitter pill to us, after having gone so far and suffered so much, but we were obliged to swallow it, and I suppose it was all for the best. I was very weak at the time we left, which was after the dangerous winds were over, though the rains still continued. We engaged the only vessel which had a cabin—the least bit of a nut-shell which you ever saw with a partition through the middle. It was just the length of a person and so low, that even I could neither stand on the floor, not sit erect on my berth—a mere box to shelter us from the rain. Here, with trunks and boxes so piled up that we could not see the floor, we slept and ate, cooking our own food and taking care of the children-ugh! There are some things you never can know. The Burmans came crowding in when it rained, hardest, squatting on our boxes in the smallest compass possible, and oh! Such smells! There were fifty-six passengers beside ourselves. The second day I was taken very ill, and I must say I never comparitively [*sic*] knew what suffering was before. I was in the most intense pain and the Doct. says in my delirium called upon him most pathetically to throw water on my head and extinguish the fire. We fully expected that I would find a grave in the ocean, but it was not so to be, though I was brought ashore more dead than alive. I was taken to the nearest mission house where I lay a week without being allowed to see anyone, and then brought to my present home. Since then, I have recovered rapidly—am now nearly as well as when we left Rangoon. But oh, you can't imagine what a treasure I have in my husband. I do not believe the world contains another man one half so kind, so patient and tender. I have no doubt I should have died but for his constant attentions—soothing the pain, bathing my head, adjusting the pillows, holding me in his arms while my bed cooled and a thousand other things. Oh you would love him *so* dearly!

Source: Hanna family files.

Mrs. Alma Sheldon Anable to Emily C. Judson, October 13, 1847— Utica

My very dear Friend

I cannot feel reconciled to letting our little box leave Utica without saying a few words to you though what I shall say may perhaps have been thrice told the story of our dear Fathers [*sic*] sickness soon after you left the country and our dear Mothers [*sic*] departure[70] for a better the spirit land were [*sic*] scenes with which you have been made familiar by abler pens than mine and the precious pouring of the holy spirit that we unworthy as we are have been permitted to enjoy during the spring months the awakening of our dear Henry[71] and Fany [*sic*][72] to newness of life with many others who evince a change of heart by well ordered lives are among the many rich blessings for had we a thousand tongues devoted to his praise we should fall very far short of what we owe to that Munificent Being whose thoughts are not as our thoughts and whose ways are unsearchable and past finding out.

I am happy in saying to you my dear E that though we have drank [*sic*] deep of the cup of affliction our joys have been at times like an over flowing stream our Church has been highly favoured [*sic*] of the Lord the young members are between 50 and 60 in number that appear to be walking softly before the Lord.

I feel for one that He has lookd [*sic*] over the mountains of our transgressions and blessed us for the sake of his son our dear Saviour [*sic*] whose blood cleanseth from all sin.

We regretted very much to part with Henry so soon[73] after he began to appreciate religious privileges but feel to rejoice in the hope that he is prepared to exert a healthful influence where it is so much needed as in the far West[.] Courtland[74] is at home and rendered himself useful here while he is engaged in studying [*sic*] the laws of his country he studies in Mr Spencers [*sic*] office

---

[70] Anna Maria Anable wrote on February 15, 1847, of Mother Sheldon's death. Deacon Asa Sheldon was the father of Miss Cynthia Sheldon, Urania Sheldon Nott, and Alma Sheldon Anable. Deacon and Mrs. Sheldon lived with their daughters and grandchildren as a part of the Utica Female Academy community. Mrs. Sheldon died January 29, 1847. Deacon Sheldon continued to have a room at the Utica Female Academy, where he died in March 1848. For many years, he led mealtime prayers for the academy family, and Deacon and Mrs. Sheldon were popular with the students, who often looked in on him.

[71] See vol. 1, "Cast of Characters," s.v. "Anable, Henry Sheldon."

[72] See vol. 1, "Cast of Characters," s.v. "Anable, Fanny."

[73] Henry had left to join his brother William in Sheboygan, Wisconsin, where Will was running a store.

[74] See vol. 1, "Cast of Characters," s.v. "Anable, Courtland."

Harriet[75] and Mary[76] were very well some three weeks since tho the yellow fever has raged sadly in New Orleans the past summer and fall.

Henry has been down for goods and returned to his new home[.] one of our very best Baptist ministers in western New York has movd [sic] to Sheboygan they find a Church all ready [sic] organisd [sic] there upon apostolic ground.

William and Olivia[77] are very happy they say she is an excellent housekeeper they need the influence of divine grace to prepare them to live right or in a manner that will glorify God in their bodies and spirits whitch [sic] are his.

Our dear Father is much more comfortable than we ever expected he could be in this world we had no hope that his days would be so kindly lengthened being bourn down with so many infirmaties [sic].

Now my dear you see that my time and paper is spent in talking about our selves [sic] I believe I can say of a truth that our hearts are often with you often do I wish while in the back pantry that I could convey to you two or three pies when of course they hapen [sic] to be pretty good but alas alas its [sic] thoughts only that can be transmitted So soon the box is packing and I must close without [ ] tax on your patience with kind regard to your very dear husband much love to your self and kisses for all the dear little ones[78] I remain your ever affectionate

friend Alma Anable

Mrs. E.C Judson

Source: American Baptist Historical Society, AJ 12, no. 339.

---

[75] Harriet or "Hatty" or "Hattie" or "Hat" Anable was one of nine children born to Joseph and Alma Anable, and was a niece to Miss Cynthia Sheldon and Mrs. Urania Sheldon Nott. In 1841, she had added a note to a letter written by Miss Cynthia Sheldon to Emily. As early as November 1842 she was away, and a letter from Emily to Catharine Chubbuck said that "she (Miss Sheldon) expected that Hat would return as accomplished as Anna Maria." Her trips away were both educational and employment, as she worked as a private tutor in families that would bring her into their homes. In August 1843, she had just returned from Beonsen, in the vicinity of New Orleans, and was engaged to go again. A letter from Anna Maria on January 6, 1845 said that she would stay South for another year. About this time Miss Cynthia Sheldon mentioned her concern for Hatty's spiritual health. In May 1845 she was in New Orleans. She was home again in summer 1846, but a September 27 letter from Anna Maria said she had been asked by Mr. Roman with some urgency to return and she thought that she should. She was to return home from New Orleans in January 1849 after Anna Maria Anable had started the Misses Anable's School in Philadelphia in fall 1848. Harriet was fluent in French, having placed herself earlier in a French environment in New Orleans. Hatty died in 1858.

[76] Mary Juliet Anable was born February 18, 1830 in Bethlehem, Albany County, New York, one of nine children born to Alma and Joseph Anable. She went to New Orleans with Hatty in 1847, but she returned home early in March 1848, and by 1849, she was working with Anna Maria in the Misses Anable's School in Philadelphia. Writing in March 1849, Hatty said of Mary, "She paints and draws, speaks French, plays the piano, sings, dances and is our mathematician. What should we ever do without her? She laughs from morning till night, and it is really refreshing to be with her." On December 26, 1860, she was married to Pierre Jacques Darey, the officiating minister being the Rev. Dr. Eliphalet Nott, her uncle. Mary died at the age of sixty-eight on April 20, 1898 in Ottawa, Ontario, Canada.

[77] Born on November 6, 1816, in Albany, New York, William Stewart Anable was the second child and the second son of Joseph and Alma Sheldon Anable. In an August 31, 1844 letter, Miss Cynthia Sheldon reported to Emily that William had returned home, having "doff'd his sailor garb for age." He married Olivia Williams on September 24, 1846, according to a letter written on September 27 by Anna Maria Anable. They moved to Sheboygan, Wisconsin, where Will opened a store. William died February 9, 1863 in Virginia, California.

[78] Henry and Edward Judson were living in Maulmain with Adoniram and Emily Judson.

Anna Maria Anable to Emily C. Judson, October 13, 1847—Utica

Dear Nemmy[79]

I have just put things in this green bag and am only sorry that I could not get the little dresses done. The flannel petticoats Jul.[80] and Sarah Bell[81] made and the big night-gown is Jul's idea of what the child will[82] be by the time the box arrives at Rangoon. Fanny[83] embroidered the blanket. The h'dk'fs are a present from Jane.[84] The spoons shawl and baby's frock are from yr humble servant Ninny.[85] If they don't make you think of me when you eat, walk or dress the baby I shall be 's'p-pointed. [*sic*]. The doctor will find a covering for his head in case of a rise of the east wind. Tho' for fear it should be too small I send some pieces to enlarge it. It fits Mr. Gratiot's[86] head. The other things that fill up the box are borrowed from Aunt C's[87] side of the house. Wish I could put myself down in our corner of the box. Adieu.

Anna M.

Source: American Baptist Historical Society, AJ 13, no. 498.

Emily C. Judson to Mrs. Mary Colby, October 18, 1847—Maulmain

My very dear Mrs. Colby:

Anna Maria—Miss Anable[88] has just informed me, under date of July 30th,[89] that you have received no letter from me. Now, that it is very strange—I wrote both you and your mother, one from Maulmain and the other from Rangoon on my first arrival there; but which was written first, I cannot say. If yours was the Rangoon letter it must have been lost in the little vessel which brought it to this place. At Rangoon I described in letter writing—various trials which came upon us—and beside, I must own, we almost began to fear that our American friends forgot us when the *Faneuil Hall* lost sight of Boston.[90] You do not know how anxiously we used to look for letters, nor how sad we felt when none came.

I first heard through Mrs. Stevens[91] of the failure of your health; and you may be assured was glad to learn afterwards that it was even partially restored. I hope it will continue to improve, and you will find your new residence in the country conducive both to health and happiness. It has quite unsettled my fancies—your leaving Pemberton Square—I do not know how to think of you now. Is Miss Roberts with you? And where is your dear good mother? How I wish I could just

[79] Emily Chubbuck. See vol. 1, "Cast of Characters," s.v. "Nemmy, Nem, or Nemmy Petty (Nemmie Pettie)." Also the chapter "Names of Endearment."

[80] See vol. 1, "Cast of Characters," s.v. "Look, Julia."

[81] See vol. 1, "Cast of Characters," s.v. "Wheeler, Miss Sarah Bell."

step in and spend this evening with you and see how you all look. Wouldn't I tell Rangoon stories—some of the dark and bloody ones—and listen to Boston stories? And wouldn't we make a very long evening of it?... you don't know how much we talk of you, recalling every thing [sic] that occurred at your house, and dwelling on it for a long time; finally concluding, with a half sigh, "Well those things are all over now." Yet we are very happy now, and comfortable, though we had some pretty severe trials at Rangoon. Imagine me in a large city under a heathen government with deeds of blood going on all around me, the house banned and watched and I unable to make myself understood to any extent even by my own servants. Imagine me in these circumstances with husband and children both dangerously ill—unable to leave on account of the Monsoon coming and no medical advisor nearer than Maulmain. One night in particular I shall never forget. Little Edward[92] screeching with pain which I suppose a man would have borne scarce more hero-ically, Mr. J. groaning at every breath, Henry[93] with just fever enough to make him irritable, and I so faint and giddy that in crossing the floor I twice fell headlong.[94] It was a dark dismal night, the rain pouring down incessantly—the winds roaring—dogs howling—a party of heathen carousing in the room below—and across the way, a hammer busy with driving nails into the coffin of a dead Moorman. I had scarce a hope that either Mr. J. or Edward would recover, and there were none in all Rangoon to whom I could look for any kind of assistance—not a lip that could pronounce a prayer over their graves but a loving Eye was on us—a kind God took care of us—and we are now—Oh, *so* well and *so* happy. I would have given any-

[82] Emily's friends at the Utica Female Academy were making clothing for Emily and Adoniram Judson's expected baby. Emily Frances Judson was born December 24, 1847.

[83] See vol. 1, "Cast of Characters," s.v. "Anable, Fanny."

[84] See vol. 1, "Cast of Characters," s.v. "Kelly, Miss Jane."

[85] "Ninny" was a name of endearment given to Anna Maria Anable by her most intimate friends at the Utica Female Academy. Emily was "Nemmy."

[86] See vol. 1, "Cast of Characters," s.v. "Gratiot, Charles."

[87] See vol. 1, "Cast of Characters," s.v. "Sheldon, Miss Cynthia."

[88] See vol. 1, "Cast of Characters," s.v. "Anable, Miss Anna Maria."

[89] During the summer of 1847, Anna Maria Anable spent the summer in Boston taking a series of medical treatments to straighten her spine and strengthen her shoulder. See "Cast of Characters," s.v. "Anable, Anna Maria."

[90] On the eleventh of July, 1846, Emily and Adoniram had sailed from Boston to Burmah on the ship *Faneuil Hall*.

[91] Elizabeth Stevens arrived in Maulmain in February 1838; her husband was Edward Stevens. Elizabeth Stevens took six-month-old Edward Judson into her home when Sarah and Adoniram had to leave for the United States in 1845, and her care and nurture saved his life. She served forty-eight years in Burmah. She had extensive correspondence with Emily Judson, and her letters spoke of everyday life among the missionaries. When Emily returned to the United States, the letters from Mrs. Stevens brought news of friends and colleagues. Mrs. Stevens had a sister, Sarah Haven, in Massachusetts, who wrote a number of letters to Emily asking for information on the Stevens family.

[92] See vol. 1, "Cast of Characters," s.v. "Judson, Edward."

[93] See vol. 1, "Cast of Characters," s.v. "Judson, Henry Hall."

[94] This unfolding story is similar to Emily's letter to Anna Maria Anable dated July 1, 1847, and her letter to her sister Catharine dated October 4, 1847.

thing in Rangoon to have had Anna Maria with me; but much as I love her, I have not felt at liberty to encourage her to come here. We are keeping an eye out, and shall try to find for ourselves a field of greater usefulness, though Mr. J. is obliged to look to those places where he can pursue his dictionary to the best advantage. Quite between ourselves, you and me—if that were finished we should be off to Arracan by the next steamer.

We shall not however, go away again unless it is obviously for the best; and in that case Mr. Colby[95] must make the Board send Anna Maria to us.[96] Will he? Make him promise, please. Give much love to all I love in Boston—remember me most affectionately to Mr. C.—kiss the children—and believe me, with a great deal of love,

Your sincere and grateful friend,
Emily C. Judson

Source: Hanna family files.

Emily C. Judson to Catharine Chubbuck, October 22, 1847[97]

Steamer arrived—no letter from you. Why don't you write every month? Anna Maria[98] writes from Boston[99] that she is sewing for me and she thinks they will make me up a box at Roxbury. I have got three people sewing for me now. One for the doc. One for Henry[100] and Ed.[101] And one helping me on small articles. I have to cut and baste for all of them.

Source: Hanna family files.

---

[95] See vol. 1, "Cast of Characters," s.v. "Colby, Gardner."

[96] For more on Anna Maria Anable and a possible call to missionary service, see vol. 1, "Cast of Characters," s.v. "Anable, Anna Maria."

[97] This letter is an addendum to a letter dated October 4, 1847.

[98] See vol. 1, "Cast of Characters," s.v. "Anable, Miss Anna Maria."

[99] During the summer of 1847, Anna Maria Anable spent the summer in Boston taking a series of medical treatments to straighten her spine and strengthen her shoulder. See "Cast of Characters," s.v. "Anable, Anna Maria."

[100] See vol. 1, "Cast of Characters," s.v. "Judson, Henry Hall."

[101] See vol. 1, "Cast of Characters," s.v. "Judson, Edward."

[102] Sarah Colby was the mother of Gardner Colby.

Mrs. Sarah Colby[102] to Emily C. Judson, October 24, 1847[103]— Roxbury

If my dear Mrs. Judson knew how hard it is for me to write she would excuse my ekeing out this old letter—now I find there will soon be an opportunity to send by ship—I spent the last few days at Newton, we talked much of you etc.—Mary[104] will write I think—our sympathies go out after you, and our prayer is constant that God will [ ] you and never suffer your per[son] to fail—much love and kind regard to your beloved husband with the hope that you will call upon me if I can serve you—and that you will always write to me when you can do so consistent with your various duties I subscribe myself your affectionate friend

Sarah Colby

Source: American Baptist Historical Society, AJ 15, no. 598.

Elnathan "Elly" Judson to Emily and Adoniram Judson,[105] October 30, 1847—Worcester

My dear father and mother,

I have long neglected to write to you but I will try to make it up in the letter I am about to write to you. I have had several presents from Miss Flag our second teacher. I will send 3 of the presents along with Mr. Simons,[106] with several other books that we have been gathering with our money and bought. Besides these I have got other books which we bought last winter. We are gaining money pretty fast, by running errands, and posting papers and selling bottles. We were promoted from Miss Flag's school into a school next to the high school. Since that time a private school has been opened, taught by Miss Albee, and as both boys and girls

---

[103] This is an addendum to a letter started September 1, 1847.

[104] Mary Colby was the wife of Gardner Colby, a prominent businessman and active Baptist layman. Mr. Colby was a member of the Board of the American Baptist Missionary Union and an avid supporter of the missionary movement. In a letter after they sailed from Boston to Burmah, Emily mentions the extravagant hospitality extended to them in early July as they waited for the *Faneuil Hall* to embark. Adoniram and then Emily stayed with the Colby family quite frequently over the years. Mrs. Colby was an active correspondent with Emily and supported her, her family, and the cause of missions.

[105] Elnathan Judson wrote two versions of this letter, one dated October 30 and one dated October 31. The second is an abbreviation of the first; both of them were sent

[106] Thomas Simons was born in Wales. He was ordained on December 18, 1831, after graduation from the Newton Theological Institute and was appointed to missionary service on March 7, 1831. He sailed for Burmah on June 29, 1832, arriving in Maulmain on January 1, 1833. On June 23, 1833, he married Caroline Jenks Harrington in Maulmain, probably the widow of a missionary who had died, and between 1834 and March 1843, they had six children, two of whom died in June 1839. Caroline Simons died on May 1, 1843. Mr. Simons returned to America in May 1846. While in the United States, he visited with Abby Ann Judson at Bradford Academy; she would have known him from her years in Burmah. He returned to Burmah in November 1847, arriving in Maulmain April 19, 1848. His second wife was Lydia Lillybridge, who had sailed to Burmah with Adoniram and Emily Judson; they were married in Maulmain in 1851.

went there Aunt Newton[107] sent us to it. The tuition is $5.00 per term we have been here about 6 weeks. Miss Albee says that she would be very glad to give us our tuition after this term, as long as Aunt Newton wishes to send us. Miss Albee hopes that the next time I write that I will write better, as we have just got our mats upon which to write. We are just learning to parse. I wish we could study your gramar [sic] I know you are an author of a gramar[108] [sic] for I have seen your name amongst the authors of gramars [sic] in the begining [sic] of our gramars [sic]. Almost every Wemsday [sic] and Saturday we go to math with Miss Albee. I have been wanting to be it Christian [sic] but have failed in it almost every time. But the last time, I have been holding the door against Satan. Several times he has broken open the door but this time I have succeeded in sending him away pouting and I hope I will be able to hold the door until I can lock it and then he can never get in.[109] Our teacher is reading *Charles Linn*[110] to the scholars and hopes that they will follow his example. I hope to see my dear little brothers,[111] if you know possibly what year they will come here. I wish next time you write I wish you would tell me about it. Farewell forever. I never expect to see you, no never.

Your Affectionate son
Elnathan

Source: American Baptist Historical Society, AJ 11, no. 460.

[107] Dr. Calvin Newton, after some theological training, went to medical school to become a physician. He apparently had differing ideas about medicine, and he became a part of what was known as the Eclectic School of Medicine; with that background, he established the Worcester Medical Institute. In 1835, Dr. and Mrs. Newton received into their home the young George Dana Boardman, just returned from Burmah for his education. Adoniram and Elnathan went there in fall 1845 when they returned to the United States with their father, and they remained there under the Newton's care until Emily's return in October 1851. At that time, Mrs. Newton had become ill, and the boys went to live with Dr. and Mrs. Edward Bright.

[108] In 1808, having graduated from college, Adoniram Judson began to teach school. Finding resources insufficient for his needs, he published both a book on mathematics and another on English grammar. *The Elements of English Grammar* by Adoniram Judson, Jun. A. B. was published in 1808 It was printed in Boston by Cushing and Lincoln and had fifty-six pages and an introduction from some of the noted educators of that time. This editor is proud to have a copy of this volume in his Judson library.

[109] The story of Elnathan's conversion can be found in letters of early October 1851. Emily had just returned from Burmah, and the pastor of the Worcester Church, Rev. Mr. Swaim, wrote (October 2, 1851) of how Elnathan had been before the deacons of the church and that they were waiting for a time when Emily was available to be there for his baptism. As to the issues of being a "good" Christian, the letters show this to be a demanding exercise for Elnathan.

[110] In the first quarter of 1841, one of Emily Chubbuck's early books was *Charles Linn; How to Observe the Golden Rule*. A perennial favorite, it was still being published several decades after Emily's death in 1854.

[111] Henry (five years old) and Edward (almost three years old) Judson remained in Burmah when Adoniram and Sarah had left for America in early 1845.

[112] Elnathan Judson wrote two versions of this letter, one dated October 30 and one dated October 31. The second is an abbreviation of the first; both of them were sent

Elnathan "Elly" Judson To Emily and Adoniram Judson,[112] October 31, 1847—Worcester

My dear father and mother,

    I have long neglected to write you but I will try to make it up in the letter I am about to write to you. I have been gathering all my pocket money together to buy some books for you and my little brothers Henry and Edward.[113] Besides these I have got some other books which I have had before. I hope that they will be very much interested when they get them all, enough to read them. When you left us you left us at Miss Flag's school but we have been promoted from that one into a higher one since that time a private school has been opened taught by Miss Albee and as both boys and girls went there, Aunt Newton[114] took us out of [ ] school and put us in that one, the tuition is $5.00 per term. We have been here about six weeks. Miss Albee says that after this term she would be glad to give us our tuition as long as Uncle Newton wishes to send us there. We are just beginning to learn to [Note: "Write" is written and crossed out.] parse. I wish we could study your gramar [sic].[115] We have been to math with Miss Albee almost every Wensday [sic] and Saturday afternoon. I have been wanting to be a Christian but have failed in almost every time I have tried except the last time I have suceeded [sic] in holding the door against Satan, several times he has broke it down but the last time I held it against him.[116]

    Your affectionate son

    Elnathan Judson

Source: American Baptist Historical Society, AJ 11, no. 459.

---

[113] Henry and Edward Judson remained in Burmah when Adoniram and Sarah had left for America in early 1845.

[114] Dr. and Mrs. Calvin Newton had earned the trust of Adoniram Judson. When George Boardman returned to America in 1834, he eventually found his way to the Newton family in Worcester, Massachusetts. Then, when Adoniram Judson returned to America in 1845 after the death of Sarah Hall Boardman Judson, Adoniram and Elnathan were placed with the Newton's home to live and to receive an education. They were there from the end of 1845 until Emily Judson returned from Burmah in October 1851.

[115] In 1808, having graduated from college, Adoniram Judson began to teach school. Finding resources insufficient for his needs, he published both a book on mathematics and another on English grammar. The Elements of English Grammar by Adoniram Judson, Jun. A. B. was published in 1808 It was printed in Boston by Cushing and Lincoln and had fifty-six pages and an introduction from some of the noted educators of that time.

[116] The story of Elnathan's conversion can be found in letters of early October 1851. Emily had just returned from Burmah, and the pastor of the Worcester Church, Rev. Mr. Swaim, wrote (October 2, 1851) of how Elnathan had been before the deacons of the church and that they were waiting for a time when Emily was available to be there for his baptism. As to the issues of being a "good" Christian, the letters show this to be a demanding exercise for Elnathan.

Emily C. Judson to Catharine Chubbuck,[117] November 21, 1847—Maulmain

Dear Kitty,

I am scarce fit to write a letter just now, and indeed, have half promised that I would'nt [sic], but as I shall not be likely to write by the next vessel, I tho't you might get a little anxious. I am getting on as nicely as could be expected under the circumstances;[118] much better than you would reasonably expect, but what with my serving people and the loss of my good Burman nurse and my domestic [ ] together, though very light, [ ] [ ] I have enough to do when I feel like busying myself. You must not think, however, that I am [ ]—I put a [ ] [ ] for everything that I do.

The Wades[119] are spending several weeks with us previous to embarking for America. He has lost the use of his eyes and is in miserable health. You must go and see them the moment you hear of their arrival in Hamilton[120] and don't be a bit prim or reserved. They can tell you everything about me, the house, the children—everything under the sun that you can ask. And whatever you ask you may depend she will tell it just as it is. I never was more disappointed in any person—I love her very much, and you must love her, and let her think you like to be where she is. I shall send you a few grincracks [sic] by the Wades—I scarce know what yet, but, if I live, I can send you an overland list before they arrive.—I am glad that you have plastered up the back room and are getting on so nicely in other respects. Is the fence begun yet?[121]

I got two letters from you by the steamer now in. There was a good long one, written as soon as you heard of our arrival, that went to London and was sent back to have the postage paid. That of course made it very late. [Note: Emily—or someone—has crossed out these next nine lines of the letter.] Benjamin[122] shall [ ]

---

[117] All together, some twenty lines of this letter are marked out with heavy ink. Some of the words can be deciphered, some not; but this explains the unusual number of unknown words [ ] in the transcription.

[118] Emily was approximately eight months pregnant at this time; Emily Frances Judson was born December 24, 1847.

[119] Jonathan and Deborah Wade were appointed missionaries to Burmah in 1823. Their relationship with Adoniram Judson was especially dear because of the early experiences they shared, including the death of Ann Judson. When she died and Adoniram returned to Amherst expecting to find her, he learned instead the news of her death. He never forgot the sight of Deborah Wade standing on the veranda holding little Maria in her arms. Much of their work was spent in the Karen jungle communities following the path of George Boardman. They returned home to America on December 22, 1847, and went back to Burmah in January 1851, just as Emily was returning to the United States. They were from the Hamilton, New York, area. They left for Burmah on July 25, 1850, and were in Maulmain by February 1851. Both died in Burmah; Deborah died at Maulmain in 1868, and Jonathan died in Rangoon in 1872.

[120] The Wades originally came from the Hamilton, New York area; Jonathan Wade graduated from the Hamilton Literary and Theological Institute. With family in that area, they would be returning to Hamilton and vicinity, where Catharine Chubbuck lived with her parents in a home that Emily had purchased for them.

[121] Before leaving in July 1846, Adoniram Judson purchased a three-acre parcel of land for Emily's father Charles Chubbuck so that he could plant a small garden perhaps or have some livestock on it.

[122] See vol. 1, "Cast of Characters," s.v. "Chubbuck, Benjamin."

[ ] [ ] [ ], [ ] [ ], and yet if there [ ] [ ] hope of his being prepared you couldn't have regretted it. But we [ ] [ ] him rest, poor fellow! He sinned and he suffered, and [ ] far his weak head and [ ] [ ] [ ] [ ] will weigh against or excuse [ ] is impossible, [ ] [ ] [ ] [ ] [ ] [ ] comfort to know that he didn't die among strangers,[123] and a great comfort that he had been as long [ ]. I quite like your taking the boy if you think [Note: Crossed out lines end.] you can manage him. He will be, as you say, a great care, but he will be a great comfort too, and but a trifling expense. I think, however, that *you* better take the principal charge of him and take all care from father and mother. Teach him to be perfectly obedient and respectful to them, but you do all the disciplining. And in that, ducky, you must be very firm and steady. Let your *no* be *no* and keep all your promises to the letter. Don't *scold ever*—whip when it is necessary, and whip so that he will remember it. Mrs. Wade will tell you that I am a good adviser, for they do say that my "boys[124] are the best behaved in the Mission." But enough of this. Mrs. Wade takes home with her a boy—son of a good Baptist deacon—to be educated at Hamilton. If it is convenient I sh'd like to have you know him and write a word about him now and then. It would gratify his mother very much.

Never trouble yourselves, you and mother, about my suffering for *anything*. We have very nice things indeed bro't from Calcutta, and altho' we of course prefer American manufactures, we could live perfectly comfortable with what we have. Then we have money enough for all reasonable wants. We know precisely our income by the month and regulate our expenses by that knowledge. If we want to launch out on one side we must pinch a little on the other which we can do with perfect ease. When my good husband wants to indulge me a little, he lives cheaper for awhile himself, and all comes around right in the end. We never get in debt and we have all we want—even to being able to hire a carriage every day that I am able to ride. Then you know I shall be likely to get presents from home. They are making us a little (they say *very* little, but valuable I have no doubt) box in N. Y. Another little one is probably on its way from Boston. They promise us a large one from Philadelphia, but I don't think it will be worth much, and it is just as likely not to come, as any way.[125] Another box is in tow at Utica, but I suppose mostly

[123] Ben died in Michigan while living with his Aunt Catharine Richards, his mother's sister. He left a wife and two children.

[124] Henry Hall Judson and Edward Judson, the two youngest living children of Adoniram and Sarah Hall Boardman Judson, were living in Maulmain with Emily and Adoniram. Henry was coming on five and a half years old; Edward was approaching three years old.

[125] On July 24, 1847, Mrs. Hannah Gillett wrote from Philadelphia, asking Emily to tell her what was needed to replace the items lost in the fire, and she would work toward finding replacements. Friends at the Utica Female Academy were working as well. The response was significant and generous from friends throughout Philadelphia, Boston, and Utica.

from our own money. Besides all this the doctor's sister[126] has sent us $100. Our loss by the fire and in other ways will not of course be fully made up[127] but we never shall feel it. I suppose there is no country in the world where people can regulate their expenses by their income, and be as comfortable as here. We can live like nabobs if we have plenty of money—if we have little, for a mere song. Food is cheap and we can almost go without clothing.

Written along the left margin of the address page: "I am very tired and it is time I was in bed. If you were only here, how I would make you sew, Missy. I have turned off my lazy tailor and sent for a new one—dare say he will be just as lazy. But no more yarns. Good night,"

Nemmy[128]

Written along the right margin of the address page: "You will not hear from me by the December steamer—by the Jan'y one either the doct. or I will write. It is not impossible you know that the next news may be of my death, though I have no serious apprehensions. If you do, don't be sorry that I married or came out here, and don't think it has been occasioned by hardships. We went through with a great many grievous things in Rangoon, but somehow the doct. managed to take the weight of them on himself, and since we came around here, I have lived like a princess."

Written upside down along the top margin of page 1: "Write to Walker.[129] (Oh, how I want to see him!) and Aunt Holland for me. The next letter I write shall be for them."

Source: Hanna family files.

---

[126] Abigail Brown Judson, the sister of Adoniram Judson, lived in Plymouth, Massachusetts. A spinster of eccentric character and behavior, she was a beneficiary of her parents' considerable wealth. She took a strong interest in Adoniram's children and offered them considerable support—though not often without complaint or comment—for their clothing and education in the years to come.

[127] On February 17, 1847, shortly after they left Maulmain for Rangoon, a fire in the mission compound at Maulmain destroyed two trunks of Adoniram and Emily's clothing and personal articles; much of the loss had been personal gifts of great sentimental value. In different letters the loss was estimated between seven hundred and a thousand rupees.

[128] Emily Chubbuck. See vol. 1, "Cast of Characters," s.v. "Nemmy, Nem, or Nemmy Petty (Nemmie Pettie)." Also the chapter "Names of Endearment."

[129] See vol. 1, "Cast of Characters," s.v. "Chubbuck, John Walker.

The Reverend Doctor William Dean to Emily C. Judson, November 25, 1847—Hong Kong

My dear friend,

I am induced to send you a page not because I have heard from you lately but because not having but one letter from you since I saw you in Ama [America] I feared you were lost in the Burman jungle or carried off by a Tyen—or had your right hand chopped off by that cruel Burmese King—or some other dreadful calamity had disabled you for writing. I have written to you *twice* since I have heard from you and sent to your good husband two or three Hong Kong News Papers. So let me just hear whether you are alive or not.

We are all pretty well here—I have since the cold weather been moving about. Last week at Canton and this week at Long Island where we have a station. I enjoyed my visit this week particularly [ ] the family of one of our church members whose wife I baptized a few months ago. Yes a *Chinese Woman* baptized—the *first* so far as I know. Another family in the same neighborhood gave me their household gods saying that they now had no further use for them as they worshipped Jesus. There are four or five at that station I hope soon to baptize [*sic*]. The town contains five or six thousand people and all appear very civil and *curious* to see and hear—a few I hope *love* the truth.

We hear that Mr. Jones and Mr. Johnson and families are soon expected here—the former from Siam and the latter from China.

The old cow is doing nicely and I have just had a present of an Arab—What have you done with your cow? How are the boys?[130]

A kind word to your husband from
Your friend
Mrs. JudsonW. Dean

Source: American Baptist Historical Society, AJ 15, no. 592.

Miss Julia A. Look to Emily C. Judson November 26, 1847

My dear dear Emily

It is not quite tea time, so I have a few minutes to talk. When your letters and notes came yesterday I looked in vain for mine—but I knew why it did not come. After this however, you will not send off a package to America without at least a line for me because you were not my debtor. Not you—Last night I wrote to

---

[130] Henry and Edward Judson were the two youngest surviving children of Adoniram and Sarah Hall Boardman Judson. Henry was almost five and a half years old, and Edward almost three.

[131] See vol. 1, "Cast of Characters," s.v. "Lillybridge, Miss," also the timeline "Lydia Lillybridge Simons."

Lydia,[131] and, after I have finished this, I'm going to write to Eloise Bacon Josslyn.[132] After school this afternoon Sarah[133] and I went to see Mary Jones.[134] She is much better than she was though not yet well. Mrs. Jone's [sic] health is much as it used to be. Nemmy[135] I do suppose that I shall spend all my time and cover this little sheet—without saying anything just because I am trying to tell you nothing but what is *thrilling*ly interesting. We are glad, very glad, you are again at Maulmain. I was afraid you would [ ] dead when I heard what pies and cooking you have over there. I heard a man once say, the nation's cooking was so bad, that the Do'ct would not eat it unless he got in a frolic, and I should certainly think the missionaries couldn't. One day last vacation as I was riding with Mr. Avery we met Mr. and Mrs. N. P. Willis.[136] They were visiting some friends near Aurora. But isn't Mrs. W. ugly? If all the pink ribbon in the inside her hat had but been bleached, it would have tied cakes for twenty weddings—but it by no means lent a bloom shade to the wearer's complexion—and she looked as cross as a sleepy child though not as innocently so—

We live on here just as we used to do—Find enough to occupy ourselves most of the time. Now Emily I'll venture none of your friends have been wicked enough to tell you what to wear or any thing. I'd tell you myself but I'm afraid your good Dr. will think it is because I think so much of such things. You know better though don't you? and you want to see us just as we look to [sic]—don't you! And how can you unless I tell you. We are all very plain this fall—for various reasons. I rather suspect Anna M.[137] is saving her funds to go missionarying on her own hook one of

---

[132] Mrs. Josslyn was associated with Emily at the Academy in Utica. Her letters are filled with references to people they both knew. At the time of the second letter, she was living in Michigan. Her husband had just sold their farm, and they were thinking of moving into town. They were uncertain about the future, but Mr. Josslyn had a business of making buggy whips. Though this letter was written in January, Mrs. Josslyn did not have any idea that Emily had been in Philadelphia for the previous two months for her health.

[133] See vol. 1, "Cast of Characters," s.v. "Wheeler, Miss Sarah Bell."

[134] See vol. 1, "Cast of Characters," s.v. "Jones, Morven and Mary."

[135] Emily Chubbuck. See vol. 1, "Cast of Characters," s.v. "Nemmy, Nem, or Nemmy Petty (Nemmie Pettie)." Also the chapter "Names of Endearment."

[136] Nathaniel Parker Willis was the editor, with General George Morris, of the *New Mirror*, a prominent literary magazine in New York. His "discovery" of Emily in the June 8, 1844 edition of the *New Mirror* catapulted her into literary fame and enabled her to command the highest prices for her articles and stories from the major magazines of that period. It began a new and glorious chapter in her life. Over the next two years, he became her friend, mentor, and confidant. His black-bordered letter of March 21, 1846, made it abundantly clear that her engagement to Adoniram Judson had come as a "death blow" and that he had expected to marry Emily upon his return that month from England. He returned several letters to Emily to demonstrate to her, lest she had forgotten, why he had felt right in that expectation. Within a few months of Emily's departure for Burmah, Willis married the ward of a United States Senator. A letter to Emily from her friends stated that his new bride had significant wealth. The *New Mirror* went out as Willis was returning to the United States, and he established another publication, *The Home Journal*, with General George Morris. See vol. 1, "Cast of Characters" s.v. "Willis, N. P." For a detailed examination of his relationship with Emily, see vol. 1 "A Timeline of the Correspondence and Relationship between Emily E. Chubbuck/Fanny Forester and Nathaniel Parker Willis: A Litany of Unrequited Romance."

[137] See vol. 1, "Cast of Characters," s.v. "Anable, Miss Anna Maria."

these days,[138] Sarah to plant herself well in Galena, I because I have none. A. M. and Fanny[139] are wearing black satin, shirred hats with white flowers in them. There—don't you *see* how they look? Sarah and I have marasine [*sic*] blue hats shirred.—Sarah's lined with the same—mine with corn color. Don't you see better how we look too? But I mustn't say anything now about *such* things while there are so many other better subjects. You don't know how many times I think of you on Friday mornings aside from all the other days. The school has now almost entirely changed so that my composition class is *fresh*. No one who will ever be a martyr to her genius adorns it, just at present though we have a great deal of good sense—and withal are getting on very well—though the "blue miss" trouble me sometimes—and the finding of subjects—will ruin me yet—positively drive me mad. Oh! I think of you *so* often—Tomorrow is Saturday—how I wish we could spend the day with you (and) your good Dr. and sweet little children.[140] We know you are happy in your own home—and that others are made happy by you—else we should wish you back—but now we cannot—then too when we remember the good you are daily doing, we wish our own path of duty were as well defined. I must close this little scrawl—if you find one interesting sentence I shall be satisfied. I know you have a whole brace of friends to write too [*sic*]—but do remember me now and then if you cannot often. Love to you and yours from

Your ever affectionate
Julia L.

Source: American Baptist Historical Society, AJ 17, no. 762.

Miss Sarah Bell Wheeler to Emily C. Judson, November 26, 1847— Utica Female Academy

I cannot tell you, my dear Nemmy,[141] how much we were delighted to get the last package of notes from you.

Each of us is anxious to hear all about you *and* your dear family whenever letters come. Their riches to us *are* treasures and I flatter myself that I am a favored one to get such good advice from you. I don't think you change any Nemmy (unless it is for the better)—Your letters read as much like yourself as when you write from Philadelphia.

---

[138] For more on Anna Maria Anable and a possible call to missionary service, see vol. 1, "Cast of Characters," s.v. "Anable, Anna Maria."

[139] See vol. 1, "Cast of Characters," s.v. "Anable, Fanny."

[140] Henry and Edward Judson were the youngest two surviving children of Adoniram and Sarah Hall Boardman Judson. Henry was almost five and a half years old, and Edward almost three years old.

[141] Emily Chubbuck. See vol. 1, "Cast of Characters," s.v. "Nemmy, Nem, or Nemmy Petty (Nemmie Pettie)." Also the chapter "Names of Endearment."

Julia[142] is in the school room this morning with her composition class. She teaches the class every Friday, for *she* thinks *she* can't do as well [ ] for it as you used to—Still I think her scholars love her much.

Oh if yo*u could* come to us once in a while we would make your stay *so* pleasant. Miss Kelly[143] is [ ] [ ]—and you will think so when I tell you that we have 50 boarders: and 40 day scholars—People talk about her getting married now and then but we have no reason for alarm now at any rate.

Has Anna M.[144] told you about her long stay in Boston?[145] We are delighted to have her with us again, and glad too that she grew so much stronger. But Nemmy I don't think she found a *beau* in B. She tries to teaze [sic] us a little sometimes, but we are not so easily fooled.

Our good Helen Blaswell [sic], is sitting with me this afternoon cutting out a smoking cap. She expects to leave us next week,—and we shall miss her so much. We have been like Sisters for the last year. The young ladies know that she is going home to be married but I think not at present. Speaking of marriage reminds me of myself Nemmy. I don't know when that happy (wedding day I mean) is coming to me. My friend is in Galena, so I know I shall live west one of these days.[146] Nemmy I hope you will pray for me that I may be a useful humble Christian. John has met with a great change and I trust he will remain steadfast to his profession.

Dear Miss Cynthia[147] has had an attack of the rheumatism this week and we were fearful that she would not recover from it for weeks. But she is *better* to day.

Dear Grandpa[148] remains very well, but I think you would find him somewhat changed could you see him. His room looks very lovely. Aunt Alma[149] is well, and

[142] Miss Look was a student of Emily's at the Utica Female Academy, and then a fellow teacher. A November 22, 1845 letter from Anna Maria, encouraging Emily to stay in Philadelphia for the winter for her health, remarks that Julia has the hardest part because she is teaching Emily's Composition Class and the students keep asking for Emily. In a September, 1847 letter, she was listed as one of the teachers at the Utica Female Academy. According to an 1849 letter from Sarah Hinckley, she married a Mr. Casswell. In one 1849 letter Julia speaks of another teacher who is teaching "our composition class." She was one of a small number of people who addressed Emily as "Emily" and as "Nemmy" in her letters.

[143] See vol. 1, "Cast of Characters," s.v. "Kelly, Miss Jane."

[144] See vol. 1, "Cast of Characters," s.v. "Anable, Miss Anna Maria."

[145] For more information on these medical treatments, see vol. 1, "Cast of Characters," s.v. "Anable, Anna Maria."

[146] "John" is likely "Cousin John Shelton," the son of John Shelton who was a brother of Cynthia, Alma, Urania Sheldon. Galena is in northern Illinois. There is another reference to John and Sarah Bell in a letter from Anna Maria Anable dated February 28, 1848; however, in 1851 Sarah Bell married a Boston widower, Charles Gould, of the publishing firm Gould, Randall and Lincoln.

[147] See vol. 1, "Cast of Characters," s.v. "Sheldon, Miss Cynthia."

[148] See vol. 1, "Cast of Characters," s.v. "Sheldon, Deacon Asa."

[149] Alma Sheldon Anable was the sister of Miss Cynthia Sheldon and Urania Sheldon Nott. Genealogy sources show that she married Joseph Hubbell Anable in Troy, New York on July 28, 1814, and that it was the second marriage for Mr. Anable. Born in 1773, he was forty-one at the time of the marriage, and Alma was likely considerably younger. He died in 1831, which explains why Alma Anable and her family lived and worked first at the Utica Female Seminary and then later at the Misses Anable's School in Philadelphia. Joseph and Alma Anable were the parents of nine children: Henry Sheldon Anable (b. June 21, 1815); William Stewart Anable (b. November 6, 1816); Anna Maria Stafford Anable (b. September 30, 1818), Cynthia Jane Anable (b. January 28, 1820); Samuel Low Anable (b. November 28, 1821); Harriet Isabella Anable, also known as Hatty or Hattie (b. December 18, 1823); Courtland Wilcox Anable (b. July 28, 1825); Frances Alma Anable, or Fanny (b. April 12, 1828); and Mary Juliet Anable (b. February 18, 1830).

all others in our great family. Mr. and Mrs. Gratiot,[150] and children are all boarding with us now, and we find them [ ] pleasant. Our dream vacation was delightful, dear Nemmy. I spent the first two weeks of it with Aunt Urania.[151] I was there during commencement and had the exquisite pleasure of seeing Prof. *Gillespie*.[152] I saw Mrs. Pearson and family very often. After those two weeks in S. I went to Troy and made my good cousins a visit. Fanny[153] was very well and happy. We spoke of you often and the little *Judson* is a bright beautiful child. She is so sorry that *she* did not see you before you left the country. Has any one [*sic*] told you that Lou Campbell is dead?—Poor child—She has suffered much during the last year.

The last two weeks of vacation I spent in Aurora with Julia at Mr. Avery's.[154] Their town is very delightful—and your mouth would water if I should tell you of all the delicious fruits we had. Susy is very happy. Little Samuel *is* my favorite. Kitty, doesn't like strangers and wouldn't say much to me—I have not *said half* I would like to, Nemmy, but I intend nothing of [ ] to you hereafter. Give my love to your dear husband and kisses to those little ones.[155]

My best wishes for you my dear Nemmy, and I pray that our Heavenly Father will bless you greatly in all your [ ].

With heaps of love to yourself I am your affectionate

Friend Sarah Bell

Source: American Baptist Historical Society, AJ 22, no. 1115.

---

[150] See vol. 1, "Cast of Characters," s.v. "Sheldon, Ann."

[151] See vol. 1, "Cast of Characters," s.v. "Nott, Urania Sheldon."

[152] William Gillespie was a professor of civil engineering at Union College in Schenectady, New York. He wrote two long letters to Emily, dated August 15 and September 11, 1845. His second letter originated from Union College where Dr. Nott (husband of Urania Sheldon Nott) was the president, and he noted that Mrs. Urania Sheldon Nott was "his special friend." In his first letter, he asked Emily if a certain poem had appeared in the New York *Mirror*, and if it had, he had identified the writer (if it was Emily) early on as one of great promise. In a time when Emily was considering a trip to the continent, he spoke to her of weather conditions in certain of the European countries. His second letter was filled with literary allusions, a long story to prove the point that "widows are dangerous," and a reflection on some of her writings. Mr. Gillespie was mentioned in Urania Sheldon Nott's June 11, 1845 letter to Emily; he had given Mrs. Nott the latest issue of the *Columbian Magazine*, which contained the first install-ment of Emily's story "Grace Linden." Then, on July 9, 1845, Emily mentioned Mr. Gillespie in a letter to her sister Catharine. Emily was speaking of going to Schenectady for the commencement of Union College, and she says, "A man there has fallen love with me—Mr. Gillespie, author of 'Rome as seen by a New Yorker.'"

[153] See vol. 1, "Cast of Characters," s.v. "Buckingham, Fanny."

[154] In Julia Look's letter of November 26, 1847, she speaks of riding with Mr. Avery while there and running into N. P. Willis and his new wife.

[155] Henry and Edward Judson lived in Maulmain with Emily and Adoniram Judson. Henry was almost five and a half years old, and Edward almost three years old.

Miss Cynthia Sheldon to Emily C. Judson, November 26, 1847—Utica

Dear dear E.

How can I make you know all we feel for you in the varied circumstances in which you have been placed the last year. How inscrutable are the ways of providence—yet we know that he leadeth in the right path—from the *top* of the hill difficulty we may look back and bless the all sustaining hand and raise our "Ebenezer" and go forward trusting, "hope thou in God" must be our motto—Dear E. do continue to write us every thing [*sic*], and every month—the long time between your two last packages seemed an age—I almost feared you would sink under the accumulated discomforts before you could get away from that dark abode—that you had not labored and endured in vain uses there—reflects light which the darkness of heathenism cannot extinguish—two such sheaves gathered into the Church—endowed with power from on high—and authority to go "every where preaching the word" may in future time pull down the strong holds of Satan's Kingdom—Then the first instrumentalites [*sic*] will be appreciated on earth—and approved of Heaven—

While I see my dear girl this self sacrificing spirit—I pray, God, to accept the willing mind—and lighten your burdens—How very glad am I to believe you now in Maulmain. The friends there have received you with open arms and now I hope your own house is made comfortable—Lydia[156] by your side—and all you hold dear wearing healthful smiling faces—

Dear Mrs. Bennett[157] has cheered us this week with long letters—Noble Woman—she expresses deep solicitude for you—and much anxiety to have you and the Doct. return to M.—there she says you have both friends who *love* and value all you say and do—she is indeed anxious to see you—a trip to Tavoy I hope will be enjoyed before you start again for Ava—

While we blush for the want of funds to carry you hence[158]—I bless God that your path to return was even thus made plain—The sin (if any) lies not at your door—you have done what you could—Well did I know you would feel deeply the

---

[156] See vol. 1, "Cast of Characters," s.v. "Lillybridge, Miss," also the timeline "Lydia Lillybridge Simons."

[157] Stella Bennett was the wife of Cephas Bennett; they arrived in Burmah in January 1830. Mr. Bennett remained the superintendent of the Baptist Press there for more than fifty years. From the Utica area, they sent their children back, and the girls were educated at the Utica Female Academy. The girls included Elsina (April 1828), Mary (November 1829), Ann (August 1833), Ellen (June 1835), and Sarah (June 1837).

[158] Emily and Adoniram Judson moved to Rangoon in February 1847, hoping it would be a stepping-stone to Ava; because of reductions in funding from the Board of the American Baptist Missionary Union, however, they were forced to return to Maulmain in September 1847.

loss of dear dear Mother[159]—poor dear father[160] is wonderfully sustained. Yet he grieves in pitiable moans for his great loss—Yesterday was Thanksgiving—O how sad to me, the first in twenty or more years that on this anniversary had past [*sic*], without my first helping dear Mother to her favorite piece of Turkey—I was really ill yesterday if it had been otherwise with me—I know not how I could have gone to the table—not a friend or even our Minister invited here—Mr. Corey[161] has a little daughter Emma. Our congregation has greatly increased. Mr. C. has lately taken up popular amusements for the evening—last Sabbath E'g—the theatre got full measure—I have felt anxiety for the result—somewhat relieved to learn a large proportion of our citizens approve—Judge Gridley and others of the same stamp have expressed high satisfaction with his efforts—a severe influenza has kept me housed the last four weeks—it run into [*sic*] inflammatory rheumatism a few days since—took me from my feet—but it is now happily arrested giving me rest at night and comfort by day—for we really feared it was a winter enemy—how much better the Lord is than our fears—poor Doct. Nott[162] has been sadly affected with this dire disease since Sep. now feels quite relieved but not well—I went there in the onset to set them to work with soot poultices and Port wine—No Homopathy [*sic*] must work its wonders—that gave place to Hydropathy some six weeks since. On Tuesday I let Urania[163] know that I had found it necessary to apply my own prescriptions—the next mail brought from her the most importuning letter to abandon the course—take a *packing* with wet towels and live on gruel. This Morn'g mail I told her we would agree to disagree on this point—my object was gained being quite myself again—to exhort her Doct. to do likewise and get well—have you been told of the death of dear Mrs. Warner—she was taken sick the 4th of July,

[159] Mother Sheldon died on January 29, 1847; Anna Maria Anable wrote of her grandmother's death on February 15, 1847.

[160] Deacon Asa and Mrs. Sheldon were parents to Cynthia Sheldon, Urania Sheldon Nott, and Alma Sheldon Anable. They had rooms at the Utica Female Academy where two of their three daughters were employed, and they were very popular with the students. After Mother Sheldon's death on January 29, 1847, Deacon Sheldon retained his room at the Academy; he died in March 1848.

[161] Mr. Corey was the pastor of the Bleecker Street Baptist Church near the Utica Female Academy, and Miss Sheldon and many of the girls from the academy attended worship there. (Cynthis Sheldon, Alma Anable, Deacon Asa and Isabell Sheldon, Edward Bright, and Horace Hawley had been charter members of the church in 1838.) In April 1844, he wrote to Emily expressing dismay that at a school program one of the girls had read a composition justifying dancing as exercise; he spoke of this as a roadblock to the salvation of many. Then, on March 10, 1846, Emily indicated in a letter to Anna Maria that Mr. Corey had been critical of her relationship and impending marriage to Adoniram Judson. Miss Cynthia Sheldon wrote a number of times expressing Mr. Corey's regret and support, and in 1847, there were letters of reconciliation between Emily and Mr. Corey. In spring 1848, letters reveal that Mr. Corey's wife had died of consumption, her condition exacerbated by recent child-birth. She had left behind four children. In July 1849, Anna Maria Anable wrote of his impending marriage to Jane Backus, a good choice for this "rising man." Mr. Corey remained popular with the Sheldon-Anable families even after their move to Philadelphia in 1848. A March 2, 1852, letter from Charles B. Stout told of Mr. Corey's call to the Stanton Street Church in New York City, which Mr. Corey did not accept. Finally, in 1854, there was a pastoral letter from Mr. Corey to Emily on her illness and her possible death. He preached at the Bleecker Street Church as late as January 1867.

[162] See vol. 1, "Cast of Characters," s.v. "Nott, The Reverend Doctor Eliphalet."

[163] See vol. 1, "Cast of Characters," s.v. "Nott, Urania Sheldon."

and lingered till Oct.—Dr. and Mrs. James[164] were in Vermont when her symptoms became alarming in Sep.—They returned—Mr. Warner was at that time taken with bilious fever—their little Lucy too—at the time dear Lulia [*sic*] died. Her husband had been ill four weeks—three of which is a blank in his existence—he was then so very low that her death and burial must be kept from him—poor Dr. James was well nigh wrecked—This painful dissembling seemed killing them all—five days passed and they ventured to tell the poor stricken husband—he is now slowly recovering a mere shadow—the little girl is still weak—poor Dr. is a mere shadow—the only light about the house is dear Mrs. James—she has been and now is all the world to them—Mother to the two little helpless ones the sick father, and staff and life to the Dr.—him I greatly fear will soon sink under the pressure of his grief—and infirmity—Do you know he had a fall on the ice on coming from his door to our sleigh when dear Mother was sick—we had not his council the last three days, only as I reported her case to him—this was a great grief to us at the time—although we have little reason to think the result would have been different—but I shall ever think under God he has been the instrument of prolonging the valuable lives of my dear parents. I shall ever venerate his memory—Mr. and Mrs. Beebee[165] are now in New York—they all mourn deeply the death of their loved one Ellen Colgate[166]—I had a beautiful letter from Mary C.[167] recently she had called here[168] a short time previous to her sister's death on a jaunt to Montreal, from which place she was summoned home to the funeral—she kindly sent me a copy of your Daguerreotype—you cannot know how much I prize it—It looks so like you in days gone by, that I can almost hear some new story from your lips—what would I not give—Oh vain thought—past 11 o'clock—the invalid should retire—Heaven bless you and yours—our unceasing prayer to God is to keep you all as in "the hollow of his hand "—ever yours

    C. Sheldon

          Copy
          Inventory of Articles sent to
          Boston to go out with the
          Missionaries 1st Nov. '47

[164] Dr. James was a trusted physician, who attended the students and faculty of the Utica Female Academy. He is mentioned frequently in the correspondence as having been consulted for varying medical complaints, and his advice was always welcomed and highly regarded.

[165] See vol. 1, "Cast of Characters," s.v. "Beebee, Alexander."

[166] See vol. 1, "Cast of Characters," s.v. "Colgate, Ellen."

[167] Mary Colgate was the name of both the wife and the daughter of William Colgate, the prominent industrialist and manufacturer. We believe that this is Mary Colgate the daughter, referenced in Miss Sheldon's letter of August 29, 1847. This reference is a bit misleading as Ellen Hoyt Colgate is here identified as Mary's "sister"; this is likely euphemistic for "sister-in-law," which was their relationship.

[168] See the letter of Miss Cynthia Sheldon to Emily C. Judson dated August 29, 1847.

1 large tin box dried fruit

2 white dresses—made

2 6 [ ] table clothes—1 piece furniture chintz

24 yds shirting—1 flannel sheet

1 thin suit for Dr. Judson, not made

1 Merno dress—2 linen suits for children

and 2 night dresses, Made—1 thick shawl

1 Green box Contents

1 Nett Shawl 1/2 doz tea spoons

1 velvet Cap—1 Muslin dress pattern

4 suits children clothes

2 flannel garments

7 yds white flannel—1 pr hose

2 pocket [ ]—1 Book

part of these from Hamilton

The residue proceed of the draft

sent to Mr. Jones—which makes

us even again My dear E.[169]

Source: American Baptist Historical Society, AJ 20, no. 1003.

Miss Jane Kelly to Emily C. Judson November 27, 1847

My dear Emily,

I have been sitting here before this blank sheet with pen in hand for the last five minutes, wondering what in the world those girls up stairs [sic] could have written you.[170] Now if I should sit here and *wonder* till dooms-day the whole thing would still be a mystery to me, and so instead of *thinking* any longer about the teachers or their communications to you, I am going to think about *you*. You did not write me a note when you last sent letters. I don't wonder at it, for I did not [ ] to be remembered, yet how glad I should have been to have had a single line. It don't [sic] seem to me half the time that you are really away off in that out of the way heathen land so many hours and miles from us. Your letters come dropping in upon us so regularly, giving us such natural life like pictures of your what-abouts, and where-abouts, that I really cannot believe they have traveled over such a waste of waters to reach us. Has'nt [sic] been in my head a hundred times, and on

[169] When Emily reached Burmah, she sent a draft for forty dollars to Miss Sheldon to help cover some of the expenses incurred in her outfitting for her new life. Miss Sheldon wrote that she was dismayed that Emily had sent the money; now she has used it for items to be sent and states that they are "even."

[170] This "grouping of letters includes Julia Look, Sarah Bell Wheeler, and Miss Cynthia Sheldon, all dated September 26, 1847.

my lips as many, to thank you for the kind feeling which prompted you to send me the gifts[171] which I have been so long in acknowledging, yet have been looking at every day since they came. The ink stand, tho' not to used [*sic*], stands, is on my table in full sight, the hat-box is placed under my new stand, and where my setee used to be. Can you see just how they look, and understand how often they remind me of you and how pleasantly?

Written in the right margin of the address page: "I have just been up to Anna M's[172] room and find that the letters are all written and quite as many as can go in one envelope so rather that they should go off without a line from me I have begged to have my half arrive [ ] [ ] instead of the envelope. I had no [ ] of being denied the pleasure of assuring you that I had followed your course as you have marked it out in your letters with the [ ] interest and sympathy. But I don't know that you are after all a proper subject of sympathy you have the power of creating some thing out out [*sic*] of darkness, and doing all [Note: Written in the left margin of the address page.] things connected with you in such an attractive [ ] that in some accounts you are rather envied. Has Anna M told you that we had more than a hundred and fifty and the school is [very] pleasant? Eugenia[173] is teaching in Mr. Abbott's school in New York—still lives at Mrs. Brown's. Mary Barber[174] has not written in a year. She might as well be in Lapland as well as Land [ ] as far as hearing from her is concerned."

Written along the left margin of page 1: "I meant to have written you a long letter [ ] [ ]."

Written along the top margin and upside down of page 1: "Remember me to your husband. I am ready to kiss him for being so good a husband to you. Believe me to be as ever your sincere friend Jane."

Source: American Baptist Historical Society, AJ 17, no. 787.

---

[171] When Emily first arrived in Burmah, she sent back gifts to her family and friends. See Emily's letter dated December, 1846.

[172] See vol. 1, "Cast of Characters," s.v. "Anable, Miss Anna Maria."

[173] See vol. 1, "Cast of Characters," s.v. "Damaux, Eugenia."

[174] Mary Barber was mentioned frequently in the Emily Chubbuck Judson letters; she was a student and then a teacher at the Utica Female Academy. There were ups and downs to that relationship; in fall 1845, apparently Mary had written to someone expressing what Anna Maria Anable called "ingratitude," and Mary had been banned from the Academy until she made proper apologies to Miss Sheldon. In a September 7, 1845 letter from Anna Maria, we learn that her remarks had been about Miss Cynthia Sheldon. In November 1847 Jane Kelly remarked that they had not heard from Mary in over a year. In 1848 Mary Barber was back at the Utica Female Seminary teaching with Jane Kelly. Though at this time Miss Sheldon had moved to Philadelphia, Mary Barber had been able to reconcile with her, and in later years we find Mary very close to the Sheldon—Anable families; later, there was considerable consternation on Miss Cynthia Sheldon's part in her correspondence with Emily about Mary's health, the seriousness of it, and Mary's impending death. These letters were written in April 1852. Miss Sheldon went to help transfer Mary to Albany in June 1852, where she would be better situated and perhaps have access to better doctors. On September 9, 1852, Anna Maria Anable wrote to Emily of Mary Barber's death.

Emily C. Judson to Wm. D. Ticknor and Co., December 1847[175]

To Messrs. Wm. D. Ticknor & Co.:

Dear Sirs:

The copy of *Alderbrook* which you were so kind as to forward, reached us some weeks since; and really it came to me, in the midst of my new associations, like a spectre from the world of the antediluvians. It seemed scarcely possible, as I turned over leaf after leaf, that I could ever have been conversant with such scenes—scenes in which not only the human face, but everything, down to the little bird and flower, were so utterly unlike those, which are here daily becoming more and more familiar. It is astonishing how many years may be lived in one.

I send you a list of corrections for a new edition. The poem entitled "The Weaver," I rewrote soon after leaving Boston;—please admit the emendations.

Of the various articles which the book contains, I am the least satisfied with "Ida Ravelin" because it verges too closely on a class of writings just now somewhat mischievously fashionable in America. Beside, it is the only article written without aim or object, and, I think, the only one which has no foundation in reality. One of the last things which I wrote before leaving America, was the "Angel's Pilgrimage"; and, as it properly belongs to this collection, I should like to see it substituted for "Ida Ravelin."

Accompanying this, you will receive several articles which should have been in the poetical list of the first edition. One of the pieces formerly appeared in the *Knickerbocker Magazine*; two or three in other periodicals, and some have never been published at all.

While I have been telling you these things, and especially while copying the old poems, memory has been practicing some very pleasing illusions; so that I seemed to be revisiting my old haunts. But now I am at home again talking across the ocean to a world which begins already to gather shadows about it; and I must once more repeat the adieu to *Alderbrook*—a final farewell.[176]

E. C. J.

---

[175] The first edition of *Alderbrook* appeared in December 1846. By April 1847, according to a letter from Miss Cynthia Sheldon, it was in its fourth edition, though she admitted that the number of copies printed in each addition had been small. Each addition likely had minor revisions. This letter and the Ticknor editor's reply are printed as a forward to the tenth edition, which was printed in 1851. It likely began to appear in editions as early as July 1848, and this would constitute a "major revision" with the addition of a number of new articles. Added to vol. 1 were "April," "A Wish," "To an Infant," The Old Man—A Fact," "Grandfather," "The Dying Exile." To vol. 2 were added "The Angel's Pilgrimage" and "To My Father."

[176] The final sketch in vol. 2 of *Alderbrook* was "Farewell to Alderbrook."

Reply to the Letter of Emily C. Judson by Ticknor, Reed and Fields, December 1847—Boston

Editors Note: We have taken the liberty to retain the story here referred to, as the objection brought against it by the author is more than balanced by the graceful beauty of style and admirable spirit in which it is written. The piece intended by Mrs. Judson as a substitute, is now printed as additional material to volume second.

W. D. T.& Co.

Source: Hanna family files; Fanny Forester, *Alderbrook*, 10th ed. (Boston: Ticknor, Reed and Fields, 1851).

The Reverend D. G. Corey to Emily C. Judson, December 7, 1847—Utica

My dear Sister Judson.

Your kind and welcome letter was recd a number of days since. Or rather a number of weeks.[177] And be assured it was read with interest, and for the single reason that it was written by one with whom I have been so familiar in days past. I very much regret that any thing [sic] should ever have occurred to create the least unpleasant feeling.[178] As you refer to the subject in your letter, permit me to say a word. There can be no doubt but that we should have understood each other far better had there been "no one in Utica but our two selves." I cherished more Christian affection for you, and sympathized with you more than you ever supposed. It is not my nature to manifest half what I feel. And for this reason I am sometimes censured even by my best friends. It is true, on some points we differed; and what two persons do not? But let me assure you Sister Judson, that no unkind feelings toward you, have a place in my heart. However much I may have been disturbed by some few circumstances, nothing of it remained. That you left your native land—father's house, and prospects of earthly fame, prompted by the purest motives, I most fully believe. Thus much, I feel anxious to say to you upon this subject. We may never meet again on earth.

I heard of your arrival in Burmah with a joyful and grateful heart. While tossed on a [ ] ocean, you were not forgotten in our social meetings, and around our family alters [sic]. Many hearts breathed a prayer for your safe arrival. But probably

---

[177] See the letter of Emily C. Judson to the Reverend D. G. Corey dated January 31, 1847.

[178] At the time of Emily and Adoniram's engagement, the correspondence from the first three months of 1846 indicates that Mr. Corey made some intemperate remarks in which he questioned the suitability of the relationship and her fitness for missionary service.

none prayed more, or were more thankful than yourselves. We were however surprised to learn so soon of your intention to locate at Rangoon. And yet we rejoiced in view of the good of which it would probably be productive. All regarded it as the stepping stone to Ava—the heart of that great empire of sin. And that you might not be driven back prayer was constantly offered. How many were heard to say, brother Judson will remain in Rangoon a few years, long enough to complete his Dictionary; and then before he dies, will go up to Ava and under God, lay the foundation for future Missionary operations. And so it would have been, had the Baptist Churches of America performed their whole duty,[179] had they been "filled with all the fullness of God." When our army in Mexico cries for help, help is rendered. Men and money are sent on in full measure. But, a soldier of the cross clad with his Divine panoply, is on his way *alone* to the heart of an idolatrous empire, there to unfurl the banner of the cross, he is compelled to turn back in silent sadness. And why? Because the Baptist Churches in this country do not furnish adequate means!! It has seemed to me from the day I heard of it, that for this thing, the curse of the God of Mission would rest upon us. Who knows how many years will pass away before Ava will be visited by the messengers of God? Or, who can tell but that others beside Baptists will go up and possess the land? "I am pained at my very heart," and have been for some weeks in view of this thing. O! May God forgive, and not punish us. The truth is, the Churches in this country are abundantly able to by Divine assistance, to keep all our present Mission Stations above embarrassment; and greatly enlarge the field of their operations. We have *men* enough, and money enough; and if we had religion enough, there would be no lack. There is a most criminal negligence, the perpetuity of which a few years longer, will be attended with the most disastrous consequences.

In our own Church, since you left, there has been a much deeper interest manifested in the cause of Missions. The Monthly Concerts have been well attended, and deeply interesting. Last Sat. Evening, being the last Monthly Concert of the year, we had not less than 600 persons present. We have raised for Foreign Missions this year, about $110. We desire that our Monthly Concerts shall be among our most interesting meetings. At least, we mean that they shall be as *prominent* as any. There can be no doubt I think, but that under God the monthly concert of prayer has contributed greatly to the promotion of this glorious work. Without Devine help all is vain, and this must be secured by fervent prayer. Money is important, but prayer is more so.

We have enjoyed a wonderful work of Divine grace. Since last April, I have baptized 57. The most of them young people, though some heads of families. It has

---

[179] Adoniram and Emily returned from Rangoon and were unable to go on to Ava because of funding cutbacks from the Board of the American Baptist Missionary Union.

been one of the most glorious revivals I ever witnessed. So far, the converts appear remarkably well. They pray most fervently; and especially for those who have gone from our Church to the heathen. Our prospects at present as a Church are quite encouraging. Most clearly, the Lord approved of our moving into the center of the city. It has increased our prayer to do good. We ask an interest in your prayers, that God will augment our number, and strengthen our graces. That we may contribute [ ] [ ] to the spread of the gospel throughout the earth.

Since you left America, some changes have taken place among us of a mournful character. Already you have heard of Mother Sheldon's death.[180] Never in my life, did I feel more [ ] the loss of a member of my Church.[181] O! with what delight did she visit the house of God and listen to the gospel of peace. And you know that it was a perfect feast to sit in her room and listen to her conversation. Nearly her last words were, "The name of the Lord is a strong tower, the righteous [ ]eth into it and is safe." Her death produced a very powerful effect upon Father Sheldon.[182] For a time, I thought that he would soon follow. But he is now quite smart. Nearly every Sabbath, he is at the house of God, and manifests his usual interest in its exercises. But he cannot long continue here. His pilgrimage will soon close. It has also been my lot to follow a Sister to the grave. My Sister Mary Ann died in the month of Oct. In Aug. during Commencement exercises, bro Torrey, Pastor of the Broad St. Baptist Church, departed this life. He was sick only four of [sic] five days. Since then, both of Eld Peck's sons, Philetus and Lewis have been removed by death. Thus God is removing his Servants in the morning of life. And in connection with these afflictive events, we learn that bro Vinton,[183] and Wade[184] with their wives, and brother Mason[185] are on their way to America. Truly God is dealing with us. But our consolation still remains "The Lord reigneth."

[180] Mother Sheldon, the mother of Miss Cynthia Sheldon, Urania Sheldon Nott and Alma Sheldon Anable, had died on January 29, 1847. See the letter written by Anna Maria Anable on February 15, 1847.

[181] Deacon Asa and Isabell Low Sheldon had been founding members of the Bleecker Street Baptist Church. Other founding members well known to readers of Emily Chubbuck Judson's correspondence include Alma Anable, Cynthia Sheldon, Mr. and Mrs. Edward Bright (founding minister), and Horace Hawley.

[182] See vol. 1, "Cast of Characters," s.v. "Sheldon, Deacon Asa."

[183] Justus Hatch Vinton was born in Willington, Connecticut, in 1806. He attended the theological school at Hamilton, New York, and was ordained in June 1834. In July that same year, he sailed as a missionary to Burmah. His wife was Calista Holman Vinton; they were married April 9, 1834. They worked with the Karens at Chummerah, Newville, and Maulmain, where he had charge of the Karen theological seminary. At the end of 1847, they left for the United States, returning to Burmah and work at Rangoon in July 1850. Justus Vinton died in Kemendine, Burmah, on March 31, 1858. His wife, Calista Holman Vinton, died in Rangoon, Burmah December 20, 1864. Mrs. Vinton taught the Karen women and was the author of several hymnbooks in their language.

[184] See vol. 1, "Cast of Characters," s.v. "Wade, Jonathan and Deborah."

[185] Francis Mason arrived in Maulmain in November 1830 and transferred to Tavoy in 1831. His first wife died, and he married Helen Maria Griggs just before leaving the United States. She died in Burmah in 1846; they were the parents of four children. A skilled linguist, Mr. Mason was fluent in twelve languages and translated the Scripture into two of the Karen dialects. In spring 1847, Mr. Mason was seriously ill, and the other missionaries were concerned about him. In September 1847, he remarried, and Adoniram Judson officiated at the ceremony. His new wife was Ellen Huntley Bullard; originally from Vermont, she was the widow of Edwin Bullard, missionary to Burmah. Francis Mason died March 3, 1874 in Rangoon.

A subject is now agitating the Baptists of the State of New York, of considerable importance, by the removal of "Madison University" to Rochester.[186] The Baptists of western New York are taking hold of the matter with great energy. Already they have raised some $50,000/60,000, to erect buildings etc. What the result will be, remains to be seen. By some it is thought necessary to save the Institution. But to my mind there are strong objections to it. The Hamilton people are much excited. They are having meetings on the subject, propose building a plank road to Utica, repair the old buildings etc—It is a very important measure and I trust God will take the supervision of it.

I need not ask you Sister Judson, if you are happy in your work. That this is the case, you have already declared. And may that happiness increase a hundred fold. May your health and life be long preserved to do good. How does your husband feel in view of returning to Maulmain! The disappointment must have been overwhelming. May God sustain him, and yet give him the privilege of going to Ava. How much of change God has permitted him to see in Burmah. May his life be long spared. He shares in my warmest affections, and prayers. Ask him to favor me with a letter. Let me also hear from you frequently. Mrs. Corey wishes to be remembered to you.

I am yours in Christ—

D. G. Corey

P.S. Dr. Kendrick[187] is still living.

Source: American Baptist Historical Society, AJ 15, no. 624.

---

[186] The school that was to become Madison University was founded in 1817 by the Baptist Education Society of New York State for the purpose of educating ministers. Two of its first students, Jonathan Wade and Eugenio Kincaid and their wives, were among the first missionaries to join Adoniram and Ann Judson in Burmah. The Wades arrived in 1823, and the Kincaids in 1830. In 1834, the school was organized as a seminary, college, and academy called the Hamilton Literary and Theological Institution. In 1846, it was chartered as Madison University, drawing upon all of the history and good will in its former existence. In 1847, attempts were made to remove the university to the more urban setting of Rochester, and after three years of stressful turmoil that did tremendous damage to the prospects of the university, the courts decided the case in favor of those who wished the university to remain in Hamilton. Letters of the early 1850s show that the university soon made a remarkable recovery, and the university and seminary were later named for philanthropist Samuel Colgate.

[187] When Emily Chubbuck was in her teens, Dr. Nathaniel Kendrick was the pastor of the Baptist church in Eaton and also a professor in a local theological school; he eventually became the president of the Hamilton Literary and Theological Institution. At that time in her life, Emily spoke with him about becoming a missionary. Dr. Kendrick gave her the wise counsel of discernment, patience, and waiting. Adoniram and Emily turned to Dr. Kendrick to officiate at their marriage. He married Adoniram and Emily on June 2, 1846. A. C. Kendrick, in the Life and Letters of Mrs. Emily C. Judson, says that the marriage of Emily and Adoniram Judson was the last service for which Dr. Kendrick was able to leave his home. Other correspondents mention his continued frailty. He died on September 11, 1848.

[188] This letter from Emily's sister Catharine to their brother Walker is included because it shares news about Emily's family in Hamilton, New York, as life went on in her absence. Catharine's description and interpretation of Emily's letters home is also interesting.

Catharine Chubbuck to J. Walker Chubbuck, December 12, 1847[188]—
Hamilton

My Dear Walky.

I didn't really intend to be so long answering your letter, but I've had so much to do that it has seemed to me that I should never get time to write anything, but it is so rainy to night that I can't go to meeting and so will write you. You were homesick last fall when you were home[189] because 'twas so rainy and muddy, and I rather think you would be sick of home if you were here now it is ten times worse than it was then. I never saw such a December as this. One day it will be warm as summer almost, and the next, cold as Greenland. The past week it has rained incessantly, more it seems to me than all the rest of the summer. We hav'nt [*sic*] had a particle of sleighing yet and I really begin to fear we shall have none this winter. Do you keep sleighing in Wisconsin? I don't know but that I shall be tempted to come out there if you do, for I'm such a friend to the article not so much because I have any personal use for it, for I don't take a sleigh ride hardly once in a dogs [*sic*] age, but it gives a pleasanter, lighter hue to the out-door-world, and I don't know but it may possibly serve to lighten up within doors a little, at any rate it saves us from hearing that continual dashing of rain against the windows that we have had for a week past. I don't know what has tempted me to scribble down a whole page about the weather. I rather think I was a little out of patience which was certainly very unamiable but I rather think you will prefer some other subject. I waited a little about writing you hoping we should get something from Emily and a little more than a week ago I received a long letter in which she gives us a pretty full account of the state of things there. In many respects it is discouraging she says, but still they have some cause for encouragement. Light seems to be breaking in upon them some, the Dr. had gone out to baptize the second convert while she was writing but they would'nt [*sic*] have it known for the world. She said they would'nt [*sic*] remain long in Rangoon for it was so expensive, and they had suffered so much with sickness during the rains, that it seemed best for them to return to Maulmain for a while, at least. She said she hadn't set up an hour at a time for six weeks, and still she had taken care of things and written a great deal. She has earned the board $150 during the past year writing in English, besides the "Memoir" of the second Mrs. Judson[190] which is now in press by Mr. Colby[191] of New York, which will probably bring a number of hundred more [*sic*]. I think their sickness was caused partly by not having things proper to eat. She says they come

---

[189] This was the first time that Walker came home since he left for the Wisconsin Territory at least as early as October 1837 when Emily wrote to him there. It was her hope that he would get home so that she could see him before she left for Burmah, but that did not happen.

[190] *Memoir of Sarah B. Judson, Member of the American Mission to Burmah* (New York: L. Colby and Company, 1848).

[191] L. Colby and Company, 122 Nassau Street, New York. The publishing date was 1848.

within an inch of starving—can't get any bread except a course heavy sour loaf at an extravagant price. O now while I think of it I must tell you about her dinner of "rats." I give it in her own words: "you must contrive to get something that Mama can eat" the doctor said to our Burmese purveyor. 'She will starve to death. 'What shall I get?' 'Anything.' 'Anything?' 'Anything.' Well we did have a capital dinner; though we tried in vain to find out by the bones what it was. Henry[192] said it was touh-tans a species of lizard and I should have thought so too if the little animal had been of a fleshy consistence. Cook said he *did'nt* [sic] *know*, but he grining a horrible grin which made my stomach heave a little notwithstanding the deliciousness of the meat. In the evening we called Mr. Bassaar-Masi. 'What did we have for dinner today?' 'Were they good?' 'Excellent.' A tremendous explosion of laughter in which cook from his dish-room joined as loud as he dared. "What were they?" "Rats." A common servant would'nt [sic] have played such a trick, but it was one of the doctor's assistants, who goes to bazaar for us. You know the Chinese consider rats a great delicacy and he bought them at one of their shops. After telling over her troubles, she says, "Now do you think I am in any way discontented and would go back to America to live in a palace?" "Not I. I am ten times happier than I could be there. It makes me happy to know that I was almost entirely the means of the doctors coming to Rangoon, and that some souls have undoubtedly been saved by it." I hope they are back to Maulmain before this time where they won't have to suffer. We sent a box of fruit to them and some clothing about six weeks ago, and they sent also from Utica and Boston.

Mother[193] and I were delighted with the present you sent in the letter. Mother says "tell Walker I thank him a thousand times." I tried to make her keep it all, but she would make me take half, so I took it and went strait [sic] up to the store and buyed [sic] me two new frocks with it—one was a real pretty one I'm going to keep it nice till you come home in the spring and see if you won't say its pretty. Mother's going to keep hers to buy medicine with. She had got a new dress a little while before and so did'nt [sic] need for that. Father[194] and Mother are about as usual. Mother rather feeble you know. She sends a great deal of love and says you must come home in the Spring. Father bought an excellent horse and only paid forty dollars for it paid *all down*. Sold the old one for twenty. We have boarders as usual, three in number which makes me step so fast that I don't [sic] get time to do nothin [sic]. I speck [sic] dad is afraid if he don't [sic] keep me busy so I can't, I'll be

[192] See vol. 1, "Cast of Characters," s.v. "Judson, Henry Hall."

[193] Emily's mother, Lavinia Richards Chubbuck, was born June 1, 1785, at Goffstown, New Hampshire, the eldest of thirteen children. She married Charles Chubbuck on November 17, 1805, at Goffstown, New Hampshire. Four of her children were born at Goffstown, and moved with Charles and Lavinia Chubbuck to Eaton, New York in September 1816; they were Lavinia, Benjamin, Harriet, and John Walker. Sarah Catharine, Emily, and Wallace were all born in Eaton.

[194] Emily's father. See vol. 1, "Cast of Characters," s.v. "Chubbuck, Charles."

cutting up with students too much, but he need'nt [*sic*] fret. I shall cut up with em just as much as I'm a mind to. They're making a great effort to move our seminary to Rochester, but I guess they can't come it, for we girls are dead set against it.[195] Wallace[196] is in his select school in Peterboro yet he has a very full school this term and is liked very much, but then you know he can't save much it is'nt [*sic*] in him some how. O, I forgot to tell you. I sung [*sic*] the "prairie song" to mother just before I commenced this letter. I can sing it like a book now, would'nt [*sic*] you like to hear me? Be sure Walk and come home in the spring, be mother's best boy till then and dont [*sic*] forget

  Your affectionate
  Kitty Chub.

Source: Jerome Walker Chubbuck Collection, Wisconsin Historical Society Archives, Madison WI.

The Reverend Doctor William Dean to Emily C. Judson, December 20, 1847—Hong Kong

My dear Mrs. Judson

  Really you have been taking a large dose of the "romance of missionary life." I can imagine a little what might have been your situation at Rangoon by your description together with some few pictures of the kind wh. have come under my own eye. But I don't see the use of hazarding health and life by going to R. or Ava just now or putting your heads into the hands of a heathen king so long as he is desirous of cutting them off. I have done with those views of life wh. cancel *years* in the future by *days* at the present, and are very likely disposed to err on the "safe side," and to be *over* cautious. Still missionaries have done so much to render popular suicidal sentiments that it may be, the cause for wh. we labor, has something to gain by a counter-current.

  Do you mean to say that you have "twenty four" misses at Maulmain without counting all the little "blue eyes"? If so you may well call the company a "world"—when I think it a large company to see *two*! Here I've been for eight months *alone*—so far as Misses from our Board are concerned but you know that I am not so hyper denominational as not to find society in members of other Churches than my own. Indeed you wld not know the differences among us until you count church business and ordinances. By the way thinking of ordinances reminds me of

[195] Madison University. See vol. 1, "Places, Events, Organizations, and Magazines," s.v. "Madison University."

[196] Born January 1, 1824, William Wallace Chubbuck was six years younger than Emily. During these years of Emily's correspondence, Wallace lived at or near home and worked at different occupations including printing, office work, and teaching. Emily wrote of him as capable in many areas, but seeming to lack ambition at times. He proved to be a strong support for the Chubbuck family over these years, and at the time of her death in 1854, Wallace had become one of Emily's primary caregivers. After February 1854, she dictated all her letters to him because of her failing strength.

my little Church wh. now numbers *fifteen* Chinese—one a *Chinese woman!*—the first ever baptized. So far as I know. I think I told you about her in my last letter.

I hear that Dr. Kendrick[197] was alive (Sept. 27th) still in great bodily suffering but in still greater spiritual joy and mind quite unimpaired—Rev. Mr. Sheldon[198] has become the pastor of 2nd Ch. in Buffalo. Linas Peck—husband of Cordelia Kendrick, as you know, was preaching in Hamilton Village. My Bro and family at Morrisville well and good news about my children. You may perhaps imagine how it is that some of the messages my little Fanny[199] sends to her "Old Papa" melt my heart and fill my eyes. The absence of my children constitutes the *only* trouble I have—and that is little compared with what it might be. They are well—under kind guardianship—and in *good hands*.

The Chinese and English at Canton are likely to have trouble in consequence of the recent murder of six Englishmen by the Chinese at a village near Canton City. The matter has been referring to Pekin [*sic*] by Keying as Sir John Davis is said to have made such demands as he neither will nor *can* grant—a Blockade or War is talked of and it may not be surprising if England shd take Canton under the *protecting wing* as she has Calcutta etc. Nothing is being done just now in a missy (sic: missionary) or mercantile way at Canton but it does not interrupt our work here. Our congregation on Sunday continues much the same—from 40 to 100—Chinese both morng [*sic*] and P.M. and the out-stations as usual.

You say "tell me all about yourself tho not asked." In this I am faultless—i.e. *not defective*. Having no one else but myself to talk about—unless it be my cow and horse (both which are prospering). I am [ ] likely to make what little I write about bear somewhat directly on my own important self.

I hear that Mr. and Mrs. Jenks have been obliged to leave Bangkok I suppose for Mrs. J.'s health. Mrs. Everett—another of my fellow passengers on the "Cohota" is now here. She and Mrs. Clopton and boy are soon to leave for America.

Our U. S. Consul here has taken a general fancy to the "woman of forty" in the "night gown" and is now reading her book. He is one of my best friends here and had some inquiries to make about your worthy self the other day and I of course had great pleasure in giving him what information I had on the subject wh. you know is super-abundant on most subjects.

I think if my paper is better than yours the writing is enough worse to make us even—so I will close by giving you to boot a kind salutation to your good husband

---

[197] See vol. 1, "Cast of Characters," s.v. "Kendrick, Dr. Nathaniel."

[198] The Reverend Doctor Clisson P. Sheldon pursued his academic studies at Hamilton; problems with his eyes stopped him, and he became the pastor of the Whitesborough Church. He returned to Madison University, graduating in 1846, and he was called to the Niagara Square church in Buffalo, New York, which he served until 1854. He returned to Hamilton, went on to Troy for a successful pastorate, and then became district secretary of the American Baptist Home Mission Society in 1875. He was the author of "Historical Sketch of the Baptist Missionary Convention of the State of New York." (Source: William Cathcart, *the Baptist Encylcopaedia*, [Philadelphia: Louis H. Everts, 1881] 1050).

to be inflated in a manner of your own choosing, besides a kiss to all the "blue eyes" you have and kindest regards to yourself from Yours [ ]

W. Dean

Written in the left margin of the address page: "May I trouble you to mention my name to Bros Howard[200] and Newton and their good wives and as many more out of your 'world of twenty-four' as may have or wish to retain any remembrance of an old friend they have in this longitude."

Written in the right margin of the address page: "Do you get the 'China Mail' I send occasionally to you and your husband?"

Source: American Baptist Historical Society, AJ 15, no. 590.

Miss Cynthia Sheldon to Emily C. Judson, December 20, 1847[201]

My dear dear Emily,

I find it will not do for me to take a larger piece of paper—I cannot begin to say what I would—On Sat'y last your dear Kate[202] sent me a sweet note your Mother[203] was much better had been to Church the previous Sabbath—This precious note contained your more precious letter to her, sent by ship—need I tell you my dear E. the tears fell fast—Oh how wonderfully you have been sustained—what a paradoxical year you had just closed—I believe your happiness real not withstanding the draw backs—eating rats!!![204]

You know not how glad we are to believe you in Maulmain now—and how much we think about you this month—What an amount of writing you have accomplished—no wonder your eyes have given you troubles—we are so impatient to have the book come out[205]—one thing my girl—in future change your motto—

---

[199] Augusta Fanny Dean was born June 3, 1842. Her parents were Theodosia Ann Barker Dean and Dr. William Dean. Theodosia Dean died in March 1843 of smallpox in Hong Kong. William Dean had five children with three different wives.

[200] Hosea and Theresa Howard first sailed for Burmah in 1834, arriving in December that year. Hosea Howard was a recent graduate of the Theological Seminary in Hamilton, New York. They were stationed in Maulmain as missionaries with Adoniram Judson, and he claimed in a letter to Emily that he had worked there with Adoniram longer than any other missionary. Mr. Howard's responsibility was to run schools that the mission maintained, a task in which he was ably assisted by his wife. Lydia Lillybridge was responsible to Mr. and Mrs. Howard when she arrived in November 1846. Mr. and Mrs. Howard left Maulmain for the United States in February 1850.

[201] This letter has an addendum dated December 21, 1847.

[202] Sarah Catharine Chubbuck, "Kate," "Kit," or "Kitty" was Emily's older sister by ten months. Outside of the two terms at the Utica Female Academy, which Emily arranged for her, Catharine always lived at home with her parents in Hamilton, New York. The letters indicate opportunities for marriage, but she, for unknown reasons, remained single. She later helped to care for Henry and Edward Judson after their return from Burmah in fall 1851 when they moved into the Hamilton home with their "aunt" and "grandparents," and she was remembered by them as "dear old Aunt Kate—a dear friend."

[203] Emily's mother. See vol. 1, "Cast of Characters," s.v. "Chubbuck, Lavinia Richards."

[204] See the letter of Emily C. Judson to Catharine Chubbuck dated June 2, 1847.

[205] Emily finished the memoir of Sarah Hall Boardman Judson, the second wife of Adoniram Judson, who had died in September 1845 at the Isle of St. Helena, as the family returned from Burmah to the United States.

work while the day lasts—for this—the world was not made in a day—write on the top page of the Doct.'s Dictionary too—I do feel seriously that you are both in a way to wear out soon. Heaven bless you—the dear boys[206] too, you almost provoke me to say at once, send them here—we know they are prodigies—with every thing [*sic*] you think—nothing shall get in the papers you would not wish to have there—the Dr.'s letter is going the rounds[207]—people must feel—the board must respond—the great good done at Rangoon will tell on future ages[208]—Steeped as the acts have been in sacrifices—and secret "The Lord will reward them openly"—the burden of this heart is sustaining grace to you ward [*sic*]. In times past it was for more consecration of the responsible talents given you—"The ways of the Lord are perfect"—"In Him there is fullness"—In this hour of your great need you will find it—long before this reaches you I trust your Ebenezer will be raised high—the smiles of the helpless will gladden your eye—Our dear Mrs. G.[209] and Olivia[210] are now bearing your company in solicitude—May the Lord be with all for good—Oh what should we do without the "Lamp of Life"—a knowledge of the omniscience and omnipresence of the "all seeing eye"—Through great mercy we are comfortable—the ther. down to zero.

Source: American Baptist Historical Society, AJ 20, no. 1002.

Miss Cynthia Sheldon to Emily C. Judson, December 21, 1847[211]

Dear Anna M.[212] is busy with her classes—she really enjoys teaching—a staying friend is reading to dear father[213]—Mrs. A.[214] in her room too—Urania[215] will be here in two hours—we do know you have the best of husbands—Heaven bless you both.

ever yours C. S.

Source: American Baptist Historical Society, AJ 20, no. 1002.

[206] Henry Hall Judson and Edward Judson were the two youngest surviving children of Adoniram and Sarah Hall Boardman Judson; they lived in Maulmain with Adoniram and Emily.

[207] Miss Sheldon was giving many of Emily and Adoniram's letters to Alexander Beebee to be printed in the *Baptist Register*.

[208] Emily and Adoniram went to Rangoon, hoping it would be a stepping-stone to Ava; the Board of the American Baptist Missionary Union, however, made significant cutbacks in financial aid to the Burmese mission, so Adoniram and Emily were forced to return to Maulmain.

[209] See vol. 1, "Cast of Characters," s.v. "Gratiot, Charles and Ann" or "Gillette, the Reverend A. D. and Hannah."

[210] Olivia Williams Anable was married to William Stewart Anable, the second child and second son of Joseph and Alma Sheldon Anable. See the letter written by Anna Maria Anable on September 27, 1846. They lived in Sheboygan, Wisconsin, where Will Anable was in charge of a retail store.

[211] This letter is an addendum to a letter dated December 20, 1847, from Miss Cynthia Sheldon.

[212] See vol. 1, "Cast of Characters," s.v. "Anable, Miss Anna Maria."

[213] See vol. 1, "Cast of Characters," s.v. "Sheldon, Deacon Asa."

[214] See vol. 1, "Cast of Characters," s.v. "Anable, Mrs. Alma Sheldon."

[215] See vol. 1, "Cast of Characters," s.v. "Nott, Urania Sheldon."

Emily C. Judson to Catharine Chubbuck, December 22, 1847—Maulmain

Dear Kitty,

I did'nt [sic] intend to write by this steamer, but the departure of the Wades[216] makes it seem necessary. They left on Monday last, and you will probably see them in five or six months. They know more about the doc. and me than anybody else in the world knows, and you need'nt [sic] be afraid to ask them anything you want to know. You will love them very much and you must act it out and act as though you expected them to love you. We sent a box by them which may serve as Christmas gifts. There is my mahogany writing-desk for you, which you had better get glued and rub up in sweet oil. Then there is a very gay muslin dress which you may wear or Sell—a large round cape that will do to walk out in at evenings—a few night-caps and several prs of coloured [sic] stockings. I sent the stockings because none but white can be worn here, and you will see that they began to spot. Perhaps some of them are big enough for mother.[217] There is a pair of kid gloves under each ink-stand, which the air here began to spoil. I send you a lace veil which I bo't in Boston—a green guaze [sic] would have answered my purposes much better. Then there are two prs of cloth shoes and a pair of bootees that would be nearly useless to me, the hot weather here swells the feet so. I believe there is nothing else for you except a mousseline delaine [sic] long shawl of Bengalee manufacture. I put a gingham dress for mother in the desk, and a silk pocket-handkerchief for father and I believe that is all it contains. Oh, I had forgot a wrought collar for you. I suppose the shape of the collar is quite old fashioned, but the work is so rich that if you can get handsome lace to trim it with, I think you will like to wear it. The doctor's present is for all of you—twelve yards of crimson cotton cloth to curtain the windows. Mrs. Wade has it in a separate package. It is very broad and in my calculation I allowed two yards for each window so that you can do the windows of both rooms, or the parlour [sic] windows and at least one couch. I would'nt [sic] have big curtains but make them just the size of the windows without lining. Then I would either get fringe of the same colour [sic]; or some gay calico—say with a yellow vine or stripe running through it—and make a border on each side just alike. I think you will like the curtains. We should have liked to send you a great many things, but we don't feel particularly rich just now, especially as the outfit of the little stranger, now almost daily expected[218] has been a much greater expense than such things at home. And it is terrible to get sewing done. I will pay you ten dollars a month to come and sew for me. Did I tell you that the Board has given us

---

[216] See vol. 1, "Cast of Characters," s.v. "Wade, Jonathan and Deborah."

[217] Emily's mother. See vol. 1, "Cast of Characters," s.v. "Chubbuck, Lavinia Richards."

[218] Emily Frances Judson was born on December 24, 1847, two days after this letter was written.

$200, in consideration of our loss by the fire,[219] and sister Abigail Judson $100?[220] I should't wonder if the entire sum sh'd in one way and another be made up to us yet, but even then this would be as far as money is concerned a disastrous year to us. Our Rangoon expenses were enormous.[221] Most of the things which we took with us were ruined, and we came around, particularly the doc. and children,[222] very nearly in rags. I have been scratching ever since to get them decently clothed, and so we have necessarily exceeded the amount of our salaries to an alarming extent. However, I understand economizing you know, and when we are once set afloat again, I shall take a nick here and a nick there, till all is right.

Speaking of being set afloat—remind me that we are likely to be obliged to *move* again, and I sbould'nt [sic] wonder if we sh'd trot off to Amherst. You know Mr. Stevens[223] house was burnt—well, he moved into ours, and so when we came from Rangoon we took Mr. Simons'.[224] We now hear that Simons is on his way back and we must send. I am dreadfully tired of moving. There is no house for us in Maulmain, unless we turn poor Stevens out of doors and so we must go farther.

This a [sic] regular business letter, but you don't deserve any other. Why did'nt [sic] you write by the last steamer, nigger, eh? And why do father[225] and Wallace[226] never write? I am so wrathy with you all that I won't write another word, except that I sort of like you in spite of your numerous failin's—'specially the elderly gen-tl'man and lady. So no more from

Your loving

Nem

Source: Hanna family files.

---

[219] On February 17, 1847, shortly after they left Maulmain for Rangoon, a fire in the mission compound at Maulmain destroyed two trunks of Adoniram and Emily's clothing and personal articles; much of the loss had been personal gifts of great sentimental value. In different letters the loss was estimated between seven hundred and a thousand rupees.

[220] See vol. 1, "Cast of Characters," s.v. "Judson, Abigail Brown."

[221] The letters written by Emily Judson from mid-February–September 1, 1847, detail their Rangoon experience.

[222] Henry Hall Judson and Edward Judson were the two youngest surviving children of Adoniram and Sarah Hall Boardman Judson. They had been left in Burmah because of their age when Adoniram and Sarah, with the older children, had returned to the United States, hoping Sarah could regain her health. She was to die on the trip home at the Isle of St. Helene on September 1, 1845, and in November 1846, Adoniram Judson was to return to Burmah with Emily, the boys' "new mamma."

[223] Edward and Elizabeth Stevens were missionaries to Burmah. They arrived in Maulmain, Burmah, in February 1838. There are twenty-four letters in the correspondence from them. Mrs. Stevens took Edward Judson into her home when Sarah and Adoniram had to leave for the United States in 1845, and her care and nurture saved his life. Mr. Stevens buried Charles Chubbuck (Emily's "Angel Charlie") in April 1850.

[224] Thomas Simons. See vol. 1, "Cast of Characters," s.v. "Simons, Thomas and Lydia."

[225] Emily's father. See vol. 1, "Cast of Characters," s.v. "Chubbuck, Charles."

[226] See vol. 1, "Cast of Characters," s.v. "Chubbuck, William Wallace."

Emily Frances Judson (Adoniram Judson) to Anna Maria Anable, December 24, 1847[227]—Maulmain

My dear Aunt Anna Maria

Well, here I am at last, safe on terra firma, or rather in a queer oval shaped basket, where my respectable Papa has placed me and covered me up head and ears to keep me warm and quiet, I suppose; but all in vain, for no sooner has he turned his back, then I slip out of the basket, and avail myself of his writing implements to scribble a line to my dear aunt. It is striking five in the morning. I am just an hour old, and I hear my Papa calling out to Aunt Lydia,[228] who temporarily occupies a room in one end of our domicile, that dear Mamma behaved magnificently in ushering me into the world. So it seems that I have got a magnificent Mamma,—and I like my Papa too, as much as can be inputed [sic] on a short acquaintance, and I like my own looks too, for to tell you the truth, I took a peep in Mamma's toilet glass, as I stepped out of my basket, and I assure you I have a fine head of hair for so young a child; and my fingers are the very pattern of Mamma's—O if I don't [sic] make a sensation one of these days! But I hear my Papa coming—so I must scamper back to my nestling place, and pretend to be asleep. Goodnight or rather good morning, for I hear the cocks crow, and I will tell you more next time. Stop—I must write just a line to Aunt Stevens.[229]

1 o'clock PM. And here is an extract from her answer to mine of this morning—"My dear little Fanny, O, if I could only write poetry, what a nice little piece would I now send you—dear small ladyship and how prettily I should like to tell your dear Mamma and Papa that I congratulate them so warmly. But I can only say, I am right heartily glad for the 'Merry Christmas and happy new year' your coming may afford them!" "Your very affectionate aunt—E. L. Stevens."

Source: Hanna family files.

---

[227] There are four addenda attached to this letter; they are dated January 1, January 2, January 3, and January 13, 1848, and appear under those dates.

[228] See vol. 1, "Cast of Characters," s.v. "Lillybridge, Miss," also the timeline on "Lydia Lillybridge Simons."

[229] See vol. 1, "Cast of Characters," s.v. "Stevens, Elizabeth 'Bessie.'"

Emily C. Judson[230]

My Bird

Ere last year's moon had left the sky,
A birdling sought my Indian nest,
And folded, O so lovingly!
Her tiny wings upon my breast.

From morn till evening's purple tinge
In winsome helplessness she lies;
Two rose leaves, with a silken fringe,
Shut softly on her starry eyes.

There's not in Ind a lovelier bird;
Broad earth owns not a happier nest;
O God, Thou hast a fountain stirred,
Whose waters never more shall rest!

This beautiful, mysterious thing,
This seeming visitant from heaven,
This bird with the immortal wing,
To me-to me, Thy hand has given.

The pulse first caught its tiny stroke,
The blood its crimson hue, from mine;—
This life, which I have dared invoke,
Henceforth is parallel with thine.

A silent awe is in my room;
I tremble with delicious fear;
The future, with its light and gloom,-
Time and Eternity are here.

Doubts—hopes, in eager tumult rise;
Hear, O my God! one earnest prayer :
Room for my bird in Paradise,
And give her angel-plumage there!

Source: A. C. Kendrick, *The Life and Letters of Mrs. Emily C. Judson*, 266–67; Arabella M. Wilson, *Lives of the Three Mrs. Judsons*, 327–28; Edward Judson, *Life of Adoniram Judson*, 524–25; Emily Judson, *An Olio of Domestic Verse*, 157–58.

[230] This poem was written to celebrate the birth of Emily Frances Judson, who was born December 24, 1847.

Anna Maria Anable to Emily C. Judson, December 27, 1847

I wish you could look out from my window this morning Nemmy[231] dear. The snow is about an inch deep and the sun is shining out most gloriously. The little boys in the neighborhood are sliding down hill before our house, very much to the envy of little Harry Gratiot[232] who sits top o' the fence (as he has been forbidden to go out) wrapped up in nuffties [sic] and mittens, crowing and hurrahing as the boys whiz by him, and occasionally pelting them with snowballs just to have a hand in the scene some way. He is a brave and good little fellow and I think his earnest tones of entreaty to Mr. G.[233] as he just passed out of the gate, of "Papa won't you buy me a sled?" will not be unheeded. This is the day on which our two neighboring brides Mrs. Dr. Bagg and Mrs. Potter receive calls. The wedding party was a very pleasant one and the brides of course had the good wishes of everybody.

Mary Spencer[234] feels about Marion's Marriage very much as I did about yours though I don't think she has any occasion to, for she is going to live here in Utica always and as a married woman her influence in Society can be much greater than it has been, and I very much mis-read her if she is going to be so engrossed by the husband as to give no share of her heart to her friends.

Now Nemmy I am afraid you and the Dr. are distressing yourselves about what shall be done with this child who is so bent on being a Missionary.[235] Pray do not, for since she has been promoted to the teaching of some English branches and drawing in the Utica Fem. Sem. she feels quite contented, and the more she hears of the state of the missions to the east the less does she feel inclined to engage in them. Ah! Me! it is a sad world we live in when so good a cause is left to languish for want of interest here at home.

Tell the Dr. I am very much obliged for his kind note dated in August,[236] he will have rec'd two from me before this,[237] which I am now almost sorry I wrote.

---

[231] Emily Chubbuck. See vol. 1, "Cast of Characters," s.v. "Nemmy, Nem, or Nemmy Petty (Nemmie Pettie)." Also the chapter "Names of Endearment."

[232] Harry Gratiot was the son of Charles and Ann Gratiot. See vol. 1, "Cast of Characters," s.v. "Gratiot, Charles and Ann."

[233] Ibid.

[234] On February 28, 1848, Anna Maria Anable wrote to Emily, saying, "Mary Spencer has just returned from Albany. It is said she is engaged to John James, a handsome young widower with three children, and two or three hundred thousand $'s."

[235] As Anna Maria struggled with her call to be a missionary, always in the background was her commitment to the Utica Female Academy, the way that her Aunt Cynthia depended on her, and her responsibilities within the family. The medical treatment for problems with her shoulder and spine made Anna Maria realize that it would be vain to think of anything but going out as a missionary. She says that she would not be criticized by her mother. Having prayed for six children all of her life and having those prayers answered in so many ways, there would be no question if God called her daughter for such service. She remarks that everyone in Boston seems to think that she will be going. A later letter from Miss Sheldon (August 22, 1847) states that she thought it utter foolishness for Anna Maria to think of missionary service. In the end, the family moved to Philadelphia in the late summer 1848 to start the Misses Anable's School with Anna Maria in charge, a responsibility of which she spoke in terms of her calling.

[236] See the letter of Adoniram Judson to Anna Maria Anable dated August 17, 1847.

[237] Anna Maria wrote letters on September 27 and 27, and October 13, 1847.

His kind predictions with regard to me I hope will prove true. I can truly say that in no previous year of my life have I felt the necessity of acting from principles; and the fact that duty so often clashes with inclination of course calls forth principles of action which can be easily applied.

I am constantly extending my circle of acquaintances among intelligent Baptists abroad, and to say that I am expecting friends to visit me, is now equivalent to saying, we are going to have some delightful people here.

I sit at Grandpa's[238] end of the table and we entertain all our friends there, and Aunt C.[239] does everything to make the house pleasant. In some respects our internal economy is improved very much.

Last week Mr. and Mrs. Rob. Raymond spent a few days with me. She is a charming little woman, and he is one of the most agreeable and wittiest fellows I ever knew—Then he sings better than any gentlemen I ever heard off of the stage. He is settled over a church in Syracuse, and is considered a devoted pastor. I like to have such persons come here, and I mean to invite friends to visit me oftener, for within society I can say that we have the resources among us to make a visit pleasant. I believe nearly all our folks are writing so I'll not wait for any messages but close with a bye, bye and a kiss if you please to the Dr.

Anna M.

Source: American Baptist Historical Society, AJ 13, no. 497.

Mrs. Mary H. Brayton to Emily C. Judson, December 28, 1847—Brooklyn

Dear Mrs. Judson,

I wrote you a note some time since and sent it to Mr. Brayton[240] to forward before he left but I fear it was lost, and now this last moment write to make one request. I am asked a thousand questions about the present Mrs. Judson. Excuse my frankness. I always freely and conscientiously advocate your cause. I one day repeated to a dear friend to the mission some of our conversation the pleasant day I spent with you, and he said do write to Mrs. Judson to repeat the same in public. You probably recollect it. It was a reference to your feelings in regard to being a

---

[238] See vol. 1, "Cast of Characters," s.v. "Sheldon, Deacon Asa."

[239] See vol. 1, "Cast of Characters," s.v. "Sheldon, Miss Cynthia."

[240] The Reverend Durlin L. Brayton was born in Hubbardton, Vermont, on October 27, 1808. He graduated from Brown University and then the Newton Theological Seminary in 1837, at which time he was appointed to missionary service. On October 2, 1837, he married Mary Hawley Fuller, and they sailed for Burmah on October 28, 1837. They arrived in April 1838 and, passing through Amherst and Maulmain, arrived at Mergui at April 1840. In February 1847, they departed Maulmain for America due to Mrs. Brayton's ill health. Mr. Brayton returned to Burmah the following November, and Mrs. Brayton remained in America until arriving back in Burmah in March 1850. They had one daughter, Mary. Mary Brayton died December 16, 1890 in Rangoon; Durlin Brayton died April 23, 1900, also in Rangoon.

Missionary also the two years you were engaged so extensively in writing for the public.[241] I can truly say myself that something of the kind might be very useful and gratifying to many. How much I should have many such particulars in regard to your children that I had in Maulmain.

Kind regards to Mr. Judson and kisses for the children.[242]

Written in the bottom margin of the address page: "Can you find time to write me, you will learn from [ ] particulars of my health. I shall never forget Mr. J's looks when he said 'you will get well and come back.' O I long to be back in Burmah again."

Written in the left margin of the first page: "Hope you are much better and wish love to Lydia[243] and a share for yourself."

M. H. Brayton.

Source: American Baptist Historical Society, AJ 12, no. 352.

Anna Maria Anable to Emily C. Judson, December 28, 1847—Utica

What shall I write about Nemmy[244] this time? I feel as if my letters were positively too stupid to send. Would you like to have me detail the events of one day? Could I do it well, you would know pretty well how all our time is spent, for one day is as like another as two peas. By looking at the date you will see that this is the recess between the holidays. Jul. Look[245] and Sarah Bell[246] are the only teachers beside myself who remain here. Fanny Buckingham[247] and her little boy are spending the holidays with us. In virtue of the superior dignity of my character and example I am appointed directress general of the young ladies in the absence of the principal! The way the girls train the streets in the day time [*sic*] and sit up for company in the parlor in the evening is beautiful to all eyes but a school ma'am's. Notwithstanding my loose discipline, I have heard as yet of not a single misdemeanor. Now to begin the day. By dint of great exertion I succeed generally in

---

[241] Emily E. Chubbuck wrote under her own name and then under the *nom de plume* Fanny Forester after June 1844. She was extremely popular with the literary magazines and her stories and sketches gained wide appeal.

[242] Henry Hall Judson and Edward Judson were the two youngest surviving children of Adoniram and Sarah Hall Boardman Judson. They had been left in Burmah because of their age when Adoniram and Sarah, with the older children, had returned to the United States, hoping Sarah could regain her health. She was to die on the trip home at the Isle of St. Helena on September 1, 1845, and in November 1846, Adoniram Judson was to return to Burmah with Emily, the boys' "new mamma."

[243] See vol. 1, "Cast of Characters," s.v. "Lillybridge, Miss," also the timeline "Lydia Lillybridge Simons."

[244] Emily Chubbuck. See vol. 1, "Cast of Characters," s.v. "Nemmy, Nem, or Nemmy Petty (Nemmie Pettie)." Also the chapter "Names of Endearment."

[245] See vol. 1, "Cast of Characters," s.v. "Look, Julia."

[246] See vol. 1, "Cast of Characters," s.v. "Wheeler, Miss Sarah Bell."

[247] See vol. 1, "Cast of Characters," s.v. "Buckingham, Fanny."

getting to the breakfast table before the others have quite finished their meal. Grandpa[248] is ready to wish me a good *afternoon*, and young Mr. Bingham who sits at my right smiles very complacently. This youth is a student from Hamilton the son of a Missionary to the Indians. He has a sister in school, and Aunt C.[249] has invited him to chum with Court[250] for a fortnight while Mr. Leach doctors his eyes.

He conducts family worship. After prayers a little knot of us gather around the dining-room stove as in the olden times, to block out the amusement or improvement of the day. My next step is to cousin Ann's[251] room to inquire after the health of Master Charley Gratiot Jr. who commenced his part in the drama of life last Thursday morning the 23rd. He is a fine fat baby and in two or three months will be quite an object of interest to the whole household. At present little Henry J. B. is decidedly more engaging. After a while we congregate in my room and we do somehow manage to extract a little fun out of one thing and another during the day, tho' we are a somewhat prosy set. If at any time [sic] we are in danger of becoming monotonous little Henry is by to tip over the stand or try to get a "drink" out of the inkstand or something of that sort. This afternoon Cousin Chas.[252] took Anna Sheldon (Fred's wife) and me out riding. He has a fine horse and beautiful little cutter and bye and bye if Mr. Corey[253] does not interfere he is going to take me out to Hamilton. By the way Fanny Corey (you remember her?) is to be married to a nephew of Dr. Spring of New York. I believe I told you that last month, but never mind. If I did just scratch that sentence out. We are all going to night [sic] to Jennie Hawley's. I don't know as I have visited her since you left. Horace[254] is making money every year and extending his business constantly, but neither he nor the old woman feel quite comfortable when they see any of us. They know we have been behind the curtain. Fred Sheldon is coming down from Rome to-night for his wife. Did I tell you he had gone into the grocery business there?[255] I have one piece of news to tell you any way [sic]. Old Dea. Bacheller of Lynn has begun trying to

---

[248] See vol. 1, "Cast of Characters," s.v. "Sheldon, Deacon Asa."

[249] See vol. 1, "Cast of Characters," s.v. "Sheldon, Miss Cynthia."

[250] See vol. 1, "Cast of Characters," s.v. "Anable, Courtland."

[251] See vol. 1, "Cast of Characters," s.v. "Sheldon, Ann."

[252] See vol. 1, "Cast of Characters," s.v. "Gratiot, Charles."

[253] See vol. 1, "Cast of Characters," s.v. "Corey, the Reverend D. G."

[254] Mr. Horace H. Hawley enjoyed a family relationship with the Sheldon family. Emily's letter on May 7, 1841, indicates that he was to marry a niece of Misses Cynthia and Urania Sheldon and Mrs. Alma Sheldon Anable, the daughter of their brother John Sheldon. Through the help of Miss Cynthia Sheldon, he was introduced into the life of Emily Chubbuck. A member of a publishing firm, he also worked with Alexander Beebee in publishing the *Baptist Register*. Beginning in 1841 with the publication of *Charles Linn*, Mr. Hawley was enormously helpful to Emily Chubbuck as she published her early stories and books. There are numerous references to his help and his generosity. In 1838, Horace Hawley had been a charter member of the Bleecker Street Baptist Church in Utica, along with several members of the Sheldon family.

[255] Fred Sheldon lived in Rome, New York, where he opened a grocery store. This is likely the next generation to Fred and Martha Sheldon from Troy.

get Ma'am Colby[256] to console him in his widowhood, but the old lady proved imperious to all entreaties. They say he bears his disappointment like a philosopher. Have you written to Mrs. Colby[257] you naughty child? and did you write a story called "The dream"? Tell me quick!

Mrs. Colby is becoming reconciled to her residence in the country, tho' she thinks the Professors at Newton[258] are men remarkable for their stillness. I tell you what Nem. They (always excepting Dr. Sears) have half the [ ] of the Hamilton faculty, and the students are all cut after the same pattern, and of course though they may have some polish they have not half the originality. So much for my observation at the anniversary this year.

I should think Mrs. C. would have a dull time of it, for whatever the professors may be their wives are very prosy sort of women. Such a time as I did have at a sewing circle at Mrs. S. F. Smith's. Had it not been for Miss Morse the Missionary, and Dr. Sears I should have run home in despair.

Source: American Baptist Historical Society, AJ 13, no. 496.

Anna Maria Anable to Emily C. Judson, December 29, 1847—Utica

You can't imagine how much sympathy your rat story[259] excited in the minds of all who heard it, 'cepting myself. Seeing you enjoyed them so much, I only wished that you could pickle for your use a barrel of these fat fellows that infest our second hall. Perhaps you would not like them pickled as well as fresh? Ah, well! Chacun a son govt [*sic*] is applicable to eating rats as kissing subjects.

Soberly, Nemmy[260] I could have cried a tumbler full of tears if it would have helped you to a good dinner, but I know you love it bravely. I am glad you are at Maulmain any way. Wouldn't I give something this drissly [*sic*] morning, if I could only saddle up the Telegraph and ride over to Maulmain to see how the baby does?[261] I did not get a letter yesterday Missis [*sic*]. Do you want me to write to you? I shall think you don't if you neglect me so.

---

[256] This reference is likely to Mrs. Sarah Colby, mother of Gardner Colby and long-time supporter of Adoniram Judson. There is correspondence from Mrs. Colby telling of her move from Pemberton Square in Boston to Danvers where she lived with her daughter.

[257] See vol. 1, "Cast of Characters," s.v. "Colby, Gardner and Mary."

[258] Gardner Colby built his new home at the bottom of the hill that housed Newton Theological Institute.

[259] See the letter of Emily Judson dated June 2, 1847.

[260] Emily Chubbuck. See vol. 1, "Cast of Characters," s.v. "Nemmy, Nem, or Nemmy Petty (Nemmie Pettie)." Also the chapter, "Names of Endearment."

[261] Emily Frances Judson was born December 24, 1847.

Give a great deal of love to Lydia.[262] I mean to write to her hoping she will receive it by this mail. Grandpa[263] and all the family are well. Love to the Dr. Adieu Anna M.

Mary Barber[264] visited Fanny B.[265] two or three days on her way to Middlebury. Fan says she is much gayer in her dress than formerly. She is going to spend the winter in N. Y. with a lady who has rooms in a public house instead of with her brother. Isn't she queer? Aunt U.[266] is most as queer, but it is in another way.

Source: The American Baptist Historical Society, AJ 13, Number 496.

Editor's Note: Emily Chubbuck Judson's correspondence from Burmah will continue in volume 4 and will take us through the death of Adoniram Judson and Emily's return to the United States with Edward, Henry, and a Malayan woman, Nancy, who was both a nurse to Emily and a governess for the children.

---

[262] See vol. 1, "Cast of Characters," s.v. "Lillybridge, Lydia. See also the timeline Lydia Lillybridge Simons."

[263] See vol. 1, "Cast of Characters," s.v. "Sheldon, Deacon Asa."

[264] See vol. 1, "Cast of Characters," s.v. "Barber, Mary."

[265] See vol. 1, "Cast of Characters," s.v. "Buckingham, Fanny."

[266] See vol. 1, "Cast of Characters," s.v. "Nott, Urania Sheldon."

APPENDIX

No 1 a

Philada Jan. 20th, 1846

I hand you, dearest one, a charmed watch. It always comes back to me & brings its wearer with it! I gave it to Ann, when a hemisphere divided us, & it brought her safely & surely to my arms— I gave it to Sarah, during her husband's life-time (not then aware of the secret); & the charm, though slow in its operation, was true at last.

Were it not for the sweet indulgences you have kindly allowed me, & the blessed understanding that "love has taught us to guess at", I should not venture to pray you accept my present with such a note— Should you "cease to guess" & toss back the article, saying, "your watch has lost its charm. It comes back to you, but brings not its wearer with it!" I first smash it to pieces, that it may be an emblem of what will then remain of the heart of

Your devoted

A. Judson

Miss Emily Chubbuck

Appendix

Letter from Adoniram to Emily - January 20, 1846

My own best-beloved,

I was ill in bed all day
yesterday or I should have written you; and in that
slight illness my heart clung to you — oh, _so_ fondly! Strange
that I should think of you, a comparative stranger, in
preference to those who have loved and cared for me
for many years. Ah, doctor dear, you _must_ love me,
whatever wise things that judgement of yours may say;
for there is no poet that could very well be trusted
to make a second version of "Love lies bleeding," after
your favourite.

Mrs. Gillette had a party on Thursday evening
at which I was, of course, bound to exert myself to
shine a little; and having taken a walk in the west
before evening came on, I found myself on the sick
list by the time the guests were gone. I have quite
recovered, however, to-day; and made a vow to be
more careful. I saw doctor Lyon, Mrs. Jewell & brother,
at the party for the first time; and he flourished
more like the gay New Yorkers than any one I
have met before in this sober quaker city. He professed
the greatest reverence for genius, and then turned
and complimented me so violently that I was fain

INDEX